Transitions

Transitions

Four Decades of Toi Whakaari: New Zealand Drama School

Bill Guest

Victoria University Press

TE WHARE WĀNANGA O TE ŪPOKO O TE IKA A MĀUI
VICTORIA
UNIVERSITY OF WELLINGTON

Toi Whakaari: New Zealand Drama School

40 YEARS OF ACTION, VISION AND INNOVATION 1970–2010
TOI whakaari new zealand drama school

VICTORIA UNIVERSITY PRESS
Victoria University of Wellington
PO Box 600 Wellington
http://www.victoria.ac.nz/vup

TOI WHAKAARI: NZ DRAMA SCHOOL
Te Whaea: National Dance & Drama Centre
11 Hutchison Road, Newtown, Wellington
PO Box 7146, Newtown, Wellington, 6242
http://www.toiwhakaari.ac.nz

Copyright © Toi Whakaari: New Zealand Drama School 2010
First published 2010

This book is copyright. Apart from any fair dealing for the purpose of private study, research, criticism or review, as permitted under the Copyright Act, no part may be reproduced by any process without the permission of the publishers

National Library of New Zealand Cataloguing-in-Publication Data
Guest, Bill, 1942-
Transitions : four decades of Toi Whakaari, New Zealand Drama School / Bill Guest.
Includes index.
ISBN 978-0-86473-642-0
Toi Whakaari New Zealand Drama School—History. 2. Acting—Study and teaching (Higher)—New Zealand—Wellington—History. [1. Toi whakaari. reo] I. Toi Whakaari New Zealand Drama School. II. Title.
792.07119363—dc 22

Edited by Ginny Sullivan
Typeset by Ahi Text Solutions
Index compiled by Ginny Sullivan

Printed by Printlink, Wellington

Contents

Preface

Just this morning at Toi Whakaari I saw students lead a large portion of the kōiwi session, no small undertaking with 160 people in the room; saw a staff member openly reference a difficult situation and place it in a context that encouraged continued engagement; watched a new student reflect on a previous session and open up the question of how we find the courage to oppose, as well as to agree.

As I write this at the beginning of March 2010, I am filled with excitement and anticipation for the work engendered by such forums. The quality of these experiences gives me fresh heart for the future of our art-form and for the leadership Toi Whakaari can demonstrate. When RADA voice and research teacher Jane Boston visited the school at the end of 2009, she was impressed with the sense of shared purpose, clearly visible when the students sang to her. Purpose freed the students from self-consciousness or a focus on perfecting their performance, and instead linked them to the grace of action and encounter, a grace fostered through this work in kōiwi.

Our engagement with the international community has grown, so that now we are a member of UNESCO's International Theatre Institute, regularly participating in international conferences and festivals as well as teaching master-classes as part of the UNESCO ITI family. This is giving Toi Whakaari an increasingly high profile in the international arena, building on the wide-ranging international exchange agreements and student internships already in place. It is stimulating to be able to place our work in an international context and this engagement is likely to continue and increase as we go into our fiftieth decade.

The school has always brought in international practitioners to benchmark, challenge and support the work of the core staff. Marking the fortieth birthday year of 2010, Harry Fuhrmann, who teaches at the prestigious Ernst Busch School in Berlin (Germany's top theatre school); Lisa Harrow, expatriate New Zealander and outstanding Shakespearean actress; Christine Adaire, master Linklater-voice teacher; and Jean-Guy Lecat, Peter Brook's theatre designer over thirty years, all taught at the school.

The school has long had a commitment to integrating a bicultural approach, but this commitment has often been confused and unsure of itself, sometimes latching onto the outward form of things Māori without a matching understanding of the values in which these practices are embedded. This was never insincere. The belief that led these practices, the idea that looking at the world through a Māori as well as a Pākehā lens would build more dynamic practitioners for stage and screen is, in my perception, correct. However, over the past two years we are now articulating this commitment in a fresh way, exploring the underlying values in te ao Māori as a framework that both interrogates our assumptions and helps us to perceive all the many other frameworks under which we operate. This is integrating our work in tikanga into every strand of the learning.

There has been an increasing consciousness about the performance work we are making and sharing with the public. In 2009 Miranda Harcourt, in a meeting of the school's Screen Advisory Panel, described the 2009 performance work as reaching new levels of achievement. We are becoming more articulate about the focus of our work, stressing that we are a school, not a theatre company, and that audiences can expect the work to ask questions of performance as well as to demonstrate the skills the students are acquiring. I expect the school to become ever more articulate about these issues over the next decade, as new courses, most likely in the postgraduate arena, are developed.

Our building of Te Whaea invites creative additions with its huge and labyrinthine sprawl. I salute the foresight of the boards that brought us into this flexible space after the long search for a home experienced by my predecessors. The completion of the Design Wing in 2009 demonstrated to us that we can continue to develop our building to meet the school's future needs, and I have no doubt that it will continue to transform and grow.

The school that I entered as a teacher in 1989 has been transformed from a sole-focus acting school into a multi-disciplinary educational institute for those preparing for careers in stage and screen. Bill Guest, my associate director for many of those years, and writer of this book, was a creative and moving force in driving this vision and bringing it to life, and I salute him for his visionary thinking and the huge contribution he has made both to this school and to the performing arts in New Zealand.

I also salute my predecessors: my own teacher, Nola Millar, whose vision began the whole enterprise, George Webby, Andrew Noble, Sunny Amey and Robin Payne. I have reaped the benefit of their great work, their struggles to find a home for the school, to secure adequate and reliable funding and to build a school that is truly of this place, Aotearoa New Zealand. The beautiful building of Te Whaea in which we live has grown and flourished and we likewise have grown and flourished with it. I am proud of my part in guiding this journey and very confident that I leave a school that is vital, highly skilled and continuing to evolve, one that will provide the industries we serve with excellent practitioners as well as challenging and surprising them. I look forward to being challenged and surprised in my turn.

Annie Ruth
Director
Toi Whakaari: New Zealand Drama School
March 2010

Acknowledgements

I owe a debt of gratitude to those who generously contributed their time in helping to trace the journey of the school. Without their input, this book would not exist. My biggest regret is that the time and space has limited the number of individual stories that I could include from the graduates, staff and current students who were approached during the compilation of this book.

Amongst those who assisted me and advised me in this project I would like to make special mention of the following: Sarah Gaitanos for the generous advice and encouragement she gave when I embarked on this project, and the permission to include extracts from her Toi Whakaari Oral History Project in the book; huge thanks to George Webby, Sunny Amey, Andy Noble, Robin Payne and Annie Ruth for their personal and candid views of their directorship; together with Grant Tilly, Erica Stephenson and Ruth Graham for their broad oversight of the history of the school.

My wife Brenda provided valuable logistical support throughout the writing of this book, helping to transcribe interviews, reading and correcting early raw drafts, and providing me with an essential and endless supply of coffee.

I particularly acknowledge the professional support and guidance of Fergus Barrowman, who skilfully steered me through the arcane publishing process, my editor Dr Ginny Sullivan for her insightful shaping of the final drafts, and to Sarah-Jane McCosh for her perseverance in the layout.

Episodes in the book are illustrated with images from numerous photographers to whom I am extremely grateful, especially Stephen A' Court, John Ashton, Simon Clark, Craig Duffy, Daphne Eriksen, Briene Lermitte, Stephen McCurdy, Bruce McMillan, Philip Merry, Michael Parrott and Derek Simpson. I also acknowledge the valuable contribution made in this regard by the Alexander Turnbull Library, Wellington. Every effort has been made to trace all copyright holders of photographs in the book; however, advice on any omissions would be appreciated.

Finally, I would like to acknowledge the financial support provided by the Stout Trust, Toi Whakaari: New Zealand Drama School and Victoria University Press in allowing this book to be written and published.

Bill Guest

Prologue

The start of each new year at Toi Whakaari is marked by a pōwhiri, in which returning students with their families and friends, and staff and graduates gather at Te Whaea, in Newtown, to welcome and receive a new intake of students into the school. The karanga that resonates throughout the building is complemented by a haka that creates a powerful sense of occasion that is clearly felt by all participants, especially the new students. Their emotional response to the pōwhiri often hovers between apprehension, awe and elation, but generally concludes with a sense of belonging as they move from being manuhiri to becoming tangata whenua.

For some, the pōwhiri may well also evoke the historical journey of Toi Whakaari, rooted in the vision and courage of those who imagined and shaped the school and fostered its development: the directors, teachers, administrators, graduates, and members of boards and advisory panels. It is a corporeal thing, this history, enshrined in the mana of the school and in the legacy of its 700-plus graduates.

Te Whaea: National Dance and Drama Centre has been the home of Toi Whakaari: New Zealand Drama School and the New Zealand School of Dance since 1998. The majesty of the building emphasises the national status of the two schools, and its resources are comparable with, and in many cases exceed, those of other leading international performing arts institutions. Te Whaea (The Mother) exudes creative energy; those who work there are justifiably proud and invigorated by the sense of purpose she bestows. The identity of Toi Whakaari is now so embodied in Te Whaea that new entrants and visitors can be forgiven for imagining the school has always enjoyed such grand facilities. In fact, for the first eighteen years of its life the school occupied far humbler premises, and the present facilities are the result of many years of searching, fighting and negotiation – by a determined group of individuals.

Toi Whakaari is a private training establishment and, unlike universities and many other tertiary institutions, it is not eligible to bid for capital funding. Therefore, the decision to take on the old Winter Show Building as a permanent home for the school was a huge financial undertaking, a gamble that Nola Millar, the founder of the Drama School, would have probably backed, in spite of the 'outside odds'.

The introduction of a technical production course in 1993, and the expansion of the two-year acting diploma into a three-year degree in 1997, caused a significant increase in student enrolments and required the school to step up its search for larger and more fitting premises. This was not an unfamiliar predicament, as much of the Drama School story entails the search for a suitable permanent home.

The move to the Winter Show Buildings was the seventh in twenty-eight years, and it provided space and resources to accommodate additional complementary courses. This in turn has created a more rounded institution, with student actors, directors, designers, technicians, managers and costumiers working together and undertaking research in a collaborative environment. The school now more accurately reflects an industry model, and is well positioned to explore exciting performance options to shape the character and the future of performing arts, both in New Zealand and overseas.

A well-designed building with world-class teaching facilities goes a long way to ensuring a supportive learning environment, which in turn helps to foster greater creative possibilities. But a fine building is no prerequisite for excellence. From 1970 to 1998 the New Zealand Drama School operated out of often inadequate premises, which clearly did not hinder the students' development or diminish their achievements. George Webby admits to having a soft spot for 'the prefab and improvised buildings', and in his autobiography he observes that 'each drama school building seemed to give a lot of pleasure to those inhabiting it'.[1] He was, of course, referring to the five 'temporary' premises the New Zealand Drama School inhabited from 1974 to 1988, when he was director.

The National Institute of Dramatic Art (NIDA), in Sydney, has a similar story to tell. It is now housed in glorious – some say luxurious – premises, though for well over thirty years NIDA got by with ramshackle, draughty sheds, previously the property of the Kensington Racecourse adjacent to the University of New South Wales. Yet hundreds of students trained, and indeed flourished, in those less-than-salubrious premises.

For all its majesty, Te Whaea is essentially a refurbished exhibition and show building with some interesting architectural features and a big heart. The true character and function of the building lie in the ground-breaking activity happening within, shaped by the energy and the aspirations of the students and staff. Toi Whakaari's ability to nurture future practitioners is defined by its clarity of purpose, which is embodied in the vision of the school, evident in the quality of teaching and reflected in the multidisciplinary student body

At the end of each year, during the summer break, Te Whaea is often inhabited by outside organisations. At this time, the wairua of the building shifts, and its main purpose is suspended until the principal players return. The pōwhiri heralding the start of the new academic year at Toi Whakaari powerfully reasserts the life-force of Te Whaea.

One of many students to greet the new intake at the start of 2010 was Jade Turrall, a third-year performing arts management student. She welcomed them with the following mihi:

> We welcome you into our ever-growing community of designers, managers, technicians, costumiers, actors and directors. The six disciplines are the solid foundations of the house that holds this school so strongly. We are diverse; we do not think the same and where would the challenge be if we did? It is through our differences that we demand growth – and we strengthen, change and evolve. We may stand as different departments; but we also stand together as a whole. Although our technical learning may be different, we have the opportunity at Toi to come together, to share a different kind of learning. And it is

> through this learning that we discover a shared vocabulary, we collaborate and we stand to support each other. This is what makes Toi so unique – the people: the people like you. Bring your differences, bring your listening and bring your strength.

That was no empty rhetoric: it reflects a heartfelt understanding of the purpose of Toi Whakaari and acknowledges what the school now represents. Its evolution, from a one-year acting course set up in the early 1970s to meet the needs of an expanding theatre, radio and TV industry, to a multidisciplinary school, is a story of courage, determination, periods of crisis and enormous vision.

Today, students and recent graduates of Toi Whakaari face a much more diverse and uncertain performing arts environment than many of their predecessors. Yet it is fair to say that the school has never been in a stronger position than it finds itself in now, in which to prepare future practitioners for the dynamic changes ahead.

This book is dedicated to the six directors who, from 1970 to 2010, have left their individual mark on the New Zealand Drama School. Their particular vision has shaped the purpose and direction of the school and the career possibilities of its graduates.

Someone famously once said 'the essential matter of history is not what happened, but what people thought or said about it'. So it seemed logical that the collective voice of tutors, students and graduates who were intimately involved in the journey of the school, as well as others who influenced its direction, should be clearly heard in this book. It is not so much a history as a collection of interwoven stories of identity and survival, which chronicle the changing focus of the school and question the very purpose of performing arts in Aotearoa New Zealand.

One

The Back Story

> *'Theatre schools seem to provoke many people, particularly theatre people, to hostility. They say that theatre schools are dangerous: either because they are conventional and academic, or because they are aggressively non-conforming and so become narrow, sectarian and theoretical, if not hysterical. I will readily agree that geniuses and various romantic artists are better off without training in any school at all.'* Michael Saint-Denis

Toi Whakaari: New Zealand Drama School had its beginnings in 1970, when Nola Millar founded the Queen Elizabeth II Arts Council New Zealand Drama Training School, more commonly known as the Arts Council Drama School, or simply the Drama School.

To appreciate the circumstances surrounding the advent of the first full-time training school for actors in New Zealand, we need to consider the position of theatre in the decades leading up to 1970.

A description of New Zealand theatre in the early 1950s, provided by E. Martin Browne, editor of the British Drama League (BDL) journal *Drama*, is very revealing. He had been invited by British Drama League (New Zealand Branch) to adjudicate the 1951 BDL Festival, and shortly after he arrived back in England he wrote an extensive report on his 'Antipodean Adventure' that included the following account:

> New Zealand is still an isolated country. The main streams of the world's culture, and particularly the British culture, have not flowed through it; and though it has the will and the energy to develop itself, it needs regular and constant contact with … Britain. In theatre, New Zealand is not an easy problem …. the whole country is only two million. Half of this is in the four [main] cities with considerable distance between them. This does not make an adequate circuit on which to finance [a tour] for visiting commercial companies and the consequence has been that visits have been sporadic.[1]

Martin Browne went on to 'encourage New Zealand to build up its own theatrical profession', although he acknowledged that with such a small population it could be done on only a very limited scale, with amateur societies continuing to provide the bulk of New Zealand's theatre experience:

> The four big cities have 'repertory companies'. These are large dramatic societies, having a loyal audience membership and a powerful producing organisation. There are [also] quite a number of reps in the medium-sized towns. These companies are associated ... with the New Zealand Drama Council, which aims at building up a national theatre organisation. So far its most important work has been supplying [annual residential drama schools] for members of amateur societies. The Regional Council of Auckland runs the only professional company in New Zealand. It is part of the Community Arts Service which takes the Arts to the people on a plan not unlike that of our [British] Arts Council. They play on a fit-up basis in all the towns of the region and do very good business. Its standards, especially in presentation (New Zealand is apt to be slapdash, we found) are criticised, but its genuineness and vigour are greatly appreciated. This surely offers the best available basis on which to build a small theatrical profession.[2]

He also pointed to a 'chicken and egg' dilemma that had to be addressed before even a *small* theatrical profession could be created, and warned against any quick fix:

> The training of recruits could not be done in New Zealand, and there is a sound system of government bursaries to the English drama schools. The problem at present is that the trainees often do not come back. As things are, there is no future for an actor in New Zealand, and until there is some prospect of regular employment all the best young people will be tempted to plunge into the overcrowded English profession ... We saw that, in New Zealand, only in teaching and radio was there a living at present.
>
> A top heavy scheme for a full-blown National Theatre company could only be launched at astronomical cost, and could hardly hope to gather enough regular support to keep it going even after several years of heavy loss. A quieter beginning, with productions of a simple but imaginative kind done really well, offers much better possibilities.[3]

Thankfully, his report ended on a more positive note:

> New Zealand is a country of the future. You can feel the lack of a past, and nowhere more than in the theatre. But that lack can be made up for by drawing on the English heritage, which New Zealand regards as belonging to. You can look forward to a future which shows every promise of being bright.[4]

In 1951 Unity Theatre entered the British Drama League Festival with the premier of *The Trap*, possibly New Zealand's first 'kitchen sink' drama, written by Kate Ross and directed by Nola Millar. The production was declared the 'best play in The Festival', bringing national recognition to Nola Millar and Unity Theatre. E. Martin Browne was so impressed by the play, he took it to England for publication. This was a considerable achievement for Kate Ross, given the dearth of New Zealand plays published in the 1950s.

Contrary to Martin Browne's sage advice, a National Theatre was created, in 1953, when Richard and Edith Campion launched their national touring company, the New Zealand Players. Their ambition was to create an 'All Black' theatre for and of New Zealanders, performing plays that would appeal to audiences from Northland to Southland. Nola Millar gave up an overseas bursary to help plan the new company, working as an assistant to Richard Campion. Her sights were set on directing; but when this did not eventuate, she instead managed the company, spending much of her

Nola Millar. Winner of finals of BDL Festival, Hawera 1951

Nolla Millar and Richard Campion. NZ Players 1953. *Alexander Turnbull Library MsPapers-1563-10-01*

time liaising with the New Zealand Players Foundation, a national organisation of volunteers who arranged hospitality and accommodation for the company when on tour.

Nola Millar left the Players in 1954 for a variety of reasons, not least of all their financial instability. She felt the company was rather grand, with a repertoire that replicated the West End, whereas her heart was more in gutsy realistic theatre and in the classics.

Despite universal support for most of their national tours, geographical isolation, a scattered population and escalating transport costs caused the Players to struggle financially as they had no government support other than Edith Campion's Hannah legacy.[5] The Campions valiantly continued until 1956, when they handed control of the Players to the New Zealand Theatre Trust, with Richard Campion remaining as artistic director. They found it no easier to balance mounting debt against artistic policy, and in 1960 the Theatre Trust collapsed. Nevertheless, during its six years, the New Zealand Players had produced around thirty plays, including five New Zealand ones, and employed over a hundred actors. Nola later argued that logistical and financial problems were only secondary causes of the Players' decline, and in an article in *Landfall* she criticised the company for other shortcomings:

> Officers of the company [New Zealand Players Theatre Trust] have laid the causes of its misfortune at many doors, but have never, I think, faced the fact that the Players had failed in this first principle; they had ceased to entertain sufficient numbers of people … The Trust Board appears to have been living from day to day, and something of this attitude is reflected in its choice of plays which seem to have been selected with little regard to policy or planning. Under the Trust's Board's regime no production has been related to the one before, and the company has developed neither a personality nor a continuing tradition.[6]

The set of principles laid out by the New Zealand Players included the formation of a 'theatre school [that would] work in close connection with the Company. The School could support a small apprenticeship scheme which would perform in schools and community centres in association of the Community Arts Service.' The Players' drama school emerged in 1959 with a one-year course for eight students, operating four nights a week.

The quest for a professional theatre continued, and Nola Millar suggested a way forward in a review of *A Survey of the Arts in New Zealand*:

> It is interesting to compare the rate and the form of progress in drama with those of music, ballet and opera. In each of them, the development has been from the amateur or the occasional professional. If this is the pattern for those arts, then the New Zealand theatre of the future should take root from some activity that already exists, not be superimposed from above as were the New Zealand Players. The future for the theatre, then, appears to lie in some form of decentralisation, and in sponsoring and encouraging the growth of what we have. Perhaps [by] some small amateur group which will be at first semi-professional, and later become a professional company backed by government aid? But intensive government aid should await a company that shows signs of flowering

> and fulfilling the needs of the community. Maybe [a professional theatre company] will emerge from one of the universities, where something like the National Institute of Dramatic Art in Australia is overdue. Until we have training facilities of the highest quality, we are unlikely to achieve a truly professional theatre of our own.[7]

That observation recognised some important theatre developments across the Tasman. Construction on the Sydney Opera House had commenced in 1959, providing a highly visible sign of Australia's growing confidence and investment in the performing arts. In the same year, Australia's first full-time acting school, the National Institute of Dramatic opened under the auspices of the University of New South Wales and the Elizabethan Theatre Trust.

Four years later, NIDA launched the Old Tote Theatre Company[8] in a converted army recreation hall located at the heart of its campus, effectively connecting its training programme to its own professional theatre company. By 1967 'The Tote' had evolved to become one of two leading theatre companies in Australia. In 1966 NIDA had also launched the Jane Street Theatre to present new Australian plays, performed mainly by students of the advanced course. With its two emerging theatre companies, NIDA played an essential role in both training and supporting a new wave of practitioners, which in turn helped to fuel the prodigious growth in Australian theatre from the mid-1960s to the late seventies. The establishment of the Australian Council for the Arts in 1967, together with huge federal and state spending on infrastructure, provided emerging theatre companies with serious funding. This was an extraordinary period of theatre history, with the 'chicken and egg' both arriving at the same time.

Meanwhile, the ongoing debate about leadership and the provision of resources needed to establish a professional theatre continued in New Zealand. In the drama and ballet section of the *New Zealand Official Yearbook for 1964,* Nola Millar signalled the many hazards of establishing professional theatre on a national scale:

> The audience is not large; the population is relatively small (and scattered); factors that combine to make professional theatre a risky business. Forward thinking in the theatre today favours regional development with professional or semi-professional companies based on the main centres with their own theatres and training courses attached. From the history of our efforts so far – and from the Australian pattern of experience in similar circumstances – it seems clear that regular and substantial [financial] support is needed to foster the growth of a native professional theatre in this New Zealand.[9]

Nola's call for an 'indigenous' theatre was partly answered with the establishment of two professional theatre companies: Downstage Theatre in Wellington, in 1964, with its commitment to New Zealand writing and experimental work; and Auckland's Mercury Theatre, in 1968, which had a more hard-nosed commercial approach to programming.

In the fifties and sixties, there were few opportunities for newcomers to receive full-time theatre training in New Zealand. To get round this, a number of aspiring actors received Arts Council bursaries to study drama overseas, including Elric Hooper. After working with Ngaio Marsh in Christchurch, he left New Zealand in the late fifties to train at the London Academy of Dramatic Arts. He then worked extensively in British theatre until he returned to New Zealand in 1969. Elric was clearly not impressed by what he found when he got back:

> As I looked around the Theatre in New Zealand I was despondent. Little had seemed to have changed in the ten years I had been away. The amateurs were still in the ascendant. The Mercury, I heard was going well in Auckland. Downstage was developing on an ad hoc basis. Television had started but most of the programmes were imported and the greater part of the local productions [were] rather funny in their incompetence. There was radio, of course. But there was still no [drama] school and still no possibility of an acting continuum.[10]

Opinion was polarised on the best method of providing professional training for actors. Don Farr, writing in *New Zealand Stage* in February 1967, offered a rather conservative view:

> The problems of establishing a school are the old ones of finance, premises and personnel. A large amount of capital is required to establish a school, let alone keep it going, and it would be expenditure that showed no return for at least three years. The supports of New Zealand Theatre are far too rickety to take the weight and cost of professional training, particularly when there is an established institute for this purpose in the universities. There should be no question of any bodies other than the universities providing training for actors, not at any rate until there is a need for more advanced training than the universities can provide.[11]

Others favoured company-based training, an opinion well argued in an article by John Kim and Jonathon Hardy in *New Zealand Stage*:

> Considering the establishment of the means of training actors and others for the theatre, the following premises seem to be important: that the strength of this development is going to lie in the achievement by each theatre company. That any company concerned with its own expanding horizons and development must also be concerned with providing its own sustenance and means of growth by training young students along the lines of its development.
>
> Therefore, the only fruitful training is likely to develop from groups philosophically and actively linked [with] the parent company where [the final results] can be experienced and assessed.
>
> In contrast, a national training school established in isolation from the companies it is intended to feed, would only ever be second-best to a theatre company school. With its philosophical and possibly practical working isolation, a national school is fraught with danger of building its own impotence by developing a diploma-minded student in an academically inclined atmosphere. If [temporary economic difficulties] force the thinking towards establishing a single national school in preference to company schools the battle to establish permanently viable companies could be partly lost.
>
> The impetus for the establishment of their schools must come from theatre companies themselves and its structure should be developed appropriate to the needs then felt. Actor training is not a matter of following any specific prescribed course, which supposedly

> carries its own guarantee of turning out a finished product ... but each [company] must proceed in the way determined by its own ideals.
>
> No full-time course should be less than two years duration, and should include progressively more practical work with the company during this time. A third year should be completed as an apprentice or student with the company. No diploma should be offered, since this provides an illusory recognition of the achievement of a set standard. In fact one must recognise the reality that in the theatre there is no means of formally assessing merit, but that the value of one's work rests in its practical recognition by usage. The provision of a diploma proceeds from the fallacious reasoning about the nature of theatre, whose primary purpose is to communicate effectively; the way in which this happens can never be codified.
>
> The theatre companies should also undertake the training of directors, design students, stage management students and executive officers. No student director should spend less than a year working with the first-year of actor training before embarking on his specialist work, while the design students would take part in selected studies, in common with the actors and stage-management students, besides linking with university design courses and practical work in the theatre.[12]

There was merit in what Kim and Hardy advocated: it had methodological diversity in its favour. But the practical difficulty of company-based training lay in its need to provide consistency within a training regime across a range of disciplines, additional to the theatre company's core business. Nevertheless, in considering the training of theatre practitioners other than actors, they clearly took a broader view of industry needs at that time.

The QEII Arts Council was established in 1964 to provide financial support for the arts, and, with the formation of a Drama Advisory Panel in 1968, the Council was tasked with raising professional standards for New Zealand theatre. Its funding policy favoured regional trusts as the best means of developing professional theatre, but this had the effect of excluding amateur and semi-professional groups. This decision was predicated on the questionable assumption that a clear distinction could be made between professionals and amateurs, when in fact many amateur (or semi-professional) companies such as Unity Theatre and New Theatre in Wellington and the New Independent Theatre in Auckland had clearly demonstrated their 'professional' credentials, producing innovative work of a high standard, including plays with a recognisable New Zealand identity.

New Theatre began its life in 1959 as an amateur company run by Nola Millar and architect/designer Ronald Parker, presenting Shakespearean productions to college students. And in 1964, Nola Millar, Rona Bailey and Anne Flannery started the New Theatre School of Drama to provide 'Theatre Classes' for young people and adults.

When Nola Millar was appointed to the Arts Council Drama Advisory Panel in 1968, she found herself in a much stronger position to argue her cause – that the development of professional standards for New Zealand theatre depended on full-time professional training for actors, *in New Zealand*.

She was convinced New Zealand could make a better job of training actors than most overseas drama schools, and that a cooperative, mutually beneficial relationship between a theatre company and a drama school was the way to go. She clearly had her New Theatre in mind as the prototype for such a school.

Largely as a result of Nola's influence on the Drama Advisory Panel, actor training moved up the Arts Council's agenda. She was supported in this by the chair of the Arts Council, Bill Sheat. He was concerned about the lack of professionally trained actors to meet the growing demand from theatre and radio and, given the imminent commissioning of the Avalon TV complex in Wellington, from television. He also believed that sending people overseas to train as actors was a waste of time:

> It was misguided, it was wrong; either they didn't come back which was a big waste of time, or they came back with a whole series of attitudes which were totally unrelated to the realities and how they would operate once they got back to their own country. We were just wasting money sending people overseas. People would actually go overseas then come back and drop out with no further part in it; that was an even greater waste than coming back with a whole lot of 'northern hemisphere' attitudes.
>
> One of the things the Drama Panel had to do was to establish professional theatre. For our first few meetings we had long and earnest debates about whether it should be regional or national. The chairman of the panel, George Swann, was a very strong national man as opposed to a regional man. I was a regional man, I was going to win and George was going to lose. George being a lawyer, he came up with a compromise and that was when the New Zealand Theatre Centre was set up with the idea that we would have some national theatre while regional theatre was emerging. It wasn't too difficult after that to advance the argument that we should set up a training school for actors in New Zealand.[13]

In April 1969, Bill Sheat wrote to Basil Potter at Wellington Polytechnic to suggest that the polytechnic take on that role:

> Such training as there exists in artistic areas tend to be the responsibility of the art forms concerned. The Ballet School is entirely supported by the Arts council, for example. On the other hand, there are plenty of opportunities for training in music and the visual arts within the State Education system. It is my strong belief that the person who wishes to seek a career in the performing arts is as much entitled to be trained as your lawyers and schoolteachers.
>
> I see this training as falling into the scope of the Polytechnic rather than the University. I have spoken to Professor McKenzie of the V.U.W. English Department, and he agrees with me that the proper place for actor training is in the Polytechnic, not the University. Graduates [from university] may still find their way into the performing arts employment pool, but there will still be those for whom a university course is not suitable, and in any event most graduates are likely to be absorbed into the education system.
>
> The average talented youngster, just out of high school, is not really much use to the performing arts industry. What is needed is a couple of year's activity and experience, before they are really ready to face the public.
>
> The [acting] course would need to be worked in closely with a local regional theatre company who could provide expert tutors and practical work, in this case Downstage.[14]

In October 1969 the Arts Council formally appointed Nola Millar to set up and direct a national drama school on a one-year trial basis, using the facilities at New

Theatre. The Council was careful to establish that the arrangements for the school were 'between the Council and Miss Millar alone', and that they were in no way involved or committed to the New Theatre or to any staff employed at the school.

Two years before this momentous decision, Bruce Mason and John Pocock had published a provocative exchange of letters in their book *Theatre in Danger*, in which Mason gave the following advice for anyone wishing to train as an actor:

> I would suggest that the ability to hold an audience by personality alone, the essence of an actor's art, is a gift from Heaven and all that anyone can do, faced with such talent, is show the fortunate person how to exploit it to best advantage. The only training that I can see any value in for an actor, consists of the following. Put him on the stage, give him something simple to do and see if your attention is held by it. If he arrests you, give him vocal and physical training; if he doesn't, suggest that he 'go and learn a trade'. This art, like all others cannot be learned but only practised and the thread which leads an artist through practice to achievement is his talent, allied to his will to achieve. If you want to act, act. If the gift is there and the end is clear, the means will be available.[15]

Nola Millar may well have raised her eyebrows and questioned the wisdom of that statement in its entirety, although I suspect she was not entirely unsympathetic to Bruce Mason's point of view, as it reflected her own down-to-earth approach to (professional) actor training.

Two

Nola Millar

'A very gentle person, quietly spoken: she had an absolute commitment to the theatre.'

In the introduction to Sara Gaitanos' brilliant and affectionate biography of Nola Millar, she summarises Nola's key achievements:

> [Nola] worked on every front to raise theatrical standards, championing local playwrights, premiering the most cutting-edge plays of their time, giving actors, designers and tutors the opportunities that started their careers in professional theatre. Her seminal part led to a new awareness as the emphasis moved away from the amateur to the professional and from the parochial to the national, and a new era in the history of the arts in New Zealand. … Her vision of a strong indigenous theatre has materialised and continues to grow in the hands of her protégés.[1]

Those protégées include four of the New Zealand Drama School's five directors who followed in Nola's footsteps: George Webby, Sunny Amey, Robin Payne and Annie Ruth.

Nola's credentials to head the country's first national drama school were beyond question. She was a leading authority on theatre training. By 1970 she had established herself as a powerful instrument of change as a major theatre director, and her achievements as a teacher, broadcaster, editor, critic and writer were openly acknowledged.

Her love of theatre was initiated in the early 1930s when she joined Wellington East Old Girls' Drama Club as an actor. Nola later discovered a stronger interest – directing – and throughout the war and post-war years she directed numerous productions with the Drama Club, many of which were entered into British Drama League Festivals and met with great acclaim. By 1945 Nola had been appointed secretary and treasurer of the BDL, becoming heavily involved with the New Zealand Drama Council as administrator and tutor, as well as editing the Council's journal, *New Zealand Theatre*.

At this time, many amateur theatre companies received support and encouragement from the New Zealand Branch of the British Drama League, and from the New Zealand Drama Council, which existed solely to support its (one-hundred) member drama societies to 'overcome their problems and improve standards'. It did this through a subsidised tuition scheme and by running annual drama schools, in which Nola played a very active part.

Wellington's Unity Theatre was one of the more steadfast theatre companies to emerge in the 1940s. It had a political bias: many of its founder members were card-carrying communists or sympathisers, and initial funding for the company came from the Wellington branch of the Communist Party. Rona Bailey was one of the early members of Unity. She had joined the Communist Party in 1943, and her socialist viewpoint was reinforced by fellow ideologues, including her first husband Ron Meek. It was through Unity that Rona later met and married her second husband Chip Bailey, also a member of the Communist Party and 'the true love of her life'.

Nola Millar joined Unity Theatre in 1946. At that time, its stated intention was 'to present the problems of today's social, political, and economic life'. Although Nola supported Unity's Soviet ideals for social change, she was beyond politics. She was aware that most propaganda plays had little audience appeal or much dramatic merit, so she worked to change the perception of Unity as a political theatre by redefining its aims to produce plays that were 'sincere in their presentation of life ... [and] having real dramatic values'.[2] The phrasing, as well as the intention, of its aims was taken from the Unity Theatre movement in the UK. It was nevertheless a more definite statement than most other drama societies in New Zealand were prepared to commit to at that time.

The first production she directed for Unity was *Our Town*, in 1949, in which George Webby – a young teacher at the time – had his first major acting role, as George Gibbs.

Shirley Maddock Easther was in the cast of *Our Town* and she later recalled the strength, shrewdness, wit and compassion that Nola brought to her task:

> She came down hard on silliness, affectation, insincerity or what she styled 'nimininy piminy ways' and the whole company became so caught up with the spirit of Thornton Wilder's play we felt ourselves to be truly the inhabitants of a small New Hampshire town

Our Town, 1949. L–R: June Delahunty, George Webby, Shirley Maddock Easther

Unity Theatre, 36 Drummond Street c1950

> called Grover's Corner. I have never known anyone like Nola who could put aside so effortlessly those aspects of life she felt to be tedious or unimportant.[3]

In 1950 Nola was appointed president of Unity Theatre, and raised sufficient funds to qualify for a bank loan, enabling Unity to purchase a permanent home at 36 Drummond Street, Newtown, for £1,150, with only a small deposit of £25. The small two-up-and-two-down house had 'doubtful piles' and had to be jacked up and strengthened before alterations could commence. Under Nola's supervision, walls were knocked out to create a theatre on the ground floor with an 'official' capacity of twenty-five, although it often accommodated over 120. Unity's new theatre opened with a production of *The Madwoman of Chaillot,* cast from many of the people who had helped to refurbish the Drummond Street premises. Shortly afterwards, Nola resigned from her full-time position at the Turnbull Library to pursue her greater passion for theatre, although this was seriously challenged at times by her enthusiasm for horse racing.

As well as directing at Unity Theatre, Nola ran acting classes from the Drummond Street premises where she encouraged members to write their own plays to further the cause of New Zealand playwriting and an indigenous theatre. Nola's vision was of a theatre that would truly reflect the circumstances of New Zealand. This view was re-affirmed in 1956 when she attended a performance of *The Summer of the Seventeenth Doll* in Sydney. The play had marked a significant turning point in Australian theatrical history, and Nola believed it offered hope of a similar development in New Zealand as well.

Some years later she wrote in *New Zealand Theatre*:

> Theatrical development in New Zealand has always followed the Australian pattern – with a time lag of about ten years. If this, as I believe, is true, we should see OUR Summer of the Seventeenth Doll in the early 1960s.[4]

Later, as the theatre critic for the *New Zealand Listener,* she wrote:

> For me, no other theatrical experience has touched this one. Too seldom do we see in our theatres people in whom we can wholeheartedly believe. How doubly welcome then was a play set in a world where the characters, their appearance, accent, and idiom, all rang true.[5]

Nola strengthened her commitment to a range of training activities throughout the 1960s, including the annual Drama Council summer residential theatre schools held at Massey University.

In 1964 she formed the New Theatre School with Anne Flannery and Rona Bailey, housed in modest premises in Arthur Street. The school offered 'training in movement, mime, improvisation, speech, voice production and acting for students of sixteen years or over', with an emphasis on practical work and a creative approach to theatre. Anne Flannery taught acting and voice, and Rona Bailey taught movement. In addition to her regular classes at New Theatre, Nola found time to run weekend acting classes for 'experienced actors and past students' at Mitchelltown School in Aro Valley.

One of her 'advanced' students was a young John Callen, aged eighteen and recently arrived from the UK:

> Knowing no-one, I joined a couple of theatre groups and I was told of some theatre classes being run in an old church hall up the Aro Valley. 'She's a bit weird', I was told. 'But she's good.' Indeed, I found Nola Millar to be more than somewhat odd. Here was I, a nervous young man, suddenly confronted by people who actually knew what they were doing. Nola had this wonderful ability to always have a cigarette in her mouth, lit or not. Never did I spot her rolling one, though she must have, yet there was always one in her mouth. As she spoke, the cigarette-butt danced on her craggy lips to a tune with a decidedly Australian strain.
>
> On the spur of the moment I was expected to ad lib an improvised something – who knew what – with no words:
>
> 'Right: silent acting; communicate without words – show me: You.'
>
> 'Me?'
>
> 'Uh-huh.'
>
> I can still recall the sweat starting to lift through my pores as I delivered a piece I knew was less than wonderful. It became worse as I noticed she seemed to be listening to the radio while I was doing what I imagined to be delivering my heart and soul. It couldn't be the horse-racing, surely? I brought my piece to its conclusion, full of earnest insistence:
>
> 'Right: something precious; protecting it, losing it. Tragedy – got that? Not very exciting though. Next.'
>
> She went back to her cigarette and her radio as the young lady following me went into a dance routine:
>
> 'No, no, no. Act it; don't dance it.'
>
> I was determined to return to prove myself. The best I ever got was 'You'll do'. Praise indeed.
>
> That was the mid-sixties. By the time the New Zealand Drama School opened in 1970, I was doing regular performances for amateur groups and had already started doing walk-ons for TV. Five years later, I was working as a full-time professional at Downstage Theatre with voiceovers, radio plays, TV and, of course, stage work to my credit.[6]

New Theatre later expanded to include a semi-professional Theatre Club, operating from leased premises at 127 Cuba Street, originally the Bristol Hotel. Later, it ran from a run-down clothing factory that Nola Millar converted to provide a classroom, offices, storage space and an intimate performance space – a 'black box', with a raked auditorium, formed by rostra supported by adjustable legs. The seating was donated by Mercury Theatre that was in the process of converting the Playhouse Cinema in Auckland into the Playhouse Theatre.

Because of New Theatre's 'semi-professional' status, it received no Arts Council funding, and relied instead on income from the meagre fees paid by students and from the New Theatre Club membership. Grant Tilly recalled that production budgets at New Theatre were 'less than optimal':

> When Nola ran the 'shoebox theatre in Cuba Street', I did a number of stage designs for her, including *A Streetcar named Desire*, directed by George Webby, for which Nola gave me five pounds to 'do the set'. So I bought a couple of pots of paint and some nails, and begged and borrowed stuff to do the rest. There was a flashing neon sign outside the window of the Cuba Street premises, so we left a clearway through to the window as part of the set, to provide 'New Orleans' with a touch of flashing neon for the production.

Nola with the model for Unity Production of *After the Wedding*, 1965

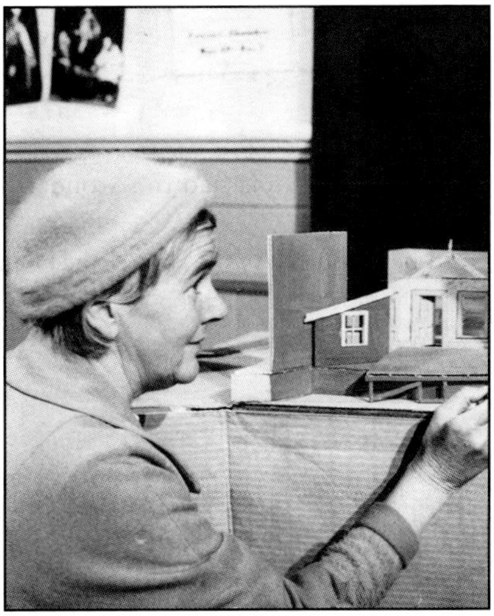

Nola and cast reading through the script of *A Dollar Bill* at New Theatre, April 1968.
ATL PAColl-0284-04-01

Nola Millar drama workshop. New Theatre, 1968.
ATL 42637-26-F

> After Downstage Theatre started, a number of people left Unity. There was no way actors would stay at Unity when they had a chance of a 'high-end' professional production at Downstage, where you could earn five pounds a week doing seven productions. I was in the first hit at Downstage, *You'll Come to Love Your Sperm Test*, by John Antrobus, in 1966.[7]

Nola continued her association with Unity Theatre and directed numerous plays for them. But she was critical of its tendency to over-commit by mounting too many productions with insufficient resources. Her idea of a professional theatre was founded on standards and training, and the provision of adequate resources, a view she was unwilling to compromise.

When Nola went to work for the New Zealand Players in 1952, she deferred a QEII Arts Council fellowship to study world theatre. In 1967 she decided to take advantage of the fellowship and embarked on a 'theatre journey' to sixteen countries, visiting theatres and schools in the USA, Canada, Holland, France, Israel and, of course, Britain.

The highlight of her time in New York was a visit to the HB Studios, in Greenwich Village, where actress Uta Hagen and her director husband Herbert Berghof ran a drama school that attracted 1500 students a year. Nola found much to interest her at the HB Studios, in particular a studio class given by Uta Hagen:

> Enthusiasm of class and teacher saw a two-hour session spill into three and a half. This was the only class I saw on my travels where *all* the students not personally involved listened and watched the whole time while others were at work being reviewed.
>
> [I also took special note of the] new equipment that the New Theatre must get, and the effective use of space, which could be copied to advantage by us at Arthur Street. This visit will bear fruit …

In England, where Nola visited major drama schools in London and the provinces, she was particularly impressed by the range of courses offered at the Central School of Speech and Drama in London. Its stage department ran a three-year diploma course for actors, with an emphasis on the core acting skills of speech and voice, movement and singing; as well as refresher and other classes for distinguished alumni, who included Peggy Ashcroft, Judi Dench, Laurence Olivier and Vanessa Redgrave:

> Yesterday I was passed by an elegant beanpole, small straw hat and long umbrella; later – transformed into flame-coloured leotard. I came across her in movement class – Junoesque, fine, couldn't make anything of her face. It was Vanessa Redgrave taking refresher classes in movement before starting a film on Isadora Duncan …[8]

Nola's response to some of the 'traditional' theatre she saw in Britain was rather mixed. After attending the Old Vic's production of *The Royal Hunt of the Sun*, she commended Robert Stephens' 'excellent, colourful and exciting moments', but thought the rest of the performance was 'rather thin really'.[9] Similarly, *Three Sisters* at the Royal Court 'just wouldn't do; all rather muted and slow, anticipating the final mood from the beginning. Poor production and an infuriating set. Royal Court really is in the doldrums.'[10] The National Theatre redeemed itself with its production of *Rosencrantz and Guildenstern are*

Dead, which Nola found to her taste: 'a mixture of theatre of the absurd and actual Shakespeare. Stunning designs; this is a real "Millar" play, which hit the jackpot more than any other.'[11]

Generally, her view of English theatre compared less favourably with the more experimental theatre she experienced in Europe and the United States. Of around sixty plays she saw during her tour, she reported that 'nothing I saw in England had the electric spark and originality of treatment of the imported American companies: the Open Theatre, the MacKayle Company of Dancers, and La Mama Cafe Company'.[12] The Traverse Theatre in Edinburgh was more to her taste: 'its miniature theatre world was most reviving and exciting, coming as it did at a point when I had become rather saturated in theatre'.[13] It had a reputation for promoting new dramatists and experimenting with dramatic and visual forms, and when Nola returned to New Zealand she incorporated aspects of the Traverse model into her New Theatre.

Despite visiting seventeen drama schools, Nola was unable to find her ideal – an integrated professional theatre school and company:

> Looking back, I think that the best work was being done at the professional theatre schools which train their students for the stage – the Bristol Old Vic, LAMDA, the HB Studio in New York and the Jacques Le Coq School in Paris. At such schools the aim is undivided. The other schools are more diversified in teaching where about fifty percent of the students are working for a teachers' course and the classes are inclined to be too large, staff and students a mixed bag, and there is a slower pace to the work.[14]

On her return to New Zealand, Nola redefined her 'ideal' drama school:

> I feel the best form of training for the professional theatre would be a school that was truly part of a professional company where school and company shared the same ideals and theatre philosophy and followed the same methods of work so that the Company was a true extension and realisation of what had been taught and practiced at the school.[15]

Given her preference for an 'integrated drama school and professional company', it seems odd that Nola chose to exclude the National Institute of Dramatic Art from her world itinerary. With its associated Old Tote and Jane Street theatres, NIDA offered a good working model of Nola's ideal drama – much closer to home.

Three

1970–1973

127 Cuba Street, 2010

'The theatre, like all arts, demands the highest possible standards. These can only be achieved by dedication and the acquisition of the necessary skills. The Arts Council's Drama Panel therefore planned a scheme to train those who want to make their life's work in the theatre. This is the beginning.' W. N. (Bill) Sheat, 1970

In December 1969 a selection panel comprised of Nola Millar, a senior representative of the QEII Arts Council and Anthony Richardson – representing 'the profession' – auditioned 'selected' applicants for the new QEII Arts Council Drama Training School. Auditions took place over a weekend at New Theatre, and included group sessions in acting, movement and speech led by Grant Tilly, John Batstone, Jacqueline Burt, Anne Flannery and Nola Millar. The tutors also acted as assessors to advise the selection panel, but they were not part of the final selection process.

Following the audition, nine candidates were chosen to attend the one-year interim training scheme, scheduled to begin in February 1970 at the New Theatre premises in Wellington. The first cohort of students was: Jean Betts, Elizabeth Coulter, Jennifer Ludlum, Denise Maunder, Joanna Miekle, John Otto, William (Bill) Petley,

Darien Takle and Bevan Wilson. The students each received an Arts Council bursary of $100–$500, and tuition fees were paid directly to the school by the Arts Council as part of the annual grant.

The nine trail-blazing students arrived at the National Ballet School in Marion Street on 9 February for an informal function to launch what was commonly known by students and staff as the Arts Council Drama School. The launch also marked the start of the academic year for the Opera School and the Ballet School – then in its fourth year. As is the case today, the 1970 drama students came from very different backgrounds, with diverse ambitions. Jean Betts (from Christchurch) had worked in children's theatre, repertory and radio. Liz Coulter (from Wellington) was simply 'passionate about theatre' and had studied dance before attending Nola's Saturday classes at New Theatre. Denise Maunder (from Australia) had an arts degree from Sydney University, where she met and married Paul Maunder, a theatre and film director. John Otto was 'tall and ethereal, in a very "I am an interesting Wellington student" kind of way'. He was not an actor, but had enrolled to study theatre design, under Raymond Boyce's supervision. Bill Petley (from Rotorua) was 'born into the wrong decade, Hollywood through and through and terribly stylish'. Darien Takle (from Auckland) 'always knew she was going to be actor' and at Auckland University 'did as-much-theatre-as-possible', performing with the Living Theatre Troupe in university reviews and outdoor Shakespeare. Bevan Wilson (from Timaru) became 'hooked on theatre' at Stagecraft in Wellington, and had attended Nola's classes at New Theatre, following a 'brush with the advertising world'.[1]

Jennifer Ludlam, 'the shy little blonde girl from Taumaranui', had performed with the local repertory society and the Children's Art Theatre in Wanganui:

> I was very keen on drama at high school and had a wonderful teacher who encouraged me and told me about Rathkeale College. I went there for ten days over Christmas, when I was seventeen, and met Paul Minifie and others who were in the Children's Art Theatre: they encouraged me to audition for Four Season's Theatre. When someone dropped out of their group, half way through my seventh-form year, I just said to my mum 'I'm leaving home', and this 'shy little girl' just hopped into the Children's Art Theatre van – and that was it. The first thing I did with them was a play at Downstage Theatre, *The Princess and the Drummer Boy*. CAT kept me on, and I toured with them in 1969. Then I heard they were starting up a drama school in Wellington. So I applied – and was very pleased to be accepted.
>
> When touring with CAT, I was paid $25 a week and we were often billeted, so I didn't spend much of my wage and was able to save. That helped to subsidise the $6 a week bursary I received from the Arts Council, plus the odd $20 note my mum sent.[2]

For Darien Takle, her first day at the Drama School was exciting – if a little daunting:

> It was a nervous bunch that fronted up to the Arts Council morning tea. Nola Millar in her cape and beret, Anne Flannery with her enigmatic smile, Jacquie Burt birdlike, Rona Bailey vibrant – arriving in her red sports car, John Batstone tall and polite, Nonnita and Phillip Mann intellectual academics bringing their experience and ideas from overseas, Deirdre Tarrant and Valerie Bayley – the dance contingent, and representatives from the Arts Council, who had ultimately handed over responsibility [for the Drama School] to Nola Millar because they believed in her ability.[3]

▲ Acting Class at QEII Arts Council Drama School, 1970. L–R: Jean Betts, Bevan Wilson, Joanna Miekle, Jennifer Ludlam, Elizabeth Coulter, Denise Maunder, Bill Petley

Caroline (Caro) Ormond 1972

The chair of the Arts Council, Bill Sheat, spoke to the students and staff about his hopes for the future of performing arts training:

> The three training courses demonstrated the Arts Council's belief that [anyone] who wished to make a contribution to the community through a career in the arts was entitled to training in the same way as [anyone] who wished to become a carpenter, teacher, or doctor. Ultimately New Zealand might have an institution adequately supported by the State, where study in all performing arts would be provided.[4]

So the Queen Elizabeth II Arts Council Drama Training School was launched, and the school year began at 127 Cuba Street. Students had classes from 9.30 to 4.30 Monday to Friday, and were on call for rehearsals and special short courses outside those hours. There were very few regulations, except that students were forbidden to attend outside drama classes or to participate in amateur or professional productions without Nola's permission. And smoking in class was *not* allowed.

Although Nola had total freedom to develop the curriculum, the teaching programme needed time to evolve. So when the Arts Council pressed her for a detailed class timetable at the start of the year, to see what was being taught, she simply (and cannily) told them that she 'liked the idea of a fluid programme'. Classes were added as the year progressed, and the timetable depended on 'the availability of tutors'.[5]

In fact, there was no need for the Arts Council to be concerned about the curriculum, as the training regime at the Drama School was rigorous. Regular daily classes included movement with Rona Bailey and Jacqueline Burt, speech and acting with Anne Flannery and Caroline Ormond (and for a while John Batstone), acting and play study with Nola, and improvisation with Grant Tilly:

> Nola didn't hire me to teach 'acting' per se; I was there to encourage students' imaginations largely through improvisational activities, in much the same way that I had studied Peter Slade and Brian Way's methods in England. Their work was largely with primary school children, freeing up their imagination using improvised drama techniques, which I had adapted for use with older drama students. They worked in their original context and I saw no reason why they wouldn't work once geared up to older students. I felt I had a reasonable handle on it, and it was a damn sight more interesting a way of engaging the burgeoning creative abilities of drama students than the way I was taught at the Central School of Speech and Drama.[6]
>
> Improvisation was always the poor relation of acting. It was done early on, and then the students moved on to text work and character studies during productions. Nola didn't appear to be confident in actually taking improvisation classes, so it wasn't used much in the rehearsal process. Instead Nola would send the students away to do 'collages' – become a collage of your character – or she would say to the student, 'Say it in your own words if you're having trouble with the text'. But that was the limit of improvisation then. Nola focused on text. She had a terrifying and annoying habit of spending a lot of time on the first and second acts of a play, without rehearsing act three, with a week to go. Her point was that by doing the ground work in terms of character, by act three the students would find it easier to learn the lines.[7]

Guest tutors included Phillip Mann, Ian Mune, Anthony Richardson, Peter Vere

Jones and Davina Whitehouse. There were other occasional sessions, or block courses, which included singing – and set construction – classes provided by New Zealand Opera; dialect with Antony Groser, the artistic director of Downstage; speech with Miss Cameron; and lighting at Downstage.

Radio drama offered real employment opportunity for Drama School graduates, and to support this Nola had persuaded the New Zealand Broadcasting Corporation to run weekly classes in microphone technique. Classes in television acting were run later on, and the NZBC acknowledged the benefit the industry derived from such activity: 'With our ever increasing commitment to locally produced TV drama we must have a continuing pool of new faces to provide diversity. With a school like this we are furthering our own future as well as the futures of the actors concerned.'[8]

John Otto, the sole design student, was without a mentor until the second term as Raymond Boyce was in Japan. So Nola set him some design and ground-plan problems to 'keep his hand in' until Raymond returned, and he also participated in all the first-term acting classes.

Undoubtedly, the Arts Council viewed the first intake of drama students as guinea pigs to test the viability of a full-time training programme before committing to a two-year programme. The students were well aware of their 'interim' status and knew they had a role to play in proving the 'experiment' worthwhile. Bevan Wilson was critical of the Arts Council's apparent lack of commitment to the school, and thought the time-frame was 'absolutely useless to allow anyone to develop [a programme]. It's as if, at the initial discussion and funding stage, the Arts Council said two years is too risky. So let's see how this year goes before we commit any more funds. We were like a trial run.'[9]

He was right: the future of the drama school and its ongoing location in Wellington were by no means secure. Mercury Theatre was hovering in the background, keen to take up the reins and establish its own full-time drama school if and when the opportunity presented itself.

If the interim one-year drama school was a test-case to assess the feasibility of a full-time training programme, what were the performance criteria by which success or failure could be measured? It is hard to say as there are no documented 'performance goals' to explain what the Arts Council required, or indeed what Nola Millar was expected to achieve in that initial trial.

Possibly, Nola saw the lack of performance criteria as a double-edged sword that was both onerous and liberating. She had almost total freedom in the way she ran the school, and was only required to make progress reports to the director of the Arts Council:

> The Arts Council didn't have any input into the course. We had total faith in Nola. In the early days it's quite clear she ran the thing on the proverbial 'oily rag'. Now it doesn't bear thinking about. But she wanted to do it and we wanted her to do it; there was a meeting of minds on that.[10]

In some respects, these were halcyon days, mercifully free of the strictures of official accountability that constantly intrude into the core business of any educational institution today.

On the other hand, the responsibility of managing the Drama School and ensuring its ongoing success fell squarely on Nola's shoulders. Her workload was intense. In addition to her considerable responsibilities at the school, she ran New Theatre courses in the evenings and weekends, and continued to direct productions at Unity and Downstage. Nola's precarious financial situation was an added burden. Although the Arts Council provided her with $7,500 to run the Drama School for the first year, she received no salary or other payments to administer the school, effectively subsidising it with income from her other enterprises.

The annual rent for the New Theatre (Drama School) premises was $3,600, of which the Arts Council contributed only $600, together with an additional $600 to cover administrative expenses, lighting and heating, and part-time clerical costs. Regular tutors were paid a 'satisfactory fee' (around $5 an hour), but there was no extra money to engage supplementary tutors to teach special topics. Nola in fact forfeited some of her own time and fees to cover these costs.

At the end of the first term, Nola reported to the Arts Council that:

> We have a group of very hard-working and conscientious students, all of whom have made progress. This has been particularly so in movement classes. Next term the emphasis will be on individual work in speech and acting when we hope to see each student develop a more dynamic and flexible range.[11]

Nola completed her report by signalling her unease about the students' future:

> I feel that uncertainty about their future clouds over the students at times. I hope that the Arts Council will consider favourably some sort of prentice year for most of them in 1971. It would be both encouraging and fair to let them know soon, what are the possibilities for them next year. The tutors show concern lest [the students] do not follow this year's basic course with some opportunity for wide theatrical experience within their apprentice year, so they can continue to grow.[12]

The students responded favourably to the tightly structured curriculum and made good progress. It is also clear that Nola and other tutors at the school were held in high regard by them:

> *Bevan Wilson.* Of all the regular tutors I liked Grant Tilly. He was always jolly, fun, and we could see him working on stage. He was what I hoped to grow into – a working professional. Ian Mune was particularly exciting. He did mask with us, and this was my first introduction to the indescribable, the sheer magic of theatre. I hated movement. God knows I needed coordination. But all that free expression through movement defeated me. I came to dread seeing either of the two Ronas greeting us on a freezing morning, leotarded and tambourined to buggery. And of course there was Nola. Teacher is the wrong word to ascribe to Nola. She never 'taught' as such – just guided, steered and directed. In her professional work, Nola always created an atmosphere of collaboration. She always seemed to be surprised by the world as if everything was new to her. She was constantly delighted by the good work of others. Little bird-like screw-up of the face – and light but heartfelt applause with clapping hand in front of her face. I know she liked my work, and

when I did well in her opinion she was never too effusive in her praise. She simply found a moment to give my hand a little squeeze and whisper 'well done'. These were glowing moments for me.

Denise Maunder. I really admired Nola. She was a legend indeed. I can simply remember the twinkle in her eye, her betting, her berets, her unusualness, her sharpness. Nola was highly regarded at the time, though her eccentric persona wouldn't have survived in the age of mission statements and accountability. She was a one-off – an original.

Jennifer Ludlam. Rona Bailey: loved her classes – loved her stuff. Throw your words, rolling, floating. Nola: blue beret, bustling, beautiful clear blue eyes – sort of lit from within and a beautiful face. She was very kind to me – nurtured me a lot. I didn't like being called into her office and being told off. Had a bit of trouble with Jacqui Burt who made me continue with a movement class when I'd hurt my back, and I've had terrible back trouble ever since.

Darien Takle. Rona Bailey came in with her tambourine and wearing black leotards and away we went with gusto and lots of action. Anne Flannery was probably the one who had the most influence on me because she was so giving and approachable and tremendously helpful when I announced I was pregnant. The main thing I remember about Anne is her huge worn tan leather bag which seemed to carry lots of milk bottles and books and a complete household. She would stagger up the steps at 127 with this 'portmanteau' and it would land clinking and clanking at her feet. Then she would give us one of her enigmatic smiles and talk slightly out the side of her mouth, but she knew her craft and was a fine actress. We all enjoyed any work of Grant Tilly because he was funny and very good at his craft – and was a professional actor. Nola knew her craft and exactly what she wanted. Although she didn't say a lot, she [guided] us in an expert way – helping us to create our own characters without imposing her direction on us. Nola was exceptionally wise and 'knew' things. She did not suffer fools gladly. I think she was incredibly shy and seemed to always be on the move, highly intelligent and not one to [accept] emotional indulgence.[13]

When Darien Takle became pregnant in her first term at the school, Nola dealt with this dilemma with great compassion, especially at a time when unmarried mothers were frowned upon. Darien was given time off school to consult a doctor and to consider her options, which she did, and decided to continue with the pregnancy. She feared she would be thrown out of the course, but Nola continued to be quietly supportive, employing her to do secretarial work at the school, something Nola could probably ill afford:

> She said it was her [school] and her decision and I could stay as long as I felt able. I wouldn't be surprised if she paid me out of her own money. I think she recognised my determination and my total commitment to theatre and acting, and the fact I was determined to be a really hard-working student. How courageous was that … to allow me to stay?[14]

Darien Takle's pregnancy wasn't the only 'pastoral' problem that Nola had to cope with during the first year. Denise Maunder had a motorbike accident and spent considerable time with her leg in plaster, Joanne Meikle broke her leg in a skiing accident and had to pull out of the school in the final term, Jennifer Ludlum burnt her face on a sun lamp and Bill Petley contracted pneumonia.

Production activity at the school was largely confined to the end-of-year graduation plays: *Suddenly Last Summer*, *Happy Haven* and *Lunch Hour*. Most of the students appeared in both *Suddenly Last Summer* and *Happy Haven*, except for John Otto who designed the sets and stage-managed all three plays, and Joanne Meikle who had by now left the school.

Jennifer Ludlum, Bevan Wilson and Darien Takle were in *Lunch Hour*. Darien Takle played the (pregnant) Landlady, with Bevan Wilson and Jennifer Ludlam as the husband and wife. Bevan recalled *Lunch Hour* as 'a three-hander comedy thing about a tryst in a hotel room. I think it was Nola's idea of a showcase for me and Jennifer's comedy skills, with lots of climbing in and out of windows.'[15]

A quirky aspect of this season of plays is that Darien Takle, almost nine months pregnant, managed to perform in all three productions, including the improbable role of a nun (Sister Felicity) in *Suddenly Last Summer*.

In addition to their graduation productions, the students joined the Ballet School as supernumeraries in *Sleeping Beauty* at the Opera House, an early inter-school collaboration that was clearly viewed by some as a mixed learning experience, in particular Bevan Wilson:

> I was taken out of the peasant's picnic scene because I could not step and skip in the right order. I ended up as a supernumerary with the very important role of the Herald. I was appalled at my costume, a little bolero tunic thing that didn't come down nearly far enough at the front and exposed all including my skinny legs. I remember trying on a pair of tights and checking myself in the mirror. I was aghast – so I secretly added five more pairs of tights until I was pleased with the way my legs had thickened up. I looked like I was getting around on a couple of telegraph poles. However, I remember the devotion and absolute focus of the ballet school students, and our collective awe of their ability to pick up steps in a flash, and my feeling of wankery that we [drama students] were farting around while all this was going on.[16]

Before graduating, the students auditioned for a group of directors from various professional theatres. The Arts Council in collaboration with some of the theatre companies had recently introduced an apprenticeship scheme to provide additional training for actors, enabling some of the students to gain employment with those companies when they graduated. Bevan Wilson joined Mercury Theatre as a student actor and remained with the company for four years. Jean Betts stayed in Wellington to work at Downstage and then moved to the Gateway Theatre in Tauranga. Jennifer Ludlum went straight to Four Seasons Company in Wanganui to work with Paul Minifie. And Denise Maunder joined the Amamus Theatre Group, founded by her husband Paul Maunder, and performed in productions at Downstage and New Theatre. Liz Coulter and Darien Takle were offered a second year at the Drama School.

Jennifer Ludlam, by her own admission a shy country girl when she moved to Wellington, used her time at the Drama School to 'grow up':

> I was far too young. But it was wonderful for me, and hugely beneficial: it's where I met my community. It was a really good introduction to the theatre world. I still use some of the voice exercises and warm-ups that I learnt then, and still have a little book that I've kept on some of the ways of approaching characters, which I still use.
>
> I remember Nola saying to me at the end of the year that I had 'travelled the furthest distance'; but then I probably needed to. I had the opportunity to go back for another year, but by then I had a job at Four Seasons, which was a great training ground anyway. Then I went to Gateway Players in Tauranga, worked a little bit at Centrepoint Theatre and then at Central Theatre in Auckland. Also in the mid-seventies TV2 started and I was in a lot of their drama stuff. From there I went to Theatre Corporate and Mercury Theatre, and in 1980 I went to Australia to work, including *Playschool* presenter: a great bread-and-butter job. I returned to New Zealand in the mid-eighties to work at Downstage and Circa, and a couple of big TV things for Gibson's: *Cover Story* and *Undercover*.
>
> The year I had at Drama School was what it was – no point in hanging on to something that was actually finished. But a year was far too short.[17]

As for the other three students from that year, it appears Bill Petley left New Zealand forever in 1979 to live in Australia and is now a newspaper columnist – who avoids theatre. Rumour has it Joanne Meikle became an air hostess, but no word of John Otto.

In any event, the Arts Council judged the first year of the Drama School to be a success and confirmed it was 'well and truly established with many candidates around New Zealand applying for the 1971 intake'.[18]

By the end of 1970 Nola's expanded workload had taken its toll, undoubtedly contributing to a decline in her health, and in December she collapsed and was rushed to Wellington Hospital. Shortly after being admitted, she underwent major surgery to remove a tumour and was not expected to survive. For a while, her life hung in the balance, and she needed many weeks in hospital and a lengthy period of convalescence to recover from the surgery.

However, Nola was irrepressible and continued to organise the 1971 school year from her hospital bed in order to ensure that it began as planned, in February, with a new intake of students. In a letter to David Peters (director of the QEII Arts Council) written from her hospital bed, she added this postscript: 'This year's class is a good one and I think it could far outshine last year's, except for Jean Betts.'[19]

During Nola's absence, the Arts Council arranged for Sunny Amey (who had recently been appointed artistic director of Downstage) to act as consultant director for the Drama School, and contracted Anne Flannery as principal tutor. Liz Coulter and Darien Takle were asked to defer until Nola returned to the school later in the year. Although Darien resumed her studies, she decided to leave halfway through her second year to devote more time to her new baby daughter.[20]

Nola managed to return to the school after Easter, and directed plays at New Theatre and Downstage, as well as the Drama School graduation production *Underground Lovers*, at the end of 1971.

Michael Nicolaidi succeeded David Peters as director of the Arts Council in October

Anne Flannery with Nola Millar at the Drama School

Happy Haven, 1970. L–R: Jennifer Ludlam, Elizabeth Coulter

▲ Above: 1971 Intake with staff (Sunny Amey as acting director). Standing L–R: Jackie Burt, Sunny Amey, David Seath, Rona Bailey, Bill Sheat, Anne Flannery, Christopher Howell (student). Front row (students) L–R: Marion Gottlieb, Stephen Crane, Ross Duncan, Anthea Harper, Roslyn Everett.

▼ Below: *Underground Lovers* 1971. L–R: Ross Duncan, Christopher Howell, Marion Gottlieb, Anthea Harper, Roslyn Everett, Stephen Crane

1971. He had previously worked with Nola at Unity Theatre, and had encouraged her to develop the school. He firmly believed the work being done in the training area of the arts was 'the most important part of all the Council's activities'.[21] The following year, the Arts Council increased the Drama School's grant to $9,000, paying Nola a salary of $3,000 for the estimated two-thirds of the time she devoted to running the school. In addition, she received $500 to hire supplementary tutors and directors. Student bursaries were also increased by $200, and it was recommended that the Drama School should be provided, as 'funds permit', with mirrors and a tape recorder: the 'CapEx' era had arrived at last.

The entire selection process for entry into the Drama School remained the Arts Council's prerogative. Applications in writing were submitted directly to the Arts Council, which then created a shortlist based on the applicants' qualifications (if they existed) and other credentials – such as prior amateur or professional experience. The shortlisted applicants were subsequently auditioned in Wellington.

About a week after the two-day audition process, which included group scene work, showings of individual audition pieces and interviews with the audition panel, candidates were notified whether or not they had been accepted.

David Broughton (who later adopted his Māori name, Rawiri Paratene) was one of twenty or so applicants selected to audition for the Drama School in 1971. He was born in Hokianga and is from the Ngā Puhi iwi. His first theatre experience was at the age of fifteen, when he attended a performance of *Hamlet* at Mercury Theatre, which proved to be a major turning point in his life:

> I went to hoon around and get time off school – I had no expectation, in other words, I went there to flirt with Catholic girls. The lights went down – and from that moment I was captivated – totally captivated. It wasn't anything I expected. This young man [Hamlet] was going through all this stuff, and even though I wasn't being put through the turmoil that he was being put through – that was me. I saw a play about me, and I identified with every single thing. I knew at that moment there was such power in theatre, and I knew I wanted to be a writer of drama. I wrote a letter to Tony Richardson, the director of Mercury and said, 'My name is David Broughton, I am a fifteen-year-old fifth-former and I want to come and work for you next year.' That's how strong it was. He advised me to go back to school and write to him again later. So I went back to school. I had a lot to say – political thoughts in my head [about] my Māori-ness and I saw that drama was a powerful way of saying what I wanted to say. The written word had suddenly become very powerful – this man who died 400 years ago had spoken to me directly, as directly as my father – and with such power – and that was for me.[22]

David then joined a local drama group, performing in *Aladdin*, *Oklahoma!* and *A Midsummer Night's Dream*. He wrote again to Tony Richardson, who told him to apply for Drama School, which he did. Thinking that his parents would not approve, he decided not to tell them he had been selected for audition. Instead he told them he was going to stay with his friend 'down the road': 'To this day they don't know that I went to Wellington.'[23]

> I [arrived at] Cuba St for the audition. I was told to bring warm-up gear. Well I was a

> rugby player, and warm-up gear was what I went to training in; big baggy shorts, ripped old rugby shirts, and I had a headband because I wore my hair long. That's what I looked like. Well, I walked into leotardville. Everyone had these leotards – I had never seen a leotard before. I felt so much the odd man out – the only Māori and the only one who didn't have leotards. It was a long day and we went through a series of improvisation and movement classes. I was so raw – it was a foreign world to me, and I felt I was going so badly. It really wasn't my cup of tea. And I thought there must be other ways of getting into the theatre and this probably wasn't going to be for me. Then we were interviewed by the panel: Tony Richardson, Sunny Amey, Nola Millar, Bill Sheat and Mike Nicolaidi, and possibly John Reid. He asked me, 'Why do you want to be an actor? There must be some pressure on you to go to university because of your academic record.' I replied, 'I want to be an actor because I want to know what problems an actor has to face because I want to write for actors.' That was the most honest thing that I could say – and I knew it would get me in.[24]

Of the twenty or so applicants who auditioned in 1971, nine were chosen for the 1972 intake. Some had previous acting or drama experience, including Patricia Birdling, who had worked with Paul Maunder's Amamus Group; Linda Sexton, who had acted with amateur theatre groups and at university; and Annie Ruth (present director of Toi Whakaari), who had recently completed her degree at Victoria University with Phil Mann. Annie was the oldest member of 1972 intake, at twenty-three; and David Broughton, then seventeen, was the youngest.

Annie Ruth was passing through a stage in her life when she wore lots of wigs, and apparently it took several weeks for other students in her class to figure out she was the same person! She was married and because of this she received a smaller grant than the others; to make ends meet she worked as a cocktail waitress. Nevertheless, unlike today, the bursaries were unconditional and tuition fees were fully covered by the Arts Council.

Morning classes began with movement, taken by Rona Bailey or Jacqueline Burt at the Dorothy Daniels Dance Academy next door to the Drama School. Annie recalled trying to navigate the stairs after her first movement session: 'A lot of us went down the stairs on our bums – we were so shocked how hard the work was.'[25] Movement was usually followed by voice, singing and text classes taken by Anne Flannery.

For David Broughton, Drama School was a whole new world:

> In that first week my whole understanding of theatre was turned upside down. I suddenly started to realise I didn't understand the half of it. I was exhausted and had never met anything as physically demanding as drama school. I thought it was going to be an intellectual exercise – a tool to develop my political feelings and I wasn't expecting something that would physically drain me. But then I thought, it was choice, this drama school thing is physical: I'm good at physical and I've got good rhythm and I can dance any step you give me. I'm going to do alright here. Rona made me feel good about myself and I loved the sweat she made us do – I lived for that.[26]

The relatively small number of students at the school meant that they appeared in all productions, which were mostly confined to studio workshop showings except for the graduation show, *The Madwoman of Chaillot*. This was the only production Nola directed at the school that year; she felt the students needed exposure to a range of directing styles. As a result, Annie Ruth worked with three other directors during that year, each with a different rehearsal methodology:

> Anne Flannery was extraordinary; we all thought she was amazing. We saw her in *Turn of the Screw* at Downstage. She was really an impressive actor and pushed us to fit more within the role. Nola encouraged me to be a bit more flamboyant. She did a lot of the choreography of stage movement and paid a lot of attention to the details of how we moved. Anne [Flannery] was much more about thinking oneself inside the role, and her own work was like that.
>
> Caro [Caroline Ormond] was Grotowski influenced; very experimental – looking at the profound connection between who you are and what you created. I remember that, for our very first class with her, we lined up outside the room and went in one by one. As part of that first assessment tutorial she gave each of us a back and shoulders massage (and massage was not the commonplace thing in 1972 that it is today) and we all fell totally and irrevocably under her spell. I remember her as golden – she brought a glow with her wherever she was and huge belief in each of us that helped us in our own self-belief.
>
> In one voice class towards the end of the year, we sat in a circle with our eyes closed and had to send sounds to someone else in the circle. With only the aural as a clue, we were able unerringly to tell who was the recipient of each sound and that seemed miraculous at the time. With Caro we gained a sense of a wider world filled with mystery and possibility – a world to which we could contribute.[27]

Nola was appreciative of people's individual qualities and observed with incredible intensity. Annie Ruth remembered one particular instance when the students played a game where they put things on a tray, and after looking at them were asked to identify them by touch:

> I remember David [Rawiri Paratene] getting freaked out touching some of the stuff. It conjured other things for him, and Nola was on to that; she clearly understood it in a way that we didn't. She really got that sense of the forbidden – spiritual or demonic aspect of the world; unseen forces. Nola was a person of huge integrity. The one major thing I learnt from her is that if you are a teacher, the people you teach are more important than you are, and with Nola that was always utterly so.[28]

Reflecting on his time at the school, Rawiri Paratene has especially fond memories of Nola:

> I've always got on well with old people and brainy people and Nola had lots of that. She had character. I liked her because she was shy ... and shyness was a big part of my life, and I didn't see that as problem. The thing I also liked about Nola was her knowledge of Shakespeare. The main skill she was interested in teaching us was observation. She gave me a keener eye than I'd ever had. She would send us out into the street and we [had] to observe [people] and their mannerisms, how they moved and their rhythms.[29]

Some students were frustrated by the limitations of a one-year acting programme. They felt the need for more time and training to decipher and practise the various methodologies they had encountered, before they could usefully apply what they were learning to their performance process.

David Broughton (Rawiri Paratene) 1972

Madwomen of Chaillot, 1972. Annie Ruth (R) and Griselda Goring-Johnstone (L).

Annie Ruth was clearly affected by this constraint. She had reached an essential point of discovery, but nevertheless appreciated the opportunity she had been given to develop her acting skills and to experience a new way of learning:

> We knew at the end, especially with the exploratory voice work we'd started to do with Caro, that we were just hitting something that could be miraculous and that we would not get the chance to open that out. So we were really quite upset about that; the sense of that possibility being opened but not being able to achieve it. But again there was no other training in New Zealand, [and] it was miraculous to get a year and we didn't have anything to compare. It was the first time that I knew you could learn through your body, your voice, your mind, your emotions and your ethics. I often went home completely at the edges of what I could cope [with]. It was a huge experience and a complete contrast to university, and to my mind much more valuable.[30]

Along with other students of their generation, the 1972 Drama School students were politically aware. Political activism had reached a peak; students openly expressed their beliefs by participating in political protests and campaigns to support various movements and to show group solidarity.

Māori protest groups formed part of the progressive social movement, and David Broughton joined the Wellington chapter of Ngā Tamatoa (The Young Warriors). They organised demonstrations and pickets to draw attention to Māori concerns about loss of culture, language[31] and identity. In September 1972, Ngā Tamatoa petitioned Parliament, requesting courses in Māori language and culture be made available to both Māori and Pākehā students in all New Zealand schools in a 'positive effort to promote a more meaningful concept of integration'.[32]

David's attention began to shift from the Drama School to Ngā Tamatoa, and he spent most of his third term in a tent embassy erected outside Parliament for the 1972 elections. This commitment conflicted with his Drama School training and he struggled to attend rehearsals for the graduation production, bringing him close to being dropped from the school. But Nola did not give up that easily: she saw an opportunity for David to gain something valuable from his recent political experience and for him to use that to determine his future.

During his end-of-year interview, Nola gave David a speech to read from *Troilus and Cressida*: it was about making choices, and it proved to be a turning point in his life:

> That piece said to me – in a military movement everyone has a role to play and that movement will not be successful if that role is not played. If I was put on the earth to play a particular role and you are now turning that role down, then the thing that has been important to you all your life will fall down. It's as if she had said to me that there are lots of people who are going to be political activists over the coming years, but how many actors – how many writers? And no political movement has ever been successful without the actors, and without the writers. What she was saying is – you are here for the same purpose that you are in Ngā Tamatoa. You are going to be one of the first Māori actors; one of the first people to speak in drama terms about the issues of [your] generation. That's what the piece said to me. I knew then in my heart that I was going to continue on with my theatre career.[33]

When David graduated from the Drama School, Tony Richardson offered him an apprenticeship at Mercury Theatre. His first role in 1973 was in Tom Stoppard's *Jumpers*, in which he played an acrobat and had to dance: David was clearly in his element.

Annie Ruth recalled that there was 'a slight sense of injustice' among some of David's classmates when they learned he had been offered work at Mercury: 'He had missed miles of school, lots of classes, and was always one foot in and one foot out because of his politics, but I remember Nola saying to us "It doesn't work that way." Of course, Nola was right, David was a young Māori guy with a very strong presence and that would have made him very attractive.'[34]

It is significant that many supporters of Ngā Tamatoa are now in the vanguard of thinking and action in the Māori world, including prominent academics, broadcasters, educators, film-makers, lawyers, scientists – and, of course, actors.

When Elric Hooper returned to New Zealand in 1972 to work at Mercury Theatre, he visited the Drama School and noticed that 'quite astonishing things had happened':

> Best of all there was a school. Nola Millar, that courageous and disconcertingly honest woman, was running a sensible full-time training scheme for aspirant actors in Wellington. Many of these actors are now the backbone of the Mercury and Downstage companies. The school's foundation was a symbol of many things but especially the acceptance of the notion that New Zealand was now mature and large enough to sustain an acting profession.[35]

Elric Hooper later returned to the school as a tutor to run various block courses; and Annie Ruth and Rawiri Paratene went on to make their own considerable contribution to the development of the New Zealand Drama School.

Narrow Road to the Deep North, Downstage Theatre 1972. Drama School students operating puppets, with Ian Mune and Janice Finn.

The Nonentity, 1972. L-R Rex Merrie, Annie Ruth, Kathryn Rawlings, Patricia Birdling, Griselda Goring-Johnstone.

Four

1973

'It should not be less than two years, otherwise best not to offer it all.'

By 1973, professional theatre in New Zealand had substantially increased, providing greater employment opportunities for Drama School graduates. Downstage Theatre and Mercury Theatre were thriving; the Court Theatre in Christchurch, Four Seasons Theatre in Wanganui and Gateway Theatre in Tauranga were now established; and Theatre Corporate in Auckland, Centrepoint in Palmerston North and the Fortune Theatre in Dunedin were about to open. And there were fringe groups, such as Amamus and Theatre Action.

For Nola Millar, 1973 was a challenging year: her health continued to deteriorate and she became increasingly fragile. Nevertheless, she managed to teach and found sufficient energy to direct *Taming of the Shrew* and *A Southerly Wind* at New Theatre, and the end-of-year graduation production at the Drama School. During this time, the Arts Council provided Nola with some additional support by persuading Mercury Theatre to release Bevan Wilson (a graduate of 1970) to work as a tutor at the school for ten weeks.

Realising that important decisions had to be made about the future of the school, Nola wrote to Mike Nicolaidi at the Arts Council to express her concern over the lack of space in the New Theatre premises: 'The School has now taken wing and needs a self-contained space of its own. The arrangements will work for this year, but there must be a change in 1974. The tutors and I will discuss what we think are the basic requirements from our point of view.' Towards the end of her letter, she signalled even more profound concerns: 'I have been proud and happy to have laid the foundations, but the fifth year should bring a new and younger director. The school is ready to leap forward and 1974 is the year.'[1]

A few months later, she wrote to the Arts Council to submit her resignation as director of the Drama School. The Council responded by convening an urgent one-day meeting in Wellington to bring together 'interested parties' to discuss a range of options for the school. In addition to the artistic directors of *all* the major professional theatre companies in New Zealand,[2] the Arts Council invited other interested parties to the meeting, including Tony Groser, ex-artistic director of Downstage; Bill Austin from NZBC; Nola Millar; George Webby, then a senior lecturer in drama at Wellington Teachers' Training College; Phillip and Nonnita Mann; and Grant Tilly. It is hard to think of a group of practitioners who could more usefully advise on the future of the school, and their willingness to attend the meeting at such short notice was an acknowledgment of the gravity of the situation.

Before the meeting, the participants were asked to consider several issues: the length of the course and the status of the Drama School, staffing and salaries, future premises and facilities, and the need for a curriculum sub-committee.[3] With this information, it was hoped the group would be able to formulate a set of guidelines that would assist them to make recommendations on the future direction of the school. And yet the over-riding issue to be dealt with was the very *survival* of the school.

George Webby had earlier visited Australia, at the Arts Council's behest, to discover what he could about the way drama schools were run there. From his observations at the Queensland Theatre Company and at NIDA, and also referring back to his experience at the Dallas Theatre Center and other travels in the USA and Canada, George produced a report, *Professional Training in Australia.* This included some general recommendations about the future of the QEII Drama School and formed the basis of the agenda for the 'Wellington meeting'. As the report also defined the future direction and status of the New Zealand Drama School, it is worth taking a moment to consider what was in it.[4]

The report commenced by observing that NIDA was offering three-year training in *all* its full-time diploma courses (acting, technical production and design), and that the acting course carried with it both prestige and excellent job prospects for graduates. The report then went on to compare New Zealand actors with their Australian counterparts and their ability and willingness to move between performance opportunities:

> Many actors [in New Zealand] do not consider work in commercials to be real acting. This distinction does not seem to apply in Australia where TV commercials bring actors recognition, and there seems to be a free exchange [between] radio and TV drama, commercials, straight theatre and musicals. There is something oddly healthy about this kind of exchange; stemming from activity that is distinctly Australian. Can we in New Zealand point to the same non-elitist interests in the arts, and in particular the arts of this country?

Part of the report contrasted NIDA's resources with those of the QEII Drama School:

> The Drama School in New Zealand is no more than a token gesture of our responsibilities towards the drama of our country. Much of it has been done almost as an act of charity by Nola Millar who has, by using her own personal resources, deluded many of us into believing that drama training is inexpensive. It is not. For instance, the amount used by the QEII Arts Council in helping to maintain its drama school would not pay the salary of John Clark – the Director of NIDA.[5]

The report recommended an increase in funding for the Drama School: 'QEII must find sources for funds – private, bequests, interested bodies (such as the Education Department, NZBC, and the professional theatres) and public subscriptions. QEII hand-outs will never be enough.' This was followed by a somewhat prescient suggestion that expenditure savings could be made through the consolidation of arts training within an 'Institute of Performing Arts in New Zealand, with the Drama School and possibly the Ballet School at its nucleus':

> The greatest argument in favour of such a centralised grouping is the saving in overhead and administrative expenses. Such a move must be made as soon as possible, for the only difference between doing it now and doing it later will be the predictable escalation in costs.

The key recommendations in the report can be summarised as follows:

1. extending the Drama School programme immediately from one year to three years, consisting of two years' training at the Drama School plus a one-year apprenticeship at an approved professional theatre or institution;
2. substantial salaries for full-time and part-time tutors, in order to provide the best available tuition for the students;
3. a certificate of proficiency at the end of two years, and a diploma at the end of the apprenticeship, to increase the status of graduates;
4. a living allowance to be paid to all students, and scholarships to be made available for students having financial difficulties;
5. the academic year to be shortened to two sixteen-week terms, with a two- or three-week break in between, which would provide students with a longer summer break, enabling them to raise money with a holiday job, rather than having to work during the school terms ('An exhausted trainee is a useless trainee');
6. QEII to set up a Board of Studies, responsible for the general conduct of the Drama School.

The report also recommended that the Drama School should be located close to a well-established professional theatre; to the NZBC, television and radio facilities; and to 'a variety of experiences, other than theatrical'. The school's location relative to the tutors' other work was considered to be important factor in giving the school access to the best available expertise.

Although a longer training programme at the Drama School was recommended, the report acknowledged that the school was 'not currently in a position to run a two-year programme with a yearly intake. Consequently there is some virtue in considering a biennial intake of students into the school.' It was also recommended that the existing (1973) intake of students be given the opportunity to re-enrol for an additional twelve months' training, in 1974.[6]

When George Webby opened the Wellington meeting, he got straight to the point by stating his view on the length of the Drama School's programme: 'It should not be less than two years – otherwise best not to offer it all.' But he still doubted that the school was in a position to run a two-year course with a yearly intake, as it would put too much pressure on the facilities and tutors. Having said that, he then proposed that a third year of training could be achieved by sending students to NIDA.

Tony Richardson's preference was for a yearly intake: 'a two-yearly (biennial) acceptance would leave some people adrift, finding themselves between intakes. It would also mean that apprentices would only come on to the market every two years.' He didn't favour George's third-year NIDA option, for he believed the New Zealand Drama School programme needed to be progressive: 'developing coherently from year to year, with reference to the local situation and the needs of the New Zealand market'. Instead, Richardson felt a better option was for a third-year apprenticeship with a theatre company, but that this needed to be in harmony with the preceding two years. He also favoured secondments to professional theatres, allowing students to 'get an idea of the conditions pertaining in professional theatre and to rub against the problems of working in a group'.

Although Nola Millar supported the idea of an annual intake for a two-year course, she insisted that the prevailing physical conditions at New Theatre would accommodate only around twelve students.

Phillip Mann also preferred a two-year programme with a yearly rather than a biennial intake, on the basis that this would feed the development of a 'continuing revolution in the thinking' within the school. The longer training programme would produce a more creative breed of graduates who could 'set up new systems and create opportunities that would change thinking on theatre, and provide a general push in the development of theatre each year: New Zealand could accommodate twelve well-trained drama school graduates coming on to the market each year'.

David Carnegie introduced a somewhat radical idea, suggesting that courses could be run in shorter or varied capsules of time, alternating with practical experience in the industry. George Webby like this idea, and felt it was similar to the practice at teachers' training college where students were sent out 'on section', a structure well-suited to the requirements of drama students and theatres.

The discussion then broadened to consider the possibility of introducing courses other than acting. Nonnita Mann did not favour an actor-oriented Drama School; she believed it ought to include designers and directors, with their training delivered in 'parallel with the school's "normal function"'. Phillip Mann added that 'drama' students would also benefit from a total concept of production and all other aspects of theatre, not just acting, as this would make them 'more useful in the theatre as they would have a total picture of what goes on'.

Nola agreed there was a basic need for training people with an interest in stage management and production, but she felt that as things were they could be 'picked out and sent to NIDA'. George totally disagreed with that suggestion: 'if a student showed potential as a director or designer [s/he] should be able to train and develop within the school, interspersed with practical work in a professional theatre company'.

David Carnegie made a case for safeguarding the status of theatre practitioners other than actors:

> We must not assume that the drop-outs from the acting school will be stage managers and so on. Directors, designers and other back-stage crew must not be considered as people working on the 'second string to their bows' i.e. people who would like to be actors but have not made it. These other skills must not be denigrated.

Clearly, this topic was divisive. In any event, it was certainly not the best time for such contentious proposals, and George Webby encouraged the meeting to return to the more immediate matter of 'how to get the drama school off the ground by next February'.

Sunny Amey called for more time to 'weigh up the present and future needs of the Drama School, including its location', and recommended that the school be 'put into recess for 1974'. A one-year holding period also struck a chord with the NZBC as it reflected the level of support it could provide to the school, as Bill Austin explained:

> The Corporation would be in a no-man's land for the new broadcasting structure in 1974, but would be in a position to be more generous to the School when the future pattern of broadcasting was clearer, in 1975.

Nola Millar felt that a one-year recess would break the continuity of the school, and agreed it could be held at its present level for one more year, 'giving the new Director time to offer [his or her] ideas about the development and expansion of the school'.

This provoked a firm response from George Webby, who reminded the meeting that they had already agreed that a one-year course was inferior. What's more, 'it is nonsense to continue this model for another year. To hold off making a decision until more research is done is exactly the way governments continue with a pattern which is proven to be bad.'

Eventually, the meeting moved on to consider less weighty matters, including the audition process and the qualification to be offered by the school. It was suggested that a diploma would recognise the standard and worth of the acting course, although not everyone agreed. With regards to the entry age, participants concurred that students should be at least 'one year out of high school', but concern was expressed about the upper age limit: if students were too old, or already had a university education, they may be 'set in their ways', 'so it would be wise to discourage potential acting students from going to university and developing an over-cerebral approach'.

George Webby closed the meeting, re-stating the fundamental purpose of the Drama School:

> It is essential that training is seen not only to feed an existing theatrical pattern, but to change the direction of theatre in this country. This means that the Director appointed must have a strong point of view and must be acquainted with the situation here. At the same time training must *not* be geared solely to what theatres think they need. I cannot stress too much that any change within theatres must spring from knowledge of theatre forms and from an established discipline. It must not be allowed to spring from ignorance.

Although some agenda items remained unresolved, there was unanimous agreement on the single most important issue: that the Drama School should offer a two-year programme starting in 1974. This agreement was stated in the final 'minute' of the meeting, short and to the point: 'It was agreed that the sum of $50,000 was the minimum sum required to set up a full-time two-year course in theatre beginning in 1974.' This gave the QEII Arts Council a mandate to proceed with plans to establish a new drama school the following year.

Transitions

So everything was hunky-dory? Well, no. During the ensuing months, there was much wrangling, with one group fighting to retain the Drama School in Wellington and another lobbying for it to be based in Auckland. For a while, the situation became very confused.

Shortly after the 'Wellington meeting', the chair of the Arts Council William (Bill) Sutch wrote to the Prime Minister (Rt. Hon. Norman Kirk)[7] recommending that the government establish a New Zealand School of Performing Arts to 'give advanced training for those who are to be professionally occupied as performers or teachers in the performing arts'. It was proposed that this should be located at the New Zealand Broadcasting facility in Avalon, a proposal endorsed by several eminent social and cultural bodies and supported by the Adam Committee on Broadcasting. This represented an ambitious amalgamation of training possibilities, all housed within the School of Performing Arts, and included advanced tuition in:

> Drama, dance – including ballet, music, costume and stage design, speech including singing, film and television production, arts administration – including art galleries and museums as well as the performing arts.

An alternative, more modest proposal was advanced for a smaller centre to house the already existing performing arts institutions: the New Zealand Drama School, the Ballet School and the NZBC Orchestra. To his credit, Bill Sutch acknowledged the benefits to be gained in the proposed conservatorium, through the 'interaction between the artistic disciplines'. It would also provide an opportunity to develop new national standards for ballet exams that would 'dispense with the existing narrow relics of the colonial days'. The Arts Council's letter to the PM urged swift action, 'lest the opportunity for a performing arts school be lost for many years'; it proposed that 'two high level committees be set up to work out the details' and to then report directly to the PM.[8]

In retrospect, it is easy to see the appeal that a School of Performing Arts had at this time. There were many examples of multi-disciplinary academies in America, and in Australia the Victorian College of the Arts (VCA) in Melbourne had been proclaimed, incorporating schools of music, dance, drama and visual arts within a single institution, and having film and television in its sights. Nevertheless, establishing a super-conservatorium is a complex and costly undertaking that requires extensive planning; it is not something to be embarked on lightly. Given the dearth of expertise in New Zealand to develop such an ambitious concept at this time, the Avalon Performing Arts School proposal was – unsurprisingly – deferred.

A key recommendation to come out of the 'Wellington meeting' was that the Drama School should be located close to the 'various idioms of experimental theatre'. Downstage Theatre fitted the bill, but it was in the process of moving into the Hannah Playhouse, and therefore 'unable to cope with the Drama School, or offer basic assistance with its running, for at least 18 months'.[9] The director of the Arts Council sent a memo to his chairman with a rationale for transferring the Drama School to Auckland, at the same time reminding the chairman that 'in accordance with Arts Council's policy of regional development, the shift of the Arts Council supported training facility to Auckland would amount to a real devolution from a centralist concept of training in the arts'.[10]

On the face of it, this seemed to be a logical move, and the Auckland Theatre Trust appeared more than willing to 'become the administrative umbrella of the drama school'. Mercury Theatre announced that it would be pleased to cooperate with and offer essential services to the school: it had operated an apprenticeship scheme for several years and was therefore presumed to have an appreciation of 'the problems involved in training and working with fledgling actors'. As an added incentive, the Auckland City Council offered to acquire a site for the Drama School, at 'a reasonably low rent'.

The Auckland Theatre Trust wrote to the Arts Council, confirming its support for the Drama School's relocation to Auckland:

> We remain passionately convinced of the rightness of the move. People wanting to go into the theatre *must* be taught by men of the theatre [*sic*], and [we] believe that in Auckland at this time we are well endowed with those rare beings, men of the theatre who are deeply concerned for the future of their profession.

The Trust also took the opportunity to express its frustration over delays in implementing what it considered to be a 'unanimous decision of all advisors and executives' to move the Drama School to Auckland, a delay that was causing the Auckland City Council to lose patience with the idea and jeopardising acquisition of the site earmarked for the school.[11]

Nevertheless, there was a growing unease within the Arts Council, with some officers concerned that the school might sacrifice its autonomy if it became closely allied to a single theatre company. They also began to review the financial cost and the educational validity of such a move. Bill Sheat, who had been chair of the Arts Council from 1969 to 1973 and was currently chair of the Drama Panel, fought valiantly to retain the school in Wellington:

> Derek Firth, a Council member from Auckland, tabled a proposal that the Drama School be relocated in Auckland and be directed by Raymond Hawthorne. The whole idea of having it in Auckland came completely out of left field; there was bit of ambush about it, the idea was tossed on the table at an Arts Council meeting, without any prior knowledge. Strictly speaking, it could not have been considered. I objected strenuously. Bill Sutch who had succeeded me as chairman of the Council in 1973 said if I wanted to present an alternative proposal I had better do it before the next Council meeting and consideration of the Auckland proposal was deferred.
>
> Next day I rang Bill Renwick who I'd worked with on the advanced training working party; so he knew what I was talking about. I told him that Auckland was trying to take [the school] over and I was personally not at all happy with that. I knew that George Webby was the drama specialist on the staff of the Wellington Teachers' Training College – I was on the Drama Panel when George applied for a bursary to go to the United States to study under Paul Baker – and I said to Renwick, 'Do you think you could get George released on salary?' This was a pretty major achievement. I had no idea how it would work, but Bill Renwick was sympathetic and he took the idea to Phil Amos, the Minister of Education. A few days later Bill rang me to say the Minister

> had agreed to release George. I don't think that I had time to ask him if he wanted to do the job before I made the approach to Bill Renwick. Fortunately he agreed. I also approached Basil Potter, then principal of the Wellington Polytechnic, to see if there could be a link to that institution.
>
> It was attractive from all points of view. George was the ideal successor to Nola and having him paid for by the state made sense. The school had been run entirely by the Arts Council; they weren't part of the education system. I felt very strongly that they should be, that if you became an actor or a dancer you had as much right to be trained by the state as a plumber or a carpenter. By being part of the education system, acting students would also have access to bursaries and equipment on an equal footing with other students.[12]

The joint Education Department/Arts Council initiative rested on the willingness of the Education Department to release George Webby from his position at Wellington Teachers' Training College to enable him to assume the directorship of the Drama School at the start of 1974. Not only did Wellington Polytechnic agree to this, but it also took over responsibility for administering the school and for servicing some parts of the teaching programme. With this final piece of the jigsaw in place and with the backing of the Minister of Education, the Auckland proposal was not tabled again. From the Arts Council's point of view, the plan made good financial sense: George Webby's salary would be covered by the Education Department and the fees for other staff would be paid by the Arts Council.

The lower operational costs associated with the Wellington option made it considerably cheaper than the Auckland bid and also enabled the Arts Council to retain overall responsibility for the Drama School. Above all, the Wellington option guaranteed the school's autonomy (not being *too* closely identified with any one theatre company) and secured the future life of the school for at least two years.

Interestingly, the Arts Council's 'new scheme' required it to rethink its previous rationale for moving the school to Auckland, which complied with the 'Council's policy of regional development amounting to a real devolution from a centralist concept of training in the arts'.[13] Instead, the new venture would now be 'consistent with the Council's policy of Arts Council/Education department co-operation in the field of professional training in the arts'.[14]

Meanwhile, the Drama School was in rehearsal for the final graduation production at the old school: scenes from *Blood Wedding,* directed by Nola Millar. A week after the production closed, on the final day of the school year, the Arts Council arranged a function to celebrate Nola Millar's contribution to New Zealand theatre with a special Achievement Award, the highest the Arts Council could give for distinguished services to the arts in New Zealand:

> The citation acknowledged Nola as a major force in New Zealand theatre since the 1930s, referring to her groundbreaking work with Unity Theatre and her stand against theatrical trivia, her success in straddling the worlds of amateur and professional theatre, her association with the New Zealand Players, her own New Theatre, and her success in the difficult task of establishing the Arts Council's drama school.[15]

Blood Wedding December 1973, Directed by Nola Millar. From left: Peter Sakey, Peter McCauley, Janet Findlay. Stephen McElrea at back. On right: Greta Campbell, Anna Campion, Cathy Downes, Ruth Osbaldstone (Pretty). *ATL PACoII-0284-06-01*

By now, Nola's health was fragile, and early in the new year she collapsed and was admitted to Calvary Hospital in Wellington, where she spent her final days. She died on 20 January 1974, the day following the 100th Anniversary of the Wellington Cup at Trentham.

There were many epitaphs written about Nola Millar and the enormous contribution she had made to New Zealand theatre; but one in particular seemed to summarise her accomplishments in terms that Nola would have possibly approved. It was published in *ACT*:

> She sought no honours, she left no monuments …. but theatre in New Zealand will long be served by those in whom she saw the necessary energies and qualities and in whose hearts she purposefully planted her own sense of dedication.[16]

Grant Tilly has fond memories of Nola; he had worked with her over many years and admired her teaching skills:

> It was difficult to know if you'd pleased her – she was of the 'school' my father came from, which was 'don't give them any praise otherwise they'll get a swelled head'. If she didn't say something, you knew you were on the right track. When working on Shakespeare or Chekhov, you threw yourself on her mercy to help you through what you didn't understand. In terms of her teaching style, she was never a 'theatrical bully', even when working with the 'raw clay' at the New Theatre School.[17]
>
> I'm sure she must have given me specific direction from time to time, but I don't remember how they influenced what I did. It was almost like creating a character with help by osmosis from the director. I don't remember her ever bullying actors, as was a popular method

> at the time, nor did she employ a raft of overt suggestions or a barrage of naked enthusiasm, but seemed to work with a subtle nudge here, the whisper of a suggestion there.[18]

It is true to say that Nola's love of theatre knew no second place, and Jack Shallcrass, who had worked with her for many years, clearly understood that:

> She didn't give a two-penny stuff about what she looked like. She would let herself go and always looked like she'd been dragged through a gorse bush backwards; she was totally unconcerned about her personal appearance. Her life was really a life of the mind and the heart and mind, and yet she lived a life that was fully in the world. Nola could perceive qualities and possibilities in people that perhaps nobody else could notice; she had a unique ability to adjust to circumstances, working not only with 'theatrical people' but also with people who could react positively to theatrical experiences.[19]

Although Toi Whakaari today has little resemblance to the QEII Drama School that Nola Millar established and ran from 1970 to 1974, Nola was well aware that she represented 'the beginning', and that it would be up to others to continue the story. The essential purpose of the school she founded remains unchanged, and its initial ambition and spirit are embodied in the present philosophy of Toi Whakaari. Nola's portrait hangs in the Nola Millar Library and is a constant reminder, to students, staff and graduates of the school, and to visiting practitioners, of their link with this remarkable pioneer.

Portrait of Nola Millar.
ATL EP-NZ Obits-MB to MI-02

Five

1974

From Savage Club to boys' hostel.

George Webby

George Webby's background was in education. He had been a lecturer in English and principal lecturer in drama at Wellington Teachers' College. This, and his work with Nola Millar on many Drama Council residential schools, provided George with a unique perspective on actor training. His directing and acting experience at Teachers' College and at Unity Theatre and Downstage also helped to shape his ideology for the New Zealand Drama School.

George was an educator – not a trainer. During the 1960s and 1970s he had been part of the liberal movement in education in New Zealand in the company of other visionary educators such as Jack Shallcrass, who was on the committee of Unity Theatre during the 1950s and early sixties. As Robin Payne later recalled, they were trained to educate, to elicit knowledge by asking open-ended questions, always putting the student in a position of power:

> George has a big thing about approval and disapproval and how damaging it is. Whether it's positive approval or negative disapproval, it is equally destructive for the student if they are dependent on the teacher's opinion: they are always there as a safety net for the students. It's much easier to be the person that is 'always right', but it is much harder to truly listen to the student and attend to their individuality – without getting impatient or smacking them down.[1]

He disliked teaching methods that were too prescriptive; he believed they presented barriers to learning. Instead, he preferred students to find their own path and favoured a structure that exposed them to a wide range of methodologies, thereby giving them choices that would encourage individuality:

> We offered no one-stop, ready-mix machine, [we were] completely opposite to [the] view

> of many other training establishments. Too many of them were preaching a single philosophy: that one alone would solve all the student's problems. In extreme this manifested itself in a single master *guru*, whose word must not be questioned.[2]

This then was at the heart of George's philosophy: by allowing students to assume greater responsibility for their own learning and development, they would be encouraged to become flexible practitioners, empowered to become agents for change. The same rationale was outlined in the initial aims of the New Zealand Drama School:

> The curriculum will introduce a wide range of experiences in which the students may initiate and be introduced to new ideas and experiences [and this] will help them to develop a theatre philosophy that is meaningful, and artistically satisfying.[3]

This ideal was later expanded in an article published in *ACT*:

> The main aim of the course is the enrichment of the students' resources, so that when they [graduate] they're not going to be channelled too narrowly .... A lot of actors lose their ability to be creative. The nervous actor falls back on what he's done before, instead of creating new solutions to the problems he encounters.[4]

The shift from a one-year to a two-year programme brought with it fundamental changes that affected not only the syllabus, but also the purpose of the New Zealand Drama School and the way it reflected the broader theatre community.

George had great respect for Nola Millar, both as a director and teacher, and also for what she had achieved with the school. Nonetheless, he believed the Arts Council had been wrong to attach the Drama School to New Theatre, and he felt strongly that the school needed to be fully independent, not tied to any theatre company whose practice was aligned to a single overriding philosophy.

As soon as he was appointed director of the New Zealand Drama School, George set about finding new premises for the school. The Arts Council had previously tried to secure the New Zealand Players' Building in Newtown, but this had been rejected by George as being too isolated. Eventually a temporary home was found in the Savage Club (now BATS Theatre) at the bottom of Kent Terrace, opposite the newly built Hannah Playhouse.

The Savage Club had a long and varied life. Originally a dance hall and a venue for amateur theatre, in the 1960s Unity Theatre used the ground floor of the building as a theatre. On the first floor, there was a smallish hall, primitive changing rooms, a kitchen, and an area that doubled as an administration office and the beginnings of a library. The one big advantage for the Drama School was the building's central location.

George Webby's next priority was to appoint tutors for the school. Grant Tilly, Rona Bailey and Anne Flannery agreed to teach the core subjects: movement, improvisation, voice and acting. Other teachers were recruited for specialist areas, including Bunty Western for fencing, and Val Bayley who taught historical movement and dance, tap dancing, Alexander Technique and jazz. She introduced George Webby to Erica Stephenson, a dance teacher with secretarial skills, whom he immediately employed as a part-time secretary/dance teacher for the school.

BATS Theatre, 2010

Erica Stephenson, 1975

Erica Stephenson and George Webby

Erica developed a unique working relationship with George. She understood his ideology and could cope with his impulsive (she would say wilful) ways, in particular, his tendency to fire from the hip when communicating with the Arts Council. George recalled, 'I could spin ideas off Erica and she kept my feet on the ground. After I wrote a letter she would often advise me to put it aside for a day or too. I would go against her advice at my peril.'[5]

Erica's secretarial responsibilities were not clearly specified, but within six months she became the school's administrator, secretary to the Board of Studies and front-of-house manager. She was also a great ear for the students and skilfully looked after their welfare as a sort of house-mother. The petty-cash tin served an additional purpose – as an emergency bank – which Erica accessed to ease students through a 'financial pickle'. She was unquestioningly an unsung (but not unappreciated) heroine in the evolution of the school, nursing it through many predicaments between 1974 and 1988.

The students about to graduate from the QEII Drama School in 1973 were given the option of returning to complete a second year in 1974. However, they had already finished a cycle of training with its own particular rhythm within a given timeframe, and the offer was considered to be less than satisfactory. What the one-year programme mostly lacked was sufficient time for in-depth study: simply to tack on another year would have merely added a sort of postscript.

Auditions for the 1974 intake were held at the YWCA in Willis Street. Applicants were asked to prepare and perform two contrasting pieces of between two and three minutes' duration. This was followed by a short improvisation session and an interview with the selection panel. Auditionees living more than twenty miles from Wellington received the equivalent of a one-way first-class train and/or ferry fare from the Arts Council to cover their travelling expenses.

Tony Richardson, from Mercury Theatre, and Raymond Hawthorne, from Theatre Corporate, were on the audition panel. They had recently started their own training school for actors in Auckland, and had a somewhat biased view of both the selection criteria and the purpose of the New Zealand Drama School training programme. This conflicted with George's more liberal approach: he was seeking students who would benefit from exposure to a wide range of philosophies and points of view:

> If I couldn't run a school with, say, fourteen independent thinkers I didn't want to run one at all. I knew that I expected each of the successful applicants to question everything, that after two years they would have been in touch with dozens of philosophies and points of view, leaving, I hoped, with a highly individual amalgam of what they had been subjected to.[6]

During the audition process, Raymond Hawthorne informed the selection panel that he could not recommend the New Zealand Drama School to any of the applicants, particularly those from Auckland, because he had not been shown a course outline or a teaching timetable for the Drama School. George later discovered that both Raymond Hawthorne and Tony Richardson had lobbied for the Drama School to be relocated to Auckland, to be closely associated with Mercury Theatre. It is therefore not surprising that they had such a particular view on the purpose and function of the school.

Interestingly, both men were later appointed to the New Zealand Drama School Board of Studies, as representatives of 'the theatre profession', Richardson from 1974–75 and Hawthorne from 1976–77.

Fourteen auditionees were selected for the 1974 intake. Each was awarded a bursary of $750 per annum in the form of a living allowance paid in monthly instalments. The students were not required to pay tuition fees as these were covered by the Arts Council's annual grant to the school.

Of these fourteen students, eleven graduated in 1975. They include Jane Waddell, Frances Edmond and Rangimoana (Gary) Taylor, the second Māori student to be selected for the school.

> *Jane Waddell.* I knew nothing of actor training, and only accidentally discovered the existence of a drama school in Wellington in 1972. I was raised in Invercargill and in my first eighteen years only appeared on stage once, in my last year at high school.
>
> I hankered to join 'young rep' and harboured a secret ambition to make a life in a profession I didn't even know existed, but my parents didn't encourage it. God knows where it came from. My parents took me to local rep productions occasionally, and I remember going to see *Porgy and Bess* starring Inia Te Wiata. When I was at Dunedin Teachers' College, I became involved in drama and took speech and drama lessons from Mary Hopewell, who was a passionate teacher and director. She encouraged me, and introduced me to Sophocles, Dylan Thomas, Edgar Allen Poe, Walt Whitman, Ionesco and a gallery of others.
>
> One of the most significant experiences I had at that time was in the dying days of the Southern Theatre Trust. I was cast as one of the witches in a budget production of *Macbeth*. Heather Eggleton played Lady Macbeth and Simon O'Connor was Macbeth.
>
> From that point I was addicted, and put in a late application to audition for the New Zealand Drama School for the 1973 intake, but I was too late. I re-applied the following year when the school had been upgraded to a two-year course under the directorship of the indefatigable George Webby. When I turned up for my audition in Wellington, I was a little bit overwhelmed and awed by the audition panel, and some of the other applicants. They seemed so sophisticated and I felt like a peasant in comparison. I remember the panel were all smoking, except for Sunny Amey, such an anathema today. I was fortunate enough to be accepted.
>
> I didn't know what to expect, but I loved my time at Drama School. I was introduced to a lot of ideas that I had no previous experience of – not just playwrights, but films and novelists and people's lives. The scales fell from my eyes as I realised what a wealth of riches existed on the pages of plays and theatre books I'd never before heard of. It seemed to me to be what education was all about; it certainly wasn't just to do with theatre, it was to do with the development of your own ideas. Of course, the main thrust was performance. The experience extended me beyond bounds I thought possible and convinced me that this was a world I wanted to be a part of. Drama School was just fantastic: the freedom, the stimulation. It was a period of great personal discovery and happiness.[7]

> *Frances Edmond.* I'm not sure that I had concrete expectations beyond wanting to be an actress and knowing that I needed training. I had begun acting with a street theatre group the Living Theatre Troupe and gradually moved towards more conventional forms through classes and workshops – Francis Batten (not that he was very conventional), Ian Mune and Raymond Hawthorne.

Raymond, and I think Ian too, advised me to apply for the new Drama School – so I did. I was passionate about the theatre and about acting and I believed this was a way to develop my skills and make a career out of it. I had only had a small amount of voice training at this point and most of my work had been on improvised rather than scripted material so I wanted more of both those things.

Our year started with seven women and seven men, but at the end of the first year we lost three men who felt that they weren't learning anything and that the course wasn't for them. There were some acrimonious scenes. However, I think that for those of us who remained it strengthened our bond and our commitment to the school.

I remember that I got a great deal out of the course. Not least a thoroughly instilled cooperative way of working that has stayed with me and stood me in good stead in many situations. It was certainly not less than I expected (though I'm not sure what I did expect). However, I know that I graduated with a very good grounding in the skills needed to become an actor. We were told that drama school was just the beginning and that it takes fifteen years to really learn to become a good actor. I regard the two years spent [there] as formative, creative and constructive.[8]

Rangimoana Taylor. I'd hated school. It was the worst time ever. I had to go to reading clinic for six months before I auditioned for Drama School to try and learn to read. But I learnt what education was at Drama School, and the difference between education and schooling, and that education could go on all my life. That was a real big thing for me. People would say to me, 'Oh, you're studying at New Zealand Drama School', and I'd say, 'No no, we don't do that there', because I liked Drama School and study was a thing I hated, so this couldn't be study. We would laugh at Drama School, and for me study had never been about laughing.

I threw a chair at the panel when I was auditioning [for drama school]. They gave me a scene to improvise – and they did this with a great deal of respect, trying to give me a chance – about one of my relatives selling a piece of land and I was to be upset about this. So I did the improvisation in Māori – and it finished with me throwing the chair. I hadn't thought I was being smart, I just thought that's what you must have to do. I could see half the panel thinking, perhaps he's not ready for us, and the other half thinking, this'll be great, he's so passionate.

I was very lucky after Drama School because Tony Richardson at the Mercury, and Raymond Hawthorne at Theatre Corporate both thought I had potential. Raymond was a tough teacher, but he had a love of theatre, a real love. Working with [Raymond] and George Webby were fantastic experiences.[9]

The school year was from mid-February to November, with three terms, each roughly twelve weeks' long. The first term started with a four-week orientation programme focusing on physical fitness, speech, movement and improvisation. These became regular core classes, more or less following the methodology introduced by Nola Millar, the major difference being the class size which had now doubled, with a longer teaching programme enabling subjects to be covered in greater depth.

Jane Waddell. We began the day with a movement class taught by Val Bayley, with George on piano. Val came from a ballet background and the classes were based on the kind of fitness necessary for dancers. (Also appropriate for actors.) Val also emphasised deportment, grace, lightness, alignment and posture. We all discovered muscle groups we didn't know we had. We learnt basic routines to help develop coordination and a sense of rhythm. Voice classes followed, taught by Anne Flannery, a mysteriously beautiful woman with a softly modulated voice, whose teaching was strongly rooted in the work of Cicely Berry, by whom Anne had been taught. We did a lot of lying on the floor learning to breathe properly, then to connect the voice with the breath, humming on the out-going breath. We did articulation exercises and learnt to use bone-props. We spent nearly the whole first year working on *Fear No More the Heat o' the Sun*.[10]

Frances Edmond. The idea of 'freeing the natural voice' was implicit. There was not a 'proper' way to use the voice, but we did a lot of work on breathing and relaxation, muscularity and diction and then connecting it all with text – learning to use the whole voice.[11]

Jane Waddell. In the afternoons, we were taught improvisation by Grant Tilly – or we had acting classes with George. Improv classes began with very simple scenarios, where we would be given a situation and maybe one or two lines of dialogue that we had to include in the development of the scene. This early work was undertaken in pairs. We would be given maybe fifteen minutes to prepare our scenes and then we would share with the class – and Grant would critique us. The scenarios became more complicated as our skills improved, and we worked in larger groups. By the end of the two years we had learnt a script: *Comings and Goings*. It was about thirty-six pages of lines divided between a 'he' and a 'she'. There were probably twenty scenes of varying lengths. It became more complicated the more expert we became. Grant would give us a 'where' (the desert, the moon, a hotel room …) or a theme (romance, horror story, comic book ...) and we would adapt the scene to suit the location or the style.[12]

Frances Edmond. We actually performed *Comings and Goings* in a pub in front of an audience several times. Grant would spin a wheel to choose the performers and the audience were asked to give us the context. I guess it was a forerunner or early version of theatre sports. It was a lot of fun and kept us on our toes. I remember improvisation classes being challenging and fun. George Webby taught text-based acting, and directed most of our productions. We worked on scenes from plays … and did quite a lot of work around developing self-awareness, and understanding motivation and behaviour. I enjoyed George's teaching style. He was funny and irreverent, but thorough and knowledgeable too.[13]

Specialist classes were introduced to strengthen the students' analytical skills and broaden their understanding of theatre practice, including theatre history, philosophy, directing, organisation and management.

Jane Waddell. The day was long enough for us – 9.00 to 4.30 – and we did little beyond that. George was insistent that the maturation that happened between classes was just as important as what happened in class.

There now seem to be much greater demands placed on the students and greater pressure on the school today to teach everything. The hours that are expected of them also mean there's not a lot of time for processing learning or to have a life outside the school.[14]

The teaching programme was laid out in (handwritten) weekly class timetables prepared by Erica Stephenson:

Most of the time there was a regular pattern to the timetable with core subjects scheduled on the same day and time throughout the term. Rehearsals occurred sometimes in the

First intake of students, two-year course, 1974. *Comings & Goings* at Downstage. Part of their Open Day to celebrate the 10th anniversary. Back L–R: Christina Milligan, Christopher Harding, Prue Langbein, Peter Kelly, Frances Edmond, Peter White (Land), Charles Hambling, Celia West. Front L–R: Rangimoana (Gary) Taylor, Peter Ackerman, Jane Waddell, Karl Bradley

Comings and Goings 1974. Charles Hambling and Celia West.

> afternoon and sometimes at night. Friday afternoon was particularly interesting: George would use the time to get visitors to come along and talk to the students. We had all sorts of people. It was extremely valuable as it brought a touch of 'reality' into what was a highly specialised area.[15]

Opinion was divided amongst those involved in setting up the New Zealand Drama School, and also within the theatre industry itself, on the purpose and aims of the school. George Webby asserted that the principal job of the Drama School was to expose students to a broad curriculum as this would equip them to work in a range of performance areas. He also maintained that the purpose of the school was not primarily to serve the vested interest of the major professional theatre companies:

> Many of those interested in theatre may want to work in areas not directly related to the [professional theatre companies]. For instance, working in creative drama with children or teaching drama. Graduates may also wish to form their own company, or freelance in any number of related fields. In the future I see the school expanding into fields other than acting, such as directing, stage management and theatre administration. All these areas are relatively weak in New Zealand.[16]

George was under no illusion that all graduates of the Drama School would find work as actors in mainstream theatre, even if this was desirable; many would develop careers in other areas of the performing arts. For that reason, he believed the school had a responsibility to ensure that graduates left it 'well-grounded in *all* those areas needed for success in whatever branch of stage, film or TV they intended to work in'.[17]

Clearly, most of the students at the school wanted to train as actors, but from time to time there were those with other goals, such as Jan Prettejohns. Although she had enrolled as an acting student, her ambition was to direct. George Webby was well aware of this and he arranged for her to enrol as a 'special case student' (although there was no such category):

> After two terms of suffering as an acting student (Mr Webby had 'smuggled me in' under this guise) George and I agreed that enough of my execrable acting was – enough: time to do some real work.[18]

Shortly after joining the school, she directed its first production for the year, John Bowen's *Trevor*, performed at Unity Theatre. It was an all-student production, with a cast of eight: those not in the cast were responsible for design, lighting, stage-management and direction. Jan had a realistic view of what she and the rest of the students could achieve and viewed *Trevor* as a learning opportunity to assess her own strengths as a director: 'the thing about directing is that you can only learn by doing. And I've got to make a lot of mistakes in order to learn.'[19]

At the end of her first year at the school, Jan received an additional Arts Council bursary, which allowed her to go 'on section' to Theatre Corporate to direct *Death of a Salesman*. The following year she directed two more productions at the school, *Futz,* and *Confessional*, which was part of a compilation entitled *An Evening of Tennessee Williams* performed at Stagecraft Theatre. Although she received no actual tuition in directing, George was always around when needed to give advice, encouragement and feedback; he also attended all of Jan's productions:

> Secondments were more like being tipped cheerfully out of the nest, clutching only a script, a return air fare and everyone's best wishes. And then, after opening nights, George's uniquely annoying and perceptive take on what I had or hadn't got marginally right. In the second year, I wasn't at the school a lot. It was a kind of crazy and oddly blessed time. For example, I remember hitching a ride with Bruce Mason from Wellington to Centrepoint to see a show. Bruce, whose brainy and insightful reviews always said so much about directing and actors ... hell, I had him to myself all the way to Palmy – and all the way back.
>
> And Downstage was just down the road – Sunny Amey was in charge, the theatre was busy and welcoming – like a second home. I made tea and coffee, ironed costumes, sat in on pre-lighting in the wee small hours, went to production meetings, technical/dress rehearsals, ASM'd *Hedda Gabler* and *Valdramar*. Meanwhile, other influences were at play. At the school there were visiting tutors – glamorous names back then. We students saw different directing styles, different ways of working with actors. You chose who to listen to; you began to figure out the path you might take as a director.
>
> George also encouraged the students to take a broader interest in current affairs. When Richard Nixon resigned in 1974, George sat all the students down to watch the event on TV. That has remained with me, as someone who is interested in USA politics.
>
> I can't imagine how it would be for a twenty-five to twenty-six-year-old trainee director now; I guess I can only hope that they are availed of some of the riches I was.[20]

When Jan left the Drama School in 1975, there were few theatre directors – especially women directors – and consequently she got 'more offers of work than you could wave a stick at':

> I graduated and freelanced at the Court, Fortune, Downstage, Centrepoint, Circa and New Theatre for two years, before washing up at Downstage for three months and staying for three years to run 'Stagetruck', Downstage's Theatre in Education company.[21]

From there she moved to Centrepoint Theatre, working first as associate director then artistic director, before joining Mercury Theatre as associate director. After that, she 'ran away to join TVNZ'. Jan is now a freelance writer and script editor, noted for her work on various TV series such as *Jackson's Wharf* and *Outrageous Fortune.*

The arrangement made between the Arts Council and the Education Department to bring the Drama School under the 'umbrella' of Wellington Polytechnic was an excellent deal. It afforded the school a degree of autonomy and allowed it to remain independent of the Polytechnic's regulatory processes, thereby avoiding educational prerequisites and formal assessment procedures, which could have constrained its early development. There remained a slight underlying risk that the Drama School could, at some future date, be swallowed up by the much larger Polytechnic, or at the very least have its independence compromised. This was a small price to pay, though, compared with the advantages of its alliance with the much larger and well-resourced institution: it gained additional space to supplement the limited teaching facilities at the Savage Club, and access to a wide range of specialist tutors from the Polytechnic, including

Colleen Reilly who taught theatre criticism and current affairs at the Drama School and got the students also to think outside the world of theatre.

The Drama School students were also affiliated with the Polytechnic Students' Association, which gave them access to 'free' medical and counselling services, the Polytechnic Library and cafeteria, and other student concessions.

Shortly after the New Zealand Drama School opened, the Arts Council approached George Webby with a proposal to set up a Board of Studies, comprised of representatives from the Arts Council, Education Department and Wellington Polytechnic, to 'study the prescription covering the activities of the School' and to 'clarify the extent of the duties expected of the Director of the School'.

But George questioned the Arts Council's 'assumption' that course prescriptions had been completed and that they were available for scrutiny. He reckoned it would take at least eighteen months to produce a comprehensive set of course outlines. After all, the New Zealand Drama School had been operating for only a few months, and Nola Millar had left nothing in the way of course prescriptions or a syllabus. His response to the Council's request was straightforward: 'it will take some time .... prescriptions should be based on our actual practice, and be a true reflection of what we teach; not what we hope to teach.'[22] He had a point.

An outline of the teaching programme was eventually produced and included in the 1975 prospectus. Yet it would be another twelve years before a comprehensive set of course prescriptions for the New Zealand Drama School was published, in 1987.

When the Board of Studies was first convened, George was invited to attend meetings in a 'consultative capacity'. He was clearly not comfortable with this, and fired one of his notorious – and lengthy – salvos, drawing the Arts Council's attention to the overloaded educational representation on the Board: 'Perhaps [the Arts Council] had overlooked the area of theatre itself in their selection of Board member?' It seemed an obvious oversight to George; he knew that unless at least one well-qualified theatre practitioner was elected to the Board of Studies to represent the professional aims of the school, the theatre profession would be slighted. In the same letter to the Arts Council, he requested clarification of the ambiguous term 'consultative capacity': did this mean he was to be a consultant or a seeker after consultation?[23]

The first meeting of the Board of Studies was in July 1974, with Bill Sheat as the chair and a membership of four: Russell Aitken, Peter Chinnery, George Webby and Miss A. Colhoun – representing M. Rickard from the Arts Council. As the Board still had no representative from the theatre community, it immediately set about putting its house in order by unanimously agreeing to appoint a 'representative from the professional theatre', and nominated Tony Richardson. In addition, George Webby was invited to become a full member of the Board, to which he agreed. Its first priority was to find and secure larger premises for the school: a second intake of students was due to arrive at the start of 1975 and the Savage Club was too small to accommodate two streams of students.

George continued to assert that close contact with the 'community' was essential, and that the school should remain close to the city centre to avoid being isolated. The Arts Council disagreed; they were worried about the high cost of city centre property.

And when George proposed a six-year lease on the NAC Building in Lambton Quay, the Arts Council swiftly responded:

> It is too expensive a proposition to be given serious consideration. It is not necessary to have the school located in the heart of town, and in [relation to] the current rental and with future predictable increases, it is too high. We feel it would be misleading for the Arts Council to lay itself open to a charge of such extravagance.[24]

The Arts Council eventually conceded to the need for new premises, however, and assigned the task of finding a location that was both central and inexpensive to a real estate agency. But when Bill Sheat spotted the Fielden Taylor Boys' Hostel as he was driving down Taranaki Street one day, he noted that it was available and immediately secured the premises for the school. The Arts Council then negotiated a three-year lease with the Wellington City Mission, the owners of the hostel, which gave the Drama School a semi-permanent home until 1979.

The hostel seemed to satisfy most of the physical requirements that George wanted for the school:

> This was a tremendous improvement [on the Savage Club] as the new premises had a large gymnasium-cum-dance studio that could be converted into a theatre, and lots of little bedrooms which students could use as studies. It was also near the City Centre and Cuba Street which meant we were close to the action.[25]

The Drama School year ended with a production of Arthur Miller's *A View from the Bridge,* directed by Anne Flannery, but this was not the only project to occupy the students during those final months:

> Any visitor to the Drama school could be forgiven for thinking that the school had gone full-time professional. One room rehearsing a TV programme [*This Afternoon*], polishing up *Comings and Goings* for presentation at Downstage, and a third group preparing a miscellany of music, poetry, and drama called *Playing Favourites* which will run twice weekly as a lunchtime programme at Downstage, and still yet another programme: a full-scale production of Arthur Miller's *A View from the Bridge* … will be presented at the end of November at Stagecraft Theatre.[26]

Immediately after the end-of-year production, the students dispersed 'to freezing works, wool stores, behind shop counters and anywhere they could earn money'.

The Arts Council wrote to George to congratulate him and all concerned on the end of year production: 'it was a clear indication of what had been accomplished in the School … and the achievements of your obviously talented students'. At the same time, it used the opportunity to reprimand George for failing to include any reference to the QEII Arts Council in the *View from the Bridge* programme. You can't win 'em all.

The future of the New Zealand Drama School now seemed secure. It was beginning to establish a unique identity through its work and through the way it related to the particular circumstances of New Zealand culture. This was acknowledged in an up-beat article on the school in the December edition of *ACT*:

> Despite the [New Zealand Drama School's] claim not to be based on a philosophy with a certain stamp, the School's approach is very much a New Zealand one, oriented towards theatre in our own country, and not the former distant shores of stardom or [a style of] work rejected in these islands.[27]

Fielden Taylor Boys Hostel

Six

1975

> *'It was the full seventies schtick with the clothes, parties, politics, drugs, values, morals and experiments. I am glad I was there.'*

The Drama School relocated to the Fielden Taylor Hostel in time for the start of the 1975 academic year. There were now only eleven second-year students, but the addition of a new first-year stream brought the total student enrolments to twenty-one. As well as the two full-time tutors, George Webby and Grant Tilly, there was also a core of permanent part-timers, including Rona Bailey, Francis Batten (mask and mime), Val Bayley, Anne Flannery, John Pike (gymnastics), Leslie Souness (singing), Erica Stephenson (who taught dance, when she wasn't wearing her executive secretary hat) and Bunty Western (fencing).

The first-year students' curriculum was similar to that of the previous year, with daily training classes and additional specialised sessions, and in the second term they rehearsed and performed their own production, *Futz*, directed by Jan Prettejohns. They also supported the second-year students in their productions, carrying out technical, design and stage-management duties. This integration was an important part of George's philosophy:

> The students had to turn their hands to every aspect of theatre: from set design and building, from ushering to publicity, from costumes to programme design. The first-years attended to all the needs of the second-year actors when they appeared in productions, and the reverse applied when the first-years faced their nights of glory.[1]

A valuable part of the second-year students' training was going 'on section', mainly with professional theatre companies, a scheme not dissimilar to the secondment programmes that Toi Whakaari now operates across all its programmes. The main difference is that students now find and negotiate their own secondments, whereas in 1975 students were offered a list of 'sections' to choose from.

Going 'on section' increased the students' awareness of the daily life of a working actor and gave them an understanding of the operation of the various theatre companies. And it worked as an informal audition process, helping students to get work with one of their host theatre companies after they graduated.

Most theatre companies participated in the scheme, including Downstage, Centrepoint, Mercury, Fortune Theatre, Theatre Corporate and Four Seasons (Wanganui). However, the extent of support they could provide was largely governed by their funding or their production schedules. The Court Theatre was interested and willing to participate in the scheme, but was unable to do so until 1976 as it was busy 'tearing the guts out' the old Christchurch university buildings to make a new theatre.

Jan Prettejohns was offered several productions to direct 'on section', including *A Scent of Flowers* at New Theatre, *Who's Afraid of Virginia Woolf* at Centrepoint and *Twelfth Night* at the Fortune. Her secondment there required lengthy negotiations between the school and the theatre to settle her accommodation, air-fare, subsistence expenses and fee. Remarkably, students sometimes received a small amount of money (not expenses) for their work when going 'on section'.

Some theatre companies chose not to participate in the secondment scheme because of the additional workload it imposed or the expectation that they would have to provide accommodation and/or a living allowance for students under their supervision. It was particularly difficult for smaller theatre companies such as the Gateway Players whose annual Arts Council grant was only $8,000. The Drama School itself had only a small budget to support students 'on section': at best, it could assist with travel expenses to the tune of a second-class rail fare or equivalent, or (for the few who had cars) petrol costs. An additional $30 was available to cover 'other expenses' for each student.

Feedback on the scheme from theatre companies and from students showed that it tended to benefit both parties. One artistic director described the experience as 'an opportunity for the students to see us head down and arse up'. Sometimes the school received negative feedback from theatre companies, although this was largely confined to a few students who reportedly lacked awareness or the ability to engage with the work.

Mervyn Thompson, artistic director of Downstage, was most enthusiastic about the students 'on section' with his company:

> We were tremendously impressed with the work of the four students to the section just concluded. They were a very committed group of actors and the impression they made was marvellous. Both Stephen Tozer and Colin [McColl, associate director] found them a joy to work with, and they created the most pleasant vibrations around the Hannah Playhouse. I would be most happy to work with any of these students again.[2]

The procedure governing the selection of students and the allocation of bursaries had, until now, been the prerogative of the Arts Council, which was an ongoing concern for the school. But in 1974 the Board of Studies gained a concession, allowing audition applications to be sent directly to the school before being forwarded to the Arts Council. Bursary applications, however, were still sent directly to the Arts Council and information contained in those applications was confidential to the Council, which meant the Arts Council continued to have more information about the students than the school.

This situation was patently absurd, as the allocation of bursaries was subject to candidates being offered a place at the school, and the dual application process, with its multiple forms, was confusing for the applicants.

George described the state of affairs as 'Gilbertian', and made several attempts to persuade the Arts Council to simplify the process, including a letter to the director of the QEII Arts Council in which he 'set down clearly, and therefore, probably bluntly, [his] feelings and thoughts concerning the manner in which students are selected for the Drama School':

> Duplication of effort and responsibility in administering the present system has been a nuisance, just as an assumption that either the School or the Council is responsible for certain procedures, resulting in neither doing anything.
>
> A student could be dismissed from the School and yet still be in receipt of an Arts Council Bursary until the Council chooses to withdraw it.
>
> Courteousness above all demands that the [Drama School] Director and the Board of Studies be kept aware of changes in the system of selecting candidates [for the school].
>
> Surely the Drama School should write its own prospectus, handle all queries, applications, and processing of those applications? If, as Director, I am considered a responsible person, I should also handle these responsibilities which are important to the success (or otherwise) of the School.
>
> Why not come out in the open and allow the School and its Board of Studies to ask for applications, to process them, audition students, and then send the recommended list to the Arts Council for semi-automatic approval?
>
> P.S Erica [Stephenson] tells me my letters have a terse quality – I am, of course, a loving person by nature and I don't meant to come across that way[3]

Eventually, the Arts Council conceded, and wrote to George in 1976 to inform him that 'the time is now ripe for the New Zealand Drama School to assume full responsibility for the organisation of their student intakes .... the Council will continue to be associated with the auditions for Arts Council scholarships.'[4] Thereafter, the Drama School issued a single application form covering both entry into the school and the bursary. Nevertheless, the Arts Council continued to monitor the recruitment process with a representative on the audition panel, and the list of successful auditionees was forwarded by the school to the Council for its final approval.

At the same time, the Arts Council agreed to shed some of its other administrative responsibility for the school, providing there was a properly constituted Board of Studies. The Board, which had been hastily formed in 1974, lacked any official or legal status and functioned more as an informal advisory panel. In a move to rectify this situation, the Arts Council approached Professor John Roberts, a political scientist from Victoria University, to chair the Board of Studies:

> The Council has decided that a Board of Studies be constituted with the necessary powers to administer the New Zealand Drama School which at present is under the direct control of the Director of the Arts Council. This is an unsatisfactory situation as we believe it is necessary that a small group of those keenly interested should be invited to exercise control with responsibility to the Arts Council.[5]

John Roberts accepted the invitation and in 1976, a Trust Deed for the Board of Studies was signed and presented to the Arts Council for formal legislation, which significantly increased the Board's responsibility for the school, allowing it to become fully independent of the Arts Council except for approval and supply of budget; Annual report and proposed Budget to be forwarded by [the director] to the Board of Studies and then to the Arts Council.[6]

John Roberts was an inspired choice as chair and proved to be a powerful advocate for the Drama School during its formative years. He was a great support for George and the staff when things got tough, and for much of his term of office he negotiated with the Arts Council and other parties to ensure that the Drama School retained its autonomy and that it remained permanently and adequately funded. He later wrote of his experience, as chair of the Board of Studies, in a general article on the state of New Zealand theatre:

> For several years in which exasperation and exhilaration were almost exactly equal I was associated in a *minor* way with the Drama School. It is not too much to say that I came to regard it as one of the key institutions – comparable to the Symphony Orchestra, the National Library, the All Blacks, Public Radio – required to sustain and improve the quality of life in this country. It seems unbelievable now that in all that time the housing of the School varied from the inadequate to the deplorable, and that our funding depended upon the goodwill of the Arts Council and the Department of Education. It was a disheartening and precarious existence. At last education in the theatre arts is recognised as essential community services with ... motor mechanics, plumbers and journalists. As the graduates of the Drama School take up positions ... their approach will spread through the country to create a secure professional theatre culture. Always providing the Drama School continues to survive and maintains its creative and liberating character.[7]

That article was written in the early 1990s, shortly after the Drama School's association with the QEII Arts Council ended and the Ministry of Education had assumed responsibility for funding the school. Hence this note of caution from John Roberts:

> There is a danger. Placed as [the school] was, in the middle of two powerful public baronies [QEII Arts Council and the Education Department] the old Drama School had a certain freedom from the intellectual strait jackets of nationally prescribed educational standards. Public funding demands public accountability. But theatre demands in its turn an inventive and creative spirit at odds with rigorous course schedules and predetermined goals. Most education is largely the product of an individual exchange between teacher and student. Education for the stage and screen is predominantly concerned with group integration of skills and personalities. For this process course prescriptions can never be more than useful adjuncts. Disasters will follow the imposition of statistical abstractions intended to increase the pay from resources. Education for the theatre must be judged by qualitative rather than quantitative assessment. Stanislavsky famously responded when asked how long he prepared a production: 'until it is ready'. This was a lie but it concealed a truth.

John Roberts remained chair of the Board of Studies until 1986, when the legal status of the Drama School changed to become a Charitable Trust, governed by a Board of Trustees.

From 1974 to 1986 the Board of Studies had a dual purpose. For most of the time, however, it functioned like a board of trustees, dealing with funding, infrastructure and governance matters, rather than as an academic board that would have focused on student-related issues. In fact, the Board of Studies had no *formal* criteria with which to assess the students' progress, or the efficacy of the teaching programme, which would have made it extremely difficult for it to fulfill any sort of academic role. Furthermore, the Drama School's two-year certificate course in acting was *not* an accredited qualification; there were no mandatory or prescribed criteria to determine the students' level of attainment, and graduates were simply awarded a certificate in recognition of having completed two years at the school. The situation stayed like this until the acting course was accredited by the New Zealand Qualifications Authority in 1990.

A major production for the second-year students in 1975 was Congreve's *The Way of the World.* George Webby agreed to direct the earlier rehearsals, but later, despite his unquestionable ability as a director, he conceded *The Way of the World* was just not his 'cup of tea':

> It took longer than usual discussing the text and the characters; anything in fact to keep me from putting it on the rehearsal floor. After a week or two of floundering, I had to admit ignominious defeat. I rang Elric [Hooper] in Christchurch who luckily happened to be free at the time. He took over ... and was able to turn [the production] into something that resembled entertainment and a truer reflection of Congreve's intent. I am grateful to Elric for saving me from what would have surely been a disaster, and giving the School a delicious success that played to full houses.[8]

Elric Hooper's knowledge of theatre history, and in particular his understanding of period style, enabled him to direct student actors in this particularly challenging genre of comedy. What is more, he could be relied on to stage *The Way of the World* with the necessary panache.

As there was no theatre space at the Fielden Taylor Hostel, *The Way of the World* was performed at Wellington Repertory Theatre. But the stage there was tiny, so Elric set the play in 1910 to 'bypass the traditional traffic problems imposed by flamboyant and bulky 17th century costuming'.

It was no secret that Elric could sometimes be aggressive and infuriating in rehearsals: he called it his 'creative rage'. During the rehearsal of *The Way of the World*, he had a mild altercation with Charles Hambling, who was playing Fainall. Charles Hambling has long legs, and Elric was trying to get him to shorten his stride on stage. Charles defended himself, claiming, 'Fainall wouldn't mince.' Elric immediately retorted: 'Well, YOU SHOULD.' An infuriated Charles responded by roaring from the edge of the stage, 'COME HERE AND REPEAT THAT!' Elric then quietly and artfully responded, 'Now I want you to take all that energy and channel it into your performance'.[9] By all accounts, Charles turned in a fine performance – and shortened his stride.

The Way of the World had a four-night season and was received with critical acclaim. Bruce Mason, in a somewhat fulsome review of the production, praised Elric and the students for 'fashioning as stylish and elegant an evening as I have seen for many a day', comparing the Drama School's production with one he'd seen at the Old Vic Theatre School in 1954, with Joan Plowright, Paul Daneman and Keith Michell in the cast, and declaring the Drama School's production was 'better'. Mason made special mention of Jane Waddell's 'exuberant' Lady Wishfort: 'she took to the stage like an obese and raddled goldfish swimming in a torrent of dotty self-esteem, inordinate, outrageous and as funny as hell', and went on to congratulate the rest of the cast who 'performed with the high mettle and bravery of old troupers'.

Mason rounded off his review with an endorsement of the Drama School:

> Not so long ago, the correspondence columns of this and other papers throbbed with denunciation of tax payers' money being spent on worthless luxuries like a symphony orchestra, with the gritty sign-off: 'let those who like this sort of thing pay for it'. Well we're paying for the New Zealand Drama School also, and I ask you to take my word that your money is being well-spent.[10]

The chair of the Arts Council was similarly impressed by the production, which caused him to retract an earlier judgement of the school:

> Elric Hooper's production was superb and the performance by every single member of the cast was thoroughly professional and engaging, and a credit to the students and the School. At the beginning of last year I had serious doubts about [the Drama School] programme. I see now how very wrong I was. The eleven characters were every inch professionals, so much so that I found it difficult to become objective about the performance for anything but a few moments at a time.[11]

Those eleven students graduated at the end of the year. They were a unified group and, for most, their time at Drama School had been a period of great personal discovery, described by one of them as 'Exploration 101'. And not all of that 'exploration' took place within the Drama School:

> *Jane Waddell.* We partied together quite a lot and inevitably 'relationships' developed. A mixed group of us used to frequent the Royal Tiger on Friday nights – where Midge Marsden and his band were resident. We'd often meet at someone's flat [for drinks] and then go on to the pub for a boogie. I was very impressed by Frances Edmond in her glamorous fur coat [and] a hat that was like a fedora. She was stunning. We went to everything that was on in the theatre. One of the first things I remember seeing was Bruce Mason in *End of the Golden Weather* – I was entranced by it, and *Well Hung* – the first New Zealand play I ever saw. We often went to The Balcony to see Red Mole on Sunday night – and see Carmen dressed to the nines come out and sing 'Blue Moon'. I was introduced to the Film Society and saw my first Fellini films.[12]

Shared student accommodation was then, as it is today, an economic necessity and an accepted part of the communal experience. It may well have been the 'psychedelic seventies', but many aspects of flatting and student life remain little changed today:

> *Charles Hambling.* I moved into a flat at the top of Cuba Street, up from the New Theatre, which had housed Peter Sakey and Cathy Downes when they were drama students in 1973.
>
> The flat consisted of a shop front with faded curtains tacked up, with the bedrooms, kitchen and bathroom upstairs and a gas-fired pottery kiln out the back. No-one dared to fire it up. The potters had been famous but I've forgotten their names. Past tenants had added to the decor by painting huge circles in the best seventies orange. I had a small

The Way of the World, 1975. L–R: Peter White (Land), Frances Edmond, Christina Milligan.

bedroom with a bed that had a wooden fireplace at its head, and I set up a stereo at the foot. Our furniture and adornments were borrowed from the recycling yard across the road in the dead of night.

It was a place with a bohemian history. Peter White, Claire Oberman, Christina Milligan and I lived there with innumerable gatecrashers. The soundscape from the street was brilliant. Passers-by, lovers, drunks, Black Power gang members from down the road, rubbish collections in the early morn and milk deliveries to the dairy next door.

It was one of the joys of youth to truck through Cuba Mall in the morning with a scarf flying back and catching time with the piped music ('The Stripper' if you were lucky). The fountain changed not with the seasons but with the party animals who tried to 'improve' it. Detergent was a perennial favourite. We must have stood out from the crowd. We tried hard enough.

Coming home we would stop at the Matterhorn Cafe who did the best coffee and the best iced in the world and the greatest banana split in any galaxy.

It was the full seventies schtick with the clothes, parties, politics, drugs, values, morals and experiments. I am glad I was there.[13]

Given that this was the first cohort of students in the newly formed New Zealand Drama School, many graduates from that year thrived in the performing arts. For example, Peter White, who later changed his surname to Land (his mother's maiden name), went on to make a highly successful acting career in the UK. In 1978 Sir Cameron Mackintosh cast Peter in the lead role of Freddy in the revival of *My Fair Lady* at the Adelphi. Peter has since achieved notable success in theatre, television and musicals, in the UK and USA. In addition to his acting work, he also helped to found Los Angeles-based Soulife Records in 1999.

Seven

1976–1977

'For $6000 per student we could send them all to RADA.'

Nowadays, all applicants for Toi Whakaari are either auditioned or interviewed, a system that has operated since the late 1980s. Before that, some applicants were rejected outright on the basis of their written application and were simply not auditioned. In 1976, twenty of the sixty applicants who applied for the Drama School were not auditioned, and of the remaining forty who were, thirteen were offered a place at the school in 1977.

The attrition rate varies from year to year. But the actual number of students who leave the school before completing is not necessarily a good indicator either of student dissatisfaction or of failure. Students up until the 1990s did not receive a diploma or degree when they graduated, but were given a certificate that simply stated they had completed a two-year course of study. So if they received an offer of employment that required them to leave the school before graduating, they had to weigh the prospect of immediate employment against the benefits to be gained from completing the course.

Understandably, some chose to leave before graduating, particularly if they were nearing the end of their second year. Of the eleven students who first enrolled in 1975, five did not complete. One left at the end of her first year to go into a TV series. Two more left in their final year to join Carlos and Rose Wedde and Sally Rodwell in Vargo's Circus, an experimental touring group. Two others from the same year withdrew before completing the course, though for different reasons.

The Board of Studies was unhappy with the high attrition rate, which it noted at its December 1976 meeting:

> It was felt that there should be discussion with the Association of Community Theatres (ACT), TV and Radio about their view on employing [drama] students – try to obtain some guarantee that students would be left to finish their training.[1]

All the member theatres of ACT had been asked to submit a report on 'how they felt about the training of the students, from what they had seen so far, both at the Drama School and [when the students were on section at] theatres'. Nonnita Mann, then a representative for ACT on the Board of Studies, reported that:

> The work habits of students were undisciplined; vocal work was not good; skills not taught in sufficient depth; lack of stage-management training and other specific skills e.g. Ballroom dancing and stage fights.[2]

If nothing else, such a comment highlights a lack of understanding by ACT of the purpose of secondments within the general curriculum of the school, and the particular responsibility of theatres for the students placed with them 'on section'.

Despite the relatively high attrition rate experienced by the 1975–76 year, the students remained a tightly knit group, and by the end of their training they had evolved a way of working together to achieve an ideal that they intended to pursue when they graduated.

This may help to explain the generosity and support that the second-year students extended to the first-years during a particularly busy period at the end of their final year. They not only managed to stage their own graduation production, *The Birthday Party* at Unity Theatre, but also stage-managed and performed minor roles in the first-year students' production of *Twelfth Night*, and found time to perform in the first-years' late-night Hollywood revue, *Soundstage 12* at Unity Theatre, during the run of *The Birthday Party.*

The number of applicants for the school increased to eighty in 1977. And for the first time, the intake was limited to applicants who were over eighteen at entry, a requirement that may have helped student retentions. Aside from one student who was found to be unsuitable in the first year, the entire 1977 intake graduated in 1978.

George Webby considered the 1977 second-year intake to be a 'high-powered' group. In August, he directed them in an abridged version of *Under Milkwood,* which they performed to two-hundred parliamentarians, including four cabinet ministers and twenty-five Members of Parliament, in the Legislative Council Chamber. This event was part of a scheme introduced by the Minister for the Arts and the opposition MP for Wanganui 'to bring a little culture to the hill'. By all accounts, the performance was a resounding success, at the same time providing a few pointers for MPs seeking to improve their oratory:

> We would go so far as to say that a little tuition in the subtle secrets of the stage could avoid tedious repetition in such Parliamentary set pieces as the Address-in-Reply debate. Why couldn't the delivery of the Budget be the season highlight, a gala occasion in the most dramatic sense of the term?[3]

This production of *Under Milkwood* also marked the start of a long association with the school for a young Miranda Harcourt:

> I remember my parents taking me to see a drama school show for the first time when I was about ten. It was Under Milkwood at the Fielden Taylor Boys' Hostel. I actually met George Webby when I was about fourteen; this enormous figure of absolute glamour, very tall because I was very short. He shook my hand and looked at me closely and said he'd like to see me in the future. Well, in my mind he said that – his gaze, you know; at that

> age you went – 'Cor, he shook my hand'. To me it was really meaningful and sealed my fate and that's when I aimed to go to the drama school.[4]

Following their parliamentary success, the students were invited to take *Under Milkwood* to the Four Seasons Theatre in Wanganui. This was a fairly costly undertaking for the school, so George Webby applied to the Arts Council for a $400 special-projects grant to cover accommodation and the hire of a truck to transport the set, costumes and equipment. In his application, George Webby took the opportunity to congratulate Michael Volkerling, the new director of the Arts Council, on his recent appointment, signing-off his letter with, 'Now give us the money'.

The Arts Council's response was a resounding 'No'. But it did offer to lend the Council's mobile van to the school and to pay for the petrol. The Wanganui season of *Under Milkwood* was a great success and played to full houses: had circumstances allowed, the theatre could have been filled for two more performances. To their delight, Four Seasons made a profit of $500 on the show.

When the students returned to Wellington, they immediately embarked on rehearsals for their graduation production, *The Cherry Orchard,* directed by Sabin Epstein, associate director with the American Conservatory Theatre in San Francisco. His travel costs and other expenses were covered by his salary from American Conservatory Theatre and a US travel grant: the Drama School certainly had no funds available to engage directors from overseas at that time.

George agreed to defer the choice of play for the graduation production until Epstein arrived, as he wanted a showcase for the students in which they could be seen to best advantage. It was a courageous decision, as the production had only a four-week rehearsal period, which was scheduled to start as soon as Epstein arrived in Wellington.

The Cherry Orchard was performed in-the-round at the Drama School, and the students demonstrated a 'delicacy of understanding and great subtlety' in their interpretation of the play. In his review, Mike Nicolaidi reflected on the students' ability to perform as an ensemble:

> The graduating students more than meet the challenge, providing many moments of considerable power. [That this was] achieved after only a very brief rehearsal period is a credit to the School and the visiting guest director Sabin Epstein, and it augurs well for New Zealand theatre.[5]

Bruce Mason also praised the students and the director on their production:

> The students coped wonderfully well with emotions one might have thought way beyond them. One's only regret, much in the light of the play itself, is that these gifted students can draw no bows on a certain future in New Zealand. If they are not employed here, it will be our loss.[6]

A way of ensuring a more 'certain future' for the graduates was the apprenticeship scheme for actors operated by Downstage and achieved largely through the efforts of Mervyn Thompson. He acknowledged the company's long-term responsibility in assuring that the graduates' training continued beyond drama school. A similar system to that at Downstage had been operating in UK theatres for decades. Subsidised by

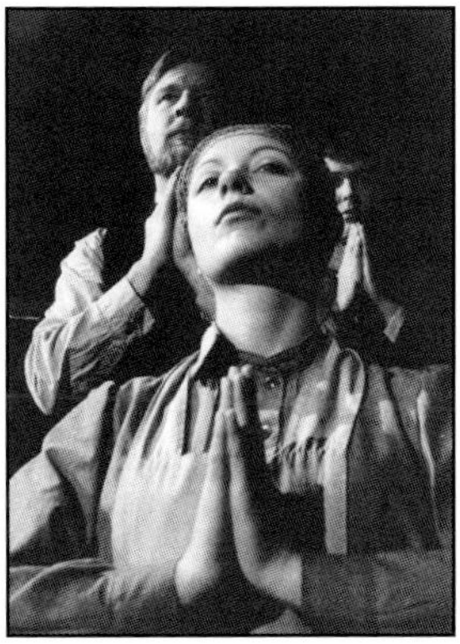

◀ *Under Milkwood*, 1977. L–R: Peter Dennett, Wiki Oman, John Godfrey.

▲ Rehearsal for *The Cherry Orchard*, 1977

◀ Rehearsal notes for *The Cherry Orchard.*
Sabin Epstein (Director). L: Maria Vlassova, R: Timothy Toye.

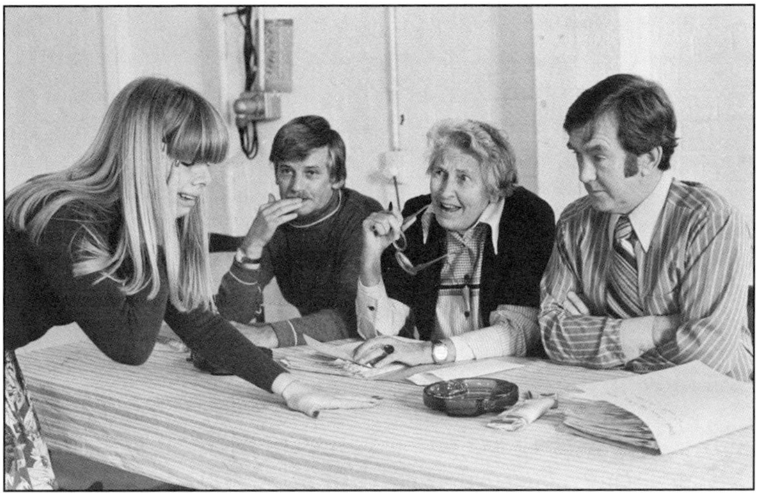

▶ Audition 1978.
L–R: Suzanne Bacon (auditionee), George Webby, Davina Whitehouse and Russell Aitken.
ATL EP/1978/3601/6a

the British Arts Council and approved by Equity, it provided opportunities for acting graduates to work in provincial repertory companies on probationary memberships.

The main obstacle to a similar scheme operating in New Zealand were the Arts Council annual grants to subsidised theatres, none of which were tagged for this purpose. Downstage was the only theatre company to offer New Zealand Drama School graduates apprenticeships in 1976. All other theatres declared that, for financial reasons, they were unable to make any long-term commitment to drama school graduates beyond the occasional short-term contract. This was a regrettable state of affairs given the relatively large number of theatre companies in New Zealand in the late 1970s and early 1980s. In many respects, it was an ideal time to introduce a postgraduate apprenticeship scheme for actors.

As there was no real financial incentive to encourage cash-strapped theatres to participate in such a scheme, George Webby asked the Arts Council to re-assess its position on actor-training: that it either provide additional subsidies to theatre companies on a dollar-for-dollar basis, or tag a percentage of the theatres' annual grant to cover the cost of an apprenticeship scheme.

In his 1976 report to the Arts Council, he included a somewhat radical proposal that apprenticeships should be allocated to Drama School graduates 'at the discretion of the Director of the School', and pointed out that 'Theatres could refuse ... but members of ACT would probably have to agree that those theatres would not offer less than equity minimum to any student straight from Drama School. Either that or they agree not to employ fresh graduates for a year.'[7]

Despite George's best efforts, no formal apprenticeship scheme was agreed. In true Kiwi fashion, the situation resolved itself with less formality, with an agreement from most theatre companies to employ New Zealand Drama School graduates at the earliest opportunity. Nearly all the twelve graduates in 1977 found work on leaving the school, and by early 1978 ten were employed in professional theatre and one in television.

Although the Fielden Taylor Hostel was a considerable improvement on the much smaller Savage Club premises, it still lacked two essential features: permanence and a theatre space. The school was on three-monthly tenure with a lease that was due to expire in 1978; the Wellington City Mission was signalling a redevelopment programme on the site. The lack of a dedicated theatre space at the hostel presented a more immediate difficulty, although the gymnasium area could be adapted as a performance space, other training activity had to be curtailed if it was used for productions.

The search for affordable premises continued for another three years, with the Board of Studies and the Arts Council inspecting over twenty properties, including two hostels, one in Boulcott Street, the other in Oriental Bay; and the old Dental Clinic in Tinakori Road. A hot favourite for a while was a warehouse/factory space with a high ceiling in Hopper Street. But the difficulty always was money, and the Arts Council found it hard to reconcile its budget with the Drama School's demand for spacious city-centre premises.

The Arts Councils' administration officer, who was also its financial advisor, considered the several relocation proposals and observed that the cost of running the school for a year would 'soon exceed $113,000 a year, or $11,300 per unit [sic] produced per annum'. He proposed an alternative solution: 'For $6000 per student we could send them all to RADA [Royal Academy of Dramatic Art] and for somewhat less we could send them to NIDA'. Other solutions considered by the Arts Council included 'relocating the Drama School to Palmerston North or Dunedin where there are other tertiary institutes and struggling professional theatre'. An earlier proposal considered by the Arts Council had the Drama School shifting to the Christchurch Arts Centre, but this plan was abandoned because of lack of space within the Centre.

In a further attempt to rein in costs, the Arts Council recommended to the school that it reduce the intake of new students in 1978 to nine, thereby saving $4,500 a year, or roughly the cost of three bursaries. John Roberts diplomatically informed the Arts Council that a reduction in the number of students was an 'uneconomic use of physical and teaching resources: the operational costs would remain the same, whether the School had nine or forty students'.[8] Furthermore, an intake of only nine students, together with the anticipated attrition rate, would reduce student numbers to a dangerously low level.

A compromise was eventually reached when the Drama School agreed to cap the *total* number of students in any one year to twenty, which allowed the school to take twelve new students a year as the attrition rate would or could reduce that number by the second year.

If nothing else, this episode reveals the considerable financial strain that the Arts Council was under in its support of the Drama School, as the administration and bursary costs continued to escalate.

Eight

1978–1980

'We had a major Sorcerer in the shape of George Webby.'

The total number of students enrolled in the New Zealand Drama School in any one year from 1974 to 1990 remained around twenty. That figure seems small when compared with the number of students now enrolled in the three-year acting programme at Toi Whakaari, which typically stands at around sixty.

One advantage of a smaller enrolment was the collaborative teaching practice that readily evolved. Tutors were encouraged to observe each others' classes, giving them a broad view of the work undertaken in the school, which led to a collective understanding that assisted them to gauge and keep watch on the students' overall progress. This was then monitored through a joint evaluation process, agreed between individual students and their tutors.

George Webby firmly believed the acting students were capable of assessing their own development, rather than depending on external grading or appraisal:

> We knew from the start that [the students] were the best judge of their own progress, and we stayed with that belief. Students were told at the beginning: that if they were still there after the first term of trial and error we would assume that the [school] suited them as a place to further their skills. Competition would be rigorously excluded from the school. Their progress was their own responsibility and, except for naughtiness or acts that impeded the progress of other students, their presence at the school was assured.[1]

Such an approach was outlined in the initial aims of the school, which stated: '[the students] will examine their own strengths and weaknesses and will seek assistance where necessary'.[2]

George felt that *Pass* and *Fail* were cruel judgments, and that both results had a deleterious effect on students, fostering a culture of 'approval' and 'disapproval' that he believed had no place in a drama school. His preferred method was to encourage students and to help them achieve their goals. To support his point of view, he referred to a passage from Viola Spolin's *Improvisation for the Theatre*:

> Our simplest move out into the environment is interrupted by our need for favourable comment or interpretation by established authority. We either fear that we will not get

> approval, or we accept outside comment and interpretation unquestioningly. In a culture where approval/disapproval has become the predominant regulator of effort and position, and often the substitute for love, our personal freedoms are dissipated.[3]

But his methodology did not always sit easy with every student:

> The students' greatest criticism is our philosophy of only working off that which is working, as against emphasising the errors. Being masochistic, they like to know what's wrong with them, but we think the faults will fall away.[4]

If George felt that a student was not suited to the school or its methodology, or if they weren't in the right space or time to be training there, he would often lead them in a conversation to the point where they could leave the school of their own volition:

> Some students wanted to leave, but the school system that they had grown up in wouldn't allow them to do that because it looked like failure. Then there was the odd one who constantly broke all the rules, and couldn't live by them because they found us wanting. It wasn't the right place for them to be in.[5]

Until 1990, there was no formal assessment process at the school, and therefore the educative values were fairly subjective: the students' 'development' was measured against their own aspiration, not through imposed assessment guidelines. Mostly what determined whether they blossomed or floundered at the school was their ability to relate to tutors and peers, or their own commitment and drive. There is little to suggest that a more rigorous *formal* assessment process would have resulted in an improved outcome for most.

> *Peter (White) Land, 1975 graduate.* I owe a debt to the bizarre esoteric teaching I received at Drama School not only in the art of acting, but also in life. We daily faced everything and it was such a shared experience that it mirrored the acting community worldwide, especially the theatre that I subsequently found myself thrown into. The real world was a little saner than the daily personal politics of drama school, but we had a major Sorcerer in the shape of George Webby – he prepared us well.[6]

> *John McDavitt, 1978 graduate.* Looking back, the structure of the course was pretty much as one would expect – for the time – but it was a practical, learning-by-doing approach … which was its strength. Overall I think the NZDS then was very much for the student to find themselves – and their own way of working. This was fine to a point, but it meant there was not much 'push' from the staff to extend a student, unless a tutor had a particular interest in them or shared interest with them.[7]

It is worth noting that a significant number of the New Zealand Drama School graduates under George Webby's stewardship succeeded in careers other than acting, including Simon Phillips, the school's second trainee-director. His first production at the school was *The Borage Pigeon Affair* at the end of 1979. All forty characters in the play were performed by seven first-year actors, with technical and front-of-house support by second-year actors. The production, described by the cast as 'Monty Python let loose in Milkwood', was performed in-the-round. It had fluid scene changes and was staged as a cabaret-circus, with Fiona Samuel cracking the whip as a Bunny Girl-cum Ringmaster.

George Webby rehearsing *What If You Died Tomorrow*, 1979. R: Philippa (Pip) Byrne, L–R sitting: Denise O'Connell and Lani Tupu.

Shadow Box, 1978, with John McDavitt and Eva Radich

The *Evening Post* review for the production made special mention of the impressive sound design, by second-year student Mark Cubey: 'The range of sound effects and music has to be heard to be believed.'[8]

After directing *The Borage Pigeon Affair*, Simon Phillips joined the second-year actors to play Jellamy the Butler in their graduation production, an adaptation of *A Family and a Fortune* by Ivy Compton-Burnett. It was performed in an elegant set (adorned with period props from family and friends) designed by Grant Tilly; costumes were provided by Gwen Kaiser and many were original garments from the Edwardian period.

Simon Phillips' portrayal of Jellamy almost stole the show (not uncommon with stage butlers). The character, little more than a device introduced to facilitate scene changes, was described by Bruce Mason in his review of the play as 'an imperious butler who rang bells and summoned maids to clear away this and restore that; thus filling out a part amounting to little more than a few coughs and spits to an image of Edwardian slyness, spying on and mercilessly leaking information from downstairs to upstairs'.[9]

The Borage Pigeon Affair was the last Drama School production at 172 Taranaki Street. By the end of 1979 the list of premises under consideration by the Arts Council for the Drama School had been reduced to two: the Engineers Building in Majoribanks Street and Sheraton House at 5 Vivian Street. A more favoured option in Hopper Street had been snapped up by another tenant earlier in the year.

The Arts Council and the Drama School agreed on the Vivian Street option. The relatively short-term lease on the property, six years instead of ten for Majoribanks Street, was a more attractive proposition for the Arts Council, as its ambition was for the Education Department to assume greater financial responsibility for the school by the mid-1980s.

In August 1980 the Drama School moved to its new premises at 5 Vivian Street. The upper floor of the two-storey building suited the purpose of the school well; it could easily be converted into studios, offices, a library and a theatre space. The premises had previously been the Malibu Supper Club, which had a somewhat shady past; eighty of its clientele had been prosecuted for illegal gambling the year before. The first floor was a rabbit warren of rooms, complete with stylish restaurant-type alcove seating left over from the nightclub. There was also a sauna and a swirl pool, but much to the students' disappointment these items were amongst the first to be removed. The Vivian Street premises were not exactly palatial, but the 8000 square feet of floor space was a considerable improvement on the cramped Taranaki Street premises:

> No expense had been spared by the previous occupants. The lavatories had almost-silver toilet-roll holders, and the 'little studies' were already furnished with comfy bean bags and tins of talcum powder. The kitchen area was well equipped and the bar area was huge with cosy banquettes and a carpeted floor that begged to be sat on. There were lots of showers and dressing areas, offices and library were all close together. Staff also had their own studies. There was a large space for movement, dance and fencing, a smaller room for general classes, and best of all, there was our own theatre space. It was a satisfying place

The Borage Pigeon Affair, 1979. Louise Dunne

Philipa Dann and George Webby painting the box office just prior to the move to 5 Vivian Street.
ATL Dom/1980/0727/1/4A

> to be in, even when the music from downstairs intruded during one of their three-minute massages.[10]

Architect Ian Athfield had the head-lease on the building and was engaged by the Arts Council to redesign the first floor of the building to create a *functional* Drama School. He generously waived his ($2,000) architectural fee. The students and staff did most of the refurbishment, cutting the cost of the conversion to $400. Just before the school moved into Vivian Street, the Wellington City Corporation Town Planning Department was alerted by an article in the *Dominion*, which revealed that the premises would have a 'theatre holding 80 people'. There had been no mention of a theatre in the plans submitted by the architects to the Town Planner, so the Arts Council responded with a diversionary tactic:

> Concerning the question of whether the premises have a theatre for 80 people. Indeed they do not. There is a large classroom which is used throughout the day for teaching purposes. On occasions the room is used for evening performances, which would not exceed 80 people. The primary means of promoting such performances are word of mouth. I hope this clarifies the position.[11]

The explanation appeared to satisfy the Town Planner, and the Drama School was allowed to settle into its interesting – but steamy – premises!

The ground floor of the building was occupied by a massage parlour, the House of Bamboo Sauna, equipped with a swimming pool, mud-bath and – of course – the essential saunas. Drama students could look down from their first-floor common room to the street below and view parlour clients as they arrived and eventually departed. Some students discovered more ambitious ways of observing the 'sauna' activity: 'One of the parlour rooms was right next to the theatre, and students would look through a little hole they'd poked in the wall to see what was going on.'[12]

To ensure the school's freedom from 'undue interference' from the Bamboo Parlour, a covenant was written into its lease, requiring the parlour 'not to do or suffer any act of omissions likely to lead to undue disturbances or annoyances to the activities of the drama school and performance venue'. Within the scope of its 'normal' activity, the parlour did its best to keep the high-jinks to a minimum, especially when Drama School performances were happening upstairs:

> It may seem odd, but there seemed to be a theatrical connection between the girls who worked downstairs and our more staid activities. They were performers just as we were and, just like us, there has to be an air of sincerity about the pleasure they are giving, or the stories we both have to tell, and the better we are it, the more money is likely to flow in from satisfied customers.[13]

For the Drama School, the most challenging aspect of the premises was the warm moist air and the level of noise drifting upwards from the swimming pool and sauna. The humidity created a particular problem for the school's performance space, situated as it was directly above the pool and sauna and completely unventilated:

> We would get all the steam and heat rising up. We had to advise people who came to performances in the winter when it was freezing cold, to dress lightly – because the theatre will be very hot. There were occasions when something very serious and of great moment would be happening quietly on stage, and suddenly there would be terrible splashes and shrieks and yells coming from underneath us. They had mud wrestling contests as well.[14]

A great advantage of 5 Vivian Street was the space it provided to house the Drama School's library, which by 1980 had around 5000 volumes. The original core of the library had been left to New Theatre by Nola Millar and was then passed on to the Drama School. George Webby also had added his books to the collection. To allow the library to function properly, all the items needed to be organised and catalogued and systems put in place. This required specialised skills, and in July 1980 Ruth Graham was appointed as the Drama School's (first) librarian. She was well qualified for the position having previously worked at the Alexander Turnbull Library and the Canterbury Museum Library. When Ruth began to unpack the books to catalogue the collection, it soon became apparent that more shelves were needed. So George immediately arranged for the students to build them.

Cataloguing the library collection was a long-term enterprise, but before she could undertake this task, Ruth had to attend to more urgent jobs such as numbering the multiple copies of plays:

> Before I arrived, the school had approached the Arts Council and said, 'Look, we've got these books, what could we do about them?' They then supplied the school with a PEP worker who had listed the books as they came in, so that was very helpful. But there was nothing to indicate which play belonged to which card.
>
> So the first thing I did was to start cataloguing and numbering the play collection, which took me years. I then put the reference collection in and catalogued it according to Dewey so that it was in a system, and then started to develop the collection from there.
>
> Cataloguing is an ongoing process and in those days before computers, cards were typed and it was quite a slow process.
>
> George's collection had been augmented a lot by that time, because of his Masters. We also acquired various big collections along the way, like Peter Harcourt's and Richard Campion's, and a wonderful collection from Jack Clay, an American theatre teacher who visited New Zealand and taught for a while at the school. After he retired, we got a letter telling us he had bequeathed his entire library to the Drama School library: well over a thousand books. So I had to organise to have that shipped out to New Zealand. His collection included a lot of material that we would never have had otherwise – a lot of publications with a focus on American theatre and on teaching practice.[15]

The library was situated in an area of the school that ran parallel with the Vivian Street frontage, a space previously occupied by the Malibu Club Restaurant. Part of the space was turned into a student common room, the remaining one-third allocated to the library. The two areas were divided by library shelving, which created a degree of separation but sadly no sound isolation. A lot of gossip from the student common room therefore floated over the wall, as Ruth Graham recalled: 'Students would forget that everything they said in the common room was perfectly audible in the library. So I learnt an awful lot – in a very short time – [about] how drama school students operate and thought.'[16]

The first production at 5 Vivian Street was *Living Quarters* by Brian Friel, which opened a few weeks after the school moved into its new home. This aptly named production was performed by the eight second-year students and directed by George Webby. Shortly after that, George left for the UK, Canada and the United States on a Fulbright Cultural Exchange scholarship, leaving the Drama School in the capable hands of Grant Tilly and Erica Stephenson. The five second-year women went on section to Mercury Theatre, to perform in *Once a Catholic*, directed by the artistic director-designate of the company, Jonathon Hardy. Technically speaking, the students were not on section: Mercury *employed* them and they each received a wage of $66.64 a week. Mercury had sought approval from Actors Equity for the students to work on the production, but the outcome of their discussions was inconclusive. To avoid a delicate industrial situation, a confidential arrangement was eventually agreed between Mercury and the Drama School. It was a good outcome for the five students: they gained valuable performance experience with a major theatre company and received $330 (tax free) each for their services.

While the women were at the Mercury, the second-year men worked on their own production of *Barbarians,* with Simon Phillips, a trilogy set in the East End of London, described in the programme as 'an unsentimental study of teenage violence and unemployment'.

Ralph McAllister's review of the play reflected a powerful and mostly positive response to the production:

> Superb teamwork, some realistic violent scenes and empathetic character portrayals make for a disturbing and provocative evening. [Simon Phillips] has wrought three powerful performances from his young actors; performances which in less committed hands could so easily have been simply distasteful.[17]

When the second-year women returned from the Mercury, they joined the three men in their group to rehearse their graduation production, *Women Beware Women.* This was also Simon Phillips' final production at the school as a trainee-director.

Women Beware Women was chosen because of the roles it provided for Louise Dunne, Georgina Monro, Fiona Samuel, Joanne Simpson and Kate Ward. It seems that Simon Phillips was fixated on theatre-in-the round at the time, and again chose this configuration, but despite making good use of the limited performance space, the production failed to please some of the reviewers:

> Once again it proves to me that old comment of Tynan's that he had yet to see an actor who worked better with his bum than his face. Working in-the-round also means a much fussier production in terms of movement as actors attempt to include the audience.[18]

And –

> I happen to loath theatre in-the-round, a convention [in which] I am rarely at my most sympathetic as a spectator in the state of acute torsion. Nor do I care to see banks of my fellows opposite, lit almost as well as the actors. [I prefer] a hospitable and anonymous darkness.[19]

Simon Phillips spoke highly of his training and endorsed the ideology that the school had fought to sustain, and for which it had sometimes been criticised. Shortly after graduating, he made the following comment about the purpose of the school:

> A criticism of the [New Zealand Drama School] has been that it doesn't turn out actors who are so technically brilliant that they can do exactly what's required without thinking about it. [The school] doesn't turn out acting machines, and some directors want people who are able to give them the goods as soon as they are told. But the School starts you on the road of growth which, if you care to pursue it will prove invaluable and stand you in good stead. Acting is a growing thing not an automatic function.[20]

Simon Phillips went on to work as an associate director at Mercury Theatre, and artistic director of Centrepoint Theatre. In 1984, he left New Zealand for Australia, and was appointed artistic director of the State Theatre Company in Adelaide. He later became associate director of the Melbourne Theatre Company, and was eventually appointed artistic director and CEO, a position he still holds.

Barbarians, 1980. L–R: Blair Park, Rob Jayne, Alexander Van Dam.

1980 Make-up class with John Banas (R). Students L–R: Blair Park, Georgina Monro, Fiona Samuel, Joanne Simpson, Louise Dunne

Nine

1981–1985

'The bully boys will now come after me with ray guns and massages.'

For most of the 1980s the Arts Council's funding for the Drama School was fairly static, apart from small annual increments to offset inflation. The only hope of a substantial increase in funding lay in the possibility of the school's being absorbed into the Education Department's budget.

Capital expenditure was virtually non-existent, and finding money to purchase much-needed equipment was a constant struggle for the school. There was also no allocation in the annual budget to mount productions, even though they were a fundamental part of the students' training. The only practical way this could be achieved was through a 'slush-fund' managed by George and Erica, for which the Arts Council was less than pleased.

When George returned from his overseas sabbatical in March, he was interviewed by Bruce Mason for an article in *ACT*. George was asked what he thought was the greatest disadvantage to New Zealand theatre; he replied: 'The national sport of throat-cutting and blood-letting. When this happens, our whole movement is diminished by just that much.' And he spoke of the community's 'ignoble delight in artistic failure. Whereas failure can be as fascinating as success; artistic experiment in New Zealand is widely equated with failure.'[1]

Clearly re-invigorated by his overseas trip, George set about strengthening the financial position of the Drama School. Perhaps inspired by a recent Telethon that had raised over $5 million ('a world record per head of population'), he embarked on his own fundraising venture by launching the second-year's production of *Fanshen* with a gala performance and wrote to everyone on the school's mailing list, inviting them to donate a 'minimum' of twenty dollars towards the purchase of new seating for the school's performance space. Confident that the cost would be covered by donations, he went ahead and ordered the lavish wool-covered seating modules. They were duly installed in time for the gala, despite only half their cost being raised through donations.

Immediately after *Fanshen*, the first-years staged an ambitious production of *Don Juan Comes Back from the War*, an adaptation of Odon von Horvath's play by

Christopher Hampton. The production was directed by Rhys McConnochie, who had made his theatre debut with the New Zealand Players in *Pygmalion* in the late 1950s. After receiving a government bursary to study in Paris and London, he joined the Royal Shakespeare Company and working extensively in the UK for many years. Rhys returned to New Zealand in 1979 to work at Theatre Corporate for six months, during which time he also tutored at the Drama School.

Rhys arranged *Don Juan Comes Back from the War* into twenty-four short scenes, giving the production a cinematic quality. The first-year cast shared multiple roles 'in the style of grotesque caricatures of George Grosz', which provided them with the opportunity to demonstrate a range of capabilities:

> They romp from street corner whores to children in the forest, from nights at the opera to jealousies in the cafe. They capture in their style that decadence which we take as an accurate reflection of the Germany of the time.[2]

In his review of the production, Bruce Mason described the first-year students as 'the most talented group at the Drama School for years, they offer in *Don Juan* the best ensemble playing in town, as of course they should'.[3]

Finding suitable plays for this group of eight women and three men was no easy task, and in their second year the school commissioned two plays for them. The first was *Today's Bay,* written by Craig Thaine. He had joined the school in May as a writer-in-residence, with financial support from the New Zealand Literary Fund and Wellington City Council's Community Development Scheme. Before coming to the school, Craig had worked as production assistant and publicity officer at Centrepoint Theatre, where he wrote his first play, *Stagger*, as well as a play for children, *Gruzzlefummit.* Both were produced at Centrepoint and directed by Jan Prettejohns.

In 1981 Grant Tilly worked with Craig and the first-year students to develop the play through a process of improvisation. It was based on Katherine Mansfield's short story 'At the Bay', which Craig used to explore New Zealand identity and the role of the artist in New Zealand within the context of Mansfield's life story.

Craig attended classes as an honorary twelfth student, and performed in the second-years' graduation production, an abridged version of *Henry V*, directed by George Webby. The play had been chosen by George to showcase the graduating students, and he later described it as one of his 'proudest'. Only seven of the eight graduating students performed on stage in *Henry V*: Fiona Johnstone's interests had shifted towards lighting and she had opted to be the production manager and lighting designer/operator for the production. She was possibly the first 'techie' to graduate from the Drama School, and went on to make a career in theatre as a lighting designer.

The first production for the second-years in 1982 was *Today's Bay* on which they had worked the previous year. It was the first time an entirely new work had been produced by the Drama School; it presented unique challenges as well as advantages for the students. Having the writer in rehearsal throughout its development allowed the production to grow organically, and improvisation techniques were used to unlock the narrative, which enabled the story to be explored in terms of action and space rather than words. It was directed by Derek Nicholson, then the director of Theatre Workshop at the Seymour Theatre Centre in Sydney:

> Derek had a very open and resourceful approach. About a week out from the show opening we thought we had reached a low point. We decided to improvise the whole thing – which we did in the dance studio without costumes or props. Somehow it released the production; and it had this amazing energy to it. At the end we sat on the floor and no one could speak for several minutes. It was a very powerful and valuable process that helped the production to gel – it was a very exciting experience. Because we'd gone through that experience together, we trusted each other on a deeper level.[4]

Today's Bay had mixed reviews. Some of the audience and reviewers were not sure if they were watching a performance or a rehearsal; and scenes set in 1982 were interspersed with scenes set in an earlier part of the century. These ambiguities were highlighted by Ralph McAllister in his review:

> Are we there, as the narrator seems to suggest, or are we not there as the unreal students seem to suggest? But then if we are not there at rehearsal, can it be a performance without us?[5]

Bruce Mason made a topical connection between the destructive behaviour expressed in the play, which 'forced the audience to recognise the sheer nastiness of our community when faced with the phenomenon of a major artist', and the partition in New Zealand caused by the 1981 Springbok Tour:

> We are a deeply divided community, existing in warring halves; almost going to war when occasions like the Springbok tour acts as a catalyst. These warring factions cannot communicate and have no interests in common, and they hardly speak the same language: one month Telethon, the next knuckle and violence. That's where we are at.[6]

When New Zealanders took to the streets in the first half of 1981 to march against the Springbok's rugby tour, Rona Bailey was in the thick of it, struck down and left bloodied in the 'Battle of Molesworth Street'. Notorious for having founded the Workers' Communist League and before that the Wellington Marxist–Leninist Organisation, Rona was referred to by Prime Minister Robert Muldoon as the 'High Priestess of New Zealand Communism', and he included her in the infamous list of twelve Communists the SIS alleged were responsible for organising the 'radical' opposition to the tour.

George Webby also encouraged the drama students to protest against the Springbok tour, and scheduled classes around demonstrations. Rachel Lang, a first-year student, and her fellow student May Lloyd were both arrested by police for obstructing the Lower Hutt motorway. Rachel and May spent several days in court before receiving community service, and as they sat in court awaiting sentence, a couple of girls asked them why they were there:

> When we said we'd sat on a road, they thought we were mental. When we explained it was because of the tour and apartheid, they had no idea what we were on about. It made me realise that I lived in a different New Zealand to these young women. I was lucky to be educated and have time to waste on political principles.[7]

Fanshen, 1981. L-R Philipa Dann, Peter East. Merfyn Owen (obscured), Heather Bolton, Mark Everton, Kerry O'Reilly, Robert Colhoun.

Today's Bay, 1982. L–R May Lloyd, Jan Fisher, Alison Routledge

Rehearsal of *Lavender Blue*, 1982. Front, standing: George Webby (director). Back row L–R: Lucy Sheehan, Ross Girven, (?). Middle row seated L–R: Stephen Judd, Michelle Leuthart. Front row L–R: Jeff Kingsford-Brown, (? obscured), Rachel Lang, Rima Te Wiata, Danny Mulheron, Ruth Dudding, Louise Green.

Meanwhile, the school was caught in a very different cross-fire. Despite having moved to more spacious (and entertaining) accommodation, the students and staff were disenchanted with some of the less desirable aspects of 5 Vivian Street:

> The premises at times had the fetid smell and humidity of a Papua New Guinea jungle, caused by the vapours rising from the saunas below. The condensation and steam from the hot pools and saunas has warped the floors, joists and ceilings, and our doors won't close. The condensation got into our switchboard and caused short circuits which put out the lights.[8]

The noise filtering up from the Bamboo Parlour below, caused by the juke box, mud wrestling, laughter, shrieks and sometimes 'terrible splashes', remained an ongoing problem for the school, particularly during rehearsals and performances. Clearly, something had to be done, otherwise the school would have to move. But despite a constant flow of solicitors' letters, little was achieved. Frustrated by the lack of action, George Webby persuaded the Wellington City Council to inspect the premises and wrote to the landlord to demand that the Bamboo Sauna 'abate the nuisance'. When George received the health report from WCC, he sent a copy to the Arts Council with the following note: 'Probably the bully boys will now come after me with ray guns and massages. Now what are you lot doing about the noise pollution and sound proofing? Signed: over-heated George Webby.'[9]

In 1982 the school again received funding from the New Zealand Literary Fund, enabling it to commission a play for the graduating year. It was *The Twelfth Man,* written by playwright/actor Jeffery Thomas:

> George Webby told me what he wanted – a play for eight women and three men. I did some arithmetic, and came up with the idea of a cricket team. It obviously had to be a women's team. And so the three men had to become women. Immediately you had a comedy, and so I took it from there.[10]

This delightfully engineered farce, directed by George Webby, is set in the changing room of a cricket club where a motley group of 'female' cricket players have gathered to play a charity match. Tolis Papazoglou designed the set for the production: a breezy indoors–outdoors affair of shifting perspectives and summer landscapes. To help the cast get a feel for the game, they were coached by the Wellington Cricket Team culminating in a match between them and the Drama School eleven – at the Basin Reserve.

In his review of the play, Mike Nicolaidi cited the production to highlight the quality of work being undertaken by the Drama School:

> Money, enough of it, will always force pressure points in the presentation of live theatre to the public. But in the end, it is the dedication of individuals working in a group, committed and full time that wins the day [regardless] of politicians, fundamentalists, philosophers and all-knowing arts administrators. This may seem an unnecessarily long introduction to what I believe is one of the finest productions yet to come from the drama school in a near decade of achievements. Yet such statements are necessary because of the depressing winds that tend to blow through the arts every 10 years. Unless we are vigilant and actually see what is happening on the escalator towards greater excellence in theatre, we could lose perspective and go down the plughole with the pessimists. The great joy

Twelfth Man, 1982. L–R: Peter Hambleton, Perry Piercy, Jon Brazier, Lucy Sheehan, Augusta McDonald, Alison Routledge, Jan Fisher, Rachel Lang, Michelle Leuthart.

Twelfth Man, 1983 at Centrepoint. L–R: Augusta McDonald, Kerry O'Reilly, Eva Radich.

> of *Twelfth Man* is that it underlines again the strength of both the individual and the ensemble of the school.[11]

Twelfth Man had a further three-week season at Centrepoint Theatre in February 1983, with most of the 1982 graduates in the cast. Centrepoint had ceased to be a production house in its own right, its Arts Council funding had been pulled and it was struggling to survive. To help the theatre through its difficulties, the cast worked on the production for very little (if any) money. George Webby and Tolis Papazoglou provided their services free to remount the production.

The second-year cohort, in 1983, was much smaller than that of the previous year, with only seven students. Simon Phillips returned to the school to direct them in their mid-year production, *Marat/Sade*. It was an excellent vehicle for the students, providing an opportunity for skilled ensemble work. The production combined verse, acrobatics, pantomime and masque, allowing them to use many aspects of their training. First-year students were roped-in to play various citizens and 'mad people', including Natasha Hay and Miranda Harcourt who had both recently joined the school:

> Natasha and I, we designed everything – sets and posters, in the two years we were at the school. For the *Marat/Sade* posters we cut off Brett Alcock's hair and stuck bits all over the posters as part of the French rosettes.[12]

The graduation production in 1983 was Simon Gray's *Quartermain's Terms*, directed by George Webby. The production marked the end of his first ten years as director of the New Zealand Drama School, providing him with an opportunity to reflect on other aspects of his extensive career. George described this time as the 'autumnal period' of his theatre work. In 1982 he had been awarded an OBE for his services to theatre in New Zealand. When he was interviewed by the *Dominion* about his inclusion in the New Years' Honours list, George used the opportunity to acknowledge the Drama School and to highlight its financial difficulties:

> It's nice to know the School has been recognised in such a way. It is an honour. But the OBE won't help us as much as a bit of money would. The two-year acting course should really be a three-year course. We'd love to be able to extend it an extra year. But, like so many areas of the arts in New Zealand, we don't have the funds.[13]

Quartermain's Terms turned out to be the school's last production at 5 Vivian Street. In January 1984 a fire was lit by an arsonist on the ground floor of the premises, in the renamed Retreat Sauna. Sixty-two firemen attended the fire and managed to contain the blaze to the ground floor, but thick smoke spread into the Drama School causing considerable damage to the library and the costume collection. Erica Stephenson was first to arrive on the scene after receiving a late-night phone call telling her the school was on fire:

> The fire had nearly burnt down, and when I went up [into the school] it was all black and disgusting. I rang a few students and asked them to get a team together to empty the school the next day. They had to wear masks as the place was still very smoky.[14]

George Webby was in the USA and not due back until February, so Erica phoned him and told him not to worry.

Quartermain's Terms, 1983. Guy Boyce and Ruth Dudding.

L–R: Miranda Harcourt, Simon Phillips, Natasha Hay - 'publicists'

The police confirmed that the fire had been deliberately lit, the most likely explanation being that the school had been the innocent victim of a massage-parlour war between rival operators. Although smoky and blackened in places, the school appeared to be relatively undamaged. The worst affected area for smoke damage was the library. Ruth Graham and a team of students worked methodically through the collection to clean and then pack the books into cartons:

> I'd previously worked at the Turnbull Library and knew the Conservation Officer – he was very helpful and came down and advised us on how to go about cleaning the books. There was a special eraser that architects use on plan drawings, a little bag with stuff in it, but in the end we reverted to methylated spirits, particularly for the book covers. And with the help of the students, we started working our way through the books before packing them into boxes.
>
> We worked in the school itself. Everything in the school was going to be cleaned and a lot of stuff was taken off shelves and packed away. The wardrobe collection was sent off to the drycleaners, and a new set of lights that the school had just acquired was laid out in the gym ready for cleaning.[15]

A second fire was set three weeks later. This time the arsonist torched the school itself, close to where the cartons of books had been stacked. The blaze was devastating, as Ruth Graham recalled:

Aftermath of the second fire at 5 Vivian St, Grant Tilly inspecting the damage.
ATL Dom/1984/0205/1/9A

> The fire completely gutted the theatre, and all the lighting equipment was lost – everything was blackened. It was like walking into a nightmare and there was no power in the building, and it was therefore very dark. The smell was horrendous: smoke and ash. The fire department had managed to contain the fire before it reached the library, so all the books were salvageable. Everyone rallied again. The first two people on the site were Liz Mullane and Mark Wright who were about to start as first-year students, just arrived in Wellington, looking for a flat. Everyone had been shattered by the first fire, and the shock of the second fire was really bad.[16]

The theatre space, the backstage area and foyer were completely gutted. The drama studios were badly burned, with extensive water damage throughout the entire building. It was fortunate that much of the school's equipment had been removed from the building after the first fire. However, the theatre seating, purchased through the school's fundraising exercise in 1981, was completely destroyed. Ruth Graham again went about rescuing the library collection:

> It looked like something out of Kafka. Everything was black, the remaining books on the shelves were totally blackened and when we took them off the shelves there were white outlines where they had been. At that point we literally had to get out of the building within hours. Quite a lot of the collection was in boxes lined up outside all along the corridor. It was a miracle they didn't all get destroyed ... because they were stored across the corridor from the gymnasium and it was in the gym that the second fire was set. Somehow these books and these boxes had missed the firemen's water. They were damp and smoky but inside they were still relatively clean. The librarian from Wellington Polytech, who'd been very helpful to me when I was first started setting up the Drama School library, came along and said, 'Write the whole lot off; those books will all disintegrate in five years.' But most of them are still on the shelves in the Nola Millar Library today.
>
> The books smelt absolutely dreadful. Anyway, we packed them into boxes and stored them across the road at Mico Wakefield's, until George or somebody organised for the books to be taken up to the old hall at Wellington High School, which was due to be demolished. We then had this entire team of students cleaning the books for the next three weeks – most of them had just arrived at the school, like Liz Mullane and Mark Wright. The students were amazing and they got to know each other very well, getting high on meths.
>
> George was on his way home when the second fire happened; a terrible homecoming. I believe his plane caught fire on the way back! It was a dreadful time, a hard time actually. John Roberts was the chairman of the Board and he was absolutely marvellous; and so was Erica Stephenson – it was just extraordinary how she managed to hold everything together.[17]

The second fire affected Erica badly and she was clearly distraught. Despite this, she diligently wrote a detailed report on the impact of the fire for the Board of Studies, in which she concluded:

> The whole building is devastated by smoke and water damage where it is not obliterated by actual fire. It is unhealthy, unsafe, and TOTALLY MISERABLE! I've had enough! I'm going to Rongotai [*the airport*] tomorrow, and it won't be just to travel to Picton![18]

Of course, she did nothing of the sort. With the help of John Roberts, Erica immediately set about finding 'temporary' accommodation for the school, and within forty-eight hours premises were located close to Vivian Street, on the first floor of 76 Kent Terrace. Although available for immediate occupation, the premises provided little more than an office space: it had low ceilings, with no area that could be used as a theatre. But given the urgency of the situation, the Board of Studies reluctantly agreed to take a six-month lease on the property.

The start of the new school year was postponed for a month to enable alterations to be made to the Kent Street premises. In the meantime, the school's library collection was again moved – to a classroom at Wellington Polytechnic – and students were once more employed to clean the books.

Other students were given the job of painting the first floor of 76 Kent Terrace to prepare for the new school year. Partitions were erected to create separate spaces for a teaching room, movement studio, common room and kitchen, library, staff room, and various small studies and offices. Although considerably smaller than Vivian Street, the premises at Kent Terrace had one distinct advantage: plenty of natural light. Thankfully, the school's insurance covered the cost of the relocation.

When George Webby returned from America he urged the Arts Council to find a more suitable – permanent – home for the school. There was a slight possibility they could return to Vivian Street when the fire damage was repaired as the owners had indicated that they wanted to restore the building. The sauna tenants had dropped out of the picture, and both floors of the building were offered to the Drama School. David Gascoigne, the Arts Council's legal advisor on this matter, advised against the proposal: '[The school] would be better off out of the premises altogether … in view of the second fire, which has now devastated the building; I think a return to Vivian Street is out of the question – or should be!'[19]

John Roberts saw an opportunity to turn the unfortunate circumstances of the fire to the school's advantage, and wrote to the Arts Council summarising the options:

> The old accommodation in Vivian Street could provide for nothing more than the present activities of the School. A third year, and a course for technicians, would demand expansion within the present building [Vivian Street] after reinstatement or a move to new accommodation. We ask only that the sponsoring bodies reinforce success and grasp this opportunity which has now briefly appeared to consolidate the School's situation.[20]

His report then itemised the *essential* needs of the school:

- A small but well-appointed and flexible theatre ... to give the students an authentic performing experience
- A large, well-ventilated and efficient movement/music room with adequate sound proofing and a good sprung floor
- Three properly equipped classrooms
- A good sized library space
- Quiet study rooms for students
- An audio visual room set up to introduce students to the techniques of screen and audio production
- Fully adequate bathroom facilities

- Adequate staff studies, and a staff common room and office space
- A large pleasant space for the students' common room with adequate facilities for preparing meals.
- Most important – the Board is persuaded that the School should be in the centre of the city.[21]

George Webby was adamant that he would not settle for yet another inadequate arrangement:

> The government, Arts Council and Education Department will have to face their responsibility and decide whether or not they are committed to the idea of a NZ Drama School. It's not enough to be given OBEs, for services rendered to the dramatic arts; it needs to be taken seriously.[22]

The Arts Council responded by offering the school space in the Odlins Building in Cable Street (now the New Zealand Stock Exchange – with scrolling electronic display). There were already plans in place to refurbish the building to house the Ballet Company, the New Zealand Ballet School, the Arts Council and other arts organisation. The area offered to the school was only 450 square metres, compared to the 1000 square metres in the Vivian Street premises, so the offer was declined.

Larger premises were needed to accommodate the proposed three-year acting programme that George had pushed for since 1974, which was urgently needed to provide space for a curriculum that had broadened to include TV and film work. The third year would also alleviate the pressure to mount 'at least' three productions over a two-year period, which in turn would allow more time for specialised courses. Not least of all, a three-year programme would raise the level of training, making it comparable to many overseas drama schools.

It had also been suggested that the Drama School would be an ideal place either to coordinate or to provide new-entrant training for theatre technicians. For this to happen, the school would definitely require larger premises and more staff.

Downstage Theatre, Maidment Arts Centre and the Court Theatre had at various times provided in-house training in technical skills, stage-management and design. But they and other theatre companies found it difficult to set up and maintain training programmes:

> Resources are not available, and the constant pressure of staging productions doesn't help to meet long-term training objectives. Trainees taken on by some theatres in the past have often been used as a source of cheap labour – the only training being the work experience. To establish a successful and ongoing programme, a separate industry-representative body is required.[23]

The Board of Studies supported George Webby's push for larger premises and for the three-year acting programme, but the Arts Council was less than enthusiastic. A letter sent to the Board of Studies in May 1984 stated:

> While we share the [school's] enthusiasm for a third-year course, we must immediately state that we see no possibility of the Arts Council funding such an aspiration, either in this year, or in the 1985/1986 year.[24]

For the next four years, the 'temporary' premises in Kent Terrace became a semi-permanent home for the school. The Arts Council set up a task-force in 1985 'to address the accommodation difficulties of the Drama School alongside the needs of the School of Dance and the Ballet Company' (by now the Odlins project had fallen over). The Dance School had a demolition notice on its premises, so its need for new and larger accommodation was even more urgent than that of the Drama School's.

Meanwhile, the Drama School continued without a performance space, and other venues were sought for upcoming productions. The first, in August 1984, was *The Skin of Our Teeth* by Thornton Wilder. Remembering the success of *The Twelfth Man* the previous year, Centrepoint Theatre came to the rescue. Its new artistic director, Stuart Devenie, offered to direct *The Skin of Our Teeth*, and Centrepoint Theatre was made available for rehearsals, with Palmerston North Teachers' College Studio as the performance venue. Miranda Harcourt and Stuart Devenie co-designed the set for the production and, with Natasha Hay's assistance, Miranda made two 'wonderful and magnificently constructed prehistoric beasties: a reptilian dinosaur and a hairy mammoth':

> In my first year I got cast in a lead role in our first-year production of *The Rivals* directed by Grant Tilly, which I shouldn't have got, because I was never there. … Then in our graduation production I got cast in a role with no words at all – in fact, it might just have

◄ *The Skin of Our Teeth*, 1984. Eteuati Ete and Miranda Harcourt

▼ *The Skin of Our Teeth*, 1984 with prehistoric beasties. L–R: 'Mammoth', Patupatu Ripley, Natasha Hay, Eteuati Ete, 'Dinosaur', Nick Farra

> been invented as a role for me to walk on, wear a wig and walk off again. I had so little to do – we were at Palmerston North for six weeks to rehearse and perform – so me and Natasha Hay designed the set and made the props, and made an amazing elephant and a Tyrannosaurus Rex. I was proud of him being made from nothing, but it didn't look as good as it should, so I phoned my parents and told them that I needed a tree that's got this fabric wrapped round it – can't remember its name but we had one in the garden. The next morning there was a call from the railway station: my father had gone out and dug it up and sent the material by train to Palmerston North.[25]

A few weeks later, the first-years performed *Taking our Time* at BATS, a play devised by the Red Ladder Theatre in the UK. The production was directed by Phillip Mann, who at that time was head of the Drama Studies Department at Victoria University and also associate director of Downstage. The set for *Taking our Time* was (again) designed by Miranda Harcourt.

Miranda's design skills did not go unnoticed. When she left the Drama School in 1984, she was employed by Tony Taylor at the Fortune Theatre where she worked for two years, half time as an actor and half as designer: 'That was really where I learned all my stuff because I was in a real environment with the real pressures.' This was a refreshing change for Miranda. As one of the youngest in her year at Drama School, she had not exactly been a model student:

> I was a very ill-focused student – that's probably a kind way of putting it; I was all over the place. Part of that was because I was very young. I went to university very, very briefly then I went to Australia and did the classic thing you did back then, that's go to Australia and get completely lost. Then I came back to New Zealand and what brought me back and probably saved my life was an audition into the Drama School. Much to my surprise, I got in. Really I was too young.
>
> In the Drama School environment, especially in the first year when you never seem to do any acting, I would spend a lot of my time hung over wearing a fencing mask and lying in a corner with Jo Briant – my evil twin. We were just useless; nowadays we would be kicked out. In fact, I spent most of my first term at the lawyers, and I tell the story in *The Biography of My Skin.* I and another student rolled a bottle store and stole heaps of bottles of alcohol. We got arrested and spent the night in the cells, then endless amounts of time going to court and going to lawyers. In the end, we were saved by Princess Diana because the policewoman who took our statements the night we got arrested was never available to go to court to be the chief witness for the prosecution; she was off on Princess Diana's security detail around the country. Because of that we got off – scot-free – and I was able to go back to school and do some work.
>
> But I never did any work, and never really knew where I was or what was going on; it was all a big mystery to me. I was surrounded by people with a far stronger work ethic than me: Patupatu Ripley was an amazing powerhouse; I think she and Eteuati Ete were two of the first Samoans at the school.[26]

Throughout the 1980s, Drama School students became increasingly concerned by the declining value of their QEII Arts Council scholarships, which barely kept pace with the growing double-digit inflation. From 1980 to 1983 the bursary level remained static – at $1,925. This represented a decrease in real value of around 30 per cent, so

George Webby wrote to the Arts Council to complain about the diminishing scholarships:

> The special nature of the course means that the students incur high course-related expenses and have difficulty supplementing their income through part-time work .... the bleak employment situation means that the chances of earning additional income are slim. A comparison with other tertiary students shows New Zealand Drama School students are now at a financial disadvantage and the scholarship to be well below the Government's minimum living allowance as set by the Unemployment Benefit.[27]

In an article in the *Evening Post*, George pointed to the financial hardship that the students were facing, and expressed his fear that 'the Drama School could become an elitist school, catering only for those students who could afford to attend, or were assured of some financial backing from their parents'.[28]

When the Arts Council eventually agreed to meet a delegation of students to discuss their grievance, it conceded that a more 'reasonable perspective' would be to base the cost-of-living calculations on the students' needs, and subsequently increased the annual bursary to $2,200.

Nevertheless, lobbying by students for an increase in the bursary became an annual task. In 1985 and again in 1986, the students wrote lengthy submissions 'in desperation' to the Arts Council, providing detailed calculations to show how the scholarships fell short of the basic cost of rent and food. In 1986 government legislation was introduced, which entitled Drama School students to the Standard Tertiary Bursary. The amount each student received depended on their age and other factors: the maximum they could claim equated to a weekly income of around $65. Without factoring in additional course-related costs, that was considerably less than the average student's weekly expenditure – of around $100 for rent, food and power.

The present arrangement of student loans and allowances makes it difficult to compare the bursary situation in 1986 with the circumstances of today. Drama School students in 1986 paid only $50 a year in fees, which also covered their membership of the Wellington Polytechnic Students' Association. Today, single students under twenty-five living away from home are eligible for a Study Link allowance of up to $160 a week, depending on their parents' income. They may also be eligible for an additional accommodation benefit. But this has to be balanced against the cost of tuition fees, student services levies and other course-related costs: a total exceeding $6,000 a year.

Training at the Drama School in the 1980s, with virtually no tuition fees, the benefit of an Arts Council bursary and no student loan to repay, was quite favourable when compared to the situation today. The appeal of the present funding arrangement is that it largely dispels George Webby's earlier fear that the Drama School could become 'an elitist school, catering only for those students who could afford to attend'.

Ten

1986–1987

'Erica and Ruth would look at us poor spotty pale students and get all motherly on us. They'd go out and buy vegetables and cook us a huge meal in the kitchen. I also remember David Geary making a stunning pumpkin pie.'

The Drama School had relocated three times since it was first housed at the Savage Club in 1974, but its accommodation was still temporary. Fortunately, the real value of a teaching institution is not the physical space it occupies, but more importantly its teachers. Despite the disruptions to the school during the previous thirteen years, the quality of the teaching was never compromised and had remained high.

George Webby and Grant Tilly were still the only full-time teachers at the school, made possible through direct Education Department funding administered by Wellington Polytechnic. Other staff wages were covered by the Arts Council's annual grant to the school. Erica Stephenson, who had taught mediaeval dance, tap and ballroom dancing part time at the school since 1974, was appointed as a 'full-time' dance tutor in 1987, in addition to her administrative duties.

New Zealand had few qualified teachers in the key areas of actor training and theatre production. Nevertheless, the Drama School had always attracted tutors of exceptional quality, a remarkable achievement given the low fees they received. Their dedication to the school and their commitment to the students are enduring aspects of the New Zealand Drama School story.

Some of the tutors who had joined the QEII Arts Council School in 1970 were still teaching at the New Zealand Drama School in the late 1980s, including Rona Bailey whose association with Nola Millar went back even further – to the 1960s.

Rona Bailey, who now taught creative movement at the school, first studied modern dance in America in the late 1930s, inspired by the work of Martha Graham at Columbia University. Rona was encouraged by the revolution that was going on in dance as a reaction to 'highbrow' ballet. On her return to New Zealand in 1939, she joined the Physical Welfare Branch of Internal Affairs in Hamilton, and incorporated modern dance techniques into physical education. She later moved to Wellington to take up a senior position as women's physical welfare and recreation officer, and later created the New Dance

Group, which helped to establish the foundation of modern dance in New Zealand.

Rona was a political animal, living her life according to socialist principles. Through her work with the Workers' Communist League, and as a long-standing Communist Party member, she was a strong advocate for many causes, including anti-racism. When, during the 1951 waterfront lockouts, the government invoked emergency regulations under the draconian Public Safety Conservation Act, Rona and her husband Chip Bailey produced and distributed the bulk of Wellington's 'illegal' bulletins.

Rona's political beliefs were closely allied to her approach to movement and dance: both were associated with real people and relevant to contemporary issues. For a time, from the late 1970s, Rona became frustrated by her self-confessed inability to make a meaningful connection between movement classes and the needs of the acting students. This was eventually resolved when Erica Stephenson gave her a copy of Jean Sabatine's *The Actor's Image: Movement Training for the Stage and Screen*. One particular passage in the book caught Rona's attention:

> The actor's only tools of expression are their voice and body, guided by their mental and emotional attributes. The relationship between the actor's physical, mental and emotional nature forms the organic whole.[1]

This affected Rona's teaching methods from then on. By appealing more to their intellect and imagination, she got the students to forget about being (often) awkward or fumbling beings, and instead to 'move to their imagination':

> You have the students very relaxed on the floor, and ask them to think about an incident in their lives – pleasant or unpleasant – and to try and absorb that incident, and when they feel they have, to start to move and explore the essence of that experience in their movement. Like improvisation, they were being asked to re-create their feelings in movement. Tied up with a kinaesthetic sense and their understanding of where they were in time and space and dynamics: from the movement point of view, without the need for any voice.[2]

Rona left in 1983 to travel overseas and when she returned the following year she resumed her teaching by complementing the movement work of Lyne Pringle and Michael Parmenter. When she stopped teaching in 1988, she continued her close association with the school by becoming a member of the Trust Board. Her long-standing commitment to the Treaty of Waitangi profoundly affected the direction of the Drama School, an influence that is enshrined in Toi Whakaari's present bicultural commitment.

George Webby claimed that during his time the Drama School students were amongst the fittest. There was certainly a major focus on physical training and an equal emphasis placed on vocal technique:

> From the very start I believed that every student should have a daily voice and movement class in one form or another, and I never deviated from that viewpoint. We increased the variety of teachers in the broader area of movement, from fencing, historical dance, through Laban theory, Alexander Technique to tap dancing and jazz. If there was an area of movement that wasn't taught at the school, it was because we didn't know about it.[3]

Speech and voice had been a core part of actor training at the Drama School since 1970, initially taught by Anne Flannery. When Anne left the school in 1976, Jane Waddell took over as the voice and speech tutor. She was a recent graduate of the school and had been taught by Anne Flannery. Apart from a break to study voice training methods in Britain between 1977 and 1978, and at other times to perform, Jane taught voice and/or speech at the school until 1992.

When Jane was in Britain, Meriol Buchanan took over as voice and speech tutor, and then Robin Payne from 1979–83. Robin had returned to New Zealand in 1979 with her partner, designer Tolis Papazoglou, to work at Downstage Theatre, she as a voice coach and Tolis as a designer for the company. When she left for Australia in 1983 to take up a position with the Melbourne Theatre Company, Nerissa Moore became the school's principal voice tutor, sharing the role with Jane Waddell, although Jane's classes were focused more towards speech.

Nerissa is a Fellow of the Speech and Communication Association, a professional body of teachers. Its membership included Robin Payne's mother Joy, who was one of Nerissa's mentors. When Nerissa joined the school, she began working with Keryn Stone to introduce integrated dance–vocal work forming a bridge between the purely physical and the purely vocal. It was 'cutting-edge' stuff at the time, and when Nerissa went on a study trip to the UK and Canada, she observed that 'no-one integrated the two disciplines as we had been doing':

> My interest in the integration of body and voice grew from my observation of my own children; they were never just voice – it was always body and voice – from go. So when I travelled overseas, that was one of my primary things, to see what people were doing to coordinate voice and physical teaching. They all said, 'Yes, lovely but we can't do it', nobody had because of timetabling and so on.
>
> Traditionally not a lot of physical activity was included in voice classes; students didn't come out of class sweating. I got the students doing physical things whilst making noises. If students are sitting on the floor holding hands with someone rocking backwards and forwards, and then running around, they end up being quite sweaty and hot and making voice all the time: that is integration. This engaged my interest in body and voice – way back then – and this has been the drive in my work ever since.[4]

The vocal–movement methodology introduced by Nerissa and Keryn was later picked up and expanded by Tom McCrory, through his 'training' classes, which he introduced when he joined the school in the late nineties. Nerissa continued to work with Tom from that time, integrating voice into the training sessions until she 'retired' in 2005.

Earlier students of the school were trained more for regional theatre where English plays were often performed, so the tendency was to teach RP (Received Pronunciation), or the New Zealand version of that. The school today is more accepting of difference, while at the same time there is an increased understanding of the need to teach actors that they cannot just use their own dialect for every role. Nerissa Moore was instrumental in advancing that particular point of view:

> The settling of New Zealand was done mostly by working class people. My parents spoke with a Lancashire accent, but I didn't inherit the accent. At that time, there was a snob

> element in New Zealand that wanted to change us to being English. It was deeply seated in our settlement, with primary school teachers trying to teach their little ones 'how now brown cow'. There was a very definite social reaction to that, a sort of reverse snobbery: if you speak properly you're putting yourself above yourself. I was known as the 'lah-de-dah' prefect at Gisborne High School, simply because I didn't sound like an east coast New Zealander, but it was just the way I spoke, and I'm decidedly New Zealand.
>
> There are many ways to pronounce 'says' other than Standard English, there's a whole variant of English now. But drama students should know that in some contexts, like Noel Coward, they should pronounce words correctly, such as 'says' – as 'sez'.
>
> But the connection between the sound people make and who they are is incredibly tight; it's part of their identity. The moment you suggest to people that they make changes, you tend to get an emotional reaction. And if you say judgmental things about Pacific Island and Māori speech, then you're going to get a *big* reaction. So when I started teaching at the Drama School, understandably some students physically resisted the idea of adapting or modifying their accents.[5]

The Drama School prospectus for 1987 boasts *seventy* tutors having taught at the school between 1974 and 1986. In addition to the many visiting tutors contracted to deliver one-off block courses, a large group of permanent part-time tutors regularly taught there. The vagaries of part-time/casual employment and incomplete records make it hard to determine exactly who was teaching at the school from month to month, but regular part-timers between 1974 and the late eighties included Val Bayley and Erica Stephenson, who between them taught dance, historical movement, tap dancing and ballroom dancing, often with George Webby accompanying classes on the piano; Phillip Mann (acting); Bunty and Brian Western (fencing); John Winera and Jim Batson (body mechanics); Flora Edwards (vocal technique); Keryn Stone (movement and jazz dance); Colleen Reilly (theatre criticism); Neil Hennessy, Leslie Souness, Murray Webb and Michael Williams (pianists and singing); Judith White (singing); John Anderson (video/screen technique); John Banas (fights and make-up); Eric Doornekamp (yoga); and Aileen Davidson (clown and mask work).

Clowning classes had been introduced into the curriculum in 1977 to help release the students' imagination and improve their ability to convey emotions simply. These extremely popular classes were taught by Aileen Davidson, who continued to teach clowning at the school until the subject (sadly) disappeared from the curriculum in 1992:

> It's important to remember what the theatre scene was like in the late seventies. 'Alternative' theatre was quite big and clowning came into that arena, as did acrobatics, street theatre, mask and cabaret, all areas I taught.
>
> Clowning was used as a way to free students up; to help them develop a complete, unique and whole character themselves from scratch. And with that character – a whole world, one the students shared with their classmates. It created a very supportive environment to work in, as one of the 'rules' was that you always help each other, that if someone called for help you always went there. To do that the students needed to know about each others' clowns and what their foibles were – that stopped any transgressing!
>
> The clown classes helped the students to gain confidence in their ability to create a character; they also found an outlet for fun, for any 'silliness'. The world they created as a

group was precious and in all the years I taught clown I never saw the same clown twice, each one was unique. Because it was all 'unrehearsed' work, it gave the students confidence to cope with whatever happened elsewhere on stage: something could go wrong, and they knew they could just carry on. You have to be prepared to be 'open' to clown, always a good thing for an actor to experience.[6]

Emma Kinnane, a 1988 graduate of the school, wrote about the joy and the total commitment to whatever situation the clowns created:

> Aileen Davidson's clowning sessions were wonderfully insane. It was like being given permission to be kids living in a fantasy world, but using adult skills to create the world. You're 'in clown' when you're wearing your nose, and you don't exist in the clown world when you're not.[7]

There were few restrictions imposed on the 'clowns', apart from 'no touching without permission' and rules relating to safety: Aileen would step in and stop a performance if it seemed unsafe. Emma Kinnane recalled a memorable class that illustrated how much the students bought into the rules of the clowning class:

> Along with half my classmates, I was sitting watching the other half playing 'in clown', and Colin Kitchingman's clown was having a really bad day so he decided to hang himself. He methodically set up a table under a roof beam and went about tying a rope up. Meanwhile, none of the other clowns in the scene had noticed. In the audience, we got more and more uncomfortable, desperate for the others to notice and help him, but we didn't feel able to intervene. But NOBODY noticed. It got more and more desperate, and eventually we were on our feet shouting and screaming until they realised what was going on. I truly believed Colin's character would have gone through with it if no-one had noticed.[8]

Clown Class 1988.
Back row L–R: Micheala Rooney, Darren Young.
Middle L–R: Simon Bennett, Tina Cleary, Katherine Mitchell, Colin Kitchingman.
Front row L–R: Dra McKay, Jonathon Hendry, Andrew Laing, Emma Kinnane.

Clown Class 1981. L–R: Rob Jayne, Simon Phillips, Fiona Samuel, (top - unknown), Blair Park, Joanne Simpson, (behind - unknown), Alex van Dam, Kate Ward, (umbrella - unknown).

One thing is certain. The quality and the range of teaching at the school were exceptional, particularly so when you consider the financial constraints, the often inadequate teaching conditions and the limited resources available at the school during these earlier years.

George Webby strove to extend the teaching programme and to include other disciplines at the school, but this was limited by the size of the annual grant. In spite of that, and in an effort to offset what he saw as a 'dearth' of theatre directors, George managed to 'officially' enrol three trainee-directors in the school in 1986: Richard Finn, Annabel Newman and Louise Tourelle. George had previously been able to insinuate the odd trainee-director into the school under the guise of being an acting student, but this was the first real attempt to deliver a structured directing course.

There had been an expectation that the school would move out of Kent Terrace in 1986 and be re-housed in larger premises. Alas, this did not eventuate, which left the trainee-directors without any dedicated rehearsal or performance space within the school. And because their work was additional to the 'normal' production activity at the school, they needed to recruit and pay professional actors to work with them. Then there were the small matters of performance rights, venue, production costs and so on. There was no budget to cover any of it.

George approached the Arts Council for additional funding, in fact, $17,350 to meet the additional needs of the trainee-directors that he regarded as being brought about by the temporary nature of their premises. The Arts Council admitted it had some responsibility for providing the students with adequate training facilities and agreed to grant the school an additional $10,000. This allowed each of the trainee-directors to direct one production, and provided financial assistance to support their secondments to professional theatre companies. Annabelle Newman was seconded to Mercury Theatre to work with Raymond Hawthorne on *La Traviata*, Richard Finn directed *Torch Song Trilogy* at the Fortune Theatre and Louise Tourelle 'spent time' at Downstage.

David Geary applied for the trainee-directors' course in 1986, but somehow missed out and was accepted instead as an actor:

> They had three [trainee directors] the year before, but no theatre to direct in, so they canned the course, and decided not to take any. We were in shitty old converted offices by the Basin Reserve. I could almost touch the roof. It had dusty threadbare carpet and ridges where the wall partitions had been. Still, it felt Bohemian and there was a pub underneath. Anyway, I applied as an actor and to my surprise got in. I'd graduated from university as an aspiring artiste, with no idea what to do with my art, and didn't want to be a lonely artist in the world.
>
> After I'd done a Samuel Beckett acting exercise not very well, George Webby came into the room and addressed the class:
>
> GEORGE: *Hello, Actors.* (PAUSE) *Hello, David.*
>
> He went on to say I talked like a director, not an actor. And I probably did. But, boy did that hurt. I wondered what the hell I was doing there. At university, and everywhere up to then really, I'd been a golden boy. Now I was bottom of the class. It was a humbling experience. One I totally needed, but there were some dark days …
>
> Somehow everything was all right after that. Drama School wasn't going to solve all my problems, but it would take me places I'd never think of going. Deep down, I think part of me always figured that struggling like fuck to be an actor would make me a whole lot better writer.[9]

The following year Simon Bennett, a Victoria University graduate, applied to be accepted into the Drama School as a trainee-director:

> I had fallen into Drama Studies at Victoria University as a way of making my BA/LLB more interesting. This quickly become a passion as I started acting initially, and then directing. The LLB side of my education fell away as I discovered a vocation for directing theatre. Phil Mann and David Carnegie took me aside and suggested I might like to consider directing as a career.
>
> Knowing that in previous years, the Drama School had accepted directing students, I applied on this basis, but I was told that there were no places for directors and that I would have to apply as an actor. I went through the audition process, interacted with cushions, and performed an excerpt from *Hamlet* (quite poorly). During the interview part of the process, Grant Tilly asked me why I wanted to go to Drama School. I replied that I wanted to work in the theatre. He repeated in his distinctive drawl, 'Wants to work in the theatre', and made a slow deliberate note on a pad of paper. I think that's what clinched my place at the school.
>
> I wanted to get a number of things out of Drama School: to immerse myself fully in the area where I had discovered a sense of vocation, and to learn as much about the craft of acting as I could in order to become the best director I could possibly be. I wanted the opportunity to learn as much as possible from leading practitioners, rather than academics. My over-riding ambition was to be the best possible professional theatre director; I wanted to be Colin McColl – who was then running Downstage Theatre. The prestigious training offered by the Drama School seemed at the time to be the best way into the profession.[10]

The Arts Council (principally Ruth Harley) acknowledged that 'training directors has got to be accorded a very high priority by the Arts Council'.[11] But the lack of resources at the Drama School excluded the possibility of an ongoing directing course. So Ruth Harley wrote to Phillip Mann, head of Drama Studies at Victoria University, to suggest a way forward:

> I wonder if you are making any provision for theatre directors at the University. The University seems to be an ideal environment for some young directors. It provides a broad range of academic opportunities including historical, literary, cross-cultural, as well as a measure of practical experiences. It seems to me that you have the basic resources for directing students.[12]

Phillip Mann was already developing proposals to expand drama courses at Victoria University. But the university did not believe it was its job to provide vocational training for the theatre: rather, its role was 'to provide an audience, to "educate audiences to the values expressed in drama", extending "the informed and disciplined intelligence" that academics practised beyond the academy'.[13]

Further progress was made in this area in the early 1990s when Drama Studies at Victoria became the Department of Theatre and Film, and again in 1997 when the department was incorporated into the School of English, Film, Theatre and Media Studies. Many aspiring actors and directors who studied drama at Victoria University have gone on to receive additional vocational training at Toi Whakaari.

It therefore made a great deal of sense when the two institutions decided to join forces to bring their unique strengths and resources together to develop a Master of Theatre Arts in Directing, which they jointly delivered from 2000.

The debate about how the school could be autonomous and yet be permanently and adequately funded continued until 1985, when John Roberts proposed a way forward to resolve the situation. His solution was to reconstitute the Board of Studies as a Trust, with responsibility for managing the affairs of the school on behalf of the Arts Council. As an incorporated society, the Trust could then seek financial support from other sponsors, and independently negotiate with other institutions and bodies to secure the school's permanent status.

The proposal was happily accepted by the Arts Council, as this would release it from its responsibility of having to closely supervise the school. In 1984 the chair of the QEII Arts Council, Sir Michael Fowler, had commented that the Council 'saw the need for this to happen as soon as possible', and confirmed that any increase in the school's funding 'could not be envisaged in the foreseeable future'. Furthermore, he insisted that the Arts Council could not possibly fund the school's proposed three-year acting diploma.

Sir Michael Fowler was clearly keen to see the school become an autonomous institution. But there was a problem: as an arts-funding body, the Arts Council was not empowered to set up a board of trustees for an 'organisation engaged in the training of students'. It got round this by selecting and approving a group of trustees, who subsequently agreed on a trust deed and then applied for incorporation of the Drama School as a Trust Board, under the Charitable Trusts Act.

Transitions

The New Zealand Drama School Trust Board was inaugurated on 23 July 1986. The chair was Sharon Crosbie, a national figure known for her work as an interviewer and commentator on National Radio, and as a journalist.

The Trust Deed provided for up to eight members of the Board, but initially there was only five. They were John Fokerd, a financial advisor who had previously been associated with the school as an accountant; Rachel Lang, a graduate of the Drama School, currently employed as a script editor for TVNZ; Phillip Mann, who had a connection with the school as a tutor and also through his association with Downstage and Victoria University; Terry McDavitt, a Wellington City councillor; and Shirley Homewood, an industrial public relations expert with a legal and managerial background. Neither the director of the school nor any staff or student representative was invited onto the Board.

At its inaugural meeting, the Trust Board established some important guiding principles:

- Its role was that of a group that would 'fight' for accommodation and finance.
- The Trust Board had the power to purchase premises.
- All the 'attributes and resources' of the school belonged to the Trust.
- The Trust had total authority to run the school in such a manner as it saw fit (within the constraints of the Trust Deed).
- The professional and curriculum side of the school remained the responsibility of the director and his staff.

The Trust Board asked George Webby to prepare a paper to summarise his ideas for a three-year course, which he duly presented at the next Board meeting. His paper explained the inadequacy of the two-year programme and how a production-oriented third-year would relieve the pressure on the first- and second-year curriculum. The lack of teaching space in the current premises meant the school could accommodate only up to thirty students at any one time. George's solution for housing the three-year course was to omit any new intake every third year, which would leave only two cohorts of students at the school in any one year.

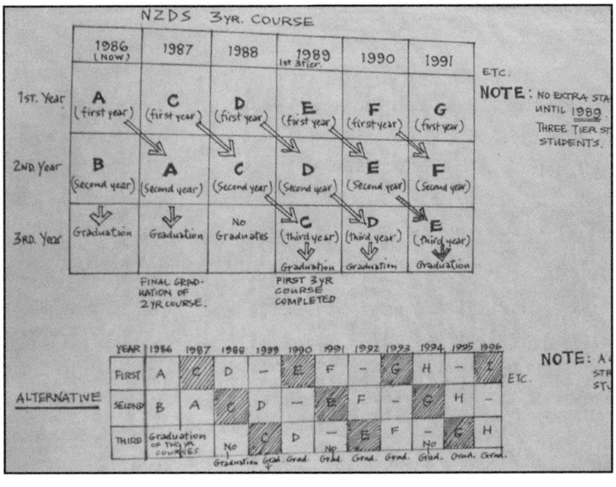

Diagram of proposed three year acting course, 1986

This idea gained the Board's approval and it passed a resolution that 'the three-year course is implemented within the next *two* years'.

George Webby's rationale for the three-year course, endorsed by the 1986 Trust Board, was fundamentally sound. But, apart from the lack of space and money, there was a major sticking-point: accreditation. Most comparable drama schools in the UK and Australia were offering three-year *diploma* courses, with degree programmes on the horizon. The New Zealand Drama School, with its unaccredited certificate course, clearly had some catching up to do if it hoped to maintain its position in the qualifications race.

It would take another decade, and the input of three more directors, before the battle for a three-year acting programme was won in 1997 when Toi Whakaari New Zealand Drama School implemented a new acting course as a degree qualification.

But in 1986, battles of a different kind were being waged as the Kent Terrace premises took on a martial atmosphere and the school prepared for war. Rehearsals were underway for two very bold productions with decidedly military themes. They were *Oh What a Lovely War,* mounted by the first-years, and *Welcome Home,* the second-years' graduation production. Both plays were performed at BATS Theatre in October/November.

Oh What a Lovely War, directed by Richard Campion, was the first musical ever attempted by the school; it was also one of the most expensive productions they had mounted, with the rights alone costing $1,000. It was an ambitious undertaking, with the first-year students (literally) being put through their paces in a couple of dozen dance routines, choreographed by Erica Stephenson; singing their way through thirty-six songs, under the guidance of musical director Neil Hennessy; and marching, drilling and being sporadically yelled at by Regimental Sergeant Major Bill Mayor from Fort Dorset: 'This broomstick is a 303. Your rifle is your best friend but I'm your worst enemy.'[14]

Oh What a Lovely War was immediately followed by the New Zealand premiere of Tony Marchant's *Welcome Home,* directed by George Webby, with set and lighting designed by Tony Rabbit. The play was chosen as a vehicle for five graduating students – all male. It tells the story of five young paratroopers returning from the Falklands War, preparing to bury a comrade killed in action. The cast of six were on stage for the entire show, and their performance was received with acclaim:

> You may wait some considerable time before you witness again such a sustained piece of theatrical brilliance. … the young actors surely have etched their own marks in New Zealand theatre history. Their ensemble playing is inspired, the team work never out of step.[15]

Welcome Home was one of George's favourite productions at the school. Annie Ruth also regarded it as one of the 'finest'. She remembers the first-year students spending a whole week breaking concrete to make 'rocks' for Tony Rabbit's set, which was installed on three levels at BATS.[16] When the production closed, Paul Riley spent many hours disposing of the concrete 'rocks' in City Council rubbish bags, a task that George knew was beyond the call of duty:

> Why he did it so willingly was either testimony to his belief in the School, or an acceptance of the madness of New Zealanders. I don't think even Tony Rabbit had calculated how heavy the concrete would be, and every night was a terrifying journey into No Man's Land.[17]

Erica's Tap class, 1986.
Back L–R: Kerry Fox, Emma Robinson, Sean Allan.
Front L–R: Peter Manuel, Jessica Wilcox, Jed Brophy, Tina Regtien, David Geary

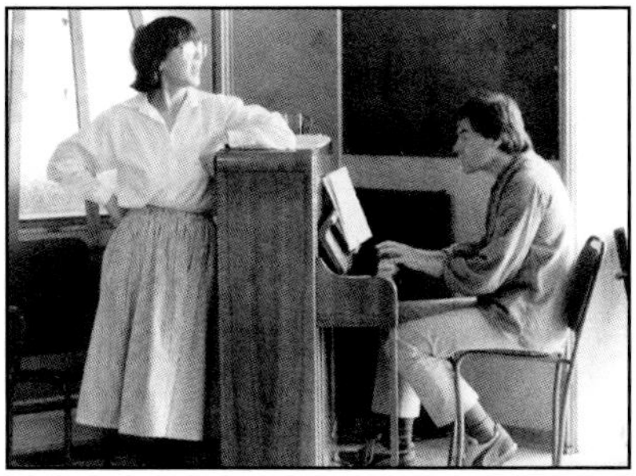

Erica Stephenson and Neil Hennessy (pianist)

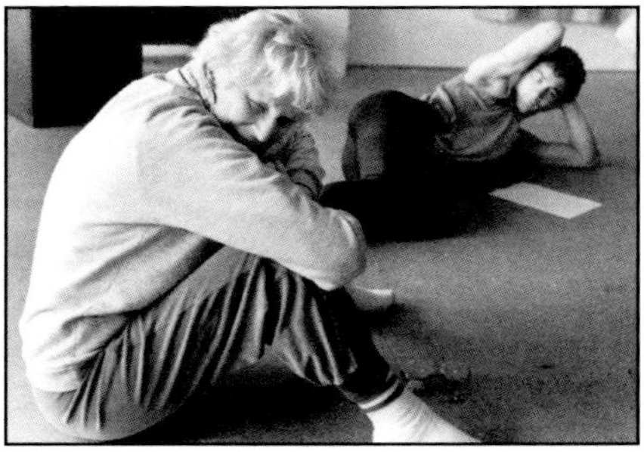

Rona Bailey movement class, 1986

Jane Waddell voice class

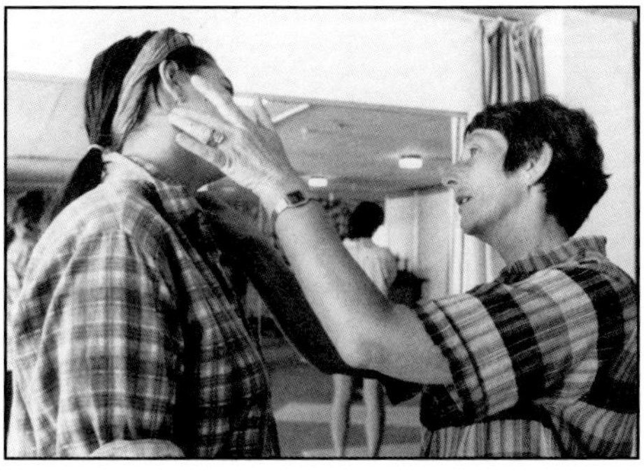

Nerissa Moore voice class

Keryn Stone movement class

▼ Bunty Western fencing class 1976

◀ Flora Edwards
singing class 1986 or 1987

Oh What a Lovely War, 1986.
L–R: Jessica Wilcox,
Tina Regtien,
Robyn Malcolm,
Emma Robinson, Sean Allan

Oh What a Lovely War and *Welcome Home* were both promoted as the fiftieth production undertaken by the Drama School. This did not, however, include the many devised works and concerts presented by the New Zealand Drama School since 1974, nor the fourteen or so productions mounted by the QEII Drama School between 1970 and 1973. *Welcome Home* was nonetheless remarkable for being the school's thirty-second New Zealand premiere.

A footnote in the programme for *Oh What a Lovely War* pointed out that after thirteen years the school was presenting its fiftieth production in the 'same venue' (Unity Theatre, now BATS) in which it presented its first:

> The School moved to Taranaki Street then to Vivian Street where it was burned out, and now functions out of a converted and inadequate office space over a motorbike shop. We are proud of what we accomplish under such awful circumstances. Imagine what we could do in a school designed to reflect the best of New Zealand's aspirations.[18]

At the end of 1986, auditions took place for the following year's intake. With over a hundred applicants to choose from, ten were selected: four from Wellington, two from Auckland, three from Otago and one from Levin. They each received an Arts Council scholarship of $2,750 a year. Amongst the successful Wellington applicants was a young Jonathon Hendry. He'd grown up in a theatre environment, with his parents involved in community theatre and he himself on stage from an early age, eventually playing the lead in *Pinocchio* at Marlborough Repertory in 1978. As with two other students from his year, Simon Bennett and Tina Cleary, Jonathon had recently completed drama studies at Victoria University. During his time at university, he had performed in numerous productions, although he almost missed out on playing Mercutio in Summer Shakespeare when he (inadvertently) plunged off Juliet's balcony. His longer-term strategy after graduating from Drama School was to work for two years as an actor and then become a director:

> The arrogance of youth! But it sort of happened that way. I wanted to work as an actor – a character actor – but I also knew that I wouldn't necessarily be employed all the time.
>
> When I met George at the Film Society, I was with my parents: he knew them. George's opening gambit was something like, 'The last time I saw you was when you were a little baby and I was bouncing you on my knee.' He asked me what I wanted to do. I told him I didn't know, but my mum replied, 'He wants to be an actor.' George's response was, 'Oh really: you should be a director.' I thought he was saying I wouldn't do very well as an actor. But looking back, I think it was just a 'George moment'. I was terrified of George in some respects because of his mana and the fact that he chose the people that got into Drama School.
>
> I'd been aware of the Drama School for years; seeing their shows – as a student at Victoria University. I got to know the drama students, as you did when up at the university: you went to the same parties, if you were keen on drama. My introduction to the Drama School was mainly through talking to students at Drama School parties, and with people who had just left. Everything seemed to revolve round George Webby.
>
> My other reason for wanting to go to the Drama School was Grant Tilly. I'd watched his work at Circa, and when I was a kid my dad took me to see a production at the Opera House in which Grant performed. I continued to watch his work when I was at varsity,

Rehearsal for *Welcome Home*, 1986. George Webby and cast.

Welcome Home, 1986. L–R: Simon Creasey, Robert Pollock, Stephen Lovatt, (lying) Tim Homewood, John Wraight

▼ Second year women outside 76 Kent Terrace. L–R: Kerry Fox, Jessica Wilcox, Robyn Malcolm, Emma Robinson, Tina Regtien, Stephanie Creed

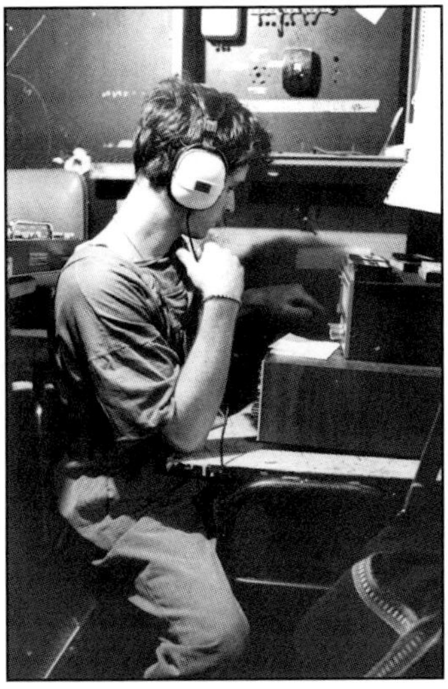

▲ *Welcome Home*, sound operator, first-year actor Sean Allan

> and I wanted to learn from him. He was extraordinary: a master. George was the person [who] everyone relates with the school, but there's no doubt that – as an actor – Grant was the person we wanted to learn from.
>
> When I first applied for Drama School they said no. When I later spoke to George about this, he said I was a bit 'too keen' and needed to grow up a bit. So I applied again the following year, by which time I'd gained a better attitude and was a bit more confident. I also had this need to get into the environment, and was desperate to be in theatre.[19]

By now, the school was entering its fourth year in temporary premises, which again forced it to postpone the proposed three-year course until a more permanent home with adequate training facilities could be found. The year before, the idea of a National Arts Centre where the Drama School, the School of Dance and the Royal New Zealand Ballet could be permanently housed, became a priority for the Arts Council. To this end, it set up a task force to locate permanent premises for the three organisations, engaging a property consultant to prepare a brief, and outlining the requirements of each organisation so that their individual and/or collective needs could be satisfied.

Included in the many proposals was part of a projected development by BP New Zealand, which contained a purpose-built 'BP Arts Centre' on the corner of Taranaki Street and Cable Street, as well as a property in Courtenay Place adjacent to the St James Theatre.

The BP proposal claimed it could accommodate the three organisations on two levels, with separate interconnection between performance, rehearsal, studio and administrative areas; whereas the Courtenay Place proposal only provided accommodation in two interconnected buildings, an arrangement that would constrain the separate identity of each organisation.

Because of site ownership and economic feasibility issues, the Courtenay Place option became less of a reality and the Arts Council opted for the BP Scheme. But when BP quoted an annual rental of $1.7 million, this too was shelved. It was far too expensive when compared to the existing combined property rentals for the three organisations, which in 1986 was only $150,000.

Given the long-term planning, construction and funding issues surrounding the Arts Centre (or Performing Arts Centre) proposal, it soon became clear that this would not solve the Drama School's immediate accommodation problem. There were also more fundamental concerns to be negotiated, relating to the disparate nature and needs of the three arts organisations. There was an obvious synergy between the School of Dance and the Royal New Zealand Ballet and they could co-exist without too much difficulty, but this was not necessarily the case for the Drama School.

George Webby was not keen on a union between drama and dance schools, having identified some fundamental differences between actors and dancers:

> Actors are noisy and vocal, dancers are graceful and quiet: they are different animals. No-one [looking at the proposed Performing Arts Centre] thought: 'Do actors and dancers gel?' Dance students are also very young – sixteen or seventeen: they are not subject to the same dynamic as actors who have to become aware and deal with their own internal neurosis; whereas dancers are not asked any of those questions; they are preoccupied with their limbs. If they have the right length of ankle and the right kind of body type, they

can evolve into a dancer. If they don't have those factors, they never can. But with an actor you never know what 'it' is. Dancers and actors only have 'performing arts' in common.[20]

Neither George nor the Trust Board was willing to accept further lengthy delays before the school could move into new premises, so they embarked on their own search for suitable (semi-permanent) accommodation. In July 1987 the first-floor of the former Gordon & Gotch Building in Adelaide Road became available. It was considerably larger than the Kent Terrace premises, with the added advantages of high ceilings and a long lease. But the annual rental was considerably more – \$377,000 compared with \$50,000 for Kent Terrace – and the estimated cost of renovating the building was around \$800,000. Although the Arts Council was prepared to consider the increased rental, it would not commit to the cost of renovations. So the plan was put on hold until a delegation could meet with the Arts Council and the Education Minister to discuss ways of funding the project. Meanwhile, the Drama School was offered another building, in Vivian Street: it was vacant and seemed a realistic proposition as an 'interim' home for the school. George Webby was asked to investigate.

While all this was happening, BP revived its scheme for the Performing Arts Centre on the basis of selling space instead of renting. But by then the Royal New Zealand Ballet and the School of Dance had lodged a submission to take over Shed 21, part of the Lambton Harbour Development. Wellington City Council, which still supported the idea of a Performing Arts Centre, then offered a number of sites to the Drama School, including the roof-space on top of the Marion Street car park. The National Museum Building in Buckle Street, which would be available when the Museum and National Gallery moved to the new 'cultural complex' on Wellington's waterfront, was also a strong contender. Again, these were long-term solutions.

There were two things George Webby badly wanted for the Drama School: a new building and a three-year acting course. But the never-ending battle to achieve these began to take its toll on him and, in the middle of 1987, he announced his retirement as director of the Drama School:

I could have gone on longer, but I find myself growing more impatient with bureaucracy. I've seen too many dear friends lost to the bureaucratic world. I have no desire to hang around. If I have to be here to see what I have achieved, then I have not achieved it.

It is ironic that my work and my dream for the students has been to create a three-year course in a satisfactory building. But it hasn't occurred; it's always just over the horizon.[21]

During his fourteen years as director of the NZ Drama School, George had confronted many changes and developments with an unswerving sense of purpose. Apart from the ongoing funding issues and the perpetual search for a permanent home, George sensed there were even greater challenges ahead, requiring him to steer an entirely different course than the one he'd chosen for the New Zealand Drama School in 1974. As he put it, it was 'the right time for one of the old school to be leaving'.

Before he left, George was determined to find a suitable home for the school. His requirements were not excessive: it didn't have to be a palace, but it had to be 'a few steps from the heartbeat of the city', with a large open space and high ceilings for a theatre. Moreover, the premises had to 'lend itself to adaptation' and be capable of 'withstanding the depredations of students'. And probably the most difficult requirement of all: an indefinable atmosphere.

When he inspected the first floor of the Gollins Building, at 36–38 Vivian Street, George felt it was capable of meeting most of his requirements – despite its being a little 'factory-ish'. What's more, it would be cheaper to renovate than the Gordon & Gotch Building. A section of the existing low ceiling could be removed to provide a performance space; and the rest of the area could then be subdivided to provide offices, studios and a student common room.

The Vivian Street property was indeed a realistic solution in the interim, at least until the school could be accommodated more permanently within the proposed National Arts Centre or the Museum Building or Shed 21 or Marion Street or – wherever. The Arts Council gave its approval for the school to take a three-year lease on 36 Vivian Street, and provided $200,000 to cover the cost of fitting out the premises and the additional rent needed for the 1987/88 year.

After George announced his resignation, the Trust Board set about finding his replacement. In September, they had a shortlist of applicants, including five overseas candidates. However, the final selection process was a more difficult undertaking as the school had no budget to fly in overseas applicants, and in 1987 there was (of course) no internet, video-link or Skype to facilitate the selection process. Despite these practical difficulties, the Board appointed Andrew (Andy) Noble as the new director a few months later. He had trained at East 15 Drama School in London. For the previous eight years he had worked as director and theatre administrator of the Coconut Grove Playhouse in Florida, and as co-founder and director of the Miami Seat, a theatre devoted to contemporary works. As Andy was unable to take up the directorship until April 1988, George agreed to remain at the school as acting director until then.

George's final production as director of the New Zealand Drama School was the 1987 graduation production, *A Midsummer Night's Dream*, at BATS. Grant Tilly designed the set (lots of beanbags), with costumes designed by Kri Leitner and lighting designed by Tony Rabbit. Jonathon (Jonty) Hendry, nearing the end of his first year as a student at the school, was the assistant director:

> Simon Bennett was expecting to be George's assistant on *The Dream* but George told him to stay as an actor in his first year, and then look at next year. Simon got very bolshie, quite rightly because he wanted to move into directing but couldn't.
>
> I think George thought that because I was very close to the new group, I would be a good person to be on the team to help. George was great; he let me in on the casting and got to see everybody's pictures: I still remember to this day Emma Robinson's picture and how she wanted to play Puck – and she did.
>
> George was retiring, so it was a magical production – and his last at the school. He talked me through the whole process. That was a very generous and formative thing that he did: I learnt a hell of a lot.[22]

The cast of eleven graduating students gave George a memorable going-away present, with their 'libidinous' and energetic performance of *A Midsummer Night's Dream*. The *Dominion* review of the production included a fitting tribute to George – and to the school:

36 Vivian Street (photo taken 2009)

▶ Performance space at 36 Vivian Street, 1988

> This year's graduation production continues the tradition and fulfils the expectations that the New Zealand Drama School had built up over the past thirteen years. As the school's director, George Webby is largely responsible for the high standards of stagecraft that have been achieved. New Zealand audiences too have become more discerning and the highly trained skill of the graduates is demanded in all areas of theatre performance. This last production for the school by George Webby well meets these demands for innovative, expertly crafted theatre.[23]

Before finally retiring, George decreed that the Drama School's library should be officially known as the Nola Millar Library in honour of his predecessor. It was a doubly fitting tribute to Nola, a major force in New Zealand theatre and a highly regarded librarian.

▲ *A Midsummer Night's Dream*, 1987. Rehearsal. Emma Robinson (standing), George Webby supporting Kerry Fox, with David Geary at the rear.

▼ *A Midsummer Night's Dream*, 1987. Cast. Back row, L–R: Stephanie Creed, Cameron Rhodes, Kerry Fox, Jed Brophy. In front of them L–R: David Geary, Robyn Malcolm (partly concealed), Emma Robinson. Front row, L–R: Peter Manuel, Tina Regtien, Sean Allan, Jessica Wilcox, Colin Kitchingman.

Eleven

1988–1989

'You've got to be game enough to reach out and when you get your fingers burnt, you have two choices – you can reach further or pull back.'

George's Farewell, with Sharon Crosbie, flanked by students and graduates

The Trust Board, staff and students organised a farewell celebration for George in the 'almost renovated' premises at 36 Vivian Street. Many of the 124 graduates from George's time attended the party, and there was a strong representation from the theatre profession, QEII Arts Council and the government: by all accounts it was a suitably riotous occasion. The redoubtable Sharon Crosbie was the compere for the evening, with Jane Waddell, Stephanie Creed and John Roberts all giving speeches in honour of George's time at the school. As a farewell gift, he was presented with an Apple Macintosh computer on which to write his memoirs, and the students then rounded-off the occasion by singing 'Somewhere over the Rainbow' in a 'tricky multiple-part harmony'.[1]

In his fourteen years as director, George had established a philosophy and an atmosphere at the school that had been respected by students and tutors alike. His sometimes flamboyant and idiosyncratic leadership style was always tempered by common sense: it was best summed up by Vincent O'Sullivan in the Foreword he wrote for George's autobiography:

Andrew Noble. Moving into 36 Vivian Street. April 1988.
ATL Dominion Post Collection

> This is the story of many things I admire – an enthusiasm that fortified generations of students; the refusal to be po-faced even about important things; a sense of proportion and scale that is intelligent and funny and gustily principled.[2]

When Andy Noble arrived in Wellington with his family in March 1988 to take up his position as director, the school was in transition between Kent Terrace and 36 Vivian Street. It was in a state of disarray, there had been no formal hand-over and nothing had been written down to inform Andy how the school operated. Nerissa Moore's memories of the turmoil are less than fond:

> Apart from Ruth [Graham] who was beautifully organised, nothing had been done in terms of organising the shift to Vivian Street. There was just a huge pile of rubbish: the filing system consisted of two cabinets in a state where they wouldn't shut because their drawers were bulging out. There was a whole lot of rubbish – I mean tip-rubbish – shifted over to Vivian Street. Andy had a really rough time, not only because of the transition, but also because it was a turbulent time in the whole of New Zealand: he couldn't have arrived at a worse time.[3]

George's departure signalled a totally new direction for the school. Throughout his directorship, it was largely monocultural, in both its curriculum and in its administration, reflecting the social and political circumstance of the time. In many respects, the New Zealand Drama School was a very 'Europeanised' institution, despite its having Māori and Polynesian graduates. George's view on biculturalism, with regard to the school and its students, was unequivocal:

> For me, the School had to remain multi-cultural and we must pay more than lip service to *all* of New Zealand's cultural interests; but it has to be expressed, like it or not, through the conduit of the English language. I don't mind taking on board the cultural world of the Māori – I welcome it – but I see no reason why I am required, except as an academic exercise, to accept its spiritual world as well. Our job at the School, surely, was to see that graduates left us well-grounded in *all* those areas needed for success in whatever branch of stage, film or TV they intended to work in.[4]

This was in no way a repudiation of Māori cultural values, but rather an acknowledgement of the more 'general skills' students had to acquire to enable them to survive as professional actors.

George never restricted entry into the school or discriminated against applicants because of their ethnicity or their cultural beliefs. On the contrary, he often spoke of his concern about the lack of Māori and Polynesian applicants. The selection process was based solely on the candidates' demonstrated ability, talent and potential, and not everyone was granted an audition. Many were culled by the screening process, broadly imposed by the Arts Council, or they were deterred by the tyranny of distance or the perceived monocultural nature of the school.

Although he resisted the trend towards affirmative action in tertiary education, and the inherent possibility of a preferential quota system, George was always ready to make provision for, and to acknowledge the distinctive qualities of, Māori and Polynesian students. This was a quality that was acknowledged by Robin Payne:

> George treated the students as individuals. I would say the beginning of the bicultural movement [at the school] went right back to George because I can remember a particular Samoan student who auditioned and did a piece of Shakespeare exceptionally badly – but then he did a piece he had written himself that was stunning, and George fought the audition panel for about three days until everyone was too tired. He was very good at cloaking the direction that he was taking people in, but he was very clear about what it was and his values.[5]

George was well aware that Māori and Pacific Island people were poorly represented in New Zealand theatre, both as practitioners and audiences. In 1982 he stated his point of view on this matter in a provocative article published in the *Evening Post*, 'Theatre Attracts Few Maoris':

> In a recent Playmarket Playwright's Workshop, there was not a single identifiable Maori observer, actor, playwright or director. Indeed, there was little indication that our playwrights were aware that a goodly proportion of our population is made up of people of Maori descent, or that there could be any dramatic material to be found in the relationship (good or bad) that exists between pakeha and Maori.
>
> Has our theatre finally limited itself to Europeans? A recent visit to Downstage (a fur coat brigade nowadays if ever there was one) or to Circa (with its trendy Tom Scott readers) would suggest this. Is our theatrical life so unpalatable that it is unattractive to the non-European? Is it meaningless?
>
> I do not like to think that it is all due to economics or to nervousness, or to ignorance. I dislike even more the thought that it is my actions that are effectively keeping Maori people out, but in what way can I make it relevant, without the charge of paternalism being levelled at me? Theatre ceases to be real when it operates for the few, or for a coterie.[6]

It is interesting to note that, as a result of George's final audition process at the school, fifty percent of the applicants accepted for the 1988 intake were of Māori or Polynesian descent: Hori Ahipene, Cliff Curtis, Julie Edwards, Toby Mills, Peter Seers and Sima Urale. Together with the Pākehā students in that year – Tim Balme, Marton Csokas, Michael Galvin, Emily Perkins, Sarah Preece and Carol Smith – they were a very wilful cohort, as Sima Urale recalled:

> We were a very stroppy group with strong personalities. Undisciplined? It wasn't discipline that Andy had to deal with, it was our fiery personalities. We weren't lazy – we did

> our work, but I think we let our passions get away from us. When George Webby left, people saw doors opening, and the opportunity to have their say about how the school should be run: that biculturalism should do this: more brown people, more this, more that. Andy got inundated with all sorts of demands, and we felt he was taking a lot of pressure.[7]

None of this had been evident to Andy Noble when he applied for the position of director. And, by his own admission, he experienced considerable 'culture shock' when he arrived at the school. But, having 'caught the ball in the air', he now had to run with it.

The difficulty that Andy was faced with in taking on the directorship at a time when young Māori and Pacific Island students were looking to establish their place within it cannot be overstated. And yet, despite his unfamiliarity with Māori and Polynesian culture, he soon began to institute a number of changes to allow students to 'learn about acting within a New Zealand, rather than a European context'. He approached this challenge with 'no baggage as far as New Zealand is concerned',[8] believing – as an outsider – that he had a distinct advantage in the current climate; it meant he could be more objective. Andy's previous teaching experience in Miami, with its large Hispanic population, also gave him an insight into multicultural interaction and the problems sometimes associated with it.

Andy Noble's willingness to take on and to advance the bicultural aspects of the school was remarkable, particularly when considered in relation to some of the more immediate pressures he had at deal with.

Just before George left, Rona Bailey wrote down some of her thoughts on biculturalism in relation to the school, which she presented to him and to the staff. In essence, she felt that, given the large representation of Māori in the current intake of students, it was the right time for the school to take some positive steps towards biculturalism and she had some particular views on how this should be achieved:

> Many people believe biculturalism is learning Māoritanga, doing some Taha Māori, learning some Māori protocol and then they are well on their way to being bicultural. I do not believe this to be so. Learning some Māori songs, while quite appropriate in itself, does nothing to re-establish the equal partnership envisaged in the Treaty, nor the ability to negotiate on equal rights. 'Why drag up the past' is a common question, but it fails to acknowledge the different approach to time of the [Māori and Pākehā] cultures. Māori face the past by bringing it always into the present, with the future unknown over the shoulder. Whereas Pākehā tend to say 'forget the past, face and look forward to the future'. This is not a value judgement, just two different ways of looking at life.[9]

With the assistance of Rona Bailey, Andy later arranged for the Drama School to spend two days examining the Treaty of Waitangi from both Māori and Pākehā perspectives. It was hoped that this would increase the staff's and the students' understanding of the Treaty, and would better support the future work and identity of the school:

> We started thinking about the make-up of the School, what our history's been and what it might be: we examined our name, the New Zealand Drama School. What is New Zealand? What is Drama? What is School? Do we fulfil that description? What are we here to do?

> We are in the business of the intangible. We don't know what the future holds, but in our hands we hold the seeds of that future. We have to allow our artists to grow and make their own statements within the New Zealand context. Their growth is the future, and they will know what to say when the time comes.[10]

There was a sense of urgency about this founded on a very practical need. The plan to re-house the school permanently in 1990 as part of a Performing Arts Centre – possibly at Shed 21 – was very much alive. This would almost certainly mean sharing the premises with the New Zealand School of Dance and the Royal New Zealand Ballet, and unless the Drama School could clearly demonstrate how it would provide for its Māori and Pacific Island students, it was facing a potentially explosive situation.

The move to 36 Vivian Street was finally celebrated shortly after Andy's arrival, with a production of Molière's *Tartuffe* performed by the second-year students and co-directed by Jane Waddell and Sylvia Rands.

Jonathon Hendry was in the cast of *Tartuffe.* Now in his second year at the school, he was very much a 'transition' student, having experienced the change in directorship and the distraction of moving from Kent Terrace to Vivian Street:

> It was an interesting time because George had put such a stamp on the school. We had also moved from cramped quarters in Kent Terrace, so tiny that David Geary would hit his head on the ceiling in the main studio. The year before us included Kerry Fox, Robyn Malcolm, Jessica Wilcox, Emma Robinson, Stephanie Creed and Tina Regtien. If someone broke down, or someone cried, it would usually be them. If George had been particularly cruel or hard there was not much privacy. One of them would go, and then they would all go, to the toilets for a cry. It was like living in a house. The library was great, though, because I would go and hide out there with Ruth; it was a nice quiet space.
>
> When we moved into Vivian Street we thought it was wonderful: all that space, we considered it to be a flash building. It was a good transitional period for Andy Noble too.
>
> He brought in a sensibility in his teaching that was structured on the much more transparent methods of Stanislavsky: all that stuff we do now. But it was new to me at the time. George had done some classes, in our first year, talking about 'units'; but it was never as systematic as that.
>
> I learned at a lot from Andy's classes about text values. He'd been asked [by the Board] to do a lot more teaching, and that's what he felt he could do well. It was particularly useful to me as a director: the structure of investigating a text, and breaking it down, and he was also strong on the 'pursuit of action'. This had not been as explicit in the language of George and Grant.
>
> George had held the school in a particular way for so long, and Andy was subjected to some quite intense pressure. I think the culture shock for him, coupled with the fact that we were in the process of re-evaluating what our expectations of the school should be, didn't help matters.
>
> Andy's personality meant that he would never come in and say 'no'. He was very quiet in his role and was cautious. He wanted to listen and understand the closeness of our community. The desire to investigate what the national drama school was striving to be was something that he hadn't anticipated: the fervour and the passion.[11]

Andy Noble's next priority was to advance the long-standing proposal for an additional third year to be added to the acting course. Although the Trust Board had passed a resolution in 1986 stating that the three-year course should be implemented within the next two years, the deadline had now been exceeded and pushed out to 1990–91.

To this end, Andy set up a curriculum review committee to develop a framework for the three-year programme. He proposed a curriculum structure with a number of common core courses developed as a matrix to allow extended options to be added, such as directing, playwriting, dramaturgy, design and teaching. Any or all of these could be developed in conjunction with other tertiary training providers.

But the increase in student numbers, tutor hours and additional resources associated with the proposal had significant cost implications. For this reason, the Arts Council decided it would be inadvisable to proceed with a third year until 'the School's new proposals have been fully costed and sources of finance secured; its proposed expansion would not fall within the present categories of Council priority'.[12] It notified the Drama School accordingly: once more the intention was put in the 'too-hard' basket.

Andy Noble's other priorities appeared to be more achievable, including an extension of film and television training in recognition of the growing career options in these areas; and, as forecast by George Webby, 'affirmative action on biculturalism as a step towards multi-culturalism in training'.[13] This priority was partly realised through the placement of audition advertisements to target 'talented students *of all backgrounds* with or without theatre experience',[14] which opened the school to more applicants. In a radical shift from previous practice, *all* applicants were given a preliminary audition, either in Wellington or in one of the designated regional centres. Regardless of the many logistical and financial difficulties associated with auditioning applicants in multiple centres, it provided a more equitable selection process.

To help raise the profile of the school within Māori and Polynesian communities, Rona Bailey enlisted the support of the Māori and Pacific Island Council (MASPAC) and her many other contacts. She was assisted in this by Harata Ria Te Uira Solomon, an accomplished singer and actor, and a member of the Māori Writers and Actors Association.

Implicit in these changes was the Drama School's unique New Zealand perspective and the willingness of the school to explore its changing purpose and identity within that context. But it was vital that this development was realised from the students' creative viewpoint. Andy Noble believed if this could be achieved, the school would be in a much better position to contribute to the future shape and practice of New Zealand theatre.

However, this proved an inopportune time to introduce such measures, let alone the development and implementation of significant changes to the curriculum and the way the school operated. Many core staff chose to review their position within the changed organisational structure and several left, including Erica Stephenson and Grant Tilly. Having inspired many students, they were a considerable loss, and their contribution to the development of the school since its inception had been enormous.

Grant's connection to the Drama School was inexorably linked with Nola Millar and George Webby, having taught alongside both of them in the 1960s as a tutor for several of the annual Rathkeale Drama Schools. Grant had also worked with Nola as a designer and tutor at New Theatre, then at the QEII Drama School; and with George

Webby as a designer and as an actor, long before he had been persuaded by George to join the New Zealand Drama School as a tutor.

When George resigned, many of the students at the school had expected Grant Tilly to take over as the director: 'We admired the work that he was doing so it was a complete surprise when he wasn't appointed.'[15]

Grant Tilly's departure was regrettably clouded by contentious litigation connected to the somewhat murky contractual arrangements surrounding the recent disestablishment of his position as senior tutor the year before, when the Trust Board had been vested with full autonomy for the operation of the Drama School. In short, the Department of Education had paid the Trust Board a lump sum equivalent to the amount previously paid in the way of salaries for the director and senior tutor. This effectively altered their status by making them employees of the Drama School Trust Board, whose responsibility it now was to negotiate conditions of employment with the school's employees. The problem was that Grant never received 'formal' notification of his changed employment status, and during the subsequent protracted litigation lawyers endeavoured to determine whether Grant's 'legal employer' was the Department of Education, Wellington Polytechnic or the Arts Council.

The matter was eventually settled out of court. But it was a sad conclusion for such a distinguished teacher who firmly believed that his strongest contribution to theatre in New Zealand was through his teaching, and whose greatest joy was being part of the growth process of young actors. As an accomplished actor himself, Grant maintained that he never taught students to 'act':

> I don't think you can actually do that. I preferred to put students in an environment that allowed them to grow, to enable them to become better actors on their own talent. … You can be a teacher of anything, if you give students a couple of years to be immersed in what you do best, and encourage them about living in the world: in the end the good ones will use that.[16]

He also believed that going to drama school was not absolutely necessary for people wanting to train to become actors, and that no amount of training could substitute for the student actor's understanding of and compassion for their fellow human beings, where everyone is a 'villain and a hero':

> Nothing for an actor can be truer than the hoary old adage that 'the study of man is man'. Just as the raw materials for a painter are paints, canvas, brushes, the raw materials for an actor are the author's words, life experience and an innate understanding of mankind. The painter combines the raw materials with his/her own imagination/vision and with a 'what if' and creates a painting. The actor follows a similar process to create the required character. The playwright in this case is only half the equation. If as an actor you don't understand what could be/is driving his characters to do what they do, say what they say, then as an actor your 'pretence' of becoming that character is lessened and is less believable to an audience. That's why there are untrained intuitive actors who are far better at this game of pretence than some trained actors who have few human skills to draw on. Some would-be actors can be made aware of this at drama school; some cannot, no matter how hard they try or how long they stay at the school or work in the theatre. On the other hand, there are some actors blessed with the ability for 'good pretending' who have no

> need for drama school. In fact it may totally confuse and/or diminish their natural talent. These latter actors should be encouraged to just get on with it.[17]

After leaving the school, Grant's acting career continued to flourish, and he remains a highly regarded and prominent actor. When he returned to Toi Whakaari in 2009 as an external assessor, he found it to be an 'interesting experience':

> I felt a 'rush of blood' to the head and thought for a moment that I wouldn't mind working with young students again. They don't seem very different to when I was teaching, but I'm not so sure about the restrictions around teaching and assessment these days.[18]

In 1988 Michael Parmenter and Lyne Pringle joined the school as movement and jazz dance tutors. Morning classes usually commenced with strenuous aerobic 'muscle and bone' classes with Michael Parmenter, followed by a voice and speech class with either Nerissa or Jane, and then singing with Flora Edwards. Improvisation, acting classes and rehearsals were scheduled in the afternoons. The second-year programme included a block course on acting for television, with John Anderson, and a Commedia d'el Art mask block course, with Ralph Johnston. Apirana Taylor also joined the school as a part-time tutor to work with the first-years on Māori theatre.

Jonathon Hendry still has vivid memories of the classes he attended when he was a student at the school:

> Rona's classes were quite challenging; but then I was never a 'good mover', I was terrified of movement. A lot of people sat out of her classes: they would sit down and say they couldn't do it: I was quite angry about that. We had an interesting time with Jane and Nerissa. Jane would often get us to work on sonnets and do things which felt more like acting. Whereas Nerissa was from a speech/communication tradition and that was really important nuts-and-bolts stuff. Michael and Lyne were really flash when they came along with muscle and bone, and hearing Michael screaming at you first thing in the morning for an hour at the YWCA gym was something. He worked us hard – he really did. Colleen Reilly would come down from the university and read a play, and follow that with a debate: a tremendous experience and a great way to get students in formulating an argument.[19]

There were only two major productions mounted by the school in 1988, apart from a presentation of Shakespeare's sonnets and a season of student-led lunchtime concerts, first introduced in 1983. Each segment generally had a student director working with a small cast to present a selection of pieces with a common theme, mainly from existing texts. In 1988 each second-year student performed a character song and a monologue, over two nights. Tina Cleary sang 'Toucha, Toucha' from the *Rocky Horror Picture Show* and a piece from *Top Girls*, and Jonathon Hendry sang 'Mr Cellophane' from *Chicago* and delivered a speech of Chebutykin's from *Three Sisters*. In some respects, the lunchtime concerts were a precursor to the monologues that were initiated the following year by Andrew Noble.

The 1988 graduation production was *The Three Sisters,* directed by John Anderson. A compelling feature of the production was the monochromatic design, featuring a stark white set designed by Tony Rabbit, and stylish black and white costumes designed by Cherie Reinschmidt. One reviewer of the production felt strongly that the design elements worked against the intentions of the play: '*Three Sisters* will be remembered for the fact that the actors had to compete with the setting and the costumes for our attention';[20] but in a letter in the *Evening Post*, a member of the audience staunchly defended the costume design: 'I take issue with your theatre critic .... In a play rich in contrast and irony I loved the white/black, close fitting/full swishy, good/evil, night/day, politically incorrect/correct, class struggle/aristocratic privilege themes.'[21]

If nothing else, these observations acknowledge a shift in the visual representation of productions at the school, from mostly representational design elements to a more symbolic or abstracted aesthetic. To some extent, this reflected a growing awareness of design as an integral part of the whole production process. Instead of costume design being little more than just a collection of agreeable images, it could be an expression of mood, and its presence could enhance or even comment on the performance.

For Jonathon Hendry the production was an extraordinary experience:

> John [Anderson] was fantastic, we trusted him. He had a wonderful manner; he was quiet and could get a little overwhelmed with things. But we had a real sense that he would be good for us. We were quite a fractious year: one of the difficulties of transition, I think. And we felt a sense that we'd lost somehow because we'd lost George. So John brought us together and made us work as a good company again.
>
> The budget for the production meant that the designers worked with calico .... it was all very moody and atmospheric. I remember people talking about the production and loving it, and what it looked like. We were really excited by it; what was done within that space blew our minds. There was this lovely sense that we were choreographed through the curtains; we never walked straight on stage, we sort of faded in and out.[22]

The Three Sisters had been successful on many counts, but for Simon Bennett it was the culmination of a difficult two-year period:

> I found myself frustrated with the lack of continuity, and what I perceived as an ad-hoc approach to the curriculum. This was exacerbated in the second year where we experienced an almost complete turnover of staff and the school seemed to enter a kind of holding pattern, until it discovered its direction post-George Webby.
>
> John Anderson created the minor miracle of bringing together a fractured group of people to work in a truly ensemble fashion on *The Three Sisters*. He taught me a great deal. I learnt about playing objectives, text analysis, character statements and guided improvisation as a tool for exploring character and character-relationships off-text.[23]

What seems particularly remarkable about this relatively unsettled period is that the school acquired a Māori prefix to its name. Part of the reason for this was to fall in line with a government policy, Te Urapare Rangpu, which required 'agencies in receipt of government funding to identify in the delivery of its service in recognition of the Treaty of Waitangi'. But the real driving force behind this initiative was Rona Bailey. Before she left the Drama School as a tutor at the end of 1988, she consulted with Timoti Kāretu, Head of Te Taurawhiri i Te Reo Māori (the Māori Language Commission) and from their discussion came the new name for the school, Te Kura Toi Whakaari O Aotearoa: New Zealand Drama School. The Māori prefix approximately translates as the New Zealand School of Performing Arts, although 'toi' as a noun also means 'indigenous' or 'native'.

The new name was adopted by the school in 1989, and the reduction 'Toi Whakaari' is now more commonly used. In recent times, this has been further abbreviated to just 'Toi' by many students and graduates, not out of disrespect, but more out of familiarity and/or affection.

Rona Bailey later came to the conclusion that the Drama School's decision to adopt the Māori name had been premature; she felt the school had done little at that time to deserve it:

> Several government departments and institutions promptly took Māori names – and for some it was just a token gesture. It would have been preferable if [the Drama School] had waited a year, and then gone for the name. You need a track record first: and to have demonstrated your commitment. The journey is a hard one.[24]

The Drama School stuck to its other main commitment by auditioning each of the 200 applicants for the 1989 intake in several regional centres, not just in Wellington. This provided easier access for auditionees from the provinces, and a more equitable selection process. Apirana Taylor was invited on to the selection panel for the Wellington auditions, his presence much appreciated by Hone Kouka who was accepted into the 1989 intake. It's interesting to note that when Hone graduated from Toi Whakaari in 1991 and started writing, Apirana Taylor directed his first script, *Mauri Tu*.

At the end of 1988, Andy Noble returned briefly to the UK. During his absence, Erica Stephenson returned to hold the fort and prepare the school for the new intake of students. She enlisted a group of students and staff and their relatives to clean and redecorate the school. They put up posters and photographs, hung curtains, re-covered furniture, reorganised the wardrobe collection, set up a video room and created a more pleasant entrance foyer to the school. Nerissa Moore's husband, John, was recruited to repair the many holes which students had 'created' in the plasterboard walls since moving into the premises. For a variety of reasons, holes continued to appear, and John kindly kept on provided his invaluable fixing service until the school moved to new premises.

Twelve new students joined the school in 1989, including two Māori students, Hone Kouka and Shane Rangi. There were also four ex-Onslow College pupils that year: Toni Gordon, Neil Holt, Larissa Matheson and Mick Rose.

Flora Edwards, who had been the singing tutor at the Drama School since 1984, was appointed head of Wellington Polytechnic Conservatorium of Music and was no longer available to teach at Toi Whakaari. Laughton Pattrick then took over that role. Like Grant Tilly and many tutors at the school, Laughton had trained at the Wellington Teachers' College,[25] and interestingly, all were taught by Sunny Amey. Laughton has a remarkable ability to empower and inspire his students, and from 1989 to 2001 he continually taught at Toi Whakaari as singing tutor and sometimes musical director. He still finds time to teach the occasional class or direct singing for graduation ceremonies and other 'auspicious' events at the school.

The Trust Board now had an increasingly important role in the life of the school, and in 1989 the composition of the Board changed. John Fokerd and Phillip Mann from the original Board remained, as did the chair, Sharon Crosbie, but there were

Grant Tilly and George Webby in the 1960s

Tartuffe 1988. L–R: Cameron Rhodes, Jonathon Hendry, Tina Cleary, Micheala Rooney (back), Simon Bennett

◀ Lunchtime Concert 1987. L–R: Peter Manuel, David Geary (scantily clad), Robyn Malcolm, Cameron Rhodes (below).
ATL Dominion Post Collection

▼ *The Three Sisters*, 1988. L–R: Tina Cleary, Emma Kinane, Katherine Mitchell.

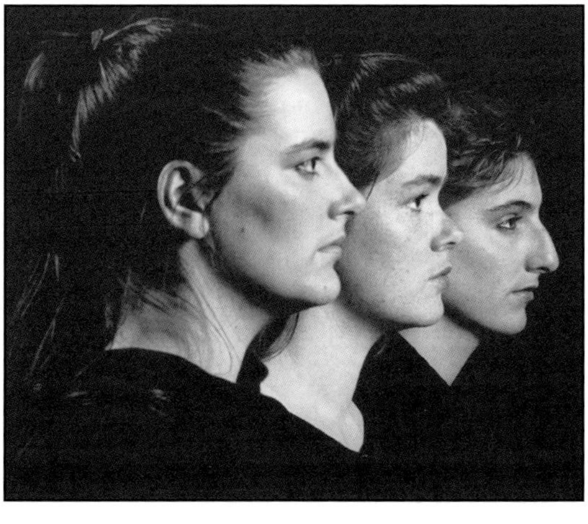

◀ Laughton Pattrick

▶ Lyne Pringle and Michael Parmenter, 1990

four new members: John Anderson, Rona Bailey, Kate Harcourt and David Jenkins.

One of the first things Rona did as a Board Trustee was to write a further paper clarifying the bicultural issues facing the school. She began by confirming that 'biculturalism is based on the Treaty of Waitangi and that this contains an invitation for Pākehā to share [Aotearoa] with Māori in equal partnership'.[26] The paper then focused on a central bicultural issue for the school: is Toi Whakaari meeting the needs of Māori students? Rona's own response to that question was unequivocal: 'I do not believe that we can even attempt to answer this question at this point in time because we do not know what those needs are, or if there are separate needs.'

Rona challenged the Trust Board to be decisive in its position on biculturalism: 'If we do not get it right, we are in trouble .... if it was decided to have Māori members on the Board, there needs to be wide consultation among Māori, and for them to choose whom they would be – not us. This is in line with the concept of partnership.' This position was reinforced with a quotation from Piri Sciasca, the director of MASPAC: 'You've got to be game enough to reach out and when you get your fingers burnt, you have two choices – you can reach further or pull back.' Later in the year, two Māori elders were appointed to the Trust Board: Puoho Katene and Thelma Keepa Grabmaier

The new intake of students arrived a week earlier than usual in 1989 to join a group of trainees on the National Theatre Technicians Training Council (NTTTC) for a technical block course. The NTTTC new-entrant training scheme had been set up in 1987 in response to the lack of formal training opportunities for theatre technicians. The Arts Council then joined forces with the theatre community to attract 'Training and Development Assistance' funding through the Vocational Training Council, that would allow a training programme to be implemented for new entrants through a combination of in-service training and block courses.

During their summer break, the second-years had been asked by Andy Noble to choose a New Zealand personality – alive or dead – and to research their background with the aim of developing a character study for a twenty-minute monologue. This visionary initiative was the precursor for what would later become the Solo Season, now an important highlight of the third-year acting programme.

This first monologue season had a generic title: *Reflections*. Most of the second-years chose characters they could identify with, admired or were intrigued by. Sarah Preece decided on Janet Frame, because she was a fan of her writing and 'admired her resilient but solitary character'; Cliff Curtis chose James K. Baxter whom he admired as a 'charismatic figure and as a gifted and complex poet'; and Julie Edwards picked Alison Holst, as she wanted to 'debunk the common perception of her as the un-liberated housewife-cook'.[27]

Tim Balme's monologue was inspired by folk-hero George Wilder: 'NZ's most famous, most successful and most friendly prison escapee'. Tim later developed his monologue into the full-length play, *The Ballad of Jimmy Costello*, which premiered at the 1997 Taranaki Arts Festival and was later performed at Downstage:

> I got a bit carried away – it was supposed to be twenty minutes, mine was forty-five. Afterwards, I realised I could do more with it. It took me quite a long time to resurrect it; but I knew it had a life as a full-length show. Without the monologue I would never have had the confidence to develop it.[28]

Hori Ahipene's monologue was based on Carmen, the flamboyant trans-sexual founder of Wellington's International Coffee Lounge, where many of her 'waitresses' were boys – or had been boys at some time. This was the mark of her establishment. Hori had grown up in a small town close to where Carmen was raised and had had similar experiences, which enabled him to draw many parallels between his own and Carmen's background.

Other students were attracted to public figures whose qualities and beliefs were (arguably) contrary to their own. Sima (Karen) Urale decided on Ngaio Marsh, simply because she felt people were expecting her to portray a Samoan character, and she didn't want to be pigeon-holed: 'Ngaio Marsh was a Pākehā – upper class, older woman: the total opposite of me.'[29] Emily Perkins portrayed Minnie Dean, the baby farmer and only women to be hanged in New Zealand, as she was intrigued by this enigmatic figure and hoped to obtain a closer understanding of her character and the question of her guilt or innocence. Through her studied observations of the trial, Emily exhibited the seeds of the renowned novelist she later became.[30]

Just before *Reflections* opened, Andy Noble announced his intention to resign, after only twelve months as director of the school. His decision had its roots in a difficult transition period, which had been compounded by logistical problems and significant cultural change. The discontinuity of support within some key areas of the school had not helped the situation, including the recent resignation of Paul Riley, administrator-secretary since the mid-1980s. These pressures had conspired to place greater emphasis on the director's role as CEO rather than artistic director, not what Andy had anticipated when he accepted the position. This left him isolated, with very little support except from Rona Bailey.

Throughout his tenure Andy remained steadfastly committed to his central aims for the school, fending off adversity to achieve a number of important and far-reaching changes. These included affirmative action towards stronger bicultural identity, en-

Reflections, 1989.
Standing L–R: Julie Edwards, Hori Ahipene, Martin Csokas, Karen Urale, Emily Perkins, Tim Balme, Sarah Preece.
Sitting L–R: Cliff Curtis, Michael Galvin, Carol Smith.
ATL Dominion Post *Collection*

capsulated in the Māori prefix, Te Kura Toi Whakaari; a more equitable selection process for applicants through nation-wide auditions, allowing easier access for applicants from all backgrounds who wished to train at the school; the introduction of a New Zealand-based monologue season; advancement towards the implementation of a three-year acting programme; and extended film and television training.

With Andy Noble's imminent departure, the Trust Board faced an extremely urgent situation: a new director had to be recruited within a few months. Under ideal circumstances, the recruitment process would be protracted, but these were far from ideal times. With the recent turnover of teaching and administrative staff, the school was now in a precarious position and was in imminent danger of becoming dysfunctional, a situation that needed to be resolved – and quickly.

The task of finding a new director who understood and could work with the complex issues facing Toi Whakaari and could also lead the school through the next stage of its development was no easy matter. So, to buy more time, the Board decided to appoint an interim director. The qualities needed to fill this position were considerable. The ideal candidate would have an established background in a leadership role in New Zealand theatre; good organisational skills; experience in dealing with the QEII Arts Council and the Ministry of Education; an understanding of and empathy for bicultural issues, particularly those relating to a performing arts school; and, most importantly, an ability to network with the theatre industry and the Māori and Pacific Island communities.

There was arguably only one person in New Zealand at that time who matched all those criteria: Sunny Amey. As 'luck' would have it, she had recently retired and was therefore (presumably) available, so the Trust Board approached her with an offer. And, after some persuasion, she accepted the position.

The Board had chosen wisely: Sunny was well equipped to assume the leadership of the Drama School, given her long association with theatre and her extensive involvement in drama in education. Sunny began her career as a speech therapist, later becoming an assistant lecturer in speech and drama at Wellington Teachers' College.

Sunny Amey 1988
NZADIE Drama Newsletter

Happy End, 1989. Sarah Preece and Cliff Curtis.

Happy End, 1989. L–R standing: Sarah Preece, Hori Ahipene (lying), Michael Galvin, Emily Perkins, Sima Urale, Cliff Curtis, Carol Smith, Julie Edwards, Timothy Balme. L–R seated: Toni Gordon, Mick Rose, Selios Yiakmis, Neil Holt (photo 1991).

In 1958 she won a travel bursary that allowed her to study theatre direction in the UK where she worked for the next ten years. Her first position was in stage management with the English Stage Company at the Royal Court Theatre, and then as assistant director. She later worked at the National Theatre as the repertory manager and assistant to Sir Laurence Olivier, and at the BBC as a trainee director.

Before she left New Zealand for the UK, Sunny performed in the Unity Theatre production of *The Good Woman of Setzuan*, directed by Nola Millar. Sunny was extremely impressed by the way Nola ran her rehearsals: 'she was meticulous, thorough, and had an eye for detail'.[31] This same quality was much needed by Toi Whakaari in 1989.

As artistic director of Downstage, from 1970 to 1975, she had managed its transition from the Star Boating Club to the Hannah Playhouse. And from 1975 to 1988, she had been the curriculum officer for drama with the Education Department, a position from which she had recently retired. During her last five years with the Education Department, she was its representative on the QEII Arts Council.

This was not the first time Sunny Amey had stepped into the breach to ease the Drama School through a difficult time. When Nola Millar was hospitalised in 1971, Sunny worked as a consultant director at the school for a term. Because she had recently retired, Sunny was not particularly keen to take on another long-term commitment. However she agreed to work as 'temporary consultant' until Andy left, and then to assume the position of acting director for up to a year. Her principal job was to oversee the management of the school, and to advise the Board on long-term planning with regard to staffing, curriculum and biculturalism. To assist her in this endeavour, Pat Holden was appointed as the new administrator for the school.

After being welcomed into Toi Whakaari with a pōwhiri, Sunny set about the task of getting the school back on an even keel and restoring a bit of discipline and cohesion. Jane Waddell remembered Sunny as being 'staunchly in command':

> She did a great job guiding the school through this difficult period. She was very sympathetic to the bicultural needs of the [Māori students] and with Rona's help she got things going enough to make those students feel that their cultural needs were being taken care of.[32]

To achieve this aim, Sunny had the support of the Māori community, including her mentor Keri Kaa with whom she consulted on Māori protocol and bicultural matters. Although Sunny was a strong advocate of biculturalism, she felt the school should learn to walk before it ran:

> It was always a bit taihoa – let's go gently here. I had hoped that when the three-year course came in, we could go more in-depth during the first year: into the bicultural thing … and into our [joint] history. The school had changed enormously – it had become many cultures and you can't attend to them all. Because the training of actors is so much about looking at your inner self, and who you are, and what your culture is, the Māori students in the school – at that time – were demanding 'Where is our culture here?' I still believe very strongly that from the bicultural you can spring off on to other cultures. It is easy for Pākehā students to feel assaulted in the school, and made to suffer, if the work is not sufficiently embedded.[33]

Transitions

By the time Sunny joined the school, the second-years were in the final stages of rehearsal for Bertolt Brecht's *Happy End*, directed by Colin McColl. He had previously directed the play as his first production after becoming artistic director of Downstage in 1985.

A key element that made the production such a success was the ensemble work, noted by several reviewers: 'The cast worked together with flawless coordination and that indefinable telepathic something which makes comedy come alive.'[34] The *Dominion Sunday Times* review was perhaps the most telling:

> [The cast] are New Zealanders, but their origins are diverse .... Some were born in England, one is of Hungarian origins, two Māori, one Samoan, another has Welsh ancestry. They work together as if there were no rivalries; creating ensemble playing that is a bonus for the audience.[35]

Laughton Pattrick, who had recently joined the school as the singing tutor, was the musical director for *Happy End.*

In the third term, both the first- and second-year students participated in a weekend workshop with Mike Mizrahi and Mari Adams, the founders of Inside Out Theatre, whose style of theatre was characterised by strong physicality and visual imagery. This had a powerful effect on Hone Kouka: 'Their work was so physical and intense; it was not text-based but image-based theatre and I could directly relate to that, and they really influenced me.'[36]

Image-based companies such as Inside Out Theatre, Theatre at Large and Paul Maunder had for years struggled to have the work of Grotowski and other European directors taken into the mainstream of New Zealand theatre. But they had a significant influence on the development of Māori and Pacific Island theatre, as noted by Robin Payne:

> The interesting thing is that this is an area where Māori and Pacific Island work has found an entrée into mainstream theatre, and it has also lent itself enormously well to that form of theatre. Particularly the sense of physicality that is incorporated in both that European work and in the Māori and Pacific Island work: the sense of non-naturalistic size of iconism, of working through symbols, of working in non-conventional theatre spaces, and the recognition and endorsement of huge emotion, and of breaking theatre convention in all sorts of different ways.[37]

After a two-week workshop in mask-making and performance with French maskmaker and performer Luc Laporte, the first-years went on the school's first-ever marae visit: an overnight stay at Ako Pai Marae at Wellington College of Education. Students and staff were accompanied at the marae by Puoho Katene and Thelma Grabmaier.

Around the same time, the second-years had a TV/film module at TVNZ's Avalon studios, led by John Anderson. The school had previously run similar but much shorter courses. This time the students had three days in Avalon's large studio with a full crew, at an equivalent cost of around $35,000. TVNZ provided the facilities free of charge as they saw actor training for television drama to be an important initiative.

The 1989 graduation production was *The Cherry Orchard*, directed by Lisa Warrington, associate director at the Fortune Theatre and a lecturer in drama at Otago University. Laughton Pattrick provided music for this production and led a group of first-year 'musicians', playing mandolin, clarinet, violin and balalaika.

Jonathon Hendry returned to the school to design the set:

> I'd got to know Lisa Warrington when I was working at the Fortune Theatre, and when Sunny said 'We'd love you to design a set for us – we know you've been interested in design', and I was, so I said yes. That was a lovely offer – and that's the way the Drama School was: the smallness of it. I had a budget of $80 or thereabouts and we scratched money together for the set: I loved the idea of space, so we used fabric to create a butterfly curtain. I seem to remember that it was the one idea that really worked.[38]

The students' ability to work as an ensemble was clearly demonstrated in *The Cherry Orchard*. Described by some as the 'Magnificent Ten', they were an exceptional group of second-years, applauded by Denis Welch in his review of their graduation production: 'All 10 students have tons of ability .... It is hard not to feel that the future of New Zealand theatre is in good hands.'[39] Their future achievements would be testament to that.

Preliminary auditions and interviews for the 1990 intake were held in Dunedin, Christchurch, Palmerston North, Auckland and Wellington, with one applicant auditioned by Sunny Amey in Tauranga: Nancy Brunning. Rona Bailey and Sunny had earlier considered the possibility of positive discrimination for Māori applicants, but

1990 intake. L–R back row: Shane Cotton, Bradley Carroll (1991 intake), Frances Kewene, Donna Muir. L–R front row: Mairanga White, Nancy Brunning, Erina Toi-Paku (photo taken 1991). Iwi Express

decided it was undesirable. Therefore everyone got an audition and the best were recalled; after that they were on their own.

Of the fourteen applicants accepted for the 1990 intake, six were Māori: Donna Muir and Shane Rangi[40] of Ngāti Porou, Erina Toi-Paku of Ngāti Kahungunu–Whanau a Apanui, Nancy Brunning of Ngāi Tūhoe–Ngāti Raukawa, Frances Kewene of Waikato–Maniapoto, and Mairanga White of Te Arawa–Ngāti Manawa.

This increased Māori presence in the school was a testament to the work of Rona Bailey, Sunny Amey and Andy Noble in spreading the word about the school to the wider community. Sunny later commented that 'this was the first time there had been this balance of cultures in our numbers, a real opportunity to achieve partnership'.[41]

Twelve

1990–1991

'I felt this need to protect the heart of the school and keep all the monsters at bay.'

Until the early 1990s, the school's growth was limited by the level of funding it received from the Arts Council. Not having a corporate identity of its own meant that it was difficult for the school to attract financial support from sponsors. The only practical way forward lay with the Department of Education; it was assumed that if it took over financial responsibility for the school, the proposed three-year acting course would soon be realised and permanent premises would be provided. But there was no legal mechanism in place whereby the Drama School could negotiate this for itself.

Since its inception, the Board of Studies had been engaged in various – and variable – negotiations with the Arts Council, the Department of Education and Wellington Polytechnic, in an effort to determine responsibility for the future of the school. The difficulty the Board of Studies experienced, in this regard, was its limited legal authority: in effect its members were servants of the Arts Council. The Board could act in only an *advisory* capacity to the school, and on its behalf to the Arts Council.

In 1994, John Roberts wrote a report on his association with the New Zealand Drama School, in which he reflecting on its financial dilemma:

> I believe the [school] has been treated shabbily by the policy makers in the education bureaucracy from the day it was founded under the direction of that great woman of theatre, Nola Millar. It had to struggle for existence in makeshift premises and beg for funding from the State and the private sector.[1]

The Drama School's grant from the Arts Council in 1989 was $400,000, and the Education Department (not yet a Ministry) contributed a further $94,000 towards salaries. The Arts Council's grant to the Drama School, together with a similar amount paid to the School of Dance, represented a fair proportion of the Council's own budget.

By 1990 the Arts Council was strongly signalling that funding for professional training in these 'art forms' should, in the future, be the responsibility of the Department of Education – or the Ministry of Education when it was formed.

Apart from Sunny Amey, the only full-time staff at the school were Pat Holden (administrator) and Ruth Graham (librarian). Ruth was supported in the library by Lisl

Hilton who, since 1983, had worked as a part-time voluntary library assistant. She was a very special part of the Drama School, as Ruth Graham recalled:

> When she started at the School, she'd recently retired as a lecturer in German at Victoria University. She was a friend of George and when she asked him if there was anything she could do at the school, George suggested that she help me in the library. From then on she would turn up at the library every Wednesday, and just charmed everybody and embraced the whole school. Lisl was an extremely knowledgeable and cultured woman, and I learned more from her than from most people in life.[2]

Indeed, any staff who worked at the Drama School on Wednesdays, particularly in the 1990s, will recall the delicious chocolate cake, cheese, paté and other 'European' delicacies that Lisl generously supplied from the Dixon Street Deli for morning tea.

Most tutors at the school continued to be employed on a part-time basis, including Nerissa Moore and Jane Waddell who jointly taught voice and vocal interpretation, Laughton Pattrick who taught singing, and Lyne Pringle and Michael Parmenter who shared movement. Annie Ruth also joined the school in 1990 as a part-time improvisation/acting tutor.

Sadly, Erica Stephenson was no longer available to teach; she had been involved in a serious car accident and needed to recuperate. George Webby returned for a term at the start of the year to take the first-years for acting classes.

Sunny Amey had been asked by the Trust Board to examine the needs of the school for the coming decade. And in 1990, a nine-member working party, which included Jonathon Hendry, was set up for this purpose. Its main focus was the structure and curriculum of the school and, in particular, the development of the three-year acting course. One of the early conclusions reached by the working party was the need to increase the number of permanent teaching staff. Consequently, the Trust Board decided that, in addition to the director's position, it would advertise for two full-time tutors to commence in 1991.

Meanwhile, the second-year students were busy, working with Murray Lynch on a devised work that developed from exercises in characterisation. Through a process of

Lisl Hilton, Library Assistant

collaborative storytelling they evolved *Roomers*, a play about mistaken identities and intentions. This production provided an early indication of a devising methodology that would eventually become a common feature at the school.

Two of the second-year productions in 1990 had a strong 'classical' bias: George Farquhar's Restoration comedy *The Beaux Stratagem,* and Garcia Lorca's *Blood Wedding.*

Rhys McConnochie returned to the school to direct *The Beaux Stratagem*. The production was strongly supported by other professionals, with a set designed by Raymond Boyce and costumes by Jane Woodall, choreography by Michael Parmenter and music by Laughton Pattrick. The play has eighteen characters, which allowed some of the cast to take on additional roles: 'maintaining a split personality under the pressures of rapid costume changes would have wearied a less professional cast … each actor, who had this task, maintained completely opposite characters'.[3]

Neil Holt had multiple roles in *The Beaux Stratagem* but suffered a severe eye infection, causing one of the performances to be cancelled. To make matters worse, his replacement fell down the school stairs and was concussed. The production also suffered the consequences of pelting rain, which rattled the roof iron, a not uncommon occurrence that made performances at Vivian Street barely audible. Undeterred, *The Beaux Stratagem* was in all other respects a great success.

This was followed by *Blood Wedding*, directed by James Beaumont. Arriving from Australia in the late seventies, he had worked as a director, writer, actor and educator with various theatre companies, including Theatre Corporate, Auckland Theatre Company and Centrepoint, and had recently been appointed artistic director of Taki Rua/Depot.

James Beaumont had chosen *Blood Wedding* because of its 'wonderful of expression of culture and community'.[4] In addition to the play itself, this expression of community was revealed in many other way ways. The first-years not only performed in the

The Beaux Stratagem, 1990. L–R: Katie Wolfe, Erik Thomson, Stelios Yiakmis, Hone Kouka, Amanda Rees, Larissa Matheson

production as Muchachas and Hombres, they were also responsible for stage-management, publicity, front-of-house, and various other technical and production duties. This was by no means unusual. Until 1993 productions were for the most part crewed by the acting students; there was no other technical or stage-management support. This was not only out of expedience, but was also seen as a beneficial part of their training, giving the students valuable experience and a broad understanding of all elements in staging a production. It also clearly demonstrated a strong collaborative culture.

Most Toi Whakaari graduates got work when or shortly after they left the school, and the 1990 graduates were no exception. By February 1991 Erik Thomson and Katie Wolfe had been contracted by the Fortune Theatre, Stelios Yiakmis had a two-play contract at the Court Theatre, and Larissa Matheson was performing in *The Seed* at BATS Theatre while rehearsing for a national tour of *Aunt Daisy.* Neil Holt was stage-managing at Circa Theatre, also developing his Len Lye solo from the 1990 *Reflections* programme for a season at the Depot theatre. Mick Rose was on a theatre-in-education tour in Auckland; Toni Gordon was rehearsing a children's play for the 'BATS Fringe Festival'; and Stuart Turner and Hone Kouka were collaborating on a writing project, *Mauri Tu*, which premiered at the Dunedin Writers' Week, directed by Apirana Taylor, and later went on to perform at Taki Rua/Depot theatre.

This was the start of a highly successful playwriting career for Hone Kouka. In 1992 he became the youngest playwright to win the Bruce Mason Award, for *Hide 'n' Seek.* His later works include *Waiora Te U Kai Po,* commissioned for the 1996 New Zealand International Festival of the Arts, and *Huia*, *Nga Tangata Toa* and *Remembrance of Things to Come.*

The campaign to recruit a new director picked up pace in the second half of 1990. The qualities being sought were extensive. Finding someone with an appreciation of the emerging bicultural issues in New Zealand, and the ability to steer the school through the many complex issues facing its future development, was no easy matter.

One undisputed frontrunner was Robin Payne. She was in her sixth year as head of voice and resident director at the Western Australian Academy of Performing Arts (WAAPA), where she also taught communication to stage management and media performance students.

Sunny sent Robin a job description, and after some deliberation she agreed to return to New Zealand for an interview. Robin was inspired by a 'wonderful and engaging but confronting series of interviews' with Sharon Crosbie and the Trust Board, and felt enthused by what she could bring to the position. But since she and her partner Tolis and their two children, Beatrice and Toby, were established in Perth, it was a big decision to make:

> Perth was a fantastic place to live and the job was very good there. I had tenure and a very comfortable life style: the children were very happy there and we were very well established. There seemed very little reason to leave Perth.
>
> But I saw the potential of bicultural commitment, and was reminded of the energy of the Drama School. And then there was the delirious freedom of the huge bureaucratic canopy that existed [at WAAPA] across the Academy; nurtured by the Edith Cowan University. There were enormous strengths in that situation: a wealth and range of

expertise, but there were also regular internecine battles about issues such as class sizes and student:teacher ratio.

Maybe the decision to return had something to do with being halfway through my life .... I felt a much stronger draw to actually stand on my earth than I had before. I started to have a heart-ache for the soil here; for the trees, for the colours that I'd never had before. That heart-ache really grew and became quite passionate. I am a New Zealander: I had my whole education, my growing up here.[5]

This connection with New Zealand and its evolving culture, coupled with an appreciation of the whakapapa of Toi Whakaari and a vision of what was needed to shape and sustain its future, helped Robin to form a vision for the future direction of the school and its capacity to affect social change:

> It's a world of horrendous civil wars and violence, where people have not learned to live with tolerance and understanding with each other. It seemed that here was an opportunity to work with an organisation that should by rights be a leader. If the role of theatre is to educate, to heal, to inspire, then what better tool was there than a drama school that was preparing the practitioners for the theatre of the future, to bring them together and give them an opportunity to understand both the cultures of this country? When I was hesitating about whether or not to accept the offer of the job, I discussed it with Tolis and he said, 'You know New Zealand can sort this out; we've got the opportunity to get it right.' So I returned home full of determination and exhilaration.
>
> I had been raised probably closer than a lot of Pākehā are to the Māori culture. Coming from Wanganui there was great integration with Māori in those days. My uncle was Walter Nash's press secretary when he was Minister of Māori Affairs because of his particular interest in Māori culture. He had married a Māori and they had four children, so we were raised alongside them. I had a personal interest in the culture and how it impacted my world: that their world of whaikōrero, of karanga, of ritual with welcome ceremonies; their pantheon, their understanding of the world seemed to have real parallels with ancient Greek times and the development of theatre in ancient Greece. So it seemed that there was a prism through which we could look at drama school, which would make the world really accessible and interesting to the Pākehā students, at the same time sharing our [Pākehā] culture with the Māori students.[6]

Robin had been 'stage-struck' as a child: 'by the age of five I knew that I wanted to be a director – not an actor: I was just so bossy'.[7] But in 1950s New Zealand, there were few models to draw on, especially female directors. When Nola Millar visited Robin's home town of Wanganui to direct a production of *The Matchmaker* (in which Robin's mother and several of her students were performing), Robin seized the opportunity to hang about rehearsals to observe Nola at work:

> I worshipped this rather strange reclusive woman who had a quiet sensitivity. She was very kind and tolerant to me; she later invited me down to various summer schools and workshops in Wellington during my secondary schooling. Nola was not only an example to me of someone who had the opportunity to direct, but she was a woman doing it, which in 1959 was unheard of ... she was her own woman – absolutely authentic.[8]

Robin's parents did their level best to dissuade her from a career in the theatre, but to no avail. At the age of seventeen she left Wanganui Girls' School to join David Smiles'

Children's Art Theatre. She was the first female to be employed by the company and toured with them for twenty months around the North Island. The following year, she enrolled in the NIDA acting course, but decided not to pursue her theatrical career as an actor. Instead, she was taken on as an apprentice director at the newly established Marion Street Theatre in Sydney. Three years later she embarked on the 'hippie trail' through Asia, stopping off to observe and teach in drama schools in Jakarta, Singapore, Bangkok and Delhi, before moving on to teach voice and speech in a drama school in Moscow, with the aid of a translator: 'Teaching in a foreign language meant that my interest in the sound of language became increasingly strong.'[9]

Robin had previously been awarded a scholarship by the QEII Arts Council to train and study in the UK, and when she was offered a place at the Central School of Speech and Drama to do postgraduate work on a course for directors and teachers, she accepted. The two prongs of Robin's work grew from this: it was her expertise as voice coach and as a creative drama teacher that provided the basis of her work in the 1980s at the Melbourne Theatre Company, and at the WAAPA.

When Robin arrived at Toi Whakaari in April 1991 to take up the position of director, she was welcomed to the school with a karanga delivered by two Māori students, Nancy Brunning and Mairanga White, together with her own cousin, playwright Riwia Brown. Robin was supported in the pōwhiri by her sister Clare, her mother Joy Payne, her Uncle Alec and her cousin Rangimoana Taylor. During the pōwhiri, Robin was described as a rangatira, which was here used in its dual meaning, referring both to a chief and also to a person who weaves together people on the move. She felt this gave her a solid footing from which to enter the school.

Robin's vision for Toi Whakaari was guided by a desire to re-establish and revitalise the links between the school and the rest of the theatre community. She saw a need to demonstrate clearly that its commitment to the Treaty of Waitangi enriched and informed Toi Whakaari, rather than compromised the school's undertaking to provide first-class training for actors:

> There was a perception that [Toi Whakaari] had become a little introverted, that it had turned in on itself and was not concerned with interacting with the rest of New Zealand theatre, and there was a sense that it had been taken over by militant Māori and that there was no place for the old tradition of professional theatre in the school. Not because of anybody's inherent racism, but because in one mode – that is, pursuing what is perceived as excellence in professional theatre – we are working from a paradigm which is clearly Pākehā – in fact until very recently, a purely British concept of what theatre is. So I put in place a series of programmes and activities to address those two perceived flaws in the school.[10]

The ideal of an intimate drama school that George Webby had so successfully created resonated strongly with Robin, and she felt responsible for maintaining what he and other directors of the school had established. Nevertheless, she was also well aware that Toi Whakaari had to expand, to move to larger premises, and to add more courses and more students if it was to survive, otherwise it would surely disappear:

> The climate was changing and that had to be responded to and I felt this need to protect the heart of the school and keep all the monsters at bay. The concept of a new building

> was already in train and couldn't be reversed, and it seemed like it would give the school greater credibility to have its own home.[11]

Sunny Amey eventually achieved her wish to retire, or at least to have some reflecting time and to 'do nothing for a long time'.[12] This was a commendable ambition but, as George Webby once remarked, 'Retirement takes some getting used to'.[13] Sunny had more than fulfilled her brief for the school: not only had she steadfastly held the students during an extremely difficult period of change, but she had also restored stability and supported the bicultural needs of the school. Later, when Sunny received the Chapman Tripp award for her Significant Contribution to Theatre in 2008, Nancy Brunning wrote this tribute to her:

> Sunny Amey was the reason I was accepted into Te Kura Toi Whakaari in 1990 – a small-town girl, straight from 7th form and with little exposure to theatre. She saw something in me that nobody else did and fought to get me a spot.
>
> Sunny Amey has been a battler for many Māori in the theatre industry for years. She has been a stern advisor to many of us, but also a support and confidante – our kuia. She taught me theatre, performance, choosing roles, understanding audiences, talked about the beginnings of theatre in this country, its potential in the future.
>
> My passion for the theatre has been steeped in me because of her. I am grateful to you, Sunny, for the courage and faith you had in many Māori who could have become invisible in this industry had you not led us. This is my personal tribute to you. Thank you. You still keep inspiring me to paddle the waka.[14]

The move to 36 Vivian Street in 1988 was intended to be a short-term solution until the school could move into new and bigger premises. That move was well overdue, and one of first things Robin did as director was rewrite the brief for the new building with the aim of drawing together the current needs of the school and providing for its expansion for at least ten years into the future. She did this with the assistance of her partner, Tolis Papazoglou. The document they jointly produced was informed by the knowledge they had gained from working at other performing arts schools, and was supported by research that Tolis had recently undertaken in the UK, Germany and Sweden.

The Trust Board's initial response was to resist the revised brief; in fact, it was seen as over-ambitious. But Robin insisted that the 'old brief' for the building was completely inadequate to meet the needs of Toi Whakaari, and that the facility needed its own theatre and had to be of a standard to train practitioners for the future – not the past:

> When I looked at the original designs for Shed 21, I knew they were completely inadequate for the Drama School of the future; that they were already too small. The designs were based on what had previously existed and were drawn up by people with little consultation.[15]

A Shed 21 Management Trust had been formed in 1989 to oversee the building option(s) for the Royal New Zealand Ballet, the School of Dance and the New Zealand Drama

School. Its initial emphasis was on a fundraising campaign. David Jenkins, the Drama School representative on the Trust, along with Mark Keyworth from the Royal New Zealand Ballet and Nonnita Rees representing the QEII Arts Council, met with the Minister for the Arts, who agreed to approach the Lottery Board to see if it would advance $3 million towards the Shed 21 proposal. The Minister of Education was also approached to gain support for the project when the Ministry eventually assumed responsibility for housing the two schools. Dave Jenkins later reported to the New Zealand Drama School Trust Board that:

> Forty or more 'rich or influential' people [had been] interviewed and 70% believed in the cause [Shed 21]. It is estimated it will cost $10.5 million for the building to be fitted out, with an estimate of $4 million to outfit the Drama School. The Lottery Board may assist with $3 million.[16]

But 1989/90 was not a good time for fundraising, given the financial climate, which was marred by inflation, the failure of the Sesquicentenary celebrations[17] and the upcoming election. The escalating cost estimates to refurbish Shed 21, which were caused largely by the need to earthquake-proof the building, was an added impediment. The Shed 21 Management Trust nevertheless went ahead and carried out a feasibility study on the needs of the two schools, commissioning concept drawings and architectural plans for the building.

The Royal New Zealand Ballet had by now taken out a three-year lease on alternative premises and made an offer to purchase the Embassy Theatre in Courtenay Place. It therefore seemed unlikely that the ballet company would have any further involvement in the Shed 21 project. On the positive side, their withdrawal from the project would allow greater flexibility in the layout of the building and free up more space for the two schools. But on the flipside, it meant there was one less organisation to fund the considerable building costs.

Accommodating the Drama School and Dance School together within a single building made good economic sense: the financial resources and fundraising capabilities of the two schools could be pooled to meet the considerable building and maintenance costs. It was mainly this uniting factor that brought them together, not any shared ideology.

In August 1991 the Shed 21 Trust withdrew its option to develop Shed 21 and continued to search for other premises. By this time, $120,000 had been spent on architects' fees for the building.

Robin Payne and the director of the School of Dance, Anne Rouse, were both appointed as ex-officio members of the Shed 21 Trust, and it was agreed the two schools should form a joint steering committee. After considering numerous properties, the steering committee recommended taking a ten-year lease on the top level of the James Smith Car Park, situated above the Betty Campbell Centre, adjacent to the Plaza Hotel in Wakefield Street. The maximum allowable budget to develop this site was $3.7 million.

But by this stage, the proposal to house the two schools within a single building was looking decidedly shaky. As Robin Payne found, it was largely through the goodwill of the two directors that the decision to proceed with the James Smith Rooftop Site was made:

> One night after work, Anne Rouse ... came into my office in Vivian Street and we talked and we had a meal together. We were both very conscious that we had the future [of the project] in our hands. We could have sabotaged it completely, or we could look at this arranged marriage and commit to make it work: and we did that. Anne needs to be honoured for that because we were both trepidatious about what compromises it may cause and what handicaps it might create. And yet we made an open-hearted decision to accept this arranged marriage – and go for it. In some respects the decision was forced too early by the Shed 21 Trust Board (but for all the right reasons), and if the people on the ground had been entrusted to work with goodwill and make it happen, we could have grown something more organic – like a blended family – where we could have found our own solutions.[18]

The Shed 21 Trust Board was then re-constituted as the New Zealand Schools of Dance and Drama Premises Management Trust (or PMT for short), with Robin Payne and Anne Rowse as two of the trustees.

An equally urgent job for Robin was the acting curriculum, which had to be rewritten to draw it up from a certificate to a diploma and then to a three-year qualification. There was also a technical course in the pipeline, which needed a curriculum to be developed from scratch.

When the school's long association with the QEII Arts Council ended in 1990, the government transferred the funding for Toi Whakaari and the New Zealand School of Dance from Arts and Culture (QEII Arts Council) to Vote Education. Toi Whakaari was then registered and accredited as a Private Training Establishment, under the provisions of the 1990 Education Amendment Act, and course approval fell under the jurisdiction of the newly-formed New Zealand Qualifications Authority (NZQA.)

Over the preceding years, the Drama School had enjoyed a high degree of autonomy, with directors having considerable freedom on how the school ran. Robin could see that this was all about to change:

> The concept of accountability and unit standards, which was racing across the world, had just reached New Zealand. As funders, the Ministry of Education found no charm in a small erratic idiosyncratic artsy school. They saw no justification for it. The funding was profoundly threatened and it seemed to me that the only way to secure the survival of the school was for it to have a large footprint. They couldn't see what type of an animal it was and they wanted to subsume it into a range of other structures – either taken over by a university or a polytechnic, institutions with which the Drama School had nothing in common.
>
> I looked at NIDA as a model, and what John Clark [NIDA's director] had achieved, and felt that was the way for survival, which did mean having visible self-importance – like a building. I fought very hard about increasing the number of students, partly on the basis that the industry couldn't absorb more than twelve (acting) graduates a year. Norman Kingsbury's response was, 'If we thought that was of any importance we wouldn't train lawyers, school teachers, and a list of other professions.'[19] Education was already on the way to becoming a commodity by that stage. The idea of a small institution, which

> was in harmony with the professional environment that it served, was an out-dated idea.
>
> So it seemed that we had to get the building, increase the size of the school and prepare a 'mission statement' – at fast speed. We became like children adopted by a stepmother who didn't want us. From having been loved and nurtured we were now having to ingratiate ourselves and claim our space and prove our viability by criteria that didn't seem to us to be useful or appropriate.
>
> It was also pointed out to us that we were the second-most expensive group to train: dentists first and then us. There was a general misconception that if you could teach several hundred business students at the same time, why can't you do that with actors? From 1991 we had to constantly re-educate officials about the importance of one-on-one work and why it was an intensive training programme.[20]

The impulse to follow NIDA's model was understandable. Since its inception in 1959 with an intake of twenty-three acting students, NIDA had worked assiduously to raise its profile. In 1962 it added a technical production course, which together with the acting course was extended to three years in 1972. At the same time, a three-year design course and a one-year postgraduate directing course were also introduced. The institute was now in the process of upgrading its diploma qualifications in acting, production and design to undergraduate degrees (NIDA's Bachelor of Dramatic Arts was introduced in 1994): it had recently introduced a two-year associate diploma course in theatre crafts, and was now in the process of developing postgraduate courses in voice, movement and production management.

As George Webby observed in 1973, NIDA had enjoyed the status of being Australia's national drama school from its inception. Yet it could not realistically be expected to remain a 'cottage-industry' drama school and survive. It had to expand to keep pace with a growing theatre, TV and film industry that was significantly larger than New Zealand's.

The growth in tertiary education in Australia had also accelerated, with vocational and academic theatre courses now available inter-state. NIDA had to compete with these institutions for students, the main competition being the Victorian College of the Arts, which was about to become affiliated to Melbourne University, and WAAPA, part of the Edith Cowan University. Both institutions were attracting an increasing number of students.

In the UK, most major drama schools were becoming multi-disciplinary and the prevailing academic drift was pushing them towards three-year degree qualifications. And in New Zealand, other theatre schools were springing up, or were about to, including UNITEC's School of Performing and Screen Arts in Auckland.

This was the 'competitive' environment in which Toi Whakaari now had to operate if it was to attract the best students. There was more choice for anyone wanting to train as an actor or in another theatre discipline, either in New Zealand or overseas.

The first production Robin directed at Toi Whakaari was Caryl Churchill's *Mad Forest*. The script had originally evolved through a series of workshops, in which Churchill and students from Central worked with their counterparts at the Caragiate Institute in Romania to tell the story of the Nicolae Ceausescu, the overthrow of his dictatorship in 1989 and the ensuing fragmentation of the country. *Mad Forest* was

Robin Payne, 1991

Annie Ruth, 1991

the first of many plays with a political bias that Robin directed at Toi Whakaari. She wanted to provide opportunities for the students to work in theatrical genres that had not previously been explored at the school, including plays from other cultures with bi-cultural themes. By performing these works in New Zealand, with a cast that included Māori actors, students could draw attention to common or shared issues.

At the start of 1991 Annie Ruth was appointed as a full-time improvisation tutor and her first performance project that year was directing *What's Bred in the Bone*. It was one of the first fully improvised productions at the school and had an innovative form that helped the cast to genuinely connect with the audience:

> We were looking for a structure for improvisation where you could tell a story that wasn't a collection of little comedy skits – like theatre sports. We were looking instead for something more considered, where you could tell a deeper, longer story.
>
> So, we took the proverb 'what's bred in the bone will out in the flesh' to tell a generation's story. It was something the students knew about – families – so we felt free to improvise inside that territory. The audience provided us with a lot of information; we would ask for the sin that beset this family through the generations – also the virtues that saved them. They wrote their suggestions beforehand and put them in a bag, and then we pulled them out. I felt that was rather graceful, rather than depending on someone shouting out stuff, like in theatre sports. We also asked them for a proverb, around which we created a myth, and often finished with the mythic theme. We then set up a tension between a 'thing of grace, and a thing of darkness'. Starting off with the family photo, we would then tell the story through the generations.
>
> The students would cast themselves on the spot; they had a whole lot of structures that they could use, so it wasn't all naturalism. For instance, they could step out and speak directly to the audience about something that was going on their mind, or they could confide in the audience – like a Shakespeare soliloquy – then go back into the scene and carry on.
>
> I think it was structurally very adventurous and I don't know why we didn't do it again. It was an original structure. But it put a lot of weight on the students. Yet the performances had great energy. I particularly remember Stephen Bain, because he took a lot of leadership in that: being such an inventive man, it was his home territory.[21]

The improvisation process helped the students later with their monologues, which before 1991 were heavily based on writing. This meant that students who found it difficult to write well often struggled and sometimes failed:

> It was such a tough experience for them. I remember a guy, I think it was Joe Conway, he really had a real flair for improvisation, and when he did his monologue it was entirely improvised. Every night it would be very different. That was his talent, his genius. It's a question that we are now only coming to grips with, how do you deal with students who have a talent but can't deal with a script. I don't think we should think, 'Oh well, then h/she's not an actor', because there's another whole sphere of 'acting' that they are very fluent in.[22]

A two-year technical course was now being seriously considered to replace the 'new entrant' apprenticeship/training scheme (NETS), previously run under the auspices of the National Theatre Technicians Training Council. That scheme was administered by a committee under the chairmanship of Jeremy Collins, and was funded by the Vocational Training Council and the QEII Arts Council. New entrant trainees were hosted by participating theatres for a two-year period, and undertook a programme comprised of 75 per cent on-the-job and 25 per cent formal training. The first intake of five trainees joined the new-entrant scheme in 1988. Pam Hindmarsh, now a senior tutor in stage management at Toi Whakaari, was one of those five:

> I was a NETS trainee undertaking an abbreviated version of the course. I started my stage management career in 1985 in children's theatre in Manurewa, and later convinced Sue Wilson to take me on as a stage manager at Circa Theatre. During this time I did the block courses up at Victoria University, with Raymond Boyce, Joe Hayes, Ian McMinn and John McKay. I went to the Court Theatre at the beginning of 1989 as the third stage manager working with their production manager, Ross Joblin. The Court was a great opportunity – it gave me a solid grounding in stage management. Unfortunately, at the beginning of 1990 I was made redundant, along with four others, as a result of Arts Council funding cuts to the Court. Tim Dowse from the Mercury Theatre then took me on as their stage manager. The course served me well: it was a good formal starting point for me, as previously I had learned informally – on the job. Importantly, I got work through the NETS scheme and it was a good way to network. As far as I am aware, the only other participant in the scheme still working in the industry is Sheena Baines, lighting designer at the Court Theatre. In 1991 I was accepted into the stage-management study programme at the BANFF Center in Alberta to gain advanced training, and the NETS training was good preparation for that.[23]

Despite the NETS scheme being well administered and strongly supported by the live theatre and entertainment industries, it turned out to be an inopportune time to launch the programme. The continuation of funding for the scheme depended on NTTTC gaining formal recognition as an Entertainment Industry Training Board, under the Vocational Training Council structure. When that was declined by the Minister of Employment in 1988, the financial viability of the new-entrant training scheme was placed in jeopardy. A growing uncertainty in the regulatory area of vocational training, education and apprenticeships compounded the problem. By 1990 the new-entrant training scheme was in serious financial difficulty and the completion of training for the existing trainees was made possible only through a one-off grant from the QEII Arts Council.

For all its merits, the new-entrant training scheme was a hybrid, and did not sit well with emerging educational and training initiatives. The 1989 Review of Post-Compulsory Education and Training, and the Vocational Training Act administered by the Ministry of Education, stipulated specific requirements concerning formal accreditation and quality assurance, requiring most training to co-exist with the new qualifications framework currently being developed by NZQA.

The new-entrant scheme was abandoned in 1991 in favour of a full-time technical course to be offered by Toi Whakaari. By 1992 Toi Whakaari was accredited as an Other Tertiary Education Provider (OTEP), allowing the school to seek approval and accreditation through NZQA to deliver additional qualifications, and then to apply to the Ministry of Education to fund the approved training programmes.

The technical course sat well with Robin Payne's goal for Toi Whakaari. The framework acknowledged the broad purpose of tertiary education: that the acquisition of knowledge and technical competencies formed only part of the picture. It also encompassed other factors that were starting to guide curriculum development, including a 'can do' attitude, flexibility, an ability to adapt, self-management and inter-personal skills, all essential attributes for practitioners in the theatre and screen arts in New Zealand.

There were sound pedagogical reasons for bringing technical and management students into the mix of Toi Whakaari. A multi-disciplinary school would enable the acting students to explore their craft alongside students from other disciplines which, it was hoped, would foster a more collaborative approach to theatre making. And by amalgamating elements of the two courses, it would provide a more balanced learning environment that would better reflect an industry model. But there were other – more pragmatic – reasons for introducing a technical training programme into the school. These were outlined in a paper that explained part of Robin's rationale for adopting the technical course:

> The first purpose of a drama school is to train actors. This, as with any education, needs to be achieved by a combination of theory, simulated experience and *real* experience.
>
> This School, with only two major productions per course, has provided limited *real* experience. The proposal to increase the productions to six per year cannot be supported by the current system of suspending all classes to allow one year to crew for another.
>
> The addition of technical students, and a staff member with relevant expertise, will reduce the enormous stress on existing staff, while still allowing acting students to participate in and learn about other aspects of production.[24]

The Arts Council supported the idea of a technical training course at Toi Whakaari, and Nonnita Rees, the manager of theatre programmes at the Arts Council, encouraged Robin Payne to take on the programme, indicating there would be funding available for this purpose.

Arts Council's support was necessary because the Ministry of Education was unable immediately to commit additional funding for a technical course. Consequently, the first two years of the programme were subsidised by the QEII Arts Council, which enabled the first intake of six students to enrol at the start of 1992. Much of the credit for transferring the new-entrant training scheme to Toi Whakaari must go to John McKay and Joe Hayes, who helped to develop the technical production curriculum for the school. To this day, they continue to provide much valued support as founder members of the Entertainment Technology Advisory Panel.

Robin later acknowledged that taking on the technical course was 'one of the best things we did'.[25] And yet she also regretted the loss of basic technical production training for acting students, which had been a fundamental part of the curriculum in George and Sunny's time.

Increased activity at the school was reflected in a changed administrative structure. In 1991 Pat Holden left and was replaced by Kern Pettigrew as the school's administrator.

She was joined by Deborah Tucker as the arts administrator with responsibility for publicity and promotions, and Moana Solomona as the clerical assistant. On the teaching side, Rangimoana Taylor was appointed as a part-time core tutor with special responsibility for Māoritanga and its relationship to theatre. There were also changes to the Trust Board: Sharon Crosbie's term of office as chair had ended, and she was succeeded by Phillip Mann. John Anderson, John Fokerd and Thelma Grabmaier also stepped down from the Board to be replaced by Dave Gibson, Michael Hurst and Keri Kaa.

The 1991 graduation production, *A Long Walk off a Tall Rock*, by Stuart Hoar, was specially commissioned by the school. Michael Hurst directed the production and also designed the set; Laughton Pattrick was the musical director. The play, an 'uncompromising story of love, avarice and survival', was set in contemporary Auckland, and was written entirely in verse. Nancy Brunning had a key role in the production, as the character Jane Suck, a prostitute. Her performance 'displayed a lightness of touch and agility that was nothing short of outstanding'.[26] By all accounts, Jane Suck's opening line, 'Get me the fuck out of here', was extremely effective in drawing the audience into the world of the play as she was 'carried shoulder high by four bearers atop a bizarrely-constructed platform like some pagan high priestess exalting in her powers as a sexual icon'.[27]

It was perhaps fitting that this gutsy graduating class should depart in such style. They were Stephen Bain, Nancy Brunning, Joe Conway, Frances Kewene, Sue Morrison, Donna Muir, Allen O'Leary, Andrew Scott, Tim Spite, Erina Toi-Paku, Mairanga White and Stephanie Wilkin.

There was praise too for Robin Payne who 'had the courage not to rely on either a classic or tested overseas play, but took a chance on a commissioned work, which makes most of other recent New Zealand efforts look very old-fashioned'.[28]

The production clearly signalled a new direction for Toi Whakaari.

Nancy Brunning, 1991

Thirteen

1992–1993

'There are theories of acting; there are no theoretical actors.'

The year 1992 heralded changes in the structure of the core teaching staff at the school. Rona Bailey had developed a methodology that allowed creative movement classes to relate more directly to actor training, but a more integrated approach was now needed to incorporate the vocabularies of body, voice, space and text. Lyne Pringle and Michael Parmenter were extremely skilled in training dancers and developing strength and stamina, but their movement work for actors only partially transferred to performance. The acting students had excellent stamina and physical courage, but their alignment and sense of space were not so well developed and they sometimes looked physically awkward in performance, particularly in dance work.

When Michael Parmenter left the school in 1991 to pursue his own performance career, Nick Blake joined the part-time core staff as a movement tutor. He was able to make a stronger connection between movement and acting through the physicalisation of character. Two Alexander Technique tutors were also contracted to improve the students' physical alignment.

The Trust Board appointed two new members in 1992: Dawn Sanders and Jonathon Hendry. Dawn was now the vice president and administrator of the Shakespeare Globe Centre (New Zealand), project manager of the Wellington Shakespeare Society Globe Theatre Project and a tutor at the New Zealand School of Dance.

Lyne Pringle in movement class - 1990

Michael Parmenter in movement class - 1990

Sixteen acting students were accepted in the 1992 intake, four more than any previous year, and six students enrolled in the first intake of the technical course. To accommodate the additional students, the existing common rooms were rearranged, but it was still a tight squeeze, requiring judicious timetabling to avoid a clash of interests in teaching activities. The technical students were the worst affected; they had no dedicated teaching space or home-room of their own, and were generally confined to a small common area adjacent to the movement and drama studios. The performance space could be used for some technical classes, but only when it was not being used for rehearsals and general production activity.

Nevertheless, despite having to grapple with logistical problems, the need for a structured training environment for technicians and stage managers had been acknowledged. And the integration of a technical training programme into a performing arts school was now viewed by many in the industry as a desirable outcome.

Clearly, the technical training programme required a substantial investment in technology and production resources, but this was hard to justify given the relatively small number of technical students. Largely due to the efforts of Nonnita Rees [Mann], the Director of the Arts Development Unit at the Arts Council, it had agreed to fund the technical course on a trial basis over two years to the tune of $130,000. But a large proportion of this was allocated to staff salaries.

What dictated the success (or otherwise) of technical training at the school was the standard of teaching and the quality of students accepted into the course. To meet their training needs, it was equally important that the integrity of the course was not overwhelmed by the voracious production activity of the school.

To safeguard this and 'to ensure that the curriculum was effectively translated into a course structure; to advise on future changes and provide informed support for the programme',[1] an industry-based Technical Advisory Panel was introduced in 1992. The panel, initially John McKay, Joe Hayes and Marc Ellis, provided valuable assistance to the school in developing the curriculum for the technical course. Given the difficulty in transferring the technical course from the NTTTC programme to the drama school, the Arts Council asked Toi Whakaari to co-opt a member of the Technical Production Advisory Panel on to the Trust Board, but the request was denied. Any further discussion of this matter was deferred until a hui between the Trust Board and Toi

Whakaari staff was held at the end of March to discuss the future role and constitution of the Board.[2] The Arts Council was clearly unimpressed by this delay:

> An effective advisory structure must have a clear relationship to the drama school. An expert group appointed without a formal brief to [the Trust] Board and staff will soon become frustrated and/or troublesome to you. It is most regrettable from our perspective that these matters have continued to drift and undermine our confidence that the school is capable of introducing and sustaining a course that meets art form and industry needs.[3]

In July the Trust Board formally recognised the Advisory Panel; this allowed the Arts Council to release $25,000 from the balance of funds held by the defunct NTTTC Committee to cover the ongoing travel costs and other expenses incurred by the Advisory Panel. The panel never achieved representation on the Trust Board, but it did form a strong relationship with the Board of Studies to whom it reported.

At the start of 1992, Ian Nicholls was appointed as the first full-time technical course tutor at the school, to coordinate the training programme and to fulfil the function of technical director. Ian's background was in theatre lighting, and during his first few months as a tutor at the school, he also worked as the lighting coordinator for the New Zealand International Arts Festival.

The technical course was the first of many new theatre disciplines to be introduced into Toi Whakaari. This commendable initiative broke the historical identity of the school; it now officially trained practitioners other than actors, though paradoxically this sowed the seeds of acrimony that began to emerge within the school as more and more courses were added. This development required judicious negotiation as the constituency of Toi Whakaari evolved.

The first 'guinea pig' technical students were Nicola Blackman, Phillip Cochrane, Sean Coyle, Craig Hunter, Kate Peters and Leanne Watkins. They came from Auckland, Christchurch, Dunedin and Nelson, and had wide-ranging interests, Nicola in stage management, Sean and Kate in design, and Leanne in lighting. Craig and Phillip's interests lay more in theatre technology, and when they were offered employment at the end of their first year, they unsurprisingly withdrew from the course.

Sean Coyle had previously studied fine arts at Otago University. After gravitating to the university's theatre department in preference to fine arts, he decided to enrol at Toi Whakaari as this would provide greater opportunity to do more theatre work:

> In our first year, we did movement every morning as well as singing and theatre history with the actors, and this helped us to be close to them. It was fortunate that most of our group were able to follow our particular interests. The equipment available to us was extremely primitive, but I maintain that this made us better practitioners and we had to be innovative with the little we had. My theory is that if you have too much technology you get overwhelmed by it, and the good ideas don't necessarily come to fruition. We did some pretty good work – with what little we had.
>
> We had drawing classes with Tommy Honey, and Raymond Boyce taught us set design and theatre history, and we did scenic painting at the Opera House with Wilf Conroy. In our first year we were seconded onto the Festival – I remember seeing a huge amount of amazing productions and doing back-stage tours and meeting various production crews.

> In my second year I designed *Romeo and Juliet* with Theatre at Large at Taki Rua theatre working with Anna Marbrook and Christian Penny. We transformed Taki Rua and did the show in traverse. After that, Kate Peters and I started collaborating as costume and set designers together. Kate is now a 'fashion mogul' running a Beyond Retro line of clothing in the UK and Scandinavia – very successful.
>
> For most of the two years at Toi Whakaari I lived across the road from the school with Dave Fane, Lucy Schmidt, Bronwyn Bradley and Damon Andrews. Drama School was like our extended living room: our bathroom was the school showers. We could wake up at 8.25 and make it to movement class for 8.30.
>
> I did a number of secondments in both my first and second years, the major one being on Peter Jackson's *Heavenly Creatures* working in the Arts Department with Grant Major the production designer.
>
> It was an amazing and really intense and life-changing two years at Toi Whakaari. It was total immersion; we lived together and trained together: a real family atmosphere.[4]

Robin Payne was keen for Toi Whakaari to have closer ties to the New Zealand International Festival of the Arts, and for the school to take a more active role in the biennial event. Following discussion with the Festival organisers, it was agreed the school would host a series of free lunch-time forums, and invite some of the Festival performers to conduct workshops and classes at Toi Whakaari. A unique aspect of the school's relationship with the Festival was the 'minders' programme' in which students were assigned to visiting companies to act as hosts and general 'gofers'. In return, the students received complimentary tickets for numerous Festival events, giving them access to shows they could not otherwise afford.

A marked shift in the teaching methodology of the school began to be apparent as various strands of the curriculum started to link up, achieving a much stronger correlation between stage-craft, theoretical studies and production activity.

Christian Penny and Anna Marbrook, from Theatre at Large, conducted a workshop with the second-year students, which also helped the students develop their monologues. Christian and Anna returned later in the year to run an intensive workshop with the first-years to lay the foundations of *Romeo and Juliet* that they would then present the following year.

Bert van Dijk conducted classes in voice and physical theatre, based on the European influences of Grotowski and Roy Hart, which introduced students to new concepts and disciplines that would later form the basis of Bert's work with the first-years on *Tungoungou/Metamorphoses*, in 1993.

Nick Blake, Aileen Davidson and Tony Wolfe conducted clown, circus and street theatre workshops with the first-years, culminating in performances at the Wellington Community Youth Festival. And the first-year acting and technical students joined forces on a puppetry workshop led by Peter Wilson, director of the Perth-based Spare Puppet Theatre.

Over the Queen's Birthday weekend, first-year students and staff participated in the National Māori Writers and Artists Hui at Omaka Marae, near Blenheim. Meanwhile, the second-years worked with Ralph McAllister on a theatre-in-education exercise with story-telling as its focus, and with Sally Rodwell on acrobatical community theatre. The second-years also had a series of intensive acting-for-camera blocks, with Ian Mune, Gaylene Preston, John Reid and Vicki Yiannoutsos.

Drew James, 1992

There were more staff changes at the school during 1992. Kern Pettigrew left in June and was replaced by Alison Smith as the school's administrator. She held the fort until Drew James was able to take up the position of business manager in November. Drew had extensive experience in arts management and had previously been the business manager for the Chrissie Parrott Dance Collective in Perth.

At the end of 1992 the school farewelled Jane Waddell, marking the conclusion of her almost continuous connection with the New Zealand Drama School over the past nineteen years, first as a student in 1974, and then as a voice tutor. Earlier in the year, she had taken leave from the school to tour in Circa Theatre's *Joyful and Triumphant,* which confirmed her decision to focus more on her acting and directing career. During her time at the school, Jane had worked with four of the school's directors.

The 1992 graduation production was *Two Gentlemen of Verona,* directed by Colin McColl. It opened at the Taranaki Stratford Festival for a week-long season in November, before returning to Wellington in December. The entire school was involved in the production, first-year actors working alongside technical students. Two of the technical students, Sean Coyle and Kate Peters, also performed in the production. And then there was Winnie, a charismatic and sometimes obedient golden retriever who played Launce's dog. For her laid-back performance as Crabb, Winnie received special mention in Laurie Atkinson's review of the production:

> The graduates will have learned by now that they must never again share the stage with an animal. Winnie … walked away with the acting honours, upstaging everyone as she yawned, wagged her tail and gazed in sad surprise at the audience when we were foolish enough to laugh.[5]

Dave Fane played the 'crowd pleasing Launce', which provided him with an early opportunity to exercise his nascent and droll sense of humour. Sarah Boddy drew the short-straw, receiving the unenviable job of 'Dog Wrangler'.

During the Stratford season of *Two Gentlemen of Verona*, the first-year actors visited schools, hospitals and various other venues to perform *Swords, Sonnets and Songs*, which incorporated sword-fighting scenes as a metaphor to explore the relationship between characters. This was the forerunner of a methodology that was later developed intensively by the school into combat metaphor, and remains a valuable part of the first-year acting programme to this day.

The 1993 intake of students was larger than that of the previous year, with seventeen acting students selected from centres across the country: four from Auckland, six from Wellington, two each from Tauranga and Christchurch, and one each from Palmerston North, Hamilton and Hawera. As well as increasing the student intake, Robin Payne had also lifted the entry age for the acting students, from eighteen to

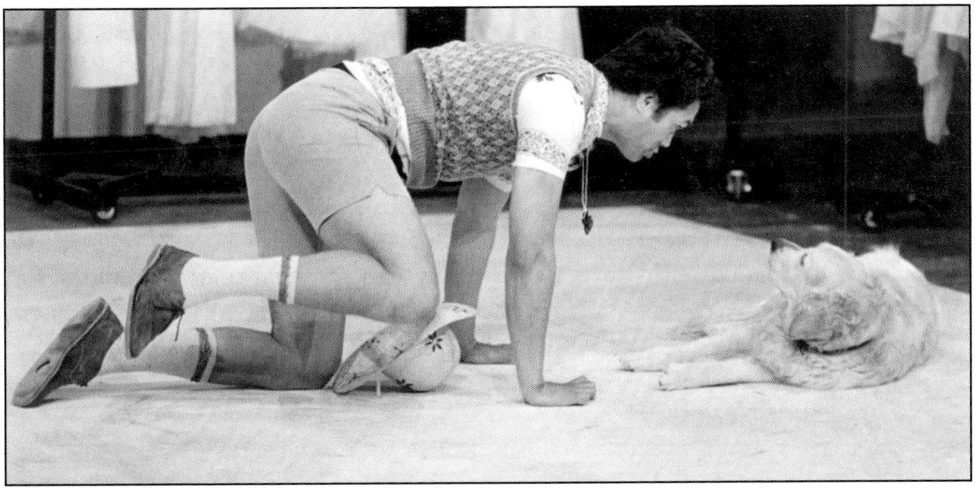

The Two Gentlemen of Verona, at Stratford King's Theatre, November 1992. Dave Fane (Launce) with Winnie (Crabb). *Taranaki Daily News*

twenty, emphasising the necessary life experience needed to enable the students to commit fully to the training provided by the school:

> It is such intensive and demanding work and the [students] need to have sorted out some of the basic things about life before they arrive at the school. If they have some sense of who they are, the work is not as potentially destructive as for a young person straight out of school.[6]

Included in the 1993 acting intake was Vanessa Byrnes, who has vivid memories of her two years as a student at the school:

> I arrived in Wellington in the distant summer of 1993. I'd just finished five years of study completing my MA at Waikato University and was thrilled to be joining an eclectic, wildly talented, diverse group of people at the school. My love affair with 'The Drama School', as it was then commonly referred to, had a long honeymoon phase. I was so excited just to be there, living my dream of learning an actor's craft. Situated, as it was then above Caffe L'Affare, the place was a heady mixture of smells and sensations; roasting coffee beans mingled with sweat from movement classes, and noises of the street below provided the cityscape backdrop for moments of silence upstairs in the varnished chipboard studios. I felt at home within its worn self; a naked architectural sense of character gave the place self-confidence and an immaterial dedication to the way of theatre. The school gave me a place where I could validate my own sense of artistic purpose in a New Zealand culture that doesn't easily put a value on feeling or sensation. Yet this was the currency the school engaged with. I think Toi Whakaari gave me a second home, a professional family, a kind of turangawaewae, or a place to stand fully in my own skin. I think many others have shared this sensation.
>
> Names remain from my days as a student in the 1990s at Vivian Street: Rona Bailey ('connect!'), Wi Kuki Kaa, Robin Payne ('Telling the truth with love'), Annie Ruth ('Amohia ...'), KC Kelly ('That's horseshit!'), Bert van Dijk ('Toss it over!'), Laughton Pattrick ('Yaaaaa!'), Lyne Pringle ('Just breathe further into the stretch'), Nerissa Moore ('What's wrong with a New Zealand accent?') and Bill Guest ('Actors can rig lights too')

> all left an indelible imprint on my mind and heart. We were lucky to be challenged by these teachers at a time when the school was still forging its identity and looking for a permanent home to lay down its roots.[7]

There was no intake of technical students in 1993 as the initial funding for the course was only for two years. Toi Whakaari now had thirty-four students, a significant increase in the population of the school that was augmented by a rise in the number of full-time staff.

Ian Nicholls stepped down as head of the technical course at the end of 1992. And when Murray Lynch joined the school in 1993, he took over the position, combining it with the job of acting methodology tutor. He somehow managed to balance his acting methodology and script analysis work with responsibilities for the acting-for-camera programme and the technical course.

As one of the country's foremost directors, Murray had played a pivotal role in developing professional theatre, first as associate director of Theatre Corporate and then as artistic director of the Maidment Arts Centre. In more recent times, he had been the founder director of the acclaimed Tantrum Theatre Company, and from 1990 to 1992 was associate director of Downstage. He had also directed productions at Toi Whakaari, including *Roomers* and *The Body.*

Later in the year, KC Kelly joined the full-time staff as an acting methodology tutor. He was a graduate of the Webber Douglas Academy in London and had also trained as an actor with Michael Howard in New York. Since arriving in New Zealand, he had taught at several universities, including Victoria and Canterbury, and as a part-time tutor at Toi Whakaari. Prior to taking up his appointment at Toi Whakaari, KC had been an actor with the Court Theatre in Christchurch.

The school also appointed a new head of movement, Bert van Dijk, brought to the school to represent modern European theatre practice and to integrate the vocabularies of voice and movement with physical theatre. His formal training included physical education, clinical and social psychology, acting and corporeal mime, and his ongoing performance practice integrated Butoh, voice and Roy Hart theatre methodology. During the 1980s Bert had been the artistic director for the Groninger Mime Gezelschap

Images L–R: Murray Lynch; KC Kelly at Vivian Street; Bert van Dijk, 1995 (Anne Nordhaus in foreground)

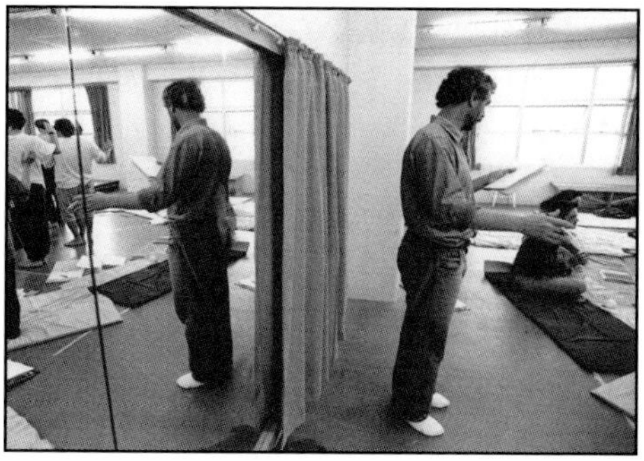

and London's Toucon Theatre, and for many years he performed with and was assistant director to Enrique Pardo's Pantheatre, in Europe and the UK. Lyne Pringle remained at the school to work with Bert, as a core part-time movement tutor.

Piripi Waretini was appointed as the school's Māori programme coordinator to advise on kawa and supervise a Māori-intensive block during the first term.

On the administration side, Sarah Griffiths joined Drew James and Deborah Tucker in the 'front office' as the secretary/receptionist. And in the library, John Snadden joined Ruth Graham to work as a second voluntary library assistant, along with Lisl Hilton. John had been an official war artist in the Second World War, and for a while had sketched movement classes at the school to get source material for an exhibition of paintings. Some of those paintings now hang in the Nola Millar Library.

The Toi Whakaari Trust Board underwent some changes in 1993. Phillip Mann stepped down as chair and was replaced by Dave Jenkins as acting chair. Rona Bailey, Jonathon Hendry and Dawn Sanders remained on the Board, but there were five new members: Giff Davidson, Gary Dyall, Terry Kilminster, Norman Kingsbury and Carrie Wainwright.

For some inexplicable reason, the school dropped the New Zealand appendage to its name and for a while became known simply as the Drama School, although the Māori prefix remained intact.

Following the earlier decision by the Premises Management Trust to proceed with the James Smith Rooftop site, the Ministry of Education indicated it would provide $1.9 million to Toi Whakaari and the New Zealand School of Dance, in the form of a suspensory loan, to assist the two schools to develop purpose-built premises. This was in addition to the $2 million already committed by the Lotteries Commission and some additional funding from Wellington City Council.

Now the Premises Management Trust was starting to have second thoughts about the James Smith site; the projected cost was beginning to escalate, just as it had with Shed 21. The original estimate for the development – $3.7 million – had increased by $500,000, largely the result of having to install lifts and hoists to allow access. At the start of the project, Tolis Papazoglou, the design consultant for the two schools and the PMT,

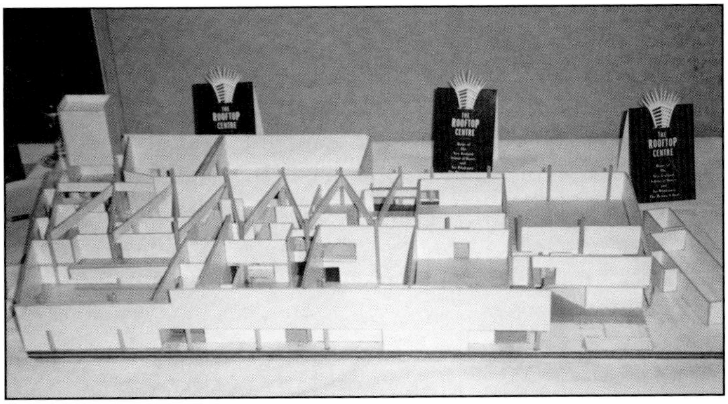

Model of proposed Rooftop Centre

had pointed out that the Rooftop site was untenable until access issues were resolved.

It appeared that some cost benefits could be achieved through economies of scale, particularly if the schools agreed to share common spaces and resources and combined some classes. But this was not an acceptable 'solution', as it would clearly restrict the individual schools' singleness of purpose and place considerable pressure on their timetabling.

These limitations were spelt out in a paper that Robin Payne wrote on the amalgamation of the two schools:

> The skill must be to establish two autonomous bodies which can share premises, some resources, some teachers and allow students and staff the enrichment of cohabitation. The students of the two [schools] are at radically different levels of emotional development and life experience. Although some social, creative and technical cross-pollination would be advantageous to both groups, neither should be disadvantaged by enforced amalgamation.[8]

As resources could not or would not be further sacrificed, the only practical solution for the two schools was to find a new location. So the PMT again began to look at other sites, including Shed 1 on the harbour and Erskine College at Island Bay. The PMT also formed a fundraising committee to find the additional money needed to meet the increased cost of the brief.

A further twist to what was already a complicated situation occurred a few months later when Anne Rouse resigned from the New Zealand School of Dance. She was replaced by Rochelle Zide-Booth as director, which meant that the Drama School, and in particular Robin Payne, had to re-establish a working relationship with the School of Dance.

The PMT had not completely abandoned the James Smith Rooftop, and after protracted negotiations to determine what was, and what needed to be, included in the purchase of the site, an offer was made to buy units in the development company that owned the site. If the offer was accepted, it would effectively give the PMT ownership of the airspace and allow the architects to proceed in their development of plans for the building.

But the feasibility of the project was still in doubt. When projected budgets for 1994–95 were completed for both schools, questions were raised about their ability to meet the projected financial commitment. Their capacity to borrow money for the proposed building development was limited, a situation that would be made worse if the Ministry of Education chose to move the schools away from bulk funding into student-component funding.

This type of funding, known as EFTS (Equivalent Full Time Student) funding, was about to be introduced as a standard for most tertiary institutions, and would be tagged to the number of students enrolled. The Ministry of Education largely thought in equations of several hundred students to one lecturer, which meant that the Drama School would have to justify its high per-capita cost of training for a relatively small number of students.

Still, the PMT decided to proceed, but with caution, by proposing the use of available funds to construct stage one of the building in the first instance, with a second stage to be completed when additional funds became available. It was hoped that such moneys would be realised through fundraising, bridging finance, naming rights or by whatever other means were necessary.

The directors of the two schools were asked to reconsider the use of fewer teaching spaces, at least until stage two was completed. It was suggested that this could be best achieved through joint scheduling and collaboration. But both directors were clearly unhappy with the staged development plan, and insisted that the entire construction had to be completed before the premises were occupied

As the year progressed, the PMT continued to grapple with ongoing building problems. They called for an engineering survey of the site to determine its 'code prescribed seismic loading', and commissioned a report on its structural integrity. But this only increased the mounting professional fees for architects and other consultants. And when the previous two-stage proposal then became a three-stage 'cost-saving option', with Mainzeal poised to sign a contract to construct the first stage, the PMT realised it had more than just a shaky building to worry about.

While all this was happening, Robin and Drew still had the ongoing demands of the Drama School to manage, a state of being that was succinctly described by Robin as 'the constantly adjusting equilibrium required to handstand on a "plank balanced over a barrel". It is difficult to divert one's attention for too long.'[9]

Following their work in 1992 with the first-year actors, Christian Penny and Anna Marbrook returned in 1993 to work with the same group on a production of *Romeo and Juliet*, with the aim of developing a piece of theatre that incorporated physical conventions and also explored something of the dynamics of biculturalism. They chose *Romeo and Juliet* because of the two warring families, seen as a metaphor for two cultures coming together in conflict and then becoming a single culture. This 'uneasy alliance' provided an opportunity to consider the nature of biculturalism rather than focusing on the specific dynamics of Māori and Pākehā relationships. When the play was performed in Taki Rua theatre, this opposing relationship was further highlighted with the two families in the play seated at opposite ends of the performance space.

A further exploration into biculturalism occurred later in the year, when Bert van Dijk directed *Tungoungou/Metamorphoses*. This totally new work, written by Vincent O'Sullivan and Apirana Taylor, juxtaposed Māori myths with myths from Greek and Roman legend. A primary aim of the production was to create a shared experience for both audience and performers, with the intention of breaking down the 'fourth wall':

> We wanted the audience to be physically involved in the unfolding stories; to get away from the idea that 'this is where the audience are and this is where the actors are'. We wanted to bring people into the play. Many Māori legends talk of food, and the Greek and Roman myths were traditionally told at feasts, so at the start of each performance the audience was invited to share a banquet and mingle with the cast, and were entertained with music that the students had composed. Then the myths began and at one point the audience was taken through a dark passage to the underworld, where one Māori and one Greek myth was performed before they were returned to the real world.[10]

Productions at the school mostly had a four-to-five-week rehearsal period, but in this case Bert chose to rehearse the cast for eight weeks, allowing more time to explore the

Tungoungou/Metamorphoses, 1993. Kirk Torrance and Vanessa Byrnes.

play in depth. More importantly, the creative process could be governed more by the students' training needs.

In many ways, *Tungoungou/Metamorphoses* was a precursor to other site-specific works that Bert later directed at the school, *Out of Space* in 1995, and *The Wild Man* in 1996, both exploring and generating performance material from original works based on mythical stories. All three productions represented a collaborative process of theatre-making, in which he developed interdisciplinary approaches to acting, using body, space, voice and text to explore intercultural and bicultural approaches to performance. He was also interested in experimenting with audience/performer relationships:

> I was brought into the school to 'represent' the Modern European Theatre practice, which was thought of as physical theatre. However, it became clear to me that physical theatre in New Zealand was and still is a marginalised term, and that my work was not considered crucial. It felt at times more like a bit of relish on the side, while in my experience my approach to theatre is mainstream and at the heart of contemporary theatre practice – at least in Europe.
>
> Acting in New Zealand, in the early nineties, focused mainly on text-based and naturalistic productions of English, American, Russian and sometimes Australian plays. The dominant acting methodology at Toi Whakaari was a New Zealand version of Mike Alfred's, and even an early version of Stanislavsky's method acting – before he abandoned emotional and sensory memory as the main tool to achieve 'truth' of emotion in favour of a physical action approach to acting. The New Zealand version of Mike Alfred's method

> appeared to me a rather intellectual exercise – using long lists of verbs and actions leading to clean-cut productions that looked good, had some emotional truth to it, but lacking depth in the physical and imaginative arenas.[11]

This viewpoint was contentious. Since the 1980s the teaching practice at school had evolved from what had largely been a single unified methodology to a more balanced approach, using a broad range of theatrical models. The prevailing acting methodology was largely based on the Alfred's technique, in reality an amalgam of other techniques including those of Grotowski, Uta Hagen, Mike Leigh and Robert Bennedetti. European physical theatre and the traditions of Māori performance work had also been adopted by the school to provide three distinct strands: Māori, European and British/American.

When Bert became head of movement and later coordinator of voice and movement, he argued for a reduction in public performances at the school, particularly in the students' first year. He felt that the pressure of public performance inhibited experimentation and risk-taking during the early stages of the students' training, denying them the freedom to fail.

But this had more to do with the brevity of the course. Public performances were included in the first year of the acting programme simply to ensure that students had a range of production experiences within the framework of a two-year course. In fact, the number of full-scale public performances for first-years had dropped significantly by the early nineties, and the trend was now towards smaller-scale studio performances, or showings, linked to methodology classes. And when the third-year acting stream was introduced in 1997, public performances were then mostly restricted to the second and final years of the acting programme.

Bert had a point, and the optimum balance between process and product remains a contentious issue between staff and between students to the present day.

Because of the strong sense of collegiality amongst the teaching staff, conflicting points of view tended to reflect engagement, not opposition. This acceptance of difference was described by KC Kelly in the Toi Whakaari Friends Newsletter in 1993. I make no apology for quoting it in full:

> Put any three of us [tutors] in a room and chances are you'll find at least two of us will end up disagreeing with somebody else on just what it is we're doing, why we're doing it or when it should be done. Call that chaos, call it deliberate eclecticism, or call it genius: the training at Toi Whakaari is crammed with such contrariness.
>
> And that, in my opinion, is what makes [Toi Whakaari] so special. There are very few 'sure things' in show business. Certain techniques work for certain people at certain times. That's really all we know. Our aim, of course, is that by exposing our students to the widest possible range of experiences, we create for them the best atmosphere for their artistic growth. Sparks from our intra-fraternal tensions, we hope, will fire the imagination of our students.
>
> In any teaching situation, it's far easier to be 'right' than helpful and everyone on staff at Toi Whakaari knows that at the end of two years, whatever's been said or done will have to be individually assimilated by our leaving students. Otherwise it won't be any use.
>
> We provide our students with a map and set of survival skills; they must find their own

> way. Graduation day highlights perhaps the most potent paradox of all: *There are theories of acting; there are no theoretical actors.*[12]

The purpose and identity of the Drama School has developed to reflect an evolving industry and social change, and to do so it has had to adapt its approach to training. Teaching methodologies and educational systems relevant to the 1970s no longer carried the same weight or had the same value. Traditionally, the core purpose of the school had been to provide students with *essential* craft skills that would equip them to work as actors within the prevailing industry. In reality, many graduates now initiated their own work, formed cooperatives, established theatres, and diversified into other disciplines, as writers, producers, film makers and directors. Toi Whakaari was now tasked with a much more difficult challenge: to equip students to make work that reflected the cultural identity and the dual cultural heritage of all New Zealanders. There was clearly a need to provide students with the survival skills to support them in this endeavour.

Graduates of the school from 1974 to 1988 were surveyed in 1989 and asked, 'For the 1990s what elements would you like to see in future training?' Their response to this and other questions in the survey[13] helped to consolidate thinking around the three-year acting curriculum. Those responses make interesting reading:

> *Christina Milligan, 1974–75.* Much more discussion was needed to thump home the realities of the profession and how to sell yourself as an actor. When I left the School I knew it was going to be hard, but I had no idea how to go about making it easier for myself.

> *Philippa Campbell, 1976–77.* My training was oriented to an industry that quickly began to disintegrate after I left the drama school. We weren't really prepared for this, or for the possibility of making our own work, which for me quickly became imperative. There was no real political analysis of our place – or potential place in the cultural life of our country. I think the kind of glorious egocentricity of our work as acting students has left a legacy of a generation that were a bit slow on the uptake: we were left winded by our changing circumstances, and have painfully had to recognise that there was selfishness about some of our work that was basically bankrupt.
>
> Workers in our industry now need to be strong and resourceful, and have business skills and the ability to combat that dreadful siege mentality that can so easily set up when your work is undervalued or questioned.
>
> Actors should be advocates of their endeavours and nudgers of bureaucracies. We had a taste of that certainly, but we were basically colonised by the dreams of plays and players. We had no sense of our history, of the beginnings of theatre – even in this country, and no sense of other cultures' performance/imaginative work.

> *Katy Beasley, 1978–79.* It is best not to pre-organise or rehearse for the future possibilities of ethnic involvement in NZ Theatre; total immersion in 'things Māori' is as undesirable as a detailed or blinkered study of Shakespeare or mime.
>
> From my current observations, the intake of Māori and Polynesian students will not only determine the needs of the students, but also the shape of NZ theatre. Let it happen: if we do, truly indigenous theatre will emerge.

David O'Donnell, 1978–79. The theatre and film industries are ruthlessly competitive for actors, and I feel that the training should contain more practical advice on day-to-day survival as a professional actor. This means marketing yourself as an actor, choosing a career path rather than relying solely on chance, finding ways of earning income and maintaining morale while unemployed, and fitting theatre in with other life ambitions. I believe strongly that difficulties in these areas have more to do with actors dropping out of the business than any problems with the work itself. Because there is no formal career structure and support network like in other professions, Drama School need to do more to prepare students for acting – as a job for life. Actors have always been keen to perform good indigenous stuff, but there's still not enough coming through. The Drama School needs to foster the potential playwright in each student, to encourage them to work towards original expression on the stage. We also need to look outside New Zealand to be able to gauge our place in the world, and to grab hold of good ideas that we can adapt to our own advantage. A lot of young actors go overseas to work; the school needs to prepare them for that by fostering standards of absolute professionalism, with good interview and audition technique and good people skills.

By moving away from the monocultural monetarist European society, towards a society that acknowledges and fosters the Māori traditions, we stand to elevate non-profit making ventures to a new status, and improve our quality of life. A bicultural New Zealand could benefit the actor enormously in that the Māori community traditionally places more importance on the spiritual artistic sides of life than the British colonial community. If New Zealand society as a whole were to accept this aspect of Māori tradition, then obviously the actor and other artists will benefit enormously. But the main challenge for theatre and for actors, as interpreters of life, is to reflect the debates as they occur and to be at the forefront of inquiry and change.

Fiona Samuel, 1979–80. More information needs to be provided about the everyday reality of an acting life. The school geared us towards a career in the community theatre, and for most of us that is what we got. Film, television, voice-over, comedy, devising original material, how to stay sane and creative when you haven't been offered a job in months, how to audition, how to write a CV: these were the key areas and questions covered barely or not at all by the training.

I would have liked more variety. With an excellent teacher, consistency is useful, but even so you are getting large doses of only one approach.

We as actors, writers and theatre workers create our times as much as we reflect them, but I feel that in the very specific environment of a drama school, exploration of social movements can be best achieved through the work, by providing tutors from across the board in terms of politics, particular disciplines, approach to creation and craft, age, race, sexual preference, you name it. … The important thing is that this can expand the students creatively, by opening up new fields of thought and practice.

May Lloyd, 1981–82. There is a need for an intensive (by no means brief) business course, covering taxation, self-marketing and promotion. How to stay afloat? This is essential in the encouragement of the autonomous actor. I believe the school should continue to develop a course which offers a basis in techniques and disciplines required in the craft of acting. Like a metal worker, a musician, a nurse etc … Without a sound working knowledge and practice in the A to Z of the trade, there is no basis for a career. I am aware that the demands from Māori and Polynesian and other ethnic groups for specific needs in their training, needs to be addressed. I feel it is up to those groups to define and lobby for that. The fundamental actor's training in movement, voice, improvisation and interpretation is common to all, regardless of their culture, and should be expansive enough to offer a very strong grounding for all students.

Actors need a continuity of work to survive, internally and externally. The school's job is to ensure that as many graduates as possible have the tools and confidence that will enable them to last the distance. Development of personal ideas and projects, emphasis on development and performance of own materials, compiling a show etc, are all important aspects of the training, as is intensive audition and film technique training – our bread and butter.

Miranda Harcourt, 1983–84. A vital element in training drama students for the future is that they must learn to provide employment opportunities for themselves. Too often drama school graduates have a 'Babes in the Wood' attitude towards their future – whereby they hope/expect some patron and/or employer to provide them with work. When that doesn't eventuate they fade away. Increasingly, employment is not available for graduates, and graduates need a kick-along to create their own work.

Eteuati Ete, 1983–84. Times have changed dramatically over the last few years, I feel now is the right time for the school to reassess its kaupapa. I would have liked to have learnt more about New Zealand, its history and its people and how it was portrayed on stage; the issue of tangata whenua and the kaleidoscope of cultures that comprise the New Zealand population, but I guess that would have been like singing in a vacuum back then, just as maintaining the same course without looking at the question of biculturalism now would be pointless. Perhaps plays by Pacific Island playwrights could have been workshopped, or a panel of elders from different cultures could have been set up to allow every student to question and learn from them. A marae visit would not have been out of the question.

Sean Allan, 1986–87. During my training it always amazed me that in Wellington there was a drama school, dance school, art school, music school, three professional theatres and a television studio, all within a few miles of each other; but contact was minimal or non-existent. A lot of ideas, experience and learning could have been exchanged through the different mediums.

Those comments represent the views of just a few graduates, spanning an eighteen-year period, but what they have in common is a clear recognition of the need for the school to provide more than a conventional or sectarian form of actor training. It was strongly apparent that the students felt the need to be prepared in a way that would enable them to adjust to changing circumstances and to manage their own careers.

Because of the large cohort of actors graduating in 1993, the school decided to mount two gender-specific plays, instead of trying to find a single play with fourteen equally weighted roles for the nine women and five men. The two works chosen were Dario Fo's *Accidental Death of an Anarchist*, directed by Murray Lynch; and Lorca's *The House of Bernarda Alba*, directed by Colin McColl. Although stylistically different,

Accidental Death of an Anarchist rehearsal. L–R: Simon Ferry, Antonio Te Maioha, Jeremy Scrivener.

the two plays complement each other thematically: each deals with oppression and a shared hatred of authoritarian power.

Both productions were mounted at Taki Rua theatre, which imposed a considerable workload on the four graduating technical students, Kate Peters, Sean Coyle, Nicola Blackman and Leanne Watkins. Between them, they designed, produced, stage-managed and operated both productions, although they did have additional support from the first-year actors.

Throughout the preceding two years, the tikanga Māori aspect of the school's curriculum had been intensified, supported by Te Roopu Tautoko, a Māori Advisory Panel, established by Robin Payne. The panel included Rona Bailey, Whetu Fala, Keri Kaa and Puoho Katene, and five Toi Whakaari graduates: Hera Dunleavy, Hone Kouka, Donna Muir, Erina Toi-Paku and Mairanga White.

At the end of 1993 Robin reported that the following year's programme would have an even stronger focus on biculturalism, with at least one suitably experienced Māori practitioner as a tutor in the performance-for-camera course. Tikanga Māori classes were introduced for all three streams at the school, including the first-year technical production course, and elements of Māori movement and voice work were integrated into the existing mainstream programmes. Voice classes incorporated both karanga and haka, and the movement programme included basic elements of taiaha training and bird movement.

Tikanga Maori session - 1993.
L–R Annie Ruth, Jack Lasenby, Keri Kaa.

Earlier in the year, discussion had taken place with Tama Huata, the head of Takitimu School of Māori Performing Arts in Hastings, to find ways for the two schools to share teaching and other resources. As a result, Takitimu had undertaken to organise and conduct the Māori intensive week at Toi Whakaari at the start of 1994. In exchange, Toi Whakaari staff agreed to teach intensive courses, in their own specialisation, at Takitimu.

Having graduated its first intake of students, the technical course had successfully passed its initial trial period. Despite having a 25 per cent attrition rate, the programme had demonstrated its capability and sense of purpose through the quality of its recent graduates. The Ministry of Education therefore agreed to fund the course from the start of 1994, allowing a new intake of students to be recruited and a permanent full-time head of technical production to be employed.

Bill Guest, 1994

I applied for and was appointed to that position in 1993. In truth, I knew very little about Toi Whakaari (there was no website to view in 1993), apart from the fact that it was moving in a new direction and that this could reinforce the school's reputation as a key player in the international forum of performing arts schools; moreover, I knew that such ideas were embedded in the school's bicultural ambition.

Since 1972 I had been based in Australia, which was very much a multicultural society, and I was intrigued by the bicultural intentions of the school. What attracted me most to the position, and what finally won me over when I visited the school, was the spirit of Toi Whakaari, conveyed through the enthusiasm and commitment of Robin and the staff, not least of all their openness to change. There was also a promise of a 'renaissance' in New Zealand theatre, of the development of a truly indigenous theatre similar to that experienced in Australia during the 1970s, fed by social change and re-evaluation of identity.

During my initial visit Toi Whakaari in November 1993, I was lucky enough to attend a performance of Bernarda Alba. I was profoundly affected by it, captivated by the way Māori and Catalan elements and cultures merged, giving an extraordinary energy to the production. The performance also revealed a level of ensemble work that I had not previously observed in any other drama school, particularly in a graduation production, as they often tend to showcase individual actors rather than collaborative work. My initial response to 36 Vivian Street was not so positive. The technical resources were clearly less than adequate when compared with those of other institutions where I had previously worked. But that could be fixed.

The big question for me was, what could I offer the school? There was my accumulated experience in a range of creative and production areas – in the UK and Australia, in theatre, film and television. I had also established technical production and design-training programmes at NIDA and at the Centre for the Performing Arts in Adelaide, which I reasoned would help me to develop similar courses at Toi Whakaari.

At the time, I was working as a project officer at Tandanya Aboriginal Cultural Institute in South Australia, alongside Aboriginal and Torres Strait Islander people. This gave me an insight into the significance of cultural expression in the lives of indigenous Australians. And yet this experience did not directly relate to the circumstances in New Zealand. After all, the legal basis of Australia as 'terra nullius' at the time of colonisation had only just been overturned, whereas Māori right to retain tino rangitiratanga had been long established in Aotearoa, with the signing of the Treaty, and was being reinforced. I was further heartened by the knowledge that, as with the Australian Aboriginal people, performance and artistic expression seemed inherently woven into Māori and Pacifika culture.

New Zealand society was at a crucial stage in its evolution, and Toi Whakaari had clearly recognised this, affirming its belief that one of the many issues to be faced in the immediate future was the nature of the country's identity. The way in which New Zealand would continue to evolve was largely a cultural question, and it was in relation to this that Toi Whakaari had a particular role to play – an aspiration that was embedded in the school's 'mission statement': 'to instil in the students an awareness of the culture of Aotearoa: New Zealand in its diversity and history as well as an awareness of their responsibility for preserving and furthering this culture'.

This was all very seductive and intriguing; it offered a range of possibilities to extend the current view and the purpose of theatre in New Zealand, which in turn would (I hoped) allow the country to reassess the value of performance as a means of social interaction. The final clincher that sold me the job was the fact that it was also very, very risky.

Fourteen

1994–1995

'I made my stage debut at five years old as Henny Penny in a paper Kleensak and a cardboard beak …'

With a new intake of sixteen acting students for the recently accredited Diploma of Professional Drama (Acting) and six students for the technical production course, the student population of the school rose to thirty-seven in 1994.

The technical production students had been chosen by Murray and Robin, and were then re-interviewed by me when I arrived in New Zealand at the start of the year. The students were Neill Bryce, Elaine Kohler, Michael Leger, Fiona McCormick, Eliza Meldrum and Nigel Scott. As with the previous intake, they had various reasons for enrolling in the technical production course: some had previous theatre experience, and several had completed tertiary education at university or polytechnic with qualifications ranging from occupational therapy and zoology through to electronic engineering. The minimum entry age for the technical production course was eighteen, two years below that of the acting course, but the average age of the 1994 intake was twenty-one.

1994 intake of Technical Production students in a sound class. L–R: Chris Ward (tutor), Fiona McCormick, Nigel Scott, Eliza Meldrum (concealed), Neill Bryce, Michael Ledger. *Photo: Simon Clark.*

The Diploma of Professional Drama (Acting) was a local accreditation from NZQA, and the school was in the process of applying for national accreditation for that qualification. When NZQA eventually approved the technical production course, in 1995, it too was accredited as a Diploma of Professional Drama, but with the suffix: technical production.

The school year was comprised of five terms, each six to eight weeks long, with a single timetable that was common to both the acting and the technical production courses. The timetable was hand-written and collated by Sarah Griffiths, the office manager. Staff often fantasised about creating a simple computer programme to allow the constantly changing timetable to be formatted and quickly modified, but the cost and effort needed to achieve such a 'luxury' were prohibitive. On the upside, having a common timetable helped to support an integrated approach to training.

Acting and technical production students participated in some joint classes, including swimming (every Friday morning at the Boys' and Girls' Institute), Cook Island dance, history of theatre, tikanga Māori, movement, and muscle and bone.

At the start of the year, the school geared up for its biennial immersion in the International Festival of the Arts. Toi Whakaari was again at the hub of the Festival, hosting public lunchtime forums and a range of other activities. The Friends of Toi Whakaari ran a shop to provide refreshments at the forums, under the guiding hand of Pat Hawthorne, the proceeds from which were donated to the school to buy much-needed equipment.

The 'minder scheme', set up in 1992 whereby acting students 'adopted' visiting Festival artists, was repeated in 1994. The rewards for the students in terms of their direct contact with Festival performers were great, but the experience sometimes tested the students' ingenuity, as Jacob Rajan recalled:

> For me it included ringing every tobacconist in town to try and find a particular brand of Cuban cigar for Wynton Marsalis's tour manager. Of course, the spin-offs for the minders were fantastic. At a concert which had sold out three days after it went on sale, I was sitting three steps away from the core of the beautiful Marsalis sound.
>
> The Royal Shakespeare Company was a different kettle of jazz. A group of fifty-four flew over from London to show *A Winter's Tale*, and a more self-sufficient, professional, tightly organised bunch you were unlikely to meet. The three minders assigned to them, myself included, felt a little daunted at the prospect of taking care of them. But the Brits took care of themselves and we just watched in awe as this lavish show assembled itself in three days, played to packed houses, packed up and left.
>
> It was a glorious time to be in Wellington, and to be a drama student. In three weeks I saw twenty-five shows, attended forums and workshops at Toi Whakaari, and averaged four inspirational chats a week with various artists.[1]

Alex Reedjick, then technical director of the International Festival of the Arts, agreed to take technical production students on secondment to work with the Festival's production department. Students were assigned to various Festival venues, where they observed and worked with experienced production crews, both local and from overseas. This scheme was a strong endorsement of the fledgling technical course, and clearly demonstrated the commitment of Alex Reedjick and others at the Festival, including

Ian Nicholls, to the training of local theatre technicians. Not only did the secondments provide first-hand experience of the Festival operation and an insight into the level of preparation and collaboration needed to produce a quality professional product, but they also gave the students a practical framework that they could refer to in their future training and work.

The school now had ten full-time and five core part-time staff. Murray Lynch was reappointed as head of directing and Annie Ruth was repositioned as head of acting. The core part-time tutors were Wi Kuki Kaa, Nerissa Moore, Laughton Pattrick, Lyne Pringle and Emile van der Mespel, the Alexander Technique tutor. Sarah Griffiths now doubled as a special projects manager and Robin's personal assistant; and Jody Garratt joined the school to replace Deborah Tucker, who'd left to pursue her interests as a writer.

Giff Davidson was the new chair of the Board of Trustees, and there were two new Board members: Gabrielle Rikihana and John Fokerd (Treasurer). They joined the remaining members: Rona Bailey, Gary Dyall, Jonathon Hendry, Dave Jenkins, Terry Kilminster, Norman Kingsbury, Carrie Wainwright and Dawn Sanders.

Dawn Sanders had recently been appointed by the Premises Management Trust as a fundraising and sponsorship manager to develop a strategic plan to try to raise the $1.25 million still needed for the Rooftop Centre project. Around 80 per cent of the estimated $5.3 million for the entire building project had already been committed, by the Lotteries Grants Board, the Ministry of Education, Wellington City Council and the two schools. However, increases in the estimated construction and fit-out costs were fast outpacing the PMT's capacity to fundraise.

Nevertheless, in April 1994, the purchase of the site went unconditional, and shortly afterwards the transfer of ownership to the PMT was finalised, allowing the Rooftop Centre to be officially launched, which in turn would enable the fundraising effort to move into top gear.

On a wet and windy morning in June, staff and students from the two schools, Trust Board members and kaumātua led by Tungia Baker gathered on top of the James Smith Car Park for a tapu-lifting ceremony. This was followed by the official Vice-Regal launch of the Rooftop Centre by the Governor General, Dame Catherine Tizard. She was accompanied at the ceremony by a large contingent of VIPs, including the Wellington Mayor, Fran Wilde and the Minister of Education, Dr Lockwood Smith.

It may well have been a defining moment in the history of the school(s), but apart from the dawn ceremony itself, the only recollection I have of the Rooftop launch is that of a large 'rock' being carried by students onto the rooftop, to signify – something. There was also my unrehearsed impersonation of Sir Walter Raleigh when I laid my coat over a large puddle to prevent the GG's shoes getting wet. I do recall that Her Excellency seemed suitably grateful.

A range of fundraising activities was initiated, under the banner of Reach for the Stars, which included an art auction, a charity ball, a Starlight Dance and a star-studded Rooftop Gala Performance-cum-variety-show featuring alumni and students from both schools. Naming rights for the Rooftop Centre also went up for sale, with prices ranging from several hundred thousand dollars for studios, down to $2,500 for four toilets. One thousand dollars would get your name on a bookshelf in the Nola Millar Library. Alas, naming rights proved notoriously difficult to sell, and consequently this aspect of the fundraising campaign had little success, although a rights pledge was received early in 1995 from the family of Mick Rose (a 1990 graduate) for the student kitchen.

The Reach for the Stars Auction was a more immediate success. It took place at the James Cook Centre in October, with over a hundred catalogued lots, including art works, various services, and a range of 'exotica' such as a Gourmet Gallery Dinner with Miranda Harcourt, Stuart McKenzie and a gallery owner:

> I don't know what we thought we were doing, we couldn't cook and neither could our friend. Eventually those people, whoever they were, came to our house for dinner; my cousin, Harriet, came to cater it because we couldn't cook. We'd lived in that house for a couple of years and when she went to turn on the oven it was broken and had been broken for the entire time we'd lived there. So she must have shipped in some food – or something.[2]

Raymond Boyce donated costume designs; Kate Hawley gave a pair of black silk evening shoes, worn by Gertrude Lawrence in *Private Lives*; a silver and paua necklet was made and donated by Jenny Pattrick; and, by no means least, four hours of chauffeuring (anywhere) by Gavin Todd in his Austin Mini was up for offer, and included the promise of champagne. The auction attracted a lot of interest. It was run by a professional auctioneer, Jack Forsyth, with Miranda Harcourt as the Mistress of Ceremonies assisted by graduates and other celebrities. Around $15,000 was reportedly raised by the auction for the building fund.

A season of four South African plays, under the common title of *From the Market*, was presented by the school early in 1994. The plays, by Athol Fugard, Barney Simon and Pieter-Dirk Uys, resonated with Toi Whakaari's bicultural exploration. They were *Statements after an Arrest*, directed by Annie Ruth; *The Island*, directed by Robin Payne and Adam Macaulay, a student director on secondment from WAAPA; *Born in the RSA*, directed by Murray Lynch; and *Just Like Home,* directed by Whetu Fala. They had initially been performed at the Market Theatre in Johannesburg around the time when Nelson Mandela was released from prison. It was therefore doubly appropriate that Toi Whakaari chose to perform the plays at this time, as South Africa had recently elected its first black government, with Nelson Mandela as President.

Because there were no second-year technical production students in 1994, the first-year technical students had sole responsibility for designing and crewing *From the Market*. They created a composite setting made from scaffold and corrugated iron to suit all four plays, and their production process was tied into and developed through formal classes, led by renowned industry practitioners Raymond Boyce, Matthew Mellor, Paul O'Brien, Claire Palmer and Chris Ward.

The school later restaged *Born in the RSA* at the Ngā Waipuna Waihanga, New Zealand Māori Artists and Writers Hui, which took place in Taranaki and was hosted by the people of Parihaka. This was the second time the school had participated in the hui: in 1993 forty-five staff and students from Toi Whakaari travelled to Te Kaha, staying

Statements after an Arrest, Jacob Rajan, 1994.
Photo: Simon Clark

▲ Annie Ruth at Parihaka, with latest cellphone

▼ Author (R) with Gavin Todd at Parihaka

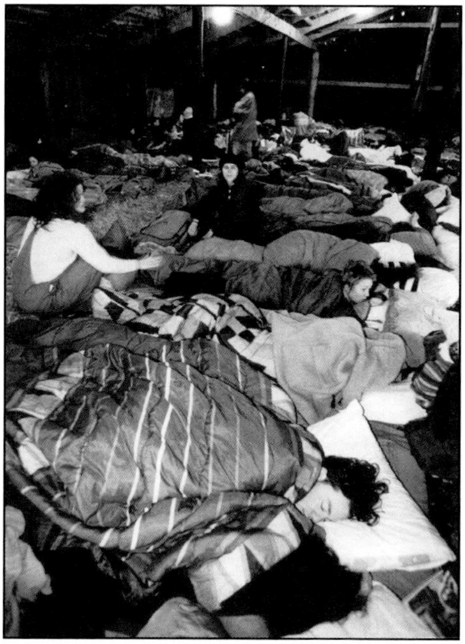

Students in the Wharenui at Parihaka

at the Whitianga Marae, to participate in the twentieth Ngā Waipuna Waihanga, along with groups from Wellington Polytechnic, the Museum of New Zealand and Whitirea Polytechnic.

The entire Toi Whakaari student body along with most of the staff participated in the Parihaka hui. It was my first visit to a marae and I was deeply moved by the pōwhiri, the openness of the tangata whenua and the willingness of the students to commit fully to a wide range of activities. It wasn't long before I was similarly engrossed, weaving flax – alongside the kuia.

When the second-year actors returned to Wellington from Parihaka, they moved into the final rehearsal for their monologues. The season followed the previous year's pattern, with an eclectic range of pieces, included Nicola Kawana's *Glamour Puss*; Anna McPhail's *The Double Life of a Hatbox*, based on the life of Minnie Dean, the Winton baby farmer and the only women to be hanged in New Zealand; and Vanessa Byrnes' *Bless me Father – 'I'm a very wicked women with a scar on me right buttock'* – which planted the seed for more understanding about her family's lineage and her own identity:

> My solo allowed me to take a punt with my taste in theatre and it connected me with my own family's whakapapa. I continue to believe that understanding your own (and family's) history is crucial to both being fully yourself and for developing empathy in the actor. 'Know thyself', reads the Oracle at Delphi, and it could surely be a maxim planted firmly above the entrance to Toi Whakaari.[3]

One of the most enduring monologues of the season was Jacob Rajan's *Krishnan's Dairy*, an enchanting and moving love story of Gobi Krishnan and his wife Zina, set in an Indian dairy and woven into the epic tale of the Taj Mahal. Jacob used masks to enable the fast transformation of characters, and I recall the great care he took in producing the masks to enable them to fit his face precisely. An extended version of *Krishnan's Dairy* was later staged by Jacob Rajan and his director Justin Lewis in 1997 when they formed the Indian Ink Company. Since then, the play has been regularly performed in New Zealand and overseas, along with Indian Ink's more recent productions, *The Candlestick Maker* and *The Pickle King*. Jacob Rajan's work has inspired many Toi Whakaari students to develop their monologues and to restage them after graduation.

Most of the technical students' involvement in production activity at the school had been in support of work initiated by others. So when they were given an opportunity to create their own performance project, they leapt at the challenge. The first such project was based on experiences at the Western Front in World War 1, requiring the students to make a piece of theatre from scratch, largely through the creative use of technology. By adopting a collaborative process, they developed skills in storytelling that helped them to translate their ideas into a theatrical presentation.

The First World War was selected as a theme because of its theatrical potential, and the wide range of literary and visual references readily available. The provocation or brief given to the students was 'to initiate a journey that identifies the stages of human experience: moving from naivety to the realisation of the futility of war'.[4] To contain and focus the project, a number of provisos were included in the brief. One of the purposes of the work was to draw in the audience and to discourage them from becoming inactive or impartial spectators. The creative team was therefore required to involve them physically in the performance. The theatre space was divided into several 'inter-active' locations, taking the audience from recruitment through to the trenches. The main tools used by the students to convey the story and to support the text were lighting, sound and projected images. Much of the historical material sourced by the students was contentious, in many instances sheer propaganda, and therefore historical accuracy in the presentation was deemed to be of secondary importance, allowing the students the freedom to present a biased point of view if it provided a more engaging piece of theatre.

The learning outcomes from this project were considerable: the students gained an insight into the complex collaborative process of self-devised work and the need for a robust framework to support the realisation of creative ideas. The project also revealed the importance of balancing artistic aspiration with available resources. But, most importantly, it was empowering; it allowed the technical production students to make a piece of theatre, mainly through the use of technology, in which they could emotionally and intellectually engage with an audience in a unified performance space. The significance of a more direct relationship with the audience was reflected in the feedback I gave to the students:

> It is quite possible that there will be an even greater emphasis on a group-devised approach to production in the future and a move away from conventional text-based work. The same approach is also likely to result in the physical/artificial barrier between audience and performer being further reduced, with both parties truly sharing the same space and experience.[5]

The value to the students was succinctly stated by Eliza Meldrum:

> World War One was our first collective project which did not involve actors. For our group dynamics, it was a turning point in communication skills, problem-solving abilities and ultimately realising we each weren't the earth's centre. The invited audience were intimately involved; victims of World War 1 propaganda and trench warfare, and witness to the awful death toll.[6]

Projects devised by technical production students continued until 2003. Their theatrical impact often depended on the students' collaborative ability, their facility for balancing artistic ambition with available resources and – most importantly – their engagement with the audience. Apart from the First World War project, for which I have a lingering affection, others were equally successful, both as theatrical events and as learning exercises.

In 1995, *Project-Ion* transported the audience on an interplanetary journey – via rocket-ship to an alien planet. Highlights of the piece included Heidi Simmonds as the air hostess, roller-skating through the rocket cabin serving refreshments to passengers as a prelude to a missile strike, through the projection screen into the cabin, that forced an emergency crash-landing onto an 'alien planet' inhabited by 'weird creatures'. As a piece of inter-active theatre, and as a learning exercise in logistics and team-work, *Project-Ion* was a triumph. In spite of the prevailing Occupational Safety and Health hazards and the (very) bizarre narrative, it had a certain madcap theatrical energy.

When other courses came on stream, opportunities for interdepartmental collaboration at Toi Whakaari increased, which effectively made the central purpose of the technical production self-devised projects redundant. There is now greater scope for technology and management students to collaborate with acting, design and directing students on inter-disciplinary devised projects. And students across all courses now have the opportunity to initiate projects and to recruit students from other disciplines to realise their creative ambitions together.

To balance their self-devised work, the technical students worked on productions with more traditional structures in 1994, including *The Caucasian Chalk Circle*, directed and designed by Murray Lynch; and *The Rover*, directed by Roger Hodgeman.

The Caucasian Chalk Circle was performed by the first-year actors and presented with the audience seated around a circular wooden revolve. Murray transposed the setting of the play from post-Nazi Soviet Georgia to the Eastern Bloc, which at the time was facing similar social and political upheaval. Murray had asked the lighting designer, Eliza Meldrum, to create a lighting rig without using conventional stage lighting, so she used hand-held lights, mostly carried by technical students, to spotlight individual performers. The narration was set to music by Laughton Pattrick, with flute and violin beautifully played by Jane Gratkowski and Kate Elliot. The production also had the backing of a three-piece band, with guitar, bass and drums played by the cast.

The Caucasian Chalk Circle, rehearsal 1994. Back to camera Murray Lynch. L–R: Gary Young, Sally Stockwell, Jeff Szusterman.

The 1994 graduation production, Aphra Behn's *The Rover*, was performed at Downstage Theatre, directed by Roger Hodgeman, the artistic director of the Melbourne Theatre Company. He had previously been the dean of the School of Drama at the Victorian College of the Arts from 1983 to 1987 and therefore understood that the training purpose of production within the context of a drama school was oriented to process, not product, a consideration not always fully appreciated by all visiting directors.

Tolis Papazoglou designed the set for *The Rover* and Jane Woodall designed the costumes. Musical direction was by Laughton Pattrick. In the context of Toi Whakaari, it was a huge production, and with just $2,000 to cover all production elements it was a triumph of imagination over budget. Tolis's colourful setting provided multistorey levels and ramps, with a vast canopy suspended over the stage; and with Jane Woodall's elaborate and rich costumes, the visual elements of the production were a testament to the extraordinary skill of the designers, who somehow managed to produce professional results on the smell of an oily rag. Lighting the production was no easy matter given the size of the acting area, with its twenty-five possible entrances and vast canopy suspended below the most useful lighting positions at Downstage. Somehow Neill Bryce, a first-year technical production student, managed to create a lighting design that was not only in harmony with both set and costumes, but also lit the cast whenever and wherever they appeared on stage.

With its carnival atmosphere, its intrigue, sex, romance, drunkenness and the opportunity for swashbuckling displays of duelling prowess and Douglas Fairbanks leaps-on-to-the stage, *The Rover* was an excellent showcase for the effervescent graduating acting students.

The individual journey of each student, up to the moment of their graduation from Toi Whakaari, is traditionally summarised in a usually brief self-described biography in the graduation production programme. Nicola Kawana's blurb in *The Rover* programme was not untypical, but it was notable for its commendable economy: 'I made my stage debut at five years old as Henny Penny in a paper Kleensak and a cardboard beak – and now I'm about to graduate from Toi Whakaari (PHEW).'

The Rover completed its season at Downstage with a Special Masque Gala Night to raise funds for the Rooftop Centre. Before the performance began, members of the audience, suitably attired and masked, were invited to 'gorge themselves on fine Spanish champagne and bountiful food', while being entertained with 'frivolous song and dance by the cast'. Following the performance, 'the revellers' were invited to join the cast onstage to consume even more champagne, before being 'poured into the blackened streets to stumble back to humble abodes'. The enjoyable bawdy event raised $2,280, a welcome contribution to the Rooftop Centre fund.

However, things were not going well for the Rooftop. The estimated cost of stage one had escalated, from $3.25 million to $4.1 million, and completion to stage two was now estimated to be $5.1 million, a far cry from the $3.7 million originally set aside to construct the centre. The increase was largely attributed to additional reinforcement needed to overcome significant structural and engineering problems encountered on the site.

To make matters worse, the Ministry of Education was querying the cost-effectiveness of the project. The $1.9 million loan it had made available to the schools was predicated on an exchange of documents that included data that had substantially changed, altering the contractual relationship between the PMT and the Ministry. There was now a real risk that the Ministry would discontinue its funding of the loan, and the builders, Mainzeal, were asked to come up with a 'guaranteed maximum price'[7] to complete the building. In November, Mainzeal advised the PMT this would be $7.9 million.

This was clearly too much, and the PMT decided it was no longer feasible to complete the current brief, or even a reduced brief that would be acceptable to the directors of Toi Whakaari and the New Zealand School of Dance. They agreed not to proceed with the project.

The directors of the two schools and Tolis Papazoglou then offered to re-examine their minimum level of requirements for an alternative site, based on available funding and any additional maximum amount likely to be raised through fundraising. But that was not going well: appeals, sponsorship, auctions and various performances had raised less than $120,000.

It was obvious that the schools would be unable to move from their current premises until at least 1996, or even later. The PMT therefore informed the Ministry of Education of its intention to construct premises at a different location, and that there was a strong possibility the two schools would not construct joint premises. The PMT invested the $4.8 million so far raised for the project with the intention of drawing on the funds when suitable premises were found.

Toi Whakaari ran its first Summer Festival of Workshops at the start of 1995. The many theatre practitioners involved in the workshops included Raymond Hawthorne, who led a week's intensive workshop on acting technique; John Paxinos from Melbourne, who ran a course in arts management; and playwright Roger Hall, who led several workshops in acting for video and film with Vicki Yiannoutsos. Miranda Harcourt, Tommy Honey, KC Kelly, Murray Lynch and Annie Ruth also presented a range of workshops.

The administrative cost of the Summer Festival was underwritten by the Dame Malvina Major Foundation for the Performing Arts. The $20,000 it contributed allowed tuition fees to be kept to a minimum for the 200-plus people participating in over twenty workshops. Many of them came from centres around New Zealand, but one travelled all the way from the UK to take part in Vicky Yiannoutsos' workshop. An even more ambitious programme of Summer Workshops was planned for 1996.

Community involvement in the school was further expanded later in the year, with an Open Programme that included workshops run by Boi Sati, Indonesia's foremost director and choreographer, and renowned voice specialist Kristin Linklater.

The intake of new students in 1995 was even larger than the previous year, with sixteen acting and eight technical production students. With two years' of students enrolled in both departments, teaching space was at a premium. To accommodate the technical production students, the school rented the first floor of a building next to

36 Vivian Street, which was then partitioned, using salvaged material from *The Rover* and some chicken wire to create a sound studio, production office and design studio.

Immediately after 'orientation', at the start of the year, the first-years embarked on a Māori intensive, which began at Takapuwahia Marae in Porirua and concluding with three days' instruction by a teaching team from Takitimu. Additional support was provided for the taha Māori programme at the school when Whetu Fala joined the core staff to assist Wi Kuki Kaa in running the course. The Nola Millar Library also got its first paid library assistant in 1995, Peter Sakey, who had graduated from the final year of Nola's QEII Arts Council Drama Training School.

Throughout 1995, Toi Whakaari's Trust Board remained under the chairmanship of Giff Davidson; Carrie Wainwright and Norman Kingsbury left, and were replaced by Gabrielle Rikihana and Gary Dyall. Rona Bailey, Jonathon Hendry, Dave Jenkins, Terry Kilminster and Dawn Sanders continued as Board members, although there was still no place on the Board for the director or a staff representative.

At the start of the year, the second-year actors began rehearsals for *Blarney, Bullets and Blessings*, a collection of scenes from Irish writers. The programme was coordinated by Annie Ruth, with past graduates Hone Kouka and Jonathon Hendry as co-directors. Following its initial season, the production had an encore performance for the Irish Society, shortly after St Patrick's Day, in which there was an extremely poignant moment when the men in the audience joined in the singing of 'The Auld Triangle' with the cast. Peace had only just returned to Ireland.

The second-year technical production students had headed off on the first of their secondments for the year, a two-week stint at the Taranaki Festival of Arts. The scale of the event is much smaller than the Wellington International Festival of the Arts, allowing the students to have a greater involvement in its day-to-day running and with a more consistent level of supervision provided by the technical director, David Innes. Eliza Meldrum (again) reflected on the benefits of the secondment:

Training course in Maori martial art of taiaha, 1995. L–R: Ben Farry, Tony Tarai, Willi Henley, Toby Leach, Mark Sant. *ATL Dominion Post Collection.*

> It was a mind-shift, but a really good learning curve due to the necessity for constant hands-on work with power tools, climbing ladders, socialising, and working alongside a new group of professionals. Their attitude, which was inclusive of actors and technicians, confirmed for me the value of team work to produce a quality show. In summary, it was a most successful training opportunity, [and] I was working against my strengths and I was trusted to use my initiative to complete tasks.[8]

This was just one of many valuable secondments undertaken by technical production students in 1995. Others included Humanimalia Dance Production, Auckland Opera, Theatre at Large, Fortune Theatre, Wellington City Opera, WingNut Films (The Frighteners), Royal New Zealand Ballet, Aotea Centre and Selecon Lighting. Nigel Scott, whose interests had shifted from stage-management to sound design by his second year, seconded himself to various sound studios and audio organisations, including Marmalade Studios. This provided a useful launch-pad for his future career, as Marmalade Studios employed him as a sound technician immediately after he graduated from Toi Whakaari.

With only a small budget to support student travel and subsistence, it was difficult to sustain the secondment programme beyond the Wellington region. Nevertheless, some organisations, including Auckland Opera, the Royal New Zealand Ballet and the Aotea Centre, generously provided an allowance to cover the students' subsistence costs.

There was no monologue season in 1995. Instead, the second-year actors broke with tradition and formed cooperatives to work on a programme of self-devised works entitled *Out of Space*. This was seen as a natural evolution from the monologues, the rationale being that students were more likely to work in a cooperative structure than to work solo after they graduated.

The students separated into five groups for *Out of Space*, and then devised a programme of image-based physical theatre pieces with Bert van Dijk. Three of these group-made works (Inner Space) were performed at 36 Vivian Street, including the basement carpark, and two others (Outer Space) were performed at Narnia Imports Warehouse on Waterloo Quay. The themes chosen by each group were diverse, ranging from Celtic mythology to boxing. The most verbal piece was the strikingly stylised *L'Aqua e le Coq*, devised and performed by Glen Drake and Georgia Duder. It explored the relationship between food and sex through a bizarre interpretation of Jeanette Winterson's *Passion*. The atmosphere of the performance was vividly evoked in Susan Budd's review of the work:

> *L'Aqua e le Coq* presents a Venetian boatwoman and French chef during Napoleon's invasion of Venice. A ladder lit with candles surmounts a bright blue paddling pool in which the gorgeously dressed boatwoman with webbed feet writhes in a sexual frenzy whilst the chef addresses and plucks the feathers of a chicken.[9]

The works performed at Narnia Warehouse were possibly the most intriguing. In Trinity, three seriously deranged sisters, Faith, Hope and Mercy, played out a ritualistic version of their lives through cyclic repetitive movement and text, performed by Claire Waldron, Sally Stockwell and Fiona 'Ofamo'oni. A second piece, Under the Influence, was loosely based on a fairy tale by Herman Hesse, and performed by Jeff Szusterman and Gavin Todd. They 'explored the struggle between personal freedom and expression'[10] as they fought each other on the concrete floor of the Narnia Warehouse, tied together with a long rope.

Unsurprisingly, *Out of Space* had a mixed reception: the audience was delighted, stunned, bewildered and amused; but mostly they were engaged. The success and value of the work was summarised by Laurie Atkinson in his review:

> *Out of Space* takes its audience out of the comfort and security of the conventional performance spaces and away from the conventional modes of theatrical storytelling and challenges the audiences as well as the students.[11]

By abandoning the successful and popular monologue season, the school had broken the tradition of text-based work, a move lamented by some who attended *Out of Space*, including tutors at the school. But Toi Whakaari stuck to its guns and persevered with the group-devised format the following year with *Mixed Lollies*, and again in 1997 with *McCahon by Numbers*.

This trend was later reversed in 1998, with a return to text-based scene work centred on four contemporary transatlantic works, under the title *Between a Rock and a Hard Place*. And, in 1999, the monologue season was reinstated for the third-year actors. This model continues to the present day, as Go Solo.

The second-year actors focused on classical text-based productions for the remainder of the year. The first of was Miller Back to Back, two plays by Arthur Miller. Half the group was assigned to *A View from the Bridge*, directed by KC Kelly; and the other half worked on *All My Sons*, directed by Michael Johnson-Chase, a visiting tutor, Fulbright scholar and associate professor in the Professional Theatre Program at the University of Wisconsin–Milwaukee. The fact that both directors were American was a bonus for the students. The rationale for taking on these American classics was clearly stated by Michael Johnson-Chase:

Michael Johnson-Chase directing
Kate Elliott and Fiona 'Ofamo'ini in *All My Sons*, 1995

> It is not unusual in the United States for drama students to cut their teeth on Arthur Miller: for American drama students to perform Miller well is regarded as akin to learning how to draw before one begins to paint. Although the general milieu for New Zealand drama training is necessarily different, the inherent challenges of [Miller's plays] for New Zealand acting students are the same.[12]

Their next encounter with a 'classic' was a completely different experience. This was the graduation production, *A Midsummer Night's Dream*, directed by Murray Lynch. He chose a Polynesian theme for the production, partly because a number of the graduating actors were Pacific Islanders, and also because 'the environment of the play is one which is very much in touch with nature and spiritual aspects'.[13]

The set and costumes were designed by John Parker, an Auckland-based designer. The exotic set design, evocative of sails and sea and a Pacific Island locale, called for a lot of non-traditional materials, which provided a major challenge for the student set builders. At the heart of the set was a large water-filled lagoon that alone would have been sufficiently challenging for professional set builders with access to a well-equipped set construction workshop. Alas, Toi Whakaari had no such resource. This was one of those occasions (and there have not been many) when the production team should have reviewed the scope of the project and called for a redesign, if for no other reason than for the OSH problems it presented. But time was of the essence and the lagoon was eventually built – out of fibreglass! The impracticality of a water-filled set surrounded by a wooden floor did not go unobserved by one reviewer:

> My principle reservation concerning the production is [the] set, which is dangerous for actors, as they attempt to leap from pools of water to a slippery wooden stage without sustaining physical harm.[14]

'Water on stage invites disaster' is a statement of fact, which (alas) this particular production confirmed. During production week, the lagoon was topped up with water from a nearby fire-hose, a very old canvas hose. Had the water supply been turned off at the main tap instead of the nozzle, this would not have been a problem. But the water pressure caused the fire-hose to expand like a bloated python during the night, eventually exploding and disgorging thousands of gallons of water onto the first floor of 36 Vivian Street, turning it into a lake. Murray Lynch and Sarah Griffiths were the first to arrive at the school the next day:

> When Murray Lynch and I arrived at the top floor of Vivian Street, during production week for *A Midsummer Night's Dream*, we found the entire floor flooded and 'live'. Murray's sense of calm was unnerving, but the show opened on time.[15]

Shortly afterwards I arrived to be confronted by a staircase turned into a cascading waterfall: it was not going to be a good day. Water had engulfed the school, it was deep and the deepest area of all was the library. Somehow, with the aid of student/staff power, giant squeegees and space heaters, the lake was drained, the school returned to a state of relative dryness and production week for the *Dream* continued. The only good thing to come out of flood was the distinct and pervasive tropical aroma it left, which was well suited to the production.

Following its season at the Drama School, *A Midsummer Night's Dream* moved to the Herald Theatre at the Aotea Centre in Auckland. The relocation of the set was its second downfall. I have a less-than-rosy memory of a not-so-minor deluge in the Aotea Centre after the lagoon sprang a leak, disgorging many gallons of water into the Green Room directly below the Herald Theatre. Needless to say, the lagoon remained sans water for the remainder of the Auckland season.

In all other respects, the production was a success – on many levels – not least of which was the experience gained by students in dealing with the practical realities of touring a show to an unfamiliar venue. The cast had to adjust their performance to the different acoustics and site-lines of the Herald Theatre, and the technical students learned how to present the essential information needed by the venue to receive the production. Two lighting designers worked on the production: Fiona McCormick for the Wellington season and Michael Leger for the Herald Theatre. With each venue offering different lighting opportunities, they had to work together to reconcile those differences in order to produce a lighting plot for both the Wellington and Auckland seasons.

A Midsummer Night's Dream was Murray's seventh major production at Toi Whakaari and the fourth in his repertoire of highly successful Shakespearian productions. It was also Murray's last production during his current tenure at the school. In 1996, he undertook a number of directing projects, including productions for the International Festival of the Arts, the Te Roopu Season at Taki Rua and a new play at Circa.

Toi Whakaari owned a costume collection, which had been made and collected over many years, but Drama School productions also relied heavily on the Downstage Costume Shop and the goodwill of Donna Jefferis who managed the collection. When Downstage was 'restructured', in 1995, it relinquished its Holland Street store, selling off a large collection of stage properties. Its costume collection was similarly under threat, which presented a real blow to the Wellington theatre community as they relied on it as a 'cheap' source of hired costumes. The collection had a reprieve in October 1995, when the Wellington Wardrobe Trust was formed to find a way of saving the costumes. But the Trust, which was represented by Downstage, BATS, Taki Rua, the Wellington Opera and Toi Whakaari, struggled to find a financial solution to balance storage costs and salaries against the projected income from costume hires. It was no easy task, as the theatre community had become accustomed to bargain-basement hire charges, but this had to be balanced against relatively high rental costs for costume storage. Both the Downstage and Toi Whakaari costume collections were eventually 'donated' to the Costume Shop, through an equitable arrangement, whereby the Costume Shop hired out, stored and maintained the collection, and those organisations that had contributed to the Costume Trust were able to hire costumes at a reasonable rate.

1995 marked the twenty-fifth birthday of the New Zealand Drama School. Preparations for the birthday bash, scheduled to take place in August, were well underway. Invitations had been sent to the 240 or so graduates and to the many staff and others who had been associated with the school. It was a considerable undertaking (in addition to everything else that was happening at the school) made possible only by a dedicated group of people, including Toi Whakaari staff, their families, friends and Board members.

1974 intake (photo taken in 1975). Front L–R: Peter Kelly, Peter White (Land), Christina Milligan, Gary (Rangimoana) Taylor, Charles Hambling, Frances Edmond, Celia West, Jan Prettejohns. Standing L–R: Jane Waddell, Karl Bradley, Claire Oberman, Christopher Harding, Prue Langbein.

The Way of the World, 1975. Jane Waddell (Lady Wishfort), Prue Langbein (maid).

Top image:
76 Kent Terrace, 2010. *Photo: Bill Guest.*

Middle image:
1994 Intake pre-pōwhiri. Waiting to be welcomed into the School at 36 Vivian Street.

Bottom image:
Artist's impression of Rooftop Centre

▶ Preparing for the Rooftop Launch, June 1994

▶ *The Rover*, Downstage, 1994. L: Eryn Wilson, R: Kirk Torrance.

▼ *The Rover*, Gala night

A Whistle in the Dark, Blarney Bullets and Blessings season, 1995. L–R: Malcolm Murray, Vela Manusaute, Gary Young, Gavin Todd. Back to camera: Jeff Szusterman.

L'Aqua e le Coq, 1995. Front: Georgia Duder and Glen Drake. Rear: Malcolm Murray and Grace Hoet.
ATL Dominion Post *Collection*

1995 Graduation Ceremony, Sarah Griffiths and Dave Jenkins (Steven Moore in background).

A Midsummer Night's Dream, 1995. Georgia Duder and Karl Kite Rangi. Photo: Simon Clark

◀ Inspection of Winter Show Building, 1997. L–R: Tolis Papazoglou, Laughton and Jenny Pattrick, Annie Ruth, first-year students.

▼ The Winter Show Building empty shell, 1997. Tolis Papazoglou (C) describing the new layout.

Both images this page: *Ornithes: Nga Manu: The Birds*, 1997.

Insurrection, 1997. L–R (rear): Tanea Heke, Grace Hoet (1995 grad), Kelson Henderson, L–R (front): Victor Rodger, Waimihi Hotere, Misa Tupou

Insurrection, 1997. L–R (foreground): Tanea Heke, Victor Rodger. Grace Hoet in background.

Te Whaea Construction, 1997. Entrance. *Photos: Bill Guest.*

Te Whaea Construction, 1997. Plaza and administration area, to the left. *NL Library. Photo: Bill Guest.*

Te Whaea Construction, 1997. Te Whaea Theatre. John McKay in foreground (back to camera, in blue shirt), Tolis Papazoglou and Bill Guest at far right. *Source: Bill Guest.*

25th Birthday reunion,
Darien Takle and Rawiri Paratene

25th Birthday reunion,
Murray Lynch and Robyn Malcolm

25th Birthday reunion,
Jonathon Hendry and Jan Prettejohns

25th Birthday reunion,
Aileen Davidson,
Rona Bailey and Mick Rose

Organising any reunion is notoriously time-consuming; the 25th Birthday Bash was no exception. Enthusiasm for the idea was not easy to sustain, as many graduates had prior performance or production commitments, were overseas or living in other centres, which made it difficult for them to travel to Wellington. Fiona Samuel and Murray Keane (from the class of 1980 and 1985) were unable to make it to the reunion because of work commitments. Along with many others, they sent a message to be read out at the reunion:

> While youth and beauty have helped us most in our careers, we are nonetheless grateful for the sterling technical training provided by the New Zealand Drama School. The medieval dances, appalling old songs and sword fighting techniques we learned have come in handy again and again over the years – perhaps not in work, but definitely in our marriage.
>
> As we enliven our domestic evenings by fencing around the lounge reminiscing about the good old days with George, Erica, Grant, Rona, Bunty and the gang, we have often had to stop ourselves from sobbing and breaking down into a rousing chorus of 'Baubles, Bangles and Beads'. That usually stems from nostalgia but oh! – What days they were.
>
> We'd be with you if only we weren't so busy and successful!![16]

After the reunion, Robin Payne wrote a report on the 25th Birthday Celebrations for the Friends Newsletter:

> Many were doubtful about the occasion. As I rang seventy-odd past grads to check on their registration, or their contribution to the Forum, I listened to the same doubts and prevarications over and over again.
>
> The truth is that we all got to laugh a lot; inordinately in fact. I certainly haven't laughed as much in the company of so many people, and so many of them friends – or with friendly faces.
>
> One reunion stretched across town (from the James Cook Centre to Vivian Street), across time from 1974–1995, and across 48 hours. Another involved the car-load of sheilas who did a Pork Pie drive from Auckland to the party.
>
> The final truth is that the event, for all the glitter, spit and silver served quite a profound purpose. The thankyou letters, phone calls and follow ups, moving in both directions, reveal that the most important achievement has been the sense of reconnection amongst the extraordinary group of people who have created and defined Te Kura Toi Whakaari o Aotearoa: New Zealand Drama School over the past twenty-five years.[17]

The year ended in usual fashion with a graduation ceremony. This time it was held at the Boatshed (previous home of Downstage) on the Wellington waterfront. In addition to the thirteen acting and five technical graduates, two administrative staff also 'graduated' from school: Sarah Griffiths (project manager) and Jodi Garratt (office assistant).

Throughout 1994 and most of 1995, Robin, Drew James and the Premises Management Trust continued their search for suitable premises, options considered including the Hannah Shoe Factory (grossly inadequate), the Odlins Building (structurally unsuitable), the Embassy Theatre (too small) and the purchase of 36 Vivian Street (far too expensive).

But one site in particular held great promise – the Wellington Show Building in Newtown – and it also appeared to be available. It had been built in 1929 by the Wellington Show Association to hold trade fairs, and was still occasionally used for this purpose and for other events. Part of the building was leased to sporting organisations by the Wellington Show Association, principally the Wellington Basketball Association and Indoor Cricket. But the Show Association was deeply in debt to the tune of $2 million, largely as a result of the failed Sesqui celebrations, and they were looking to rid themselves of that financial liability.

Warren and Mahoney, the architects for the now-abandoned Rooftop site, were given a brief to inspect the Wellington Show Building and to produce preliminary drawings for a 'National Performing Arts Centre'.

It was envisaged that roughly half the complex would be refurbished as a Performing Arts Centre; the other half would remain as an indoor sports centre. But if Toi Whakaari and the School of Dance were to go ahead with their bid for the building, there were lengthy and complex matters to be considered – and completed. The Wellington Show Association stipulated that there was to be no adverse impact on the existing tenants. How that was to be managed, and how the transfer of the lease from the Wellington Show Association to the PMT would be achieved, was anybody's guess. Preliminary investigations on the viability of the Wellington Show Building as a home for the two schools indicated a shortfall of between $850,000 and $1.5 million before a contract for construction could be considered. It was hard to predict how much of this amount could be raised through fundraising and/or a bank loan, as fundraising

Images clockwise from top left:
Winter Show Building under construction 1928;
Winter Show Building 1928;
Winter Show Building interior 1928

was constrained until the PMT could announce a confirmed site. Detailed architectural drawings were also needed to determine the actual building costs and to obtain resource consent.

Then there was the small matter of financial sustainability. Could the schools afford the rental and operational cost of such a large building? The Wellington Show Association was seeking assurance from the PMT that the schools had sufficient income to meet those costs before they were prepared to commit to a deal.

Although there was no official announcement of the school's interest in the Wellington Show Building, in 1995 Mark Blumsky, the Mayor of Wellington, publicly stated his support for a National Performing Arts Centre.

Robyn Cockburn resigned from her long-standing position as chair of the PMT towards the end of 1995 and was replaced by Peter Quinn. A notional deadline of February 1996 was then set for a decision to be made on the future of the project. There was clearly a lot of work to complete, along with some tough decisions to be made by the PMT and the schools, if a predicted occupancy date of October 1997 for the move into the Wellington Show Building was to be met.

Chapter 15

1996–1997

'Theatre is not an end, it's a means: it can make contact with people, and show them another reality.'

Toi Whakaari now faced a major upheaval and significant changes to its identity and purpose. The acting programme was about to step up from a two-year diploma to a three-year degree, accompanied by a real tension about the way actors were being trained – or would be trained – to meet the future demands of the theatre and screen industries. The school had made a substantial financial investment through its commitment to provide suitable and permanent premises, not only for existing courses but also for courses projected to come on stream within the next decade. To add to this pressure, the Ministry of Education was reluctant to commit any funding for the third year of the acting programme until the school received formal NZQA accreditation for the qualification.

Toi Whakaari ran a second Summer Workshop Festival in January 1996, with over thirty-nine week-long and weekend workshops. There was a Master Series for professionals and graduates, an Open Series for young people over sixteen, and a Young and Hungry series for anyone from ten to twenty-five to develop drama skills. There were also a number of workshops in performing arts management and writing.

Clearly, 1996 was going to be a very busy year for the school. For a start, it was a Festival Year, which intruded in the nicest possible way, but nevertheless disrupted the regular teaching pattern of the school. Then there was the Fifth Australasian Theatre Training Conference, which Toi Whakaari had agreed to organise and host in July, with participants arriving from various theatre schools and university drama departments in New Zealand and Australia.

On top of that, there were some significant changes to the structure of the teaching and administrative staff at the school. Annie Ruth was now head of the acting department, and KC Kelly was appointed as an acting methodology and stage combat tutor. Eru Tahuri, who had been working at the school as a taha Māori tutor, was appointed as a part-time coordinator of the Māori programme, replacing Wi Kuki Kaa and Grace Hoet. Two new full-time administrative staff also joined the school: Shona Pattison as the projects officer and Leah Perkins as the office assistant. And Alison Smith was employed as a part-time accountant.

In the Nola Millar Library, Deidre (Dee) O'Connor was appointed as a library assistant, allowing Ruth to take four months' much needed long-service leave. For many years Dee had worked as an actor in theatre and television, and in 1989 she enrolled in a postgraduate Library Diploma Course at Victoria University, which provided her with the qualification needed to work as a librarian, most recently at the Ministry of Māori Development. Dee's father, Dan O'Connor, had been an influential theatrical impresario in New Zealand from the 1920s to the mid-1960s. In 1948 he brought the Old Vic Theatre Company with Laurence Oliver and Vivien Leigh to New Zealand. And in the 1950s he arranged a New Zealand tour by the British Commonwealth Theatre Company directed by Ngaio Marsh.

When Ruth returned from her long-service leave, she persuaded 'the management' to keep Dee on half-time:

> It was always a bit of a struggle to convince anybody that I really needed some help. Dee was a fantastic addition to the library, because she was an actor, a theatre person, and she had complementary skills; she was more computer literate and systems-orientated than I was, and brought in all that expertise. Her arrival coincided with being able to get the software and for an online catalogue. Any computer developments in the library, Dee was the one who did them. She's continued to develop that whole area way beyond anything I could have done.[1]

In May, there was a significant change in the school's administration when Drew James resigned and Biddy Grant became the new business manager. Like Drew, Biddy had a wealth of experience in theatre and in arts management, having recently been the manager of community programmes with Creative New Zealand and the events and promotions manager for the Christchurch Arts Centre. Her arts management expertise was backed by extensive theatre experience as an actor, production manager, designer, mask-maker, craft workshop manager, and tutor in physical theatre and mask.

Dee O'Connor. *Photo: Philip Merry*

Biddy Grant (L) and Ruth Graham (R) in the Nola Millar Library

Over the previous year, dissatisfaction had been growing amongst Toi Whakaari staff over the composition of the Board of Trustees, principally its constituency, which excluded current staff and students. Another point of issue was the Board's intention to abandon the requirement of having at least two Māori trustees, in favour of 'a new form of expression of partnership arising from the dialogue with its Māori constituency'. The Board believed this would allow it to 'explore with vigour and some urgency a relationship with Ngāti Poneke', and that this might result in 'an appropriate expression of the partnership ideals expressed by the Treaty and sought by the School'. Although this recommendation had been considered by the Board at its September 1995 meeting, it had *not* been approved.[2]

What precisely the Board hoped to achieve by this is not entirely clear. Its members were not necessarily opposed to the school's bicultural intentions. In fact, a Treaty Policy Working Party had been set up by the Board in 1995 to look at this very issue, and Gabrielle Rikihana and Terry Kilminster presented a draft policy paper on the Treaty partnership, confirming that 'The School's expression of the Treaty partnership will be reflected in all aspects of the School's operations including the curriculum, staffing and Board composition and policies.' The paper also stated the school's intention to provide students with a *drama* education of the highest calibre, confirming that the school 'would continue to explore and celebrate the theatre and performing arts and other cultures and races of Aotearoa: New Zealand'.[3]

The paper then proposed a 'Māori/Pākehā Nominations Subcommittee', headed by the chair of the Trust Board with one Māori member and a further Board member who were to be empowered with the authority to nominate candidates for Board membership, such as the director of Toi Whakaari. But some Board members were opposed to the director being on that committee. As they were the director's employer, they felt there was an obvious conflict of interest in the director being involved in the selection and appointment of Board members. Another suggestion, to include a member of staff and/or a student on the nominations sub-committee, was also opposed – for similar reasons. Dissatisfied by the Trust Board's decision to exclude staff and students, the full-time staff of the school wrote a letter to them in November expressing their disappointment. It was in effect a vote of no confidence in the Trust Board.

One Board member in particular was vehemently opposed to any move to diminish the Trust Board's authority – or its responsibility on behalf of external stakeholders – by broadening its composition:

> I have, on more than one occasion, picked up a wish expressed by some members to return to a sort of cosy and comfortable setting reminiscent of 'the old days' when there was little accountability and when the Board and the Director worked together to manage the School. An outcome of this way of working was the out-of-court settlement paid to a past staff member.
>
> I would be greatly saddened to see the Board reduced to an ad hoc and disparate group appointed by various outsider groups who have no ongoing accountability to the School.[4]

The challenge to the Trust Board's authority came at a critical time, when it was facing some tough decisions on the purchase – or lease – of the Winter Show Building and the relocation of the school, not to mention the $1 million it still had to raise to allow the project to go ahead.

It therefore came as no great surprise when, at the beginning of 1996, a new Trust Board was appointed – by the old Trust Board. Giff Davidson stood down as chair, and was succeeded by Jenny Pattrick, an accomplished jeweller, writer and lyricist. She had considerable experience in leading committees, having been chair of the QEII Arts Council and before that chair of the Craft Council. New members were Carla van Zon, executive director of the New Zealand International Festival of the Arts; Peter Quinn, a former chief executive of Creative New Zealand and current chair of the PMT; Murray Lynch, who had been a full-time tutor at the school and was now a freelance director; Ross Himona, a retired New Zealand Army officer, business consultant and member of the Takitimu Performing Arts School Board; and Mere Boynton, singer, actor and joint programme manager at Taki Rua.

At their first meeting, Gabrielle Rikihana welcomed the new Trust Board, in particular Ross Himona and Mere Boynton, and commented on the challenging time they would have as Māori and as individuals on the Board. Terry Kilminster personally thanked Giff Davidson and reflected on his perseverance and skill as chair, and 'the way he pushed things through'.[5]

The number of new students enrolled in 1996 was the same as it had been the previous year, with sixteen acting and eight technical production students, including Kieth Walker, the first Māori technical production student to be enrolled in the school.

Immediately following the orientation process, the second-year actors and techs began preparing for *The Wild Man*. This project was an unusual departure from more traditional productions at the school; it was a piece of site-specific physical theatre, performed in and around a derelict Olympic-size swimming pool in the grounds of Wellington College. *The Wild Man* was directed by Bert van Dijk, his final production before leaving Toi Whakaari to form his own theatre company, Pantheatre/Poneke.

Because the second-year technical production students were seconded to the 1996 Festival, they had very little time to prepare for *The Wild Man*. It was a huge undertaking, in particular for Nicole Cosgrove who was tasked with designing the large number of exotic costumes. The lighting designer, Joanne Bunce, was also faced with the challenge of having to light a vast performance area with only restricted electrical power from a portable generator.

The production required a flying-fox to fly one of the main characters into the swimming pool from high above the performance area. Specialised 'flying' equipment had to be sourced and then safely installed: this tricky element was supervised by Greg Smale (who later changed his name to Justin Gregory). He first approached the New Zealand Army, New Zealand Navy and then the Boy Scouts, but they all declined his invitation to participate in this seemingly hazardous feat. Greg eventually managed to persuade, cajole or hire a team of professional adventurers to erect and supervise the operation of the equipment.

Before on-site rehearsals could begin, *The Wildman* cast and crew spent several days removing skip-loads of rubbish from the swimming pool. Not only was this an excellent 'bonding exercise', it also helped to build stamina for what was to be an extremely

The Wild Man, 1995. Cast rehearsing in the cleaned-up swimming pool at Wellington College. *Photo: Bill Guest*

The Wild Man, 1995. Rejected publicity shot. Top: Victor Rodger, bottom: Hone Katipa.

physical production. It was performed at night, and much use was made of fire-sticks set around the pool, as well as flaming torches, braziers and fire-balls.

Some productions at the school are well-suited to the character and talent of a particular group of students. This can be the result of good planning, at other times it is serendipity, but it is not always easy to predict with devised work, given the high level of collaboration needed, particularly in the development process. In *The Wild Man,* the essential link between concept and realisation worked well, with a strong buy-in from the students. Their energy and enthusiasm for the project came partly from their ownership of the work. They were also given a lot of freedom to interpret the story and to create their own characters. Not least of all, there was something very special – and even perilous – about staging the work in a site-specific performance space, and at night.

For security reasons, and as a precaution against bad weather, the technical crew de-rigged the lighting equipment after each rehearsal and performance. The electrics crew then stayed overnight at the site in a tent to guard the equipment, which included a valuable but extremely temperamental generator. For no apparent reason, it often stopped working at key moments during a performance, resulting in sudden if not entirely unexpected black-outs. Although this stressed the stage manager and electrics crew, the cast remained unperturbed by the frequent plunges into darkness. They simply carried on with the performance, instinctively making use of the ambient light from the flaming torches. The combination of a dodgy generator *and* an ominous storm-and-gale warning for opening night did not bode well. But thankfully the weather gods looked kindly on the production and the flame-dousing rain stayed away.

The success of performance projects at Toi Whakaari can be determined by the level of learning achieved. When students are encouraged to create their own structure, with the time and freedom to explore ideas, there is often a positive outcome. On the other hand, the opportunity for learning can be diminished if the director's ambition – or that of anyone leading a project – fails to support the training needs of the students.

In the case of *The Wild Man*, the students embraced the devising process and responded well to Bert van Dijk's direction. And through their own discipline, skill and imagination, they created a highly theatrical and exhilarating production, which was reflected in some of the reviews:

> Startling images abound: characters flying out of the darkness and dangling upside down over the pool; a fire dance with flames spinning through the blackness; and a poor lame horse struggling with its burden. The style is reflected in the colourful story-book costumes; and it strongly reminds one that not all outdoor productions have to be taken from the Shakespearian canon.[6]
>
> In the pool space, in which blazing braziers stand, at one end the Queen stands, resplendent in a red gown which shapes her body to that of a Neolithic Venus with huge hips and belly, and lesser queens sport on a barge in the water. It is a scene of strange beauty. The wild men dance an awesome haka and their handling of the Boy displays utter trust on his part and control on theirs. The men's dancing is terrific, displaying the same strength and control, and their fire dance on stilts is tremendously exciting, showing cool control of dangerously flaming brands.[7]

On a more prosaic, but no less dramatic level, the Premises Management Trust was still chasing a million-dollar underwriter to bridge the gap between the (almost) $4 million that they'd accrued and the $5 million needed to refurbish the Wellington Show Building. Despite the PMT's fundraising efforts, the amount accumulated for the project had changed little from the previous year. However, these efforts received a boost when the Todd Foundation donated $25,000 towards a new dance studio, and Dame Kiri Te Kanawa agreed to give her support to the site by becoming a patron of the New Zealand School of Dance and Toi Whakaari.

In an effort to raise the profile of the schools' intentions for the building, the PMT engaged an advertising agency, Mojo NZ, and asked them to devise a logo for the project and a suitable name for the building. The first name they offered was 'Muse', which they felt had a classical feel and encompassed the non-acting sector, for example, technicians and teachers. The School of Dance had no objection to the name, but Toi Whakaari did: they felt 'Muse' had connotations of the 1920s and failed to reflect an image of the present culture of the school. So 'Muse' was ditched in favour of 'The Show Building', which was much less pretentious. It also had a useful double-entendre, which meant the building could avoid a name change. But Mojo disliked 'The Show Building' as they felt it was too parochial: it was not international and was far too 'Wellington'. So, instead of renaming the building, Mojo chose to come up with a name for the project, The Site, which embraced all participants.

Very little formal discussion had taken place on how the PMT and the schools intended to meet their obligations under the Treaty partnership to provide bicultural input into the development of a new home for the school. But some consideration of cultural matters had previously been specified in the initial architects' brief for the building:

> Dance & Drama are the national vocational Performing Arts providers to a New Zealand society which is developing a bi-cultural/multi-cultural character, aspects of which ought to be considered in developing this unique building.[8]

Mojo then came up with a logo for the project, and the directors of both schools were asked to comment on it. Speaking on behalf of the Toi Whakaari Board and the school's community, Robin Payne felt it lacked any Māori shape, symbol or graphic; what's more, the logo (an abstract figure) looked remarkably like a dancer. Unsurprisingly, the School of Dance had no objections to the logo. As agreement could not be reached, it was suggested that Puoho Katene, kaumātua for Toi Whakaari, would be an appropriate person to consult and to advise the PMT on such cultural matters.

The Site went public in May with an up-beat front-page spread in the *Evening Post*. The article spoke positively about the new lease of life for the Show Building and how the proposed deal would 'save the city maintenance costs'.[9] An article in *City Voice* was less favourable,[10] much of it taken up with comments from Bill Mahon, an amusement operator. He had a long-standing agreement with the Wellington Show Association that allowed him to use areas in and around the building for a number of weeks each year to operate his rides and side-shows. Mahon argued that there was no other suitable venue in Wellington for his annual fair, and was therefore lobbying the Show Association to block the takeover.

1996 Street Appeal for funds,
Adam Brookfield and Jane Gratkowski

Nerissa Moore, 1996

Indoor Cricket, a major tenant of the Wellington Show Association, also objected to the project. They occupied one-third of the building and started a petition against the two schools in an attempt to stop them leasing the remaining two-thirds. They also proposed using part of the building for 'a children's playground similar to "Lollipop Land" in Lower Hutt and – if space allowed, tenpin bowling'.[11]

Before a building contract for The Site could be signed-off, the PMT still had to raise $1 million.

In July, the Fifth Australasian Theatre Training Conference (ATTC) was hosted by Toi Whakaari at Vivian Street. The previous four conferences had been successively hosted by the National Institute of Dramatic Arts, Western Australian Academy of Performing Arts, Victorian College of the Arts and the Queensland University of Technology. The conferences had proved to be invaluable in making connections between institutions and teachers involved in training actors, managers, designers, directors and technicians.

The event was a major undertaking for Toi Whakaari, which lacked many of the resources previous ATTC hosts had been able to draw on. But the school did have a very special resource in Nerissa Moore, the conference coordinator. Not only was she an excellent voice tutor, she was also a veteran conference organiser, skilled in maximising and harnessing resources. She worked through the summer with a large planning team led by Biddy Grant, and together they made the conference a success. When they discovered that there was very little accommodation available, because the conference coincided with the Bledisloe Cup match, they managed to avoid catastrophe by enlisting dozens of Toi Whakaari Friends who came to the rescue and provided beds for the visiting delegates.

The Friends had about around 150 members and was run by a small but dedicated informal committee. The Friends had been formed in 1988 by Ruth Graham, Erica Stephenson and Rona Bailey, bringing together the people who had supported, or were connected to, the school after George left. Kate Harcourt also played a major part in establishing and organising the Friends, contributing in a big way to fostering and promoting the interests of the school.

The title and theme of the conference had been chosen by Robin Payne: Tatou Kia Tahi: Together as One. It was to have two main purposes: to introduce New Zealand and New Zealand theatre to the visiting Australians, and also to address some of the theatre training issues that New Zealand and Australia shared.

Highlights of the conference included Encounters of the Theatre Kind, which explored ways of working and training for the future; The Great Debate: quality assurance versus theatre trainers, chaired by George Webby; From Past for Present, a multidisciplinary/cross-cultural dialogue on the 'classics' in the nineties; and Designing the Future. Each day commenced with breakfast meetings for special-interest groups, and ended with a Supper Series of performances and storytelling.

The strong presence of students at Tatou Kia Tahi was an important aspect that had not featured highly at other ATTC conferences. Students from Toi Whakaari teamed up with their counterparts from the National Academy of Singing and Dramatic Arts and Takitimu to perform at the conference. And students from three Australian drama schools worked with students from Toi Whakaari, sharing experience and skills on a pre-conference project that culminated in a piece of devised theatre. This was coordinated by two Toi Whakaari graduates, Jeff Szusterman and Grace Hoet.

Trans-Tasman air fares were much higher in the 1990s than they are today, making the distance between Australia and New Zealand seem greater. And initially it seemed doubtful that all the Australian schools invited to the ATTC Conference would make it to Wellington. But, in fact, attendance exceeded expectations, and Robin Payne's vision for the concept of Tatou Kia Tahi: Together as One was fully realised with four days of stimulating debate, discussion, theatre and workshops. Major issues flagged for ongoing debate in subsequent ATTC conferences included the future of Māori and bicultural theatre, revising methods of directing and teaching, accommodating the needs of the students and the role of theatre in an electronic world.

Halfway through 1996, the second-year actors wrote and performed *Mixed Lollies* under the guidance of the writer/director Gary Henderson. Gary ran Strawberry Theatre where he had staged his own work – most famously, *Sunset Cafe* and *Skin Tight.*

Unlike the image-based self-devised *Out of Space* programme in 1995, the principle medium of *Mixed Lollies* was spoken text. Five pieces were created by the students: *Numb, Gallery, Tricycle, Episode* and *The Heart of Hamatsa*, the last a bizarre pythonesque romp about a fool, a Scottish warrior and a monk. The three characters in the work spoke in 'a delightfully awful doggerel of appalling rhyming couplets'.[12] *Hamatsa* was remounted in 1998, when the trio received an invitation to perform the play at La MaMa Experimental Theatre in New York.

The 1996 graduation production was David Edgar's *Pentecost*, directed by Robin Payne. Just before rehearsals started, Robin announced that she would not be renewing her contract and would be leaving the school in Easter 1997. The reason behind her decision was briefly explained in a letter she wrote for the *Toi Whakaari*

Friends Newsletter: 'I feel that the six years have taken their toll and it's time for someone else to pick up the yoke here.'[13]

It may seem odd that Robin chose to resign at a time when a new home for the school appeared to be within her grasp. But many factors affected her decision, not least of all her growing dissatisfaction with the development process for the new building and the compromises that had been made along the way.

With Tolis's help, Robin had established a clear brief for a building to accommodate the two schools. But, as George Webby had often argued, drama and dance were unnatural bed-fellows, brought together by an historical accident when the QE11 Arts Council decided it was expedient to house the schools together. George had reiterated his concerns in a letter that was published in *The Listener* in 1995:

> I am a great supporter of the direction the school has taken, and my admiration – tempered by awe – for the incredible hours put in by the present director Robin Payne, also carries with it a warning: such talented people are rare and need to be nurtured, or we can lose them.
>
> I would like to go on record as being a vigorous opponent of an amalgamation with the School of Dance, no matter how much it may have a cosy ring to it for the bureaucrats. The sole thing that they have in common is that they are both part of the performing arts. In every other respect, apart from what is seen as convenience, the uniqueness of each school should remain untouched by the corrupting influences of what I – in shorthand – call the Business Roundtable philosophy.[14]

When the Ministry of Education assumed funding responsibility for both schools, it readily adopted the idea of housing them together. But, by 1996, it was clear the two directors had disparate needs and agendas, with particular priorities that were not always compatible. The different priorities were clearly evident when it came to shared spaces, and in matters relating to the performance and production areas.

Jenny Pattrick, the chair of the Toi Whakaari Board, was also the Board's representative on the PMT, and she recalled that '[PMT] meetings, when we were looking at plans, were a nightmare. Of course, the two directors had the best intentions; they were fighting for the best conditions for their own schools.'[15]

The growing list of building deferrals added to the tension between the two schools. They were the consequence of increased building costs and a shortfall in funding, but were nonetheless disheartening. Many of the items deferred were essential to the operation of the building, and Robin Payne fought hard to retain them. A catwalk/bridge system, which had been in the original brief to allow safe and easy access to the lighting bars in the theatre, appeared on the deferral list, along with a trapdoor system and other 'essential' items needed to operate the venue. The theatre space was over seven metres in height and the catwalk/bridge was needed to provide direct and safe access to the lighting grid.

The Drama School's response to this particular deferral was simple: 'If you can't afford the lighting bridge – don't build the theatre.' This was based on the fact that Toi Whakaari is a teaching institution, with a responsibility to train New Zealand's future theatre practitioners towards good and safe working practices. Robin battled for the catwalk – and won, but not the trapdoor system.

Robin had endured ongoing negotiations and accepted many compromises over the building specifications in an effort to retain the essential elements that Toi Whakaari needed, first with Shed 21, then with the Rooftop project, only to see both projects fall over. That battle had continued throughout the planning stages of the current project, with Robin fighting to hold the PMT and the architects to the initial brief and building specifications.

Possibly the final straw for her was the debacle between the PMT and Mahon Amusements when they threatened the PMT with a High Court injunction to retain their right to bring their fairground to the Show Building. Unfortunately, the area claimed by Mahon for the fairground was in a part of the building (the Madgwick Stadium) designated for two dance and drama studios, which gave Mahon the power to stop the whole project. This left the PMT with few options: it could engage in a costly court case, which it was unlikely to win as legal advice indicated that a court injunction would be granted in favour of Mahon.

Peter Quinn, the chair of the PMT, eventually made a deal with Mahon, allowing him to use part of the building – the Mahon Space and part of the Basketball Courts – for seventeen days a year for the next five years. In return, Mahon agreed to pay $40,000 per annum to rent the space, an amount that would be fed back into the schools to subsidise their operation and to provide funds to maintain the building.

This solution appeared to be the only one that would allow the building project to continue. But in fact, one problem had simply been traded for another. The displaced dance and drama studios now had to be located in another part of the building, the difficulty being that there was no more ground-floor space available. And the only way to accommodate the two studios was to build a mezzanine floor at a capital cost of $300,000. Alas, this did not tally with the anticipated rental recoverable from Mahon over the agreed five-year period, which was predicted to be around $200,000. The cost of an additional mezzanine floor meant funds would have to be diverted from other areas of the building project.

The decision to continue with these fundamental design changes was made solely by the PMT: the directors of the two schools and the design consultant were not included in the negotiations. Robin, for one, was extremely unhappy with this decision, and believed it compromised the credibility and excellence of the building as a home for the Schools of Dance and Drama:

> The failure to adhere to the brief – the loss of two ground floor studios, immediate access to the outdoors, a wall of west facing windows and the sound isolation buffer between the two studios – all combined to an unacceptable level of compromise.[16]

Robin was right, and so was the PMT. Yet there appeared to be no other way that the impasse with Mahon could be satisfactorily resolved without causing further costly delays to the building project.

One of biggest problems facing the PMT was the requirement for someone to underwrite – or guarantee – a loan for $1 million that was still needed to complete the building. Of the two funding proposals under consideration, the most favourable was with the Bank of New Zealand, but this option needed the Wellington City Council

Robin Payne in graduation party mode

Robin Payne performing 'other Director duties'

to act as a guarantor, and that was still under negotiation. The situation was not helped by the School of Dance; it was not keen to commit to a large mortgage, and pinned its hopes instead on being able to bridge the gap through fundraising.

To make matters worse, the Ministry of Education had begun to query the $380,000 interest that the PMT had earned on the $1.9 million suspensory loan since it had been granted, two years previously. The PMT had, in all good faith and with the full knowledge and consent of the Ministry of Education, retained the $1.9 million to apply it to the Wellington Show Building project after the Rooftop project collapsed. In fact, the PMT had made no provision for the repayment of the accrued interest; much of it had been consumed by consultancy and other professional fees. Not wishing to further jeopardise the viability of the project by asking the PMT to return the funds, the Ministry agreed to a 'staged repayment' of the interest, achieved by reducing the annual grants to the two schools by $126,000 a year over the next three years. But this would affect the schools' abilities to fund their day-to-day operations, not to mention the additional cost involved in occupying bigger premises and paying off a $1 million mortgage.

Apart from the building problems and mounting financial pressures, there was a more fundamental reason behind Robin Payne's decision to resign. There had been a huge expansion of activity at Toi Whakaari over the previous six years that would inevitably continue into the foreseeable future. In some respects, this expansion conflicted with Robin's deeper instincts – and her aspiration – for the school.

When she arrived in 1991, she had a ten-year plan, which included a design course, a directing programme, the implementation of the three-year acting programme and new purpose-built premises. But for Robin, this expansion and the sharing of premises had its price. She felt that the much-treasured sense of cohesion, of family, which had been at the heart of the school since Nola's time, sustained by George Webby and Sunny Amey, was likely to be compromised – or, even worse, sacrificed.

Despite the acknowledged lack of money, the fact that two years was not long enough to deliver a comprehensive training programme for actors and the ubiquitous housing problems for the past twenty-six years, the New Zealand Drama School had been an idyllic environment in which to nurture the talent and aspirations of a select group of students. The intimacy and the familial atmosphere of the school had been one of its greatest strengths: a rare quality seldom encountered in other drama schools. It was unique and highly appropriate to New Zealand.

Given the issues the school now faced, Robin's uncertainty about her future role as director of Toi Whakaari is perfectly understandable:

> My plan included the head of the technical department being parallel with the head of acting, with different departments coming out from underneath those two areas. Everything that exists now – with the exception of the costume construction course – was included in the ten-year plan. I had to do that plan to try and persuade people of the credibility of the school. Not necessarily because that's where I wanted the school to go, but it was a compelling argument for wanting a bigger building. It was more a response to people who were making decisions but clearly didn't have enough information to make those decisions.
>
> I felt that I had failed to protect everything I had been entrusted to protect and care for. … I didn't want the acting programme to be a three-year course or a degree and yet I willingly set that in place. I didn't want the school to grow so big that the right hand couldn't see what the left hand was doing.
>
> I believed the school needed to move into the twenty-first century to be competitive with other institutions such as NIDA, and yet I didn't want to let go of the little cottage industry microcosm. There are many things I would have done differently if I could have got over that internal rift in my heart.
>
> The plan to amalgamate [the two schools] to a single Board also provided a reason for me to resign. I could see that both schools needed a period of stability and the Drama School, in particular, had had nothing but change for the past seven years and we were rocking with the change: we needed time to let the boat stabilise and for the waves to settle down, to allow us to find an easy course through the water. I thought the two Boards would eventually amalgamate – because [they] had chosen to, not [because they were] forced to.[17]

Had she been allowed time-out to recharge her batteries to reconsider the future direction of Toi Whakaari, and to reflect on what she had accomplished during an unprecedented period of growth at the school, Robin may have found the strength and determination to continue as director. But as there was very little possibility of her taking extended leave in the immediate future, she felt it was better to hand the directorship to someone else, someone who, it was hoped, would bring a fresh energy that could take the school through the next stage of its development.

Although Robin never directly harvested the results of her efforts to get the school into new premises, she nevertheless reshaped the school, enabling it more readily to confront the many complex and primary issues relating to the future direction of theatre in New Zealand. Her many achievements include the accreditation of a three-year acting degree, the introduction of the technical production course, the increased international profile of Toi Whakaari, and the provision of a much-needed permanent home, befitting the aspiration and status of New Zealand's national drama school. Above all, Robin's most profound contribution to the school was the advancement of the bicultural purpose of Toi Whakaari:

> For philosophical, humanitarian and the ideological reasons, I was passionate about the bicultural work and the possibilities of that and where it could go. I felt with a real zeal that it was essential; that the school carried an enormous load as well as a privilege to work out how to expand the world: how to literally double the world that we are standing in; at the same time as educating for a specific vocation. Pragmatically there was every argument for doing it. The Māori renaissance had already begun in the 1970s and was gaining momentum. Our graduates were going to have the opportunity to work in Māori theatre, in blended theatre, in theatre forms that we didn't even envisage, and they needed the skills to do that. For employment within New Zealand there was a pressing argument for them to become more Māori literate and versed in the ways of theatres like Taki Rua, and other Māori theatres that already existed and were burgeoning. Internationally, the ethnic offerings are the most marketable. It is patently clear that Māori performance troupes travel [overseas] with an ease and with an acceptance that we [Pākehā] can't. The bicultural movement at the Drama School had its genesis with Nola, it gathered momentum when Sunny stepped in with a clear agenda and began to implement it. I was passed a little bush that was already alight.[18]

Having announced her decision to leave, Robin began rehearsing *Pentecost* and was clearly in her element. For a while, at least, she could focus on what she most enjoyed. Annie Ruth observed that 'Robin is so happy now – directing *Pentecost*. She is fantastically happy and she needed a lot more of that along the way. I believe the reason for the burn-out for Robin is that she hasn't been released often enough to direct.'[19]

Pentecost takes place in an unnamed eastern European country and is set in an abandoned Romanesque church in which a fresco is discovered: it appears to predate any other known renaissance painting and could permanently change art history. The church is occupied by refugees who have taken hostages in their effort to gain asylum. Ten different languages and thirteen different nationalities are represented in the play, providing an interesting challenge for the cast.

The production was performed at Taki Rua theatre, with a set designed by Tolis Papazoglou, transforming the venue into the interior of an Eastern European Church. The costumes were designed by a second-year technical production student, Ross Gibbs. The set construction proved to be a demanding assignment for Brett Tompkins, the construction manager, and for Nicole Cosgrove, the scenic artist. During the course of the play, a large fresco on the end wall of the church is slowly revealed. And in the penultimate scene it is demolished by a huge explosion when commandoes abseil into the church – guns blazing to end the siege.

To allow the wall to be 'demolished' and then reassembled after each performance, it was constructed like a huge jigsaw puzzle. The task of reconstructing the wall was carried out by Toby Papazoglou, who spent many late nights and early mornings fitting the huge jigsaw back together.

Earlier in the year, the first-year students performed Edward Bond's *Human Cannon*, directed by Annie Ruth and designed by Nicole Cosgrove. The play takes place during the Spanish Civil War and its aftermath, following the tribulations of a group of women in a remote mountain village as they face the moral dilemmas and horrors of war. The extensive list of characters in *Human Cannon* allowed each cast member

Pentecost, 1996.
Richard Edge (L) and
Steven Moore (R)

Human Cannon, 1996.
L–R: Matthew Sunderland,
Vanessa Rhodes, Mitch
Thomas, Rhys Morgan,
Lynette Crawford-Williams
(in wheelchair).

to take on several roles. Technical production students were also recruited as villagers, soldiers and prisoners. A central feature of the production was a large realistic-looking cannon that had been beautifully crafted by Juliette Howard, a first-year technical production student.

There were more staff changes at the school during the year. Bert van Dijk left, and the position of head of movement and voice was temporarily filled by two visiting tutors, Keely Eastley, a voice teacher from the USA, and Janet Robertson, an Australian movement tutor. Shona Pattison resigned from her position as projects officer and was replaced by Matthew Savage, who had been the projects officer and theatre manager for Gecko Theatre. Sarah Griffiths returned to assist with the final productions, and the school got a much-needed audio-visual technician, Tam Webster.

At the start of 1997, a third series of Summer Workshops was held at the school, coordinated by Damien Kelly. The sixteen workshop tutors included Vadim Ledegrov, a Russian specialist in the Stanislavsky System; Sue Ingleton, an Australian who ran a workshop on writing for monologue performance; Sylvia Rands on the voice in theatre; and Gaylene Preston, who ran a screen performance class. An extended Young and Hungry series of acting workshops was also offered, in association with BATS theatre.

The first day of the first term of 1997 heralded another first. It was the first day for the first-year students enrolled in the new three-year acting course. But the accreditation process for the qualification had not yet been completed; agreement still had to be reached on whether it would be a diploma or a degree.

The three-year acting course provided more time and opportunity for specialisation than the whirlwind two-year diploma course. The 'basic training units' now extended over the first two years of the course, reducing some of the pressure on production activity. A series of optional units in the third year also gave students greater autonomy in choosing and structuring their own training. The new curriculum included the return of the monologue season, expanded film and television modules, and a major graduation production. Woven into the third year were cooperative productions, secondments and specialist block courses.

The 1997 intake of students had a distinct multicultural flavour, with Bjorg Halldorsdottir, the school's first Icelandic student enrolled in the acting course; along with technical production students Pornsupasri Berrigan (Pook) from Thailand, and Geina Toscano, Janice van Rooyen and Matthew D'Herville, of Italian, Dutch and French parentage respectively.

There were a number of staff changes at the start of the year. Lyne Pringle became the movement programme manager, Simone Lourie was appointed as the new programme manager for voice and Rangimoana Taylor joined the school as the new taha Māori programme coordinator.

Simone Lourie was a recent graduate of the NIDA voice studies programme. She had a background in acting and directing, and had been a voice coach and teacher with the New Theatre in Sydney. The year before, she had been seconded from NIDA to Toi Whakaari to observe the voice programme and to contribute to the *Mixed Lollies* self-devised programme.

Since graduating from the school in 1975, Rangimoana had over twenty years' experience as an actor and director in theatre, and had worked in television production and presentation. This broad experience enabled him more easily to relate the taha Māori programme to the students' performance work.

Part-time tutors at the school now included Glen Birchall and Kate Hamblin, both movement tutors. Recent additions to the technical production department were Stephen Blackburn (production management and lighting mechanics), Dorita Hannah (theatre architecture) and Helen Todd (lighting design).

The recruitment process to find a new director had commenced towards the end of 1996. But with major decisions still to be made on the building project and the three-year acting programme to be bedded in, it was crucial the school didn't go into a holding pattern. The Board was urged to appoint an interim director until an appointment could be made. Murray Lynch and Annie Ruth, who worked well together and had complementary skills, applied to be co-directors of the school, but the Board rejected their application, believing it would be difficult to relate to more than one

▲ Annie Ruth

◀ Staff Photo, 1997. Standing L–R: Matthew Savage, (?), Ruth Graham, Dee O'Connor, Bill Guest, Biddy Grant, Simone Lourie. Sitting: L–R Murray Lynch, Annie Ruth, Lyne Pringle, Tam Webster, Rangimoana Taylor.

director. And early in 1997, Annie Ruth alone was appointed as the new director of Toi Whakaari, which gave her the distinction of being the first graduate of the school to hold this role.

Annie was well positioned to take on the directorship of the school; she had been a full-time acting and improvisation tutor at Toi Whakaari since 1991 and head of acting from 1996.

The burden of managing the school had previously fallen heavily on the director. Now that Annie held that position, she was interested in closing the gap between herself and the heads of department, in order to give them greater autonomy. To achieve this, she and the heads of department began to meet each week to discuss strategic and philosophical issues relating to the management and future direction of the school. This process of consultation and shared decision-making was further extended when I was reappointed as an associate director in 2002, assuming responsibility for curriculum matters. And again in 2007, Christian Penny was appointed as an associate director, with responsibility for strategic planning.

Annie's 'formative educational experience' had been at Sacred Heart College in the late 1950s. By her account, this had been a mixed blessing: either inspirational or loathsome – depending on the teachers. She then went on to study political science and drama at Victoria University and joined the women's liberation movement. But her true passion lay in theatre, and in 1970 she auditioned for Nola's fledgling drama school and was accepted. Rawiri Paratene, the youngest in her group, recalled her as being 'very much the oldest. She was really strong, and bubbly and bouncy, just exactly like she is now … and Annie introduced me to yoghurt and muesli and other foods.'[20]

In 1974 Annie travelled to Greece, where she taught at the Montessori Nursery School in Athens, returning to Wellington in 1984 to give birth to her son, Alexi, before enrolling at Teachers' College where she came under the influence of Ralph McAllister, her drama tutor:

> He brought back my joy in theatre, and the knowledge that that's what I had to do. Through him I learnt about asking questions in an open-ended way that lets others own the drama. I could begin a situation where I would genuinely not see what the end was going to be, and help guide people through those situations. That was a huge skill.[21]

After graduating from Teachers' College, Annie spent a year with the Town and Country Players, confirming her commitment to theatre. She had also helped to get theatre sports started in New Zealand and, in 1988, was a member of the New Zealand team at the Festival of Theatre Sports in Brisbane:

> That was an amazing experience because we were so bad. We had no idea. We'd planned in a very rigid structure, here in New Zealand. But all the international people played much more fluidly and openly, and without those tight structures you've got to be a whole lot better. It was the most humiliating experience, and so difficult to get up and do it again .... Others were falling about and weeping and refusing to go on. But I decided that I wouldn't do that, that we would just do it anyway and learn, and we did get better. By the end we got into the final round and they gave us the 'Culture Shock Cup for Coping'.[22]

When Robin Payne was farewelled by Toi Whakaari staff, students and the Board in March, Robin asked Annie and Sunny Amey to join her. For Annie it was an amazing moment – to have three directors of the school standing together. Robin's leaving was in fact a sort of 'Clayton's Departure', as she was to return in August to co-direct *Ornithes: Nga Manu: The Birds*.

Her going more or less coincided with the deadline for the PMT to sign off unconditionally on the National Dance and Drama Centre with the Wellington Show Association and the City Council. If the deadline was missed, the Lottery's grant to the PMT would be forfeited. But the PMT still had some serious financial hurdles to jump before it could fully commit to the project. The Ministry of Education had reconfirmed that the $380,000 interest, which had accrued on the suspensory loan, could be paid off over three years. This gave the PMT and Toi Whakaari some difficult options to consider. There was the possibility that they could reduce the cost of the project by revisiting the list of building deferrals, but this had already been pared to the bone. Or they could increase the student fees by $1,000 a year to cover the additional cost, seek a $380,000 increase in the BNZ loan or pull the plug on the entire project.

In fact, the PMT chose none of those options, and instead engaged in a bit of brinkmanship, notifying the Ministry of Education that it was *not* prepared to consider any additional cost to the current project, and that unless the Ministry reversed its directive on the interest repayment the two schools would abandon the project. The PMT minutes for the meeting on 2 March noted that:

> The inevitable effect of this action would be the winding up of the PMT and the cessation, for the foreseeable future, of any further similar joint initiatives by the School's Boards to address the chronic and critical accommodation problems.

This ultimatum had the desired effect. Wyatt Creech, the Minister of Education, intervened and a compromise was reached, allowing the interest to be repaid over five years instead of three, which reduced the annual payment by each school to $38,000. The belief was that this amount would be offset by a compensatory increase in the Ministry's operational grants to the schools.

With these final obstacles out of the way, the building project went unconditional, allowing the Wellington Show Association's lease to be reassigned to the two schools. Wellington City Council then agreed to stand as a joint guarantor, along with the Boards of the two schools, enabling the $1 million bridging loan to be secured from the BNZ.

But it was a close call. At the last minute, Jenny Pattrick had to intercede to make sure both Boards were in agreement:

> I particularly recall the day we finally signed off on the Winter Show Buildings site for the two schools. We had to take a risk, in that the funding from various sources – especially Lotteries commission money – was well short of the sum needed to convert the building. If we didn't take the decision that day, the Lotteries money would be withdrawn. Toi Whakaari Board accepted the need to go ahead but there was not a majority in the Dance School Board willing to take the risk that the remaining million dollars could be raised. I spent the day ringing each Board member and talking them through the options – trying not to downplay their real concerns, but also desperate to secure the Winter Show Building. Finally we got the majority, with one valuable and necessary Board member agreeing to abstain rather than resign.[23]

The PMT was still pinning its hopes on the fundraising committee being able to raise a proportion of the additional $1 to $1.7 million still needed to complete the building. The school would not then have to draw down the entire BNZ loan. In agreeing to go unconditional, the School of Dance Board had prudently asked for contingencies to be put in place in case fundraising fell short of the loan amount, which gave it greater control over the extent of the staged development and enabled its Board to manage the school's exposure.

A contract with Mainzeal Construction was signed off, with a projected completion or handover twelve months away. In June 1997, the first 'brick was laid', which, in reality, meant the first bit of the Show Building's Festival Hall was demolished.

The building contract included four drama and five dance studios, an assortment of smaller studios or classrooms for each of the two schools, a large 400-square metre performance space with a loading bay, the Nola Millar Library to house the collections of both schools, a spacious central common area, costume and props stores (destined to become workshops), two small audio-visual studios, a commercial kitchen, a refurbished common room, two changing/locker rooms, a lift and an administration/office area. Languishing on the deferral list was a TV studio in the basement, though this was never completed.

When Annie took up her appointment as director, Murray Lynch was appointed head of actor training and productions. He had recently remounted *Waiora* at Downstage with mostly Toi Whakaari graduates in the cast, and the production was scheduled to tour New Zealand before going to the Brighton Festival in the UK.

To bolster the number of teaching staff, international tutors were invited to work at the school in 1997, including Michael Johnson-Chase and James De Paul from the University of Wisconsin–Milwaukee to teach acting methodology. Sue Western, a director/choreographer and movement tutor from the UK, also worked with the first-year actors. And Timothy Douglas was due to arrive from the USA later in the year to direct *Insurrection: Holding History*.

The second-year techies embarked on their individual industry secondments at the start of the year. Possibly the most adventurous secondment – and apparently the most fun – was the 1997 Taranaki Festival of Arts, which involved all the second-year technical students, the merits of which are best described by Jane Chewings, in her 'poetic' secondment report:

> From rigging lights in mosquito infested venues, to creating art exhibitions, to doing time up castles and cherry pickers, to making trees out of drainage pipe, to selling programmes amongst the hordes at ENZSO, to taking a show to Hawera – the town of hellish food places and slapped-in-the-face-with-a-cold-wet-fish customer service, to hanging around in haunted old ex-hospital buildings, to living in shoe box style accommodation in a motor camp squeezed between the Tasman Sea and the alarm-clock railway, to driving around the legendary 'Theatre Lamp and Lighting' van – Wahoo!; to making our intimate acquaintance with the roofs of New Plymouth, to cabling and de- or dis-cabling the mother of all cables at Rugby Park, to hanging with the Army boys and girls, to packing out the Searchlight Tattoo 'till the wee small hours; yes we did it all. Life was bliss with a candy-coated motel room to round off our R & R at our sea-side industrial resort.[24]

Jane Chewings and Heidi Simmonds, Taranaki Festival. *Photo: Bill Guest.*

Ross Gibbs, Taranaki Festival. *Photo: Bill Guest.*

From a fleeting visit to inspect the troops at the Taranaki Festival, I do recall that the 'box style accommodation' had a certain candy-coated charm.

The 1997 graduating year of technical production students – Jane Chewings, Ross Gibbs, Juliette Howard, Kate Robertson, Heidi Simmonds (the dancing tech) and Kieth Walker – were an exceptionally close-knit group. Together, they had coped with some difficult issues in their first year but benefited from their mutual strength. Two students from that cohort now teach at Toi Whakaari: Kate Robertson is head of entertainment technology and performing arts management, and Jane Chewings teaches marketing and promotions in the performing arts management programme.

Although this was an exceptionally unified group of student, it is not always the case. Each technical production (or entertainment technology) cohort has its own distinctive style, reflected in a diverse range of interests and ambition. The students spend two years working in close proximity, often under intense and pressured circumstances; and because of this and their often disparate temperaments, they don't always see eye-to-eye. Divisions sometimes occur but this rarely affects their ability to work harmoniously on performance projects. The working environment at the school is not dissimilar to the one they will encounter in their future practice, where any underlying personal differences – or dislikes – become secondary to the demands of a production.

The first production for the second-year actors in 1997 was *Mind Your Manners*, a compilation of scenes from late nineteenth- and twentieth-century comedies. The five scenes were each directed by Roy Ward, Jane Waddell, Murray Lynch, Bill Guest and Raymond Boyce, who directed a scene from that quintessential of English comedies, *Pygmalion*. Tanea Heke was in the cast of *Pygmalion* and recalled some unintentional humour that emerged within the production:

> I'm sure someone must have given Raymond a bit of a warning that he'd be working with all the brown students on *Pygmalion*. For some unknown reason they found that an amusing way of casting. I don't know. Professor Higgins was played by Victor Rodger, Waimihi Hotere played Mrs Eynsford-Hill, Mitch Thomas was Pickering and Lynette Crawford-Williams played Eliza. Terrible things happened during some performances; there was a bit when I was playing Mrs Higgins, and Waimihi had forgotten her lines; I remember we were all sitting on a chaise-longue and Waimihi sat deliberately on top of someone so that they would say something and cover for her. She did it every night; there'd be something she'd completely fluff onstage but being the competent 'professional' she was, it never looked like her, it always looked like one of us – ghastly, ghastly creature! I can still see her doing that, with a big feather boa. But it was a lovely production and Raymond was very patient. It was very funny and I loved it.[25]

The NZQA approval process for the three-year acting qualification was finally completed in August 1997. It was accredited as a Bachelor of Performing Arts (Acting), and was notable for being the first-ever degree in acting in New Zealand. In its accreditation of the degree, NZQA acknowledged the holistic nature of the qualification and the rigorousness of the training offered by Toi Whakaari. Although the acting course is unit-based, none of the units stands alone; they are intrinsically linked and interdependent. As there is little value in gaining credits for part of the training or for previous qualifications, students have to commit to the entire three-year training programme.

Halfway through 1997, rehearsals commenced for *Ornithes: Nga Manu: The Birds,* directed by Robin Payne, Tolis Papazoglou and Rangimoana Taylor. The production was supported by a number of specialist tutors, including Paiki Johnson whose extensive knowledge of taiaha and bird movement provided a specific focus for the work. Each actor was cast as a bird, as well as a god or a human, and explored and adopted a range of bird movements under Paiki Johnson's guidance. For several weeks, the school was transformed into a large kōhanga ngā manu, reverberating with the sounds of 'exotic' birds, and resembling an aviary inhabited by half-bird-half-human beings.

Rangimoana Taylor worked closely with Hone Hurihanganui to translate the Greek chorus into te reo Māori, and to set the haka and poi sequences against Greek footwork. Other specialists joined the team later, included Mark Newman, a trapeze tutor; Peter Wilson, a puppet specialist; and Tom McCrory and Beatrice Papazoglou, who worked on chorus movement and choreography. The musical director was Laughton Pattrick, and Debz Ruffell constructed an extraordinary range of bird and other costumes.

Jane Chewings, the set designer for *Ornithes*, created a large scaffold framework to provide a three-dimensional performance space for the cross-cultural collection of gods, humans and birds. The audience also inhabited the entire performance space and was integrated into the mythical world of *Ornithes: Nga Manu: The Birds.*

At the end of the year, the second-years began work on their graduation production, a double-bill of historical plays: *Insurrection: Holding History* by African-American playwright Robert O'Hara, and Caryl Churchill's *Vinegar Tom*. Both were performed on the same set at BATS theatre.

Insurrection was directed by Timothy Douglas. He had previously directed a reading of the play when working at the Mark Taper Forum in Los Angeles as resident artist in directing. Robin Payne first met Timothy in Los Angeles, and when they later met by chance in New York, she invited him to direct *Insurrection* at Toi Whakaari. The story is based on a slave uprising in Virginia in 1831, and as an African-American Timothy Douglas was fascinated by the play. In its first performance it was 'greeted with howls of recognition by black Americans in the audience, and stunned silence by the white Americans'.[26] The Toi Whakaari production was only the second time *Insurrection* had been produced in its full version.

Timothy Douglas was amazed that the play was being done in New Zealand – 'America is not yet ready for plays about slavery'[27] – and it was a remarkable journey for the eight, mostly Māori or Polynesian Pacific Island, acting students as they explored the volatile issues with Timothy Douglas. Tanea Heke's outrageous performance as the Southern Belle, Mistress Mo'tel, was straight from *Gone with the Wind* and will be long remembered, as will the haunting music, composed and directed by Janet Roddick.

The other half of the 1997 graduation double-bill was *Vinegar Tom*, directed by Murray Lynch. Apart from being an excellent companion play, *Vinegar Tom* was chosen for the substantial female roles it provided for the remaining six students in the class. The composer and musical director for this production was Charlotte Yates.

Throughout the year, the acting students had a series of performance-for-camera

Timothy Douglas and Jane Chewings, *Insurrection*

blocks, which provided them with the opportunity to work with an impressive line-up of industry leaders, including directors Ian Mune, Aileen O'Sullivan and Vicki Yiannoutsos; cinematographer Waka Attewell; film editor John Gilbert; and John Callen, who directed a fast-turn-around television drama workshop with the third-years at Avalon Studios.

Performance for Camera Class – Aileen O'Sullivan and Cliff Curtis

Other innovative projects introduced in 1997 included combat metaphor with KC Kelly, and *The Grand Sweep*, a culmination of history-of-theatre classes. There was also a series of technical design blocks with Tolis Papazoglou, Helen Todd and Dorita Hannah.

The final graduation ceremony at 36 Vivian Street took place in November before the school moved into the newly named National Dance and Drama Centre, no longer the Winter Show Building. Construction was progressing fast, the interior and exterior demolition work was complete, studio and theatre walls were up, and a maze of streets and walkways formed a network between the various areas in the building. The completion and grand opening for the National Dance and Drama Centre was scheduled for May/June 1998.

Sixteen

1998–1999

'Board discussion got bogged down in the nitty-gritty too much, instead of dealing with common issues relating to both schools.'

The pōwhiri, held at 36 Vivian Street at the beginning of the 1998 school year, heralded two 'firsts': Annie Ruth greeted the new Toi Whakaari students in her capacity as director, and the School of Dance welcomed its new director, Garry Trinder. This important stage in the journey of the two schools and their future shared relationship in Te Whaea was reinforced when the dance students participated in the karanga and sang a waiata to support their recently arrived director.

Garry Trinder had previously been head of dance at UNITEC's School of Performing and Screen Arts. Before that, he was director of the Hong Kong Ballet, director of dance at South Africa's NAPAC Dance Company and lecturer in dance at the Newcastle College Centre for the Performing Arts in the UK.

Toi Whakaari received twenty-six new students in 1998, with a similar number enrolled in the second year. This would significantly increase the following year when for the first time there would be third-year acting students. To meet the current and anticipated teaching load, the school set about increasing the number of tutors and ancillary staff.

A new full-time position, programme coordinator for theoretical studies, was created, partly to meet the requirements of the new three-year acting degree, but also to advance the history, theory and philosophy of theatre programme as core training elements for all courses. Vanessa Byrnes was appointed to that position. As a student at Toi Whakaari from 1993 to 1994 the school had 'opened a gateway to the world of the professional practitioner',[1] for Vanessa. Since then she had performed in theatre and on screen, had directed theatre and radio, been a dramaturge for new plays, produced theatre and short films, and had also taught.

Miranda Harcourt also joined the school in 1998 as a full-time tutor in the acting department. After graduating from the New Zealand Drama School in 1984, she had become something of an entrepreneur, often creating her own work:

> I was always looking for plays, or buying the rights to a novel, or touring plays like from

Miranda Harcourt

> *Children of a Lesser God* all round the country. I went on endless national tours playing to huge houses of these plays and no idea where the money was going to. I had a series of unscrupulous producers who took it all. Then I moved on to devising my own work after I did my postgraduate work at Central School in London in 1990–92.[2]

On her return to New Zealand, Miranda used those skills to teach in prisons and on various drama courses. Her many accomplishments as a stage and screen actor included several short films, TV drama and radio. She toured various productions, including *Flowers From my Mother's Garden*, which she wrote with Stuart McKenzie and had recently performed with her mother Kate at the 1998 International Festival of the Arts.

Other new staff appointments included Anne de Geus, who joined the core staff of the technical production department as a costume tutor and wardrobe supervisor. For a number of years, she had worked at the school as a part-time costume tutor and costume maker. She also taught in the fashion design department at Massey School of Design. Tam Webster, who had previously worked at Toi Whakaari as part-time audio-visual tutor and technician, was also appointed full time. When the school moved into its new building later in the year, Tam played a pivotal role in setting up technical and computer facilities for the technical production department.

The structure and governance of the school changed as well. When the New Zealand Drama School became a Charitable Trust with a Board of Trustees in 1986, it relinquished its Board of Studies. But in 1997, when the three-year acting degree was approved, a Board of Studies was reinstated; it had been an NZQA requirement.

This new Board of Studies had its inaugural meeting at the end of 1997, with Annie Ruth as acting chair. The membership comprised Steve La Hood (who took over as chair in June 1998), Ruth Graham, Bill Guest, Tanea Heke (a recent graduate), Murray Lynch, Mick Rose (1990 graduate) and Tama Smith (student representative). David Carnegie from the Department of Theatre and Film at Victoria University joined the Board a little later.

This first meeting was taken up mostly with reports from various advisory panels. They had been established during previous years to function as informal committees, made up of industry and staff representatives acting in an advocacy or consultancy capacity to support the various disciplines. There were six advisory panels: acting, movement, voice, cultural studies, Te Roopu Tautoko and technical production. The latter was particularly active. In addition to its founder members John McKay and Joe Hayes, the panel now included Piet Asplet, Nicola Blackman, Stephen Blackburn, Stephen Fairweather, Ian Hull-Brown, Rob Peters and Helen Todd. Although the advisory panels had no regulatory powers, they could and did make recommendations to the Board of Studies on matters relating to new initiatives and curriculum development.

The principle purpose of the Board of Studies was regulatory, to provide a flow of information between the school and the external stakeholders regarding the quality and effectiveness of the teaching programme. Its intended role was to ensure that approved courses being delivered by the school met NZQA requirements, as well as 'industry' needs (potential employers of Toi Whakaari graduates) and, of course, the needs of students. The Board also had a key responsibility for developing and establishing new qualifications at the school, and for monitoring assessment criteria and procedure.

With such a large representation of Toi Whakaari staff and graduates on the Board of Studies, it could be argued that its purpose would have been better served had it included more outside practitioners to provide a broader educational and industry perspective. Unlike the Board of Trustees, which had a formal constitution to guide and govern its activity, the Board of Studies had no formal protocol of its own (at least none that was recorded). Its terms of reference were in fact incorporated in a Board of Trustees' policy, thus effectively making it a sub-committee of that Board, to whom it reported.

From 1974 to 1986 the previous Board of Studies had a dual purpose: governance and academic scrutiny. When it was dissolved in 1986, the school was left with a *single* Board of Trustees, and it is possible that, in transferring responsibility from one Board to the other, the separate purposes of the two Boards were not fully understood, an ambiguity that became embedded in the institutional memory of the school.

As later events revealed, it was unfortunate that the precise relationship of the two Boards was not more clearly defined when the Board of Studies was re-established. The only requirement in the Trust Board's policy directly relating to this relationship stated that the Board of Studies should 'report … annually to the Trust Board on the adequacy of relevant resources, facilities and services for courses offered at Toi Whakaari'.[3] Whether the two Boards were intended to function as single or separate entities, or how much autonomy the Board of Studies had, were never stipulated. When their separate interests overlapped or appeared to clash, this sometimes led to misunderstandings.

The principle responsibilities of the Toi Whakaari Board of Trustees included the overall financial management of the school and the development and approval of policies for its strategic direction and good management. The Board was also expected to act as an ambassador for the school; to raise its profile with government and in the wider community; and to support the director with advice regarding legal, financial and business matters. Most importantly, the Board had a major responsibility to resource and to attract financial support for the school through personal networks, fundraising and other endeavours.

At the start of year, the building complex gained a Māori prefix, *Te Whaea* – the mother, the nurturer – and a date was set for a dawn ceremony and blessing for the building in April, followed by an official opening ceremony in June.

Jenny Pattrick and Graham Oldershaw, the fundraising coordinators for the project, had spent a great deal of time and effort in chasing corporate sponsors and/or wealthy individuals to support the cost of the building in exchange for naming rights. Yet their attempts had met with little success. This was not surprising as the amounts they were seeking ranged from $1 million for the naming rights on the entire building to $50,000 for each of the two main studios.

From her experience with Creative New Zealand, Jenny Pattrick knew that many arts organisations were chasing the same dollars:

> It's quite common for potential sponsors to say that you are being funded by the education department and therefore they should give you the money. You might get bits of money for special projects but a school is never going to attract big sponsorship. I don't think they are prime subjects.[4]

She therefore chose to direct her energies to a more realistic campaign: Club 100. This group of a hundred individuals and organisations were each asked to donate between $1,000 and $5,000 to the building project. In return, Club 100 members were entitled to various benefits relating to performances and other activities at the school. They also received a beautiful silver and paua lapel pin, designed and made by Jenny Pattrick.

By October 1998, over twenty Club 100 members had been recruited, many of whom were also Friends of Toi Whakaari. The Friends' contribution had already been enormous; whenever the need arose, they provided support and assistance, and organised fundraising events for the new building. When the school moved into Te Whaea, they donated $7,000 to pay for shelving in the Nola Millar Library.

There was no denying that Te Whaea provided a magnificent home for the two schools, but it was still a shell – albeit a very striking one. The fit-out included only essential equipment needed to operate the building, leaving the schools with little option

Jenny Pattrick (R) and Kate Harcourt (L) - 1993

but to move their mostly old and dilapidated equipment from their former premises into Te Whaea. The lack of office furniture was partially resolved with a consignment of second-hand desks and screens, donated to the schools via the PMT.

For Toi Whakaari, the dearth of *new* furniture did not present a major problem; the school had lived with its motley collection of furnishings for years, and the disparity between the 'op-shop' furniture and the sparkling new architect-designed, world-class facility could be overlooked, at least for a while.

The bigger problem was the lack of operational equipment in the technical production areas of the building. The shortfall in funding meant that no expenditure had been factored in to fit-out the performance space. Te Whaea Theatre is essentially a multi-purpose performance and teaching facility: a large 'black box' (actually brown) venue, with a grid-shaped catwalk above to provide access for rigging mainly stage lighting equipment. The only other items specified in the building contract for the venue were lighting and audio circuits, wired to separate patching systems. In short, it was simply a bare-walls venue with some very useful lighting and audio circuitry.

The theatre had a dual purpose, primarily as an exploration and performance space for training actors, dancers, technicians and designers, and secondly as a user-friendly venue for community use. It had intentionally been designed with few physical or architectural limitations to allow it to be both functional and adaptable. But, as a bare walls venue without a seating system or drapes for masking and sound attenuation, it seemed doubtful the space would be used by the community. And without essential lighting and sound equipment, its use as a performance and teaching resource for the school would be severely limited.

Fortunately, a number of benefactors came to the rescue. Jenny Pattrick and Graeme Oldershaw had earlier applied to the Community Trust of Wellington for a major sponsorship of $1.3 million. Although this amount was not realised, the Community Trust did agree to provide $100,000 to purchase essential equipment for Te Whaea Theatre, which it was hoped would allow income to be generated from hiring the venue to the community.

Adaptability was a major consideration in the concept of theatre, and a vital element that supported this was an ingenious seating system designed by Tolis Papazoglou. It was made up of independent modular units that linked together to form multiple seating or staging configurations. This offered a range of options, from end-stage (200 seating capacity) to arena, in-the-round, traverse, diagonal axis and even suspended in space, giving students the opportunity to explore a wide range of performance possibilities.

The lack of lighting equipment for the venue was solved by Selecon NZ, largely through the intervention of its managing director, Jeremy Collins, who generously donated a range of Selecon's latest equipment to Toi Whakaari. For many years, Jeremy had demonstrated his commitment to technical theatre training, first as chair of the National Technical Theatre Training Council, and more recently in support of Toi Whakaari's technical production course when it replaced the NTTTC new-entrant scheme.

Kenderdine Electrical came to the party too when, in collaboration with Strand Lighting, it came up with a sponsorship deal that enabled the school to purchase the very latest in computerised lighting desks.

Computer technology now played a vital role in performing arts production. Students working in this area needed to be provided with a level of competency in computer-aided drafting to support their training in set and lighting design, and in audio and multi-media editing. The school therefore did a deal with Apple, allowing a 'pod' of computers to be purchased and installed in the new Computer Lab in Te Whaea. Sadly, the day after they were installed, the Lab was burgled and a number of high-end Apple Macs were stolen. Fortunately, though, they were covered by the school's insurance and the computers were eventually replaced.

Until April it was business as usual for the school at Vivian Street. The new intake of students started their year with the orientation programme, followed by a four-day Māori intensive led by tutors from Takitimu Māori Performing Arts School.

With the three-year acting degree now in place, a new framework of training began to evolve for the acting students, integrating movement and voice work, acting methodology, improvisation, speech and singing. One of the first students to experience this new regime was Simon Vincent who had joined the school in 1998 after studying at university, where he'd 'done some Shakespeare and some practical stuff'. He found his first year at Toi Whakaari somewhat difficult:

> The first year is hard, you are constantly in fear that you won't get through to the second year. I believe our year had the highest attrition rate ever at the school. We started off with eighteen in our class, six guys and twelve women, but by the end of the third year we were down to twelve: four guys and eight women. I think I was lucky that I was very green when I started at the school, whereas some others in my year were a bit older, experienced – and perhaps jaded. There were also quite a lot of strong women in the class, which was quite full-on for us guys. But I was open to anything, a bit of sponge, and I benefited from that because I didn't get cynical.
>
> In my second year, I became much more confident in my ability. I had so many performance opportunities during that year, particularly *Translations* where I was able to play to my strengths. In a way this ran counter to the other side of the training, which I found quite hard, where you need to become aware of your 'weaknesses'. I felt I was not at drama school to work out how to be a better person and that working with weaknesses was not necessarily the best way to reveal strengths. We're all messed up people and we've all got our own issues and crosses to bear … that's not my job; my job as an actor is to play the part. The other stuff – I'd prefer to leave that to my psychologist, if I had one.
>
> The way I now try to work is to focus on the text; that comes through my own experience, that's who I am. Your work as an actor is always to do with who you are.[5]

At the start of 1998, the school again participated in the Festival of Arts, hosting Festival Forums and 'minding' visiting artists in exchange for a generous supply of tickets for around fifteen shows.

During the Festival, a symposium on theatre design, Out of the Dark, was held at the Wellington School of Architecture and Design. It was an initiative of the newly formed Performing and Interactive Design Guild and was coordinated by Dorita Hannah. The symposium brought together a mix of theatre/design practitioners: architects, theatre critics, students and overseas artists involved with the Festival. Its aim was to provoke theatre audiences, actors and directors into revaluing performance design in an age increasingly concerned with new technology and moving image. Festival events, such as Ex Machina's *The Seven Streams of the River Ota* and the Live Ambient Graphic Opera *Lago*, offered excellent examples of new media/performance work, integrating traditional forms with projected computer imagery.

One of the Talkfest Forums held at Toi Whakaari was Technology in Performance, in which design and technology as drivers to extend the boundaries of performance was debated. This forum complemented ideas raised during the Out of the Dark symposium, and helped to consolidate thinking around the scope and form of a new design qualification currently being considered by Toi Whakaari.

Meanwhile, preparations for the move to Te Whaea continued with military precision under the direction of Biddy Grant. But the refurbishment of Te Whaea was only partially completed. Wall surfaces remained unpainted, although some offices and the library were eventually painted by staff, Board members and Friends in the weeks leading up to the move. Windows were without curtains, technical areas were incomplete and the theatre still had to be commissioned.

Regardless of its unfinished state, Toi Whakaari and the New Zealand School of Dance moved into Te Whaea at the end of April. This momentous occasion was commemorated with a dawn ceremony, attended by students and staff, Board members, advisory panels, VIPs and graduates. This was the first time such a large gathering had assembled inside the refurbished building and their presence immediately reinforced the scale and the possibilities offered by Te Whaea. It was clearly a far cry from the cramped Vivian Street and Cable Street premises, and with a sense of awe, the staff and students took possession of their new home.

Te Whaea is a testament to the perseverance of those who fought to achieve the potential of this remarkable building to provide a permanent home for the two schools. At just over $5 million, its refurbishment was a bargain. Te Whaea could not have been realised without the courage and acumen of the Premises Management Trust, and the vision and the persistence of Robin Payne and Tolis Papazoglou. As for the refurbishment itself, credit must go to Warren and Mahoney, especially the architect Peter Rowbotham for the inspired design, and Ian Maskill and Brendon Hogg for their project management. Not least in the collaboration was the construction company Mainzeal, who went the extra mile to ensure that the schools got value for money.

Following the dawn ceremony, entertainment was provided by students and staff from both schools, and students from Takitimu. Classes were then held to launch the studios and classrooms, and students bonded with Te Whaea by sleeping overnight in the studios.

Shortly after, the school staged its final production at 36 Vivian Street, *The Crucible*, directed by Christian Penny and performed by the second-year actors with a second-year technical production crew. They were now the only students remaining in the old school. The performance space was gutted, and the floor and walls sandblasted by the production designer Janice van Rooyen to create a stark, grey narrow pathway, with audience seating down each side. This sense of austerity was enhanced by Matt D'Herville's harsh monochromatic lighting, inspired by the photographs of Richard Avedon that depict people against a white background.

Students relaxing in the common room at 36 Vivian Street

Te Whaea. Shortly after the Schools moved in

Christian Penny rehearsing *The Crucible,* 1998

When Toi Whakaari vacated the Vivian Street premises, it was left in a very clean state. The performance space had not only survived a flood in 1995 (*Midsummer Night's Dream*), but it had also recently been sandblasted and cauterised by fire – an exciting performance element of *The Crucible*, which, alas, would not be permitted in today's less forgiving OSH environment. 36 Vivian Street was again inhabited by drama students when the Wellington Performing Arts Centre took over the premises shortly after Toi Whakaari moved out.

Te Whaea: National Dance & Drama Centre was officially launched at the end of June by the Governor General, Sir Michael Hardie Boys. In his opening speech, he honoured the history of the building and spoke about the promise that Te Whaea held for the performing arts in New Zealand:

> Talent withers and dies unless it is nurtured and exercised. Sporting talent has always had every encouragement here. Yet those talents expressive of mind and spirit have not been fostered so well. Now there is a growing awareness that this is not as it should be; a dawning realisation that we as a nation have a culture and a cultural identity that go well beyond the sports field and of which all New Zealanders can be proud as we are of our sporting prowess.[6]

The ceremony concluded with a moving rendition of 'Purea Nei', sung by students and staff of the Dance School, and then a resounding 'E Te Whaea E' from students and staff of both schools. After a tree dedication by the Mayor of Wellington, Mark Blumsky, the guests were invited to drink and be merry. Te Whaea: National Dance and Drama Centre was now well and truly launched.

The move to the new premises brought with it staff changes for both schools, particularly in the combined reception and administration centre. Gillian Jefcoate was appointed as the receptionist for Te Whaea and the schools; and Susanna Briggs, formerly the secretary for the School of Dance, was appointed as the administration clerk.

Directly opposite the reception area is the Nola Millar Library, with its architecturally interesting glass walls and beautifully polished wooden floor. It now housed the book collections of both Toi Whakaari and the New Zealand School of Dance, which would eventually be integrated into one system.

As well as ensuring the satisfactory completion of Te Whaea, the Premises Management Trust had responsibility for managing the entire complex, including the sports areas and the surrounding grounds. To assist with this, and to ensure the financial sustainability and the longer-term maintenance and development of Te Whaea, the PMT appointed a facilities manager, Jeff Williams. He also had the task of generating income from Te Whaea to support the financial operation of the two schools. Jeff's extensive knowledge of accountancy, building systems and building regulations was extremely helpful, particularly when it came to conjuring up new structures within Te Whaea. His ability to do this, often at very little direct cost to the schools, was remarkable. Jenny Pattrick had previously worked with Jeff at Creative New Zealand and she described him as 'best thing that ever happened to the two schools'.[7]

Toi Whakaari mounted its first production at Te Whaea in July with *Between a Rock and a Hard Place*, in which five directors worked with the second-year actors on scenes from plays by Pinter and Mamet. Later, in September, the second-year actors were again split into groups for their self-devised projects, with each group devising a twenty-minute piece to cater for a specified age-range of school children, from five to seventeen years. The programme, facilitated by Miranda Harcourt, was presented to school audiences throughout the Wellington region.

Meanwhile, Te Whaea Theatre underwent a hectic commissioning process, in which seating modules, curtains, lighting and sound equipment were installed just in time to stage the end-of-year production, Brecht's *The Threepenny Opera*. The musical had been chosen to display the talents of the second-year technical production students, as they were the only students to graduate from Toi Whakaari in 1998; the current second-year actors were enrolled in the three-year degree and would graduate in 1999.

The Threepenny Opera was directed by Murray Lynch with musical direction by Laughton Pattrick. A futuristic dystopian world was created by Dion Boothby's set, with lighting and projection by Rachel Butler, Tama Smith and Matt D'Herville. It was an excellent vehicle to launch Te Whaea Theatre, making full use of the height and width of the venue. In keeping with Brecht's theatre of alienation, the audience was seated on both sides of the acting area, confronting each other. The huge double doors at either end of the venue were used for dramatic entrances and exits, including the arrival of a vintage car for Macheath's entrance. The height of the venue provided Macheath with a very dramatic exit at the end of the performance, as he was carried high above the audience on an elevated work platform.

Technically ambitious projects are often fraught with teething problems and *The Threepenny Opera* was no exception. On opening night a chain-saw refused to start and padlocks refused to open. But within such a powerful production, these difficulties seemed insignificant.

In her review of *The Threepenny Opera*, Lynn Freeman concluded:

> [This was] a production of Brecht as it should be played, on a grand scale and totally over the top. The set and fabulous costumes made this one of the most distinctive looking productions of the year. It's also got guts, vision and relevance and everyone involved should take pride in this achievement. The future of NZ theatre is in skilled hands.[8]

At this time, Toi Whakaari still had no design course. Most productions were designed by the technical production students, many of whom have since continued their careers as designers, including Nicole Cosgrove, Sean Coyle, Ross Gibbs and Dion Boothby, who went on to work as an art director on numerous BBC and ITV productions, music promotions and commercials.

The first graduation ceremony in Te Whaea was held shortly after *The Threepenny Opera* closed, and the entire school gave the seven technical production graduates a magnificent farewell.

A condition of NZQA's approval for the three-year acting degree was the appointment of an external monitor to scrutinise the delivery of the qualification. Dr Geoff Gibbs was appointed to this position: he had been director and dean of drama at WAAPA for eighteen years and was chairman of the International Foundation for Arts and Culture. His first monitoring visit to Toi Whakaari was in December 1998. In his favourable report, he concluded that 'the degree programme was working well and that there was significant student, staff and industry satisfaction with the course'. He noted as a particular area of strength that:

> The bicultural approach [of the school] is a special quality and an enriching feature, without its dominating the final outcome of the education and training of the students. The spiritual and cultural underpinning that that provides makes the programme unique.

He was equally impressed by the new building:

> The monitor considers [Te Whaea] to be one of the best teaching facilities in the world for arts training with the size of the studios, the provision of student spaces and the sensible integration of dance and theatre teaching spaces.[9]

The only areas of concern expressed in the monitor's report were to do with the lack of computers for staff and students, and the need to increase staffing levels to support the delivery of the new acting degree. The report also recommended an increase in staff research, in order to investigate and record some of the more unique aspects of the acting programme. But it contained no 'requirements', which signified that the acting degree had passed its first major test – with flying colours.

Toi Whakaari had undergone much change during the previous twelve months, and the school was hoping for a respite the following year before launching into any new initiatives. Unsurprisingly, the pace did not slacken in 1999, although it did allow time for some consolidation and staff restructuring.

At the end of 1998, Tam Webster resigned, after which his dual roles of audio-visual technician and technical production tutor were split to create two new full-time positions: Chris Winter as an audio-visual/theatre technician, and Stephen Blackburn as a technical production tutor and technical director.

Stephen was the ideal person for this relatively new and challenging role. He had previously been production manager for the Royal New Zealand Ballet, and had been on the Technical Production Advisory Panel and taught part time at Toi Whakaari. He firmly believed New Zealand theatre required technicians with well-rounded holistic training, coupled with key competencies, qualities that also made New Zealand technicians highly employable internationally.

His pedigree was undeniably 'theatrical'. Actor Ken Blackburn is his father, his mother Suzanne Blackburn is a mezzo-soprano and his brother Phil is a lighting designer. Stephen's own theatrical career started in the early 1980s at Downstage Theatre. He worked there as technical director and as a lighting designer for a number of years, including a stint managing the Memorial Theatre at Victoria University. During that time, as secretary of NZATT, he'd been involved in setting up the 'new entry' technical theatre training programmes. Stephen then headed overseas, first to the USA for six months then to the UK for ten years, as a lighting designer and production manager.

Toward the end of 1999, Tom McCrory also joined the core staff as an acting and physical theatre tutor. Before moving to New Zealand in 1996, he'd co-founded the London-based Spiral Theatre Company and had been the senior movement teacher at Mountview Drama School. He had earlier trained and studied at the École

Left: Stephen Blackburn, middle: Tom McCrory, right: Rawiri Paratene *(Rawiri's photo: Karen Kay Management)*

Internationale De Theatre Jacques Lecoq in Paris. This experience, together with the study of other intercultural training traditions at the London School of Capoiera and the South Indian martial arts centre in Kerala, provided Tom with the basis of a unique training programme, essentially a research-based methodology involving a process of discovery driven by questions. Shortly after arriving at the school, Tom began to introduce his training methodology:

> You have a hunch; like any research you have to cast a net out into a certain territory and then start to map that territory, and as you proceed you become aware of certain parts of the landscape that you are exploring. A form then emerges with a whole series of original exercises, and a process.[10]

His methodology helped to integrate movement, voice, singing, acting and dance. Tom believed these skills had often been taught in a fragmented and compartmentalised way, often with no common thread, and that this instilled a sense of disconnectedness within the performer's body: 'it just defeats and decapitates our art and reduces it'.[11]

Rawiri Paratene returned to the school, replacing Rangimoana Taylor, to coordinate the taha Māori programme and to teach acting. Since graduating from the QEII Arts Council Drama School in 1973, Rawiri had performed with most professional theatres in New Zealand, often in principal or lead roles, and had become one of New Zealand's best know and versatile actors. From 1976 to 1999 he'd worked extensively in TV and film and taught drama and other related subjects in various educational institutions. From 1982 his focus had shifted to writing for television. He ceased to work in theatre for a number of years, and made his comeback in *Waiora* at the New Zealand Festival of Arts in 1996.

To streamline decision-making on issues affecting both Toi Whakaari and the School of Dance, their Trust Boards began meeting together. This arrangement made a lot of sense, given that the two schools shared the same premises. In 1999, both Boards agreed to enter into a memorandum of understanding in relation to the governance of the two schools, formally allowing them to meet jointly as a single entity while still retaining their separate legal status. It was hoped the merger would facilitate their common goals and advance their shared objectives, particularly the management of shared facilities and joint administration. However, the first hurdle was to get equal representation from the two schools onto a single Board, in order to create a single non-partisan governing body. This proved to be a challenging task, in particular for Jenny Pattrick, the chair of the joint Trust Board:

> Individual members were appointed to the Board because they were either a ballet/dance person or a theatre person. Maybe the individual Board members' interests were too partisan rather [than having] a general interest in arts and in education. Because of this, Board discussion got bogged down in the nitty-gritty too much instead of dealing with common issues relating to both schools.[12]

The Premises Management Trust was the head lessee of Te Whaea, which also made it the landlord of all the tenants in the complex. One of the PMT's prime objectives was to maximise rental income from Te Whaea, including the sports areas sub-leased to the Indoor Cricket and Wellington Basketball Associations. The income from that would then financially benefit the schools, covering some of the maintenance costs of the building; it would also help to eliminate debt. By 1999, the PMT had been reduced in size to just three: Bernard (Bernie) Te Uira Harris, who had replaced Peter Quinn as the independent chair, and two members who were nominated by the joint Trust Board to represent each of the schools, Roy Cowley and me.

In marked contrast, the Board of Studies had significantly grown; in addition to four staff and two student members, it had acquired four industry and academic members. One of their key responsibilities was to consider recommendations from advisory committees on the introduction of new qualifications at the school. The lack of space in the old premises, which had previously inhibited the introduction of new courses at Toi Whakaari, was no longer a problem, and the improved and much larger facilities at Te Whaea allowed a batch of new qualifications to be advanced. One of those was a Masters degree with two streams, one in directing and one in design, possibly to be delivered in partnership with Victoria University. This was in the early stages of development, and extensive consultation between Toi Whakaari and Victoria was still required before a curriculum could be agreed and approval for its delivery granted.

In response to discussions on the proposed Masters degree, Creative New Zealand acknowledged directing and design as priorities for professional development, but had also listed the role of the producer as an equally significant priority. It was therefore pushing Victoria University and Toi Whakaari to add production as a third strand:

> The lack of skilled producers is a major gap in the performing arts in New Zealand and is regularly identified by our leading creative artists as an urgent need. Arts organisations, festivals, touring companies all require the skills of a creative producer who marries artistic and business knowledge and experience.[13]

For some time, the Technical Production Advisory Panel had been considering several options to extend the scope of the existing two-year technical production course, including its re-accreditation to a three-year diploma/degree qualification. Eventually the panel decided the most useful and practical proposal was an additional postgraduate qualification, an Advanced Diploma in Technical Production, which would provide an optional extension to the two-year diploma and allow for advanced training in specialised areas of performing arts technology.

This was immediately put forward, and approval and accreditation was granted by NZQA in July 1998. It was evaluated by an industry-based committee under the guidance of NZQA's quality systems analyst, Ken Millar. He both understood and was sympathetic to the academic aims of Toi Whakaari, and later involved himself in the evaluation of most of the qualifications submitted by the school to NZQA.

At the start of 1999, the first intake of students since the school moved into Te Whaea was welcomed, with a pōwhiri in the newly named Mainzeal Plaza. There were thirty new students across the acting, technical production and advanced diploma courses, increasing the student population of the school to over seventy.

The first Advanced Diploma in Technical Production students were Pornsupasri 'Pook' Berrigan and Juliette Howard. Pook had graduated from the technical production course the year before and had re-enrolled in the advanced diploma to further her interests in puppetry and tour management before returning to work in Thailand. Juliette had graduated from the technical production course in 1997 and was the first student to receive a scholarship from the Performing Arts Foundation of New Zealand, which had been recently established by the St James Theatre Charitable Trust to foster excellence in all areas of the performing arts. Juliette's specialisation was lighting design, not just stage lighting but also architectural lighting, as she was interested in exploring the intersection of the two technologies. One of her greatest ambitions was to create a multicoloured lightscape within the ice flows in Antarctica; she found their pure blue-white surface irresistible. During her advanced diploma year, she received financial support from Meridian Energy to illuminate the wind turbine on top of Brooklyn Hill. Her design for this incorporated an array of colours that changed with the mood of the day. Alas, the local residents objected to the idea so the project was shelved.

The first production in 1999 was *The Love of the Nightingale* by Timberlake Wertenbaker, directed by Annie Ruth. This was a joint second-year acting and technical production project, incorporating songs by Charlotte Yates. Shortly afterwards, Annie travelled to the USA and the UK, visiting drama schools to open up opportunities for student and staff exchanges. This led to formal exchange agreements between Toi Whakaari and the California Institute of the Arts (CalArts), the University of Wisconsin–Milwaukee and the design school at Nottingham Trent University in the UK. Exchange agreements were already in place between Toi Whakaari and two Australian schools: NIDA and WAAPA.

The monologue programme was reintroduced in 1999 for the third-year actors. This was followed by a Celtic Lands season, which comprised two Irish and Scottish plays that had not previously been performed in New Zealand: Brian Friel's *Translations*, directed by KC Kelly; and Sue Glover's *Bondagers*, directed by Vanessa Byrnes. The plays were first presented by the second-year acting and technical production students in Te Whaea Theatre in May, followed by an Auckland season at the Herald Theatre in the Aotea Centre.

As Toi Whakaari and the New Zealand School of Dance settled into Te Whaea, the process of moving the two schools together continued. The Board of Trustees instigated a restructuring of the administrative services by creating a single administration centre to service both schools and Te Whaea. This 'shake-up' gave rise to a number of resignations by administrative staff, including Matthew Savage (projects coordinator), Susie Briggs (administration assistant), Gillian Jefcoate (receptionist) and, most significantly, Toi Whakaari's business manager, Biddy Grant. As well as having a background in arts administration, she had also been a qualified nurse. It was undoubtedly the unique combination of those two skills that enabled the transition of the school from Vivian Street to Te Whaea to happen with such relative ease. Her three or so years as Toi Whakaari's business manager had not been without their stresses and strains, spanning a difficult period during which the school faced severe financial hardship, yet she constantly nurtured the staff and students during this time, even ushering the first of the school's new qualifications, the Advanced Diploma in Technical Production, through its NZQA accreditation process.

When Biddy Grant left, Chris Goldsworthy was appointed as the business and strategic manager for both schools. He had recently graduated from Bond University in Australia with an MBA, and before that he'd been a ballet dancer. His partner, Fiona Tonkin, was the rehearsal director for the Royal New Zealand Ballet. Other administrative appointments were then made, with staff working across both schools: Meredith O'Brien as office supervisor and Ann Hunt as receptionist. And Toi Whakaari appointed a new project coordinator: Nicky Nikolaou.

One of the mutual benefits of sharing Te Whaea was that it enabled Toi Whakaari and the New Zealand School of Dance to collaborate on joint performance projects. The first of these was a lighting/choreographic workshop in 1999, led by Helen Todd, a leading New Zealand lighting designer who specialises in dance and physical theatre. She worked with the students to explore the relationship between light and movement, and then, to encourage a greater understanding of each other's practice, the dancers were asked to design lighting and the technicians to choreograph. This collaboration was extremely successful and laid the foundation for the annual Choreographic Season, a joint venture between Toi Whakaari's technical production department and the contemporary department of the New Zealand School of Dance.

In the middle of the year, the third-year actors embarked on four cooperative projects as part of their final-year electives. Each group received a $500 budget to produce their chosen play and were then left to their own devices. Essentially, it was a crash course in producing. The students were entirely responsible for realising their own production: they had to choose a script; secure a professional director; negotiate a performance venue; find or make their own costumes, sets and props; and, and where necessary, gain additional sponsorship.

Two cooperatives were performed at BATS Theatre: Christopher Durang's *Laughing Wild*, directed by Jonathon Hendry; and *Burn This* by Langford Wilson, directed by Murray Lynch. Rather than choosing an existing play, the third group devised its own piece, *Elvis Was a Coconut*, directed by Richard Damon. The work, which traced the career of Elvis (Rarotonga's superstar) and a bizarre love triangle, somehow came

Elvis was a Coconut, 1998. Nigel Collins and Tausili Mose

together to explain also the 'origins of Viagra and the future Antarctic discovery of the Missing Link'.[14] It was performed at the Sunset Palms, Wellington's only Pacific Island nightclub, giving the production added authenticity.

The other cooperative chose a play by Sam Shepherd and Patti Smith, *Cowboy Mouth*, directed by Cameron Delaney and performed at the Phoenix Theatre.

The students' initiation into the 'harsh reality of producing' provided them with some useful survival skills. Karl Drinkwater was in the cast of *Burn This* and found the cooperative experience empowering: 'It was a fantastic chance for us to get out there and show ourselves off, and impress people with our enthusiasm and passion.'[15]

The next project for the third-years was *The Big Game,* the first fully fledged short film commissioned and produced by Toi Whakaari. It was also the first short film to be shot entirely on 16mm film at the school. The screenplay for *The Big Game* was by Rawiri Paretene, the producer was Di Oliver, it was directed by Ian Mune and Waka Attewell was cinematographer. Under the guidance of Alice Tinning, the students' common room in Te Whaea was turned into an impromptu set. Because of its high production values, *The Big Game* established a new standard for the screen component of the acting course and a benchmark for others to follow.

When Miranda Harcourt joined the school as a full-time tutor, the development of a professional-based screen programme had been the focus of her ambition. She had some very firm ideas about how this could be achieved:

> Up to now the school had managed to get screen included in the acting programme, but only by hitch-hiking on someone else's expenditure. It became clear that we should be investing more time and money on our own account and that we were spending money on screen training in an ill-advised way.
>
> The school would hire someone who would come in and direct something for the students in a teaching environment. Often in a 'teaching environment' there's no pressure to make something good, because the director who's been hired is being paid [very little] for the two-week period to make a film. He says, 'I can't do anything good because

> these students aren't any good, they're not very experienced, there's not enough money, we can't go on location, it's a studio-based thing, so we'll make something crappy and the experience of doing it will teach them something.'
>
> The students were also being sent out to Avalon. I think it was $24,000 for a two-week block to do an in-studio shoot with a couple of Avalon directors and have the experience of meeting the big cameras. But sending them out to do the 'screen experience' way out at Avalon was disconnected to the students' own experience and it was something that gave them little ownership. I didn't subscribe to that, it was not good value and I felt strongly that we should spend that money ourselves. I proposed that we should no longer hire Avalon; instead, we would use that money and put the project up for tender. This would happen over a couple of years, whereby a number of film makers would pitch for the opportunity to use that $24,000 to $30,000 to do whatever they wanted.
>
> *The Big Game* was the first step on the journey towards putting it out there, in our film magazine and through the Screen Directors' Guild. Putting the information out there and saying, 'Hey guys, there's $30,000, whoever you are you can come in and make something good. The only rule is that every single student has to be in your film. You can make a five-minute or a forty-five-minute film, do whatever you want, but everybody has to be in it.' We had five years of really great film product. We were again hitch-hiking but we were hitch-hiking on the passion of film makers who wanted to pick up that opportunity and make something really good. So their ambition was engaged in the process, as opposed to them just coming in for hire and being let off the hook to make something crappy, because it was in an 'education environment'.[16]

Earlier in the year, Murray Lynch had worked with the second-year actors and the first- and second-year technical production students to direct an ambitious production of *The Tempest*. The play was cast blind to gender, although it retained the original gender language, with two Calibans and two Ariels. Murray drew on his broad knowledge of all production elements to empower the cast and production team, encouraging them to contribute their skills to his overall vision. The production was designed by Van Locker, a second-year technical production student, and it was his first-ever production design, relying heavily on visual projection, lighting and sound to create a variety of different performance environments. Murray Lynch put a great deal of trust in Van's unorthodox design and encouraged him in his endeavour. Rightly so: Shakespeare wrote *The Tempest* to appeal to a range of senses, with practical sound effects and music, and would have undoubtedly approved of Van's design concept. But then, Van knew that.

The Tempest provided the cast with an opportunity to exercise their comedic skills. This was very evident in the scenes between Stephano (James Insley), Caliban (Jerome Leota and Robbie Hunt) and Trinculo (Nikki MacDonnell). Nikki's inspired performance was engaging the moment she entered the stage to deliver Trinculo's 'man or fish' monologue.

This innate flair for comedy was also displayed by the first-year actors when they presented *Social Disorder*, a compilation of scenes from contemporary British comedies of manners, including *Table Manners*, which is part of Ayckbourne's *Norman Conquest* trilogy that, although fundamentally tragic, has a subtext of essential humour. Balancing tragic and comic elements is not always easy for student actors; if they play the comedy rather than revealing the authenticity of a character, the performance lacks truth. Julian Wilson, who played Norman, the main protagonist in *Table Manners,* clearly demonstrated his natural instinct to get to the heart of a character, revealing both humour and pathos.

Timothy Douglas returned from the US to direct the final production of the year, *The Three Sisters*, which marked the completion of training at Toi Whakaari for the first cohort of three-year acting students. It was also the second-year technical students' graduation production.

Finding a play to showcase the talent of each graduating student is a hard task, no less so than for the 1999 graduating acting year that included eight women. With only five female roles in *The Three Sisters*, the principle characters including the three sisters were doubled, allowing the cast to play various roles throughout the season. However, this adversely affected the amount of rehearsal time available for the cast, a difficulty acknowledged by Lynn Freeman in her review of *The Three Sisters*: 'Fortunately the true – and considerable – talents of the actors were more truly reflected in the series of productions they performed in various Wellington venues earlier in the year.'[17]

Similar casting problems had previously been solved with a double-bill: in 1993 *Bernarda Alba* and *Anarchist*, and in 1997 *Insurrection* and *Vinegar Tom*. This provided a degree of flexibility in casting a relatively large and diversely talented group of acting students, particularly in their final stage of training.

At the end of the year, a splendidly themed graduation ceremony took place in Te Whaea Theatre to farewell the first graduates of the Bachelor of Performing Arts (Acting) and Advanced Diploma in Technical Production. It was both joyous and celebratory. As befitting a performing arts school, the ceremony had a distinct theatrical flavor, with whanau and friends openly acknowledging the achievements of graduates with a mihi and haka, clearly expressing the spirit – the wairua – that pervades Toi Whakaari.

It was thirty years since the inauguration of the Drama School; and 1999 also marked the end of the millennium. With an impending Y2K bug predicted, the staff of Te Whaea diligently backed up their computers before leaving for a well-earned rest. Toi Whakaari's transition into a new century was best summed up by John Smythe in his review of *The Three Sisters*:

> They left me believing more than ever, the new millennium will belong to those with the creative vision, the motivation and the skills to make it happen – and those with the human decency and sense of justice to make it all worthwhile.[18]

Amen to that.

Seventeen

2000–2001

'Quite a weird piece really. You have to play it truthfully, but you also have to have a sense of taking the piss out of yourself. It's got some quite cheesy comedy.'

With Y2K pundits and the associated dire predictions now a bygone memory, and with hard-drives still intact, Toi Whakaari confronted the new millennium with a Futures Day to consider the direction of the school.

The forum was not expected to resolve any burning issues; it was more an opportunity for staff, the Boards, advisory panels and others associated with the school to share ideas. Nevertheless, some 'burning issues' were strongly debated. After discussing the value of expansion and the future identity of the school, attention turned to a proposed Master of Theatre Arts in Directing that was under development. It was generally felt that an increase in the number of trained directors would help to lift the standard of theatre in New Zealand, and the fact that the proposed directing qualification was an applied or taught degree, not an MA by written thesis, was commended by the forum.

Those at the forum with a particular interest in television and film discussed actor training for screen and stage. Given the increasing number of Toi Whakaari graduates now earning their living in this area, it was seen as a particularly worthwhile topic.

The idea of a graduate company at Toi Whakaari was also raised, although opinion on this was decidedly mixed. Some believed it would help to stimulate the growth of theatre in New Zealand, and the idea therefore had merit. Others felt the purpose and structure of a graduate company needed careful consideration, and questioned how the work produced by it would differ from that at Downstage or any other professional company. In fact, the school had no intention of setting up a 'rival' theatre company: the proposed graduate company was envisioned more as a place for performance research doing the things that most theatres couldn't do, and as a vehicle for staff and graduates of the school to seed work.

This led to a discussion of the purpose of productions at Toi Whakaari, and the need to balance training requirements against audience expectation. Unsurprisingly, few conclusions were reached as this topic was essentially a reiteration of the ongoing process-versus-product debate. The 'serious' nature of Toi Whakaari productions was also raised, with the question asked: *is comedy being neglected?*

A particularly vigorous discussion ensued over the drop in applications for courses at Toi Whakaari. Some participants at the Futures Day felt that the school needed to take a more aggressive approach in its marketing, as there were now around twenty drama (acting) courses available in New Zealand, many of them accepting younger students than Toi Whakaari. It was also felt that the current demands of the film industry for younger actors meant that careers, in certain areas, were over by the time actors were thirty. A proposal was therefore made to lower the age limit for entry into the school for the acting course from twenty to eighteen.

In fact, the more pressing recruitment difficulty lay with the technical production course. There was a relatively small pool of candidates to draw from, and Toi Whakaari had to compete with other institutions for students seeking technical production training, particularly UNITEC, which was now mopping up most of the technical production candidates in the Auckland region. The technical production course also lacked the 'allure' of the acting programme, although this was starting to be reversed through the efforts of the National Drama School in Havelock North, and the excellent foundation drama course run by Cameron Mattox at the Hagley Community College in Christchurch.

The new millennium was heralded by the acting students when they teamed up with students from the New Zealand School of Dance and community groups to perform in the Newtown Festival. They formed a cavalcade, with stilt-walking, dancing and percussion, which travelled from the Wellington Zoo through Newtown then on to Te Whaea.

Acting students at the 2000 Newtown Festival

At the start of 2000, Jude Gibson was appointed as an acting tutor, replacing Miranda Harcourt who had resigned at the end of 1999 to fulfil other commitments, although she planned to return during 2000 to take block courses and to direct the graduation production, *Into the Woods*.

Jude Gibson had trained at Theatre Corporate in the mid-seventies and had since worked as a freelance actor and director for Theatre Corporate, Court Theatre, Auckland Theatre Company, Watershed Theatre, Downstage and Circa, as well as acting in film and television. During that time she'd also taught movement and acting technique at Theatre Corporate, Auckland Performing Arts Centre and UNITEC.

When, a few months later, Murray Lynch left the school to take up an appointment as artistic director of Downstage, Miranda Harcourt was appointed as Toi Whakaari's new head of acting:

> At my interview I remember talking a lot about the idea of convergence, which would bring in the visual arts and contemporary music, bringing together a whole lot of experiences that drama students didn't experience. I believe that's what got me that position as head of acting, an attitude to opening their eyes to a number of other practices, not just our one.[1]

Because Miranda was due to give birth in October, she could only work at the school on an occasional basis for the remainder of the year. So Murray agreed to stay on until the middle of 2000 to supervise the third-year acting programme and to direct *Lovelock's Dream Run* in June.

Lyne Pringle had also resigned at the end of 1999, and Tom McCrory was appointed full-time as coordinator of the movement programme at the start of 2000. This provided him with a greater opportunity to advance the 'training' model that he'd been developing at the school:

> A form had emerged with a whole series of original exercises and a process and a journey. It's been part of a growth in the school towards integrative thinking; providing a model of where we want to go as a school. It also gives students a way to explore points of connection in their work. Training has gone through periods of feast and famine, but I think those things are true of any theatrical developments.[2]

Other new staff appointments included Rawiri Paratene, who was contracted on a full-time basis as the taha Māori coordinator and acting-for-camera tutor; and Sally Barratt-Boyes joined the school as a singing tutor, to complement the work of Laughton Pattrick.

The trustees of Toi Whakaari and the New Zealand School of Dance now met as a (rather large) joint Board, with Graeme Oldershaw as the new chair, and Board members Doug Brown, Ariane Burgess, Neville Carson, Roy Cowley, Christopher Goldsworthy, Geoff Husson, Helen McQueen, Jean Packman, Annie Ruth and Garry Trinder. Staff representatives on the Board were Christine Gunn and Bill Guest, and the student representative for Toi Whakaari was Nyree Andrews.

The Masters of Theatre Arts (MTA) in Directing was now in the final planning stage. When accredited, it would be the first and only full-time postgraduate course in

New Zealand exclusively for theatre directors. Toi Whakaari and Victoria University's School of English, Theatre and Film had agreed jointly to deliver the degree, providing a partnership that gave a unique combination of academic and professional credibility to the qualification, which could be taken full time over two years, or part time over three to four years.

Other specialist streams were being considered as part of a wider Masters of Theatre Arts programme, including scriptwriting and critical dramaturgy. These could possibly be taught in partnership with the creative writing programme and English at Victoria University. And in 1998, Victoria's School of Architecture and Design had declared an interest in participating in the MTA programme: it was in the process of developing a Bachelor of Design, Performing and Interactive Arts and it was thought this could possibly feed into or become part of the MTA.

Following discussion between Toi Whakaari and Victoria University in 1999, draft plans for the MTA contained options for both directing and design courses. Because of the essential synergy across the two disciplines, it seemed logical to deliver a design strand alongside the directing programme. At that time, there were no other theatre/performance design programmes in New Zealand to which the MTA directing students could relate, either at undergraduate or postgraduate level.

It was also clear that the area of greatest and more immediate need, with the highest student demand, was the Masters of Theatre Arts in Directing. This would provide an extension to the existing undergraduate programme in theatre studies at Victoria, as well as to similar programmes at other universities. Because the task of developing design and directing programmes in tandem would be a much bigger undertaking, it was agreed that additional streams of the Masters programme could be introduced later, when and if their justification was established.

In fact, the idea of a postgraduate performance design qualification in New Zealand posed a number of as-yet unresolved philosophical questions concerning its purpose and scope. Postgraduate theatre design at most overseas universities and vocational training institutions contained a synthesis of practical design and academic studies, often linked to study and research in other disciplines such as architecture, engineering and archaeology. Those institutions generally offer both undergraduate *and* postgraduate theatre design courses, with admission into the latter requiring an undergraduate qualification in design, fine arts or a related subject, although not always theatre design.

This brought into question the concept of a postgraduate performance design qualification in New Zealand before a similar course at undergraduate level had been established. In some respects, it would be 'putting the cart before the horse'. In any event, the decision to defer the MTA design stream turned out to be providential.

Although Toi Whakaari had run a sort of de facto performance design course for many years via the technical production programme, in which students were designing most of the school's productions, some areas such as lighting and sound design were well supported within the curriculum while others were not. Set and costume design modules were included as components of a broader holistic programme and to provide a basic understanding of design principles and process, not to give comprehensive set and costume design training. That was simply not possible within a two-year technical production programme, even with an advanced diploma year that would allow additional design training. Undeniably, the technical production students put forward some outstanding designs, but as an ongoing strategy it was unsustainable.

By 2000 it was clear that the two-year technical production course needed to be restructured, and one idea being considered was the provision of additional parallel courses, with performance design and technology as a possible option.

In addition to the Masters in Directing, now in the pipe-line, Toi Whakaari had a three-year acting programme, an Advanced Diploma in Technical Production and a two-year Diploma in Technical Production. There were obvious advantages to be gained by adopting a more unified and collaborative learning culture within the school, not least of all because it would help promote a wider vision of what could be achieved by the performing arts in New Zealand. Yet a vital ingredient was missing: a comprehensive and broadly-based performance design programme. This was a remarkable omission given the growing significance of the designer as visual director or prime collaborator with the production process, the advantages of which had been clearly highlighted in the design-oriented work of most European theatre companies that took part in the recent Festival of the Arts.

My particular interest in the pathway between undergraduate and postgraduate design programmes had been advanced the year before when I was invited by a number of key performing arts institutions in the United States to observe their Masters programmes in performance design. So, early in 2000 I set off to visit programmes at Yale and in Washington, Texas, Illinois, Indiana and Pittsburgh. I also visited CalArts, which is essentially a conservatorium with an academic framework and purpose in some ways comparable to Toi Whakaari.

Most of the major drama schools in the USA are attached to universities, where students study acting, stage design, theatre technology and management as a major, along with non-theatre electives. Undergraduate degree programmes are usually for four years, although as a general rule theatre training is less intensive at a university than it is in a conservatorium school. Production activity is not always integrated into the main curriculum; rehearsals are often scheduled in the evening, sometimes with an associated theatre company. Students in the undergraduate theatre design programmes are rarely given a full-scale production to design; they mostly work as assistants to postgraduate design students. Graduate schools also rely heavily on apprenticeships and internships with regional theatres to provide students with an essential link to the professional world.

Theatre students in the USA seriously contemplating a professional career complete both an undergraduate and a postgraduate degree, requiring six or seven years of study at one or more universities. In terms of professional employment, the ranking of a postgraduate programme is paramount: there is stiff competition to gain admission into the more prestigious graduate design programmes, particularly Carnegie-Mellon and Yale.

Many of the theatre design programmes I visited were excellent, yet there seemed to be a degree of conservatism or orthodoxy about the students' work. This is understandable when you consider that most postgraduate students in the USA are preparing to work in the commercial theatre or film sectors.

It came as something of a surprise to discover that many design students felt that production design should be subservient to the directorial concept. On my visit to Yale I was able to meet with the adjunct professor of theatre design, Ming Cho Lee, who invited me to observe one of his regular tutorials. I was told it was not uncommon for him to travel from Europe to lead these sessions. Each student was given thirty minutes to present his or her design, which included a detailed 1:100 scale model. Ming Cho Lee then assiduously critiqued each design, removing all non-essential items from the model and leaving only the very essence of the design concept. On several occasions, all that remained was a bare stage or a single item of scenery or furniture.

I later met Ming Cho Lee to discuss my as-yet-embryonic thoughts on a theatre design course for Toi Whakaari. He immediately informed me that I'd probably been 'wasting my time' looking at the American model and recommended instead the greater value in considering theatre practice of Korea or Japan, which he felt were more 'culturally aligned' to the New Zealand national ethos. He was, of course, quite right.

In addition to its postgraduate theatre design course, Yale Theatre School has two other highly prestigious programmes: theatre management and design technology. The latter was led by Professor Bronislaw Sammler, a foremost authority on design technology and stage mechanics. Students in his programme worked closely with the theatre design students, collaborating on projects to develop common design solutions: it was very exciting. I sat in on several classes, and it came as no surprise to learn that many design technology students at Yale had backgrounds in non-theatre areas, such as mechanical engineering, aero-space technology and medicine.

In fact, graduate theatre design schools in the USA generally prefer to take students with a broad educational background rather than those from undergraduate theatre design programmes. Yale is no exception, as Ming Cho Lee affirmed:

> The student who is interested in theatre should take as many 'intro' courses as possible: history, political science, economics, psychology and sociology, and literature, history of music or music appreciation. This aside from the requirements of mathematics or natural sciences should occupy a student fairly heavily for at least two and a half years.[3]

Susan Tsu, head of Graduate Design and Technology at the University of Texas at Austin, had a similar view: 'Designing is about the human experience, living in the world and being a thinking person who delves into all the complexities of what it is to be human.'[4]

The splendidly endowed theatre department at the University of Texas is ranked amongst the top eight in the USA, with a faculty of forty to supervise the work of 350 undergraduate majors and a hundred graduate students. I was enormously impressed by its super-sized lighting laboratory, equipped with an enviable array of programmable lighting units, all freely donated by Texas Instruments.

My next visit was to the University of the Incarnate Word in San Antonio, where I caught up with Robin Payne and Tolis Papazoglou who were teaching there. Because San Antonio is close to the Mexican border, the majority of students at Incarnate Word are Latino, giving the institution a bicultural feel similar to that at Toi Whakaari. On my arrival I was welcomed with what can best be described as a Spanish pōwhiri: I sensed the strong influence of Robin and Tolis.

Before leaving the USA I met up with Dorita Hannah in New York, where she was teaching and studying for her PhD at Tisch University. Before taking leave from her position as senior lecturer at Victoria University School of Architecture and Design, she had been developing an initial proposal for a performing and interactive arts design degree. It had soon become clear that there was potentially a lot to be gained if our two institutions could jointly develop and then deliver a performing arts design qualification. Anyway, it was certainly worth investigating, as it was clearly nonsensical for Toi Whakaari and Victoria to offer competing design degrees. Dorita had no immediate plans to return to New Zealand but we agreed to continue our discussions via email.

The USA visit confirmed my belief that if Toi Whakaari were to introduce a design programme, it had to be tailored to the unique circumstances of New Zealand. I was equally convinced that performance design students should learn their craft alongside students from other theatre and design disciplines, certainly within a theatre training school and possibly in partnership with a university school of design. A jointly delivered programme would not only develop practical performance design skills, it would also foster research and provide the necessary academic rigour. In addition, it would allow greater opportunity for performance design students to work with students from other visual and creative arts disciplines.

This model exists in many theatre design courses in the UK, particularly those attached to fine arts programmes at schools of design, such as Wimbledon College of Art, Nottingham Trent University and St Martin's College of Fine Arts. Some are not directly attached to drama schools (although St Martin's is now affiliated with the Drama Centre in London), and students in those theatre design programmes have little or no regular contact with students from other theatre disciplines.

New Zealand was now at a point where it needed to revitalise and re-establish its own viable theatre industry. A much more inclusive approach to theatre training was therefore needed, one that would empower all practitioners to initiate work in order to achieve a sustained and integrated creative process. To achieve this, the design curriculum needed to balance practical training with academic study, and any pressure on the theatre design programme to fully service production activity at Toi Whakaari had to be skilfully managed.

A three-year degree design programme at Toi Whakaari would mean an additional influx of students, which would inevitably stretch the physical and staff resources of the school – and Te Whaea. Moreover, the successful delivery of a top-quality theatre design course relied on the availability of teaching staff and on their vision and expertise, in particular that of the person leading the programme. But at this stage, there was no-one fulfilling this role. Ideally, the head of design would participate in the development of the new design programme to determine its philosophy and structure, but it seemed unlikely that an appointment would be made until *after* the course curriculum had been written and accredited. This would leave little opportunity for that person to influence or shape the initial programme.

On my return from the USA, I was launched into *The Mysteries*, a grand performance project based on adaptations of various English Mystery Cycles, involving the first- and second-year actors and technical production students. I worked on *The Mysteries* with three other directors: Annie Ruth, Larry Rew and Vanessa Byrnes. The production had twelve scenes performed on seven different stages throughout Te Whaea, a piece of promenade theatre with the cast and audience travelling through a range of performance venues.

Textile design students from the Massey School of Fine Arts and Design collaborated in *The Mysteries*, creating fabrics for the costumes designed by Alice Tinning, an advanced diploma student. Two other advanced diploma students, Pook Berrigan and Stacey Merrifield, worked on the production as designers. Student composers from Victoria University School of Music contributed as well, playing music throughout much of the performance.

The Mysteries was the largest work the school had mounted and produced. It was a testament to the collaborative ability and the shared vision of a large team of directors, actors, designers, technicians, musicians and puppeteers who worked in harmony to overcome the logistical challenge of presenting a highly theatrical work to a mobile audience in multiple venues. The entire cycle took around four hours, though the audience seemed unfazed by this, enjoying instead the close proximity of the performance and the opportunity to move through a variety of different locations.

After *The Mysteries*, two other plays went into production to celebrate the thirtieth anniversary of the New Zealand Drama School, both written by graduates of the

The Mysteries, 2000. Top: Julian Wilson. (L) Mark Ruka, (R) Jarod Rawiri

school: David Geary's *Lovelock's Dream Run*, directed by Murray Lynch; and *Ophelia Thinks Harder* by Jean Betts, directed by Annie Ruth. Jean Betts graduated from the Arts Council Drama School in 1970 and David Geary from the New Zealand Drama School in 1987. The plays were performed by second-year acting actors with a second-year technical/design crew. Following its season at Te Whaea Theatre, both plays toured to Auckland.

As part of its broader approach to actor training, the acting department increased its efforts to foster a stronger sense of independence in the students, giving rise to a pattern of exploratory work. In addition to industry secondments and self-devised solos, third-year students embarked on a series of laboratory projects and cooperatives. *He Kore Te Wiwia/A Space Without Boundaries/Avanoa Leai Se Mea O Iai* blended Polynesian and European cultures. The production, directed by Helen Todd and Nina Nawalowalo, was performed at BATS with three actor/dancers. Two of the cast were Samoan: Anapelo Palataivao and Jerome Leota; the third, Kayte Ferguson, was Māori (Tainui). Design, lighting and music were major performance elements in *He Kore Te Wiwia.* To support this, Helen Todd and Nyree Andrews, a second-year lighting designer, led the cast in a laboratory project to discover how light could inspire the work and define the actors' movement within the performance space. This effective collaboration was described in the programme notes:

> The process we adopted demanded a redefinition of roles and a high degree of trust and support. By placing equal value on one another's experiences and contributions we view each artist working on the project as a collaborator; it is vital that each person feels able to contribute freely to the creation of the work.[5]

Jennifer Shennan, in her review of *He Kore Te Wiwia,* responded positively to the visual imagery:

> I could write for days about the layers of meaning woven into this intriguing work, but I might as well try to describe the fragrance of a frangipani flower, the fury of a tropical storm or the burnished beauty of a 180 degree latitude sunset. Better you just go along to the show.[6]

A second cooperative, *Faultline*, based on physical theatre principals, was performed at Victoria University's Studio 77. The production had a cast of four: Simon Vincent, Rosella Hart, Olivia Robinson and Nikki MacDonnell, directed by Tom McCrory:

> It was a group of students that I'd done a block of physical theatre with and they wanted to extend the experience. They'd enjoyed the devising process of making a piece of physical theatre and they approached me to make something with them to take the work further into production. I don't go for separate definitions between physical and naturalistic theatre; it was a combination. Some parts were expressed physically, but it had a very strong naturalistic quite filmic mix.
>
> Students from different disciplines in the school worked on the production. This is part of what I was attempting through training; to get people to think in a more company-based model. That's the way I think theatre advances, through extended periods of creative collaboration, between different disciplines. It's a way in which things can be thrashed out – worked out and new models of working forged.[7]

The set/costume and audio-visual designers for *Faultline* were Alice Tinning and Stacey Merrifield, both advanced diploma students. Music for the production was composed by Peter Edge, a second-year technical production student: he made a significant contribution to the work and 'crafted an evocative soundscape confirming him as one of the most exciting local composers of live theatre'.[8] Tom McCrory's partner Nina Nawalowalo also worked on *Faultline* – as a 'Magic Advisor'.

Later in the year, Tom directed *Whatu/Weave*, a joint project between Toi Whakaari and Takitimu Performing Arts School. This was a 'bicultural production' in the sense that it explored similarities between Māori and Celtic cultures, rather than what divided them:

> At the time there was a lot of heat around biculturalism. I was a relatively recent arrival in New Zealand, and a bit naive about everything. But I kept meeting these incredible cocktails of human genetics that made me see that the [bicultural story] is not all about conflict. My own family, me and my wife are bicultural, in a sense that she's Fijian and our kids are these genetic cocktails. So I got very interested, particularly the relationship between the Irish and the Scots, and Māori: the whole thing of the Land Wars when Highlanders deserted from their regiments and went and fought for Māori. They had recently been cleared off their own lands; the Highland Clearances were happening at the same time as the Treaty of Waitangi was being signed. Having Irish and Scots ancestry, I felt an affinity with many things here: politically, socially and culturally.
>
> I was interested in looking for celebration of likeness, rather than this constant picking of a scab – of a wound. There's a heartbeat here, practically everybody in the Toi Whakaari cast of *Whatu/Weave* had some Scots or Irish ancestry and I was sick of hearing Pākehā students bemoaning the fact that, unlike the Māori, they had no 'culture'. When in fact they've been on a bloody hard journey to find out who they are, they have a name that comes from another place and therefore they have a connection to a culture.[9]

The production was created from scratch through a process of devised choreography incorporating live music and songs from both cultures. This was strikingly demonstrated by a male chorus performing the haka against the swirl of the bagpipes. Rehearsals for *Whatuweave* were completed at Takitimu in Hastings, where the production opened before returning to Wellington for a season at Te Whaea Theatre.

One of my long-standing ambitions was to direct Alan Ayckbourn's *Mr Whatnot*. First performed in the 1960s, it remains one of Ayckbourn's lesser known and seldom produced farces. There is good reason for this: it is technically complex and the narrative is precisely choreographed to an elaborate soundscape and governed by detailed stage directions. When *Mr Whatnot* was first produced, only reel-to-reel tape recorders were available on which to play back the complex sound track, and the operational difficulties were considerable. Recent advances in computer and sound technology made the realisation of the work much more possible, but the equipment we had in 2000 was still relatively primitive when compared with today's.

Although it seemed unlikely that *Mr Whatnot* would ever be considered as a mainstream production at Toi Whakaari (or indeed anywhere in New Zealand), it was an ideal laboratory project, the tightly scripted sound-score demanding precise timing from the both cast and crew.

Mr Whatnot, 2000. Nikky MacDonnell and Simon Vincent

The play is a blatant attack on the British aristocracy and its obsession with order and social distinction. Mint (Mr Whatnot), a mute piano-tuner, sits outside that social circle: he is besotted with Amanda Slingsby-Craddock, an unrequited love he is determined to pursue. Because Mint is mute and appears in virtually every scene, the actor playing the part needs well-developed physical and mime skills. When I saw Nikki MacDonnell perform Trinculo in *The Tempest* in her second year, I'd been impressed by the Chaplinesque quality of her work, and it was this performance that finally convinced me to take on *Mr Whatnot*. Nikki had also trained as a dancer, and when I suggested the part to her, she not only accepted the challenge but also offered to direct some of the precise choreography needed for the production. The remainder of the cast then magically fell into place.

Peter Edge and Hadley Thomson accepted the formidable task of sound design and operation. And Sefton Bates created the exacting lighting design, supported by Helen Todd as his mentor. Stacey Merrifield designed the set and costumes.

Mr Whatnot was under development right through to the final performance. Many of the ideas tested in rehearsal were discarded whereas other scenes were refined in performance. The tennis match was totally mimed and synchronised to sound effects, demanding meticulous timing between cast and crew. Above all, this 'risky' venture was a demonstration of the students' willingness, courage and determination to explore complex technical challenges – a level of collaboration that is now commonplace at Toi Whakaari.

With only a brief end-of-term break in October, the third-year actors and second-year techs embarked on a short film, *The Sweet Singers*. It was similar in process to the previous year's film, *The Big Game*, directed by Ian Mune with cinematographer Waka Attewell. They both returned to work on *The Sweet Singers* with writer Stuart McKenzie and producer Di Oliver.

A much more ambitious film project was proposed for the following year. Maurice Murphy, an Australian film maker/director/writer/auteur visited the school in October to work with the second-year actors in preparation for a full-length feature to be shot with a professional crew in 2001. The film, a science fiction/fantasy set in a futuristic world where the main heroes are actors, had no title as yet, though it did have an intriguing draft synopsis: 'It's a world where the main heroes are actor-soldiers, who go out and do the most heroic things. They are human beings, not troglodytes or people out of *Star Trek*.'[10]

More staff changes occurred towards the end of 2000. Charles Norwood replaced Eloise Hinkley as project coordinator for Toi Whakaari and marketing coordinator for Te Whaea. And KC Kelly returned to coordinate the combat metaphor programme with the first-year acting students. The school also got a much-needed teaching and resource technician, a newly created position that required someone with wide-ranging responsibilities including a good understanding of audio-visual technology. More importantly, it needed a person who could anticipate and be sympathetic to the disparate learning needs of the students (and staff) confronted by fast-changing technology. The school was extremely fortunate when it chose Tony Toufexis to fulfil this role. He'd previously worked as an audio-visual technician at Wellington Festival and Convention Centre and for Multi-Media; it was this combination of technical expertise coupled with his strong creative ability that enabled Tony to manage this multifarious role to perfection: an absolute gem.

Another gem to join Te Whaea staff in 2000 was Priscilla (Cilla) Gough. She was initially appointed as the student administrator for Toi Whakaari and the New Zealand School of Dance, but when the job of reporting to government and working as an administrator for both schools became too big for one person, the position was split into three: office manager, dance administrator and drama administrator:

> I was offered dance administrator or office manager. Because I loved the balance between the two schools and didn't want to work for one school alone, I opted for the office manager position. This entailed 'bits and pieces' of the reporting to government on student matters. Also venue hireage and security, and cleaning; by then we'd gone into commercial cleaning companies. When I started we had an accountant for just four half-days a week, so I also did some of the invoicing.[11]

◀ Tony Toufexis

▶ Priscilla Gough

Both photographs by Philip Merry

Into the Woods, rehearsals. Left: Rosella Hart with puppet; Middle: Miranda Harcourt and Hadley Thomson (SM); Right: Olivier Robinson-Falconer, Kayte Ferguson, Heather O'Carroll.

The Master of Theatre Arts in Directing was finally approved by NZQA in October. This was a groundbreaking achievement, the first time in New Zealand that a university had joined forces with a private training institution, as equal partners, to offer a jointly taught Masters programme. The first year of the MTA was scheduled to commence in 2001, with four theoretical and practical papers delivered by the Department of Theatre and Film at Victoria University. The second year was based on a series of practical assignments that would be delivered by Toi Whakaari from 2002. NZQA's approval for the qualification was contingent on Toi Whakaari employing a full-time supervisor for this second year of the course.

The Master of Theatre Arts in Design, on the other hand, was indefinitely deferred and Toi Whakaari began instead to focus on an undergraduate design degree. With this in mind, revisions were made to the technical production course to provide a modified programme, offering a range of electives in the second year and greater depth in core subjects.

In the final term of 2000, rehearsals began for the graduation production, Stephen Sondheim's musical *Into the Woods*, directed by Miranda Harcourt with Mark Lipman as musical director. With its mixture of naturalism, burlesque, puppetry, music hall and illusion, the production drew upon the wide range of skills the students had acquired during the previous two to three years. It was big, with a cast and crew of nearly fifty, including four designers: Sefton Bates (sound design), Natasha James (lighting design), Miranda Luxford (costume design) and Alice Tinning who designed a colourful 'story book' set within a Victorian music-hall proscenium. A band provided the music for the production, led by musical director/pianist Mark Lipman. He had only recently arrived from New York and this was his first time working with students at Toi Whakaari. He was suitably impressed:

> I treated the situation as if I were doing a professional show based on my experience on Broadway and in New Zealand professional theatre. I expected discipline and professionalism from everyone involved. I ran a tight ship and the students responded with great energy and enthusiasm. They were a wonderful class to work with and I felt a connection with each and every one of them and the time I spent on the show.[12]

The school year finished in style, with a bumper graduation ceremony for twenty-four graduates across three courses. Stephen Blackburn took charge of the substantial production/design elements for the ceremony that, in addition to Te Whaea Theatre, included a highly themed Plaza and a pre-ceremony chill-out space for those graduating.

Although Toi Whakaari celebrated its many accomplishments in 2000, there was growing anxiety over the school's financial situation. A forecasted income of $300,000 from sponsorship/fundraising for loan retirement had been optimistic, and the cash flow projections for Te Whaea revealed a shortfall in expected revenue.

Toi Whakaari and the New Zealand School of Dance had secured a Smokefree sponsorship, providing each school with around $25,000 towards debt retirement. In exchange, Te Whaea became a smoke-free zone. Thereafter, staff and students wishing to 'have a smoke' were consigned to a rear entrance of the building, out of sight – but not beyond the reach of the smoke police.

Club 100 donations also provided a similar amount of financial support to the two schools, although this came with no strings attached.

Despite these welcome contributions, Toi Whakaari struggled to repay its share of the bank loan, and was able to do so only by severely depleting its financial reserves or by running a deficit budget. To make matters worse, the Ministry of Education informed the school that there would be no increase in its funding in 2001.

Although there were more full-time staff and the school needed to invest in equipment to meet the requirements of new courses, Toi Whakaari's funding base had remained static since 1998. The current budget severely limited any further capital expenditure, increase in staff levels and purchase of essential teaching equipment. The building itself was still a work in progress, with extra funding needed to resurface floors, line walls and paint studios. Some cost-savings had been achieved by appointing joint operational staff, and both schools now shared a business manager, office manager, communications coordinator, development coordinator, receptionist and library staff.

The cash-flow difficulty was not helped by a shortfall in income from Mahon Amusements for their rental of space. Expensive litigation was underway to recover some of the outstanding debt, but by September 1999 the PMT had accrued legal costs of $14,000 without any satisfactory conclusion.

When the lease on the Wellington Show Building was transferred from the Show Association to the PMT in 1997, the peppercorn rent of 10 cents a year previously paid by the Show Association to Wellington City Council was increased to $87,000 per annum. This was considered to be a reasonable market rental. At the same time, the Council withdrew from its obligation to subsidise the Show Association to the tune of $100,000 a year, which the Show Association used to pay off the interest on a debt of nearly $2 million they'd accrued because of the 1990 Sesqui Trust failure.

So, from a position of having to pay $100,000 a year to the Wellington Show Association, the City Council had an agreement from the PMT to upgrade the building to the tune of $1.65 million over five years, in addition to the $5-million-worth of improvements the schools had already made to the building. On top of that, the City Council received rental income of $87,000 a year from the schools for Te Whaea, which was set to increase to $150,000 after five years.

The new chair of the Premises Management Trust was Bernie Harris, an astute business man with a background in senior management in Shell, Rank Xerox and Price Waterhouse. Bernie is a tenacious negotiator: some might say a terrier. As soon as he took up his appointment with the PMT, he began to renegotiate the lease arrangements for Te Whaea with the City Council. He presented a formula that recognised the capital improvements made on the building by the schools, improvements that the Council would inherit at the termination of the lease. And, by drawing its attention to the 'inequitable rent' paid by the two schools, he put forward a very compelling argument that the Council found hard to ignore.

In February 2001, the Wellington City Council agreed to give Te Whaea an immediate payment of $130,000 with similar payments over the next four years. In effect, this would be used to purchase some of the improvements that the PMT had made to the building since taking over the lease. It was a form of rent relief for the duration of the bank loan, with no actual cash changing hands. This was a major victory for the PMT, in particular Bernie Harris. Wellington City Council graciously acknowledged that it was also a 'good deal' all round:

> If [the schools] had not moved into the building, it would have been a real burden on ratepayers. We wind up with an asset that was splendidly restored and renovated, and we are buying from them some of the work that we should have really paid for. It is quite right that the council works with [the schools] to ensure they have a long-term viability.[13]

But this was not the end of the financial woes for the two schools; they still needed an additional $300,000 a year if they were to survive. In March 2001 their financial predicament was made very clear in an article in the *Sunday Times* under the dramatic heading, 'Performance Schools Near Final Act': 'the New Zealand Schools of Dance and Drama could close in less than two years due to the worsening financial situation, and would "hit the skids" in just over a year'.

Annie Ruth came out fighting, declaring Toi Whakaari's plight in no uncertain terms:

> [Te Whaea] is a world-class space and these two schools are like national treasures. We are utterly fiscally responsible; there is no fat whatsoever in our budget, we can't fix the building, there are no extras. Local film companies have helped us out but we can't keep going along by grace and favour. We've reached the point where we can't just pull any more miracles out of the hat.[14]

And George Webby put forward an opinion that many thought but few feared to say:

> Both Schools are so well established and turning out superbly skilled graduates that it would be an absolute calamity if they went under now. But maybe the cost of the building was too much in the first place, and the [Drama] School has bitten off more than it could chew.[15]

In 2000, the Prime Minister and Arts and Culture Minister Helen Clark stunned the arts community with an arts recovery package of $80 million. This was the biggest one-off financial boost to the arts in New Zealand. Sadly, none of the cash found its way to Te Whaea. This was particularly ironic, as many performing arts organisations benefiting from the 'arts recovery' windfall relied on Toi Whakaari and the New Zealand School of Dance to train their future performers and technicians.

The pōwhiri at the start of 2001 welcomed a new intake of eighteen acting and seven technical production students, including Toby Papazoglou, the first (but not the last) of Robin Payne and Tolis Papazoglou's children to study at Toi Whakaari. The inaugural intake of MTA directing students was also welcomed into the school. They were Jacqueline Coats, James Hadley, Rachel More, James Sutherland and Madeline McNamara, a part-time MTA student. Although they were based at Victoria University for most of their first year, they would spend some time at Toi Whakaari working on their practical papers.

To provide the MTA students with a home base and a performance venue, the school rented additional space in the Te Whaea basement from the Premises Management Trust. The venue required upgrading with acoustic isolation and lighting bars, and Tolis Papazoglou was engaged as a consultant and project manager to supervise the work.

The MTA programme now had its own Board of Studies, chaired by David Carnegie from the Department of Theatre and Film at Victoria University. The other members were John Downie and David O'Donnell from Theatre and Film, with Annie Ruth and me representing Toi Whakaari, and Murray Lynch as the industry representative. The Board of Studies later included first- and second-year MTA student representatives.

There were many staff changes in 2001, including the departure of Ruth Graham, who was leaving the school after twenty-one years. She and her partner Peter had bought a property in the Wairarapa with the intention of growing olives and harvesting them for oil.[16]

Since establishing the New Zealand Drama School library in 1980, Ruth had diligently built and managed the collection, rescuing it from disaster on at least three occasions to finally establish the Nola Millar Library at Te Whaea. Amongst her many accomplishments was the *Friends Newsletter*, which she wrote and distributed three or four times a year for more or less the entire time she was at the school. It remains one of few reliable records of Drama School activity during that time. For that, the author of this book is eternally grateful. Ruth's personal philosophy for the library had been entirely governed by the learning journey of the students:

> The library was there to support the curriculum and my job was to create an environment for that, not just about coming in to borrow a book, but a space within the school that gave the students and staff something different than what they experienced elsewhere: peace and quiet if nothing else.[17]

▶ Ruth Graham and Dee O'Connor, 2008

When Dee O'Connor took over as library manager, she summarised Ruth's contribution to the school:

> Ruth Graham's management style has been described by one frequent borrower as 'exquisite' – a word that also describes the quality of resources she has created. She has provided a constant, calm (but not soft) centre in all the premises the library has inhabited, and staff and students over the last two decades have benefited from her unfailing support and counselling.[18]

Staff arrivals included Karl Kite Rangi (1995 graduate) and Waimihi Hotere (1997 graduate), who were appointed jointly to the taha Māori position for the remainder of 2001. Virginia Earle joined Dee O'Connor in the Nola Millar Library as librarian. Before coming to Te Whaea, Virginia had worked at the National Library and the Open Polytechnic as a cataloguer and education librarian.

Jean Packman now chaired the joint Board for Toi Whakaari and the New Zealand School of Dance, as Graeme Oldershaw's term of office had come to an end, although he remained as a member of the Board. Simone Lourie joined the Board as the Toi Whakaari staff representative and Aaron Alexander was the new student representative.

2001 heralded a new collaborative venture between Toi Whakaari and the New Zealand School of Dance in the form of a joint performance project, *Who Needs a Vespa*. This was not the first joint project undertaken by the two schools, as the contemporary dance and technical production courses had previously collaborated on numerous lighting and choreographic workshops. But *Who Needs a Vespa* was the first public performance project to involve both second-year acting and technical production students from Toi Whakaari, and final-year contemporary dancers from the New Zealand School of Dance.

Who Needs a Vespa was directed by Jude Gibson and choreographed by Wendy Wallace. Since joining the New Zealand School of Dance as head of contemporary dance in 1999, Wendy had advocated a closer alliance between the contemporary dance and drama students. Although the disciplines of the two schools are in many ways different, the creative and devising process of an actor and choreographer are not dissimilar. Wendy was therefore keen to bring the two schools together and to collaborate on performance projects.

Vespa was a bold step for both schools, requiring an exchange of skills, with dancers acting and actors dancing. For many, it was a totally new experience: literally, a leap into the unknown. The devised production was loosely based on the work of film maker Federico Fellini, with students drawing upon themes and images from his films for inspiration. They then gathered their collective responses and workshopped them to come up with an extraordinary Fellini-esque theatrical journey. Peter Edge returned to the school to compose the music:

> Seeing Fellini's *Casanova* and hearing Nino Rota's marvellous score, I knew I'd have a lot to live up to. *Vespa* has seen the fulfilment of several 'Hey! Wouldn't it be great if I could...' ideas that have been buzzing around in my head for a while.[19]

Some of the cast, including Amy Tarleton, found the business of learning to dance alongside dance students to be a challenging experience:

> The first time I heard the music I thought 'that's too fast. There's no way I could dance to that'. But the dance students were really cool … a lot of what we were doing was movement-based, but I wouldn't necessarily call it dance. I thought, 'If it all turns to custard, the drama students can at least act as if they know how to dance'. Fellini's films are about image rather than story. That's the approach we took for the show.[20]

The students successfully merged their dance and drama skills to create a very stylish work, with sexy choreography full of symbolic imagery. They also demonstrated a unity of purpose that connected all the performers, and this opened up possibilities for future collaborations between the two schools.

Throughout 2000, Dorita Hannah and I continued to discuss the possibility of a performance design programme. During that time, discussions also took place between Toi Whakaari and Massey University School of Design and Fine Arts, which was showing a strong interest in developing closer ties with Toi Whakaari, as it was considering the possibility of a costume design course as part of its textile and fashion design programme. Victoria University was also demonstrating an interest in investigating a possible liaison with Toi Whakaari on a design degree, but seemed to be leaning more towards performance studies rather than theatre design practice.

An 'extraordinary meeting' of the Toi Whakaari Board of Studies was convened in March, specifically to discuss the proposed design degree. Members agreed in principal that the school should pursue the undergraduate design qualification with both Massey and Victoria University, and instructed me to write a draft proposal to represent Toi Whakaari's point of view in relation to the degree. Interestingly, the Board of Studies also recommended that Toi Whakaari and Victoria 'push ahead' with planning for a Masters in Theatre Design, which would then be considered in parallel with the proposed Bachelor of Performing Arts Design.

As requested, I wrote a background paper in support of the undergraduate design degree, which included a draft programme based on a four-year Bachelor of Performance Design. This assumed a joint partnership between Toi Whakaari and a (as yet unspecified) university school of design, with the option of taking an initial intake of twelve students in 2003. The paper emphasised the importance of appointing a head of design *before* proceeding too far with the development of the qualification, to enable that person to shape the philosophy, structure and objectives of the degree. Inevitably, the introduction of a design degree would bring about major changes to the traditional structure of the school, and I felt it was important to flag this:

> If the proposed Performance Design student numbers are realised, the student population of Toi Whakaari will increase by 50% by 2006. More significantly the combined number of students in the design and technical production programmes will equal the number of students enrolled in the acting programme. I anticipate there will be renewed pressure to form two independent divisions within Toi Whakaari, if the generic 'Drama School' title ceases to precisely describe the extent of all activities undertaken by the School.[21]

Toi Whakaari was now faced with a tough decision: two potential partners were interested in forming a relationship with the school to deliver a joint performing arts design degree, each with different but equally valid strengths. Although design and directing courses could be jointly taught by Toi Whakaari and Victoria, enhancing the collaboration between the two disciplines, Massey's School of Design offered a range of teaching programmes that were more closely aligned with the craft-based performance design programme Toi Whakaari had in mind.

There were clearly distinct advantages in a partnership with either university. However, the key question for Toi Whakaari was: which of the two universities would provide a *truly* equal partnership? The person appointed by the partner university to lead the design programme on its behalf was also an important factor to be considered. S/he would have to have a broad working knowledge of the performing arts, and an awareness of the complex cultural and industry needs relating to the development of theatre and associated arts in New Zealand.

Victoria's involvement in the development and delivery of the joint Master of Theatre Arts in Directing had demonstrated the university's commitment towards an equal partnership with Toi Whakaari, and it therefore seemed sensible for Toi Whakaari to discuss the possibility of a joint design degree with Victoria. In June the head of Victoria's School of Design met with Annie Ruth, together with staff from both schools, for a preliminary discussion. Out of that meeting came a draft curriculum framework for a jointly delivered performance arts design programme.

The matter was resolved in July, when Dorita Hannah accepted an associate professorship at Massey School of Design. Not only was she an established and highly regarded theatre and stage designer, with the right academic background, vision and rigour needed to support the type of innovative design programme Toi Whakaari had in mind; her approach to stage design was also unequivocal. She saw the role of designer as an initiator and prime collaborator in the directorial process, and this was also Toi Whakaari's view.

The school's draft proposal for a design degree focused mainly on set, costume and lighting design; and Dorita Hannah recommended a broader curriculum to include exhibition, film, video, multi-media and events design. This made sense, given the real possibility of a partnership between Toi Whakaari and a design school.

Another factor that swayed Toi Whakaari towards Massey was the close proximity of its campus to Te Whaea. Given the likely interaction of the two institutions, this was an important consideration. There was also a strong historical connection: Massey's Wellington campus had previously been the home of Wellington Polytechnic, which had been closely associated with the New Zealand Drama School from 1974 until the early nineties. And there was the important matter of Toi Whakaari's autonomy, which arguably would be better served by having a diversified partnership with both Victoria and Massey.

In August, Dorita Hannah returned to Wellington from New York to attend a series of meetings between Toi Whakaari and Massey College of Design Fine Arts and Music. Discussions were centred on the various options for a jointly delivered design degree, including possible interactions with other departments within the School of Design. It was a very fruitful exchange that resulted in a draft agreement being reached by the two institutions to develop and deliver a Bachelor of Performance Design, jointly taught and awarded by *both* Toi Whakaari and Massey University: in other words, an *equal* partnership. It was agreed that the design degree would have a framework similar to Massey's four-year Bachelor of Design, and a draft memorandum of agreement was drawn up, defining responsibility for delivering the various components of the programme, and the provision of facilities and resources.

The proposed start date for design degree was 2003. To enable the accreditation process to proceed in 2002, a draft proposal with course prescriptions had to be completed by the end of the year. Dorita returned to New York and the development of the necessary documentation for accreditation was continued by email correspondence. Thankfully, Judith Nathan, the academic director of Massey School of Design and Fine Arts, supported us in this endeavour.

Meanwhile, in June, a fundraising concert was jointly presented by Toi Whakaari and the School of Dance to raise money to enable two dance students to attend the Asian Pacific International Ballet Competition in Tokyo, and to purchase a much-needed digital video camera for Toi Whakaari. The concert, which included a programme of duets and trios from musical theatre, was directed by Sally Barratt-Boyes with Wendy Wallace as choreographer and Nicola Lynch-Reeves as accompanist. It was performed in the Purple Hatch cafe, which operates from a commercial kitchen adjacent to the student common room in Te Whaea. The Purple Hatch is run by Dusted and Delicious and is a veritable life-saver for staff and students, serving wholesome organic food and superb stamina-building coffee. It also caters for special events and formal occasions at Te Whaea.

This initial concert idea was later developed by Robbie Warwick to become Toi Whakaari's cabaret season, now an established part of the second-year actors' syllabus. The first was held in 2002, in Te Whaea Plaza, and subsequently cabarets have been performed in the student common room, the Jimmy Bar, the Big Kumara and the Museum Hotel in downtown Wellington.

The second-year actors faced an entirely different challenge in June, when they focused on a compilation of scenes, poetry and prose by South Island writers under the title of *Southern Lights*. Songs from the legendary Kiwi label Flying Nun formed the backdrop for works by James K. Baxter, Denis Glover, Gary Henderson, Keri Hulme and Hone Kouka. The production was coordinated by Miranda Harcourt, with Annie Ruth, Simone Lourie, Tom McCrory and Karl Kite Rangi as directors, and Janet Roddick as the musical director.

The third-year actors were mostly on secondment or working on cooperatives and laboratory projects for the first half of the year. One of the labs, *I am Me*, was led by Vendula Prager, a Paris-based Czech performer who had worked with the Philippe Genty Company during the 2000 International Festival of the Arts. She remained in Wellington after the Festival to work at Toi Whakaari, helping with classes, workshops and *The Mysteries*.

I Am Me was staged at Circa Studio with a cast of third-year students and some recent Toi Whakaari acting graduates. A devised experimental work, it was based on the story of Echo and Narcissus, and had few words: the narrative was explored through movement and the manipulation of materials such as mirrors and other reflective surfaces interacting with light.

The other third-year cooperatives were *Cooking with Elvis*, directed by Vanessa Byrnes, which performed in Te Whaea Basement; and Steven Berkoff's *East,* directed by Ralph McAllister, which performed in Circa Studio. Ralph McAllister had worked in the East End of London in the 1960s and 1970s, the period in which Berkoff's play is set, and understood the harsh humour and the violent world of *East*. The *East* company formed the Petrol Cooperative, co-opting Kenny King (2000 acting graduate) as their production manager and Steve Gallagher to perform music. The cast was keen to continue the Petrol Cooperative when they graduated, and in 2002 they re-formed for a return season of *East*, and Jean Paul Sartre's *No Exit*, at Circa Studio.

There were two major productions in the final term: *Orpheus Descending*, a second-year acting project directed by Miranda Harcourt; and the graduation production, *The Cook, The Thief, The Wife and her Lover,* directed by Jude Gibson. Each production involved only one year of acting students, but both were designed and crewed by the second-year technical production students.

With the introduction of the third-year acting stream, the technical production students' journey no longer paralleled that of the actors except a few performance projects in their first and second years. So, when the two streams joined forces on their graduation production, they did so with very little insight into each other's practice. This inconsistency remained until the three-year performing arts management and design degrees were introduced.

The Cook, The Thief, The Wife and her Lover was an adaptation of Peter Greenaway's film script. In an attempt to match the film's visual impact, the production team transformed the basement of Te Whaea into a 'restaurant and commercial kitchen', with a large roller-door leading to the 'outside world'. The audience was seated at tables in the centre of the 'restaurant', surrounded by numerous stages.

Unlike film, audience focus in live performance tends to be arbitrary, particularly if they are given options. In this regard at least, the translation of the filmic quality of *The Cook, The Thief, The Wife and her Lover* into live performance was never fully

The Cook, The Thief, The Wife and her Lover, 2001. Fiona Collins and Julian Wilson

resolved. However, the production was particularly successful in its bold exploration of collaboration that was openly encouraged by the director. This example opened up further creative possibilities for students at the school, across all disciplines, to initiate and present work.

This was not the only voyage into the realm of film for the third-year actors in 2001. For most of August and September, they were immersed in Maurice Murphy's wacky science-fiction full-length feature, *Aliens 'R Us'* aka *Zenolith*, directed by Maurice Murphy, with a professional film crew. Maurice had workshopped various ideas for the movie with the cast the year before when they were in their second year.

The school had previously produced several low-budget short films, but *Zenolith* was the first time it had invested in a full-length feature, which was a remarkable opportunity for the students:

> In a way that kicked off that new screen programme, like let's really commit to the genre of short film where you can realistically make something good with $30,000. And you can, because Toi Whakaari has proved that to be the case. Also the tender system now reaches out beyond the school into the actual community. Film makers are aware of the school: they think about it and they submit. One person gets the money, and then comes to the school and thinks, 'Wow, I can work with actors in a different way', so it starts the change in a small way, creating an interconnected flow of learning opportunity. The success of the product depends on how well the director can work with actors, and often that skill is very low, because in the narrative or story-telling they often work with very talented people in CGI – or cine-photography, but they rarely get the opportunity to work with actors.[22]

To say *Zenolith* commandeered Te Whaea is an understatement; virtually every part of the building was inhabited by the art department and the film crew for the entire shoot. This required the school(s) to frequently 'freeze' and stop whatever they were doing, or face the rebuke of the sound department – or an irate assistant director. But then, that's the nature of the beast.

Zenolith is part love story, part fantasy, part satire, set in a drama school 'sometime in the future'. Dena-Marie Kennedy, one of the cast members, described the storyline as: 'Quite a weird piece really. You have to play it truthfully, but you also have to have a sense of taking the piss out of yourself. It's got some quite cheesy comedy.'[23] Lauren Jackson (Ethel of Aramathea) had a more ethereal view of the film: 'Colour is a really good word for this film. Colourful costumes – colourful sets – colourful music – big splashes of everything. All mixed up together.'[24]

Technically, *Zenolith* was a polished film, supported by first-class professionals. The soundtrack was composed and arranged by Gareth Farr and performed by the Tasmanian Symphony Orchestra, the cinematographer was Wayne Vinten, the art director was Mike Gibson and the fantastical costumes were designed by Janet Dunn. It appears that the movie is still doing the rounds of film festivals, promoted as a 'multi-layered kaleidoscopic rock opera'.[25] One piece of set-dressing from the film remains suspended in Te Whaea. It resembles a decorative sputnik and is a constant reminder of *Zenolith* and its world of turmoil.

With movies still in the air, and following the success of *Who Needs a Vespa,* I floated an idea for a joint Drama/Dance School collaboration. I had in mind a *film noir*-style (stage) production, incorporating music and dance. Annie Ruth had been looking for a work similar to *Vespa* but one that was more text-based, and my proposal seemed to fit the bill. With the backing of Annie and Wendy Wallace, I set about writing *Hollywood Combo* for the eighteen second-year actors and fourteen second- and third-year contemporary dance students.

A singular advantage of a commissioned work is that it overcomes the need to find an existing play with substantial roles in order to meet the individual needs and abilities of a large group of students. Having seen the acting students perform in their first year, I was impressed by their virtuosity and innate sense of comedy. And knowing their range and their personalities, I was able to tailor the play for a known cast; this helped me to form the characters in the play.

Hollywood Combo is an evocation of the writings of Raymond Chandler and Dashiell Hammet: it is certainly not a literal representation of their work, or in a cinematic style; it is more a theatrical pastiche.

The key protagonist in most Chandler mysteries tends to be a hard-boiled, cynical, disillusioned but otherwise likeable private-eye. In a rare moment of political correctness (and because I could) I created a female counterpart: a sassy, independent and altogether smarter female detective. I cast Louis Sutherland as the 'loveable gumshoe' and Nicola Colson as the irascible female detective. In structuring the play, I was heavily influenced by Chandler's Ten Commandments, which he formulated as the basis for his detective novels: 'It must baffle a reasonably intelligent reader and it must have enough essential simplicity to be explained easily when the time comes.'[26] Thematic unification: absolutely not.

Creating *Hollywood Combo* gave light relief to another form of writing that occupied my time: the course outlines and draft structure for the Bachelor of Performance Design. Massey had decided to speed up the accreditation process in order to submit a draft degree proposal to the College Board, which would allow the university to submit an application for approval to both the Committee on University Academic Programmes and NZQA in May 2002. This unexpected pressure coincided with an equally unforeseen event in New York: 9/11. Dorita Hannah was living in Manhattan at the time, and after the collapse of the twin towers she was understandably having difficulty focusing on the design degree. Nevertheless, with expert assistance from Judith Nathan, we managed to produce the required documentation that allowed us to submit a partial degree document to the Massey College Board by the due date.

It was also necessary for the Toi Whakaari Board to give its approval before the dual process of accreditation could proceed, so a special meeting of the Toi Whakaari Board of Studies was convened in December to deliberate on the performance design degree.

The Board of Studies had substantially increased in number; it now had a chair, Steve La Hood, and fifteen members: Vanessa Byrnes, David Carnegie, Bill Guest, Miranda Harcourt, Tanea Heke, Dee O'Connor, Jean Packman, Robin Payne, Perry Piercy, Annie Ruth, Rangimoana Taylor, Helen Todd and Lani Tupu; and two student reps, Ian Leslie and Fiona Collins.

All but five members of the Board of Studies attended the December meeting. After considerable debate on the pros and cons of the Victoria and Massey proposals, it seemed likely the Board of Studies would defer its decision until further substantive negotiations with Victoria University had been completed. Some members felt a decision to form a partnership with Massey could jeopardise plans for an MTA in Design. Yet there was little chance of that happening in the foreseeable future:

> The current MTA partnership with Victoria University would not be aided by Toi Whakaari going into an undergraduate partnership with Massey; and that a Design stream for the MTA would be significantly more difficult to achieve.[27]

When a motion was put to the Board to defer the proposed performance design degree, there was no seconder and it lapsed, allowing a formal recommendation to be made to the Board of Trustees 'that it progress a Bachelor of Performance Design degree with Massey University'.[28]

With the approval of the Board of Studies and an 'acceptable' draft degree document, Toi Whakaari set about seeking endorsement for the qualification from industry practitioners and performing arts organisations.

More staff departures occurred at the end of 2001. After five years as Toi Whakaari's voice programme manager, Simone Lourie resigned and returned to Australia to work, and also to study in the area of directing. At her farewell do, she rode into the school on the back of a motorbike to bid her last goodbye. Chris Goldsworthy also resigned from his position as Te Whaea's business and strategy manager to join his wife Fiona Tonkin in London; she had left the Royal New Zealand Ballet to take up a position with the English National Ballet. In some respects, Chris had never been entirely comfortable with the Drama School, perhaps not helped by his dance background. He found the acting students less compliant and more boisterous than their classically trained counterparts: they are indeed very different creatures. Nevertheless, Chris gallantly held Te Whaea's business centre together during the first three years of its life.

2001 had undoubtedly been a very busy year and it was certainly time for a well-earned break before embarking on what would be an equally challenging 2002.

Eighteen

2002–2003

'This scenario clearly opens up exciting interdisciplinary possibilities …'

A hui was held at Toi Whakaari at the start of 2002 to discuss the proposed Bachelor of Performance Design. Twenty-six 'stakeholders' attended the meeting: a cross-section of designers, academics, directors, technicians and students. The key themes of the meeting included training versus education, focusing on the ability of the programme to open minds and make smart designers, and the need for the academic programme to be supported by hands-on learning.

The level of representation at the hui assured an informed and wide-ranging discussion of the value of the proposed qualification, and some deeply held feelings were expressed. Most designers work on a freelance basis; for this reason it was recommended that the course include survival skills, such as financial management and contract law. Raymond Boyce raised the seemingly contentious topic of text analysis; opinions on this were divided, ranging from the traditional view of text as the basis for performance to the designer's perspective on non-text based work. Sally Morgan, Massey's head of Fine Arts, felt the degree needed to teach collaboration, to break down hierarchy. Steve La Hood, representing the film industry, proposed an increase in the film and video elements within the (draft) design degree curriculum on the basis that 'film is overtaking live performance in New Zealand'.[1]

Despite some opposing views on the purpose of the qualification, the opinions expressed helped to clarify the structure and purpose of the design degree and, overall, there was a generosity of spirit and strong support for the proposal. This was enormously encouraging: without the backing of peers and acceptance by the industry the design degree would be difficult to implement.

A few weeks after the hui, a memorandum of understanding was signed by Toi Whakaari and Massey University to formalise the basis of their partnership to deliver the proposed Bachelor of Performance Design. To mark the occasion, a ceremony was held in the Tea Gardens at Massey, and the Pro Vice-Chancellor, Dr Duncan Joiner, spoke of the benefits the design degree would bring to New Zealand theatre, film, television and music:

> Performance designers will now have an internationally recognised university qualification enabling them to become an equal part of that triumvirate of directors, performers and designers.[2]

Annie Ruth spoke of the impact that the performance designers would have on the industry, and of her expectations of the degree:

> When the first graduates are within the industry and collaborating with directors, the shape of New Zealand theatre and film would be changed forever.[3]

Design Degree MOU signing at Massey, 2002. L–R: Professor James McWha, Jean Packman, Annie Ruth, Dr Duncan Joiner (rear), Dorita Hannah, Bill Guest.
Massey University, Massey News (2002).

On this very positive note the year got underway, with a pōwhiri to welcome a new intake of students – across three disciplines. It also included the first group of New Zealand Drama School/Toi Whakaari graduates returning to upgrade their diplomas to degrees: Michell Amas, Anna McPhail, Denise O'Connell, Perry Piercy and John Wraight. There were four new staff arrivals in 2002: Christine Richardson, Robbie Warwick, Christian Penny and KC Kelly, making a welcome return to the school as an acting tutor.

Christine Richardson had been appointed as Te Whaea's new business and strategy manager. She had previously worked with Amnesty International and there was a certain logic in her decision to move to a performing arts organisation:

> The roles are very similar in many ways: and at Amnesty International I was working with people who were passionate about what they did, and similarly my colleagues at Toi Whakaari are passionate about their work. Both roles are within organisational structures that need good, solid foundations and resourcing to enable the core work to happen. After five years at Amnesty International I was ready to move on from an environment which was focused on trying to prevent terrible things from happening, to working in an environment where people are creating work in the performing arts – and I have always been a great fan of theatre.
>
> The greatest priority that I saw as Te Whaea's business manager was resourcing. There was a need to take the building on to the next stage, and I also wanted to create as much

stability (even growth!) around funding as possible, and armed with that information and certainty to enable informed financial decision-making by the school. I wanted to implement good processes around financial and human resource management, and to clarify the role of administration within the structure of Te Whaea. I believe that good administration at the school is about creating a sound framework and removing unnecessary barriers in order to allow greater focus on teaching and learning. My way of working is to try to instil an attitude of 'let's see how we can make it happen', a 'yes' culture, and by introducing processes to keep everyone safe.[4]

Christine's 'can do' attitude and her smart negotiating skills had a very positive effect on the financial viability of the school.

The new voice tutor, Robbie Warwick, had over twenty years' experience teaching voice at VCA in Melbourne, WAAPA in Perth and at various other performance programmes. She believed voice to be an expression of the whole self, a view that matched the integrated 'training' methodology of movement/sound exploration developed by Tom McCrory and Nerissa Moore at Toi Whakaari. Robbie's training as a Feldenkrais practitioner and at the Central School in London gave her a profound understanding of how the whole body is involved in the creation of voice:

The ethos and philosophy of Toi Whakaari agreed with my own .... It was my mission to provide a serious skill-based methodology for performers, based on experiential learning in a structured and sequential development, to allow them to have a greater chance of long-term careers and greater versatility across practice.[5]

Christian Penny's appointment as the head of directing at the end of 2001, to coordinate and supervise directing students in 'part two' of the MTA directing programme, coincided with the arrival of the first group of second-year students based at Toi Whakaari. Christian had trained at the Drama Action Centre in Sydney, followed by further study at Auckland University. In 1990, he started Theatre at Large with Anna Marbrook, and in 1993 they directed *Romeo and Juliet* at Toi Whakaari. He later returned to the school, in 1997, to direct *The Crucible*.

When Christian saw the head of directing position advertised, he immediately sensed that it was the job for him:

Christine Richardson

Christian Penny
(photo: Philip Merry)

> I could just feel it. Not only that, I wanted to, and should do it. It's a calling on that level, when one feels something that strongly. Since Theatre at Large, I had been freelancing. I wanted to build something again, and I knew I had to either start another company or contribute to something more long term. The main thing I remember about my first year at Toi Whakaari was that none of the briefs were written for the second-year MTA projects, so I worked on those. It was quite challenging for the [second-year] students because they'd had the university year and I arrived with a whole other take on what I thought they ought to be learning. I remember them reporting to me that the second year was a bit shocking, that I was a bit shocking.
>
> I was shocking – to the extent that I made the students take responsibility for what they were doing: to be responsible in their role of director. I realised that I needed a vehicle to change that, so I began a system of shared tutorials, putting part-one and part-two students together, and ran them as an open forum for questions. That allowed the part-one students to come in contact with me more and to see how I was working with the part-two students. It became clear at the end of the first year that I needed to work with the part-one students to build enough of a relationship so that when they got to the second year they were clear about how and what they wanted to learn.
>
> In that first year there were mostly learning questions. The part-two students were just trying to come to terms with a very different learning process. And we had no contract when I arrived: I didn't pick them and they didn't choose me.
>
> The first cohort of MTA students was great, they were also brave. A student who takes on a new programme like that in the first year is always a brave student. They have all since gone on to work in different fields and with different focus, mostly in positions of leadership.[6]

In 2002 Rachel More was one of the first directing students to undertake part two of the MTA. But her first year at Victoria had been a 'bit bumpy':

> It was all over the show really. We kept turning up for classes and no-one knew who we were. We were often sitting up at Victoria when we'd get a wistful phone call telling us we were supposed to be down at Toi Whakaari. None of us had cars so we were often about forty minutes late for class. We blundered around in the dark a bit in our first year and nobody really focused on us – we had little bits of attention. In the second year, we suddenly had Christian completely focused on us and that scared us.
>
> It was a terrible shock. Christian was very provocative and confrontational and seemed to want to shock us – for the sake of shocking us. We were terrified of him at first. Sometimes it was like the inquisition. It was nothing to do with his intent: he'd been working with his own theatre company in Auckland and had set up a certain way of teaching or confronting students that didn't quite mesh with where we had come from. That blend now happens much easier.
>
> I don't think Christian had an easy time with us either. Our group had all come from university and in our first year we were working very much in a university-type model. So the change for us was quite dramatic. But we learnt a hell of a lot more in two weeks with Christian than we did in the entire year puffing around on our own. Although, in that first year, we had some beautifully intensive stuff that set us up for our second year. We were let loose in the theatre with a two-week lighting block, playing with lights and sound. It was extremely valuable and I now have a lot more technical knowledge.
>
> It was a great thing that Christian was brought into the school. It was just that we

Rachel More.
Photo: Philip Merry

> hadn't had him the whole time and he was challenging us on bigger things, especially actors' connection and connection to audience; stuff we would have got away with had Christian not come on board. I was lucky because I had a real speed-bump half-way through and I had my biggest learning experience for the whole two years on my first project: an actor threw a tantrum and stormed out. She couldn't get something and I approached Christian complaining about my actor and suddenly realised if you keep asking 'why' in the rehearsal room, why something went wrong until the question is answered, it's usually going to be something that you [as the director] initiated. I wanted to be liked too much and it was impeding me getting on with the job. Having that sorted out early on helped me through the rest of the year, particularly *Speed the Plough*, which I did as my major project with Toi Whakaari grads Paul McLaughlin, Simon Vincent and Lauren Jackson.
>
> Above all, the MTA gave me confidence and I have pretty much worked full time since graduating, directing back-to-back. My greatest joy is getting a performance out of an actor – that's always been my buzz.[7]

With the introduction of the acting degree at Toi Whakaari, the need for full-time tutors to undertake research increased: as with any degree-awarding institution, it was a requirement. Because the business and purpose of Toi Whakaari is performing arts training, research in this context is mostly expressed through performance, achieved largely through professional work or through study as part of professional development.

In 2002 a range of professional development projects was undertaken by tutorial staff. Tom McCrory travelled to Paris to work on the development of a piece of underwater theatre. He also performed in TV commercials, and worked with his wife, Nina Nawalowalo, to set up the Conch, a Pacific Island theatre company and then to perform their first work, *Vula*. Annie Ruth took part in a directing symposium at La Mama in Spoleto, Italy, and later travelled to Los Angeles to further the school's relationship with CalArts, and to teach. Miranda Harcourt co-directed a short film with Rawiri Paratene. She also took her production *Flowers From My Mother's Garden*, with Kate Harcourt, to the Taranaki Festival. Christian Penny worked with Touch Compass to direct their new show *Lighthouse* at the Aotea Centre, and Karl Kite Rangi travelled to Ireland to participate in the Youth Theatre International Conference.

Given the relatively small team of full-time core teaching staff at the school, procedures for managing staff absences were rudimentary. Requests for professional development leave were often associated with performance projects, the timing of which were sometimes hard to predict and created problems for the remaining staff who often found it difficult to take on additional teaching or administrative duties when their colleagues were away. The degree-monitoring report, in 2000, noted this as an area of 'weakness and concern',[8] and recommended that the school develop a policy and procedure to deal with the problem, although there was no quick fix. Performance research was an acknowledged priority and teaching staff were entitled to professional development leave. Yet the financial resource to support professional development leave was severely limited.

The degree monitor's report also identified the need for someone to deputise for the director in her absence to ensure continuity. This was resolved by the appointment of an associate director, a position I held from 2002.

The Board of Trustees now had two new external members, Simon Bennett and Carolyn Henwood NZCM – a lawyer and district court judge. Simon's appointment provided a much-needed Auckland presence on the Board. Carolyn Henwood, and her husband, actor Ray Henwood, had both been pivotal in establishing Circa Theatre; she was also a founding member of Circa Council. The new staff representative on the Trust Board was Tom McCrory and Angela Green was the new student representative for Toi Whakaari.

Tuition fees for Toi Whakaari students were approaching $5,000, increasing the need for more scholarships to support the students' training. The Aotea Trust had recently begun awarding scholarships for students in the performing arts, but they were hotly contested. Toi Whakaari's success in securing grants from the Aotea Trust was variable, although 2002 was a particularly fruitful year: two acting students, Tim Foley and Amy Tarleton, and one technical production student, Melinda Brown, received Aotea scholarships to support their study and secondments.

The Performing Arts Foundation of New Zealand, which is funded through a ticket levy imposed by the St James Theatre Trust, also provides grants to performing arts students. They have been particularly generous in their support of Toi Whakaari, and in 2002 they awarded six scholarships to acting and technical production students to assist with tuition fees and airfares for overseas secondments.

A particularly generous scholarship was inaugurated in 2002 by Chris Parkin, the owner of the Museum Hotel, in collaboration with Dawn Sanders, the CEO of the Shakespeare Globe Centre in New Zealand (SGCNZ). The Museum Hotel scholarship included a lump sum to cover tuition fees and a monthly living allowance for the recipient's second or third year at the school, fostering excellence rather than hardship. It was open to Toi Whakaari acting students who had previously participated in the SGCNZ Sheilah Winn Shakespeare Festival and recipients were selected by Dawn in close consultation with tutors from the school. The first to receive the Museum Hotel scholarship was Angela Green: she had performed in the Sheilah Winn Festival in 1996 and had then joined the SGCNZ Young Shakespeare Company, touring with them to California the following year. Subsequent winners of the scholarship have been Matu Ngaropo, Kate Prior, Dan Musgrove, Brooke Williams, Dan Caddy, Cian White, Sophie Lindsay and, in the fortieth anniversary year of Toi Whakaari, Chelsea Bognuda.

Smaller grants were occasionally awarded to students by various charitable trusts. Nathan Meister, a final-year acting student, received a Rotary Goal Setters Award in 2002. He had an interest in dance and movement, and he seconded himself to the New Zealand School of Dance, working with the contemporary dance students in their 2002 Choreographic Season, *Finding Jimmy*. Nathan was one of the first Toi Whakaari students to make the transition from drama to dance; after graduating from

Angela Green receiving the Museum Hotel Scholarship from Christopher Parkin. *Photo: Dawn Sanders.*

Toi Whakaari he returned to the school as a tutor in the training programme, with Tom McCrory.

Around a third of the final-year students, across four courses, secured scholarships in 2002, assisting many to embark on international secondments.

Emma Deakin, a third-year acting student, travelled to Chile for her secondment with La Mancha International School of Image and Gesture, where she explored a range of theatre styles, including Commedia Humana: 'I felt like I'd had a huge feast. Every moment was new and upside down compared with anything I had ever experienced before.'[9]

Sarah Feely, a second-year technical production student, headed to Milwaukee in the middle of their winter, for her secondment at the University of Wisconsin to extend her stage management expertise. This was mostly achieved within the university's Professional Theatre Training Programme where she stage-managed a production of *Everyman*. She later toured the production to Shanghai and Beijing in the final two weeks of her secondment.

Other international secondments in 2002 included CalArts, Odin Teatret in Denmark, Yellow Earth Theatre Company in London, International Acting Laboratory in Seville, John Bolton Theatre School in Melbourne, and the University of the Incarnate Word in San Antonio, Texas. Students also completed over thirty secondments with performing arts organisations within New Zealand

Since 2002, student numbers have significantly increased, yet the availability of scholarships has not. Students now find it increasingly difficult to obtain financial support for their secondments, particularly when travelling overseas. Yet secondments are not optional; they are an essential part of the core curriculum for all courses at the school, exposing students to a broad range of performing arts practice and providing specialist skills that often validate the students' direction and clarify their sense of purpose during the final stages of training.

There was a marked improvement in Toi Whakaari's relationship with the International Festival of the Arts in 2002. Having lost the lunchtime Artists' Forums in 2000, the school again hosted them, and a number of visiting artists ran workshops at the school, including Max Stafford-Clark, the artistic director of Out of Joint Theatre Company, and Yves Jacques from Ex Machina and a performer in *The Far Side of the Moon*. As in previous years, Toi Whakaari students hosted international guests. And, during the opening of Writers' and Readers' week, they sang Nigerian songs to support Nobel prize-winning playwright Wole Soyinka. Some of same students then presented a rehearsed reading of Soyinka's play *King Baabu,* directed by Nina Nawalowalo.

Immediately after the Festival, the second-year actors, second- and third-year contemporary dance students from the School of Dance, and second-year and advanced diploma students began rehearsing *Hollywood Combo.* I co-directed with Wendy Wallace as dance director. The production was blessed with a 'dream team' of professional designers: Stephen Blackburn (lighting design), Nicole Cosgrove (set and costume design) and Peter Edge (sound design). The technical director was Tamsin Lakeman, an advanced diploma student, and the production manager was Laura Staples. Sarah Feely, who'd recently returned from her secondment in China, stage-managed the production.

Hollywood Combo had forty characters, thirty-five scenes (the final one written entirely by the cast) and twelve dance sequences. The plot was suitably convoluted, but this was par for the course. When filming *The Big Sleep*, the director asked Chandler to explain the plot and allegedly received the response: 'How the hell do I know – I only wrote the goddamned book.'

With such a large number of characters, scenes and dance numbers, *Hollywood Combo* turned out to be long, and with only five weeks to rehearse the production, it was hardly a true ensemble work – more a logistical exercise. Yet, in every sense, it was a cross-disciplinary exercise: actors performed dance sequences with the dance students, and the dancers each had a speaking role and quickly discovered their 'acting' talent. With the support of a skilful stage-management/design/technical team, logistical problems were resolved and the production somehow came together. *Hollywood Combo* was a tribute to the proficiency and willingness of cast and crew to collaborate as a company, and to Wendy Wallace's remarkable choreography – and her unending perseverance.

Hollywood Combo, 2002. Tahi Mapp-Borren.

The final dance sequence from *Hollywood Combo* was later restaged to launch the refurbished State Opera House, and in 2003 the play was reworked by the Hagley Theatre Company – alas without the dance sequences.

Many Toi Whakaari graduates work between live theatre, film and TV; for some, screen work is their primary area of professional practice – and income. The amount of screen work at the school had significantly increased in recent years, largely as result of Miranda Harcourt's refocus of the acting curriculum. This development was assisted by the arrival in Wellington of the Film School, as well as the new relationship between Toi Whakaari and Massey School of Design.

Some Trust Board members had previously resisted an increase in screen work at the school, but when the 2000 degree-monitoring report recommended that the school develop a performance-for-camera programme, the Board's attitude softened. This recommendation was further endorsed by the Acting Advisory Panel in 2001,[10] resulting in the formation of the Acting for Camera Advisory Panel, which included Ian Mune and John Callen. By 2003, performance-for-camera was truly embedded across all three years of the acting programme, camera-related teaching hours had significantly increased, and it was firmly established as an essential and valuable component of the actors' training.

In July, the second-year actors joined students from the Film School to make a series of short films, supported by tutors from both Toi Whakaari and the Film School. The joint arrangement made the most of scarce resources and established a beneficial partnership between the two institutions. It also provided the acting students with valuable camera experience, and prepared them for more advanced work in their third year.

Earlier in 2002, the third-years had worked with Aileen O'Sullivan to seed *Spring Flames*, a short feature based on the devastating 1940s Ballentyne's fire in Christchurch. Aileen O'Sullivan is an established and renowned film director and also a tutor at the Film School. She both wrote and directed *Spring Flames*, which she shot later in the year under the auspices of her production company, Seannachie Pictures, assisted by production coordinator Tamsin Lakeman, an advanced diploma student. The music score for *Spring Flames* was written by Gareth Farr.

Following the recommendation of the Board of Studies, the Trust Board gave its approval to proceed with the application to NZQA, allowing the jointly delivered Bachelor of Performance Design with Massey University to proceed.

An important stage of NZQA's validation of the design degree was an evaluation panel, led by an independent chairperson and evaluator (Ken Millar) appointed by NZQA. This included two university academics, an industry representative, a senior representative from Toi Whakaari (but not the co-author of the degree) and one Māori representative.

After several days of careful deliberation, the majority of the panel recommended to NZQA that they approve and accredit the design degree as a jointly awarded qualification with Massey University. The panel also made a recommendation that Toi Whakaari appoint a head of design as soon as possible.

Not every member of the panel was in favour of a jointly awarded Bachelor of Performance Design, and one submitted a minority report opposing the degree. In essence, it expressed a concern that the theatre industry would view the degree as a qualification fundamentally in live theatre performance design, and that there would be insufficient employment opportunities in this area in New Zealand for graduates of the broadly-based performance design programme. This view was apparently predicated on the view that the specific practices of Toi Whakaari and Massey School of Design were incompatible: Massey trains designers, whereas the more discipline-specific Toi Whakaari trains theatre practitioners. Furthermore, it was asserted that this 'mismatch' in the joint delivery of the degree would (not could) compromise the standards of professionalism in New Zealand's theatre industry. And because the performance design programme would create opportunities for 'other related design disciplines to impose inappropriate principals on the art of theatre design', Toi Whakaari would have to significantly modify the work generated by the school in order to accommodate the degree.[11]

There is no doubting the validity of the minority report, but the central arguments contained within it only held if the intention of the performance design degree had been to maintain the status quo of theatre in New Zealand. In fact, the current state of affairs was partially served by the degree, which, in its aims, clearly acknowledged essential competencies fundamental to an undergraduate theatre design programme, and the focal point of the programme was live performance, principally dramatic theatre. In terms of its scope, it was not dissimilar to the acting degree: its main focus was on live theatre, but it incorporated other aspects of performance such as screen and corporate work.

The purpose of the performance design degree was to educate designers who could then either specialise or diversify, and its main strength lay in an integrated approach to design that, it was hoped, would broaden the performance possibilities for both acting and design students and thereby redefine theatre in New Zealand. So, where better to explore this 'outrageous' idea than in an environment where designers, directors, actors, dancers, technicians and managers collaborate to explore the future direction and possibilities of performance? It was perhaps a radical concept, but drastic measures were needed if a viable live performing arts industry in New Zealand was to be assured.

It was clear that Massey and Toi Whakaari would have to adjust their structures to allow the collaborative partnership to work effectively. But we were all confident that any problems concerning the integration of different teaching practices and curricula would be creatively resolved by the inter-institutional Board of Studies.

In the meantime, the technical production students continued to design most of Toi Whakaari's productions. In June, they designed the set, costumes and lighting for the second-year acting production of *Mother Courage*, directed by Miranda Harcourt. Andreas Lepper, a Wellington composer, created a percussion score for the production, generating sounds through the use of found elements and bodies as 'musical instruments'. Mother Courage's daughter Kattrin is mute, and for this role Miranda chose a guest actor, Amy Szostak. Like Kattrin, Amy Szostak was also physically disabled. She had previously worked with Miranda on several projects at the Lower Hutt-based Acting Up Theatre Company, whose members mostly have physical or intellectual disabilities.[12]

The second-year MTA directing students began to make their presence felt in the school, embarking on a series of performance projects, each with a different focus. They included technical directing, community/corporate projects and major full-length productions with each director exploring a particular style of theatre. Rachel More directed Mamet's *Speed the Plough* with original music by Gareth Farr; James Hadley directed Howard Barker's *Women Beware Women;* Jacqueline Coats directed *A Despoiled Shore*, a cast-devised work with a combination of music, movement and Middle English text; and James Sutherland wrote and directed *DSCH*, a work based on a variety of found texts.

With the arrival of a second year of MTA students, production activity at the school began to escalate, which in turn increased the workload of the technical production department. The relatively small intake of technical students in 2002 meant that graduates and other professional technicians had to be employed to service shows mounted by the school, which led to a significant increase in the overall production budget for the year.

Despite various promotional initiatives targeted at increasing the pool of applicants for the technical production course, recruitment remained disappointingly low. The selection criteria could be relaxed, but it was feared that this would inevitably create unrealistic expectations for applicants unsuited to the demands of the training programme. It could also endanger the standard of the course. The name of the qualification appeared to be an obstacle to recruitment. In some respects it was anachronistic, in that it no longer fully described the nature of technical training delivered by the school. The Technical Production Advisory Panel therefore recommended changing the name of the diploma to entertainment technology, as they felt this described the content and scope of the course more accurately: it was also more 'marketable'. The Board of Studies endorsed this recommendation, and entertainment technology was adopted in 2003. To help market the 'new' course, a DVD was shot and compiled by Tony Toufexis and edited by Alan Smith, a producer with the Gibson Group, which proved to be an extremely effective promotional tool.

The Entertainment Technology Advisory Panel then recommended extending the two-year diploma to a three-year degree, to bring the qualification in line with the acting degree. It would also have the added advantage of giving entertainment technology graduates an internationally recognised qualification, an important factor for those seeking employment in the UK or Europe, where many technical and stage-management graduates have advanced academic qualifications. A three-year degree could potentially attract more overseas applicants to the school, particularly those seeking training in performing arts management.

However, the panel felt the existing two-year diploma served an established need, and if there was to be a three-year degree, they preferred the additional option of a two-year diploma opt out. But this was *not* a model traditionally favoured by NZQA.

The 2002 graduation production was *The Rover,* directed by James Beaumont. It was, however, a very different version of Aphra Behn's play than the one produced by the school in 1994. This time, scenes were rewritten and adapted by James Beaumont to suit the requirements of a large cast of ten women and seven men from the third year, plus seven second-year acting students and two on secondment from CalArts. Alice Tinning (2000 graduate) designed the costumes and, interestingly, Toby Papazoglou designed the set, following the footsteps of his father, Tolis, who had designed the set for Toi Whakaari's 1994 production of *The Rover*. Like the earlier iteration, the 2002 version was an excellent vehicle for the graduating students, particularly the men, who displayed their sword-fighting skill in superbly choreographed scenes.

Enrolments for both the MTA directing and the performance design courses were processed by Victoria and Massey universities respectively. The selection process for the first intake of performance design students was therefore held at Massey at the end of the year. But unlike the MTA selection process, which was governed largely by the MTA Board of Studies, the Bachelor of Performance Design process was subject to a portfolio selection and this was not, in the initial stage, specific to design disciplines.

This presented a problem for Toi Whakaari, its selection criteria across all courses being predicated on a range of factors, not simply 'artistic talent' or academic ability. To ensure the integrity of the design process within a production, performing arts designers not only have to communicate abstract concepts, but also have to collaborate effectively with the entire production team. Being a talented artist is no guarantee of collaborative ability. For this reason, a requirement was introduced into the selection process stipulating that *all* shortlisted applicants for the Bachelor of Performance Design had to be interviewed by a selection panel. In 2002 this comprised Dorita Hannah, Tommy Honey and me. Some of the previously rejected portfolios were reviewed by the panel, including those submitted by applicants lacking the necessary university entrance qualification, which revealed a number of interesting candidates who might otherwise have been overlooked.

First-year students enrolled in all disciplines at Massey's College of Design, Fine Arts and Music complete what is effectively a foundation year. At the end of that year, they can then apply to re-enrol in a different discipline in their second year. This made it difficult for Toi Whakaari to determine the actual number of students continuing into the second year of the performance design degree as it was possible some would transfer to another programme. On the other hand, it provided an opportunity for Toi Whakaari to recruit or seduce students from other design disciplines into the performance design degree at the end of their first year.

With around thirty design students to be accommodated in Te Whaea by 2005, Toi Whakaari was faced with an urgent logistical problem. To cater for this, and for other courses that had been flagged, a Concept Development Plan for Te Whaea was prepared by Aonui Architecture. They came up with an imaginative and ambitious solution to resolve the future accommodation needs of Toi Whakaari and the School of Dance but it was expensive: between $1.4 and $6 million depending on the option chosen.

The Trust Board considered the proposed development plan and noted that the existing loan on the building would not be paid off until 2005. This meant additional funds would have to be borrowed to pay for redevelopment, and it was unlikely the schools would be able to service a loan of the size needed. Nevertheless, the Board endorsed the concept development plan (in principal), and the architects proceeded to draw up plans for stage one. The Board set up a working party to consider the proposal further and instigated a 'fundraising scheme' to meet the cost of redevelopment.

At the start of 2003, the entire school gathered for a shared week of orientation. Each new student was given a provocation to deliver a five-minute piece, 'Something from My Culture', and the returning students were asked to prepare a presentation based on 'This Moment Now'. This resulted in a much more balanced and objective view of each student than had occurred in previous orientations: it was more revealing of the students' relationships with the school – and with their training.

There were also more administrative and teaching staff changes at the start of the year. When Jami Kimbrough moved into a new position in the Nola Millar Library as an administration support officer, Annabelle O'Meara replaced her as the receptionist for Te Whaea. Charles Norwood left to take up a position with a computer software company, and the position of marketing manager was then filled by Ceridwyn Roberts, previously employed by the Fringe Festival and Rape Crisis doing a similar job:

> Toi Whakaari was the most challenging because I was challenged to be myself within a creative industry full of eccentrics, talents, madmen, geniuses and evolved human beings.
>
> Personally, I work in the arts because I believe that stories change the world for the better and I want to be a constructive part of that change. I know the odds of success within the creative industries, but to find your passion it is important to both dream and plan. In an ideal world Toi teaches its whanau to do both.[13]

The position of head of performance design was finally filled by Penny Fitt. She had visited Toi Whakaari the previous year when on vacation with her family, and had been excited by school and the scope of the proposed performance design degree. At that time she was head of theatre design at the Bristol Old Vic Theatre School.

Penny had initially studied theatre design under the legendary Percy Harris at Motley, in London, before establishing herself as a highly regarded stage designer and teacher in the UK. Her early designs include *I Miss My War* at the Almeida, *Street Scene* in Brixton Prison for the English National Opera, and *Fools' Mate* at the New End. Later, as resident designer at the Octagon Theatre in Bolton, she designed *Blue Remembered Hills* and *Death of a Salesman.*

Penny Fitt, Head of Design. *Photo: Philip Merry*

As with any new qualification, the performance design programme was a considerable undertaking. Nonetheless, Penny's inclusive and practical approach to performance design suited the requirements of the course admirably, and from Toi Whakaari's perspective she was ideally suited to the position.

When she arrived at Toi Whakaari in July, Penny had to quickly familiarise herself with the complexities of the dual Massey/Toi Whakaari administrative structures and establish resources for the first intake of second-year performance design students in 2004.

Fleshing out the curriculum from the brief course prescriptions, which had been developed mainly for the purpose of degree accreditation, was also a high priority.

One of the more urgent papers for Penny to develop was 'Introduction to Theatre', an elective open to all first-year Massey College of Design and Fine Arts students. This paper was a great success: not only did it help to confirm existing enrolments in the Bachelor of Performance Design; it also worked as a recruiting mechanism to attract students from other disciplines at Massey into the second year of the performance design programme.

A few months later, Penny's husband Derek Simpson arrived with their two children. Derek is an experienced production manager, a role he'd previously held at the Bristol Old Vic Theatre School. This skill would again be put to good use when he was later appointed as Toi Whakaari's production coordinator.

At the request of the Entertainment Technology Advisory Panel, I wrote a discussion paper to outline various options for a three-year technical or management qualification. Although the panel had already stated its preference to retain the existing entertainment technology diploma, it was open to the idea of a separate performing arts management degree, particularly one that incorporated major elements from the diploma course, in order to provide an opportunity for students to articulate between the two qualifications. This was an important consideration as it is not uncommon for entertainment technology students to realise their management potential part way through their training. Likewise, performing arts management students could well discover, in the early stages of their training, that they had stronger technical or design skills. The panel also asked for the existing advanced diploma to be retained, as this provided an option for two-year diploma students to gain specialist technical training and for existing practitioners to upgrade their skills.

The Advisory Panel approved those ideas and recommended to the Toi Whakaari Board of Studies that the performing arts management course be developed for delivery in 2004.

It is worth noting that the 'Background and Discussion Paper for the Bachelor of Performing Arts Management', which was approved by the Advisory Panel and presented to the Board of Studies, included the following impact statement:

> If the anticipated numbers of Performance Design students are enrolled in 2004 (20) and the Entertainment Technology/Performing Arts Management student intake target is achieved, there will be a significant increase in the undergraduate student population at Toi Whakaari by 2006. The combined number of students enrolled in these three courses could then equal, or exceed, enrolments in the Bachelor of Performing Arts (Acting).
>
> This scenario clearly opens up exciting interdisciplinary possibilities. It also requires a major philosophical re-evaluation of curriculum delivery methods, and the system/rationale for programming productions and projects.
>
> If this unique opportunity is not openly embraced and explored by all disciplines at Toi Whakaari there could be increased pressure to form two independent divisions within the School.
>
> The long-term impact of the introduction of the Bachelor of Performing Arts Management and Performance Design programmes needs to be fully discussed by management

> and tutorial staff to clearly identify problems and opportunities. These already overdue discussions need to take place as a matter of urgency as certain fundamental issues need to be resolved before the accreditation process for the Bachelor of Performing Arts Management can proceed.[14]

The first production in 2003 was *Memories for Tomorrow,* directed by Miranda Harcourt and choreographed by Wendy Wallace. This was the third major collaboration between Toi Whakaari and the School of Dance.

The *Memories for Tomorrow* cast had been asked to return from their summer break with stories from their family history. These were then used to seed the production, forming the foundation for the rehearsal process. Alice Tinning worked with the company to design the set and costumes, and Steve Gallagher translated the performers' work into a music score for the production. The work was entirely written and choreographed by the students, highlighting the importance of ownership when both process and product are student-driven. But it appears this particular collaboration benefited the acting students more than the dancers:

> Wendy and I had a great time making it and the show was really good, beautifully designed, it all came together. But it was very interesting in that the dancers were dissatisfied with that show and they felt a bit lost, because they wanted to learn how to act, and they had a very concrete and out-of-date concept of what acting is. What they wanted was speech and drama, that's what they understood would help them in their career as dancers. So they were dissatisfied with the process, they wanted stuff written down in a script and I can understand that.[15]

Later in the year, the second-year actors performed *The Gentleman from Olmedo*, directed by Tom McCrory. It was the first time Lope de Vega's play had been performed in New Zealand. Nicole Cosgrove designed the set, using the entire theatre space to create a U-shaped amphitheatre, suggesting both a bullring and the staging in which the play was originally performed. The appeal of the play was that it offered the ensemble the opportunity to explore the body of possibility that had been generated through 'training':

> The students could actually move as one body; they had all these movement skills and *Olmedo* provided the possibility to explore the application of that through rehearsal to performance. The poetic nature of it, the interpenetration of a metaphysical world with the everyday world and the visceral aspect of it, lent itself to a movement-based exploration.[16]

The third-year actors performed their Go Solo season early in 2003, in March. They each chose a twenty-minute piece based on a New Zealand or Pacific personality. As with previous solo seasons, there was a broad mix of work, ranging from Andrew Ausage's depiction of David Tua in *Lumana'I*, combining English and Samoan language, to Nick Dunbar's tribute to his uncle Les 'Chalky' who had been stranded in occupied France during the war. Go Solo also included James Ashcroft's extremely humorous *Sorry I'm Out, but I Can be Booked*, the story of a young video-store worker; Matu Ngaropo's *Te Kuraroa*, an examination of Hirini Melbourne; and Jean Copland's *Polly Want a Cracker*, a pirate adventure based on the story of escaped convict Kitty Haggerty.

Following its Wellington season, Go Solo played at the Auckland Art Gallery, providing the students with valuable exposure to Auckland agents and producers. Jude Gibson coordinated Go Solo and the production/tour manager was Lynley Hill, a second-year technical production student.

The third-year actors then embarked on a fifteen-minute short film, *Dead End*, written by Louis Sutherland and directed by Mark Albiston of Sticky Pictures. The film's narrative relied on visual imagery with very little dialogue. For this reason, and also the excellent acting, cinematography and editing, *Dead End* was extremely successful. It has since been shown in several international film festivals, including the Sydney and Commonwealth Film Festivals. Unsurprisingly, the writer/director team of Louis Sutherland and Mark Albiston went on to win accolades for their later films, *Run* (Jury Prize – Cannes Film Festival 2007); and for *Six Dollar Fifty Man*, which received Special Distinction at the 2009 Cannes Film Festival, Best Film at the Expresion en Corto Short Film Festival in Mexico and Best Short Film Jury Award at the prestigious Sundance Film Festival in 2010.

The 2003 graduation production occurred much earlier in the year than usual. This was *Troilus and Cressida* co-directed by Annie Ruth and Rangimoana Taylor. Geoff Pinfield, a second-year MTA directing student, was the dramaturge. The production was designed by Toni de Goldi and music was composed by Gareth Farr.

Some of the text was translated into Māori by Te Kohe Tuhaka, a second-year acting student, with the help of his uncle. It was later reported by Māori speakers that his translation was extremely elegant.

It was decided to set *Troilus and Cressida* sometime during the Land Wars in the 1860s. This allowed scope for the company to work in two languages: the Trojans were played as Māori, and the Greeks as British-backed government forces:

> The production raised some hard questions for us to ask ourselves as New Zealanders. It was a complex thing to do, to cast racially with brown against white. And I think that was the first time the students had looked at each other in this way and that was very uncomfortable, of course. And that brought up a lot of issues around colonisation, not just around the Land Wars in New Zealand.[17]

Prior to rehearsals, the directors and cast spent five days on a marae with the people of Parihaka to seed the production and undertake research on the Land Wars.

> We went to Parihaka because that was the place of peace: the whole play is about war so we thought let's go to a place that is absolutely dedicated to not taking that route to solve disputes.[18]

The company later returned to Parihaka to complete rehearsals, and then opened *Troilus and Cressida* there.

Troilus and Cressida is essentially about the futility and absurdities of war and the deleterious effect it has on the combatants. By adding the image of New Zealand history to the production, the audience was enabled to view the play more clearly. The themes explored in the play resonated with many recent political events, as John Smythe pointed out in his review of the production:

> Right now, to us, the production might say as much about the foreshore and seabed debate or the US/British response to Afghanistan and Iraq or the Israel/Palestine conflict as the land wars of 140-odd years ago.[19]

It also resonated strongly with Māori audiences, both at Parihaka and Ruatoria:

> We took the production to Ruatoria, staying with Keri Kaa on her marae, and performed in the school hall. There were people in the audience who were in their seventies and kids as young as two; it was like the whole community was there. What was amazing was how partisan they were, they were up on their feet screaming at Cressida: 'Don't do it girl, don't do it!' It was fantastic. And when some of the fighting in the play went down the aisles, the audience intervened to get between the Māori and the Brits. So that was a huge experience for the students.
>
> Neither the Parihaka audience, who saw the show on opening night, nor the Ruatoria audience had any problem understanding the story. But some of the Pākehā audience had difficulty with it: it was as if they couldn't trust what they saw, and so when they heard Greek names they were going 'What's that?', whereas for the Māori it's all strange, they were going 'Well, that's clearly Māori and that's clearly British', and so they just followed what they could see and let the language flow from that.[20]

When Annie Ruth approached the Globe Theatre in London to discuss the possibility of Toi Whakaari performing its production of *Troilus and Cressida* there, the school was invited to perform at the Globe in 2003. But funds to cover the air fares could not be raised, which was a great pity, if for no other reason than the one given by John Smythe in his review:

Troilus and Cressida, 2003. L–R: Rashmi Pilapitiya, Paul McLaughlin (1996 graduate), Louis Sutherland. *Photo: Michael Parrott.*

> Given Shakespeare's habit of plundering stories from around the globe to fuel his creative genius .... there is something immensely satisfying about the prospect of his Troilus and Cressida returning 'home' so profoundly filtered through a Kiwi perspective.[21]

Brian King was the assistant designer for *Troilus and Cressida.* After twenty-one years as a general medical practitioner, he had decided to do something 'more creative': to follow his passion for opera and theatre. So he sold his share in a central Wellington practice and enrolled in the second year of the Bachelor of Performance Design, due to commence in 2004. In the meantime, he'd enrolled in Toi Whakaari's advanced diploma to gain background knowledge of the technical aspects of theatre. Brian's dedication to becoming a professional stage designer was evident from the outset, in every aspect of his work.

Toi Whakaari's first ever research conference was held in November. This new initiative brought together theatre and screen research undertaken by most final-year students, and included research papers from a number of Drama School graduates who had re-enrolled to upgrade their previous qualification to a Bachelor of Performing Arts.

The final 'event' of the year was the graduation ceremony, a grand and celebratory event launched by Peter Biggs, chairman of Creative New Zealand. Each graduating student was presented with an individually designed cloak made by their peers. This had now become a central feature of Toi Whakaari graduation ceremonies, with cloaks featuring ornate motifs and decoration, acknowledging the character and/or specific achievements of each graduate. The 2003 graduates included eight upgrade students: Vivienne Aitken (1978), Peter East (1981), Dave Fane (1992), Johanna Smith (1992), Simon Ferry (1993), Lyndee-Jane Rutherford (1993) and Kirk Torrance (1994). Also graduating in 2003 was the second cohort of MTA directing students: Jade Eriksen, Kerryn Palmer, Geoff Pinfield and Kristin J. Smith. They would later participate in a somewhat less theatrical graduation ceremony at Victoria University, in 2004.

Toi Whakaari graduates also had a strong presence in the 2003 Chapman Tripp's, with eleven awards presented to Toi Whakaari alumni, including a newly graduated director and an actor-turned-writer. Some other graduates received international tributes too, in 2003. Nigel Scott (1995 technical production) was part of the sound-editing team from Park Road Post that received an Academy Award for *Lord of the Rings*; Emma Deakin (2002 acting graduate) scored a major role in *Return of the King*; and Rawiri Paratene, Cliff Curtis and Rachel House were integral to the international success of *Whale Rider.*

At the end of 2003, Stephen Blackburn resigned as entertainment technology co-ordinator and technical director to take up the position of general manager of the National Theatre for Children. Since joining the school in 1999, Stephen had made a huge contribution to the advancement of the technical production programme, including major advances in health and safety, both within and outside the school. He was instrumental in the development of a much-needed set of safe working practice guidelines, now a standard within the New Zealand theatre industry. More importantly, Stephen practised his ideals and taught by example. Many technical production graduates have good cause to be thankful for his sage advice, and for the technical knowledge and sense of professional disciplinc that he engendered.

Nineteen

2004–2005

'What a woman she was! We shall not look upon her like again.'

The decade leading up to 2004 had brought with it enormous expansion at Toi Whakaari. A three-year acting degree and the MTA in directing had been established, and performance design and performing arts management degrees were in the pipeline. These initiatives had increased the student population at the school to ninety-five.

It was a far cry from 1970, when Nola Millar had an Arts Council grant of just $7,500 to set up and operate the first year of the QEII Arts Council Drama School. With the inauguration of the New Zealand Drama School in 1974, under George Webby's directorship, annual funding increased to around $50,000, provided by the QEII Arts Council and the Department of Education. Of that amount, around $15,000 was allocated to operating expenses; the rest went on salaries and premises. In addition to its annual grant to the school, the Arts Council provided students with bursaries.

It is difficult to compare the financial circumstances of the Drama School in 1970 with that of Toi Whakaari in the early twenty-first century. However, it is interesting to note that in the fifteen years leading up to 1988, the annual 'grant' received by the school grew from around $50,000 to $490,000[1] without any appreciable increase in student enrolments. By this time, a much larger proportion of the Arts Council grant was needed to cover the cost of premises.

From 1990 to 1996 there was no significant increase in Toi Whakaari's core funding from either QEII or the Department of Education, except for 1992 when the annual grant increased to $716,000 with the introduction of the technical course. In fact, the school's annual grant actually dropped to $682,000 between 1993 and 1994. To compensate for this and the cost of additional full-time staff, tuition fees were increased from $1,000 to $3,000, which provided additional income of $108,000. It was the largest one-off increase in student fees in the history of the school.

From 1994 until 1997, the Ministry of Education's funding for the school remained more or less static until the three-year acting degree was introduced when tuition fees were again increased. Then, from 2001 to 2004 the annual grant for the school rose from $890,000 to $1.095 million, and the total income from student fees increased from $297,000 to $397,000, largely due to higher student enrolments.

In order to manage this increased fiscal responsibility, more sophisticated financial reporting was introduced, and accounts and financial decisions were monitored on a regular basis by the Trust Board's audit and finance committee. The task of managing the school's income and expenditure in 1974 or even 1994 was no less daunting then than it was in 2004. Even though there was far less money involved, it still required considerable acumen to balance the books – an ongoing battle between ambition and revenue. However, an area that had considerably increased over the years was the extensive and often complex wrangling that now took place between management, the Trust Board and the Tertiary Education Commission (TEC) to secure the school's annual operational budget.

The establishment of the TEC in 2003 was seen as critical to the 'new direction for tertiary education' that had been promoted by the Labour government when it came into office in 1999. The government wanted increased collaboration and stronger links between tertiary education providers, stakeholders and communities, with a greater focus on quality and excellence. This initiative was central to the government's growth and innovation strategy to ensure that 'New Zealand stands tall in the 21st century as a confident and dynamic nation'.[2]

In leading the government's relationship with the tertiary education sector, the TEC assumed responsibility for funding the government's contribution to tertiary education providers, including Toi Whakaari. That, and the other changes introduced by the TEC, began to have a profound effect on the prospects of the school.

Toi Whakaari's budgeting and financial management systems have increased in complexity in recent years, along with the myriad of governance, management and academic structures seen as essential to sustain the operation of the school. Undoubtedly Nola Millar and George Webby would have been horrified had they been confronted with such labyrinthine governance.

Nola Millar, in particular, had almost complete autonomy over the philosophy, methodology and management of the QEII Arts Council Drama School. She was answerable only to the director of the Arts Council, mostly on matters relating to funding. Similarly, George Webby had considerable directorial discretion, except that he was accountable to a Board of Studies. Their initial responsibility had been the academic direction of the school, and later they took on other responsibilities to secure financial support and other resources for the school. When the Board of Studies was replaced by a Board of Trustees in 1986, George still had only one level of governance to contend with. The Board of Trustees' principal function at that time was that of an advocate body, for accommodation and finance and for securing the status of the school, and its Trust Deed clearly determined that the professional and curriculum side of the school was the responsibility of the director and staff.

Little had changed in the way of governance by the time Robin Payne was appointed director, but between 1998 and 2004, the 'controlling' and support structures surrounding Toi Whakaari increased substantially, with numerous reporting bodies now orbiting and having an impact on its core operation. When the school moved into Te Whaea in 1998, the Premises Management Trust assumed direct responsibility for management and maintenance and in effect became the school's 'landlord'. A separate body, Te Whaea Management Services, was then established to provide administrative support to Toi Whakaari and the School of Dance, charging a levy to administer the shared facilities and staff.

By 2004 there were *three* Boards of Studies scrutinising and overseeing the academic programmes of the school: Toi Whakaari, MTA and performance design. The Toi Whakaari Board of Studies had a wide-ranging brief to ensure that *all* qualifications delivered by the school met NZQA requirements. In practical terms, it presided over the continuing improvement of existing courses and curriculum, made recommendations to the Board of Trustees on the development and establishment of new programmes, and considered educational policy issues.

The MTA in directing and the Bachelor of Performance Design programmes had their own Boards of Studies, with membership drawn from Toi Whakaari, Victoria and Massey respectively. Unlike the Toi Whakaari Board of Studies, the MTA and Performance Design Boards were aligned with the academic procedures of the two universities, with a greater focus on curriculum development and on student evaluation.

Each governing body associated with Toi Whakaari has its own terms of reference, filtering and interpreting information in different ways, each ultimately affecting the delivery of training at the school. At the centre of all this 'governance' sits the director of Toi Whakaari, faced with the task of reconciling the requirements of the various boards with the delivery of quality teaching programmes, and integrating those demands with the over-arching vision of the school. It is probably fair to assume that apart from the director and key management personnel, few staff or Board members fully comprehend the connectivity of all the constituent bodies that variously impinge on the day-to-day running of the school.

The biggest change at Toi Whakaari between 1994 and 2004 was its growth, which in itself was a necessary strategy for survival to enable the school to 'stand tall in the 21st century' and to be competitive with other institutions. The next stage of Toi Whakaari's development was one of consolidation. An accelerator for that was the new TEC structure. To justify its ongoing funding and – ultimately – its continuing existence, the school had to evaluate its position, then state its strategic direction for the ensuing five years. This 'strategic direction' was articulated through a Charter, essentially a statement of values supported by a series of 'profiles' to demonstrate how the school would adapt its education and operational structure to meet the needs of its learners and other stakeholders. Before this could happen, the school had to be clear about both its vision and its purpose.

This was partially achieved through a vision plan for Toi Whakaari entitled *The Next 10 Years 2004–2014*, published in 2004 and guided by the school's internal organisational goals. A key goal was the need 'to respond to the increasing diversity of training offered at Toi Whakaari by promoting integration across courses to maximise possibilities'.[3]

The vision plan for 2004–14 was superseded in 2006 by a more comprehensive document, a *Strategic Plan*,[4] intended to provide a framework for the activities of the Toi Whakaari management structure for the five years from 2006 to 2011. It contained a much wider strategic context than the previous 'vision', with more detail on the way the school intended to fulfil its future purpose. At the heart of this sat 'convergence', which echoed the 2004 goal of 'promoting integration across courses to maximise possibilities'. This seemingly simple aspiration would ultimately trigger the greatest challenge to Toi Whakaari since its inception, affecting the identity and the cohesion of the school.

One of the organisational goals for 2004, 'to bring the Bachelor of Performing Arts (Management) into effect so that it can be offered in 2004 and to continue to investigate offering craft based courses', had already been partially implemented. The curriculum documentation and NZQA application for the Bachelor of Performing Arts (Management) had been completed in October 2003, under the guidance of NZQA's evaluator Ken Millar, and the degree was finally approved and accredited in June 2004.

Despite this delay, the first cohort of performing arts management students were 'unofficially' enrolled in February 2004 by including them in the entertainment technology course intake until they could transfer into the performing arts management programme in their second year.

Also floated in 2004 was a proposal for a two-year diploma in costume construction. The school regularly received enquiries from people wishing to undertake a specialised costume-making course, and this had been identified as an area of high demand. There was no existing full-time course in New Zealand that covered the broad range of costume-construction skills required for professional employment in theatre or film, and yet there was an acknowledged need for skilled costume makers and costume specialists in the local theatre, film and television industries. Through discussion with leading costume designers and makers, it was evident that up to six graduates a year with the necessary specialist costume skills could easily be absorbed by those industries. The recent introduction of a Bachelor of Performance Design had expanded the design output and production activity of the school, which was in turn likely to bring about a greater demand for skilled machinists, pattern makers, cutters and other costume specialists.

When the Toi Whakaari Board of Studies looked at the initial proposal for the costume construction course, it had some concerns over resourcing issues and the pace with which the course was being introduced. Nevertheless, it agreed to support the proposal and recommended to the Board of Trustees that it approve the introduction of the course in 2005, providing adequate resources were available. James Acheson, a three-time Oscar-winning costume designer[5] who would later teach on the performance design course, was co-opted on to the Board of Studies as an ex-officio member, specifically to comment on the proposal for the costume course, and his endorsement provided considerable clout.

Other key objectives in the 2004 to 2014 visioning plan included a review of the acting course to permit greater flexibility and specialisation, and consideration of further possibilities for integration with other courses, along with an alliance with a film school.

It was hoped the informal association that Toi Whakaari had with the Film and Television School could develop into a more formal arrangement and a closer physical relationship before 2014. The Film School was looking for a more permanent home and was considering space in Te Whaea. Mahon Amusements Ltd had relinquished their occupancy of the Indoor Cricket area, and this seemed a possible location. However, it proved too expensive and the Film School later abandoned the idea, relocating instead to premises in Vivian Street. Nevertheless, Toi Whakaari and the Film School retained a strong relationship and still continue to explore other avenues to strengthen links between the two institutions.

At the start of 2004, Toi Whakaari experienced its largest-ever intake of students. There were fifty-seven new enrolments over five courses: twenty-two actors, six MTA directors, eleven entertainment technology and management students, and eighteen second-year designers who were now 'officially' at the school, having completed their first year at Massey. But they didn't fully arrive at Toi Whakaari until later in the year, as the first semester of their second year was undertaken at Massey. This gave Penny Fitt time to convert a drama studio into a design studio as an interim measure until design-specific studios could be afforded.

Two design studios had been included in the school's 2004–14 visioning plan, together with a lighting laboratory, a shared studio for the acting and directing students, an extension to the existing costume workshop, and a workshop for set and property construction. But, unlike universities and polytechnics, Toi Whakaari received no targeted capital funding, requiring the majority of the equipment and building needs to be met from the school's operational budget or from its reserves. The school was unable to raise a bank loan to improve the premises because it was only a tenant of Te Whaea; it had no equity in the building despite having invested much of its reserves in redeveloping it.

Toi Whakaari therefore took a more pragmatic approach in proceeding with the architectural journey of Te Whaea. As part of its normal production activity, the school built temporary performance environments: sets. That expertise was put to more permanent use to create structures in Te Whaea, aided and abetted by Jeff Williams, the PMT's property and building manager. He knew the building like the back of his hand. And, with the blessing and support of Te Whaea Management Services, he extended the facilities in Te Whaea in a very cost-effective way – often by sourcing second-hand building material.

By excavating a disused tunnel connecting the basement area below Te Whaea Theatre to the basketball courts, a scenery workshop was created. A mezzanine level was constructed within the costume workshop to provide teaching and storage space, and additional teaching space was created above one of the technical production classrooms. The Nola Millar Library also gained an office, which in turn released more space for the library collection.

Much of the teaching equipment for these refurbished areas was obtained through one-off grants from various charitable trusts. In 2004 the joint Boards' audit and finance committee reported a surplus of around $14,000 for the 2003 year in Toi Whakaari's fortunes, which was also made available to purchase much-needed capital equipment.

When Miranda Harcourt took professional development leave at the start of 2004 to direct major projects at Downstage and Circa, Aileen O'Sullivan took over the role of head of acting. Other new appointments included Ross Joblin as the new entertainment technology coordinator and technical director; Vanessa Byrnes returned as the acting course manager; and Barry O'Connor, Robbie Warwick's partner, was contracted to coordinate history of theatre classes. A few months later when Robbie resigned from her position as voice programme coordinator for health reasons, Barry returned with her to Australia, and Robin Payne was then appointed until the end of the year to teach some history of theatre and to 'upgrade' classes; Vanessa Byrnes resumed responsibility for coordinating the history of theatre and philosophy programme, as well as continuing as the acting course manager.

With an increased administrative load brought about by new courses and larger student enrolments, Annabelle O'Meara was reappointed as the school's inaugural drama school administrator. Her previous baptism of fire on the front desk at Te Whaea no doubt helped to ease her transition into this role, as did her previous experience as parliamentary agent looking after the Lake Wakatipu electorate in Otago.

In the second half of the year, James Acheson and Kasia Pol were appointed by Massey and Toi Whakaari to teach papers in the Bachelor of Performance Design.

The 2004 production season at Toi Whakaari commenced with *Dead Friend*, a piece of devised surrealist theatre based on Alfred Hitchcock's 1958 movie, *Vertigo*. It was performed by the second-year actors and directed by Andrew Foster, who described the work as being like a massive collage. The narrative was conveyed with minimal dialogue and with inter-linking but sometimes unrelated scenes that were used to explore the difference between reality and perception. The performance opened with one of the cast hanging upside down high up on a wall, throwing baby dolls to the ground.

This was followed a few months later with *Great Expectations*, an adaptation by Simon Phillips of Dickens' novel, originally produced by the Melbourne Theatre Company. Toi Whakaari's production was co-directed by Miranda Harcourt and Tom McCrory, they made a conscious decision to approach the production very differently, combining Tom's Bouffon technique and Miranda's psychological naturalism. The production was performed across two venues, Drama One and Two, which reinforced the experimental nature of the work. Six actors played the main characters in the play, with the remaining 117 roles filled by twelve other members of the cast. The production had very few scenic elements; instead, it was performed both in traverse and in-the-round as a way to heighten the sense of character and to focus on their physicality. It did, however, have some splendid costumes that were made for the Court Theatre's 2003 production of the play.

Dan Caddy who played Pip, the central character in *Great Expectations,* was on stage for all but ten seconds of the entire three-hour performance. Before joining Toi Whakaari, he'd trained as a singer and also appeared in cameo roles in the TV series, *The Strip*. Dan's ultimate ambition was musical theatre, which he advanced in his third year by seconding himself to the New Zealand School of Dance to perform in the Choreographic Season. When he graduated from Toi Whakaari in 2005 he joined the School of Dance as a full-time student in the contemporary programme.

The final production in 2004 – for the second-year actors – was *Pericles*, directed by Peter Hambleton (1981 graduate) and designed by Tolis Papazoglou. The production was set in the 'Pacific of the imagination', complete with surfboards and wetsuits. Surfing elements inhabited every element of the production, from the costumes to music, played live on stage by Gareth Farr and members of the cast. It is interesting to note that Nathaniel Lees was co-opted onto the production, playing Gower as a narrator/MC.

Earlier in the year, the third-year actors worked on *The Rules of Dogs and Men*, a forty-five-minute location-based mini feature set in the downbeat world of dog racing in Petone, directed by Anna and Jim Marbrook. Every third-year student had to be in the film, and when an entire storyline was cut, including the character played by Kate Prior, Miranda Harcourt insisted that the directors go back and reshoot with Kate to get her back into the film.

By far the largest project for the third-year actors in 2004 was *Penumbra*, initiated by Christian Penny and David Geary and in development in 2001 under the working title, *Point on the Hill.*

After graduating from the New Zealand Drama School in 1987, David Geary had established himself as a writer, winning both the Bruce Mason and Adam Foundation playwrights' awards. Among his television credits are *Shortland Street, Jackson's Wharf* and *Mercy Peak*, and his theatre writing includes *Pack of Girls* and *Lovelock's Dream Run.*

Penumbra, 2004. Abby Marment, Jade Daniels, Kate Prior. *Photo: Michael Parrott.*

Dead Friend, 2004. *Photo: Michael Parrott.*

David Geary described the *Penumbra* development process as a creative conversation: 'rather than me writing a script and giving it to a director who finds actors, there's a whole lot of ways to make plays now. Unlike the previous culture of writers, and directors, everybody's a maker.'[6]

Jade Eriksen joined *Penumbra* in 2003 as part of her Master of Theatre Arts, and Penny Fitt agreed to design the show. Christian and Jade then led a two-week development workshop with the cast in their second year, meeting each fortnight to share ongoing research, which culminated in a further week of research, presentations and composition in December.

Before the students left on their secondments around New Zealand and overseas, improvisations were set for the *Penumbra* cast at the start of 2004, based on provocations from Jade, Christian, David and Penny. The cast then remained connected through an e-mail diary, 'Collected Thoughts', enabling the show to continue as a dialogue between individual company members. Secondment experiences were also fed directly into the work:

> No actor knows what the others are developing. Students travel to different cities to develop work. Provocations include working with a Māori private training provider on the East Coast, in Access Training Centres, with Aged Care, studying the movement patterns of international flight attendants, filming a day in the life of an ex-pat artist based in Amsterdam, and a range of other diverse investigations. The labs produce the beginning of the character journey – and tempo. A few of the characters are brought together blind; instructed just before meeting about the nature of their relationship. Long format improvisations are filmed and then scripted. The core points of the journey emerge.[7]

Penumbra was the first fully-devised graduation production staged by Toi Whakaari. Creating devised work in this way was also a new way of working for Penny Fitt, different to the design process she'd previously experienced in the UK:

> I was aware from my previous visit how little theatre there was in New Zealand. So there was much less opportunity for me to design shows, as I had done when I was teaching at Bristol Old Vic. I then realised there was a different way of working than just selecting the show that I wanted to do. *Penumbra* was a completely new way of working for me. Books of my work from that time are mostly filled with 'How on earth do I operate as a designer, and how does a designer contribute, and provoke questions around design when the whole piece is being formed?' Much of my time on *Penumbra* was spent with Christian, David and Jade as we formed and reformed questions around the whole structure of the piece, which we looked at through various different perspectives of characters, and how to get those to interweave. I remember being pretty exasperated by the process, feeling that I couldn't do the thing I was skilled at doing: I couldn't actually be a 'designer' – and design. But the methodology we used on *Penumbra* now affects the way I design – even if it's scripted – also the way I teach: an investigative method that gets to the question of the piece, rather than solving the locations and the period of it.
>
> I wanted quite a few elements built for *Penumbra*. But I had to come up with something that would be flexible enough for us to work all the things that we were going to work into it. In fact, it was more of a structure or framework to hold the piece, rather than a design for a *set* that would illustrate parts of the play. We also made an operations booth

> because I came with my European ideas of not wanting to see any of the technicians, or to have them seated within the audience.
>
> For me, the big question was how to ensure a professional standard of finish in the costumes and props etc. if they are forever changing [in the development process]. We had a large team of students on *Penumbra*, and we used them in a different way as well. We got the stage-management students to ask the same question that I was pondering, which was: 'How do you do your job given this is the structure, rather than having you try and do your job based on a different model and try and force the thing into it?' – which is what usually happens with devised work. That was an eye-opener.[8]

The cast returned to Toi Whakaari in August, and as they resumed rehearsals based on further provocations, the bones of the story began to emerge. The title was also changed from *Point on the Hill* to *Penumbra*,[9] for reasons best described by Christian Penny:

> We live more of our lives in this space, framed by a collection of shadows cast by our forebears – parents, communities and the political forces that have preceded us and affect us in the present.[10]

When final rehearsals commenced in October, the core story of *Penumbra* was revealed to the company. The work was then divided into five 'contacts', and final changes, additions and adjustments were made before it opened in November.

The journey of *Penumbra* links the lives of over forty characters, spanning three generations of a family and fifty years of New Zealand history. Stylistically, the structure of *Penumbra* resembled Robert Lepage's *Ex Machina* work, such as *Seven Streams of the River Ota*, with its narrative technique spanning several timeframes, chance encounters and parallel events linking interrelated stories.

Penumbra was performed in the MTA Garage space and an adjacent basement storage area, with a technical/management/design team comprised of performing arts management, entertainment technology, MTA directing and design students. The production team was led by Shelley Irwin, with Nga Larsen as the stage manager. Three student designers from MTA directing and entertainment technology assisted Penny Fitt on the production: Laurie Dean (lighting design), Leo Gene Peters (sound design) and Veialu Aila-Unsworth (audio-visual design.)

Another interesting collaborative/devised work in 2004 was *Shifting*, directed and designed by Leo Gene Peters, his major performance project in his final year of the MTA directing programme. The production followed the lives of four characters as they shifted houses, relationships, countries and emotions, and intersected 'on the path to change'. The director, cast and crew used around 5000 cardboard boxes to create a set, which 'transformed' itself during the action of the play from a university lecture theatre to a biochemistry lab, a kitchen, a bar and a student flat.

Eleanor Bishop, in her review for *Salient*, described *Shifting* as 'one of those rare plays that is highly entertaining, seemingly about nothing, yet extremely thought-provoking at the same time'.[11] Like most devised work, the production was very much a work in progress, and the audience was encouraged to return during the season, paying only a koha, to see the show evolve.

Shortly after the 2004 graduation ceremony, many of the graduates returned to join with students and staff in a poroporoaki. This was a new initiative for Toi Whakaari, providing students and staff with a final opportunity to farewell the graduates personally and, through an exchange of thoughts and feelings, to acknowledge their changed relationship.

The move from a fairly regulated lifestyle at Toi Whakaari into a more self-directed practice in the industry is an anxious time for some graduates, many experiencing a sense of loss made especially poignant because of the clear sense of whanau at the school, and the close bonds developed within and across particular cohorts of students. The poroporoaki fulfilled a useful function in this regard, and for many it was clearly a liberating experience, marking the conclusion of their initial training at Toi Whakaari and their exit from the school.

Tutors leaving Toi Whakaari at the end of the year were also acknowledged during the poroporoaki, as the school said farewell to Karl Kite Rangi, Ross Joblin and James Acheson, who was off to Australia to work on *Spiderman 3* as the costume designer. Ross Joblin was not replaced immediately; instead, the position of entertainment technology/ performing arts management tutor was advertised with the aim of appointing someone towards the end of 2005. This released funds to enable Derek Simpson to be appointed as a production coordinator for part of the year. With his extensive background in production management and in teaching, Derek was the ideal person to trial this new initiative.

With much of the creative practice at Toi Whakaari expressed though production activity, the school had earlier set up a production unit in order to provide greater clarity for the entertainment technology and management students, and to safeguard their learning when working on productions. This unit is led by a coordinator who supervises the work of students when they are assigned to productions. During that time, they are answerable to the production coordinator and their production responsibilities are focused through the production unit. This allows them the freedom to develop their own methodology and to adapt what they have previously learned to the production environment. The coordinator also provides the students with individual contracts to describe the scope of their work, reducing the possibility of a potentially damaging and unproductive push-me pull-you relationship between students and their head of department. More importantly, it provides a clearer delineation for the students between their general course work and production duties.

Derek Simpson
Photo: Philip Merry

When technicians, designers and managers graduate and enter the industry, their opportunity to exercise creative risk is often limited by commercial factors. But, as students, they are encouraged to take creative risks and to accept the possibility of failure as an inevitable part of the learning process. This does not always sit easy with artistic ambition. Failure to meet expectations may simply be the result of mistiming, over-zealousness, inexperience or – quite commonly – miscommunication: it is never the intended outcome of risk.

The Entertainment Technology Advisory Panel had become increasingly concerned by the expansion of production activity at the school, regarding it as sometimes detracting from the core objectives of the technical training programme. They therefore recommended that the scope of the technology students' involvement in productions be reviewed, and as a result production activity for first-year technology students was confined to the second half of the year. This gave more time for essential core units to be completed before the students embarked on production practice.

An elective programme was also introduced for the second-year technicians to give them greater scope for specialisation. To accommodate this, the number of productions that students had to complete in production practice was further reduced. The downside of that was a significant reduction in the availability of second-years to crew Toi Whakaari productions. This was partly resolved by scheduling one 'technically unsupported' production each year. Just like the 'old days', the acting students sometimes provided their own technical support, and at other times the school employed additional technical staff to coordinate the 'unsupported' work.

The elective programme created an important point of difference between entertainment technology and acting students. They had few elective options and those they did have were mostly in their third year. The effect of this was especially evident within production practice. Whereas acting students are often assigned performance roles by a director or their head of department, technology and management students negotiate production assignments from their second year.

The big advantage of this for the entertainment technology department is the degree of flexibility it provides to tailor the students' training needs to their individual interests or ambitions. But it comes at a cost, requiring detailed and often protracted negotiations between staff and students. It is a complex logistical exercise, requiring production assignments, secondments and course work to be juggled and rejuggled in order to match the needs of individual students with the availability of tutorial staff, a process that remains in a state of flux for many months.

Where circumstances allow, production assignments are matched to the specialist interests of individual students, particularly in their second year. The option of selecting performance projects that are aligned to the students' creative ambition, or fulfil a particular training need, tends to foster a more collaborative approach to theatre-making. Recent initiatives such as MTA productions and third-year cooperatives have also broadened those options. An associated problem is that it further reduces the number of technical and management students available to work on 'mainstream' productions, again requiring production crews to be augmented by professionals from outside the school, at a cost.

Towards the end of 2004, Dave Gibson and Stuart McKenzie were invited to make a presentation to the Trust Board for a proposed documentary film that would follow the acting students' journey through the school. They pitched for a series of between seven and ten half-hour episodes, which would be aired on TV2 either late in 2005 or early in 2006 under the title of *Tough Act*. Stuart McKenzie would direct the series and Gibson Group would produce it.

Many reasons were given for making the documentary. TVNZ believed the series would provide an opportunity for an audience to understand the value and discipline

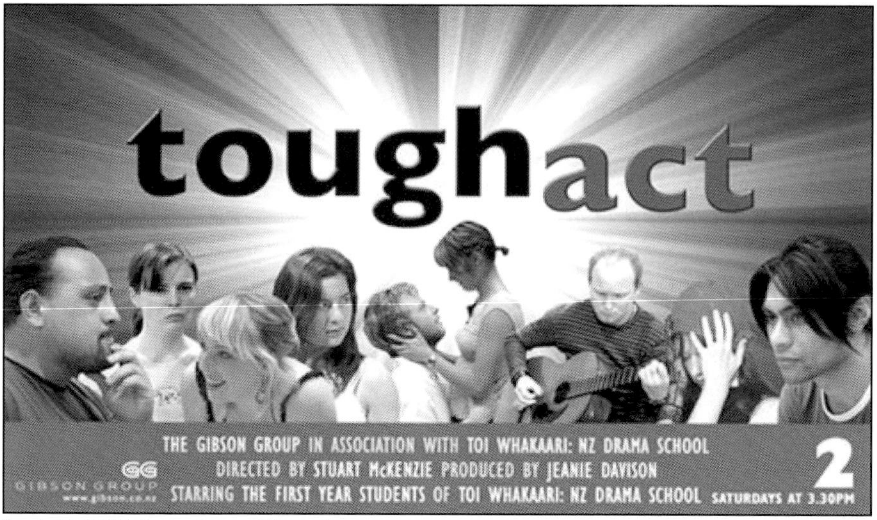

Tough Act. 2004 Poster. Source: Gibson Group

of the arts within society, disabusing the public of any misconceptions about actor training. In a similar vein, Stuart McKenzie's objective for the series was to 'show the "outside world" the magic and creativity that is Toi Whakaari, and to celebrate what goes on at the School in all its different facets'.[12] It was also felt that the doco would provide a 'warts-and-all' record of the acting students' journey through their arduous first year at the school, showing how they grew and changed through this experience.

A particularly compelling argument in favour of the doco was the benefit it would provide to the students, by 'having their training and dedication valued in the wider community, and the satisfaction of allowing a wider audience to appreciate the rigors and sacrifices involved in training to be an actor'. Perhaps the most convincing reason for the documentary was the fact that it would bolster the public's perception of Toi Whakaari as a place worth preserving and investing in. Viewers would undoubtedly 'admire the dedication, creativity and professionalism of both staff and students, boosting the school's reputation in the public arena', which in turn would cement its 'reputation as one of the country's top creative establishments ... at a time when institutions are struggling to embrace and practice multiculturalism with integrity'.[13]

Filming for the doco started at the end of 2004, tracking acting auditionees through to the recall weekend. It then resumed at the start of 2005 to follow the progress of the first-year actors through their initial year. In addition to Stuart McKenzie, the film crew included a camera operator and a sound engineer, who responded with great sensitivity as they melded into what was often a highly-charged and sometimes emotional training environment.

Miranda Harcourt felt that the outcome of *Tough Act* was very positive for the students:

> It was of enormous benefit to those kids to have 500 hours' camera exposure as part of the screen programme. You can see that a number of them, like Dan Musgrove, Matt Whelan and Sophie Roberts in particular, have had good screen careers since then, and they could walk into an audition room and not be overwhelmed.[14]

Likewise, Annie Ruth saw the potential of *Tough Act* to raise the profile of the school and was in favour of it:

> I don't regret it: we've now got much stronger brand recognition than we had then, and along with other things that were happening at the school at that time, it really 'rocketed' us. However, I think we've since moved on as a school, our teaching is way less personal now than it was when *Tough Act* was made. The film allowed us to look at our teaching practices and to say 'We don't want to keep on doing that', and I think that's been really good for the students.[15]

Responses to the documentary were polarised. Some questioned the wisdom of exposing a group of students in their first year of actor training to an intense public gaze. Others were worried that the documentary portrayed Toi Whakaari as an academy that trained only actors and not as a multi-disciplinary school. Jane Clifton applauded *Tough Act* in the arts and entertainment column of the *Dominion Post*:

> Here at last is a show of vital interest to most children and young teens … which their reality-TV averse parents would also enjoy watching because it's not schlocky or artificial and follows a process which is genuinely fascinating: how do you teach people to act? What is best about the programme is that even those who might roll their eyes at the thought of watching acting luvvies training try-hard youngsters with probably unrealistic dreams of stardom will have their prejudices assaulted.
>
> This School is tough. It's like being perpetually subject to the judging panel from *New Zealand Idol* only without the one nice judge. This is not a million miles from army style discipline, only the sergeant major is roaring at you for your lack of authenticity rather than your grubby boots.
>
> It's crisply directed and edited .... the original music is furnished by Barnaby Weir, which is a bit of a coup; and, most winningly, it's an incidental celebration of Newtown, where the School is located.[16]

Negative comments in her review were directed at TV2 for screening *Tough Act* at 3.30 on a Saturday afternoon:

> The stupidity of it is gobsmacking: TV2 commissioning an intelligent, engrossing series that would hook in children and parents in mega numbers [at a time] when it will be really difficult for most viewers to watch. This is just the latest in a long line of good local programmes wasted in hopeless time slots.[17]

That view was shared by Stuart McKenzie:

> *Tough Act* was commissioned for a prime-time audience. That's how we conceived, shot and edited it. The possibility of it not being in primetime was never discussed. We kept on cutting it for primetime … It was complete news to me that they were putting it on at 3.30 on Saturdays.[18]
>
> This is not the first time programmers have misread New Zealand audiences' desire to see strong local product celebrating achievement at primetime.[19]

Jane Bowron, in her article in the *Dominion Post*, focused more on the ethics surrounding the making of the series:

> The whole thing stinks like yesterday's diaper and is deeply exploitative of the vulnerable

> young. Even the name *Tough Act* is suspect, for the tutors appear to be doing their best to behave like Simon Cowell from *American Idol.*
>
> One would have thought that a drama school in the noughties [2006] would be enlightened enough to know that a student learns very little when they're being castigated and it's all being recorded for our entertainment.
>
> What exactly are these students being toughened up for might I ask? The concept of having to learn the hard way or the highway is so 1980s school of *Fame*; it's laughable seeing the reality of the 'training' being carried out at the national boot camp for thespians.[20]

So, how did this lengthy exposure to being 'toughened up' affect the students? Sophie Hambleton, the daughter of Aileen Davidson and Peter Hambleton, appeared in the documentary. Being the first child of a graduate of the school to study at Toi Whakaari Sophie had a personal insight into the changes that had taken place in the acting course since the 1980s. And this was a factor in her evaluation of the group's response to *Tough Act*:

> When Dad was a student at the drama school, it was more 'old school' in terms of the core fundamental practical skills they learned. We were exposed to a much wider range of subjects, with a greater focus on us as individuals: who you are and what you bring with you and where you are going. The acting course was more emotionally and psychologically driven. But there has to be balance: it is very easy to go too far down that track and lose sight of why we are at the school. We were, after all, training to be actors and we didn't need to unpack everything, particularly as there were twenty-two of us. In my dad's day there were only eight: that changes everything.
>
> Most of the time, I loved *Tough Act.* I was so young – we all were – and I was going to be on television. There were cameras, it was a completely new experience and I thought it was fantastic. It never occurred to me that I would undergo a very personal, private or confronting experience and that maybe exposing myself to twenty-one strangers, who I had only just met, would be difficult. Rather I felt, 'Well, why we are in this business if we don't want to experience something like that?' At first, I was not concerned about having cameras in the classroom. I didn't necessarily agree with the view that 'you'll be totally comfortable in front of cameras' because it's a completely different experience to *act* in front of a camera than it is to pretend the camera is not there. But I soon forgot about the film crew and it wasn't until later in the year that I became less comfortable with the situation: I didn't know what was going to come out of me, I had so little control of the situation and I no longer felt safe. But by that stage it was too late.
>
> When we saw the finished product it was very different than I what thought it would be. It was interesting to see the amount of relationship coverage in *Tough Act.* So much time seemed to be taken up with who was going out with whom, and who was crying about what, and other personal stuff. A lot of what I thought was magical about the school was missed. There was so little of the work we did or the moments of epiphany for people in the classroom that I thought the viewers watching *Tough Act* would think that actors are all wankers. I realised the [producers] needed to take that approach for television; the general public weren't really interested in [voice classes]; they didn't really understand it. On the other hand, viewers needed to understand the people in the film, so that when they saw the students in class or something amazing happened – they could see that they were learning and that they were actually changing. But it seemed certain

things were portrayed specifically for television. I was so honest with that programme – with the camera, and towards the end of the series I felt quite betrayed.

But *Tough Act* unconsciously tightened us up as a group, especially when we watched it together. It was the 'big reveal'. There were things in the film that weren't pleasant, things that people had said about other people that they'd never said to their face, which created an interesting vibe.

I don't think the experience impeded our training, quite the opposite. I believe it made our group much stronger and tighter because we were all in the same boat together: it was very weird and foreign. No-one was pressured into appearing in the film. We had the option of saying no when asked to be interviewed; therefore some people in the group had less exposure than other people. But no-one left in that first year. I suspect it had something to do with the fact that nobody wanted to be the one who left on camera.[21]

As if to prove their point, the entire 2005 first-year acting intake graduated in 2007, aside from one student who left to have a baby.

Tough Act has been screened at least twice since 2006, and was nominated in the Qantas Television Awards in 2007 in the 'Best Observational Reality Award' category.

At the start of 2005 there were 115 students enrolled at Toi Whakaari: fifty-six actors, seventeen technicians and performing arts managers, twenty-two designers, twelve directors and nine upgrade students (including Rawiri Paratene). This was a record number, and yet it would be further exceeded in 2006.

New staff to join the school in 2005 included John Senczuk, who was appointed as a design tutor for the first half of the year to work with Penny Fitt on the performance design programme. John had recently developed undergraduate programmes in scenography and dramaturgy at both the University of Wollongong and the Western Australian Academy of Performing Arts. John is also an established and highly regarded designer, director, dramaturge and writer. The combination of all these skills, and his intellectual rigour, provided a timely boost to the design programme.

Rangimoana Taylor returned for a while to teach tikanga until Keriana Whati took over as the taha Māori coordinator in May. Peter Rowlands was appointed to coordinate and teach history of theatre across all undergraduate courses at the school. Salesi Le'ota (2002 graduate) joined the Te Whaea management team as receptionist and to

Images left–right: Sophie Hambleton; Salesi Le'ota; Tamara Aluwihare *(photo: Philip Merry)*.

work in other administrative roles. Tamara Aluwihare, who had worked for Te Whaea Management Services as an accountant on a half-time basis in 2004, was reappointed full time as a finance officer at the start of 2005. Besides being a financial wizard with an eagle-eye for figures, Tamara has a theatrical background. As a child growing up in Sri Lanka, Tamara shared her father's passion for musical theatre, and later when she arrived in New Zealand, she continued her interest in the performing arts. Tamara is one of those rare accountants who has the ability to understand and (even more remarkable) accommodate the sometimes quixotic temperament of performing artists.

More staff changes occurred later in the year. Nerissa Moore decided to 'retire' (but not quite) after twenty years teaching voice at the school, and Sylvia Rands was then appointed as the voice tutor. Sylvia has had an extensive acting career, both on stage and screen, and is one of New Zealand's most experienced teachers of voice, having taught for eight years at VCA in Melbourne, the Actor's Centre and the University of Western Sydney. She developed a method that integrates a range of vocal techniques that include Hakomi Bodywork, metaphysical teaching, and the practice of Frankie Armstrong, Roy Hart and Kristin Linklater.

And the school got a new singing tutor: Jane Keller. She was classically trained, with over thirty years' operatic experience in the USA. Her real passion is musical comedy and she is also a highly regarded jazz singer. That and her remarkable ability to teach the singing styles and repertoire of musical theatre proved enormously valuable in Toi Whakaari's annual cabaret seasons.

At the start of the year, Toi Whakaari embarked on yet another major collaborative project with the School of Dance, involving second-year actors, contemporary dancers and second-year entertainment technology students. The 2005 production, *Pegasus Moon*, was essentially a physical theatre/dance work in two halves. The first half, *Pegasus*, was led by Tom McCrory and Wendy Wallace, and drew parallels between the behaviour of horses and humans in relation to conflict, herding and courtship. The second half of the programme, *Moon,* was led by Jude Gibson and Paula Steeds-Huston.

This was followed by the second-year actors' first major screen project, *Accident and Eternity*, a short horror film directed by Charlie Bleakley and jointly produced with the New Zealand Film School. It was set in an emergency ward, an A&E for the dead, where 'patients' were processed before they were dispatched to heaven – or hell. Shot entirely in a disused ward at Kenepuru Hospital in Porirua, *Accident and Eternity* provided students with an excellent opportunity to gain film-making experience on location.

Returning from this 'deadly' experience, the second-years embarked on a remarkable production, *Battles of the Heart*, a compilation of three New Zealand scripts celebrating the contributions of Kiwi men and women in World War II. KC Kelly came up with the initial idea and Miranda Harcourt negotiated the rights to work with material, including *War Stories Our Mothers Never Told Us* edited by Judith Fyfe, from the film by Gaylene Preston; and verbatim stories from *Silent Casualties* by Alison Parr. Other stories came from oral archives.

The students had previously worked on *Battles of the Heart* with Gaylene Preston and the director, Aileen O'Sullivan, at the start of the year. They were later joined by

Jane Keller. Photo: Philip Merry.

Moon, 2005. Entire cast.
Photo: Michael Parrott.

Battles of the Heart
2005, Arthur Meek and
Mrs Flo Small.

Sally Barratt-Boyes as the musical director and Jane Keller as accompanist. Sally Stopforth was the choreographer and the producer was John Senczuk.

The characters portrayed in *Battles of the Heart* were real, not 'fictional', and for that reason it was particularly important to honour and treasure their memories that, for many, were still a reality. There was also a strong possibility that some of those portrayed in the production would see the finished product.

Battles of the Heart was performed in-the-round at St Andrew's church hall on The Terrace, which the students set up to replicate a dance night from the 1940s. Because the hall was fairly small, the cast had a fairly intimate relationship with their audience:

> *Laurel Devenie.* Seating the audience round the entire wall of the hall gives us such a scope of possibility – it will definitely keep us on our toes: there is a kind of nakedness that comes with that. Everything can be seen by the audience from [many] angles – there is no room for bluffing.[22]

It was a 'technically unsupported' production, which meant the cast had to hire or somehow find their own costumes and props; they also made ninety cushions for the seating, designed the programme, rigged supplementary lighting (with the assistance of Tony Toufexis), and during the performance served lamingtons and tea to the audience. The old dining hall was well-suited to the production, requiring little in the way of technology or design to support it:

> *Chantelle Brader.* It's dinky, run-down and complete with old-school lighting hanging around the walls, but with so much 1940's charm, perfect for this play. The first thing that struck me was the acoustics and how it can swallow up the sound if we don't articulate clearly. Aileen said the hall had 'echo fairies' that we want to call on when we are singing and let them rest when we are speaking.[23]

The rehearsal period proved to be an emotional journey for the cast, many of whom were profoundly affected by the experiences and stories of their 'characters' who, during the war, were roughly the same age as the students:

> *Arthur Meek.* I stumbled on to Peter Fairlie's story while looking for accounts of shell-shock. I found [Peter's] almost clinical description of the symptoms of fear extraordinarily moving. I have probably never rehearsed a piece of text less than I did this one. The words just sank into me without any effort and they seemed to perform themselves, requiring only the slightest control on my part. The *duende*, the spirit that Peter had described so brutally, came and sat in me for those few minutes every night .... It was as if I was hanging on by my bootstraps while the words and emotions flowed out into the audience.[24]

Gareth Williams was similarly attached to his character, Jack Williams, an airforce rear-gunner who'd flown many sorties over Germany:

> Having the audience in the round only boosted Jack's story further. It allowed me to imagine the almost 360 degrees he would have had to try and scan, night after night, for enemy fighters. It made the situation much more alert. Being able to just talk to people and tell a story of coming to terms with loss and having your life spared for an unknown reason was something special. There was ultimately a sense of complete listening from the audience each night. Now that's theatre. That's storytelling. It was an absolute gift and pleasure.[25]

Research was a major part of the rehearsal process. Serena Cotton played Flo Small, 'a carefree Newtown girl with a mischievous grin and daring red shoes', and scanned newspaper articles for stories of Kiwi women's experiences with American soldiers. A few weeks before the show opened, she had the opportunity to meet Flo:

> I fell in love with her the first time I watched Gaylene Preston's film, and as soon as I heard her call out from her kitchen, I fell in love with her all over again .... I found her to be even more sprightly and funny and delightful and generous in person. Her giggle was contagious and, at ninety, she still had a mischievous gleam in her eye.
>
> Performing *Battles of the Heart* was an extraordinary experience. It was hugely rewarding to have an audience so engaged, so reluctant to leave, so inspired to stick around and share their own stories. Closing night was so special, all our ladies were there. It was difficult to keep a lid on the swelling emotion that came from seeing the women and their families through their young eyes. I found myself gravitating towards Flo during my monologue, and during the rendition of 'White Cliffs of Dover' I clung to her and we both had a big old cry. It was such a privilege and honour to perform this work and to meet these wonderful, open, generous, brave women.[26]

Other members of the cast had similar stories to tell about their journeys on the production and their connection to the audience:

> Laurel Devenie. Performing *Battles of the Heart* is an experience I will never forget and one that we will not ever get much chance to revisit. That kind of precious and visceral material, which is the lives of a lot of the audience, is something quite phenomenal. Performing with the lights on – seeing the recognition in people's faces as they watched – made one realise this project was not about bettering our acting skills but about telling their stories effectively. As I spoke Ali Doyle's monologue, I could feel the listening in the room. It was incredible – you could feel it in all the monologues because of these amazing stories that New Zealanders are close to.[27]

The second-year actors' remarkable range of performance opportunities continued later in the year with *Small Lives, Big Dreams*, a work created by Anne Bogart and SITI Company, and directed at Toi Whakaari by Annie Ruth. She made huge physical demands on the cast, inviting them to go on a journey without the usual anchor of a linear narrative. John Senczuk designed the set, with the audience seated on a 'revolve' that rotated to reveal new locations, allowing them to follow the fluid action of the play. John's set design was realised by Laura Nicholls and Dan Williams, both second-year performance design students. Katie Fletcher, a second-year technical student, created a continuous soundtrack (complete with realistic earthquake); and Paul Evans, a performing arts management student, designed the lighting. *Small Lives, Big Dreams* epitomised the way in which actors, designers, managers and technicians were now collaborating in a highly integrated way to explore the possibilities of theatre. This, in hindsight, seems the more remarkable, given its proximity to the ensuing examination and later denigration of integrated teaching practice at the school.

In marked contrast to anything else, the second-year actors' final production for the year was the Toi Cabaret, which they performed at the Big Kumara in downtown Wellington. Described in the programme as 'raunchy and sinfully salacious', the cabaret was indeed 'an expression of every kind of sin through songs from musicals, cabaret and burlesque'.[28] Coordinated by Australian director Adrian Barnes, this 'decadently in your face' cabaret provided an excellent opportunity for the musical director, Jane Keller, to indulge her love of musical theatre.

Meanwhile, the third-year actors were in rehearsal for their final production, David Williamson's *Jack Manning*, directed by KC Kelly and designed by Penny Fitt. The play, which was based around the world of work, business-related disputes and restorative justice, had an excellent range of acting roles; it was therefore a good vehicle for the graduating actors.

In earlier years, it had been difficult enough to find a single play to showcase a relatively small number of students. Now, with around thirty students graduating each year across a range of disciplines, equality of opportunity within a single graduation production was even harder to achieve. But as other performance projects were available that could equally engage or cater for the specialised interests of final-year students, the graduation production became less of a priority. Some technical, management and design students chose to work with second-year MTA directing students on a wide range of projects, not all of them 'text-based' (in the conventionally accepted sense of the word). For example, Pedro Ilgenfritz Silva created *The Spot*, a devised clown work:

> Making *The Spot* was the highest point of my journey at Toi. I had the opportunity to rehearse for twelve weeks and create a comedy with four actors and one musician. The show was based on clown language (which is my area) and the basic elements of game.
>
> I set out to create a show that would be read by the audience in its details, a non-psychological show where the physical action is dominant over the text, a spectacle that would entertain the audience and display a very high level of acting. The actors were totally in control of the score, actions, the space, characters, the audience and text. They improvised with confidence and economy in a way that I hadn't seen before in other shows in New Zealand. *The Spot* was very close to the essence of theatre and popular forms of drama. It had a very simple story, showing the paradox of homelessness in contrast to our respectable working lives. We wanted to celebrate the street personnel with due respect for their (seemingly useless) role in our society, rather than presenting their drama and our pity towards them.[29]

There were other MTA productions in 2005. Thomas Beauchamp's *Plunge*, a piece of aerial theatre performed by students from the School of Dance, explored the relationship to Wellington's coast and sea. Veialu Aila-Unsworth made a five-minute animated film, *Blue Willow,* in which she aimed to reveal the original elegance that inspired Minton to create his enduring Willow Pattern design. The film was later accepted into the prestigious Berlin Film Festival and was also nominated for two New Zealand Film and Screen awards for Best Short Film and Best Script. Other MTA productions included Julie Noever's devised work, *Girls, Suitcases, Highways & Wide Open Spaces;* a production of *Nga Po Wahine* by Briar Grace-Smith, directed by Tina Cook; *Endgame* by Samuel Beckett, directed by L'Hibou Hornung; *The Play About the Baby* by Edward Albee, directed by Penni Bousfield; and *Attempts on her Life* by Martin Crimp, directed by Steven Whiting.

Toi Whakaari and the New Zealand School of Dance had been lobbying the

▶ *The Spot*, 2005. Brian Hotter and Rina Patel

▼ Prime Minister Helen Clark with dance and drama students, 2005. Toi Whakaari students L–R: Dan Caddy, Aaron Cortesi and Michael Whalley.

Labour government for a number of years to increase the schools' baseline funding. And in August 2005, they received a much needed boost to their coffers, when Prime Minister and Minister for the Arts, Culture and Heritage Helen Clark announced a $1.8 million funding increase for Te Whaea. The government's media release announcing this increase acknowledged the distinctive and highly intensive nature of the education and training provided by both schools:

> This is why we have decided to increase funding so they can continue to deliver the high quality training required by the creative arts industry.
>
> Both Toi Whakaari and the New Zealand School of Dance have a vital role to play in supporting the performing arts. The government wants to ensure the schools continue to offer opportunities for realising the potential of the incredible pool of talent we have in New Zealand.[30]

The liability of $228,000 that related to the outstanding interest owed to the Ministry of Education could now be removed from Toi Whakaari's balance sheet. No actual cash changed hands; it was a sort of technical adjustment, allowing the outstanding loan to be 'forgiven'. However, Toi Whakaari received an additional $150,000 in its annual grant for operational and capital development funds over the next five years, with a further increase in Consumer Price Index adjustments. That equated to approximately $1.8 million across the two schools.

The additional funding strengthened Toi Whakaari's case for the proposed costume construction course. Although approved by NZQA, it had been postponed until term 2 of 2006 because of a delay in getting formal confirmation from the TEC on the level of student component funding for the course. The vital matter of a tutor to lead the costume-construction course was resolved in December, with the appointment of Kaarin Macaulay. She had, fortuitously, moved to New Zealand from Australia when her husband, Adam, was offered work as a producer with Radio New Zealand.

Writing a new course and getting approval for its delivery is one thing, bringing it to reality is an entirely different challenge. It requires a person with the right level of experience to lead it, someone with passion, determination and vision who can develop the programme and also inspire the students. Kaarin Macaulay has all those qualities, in abundance.

After studying media and theatre studies at university, Kaarin worked for five years as a freelance costumier with the Australian Opera and other major Sydney theatre companies. She then moved to Perth to work as a cutter for the West Australian Opera and the Black Swan Theatre Company, later returning to the east coast to work as the principal costumier for Disney's *Beauty and the Beast* in Melbourne, and a range of musicals, including *Phantom of the Opera, Les Misèrables* and *Sunset Boulevard*. For the previous ten years she had worked for the Australian Opera as a cutter, and had also obtained a teaching qualification. Kaarin's insistence on the very highest standard of work, and her students' ability to achieve that, has made the costume-construction course one of the jewels in the crown of Toi Whakaari.

The costume course was approved for six students to be enrolled in each intake of the two-year programme. This was considered to be a realistic or optimum number to ensure graduate employment across theatre, film and TV. Also, the intensive teaching load limited the total number of students to twelve over two years.

The existing costume workshop was just large enough to accommodate the first intake of costume construction students, and preliminary plans had been developed to expand the work room into the space occupied by the theatre loading-bay. If the estimated cost of around $50,000 could not be raised, the costume course could be offered only every two years, with a single cohort of students enrolled at any one time. This was undesirable academically and would also halve the income that was needed to cover the cost of building the extension – something of a Catch-22.

What's more, there were other building priorities competing for funds in 2006. A new floor was needed for Drama Nine to make it usable as a classroom, and a lecture theatre was planned to allow a classroom, currently shared by Toi Whakaari and the School of Dance, to be freed up so that it could be used as an additional studio to house the increasing number of design students.

After nearly a year, the recruitment campaign for an entertainment technology and performing arts management tutor was successfully concluded with the appointment of Emma Weston. She is a graduate of the Royal Welsh College of Music and Drama where she studied stage and events management; after that she worked extensively as a freelance stage and events manager mainly in the UK. Emma's job description later changed to senior tutor in stage, events and production management to reflect her actual teaching responsibilities. She was in her mid-twenties, which meant she was close in age to many of her students, which she saw as a distinct advantage:

> I could understand where they were coming from, as I had recently been through drama school myself. I identified the students' interests really easily and we would discuss the application of a new technology, good gigs to work on and inside stories of accidents – dodgy rigging, poor management and overtime.
>
> Primarily I taught in the areas of stage, events and production management. But there was more to the teaching than mere skills acquisition and the development of technique. My teaching methodology was based on the idea of maximising the students' potential to communicate with one another, and inevitably to communicate with an audience.
>
> For events management, I taught mainly from experience: stories of muddy

◀ Kaarin Macaulay

▶ Emma Weston.
Photo: Annie Ruth

> Glastonbury, fire scares at Winchester Cathedral, and working with fireworks and water. I would get the students really excited about performance outside of the black box, then hit them with a major project that would see them indulging in late nights, coffee and stress over detail, much like the 'events industry' itself. The students got excited by ideas of rock and roll, of late night street theatre, parades through city centres, weddings and conferences. For me, the fundamental purpose of their training was to enable the students to realise the differences between their theatre practice and a wider entertainment industry, and to gain some sense of what it meant to work in [a broader] context.[31]

The number of qualifications delivered by Toi Whakaari had now increased to six, which meant the school no longer had a singular focus. It had truly become multi-disciplinary. This opened up possibilities for greater inter-disciplinary work, which it was hoped would eventually challenge traditional boundaries and widen the students' perception of performance and the nature of theatre. Apart from productions, inter-disciplinary activity at the school had been mostly confined to taha Māori, history of theatre and philosophy, and singing. Toi Whakaari was now looking for ways to extend this inter-activity into other teaching areas to allow students to benefit from the thinking and creativity of students from other disciplines, and in a context not necessarily driven by production deadlines.

Production timelines at Toi Whakaari generally paralleled those of the industry, but this rarely allowed sufficient time or opportunity for students to explore the collaborative process fully, nor did it necessarily foster effective communication or help the development of a common language between the various disciplines. In a response to this, and in a move to promote integration and to maximise possibilities across the courses, a series of half-day visioning meetings was held at the end of 2005. To provide space for all Toi Whakaari and Te Whaea Management Services staff to reflect on and examine their vision for Toi Whakaari, it was decided to end the school year a month early.

Some of the thinking around creative relationships at those meetings was inspired by Sir Ken Robinson, an acknowledged expert in the field of creativity and innovation in business and education. His report, *All our Futures: Creativity and Education*, written in 1999 and commissioned by the Blair government and dubbed the 'Robinson Report',[32] had a huge impact on both government and corporate attitudes towards creativity. A passage from a speech that Robinson gave at a mini-summit on arts education in Melbourne in 2005 seemed to resonate with some of Toi Whakaari's future ambition:

> The most creative periods in history have been when conventional boundaries between disciplines and ways of thinking have become permeable or have dissolved altogether. It's about identifying relationships between ideas and processes that were not previously related. Most creative thinking is driven by group activities; and the reason is this: good groups model the human mind. If you drive creativity, drive it through collaborations [to achieve] a constant cultural interplay.[33]

Here was an 'ideal' that seemed to offer a desirable (and achievable) aim for a multi-disciplinary performing arts school in the twenty-first century: 'to routinely make what has never been done before'. It also reflected the changing purpose of Toi Whakaari and provided a sense of exploration and delight in the future possibilities of performance.

That along with other ideas were explored in the November/December visioning meetings with the aim of promoting an integrated teaching structure at the school. But to achieve that ideal, Toi Whakaari needed a collective vision, one that would respect and support diversity and allow the various departments of the school to sit comfortably with difference and to co-exist without fear of 'appropriation.'

In some respects this concept was much easier for the 'new kids on the block', the design, directing and performing arts management students. They already had a common purpose and a shared vision, and they acknowledged those attributes as necessary prerequisites for collaboration and as essential elements of production practice. The synergy between those disciplines and the acting course had been carefully considered and clearly articulated as part of the accreditation process for all new qualifications at Toi Whakaari, and was readily understood. On the other hand, there had been no major review of the acting curriculum since it was first accredited in 1997 and it contained no reference or requirement relating to interdisciplinary collaboration.

The lack of a common vision across all the disciplines at Toi Whakaari made the task of aligning discussion around mutual co-existence that much harder. Nevertheless, many fundamental issues and concerns were vigorously debated in the end-of-year visioning meetings, including the essential purpose of Toi Whakaari as it moved from serving training needs to focus more on its broader educational purpose.

Some staff argued for increased opportunities for diversity of opinion as a means of encouraging and fostering independence and exchange, with a greater focus on questions instead of answers: 'if theatre chooses to stand in the question, so should the School'. Others felt students needed to take more responsibility for their learning, as this would help them to become independent practitioners who 'would grow the industry, instead of just filling it'. There was general consensus that Toi Whakaari was now an acknowledged centre of performance research, although there needed to be greater focus at the school within that. However, finding the right balance between skills, reflection, critical thinking and process was a work in progress.

The exchanges of views at these meetings were mostly positive: there was a great sense of optimism and it was clear the staff wanted the best for the students, and to see Toi Whakaari reach its full potential.

Emma Weston, who had just joined the school, later reflected on the changes that were happening at that time:

> I arrived at the school during a period of growth and reflection. The school had developed from a school that delivered an acting diploma and a technical production course, to a school that teaches actors, directors, designers, costumiers, technicians and performing arts managers. Of course, with this growth came some significant identity 'crises'. There was intense debate about what the school was, what it was for, who it was for, who was leading it and its future direction; all at a time when a large turnover of tutorial staff occurred.[35]

After the final meeting, an upbeat draft statement was prepared, highlighting the vision and purpose of Toi Whakaari. It captured some of the optimism and the aspirations expressed by many of the staff at those visioning sessions:

- We celebrate collaboration and innovation.
- We embrace the talents of designers, directors, technicians, actors, playwrights, film makers, dramaturges and scholars. We encourage collaboration among disciplines. We promote new and exciting work.
- [Toi Whakaari] staff are practising theatre and screen professionals and our Kura provides a stimulating and supportive learning environment. We are students. We are teachers. We learn from each other.
- Drawing upon a wealth of expertise and collaborative talent, we use a process of skills development, provocation, reflection and analysis to encompass a structured, interdisciplinary approach to the work of making theatre.
- We are a catalyst for change.[36]

While there were many gains at Toi Whakaari in 2005, sadly there had been one significant loss: Rona Bailey passed away in September, at the age of ninety-one. A memorial ceremony was held at Te Whaea with close to 400 people, not so much to farewell Rona as to celebrate her life and work. Jan Bolwell was one of the many speakers at the ceremony and in her valediction spoke about Rona Bailey's valuable contribution to the Drama School and her extensive contribution to biculturalism in Aotearoa:

> With her work as a movement tutor at the New Zealand Drama School, Rona influenced generations of actors. It was at the 1964 Drama Council's Summer School that Nola Millar, that doyenne of the theatre, pushed Rona into exploring the teaching of movement for theatre. Some years later when a national drama school was established, Rona became one of the core movement tutors with Jackie Burt. When George Webby took over the Drama School in 1974 he asked Rona to work as movement tutor with Erica Stephenson. She continued to work in this capacity for the school right up to 1988, retiring at the age of seventy-three.
>
> In 1987 at a conference in Wellington Rona introduced the New Zealand dance community to the basics of biculturalism. I will never forget the sight of this feisty seventy-three-year old socking it to the dancers about race relations in New Zealand. Courageous, passionate, brilliantly articulate and teaching superbly, it seemed to me on that day; it was the culmination of all that Rona had worked for in her life as she brought together her twin passions – the arts and politics.
>
> What a woman she was! We shall not look upon her like again.[37]

Rona Bailey. *Photo: Simon Clark*

Twenty

2006–2007

'It's not about losing anything, it's about actually engaging in collaboration and interdisciplinary activity.'

The healthy and robust discussion at the 2005 visioning sessions helped the school to examine the many options and questions surrounding its future direction. Some of the excellent ideas from those meetings were put into practice in 2006. They included ways to increase collaboration across and within the various disciplines, along with 'new' teaching methodologies to support the students' learning and strategies to empower them as practitioners.

A term adopted during the visioning session to encapsulate some of the ideas explored was 'convergence'. It had been used earlier by Tom McCrory to support his concept of a more integrated approach to teaching within the acting programme. In that context, it made a lot of sense, particularly as the acting curriculum was under review:

> It's something I had been working [on] with the acting department since I arrived. Essentially we are a collaborative art form. That's always been true of theatre or film; therefore the practice of the ability to collaborate and the exploration of the meeting of our different skills, ideas and values, is a most important educational model: more importantly it reflects the realities of our craft. We have to reflect that as a school, not only as a philosophical idea, but in our professional practice.[1]

The scope of convergence now being considered and implemented was far wider. It implied greater collaboration across *all* departments at the school. Initially, this was seen by most teaching staff as desirable, but when the fundamental purpose of 'convergence' was misconstrued by some, it caused divisions within the school.

This partition was not helped by the very mutable nature of the word, the problem being that 'convergence' literally has *too many* meanings. But the generally accepted (OED) meaning is quite explicit: *to come together from different directions so as to eventually meet* – the emphasis here being on *meeting* rather than merging, which is certainly *not* what the school intended. But combining disciplines at the school into a unified whole was seen by some as a likely, undesirable, outcome.

In 2006 the concept of 'convergence' was used as something of a blanket term to cover many different ideas and innovations emerging out of a number of inter-disciplinary projects.

The creative synergy suggested by convergence in its initial usage was manifest when third-year design and management students joined the first-year directing students for management and leadership classes led by Lani Morris. Design, management and directing students teamed up to collaborate on a studio design project for the opera *Faust*. First-year directing and second-year design students worked together on an audio-visual block taught by Stephen Bain; and design and management students shared film production management classes run by Jo Hiles for an entire term. These and other collaborative projects strengthened the students' ability to perceive the production system as a whole, and also their part in it. The cross-disciplinary activity also helped them to forge relationships, which would assist them in their future work.

Other new initiatives to explore the idea of convergence included shared voice and movement classes, involving first-year acting, directing and entertainment, and performing arts management students, led by Tom McCrory. Although successful in integrating new students at the school, these classes were not continued beyond term 1 for logistical reasons. On the other hand, Annie Ruth ran a series of 'viewpoints' sessions throughout the first half of the year, bringing together students from all courses, and culminating in a laboratory or critique. These were extremely valuable in providing students with a common understanding of how to make work together.

Later in the year, Michael Giannitti, a visiting Fulbright Scholar from the USA, led a major three-week lighting design and devising collaboration. He is a highly regarded lighting designer, and is on the faculty of Bennington College in Vermont where he teaches lighting design to students from a range of disciplines. The collaboration between the first-year acting and entertainment technology students was based on a theme of light and dark, an improvised/devised work that the students had previously developed with Leo Gene Peters (2004 MTA graduate). Michael Giannitti also ran specialised lighting design block courses with the design and directing students.

Earlier in the year, a particularly bold exploration of 'convergence' provided a unique opportunity to extend practice around collaboration. This was *Chance*, a design–acting project with 'chance' as both the theme and the methodology. Second-year actors and third-year designers were split into groups to work on independent projects, with some direction from Penny Fitt, Annie Ruth and Tom McCrory. But essentially the students were 'thrown in the deep end' and given the freedom to explore independently the relationship between design and performance. Unsurprisingly, the project had mixed outcomes. This was, after all, the *first ever* design–acting fully devised collaboration at the school: it was a total voyage of discovery for everyone involved.

Sophie Hambleton recalled that her group of four actors and two designers had a 'fantastic time' working on *Chance*. They created *Light Splashes* that explored the idea of chance moments of action captured within a flash of light:

> We made the whole piece behind transformation gauze using a range of light sources. We had a story; but each performance was different because of the variables of light, so

> the audience would interpret the story differently depending on what they happened to see in the flash images. Because the project wasn't tutor-driven, we were able to do our own thing. We had a wonderful relationship with the two designers, but we didn't rely on them for direction. It was interesting – actors and designers coming from two different worlds to make a work without much supervision or structure, but nonetheless a very valuable exercise. We were talking two different languages which we hadn't really encountered before. The project was also pitched as a 'burning exercise' rather than an opportunity to just work together and make a piece of work. I suspect the objective of *Chance* was a bit confusing, but I thought it was a fantastic exercise. We had to make a piece of work; we had to figure out a company; we had to do everything. Had it been more structured, we may not have discovered quite as much.[2]

Toi Whakaari was now venturing into unknown territory, and variable outcomes in collaborations and teaching innovation were to be expected, given a lack of familiarity in dealing with many of the inter-disciplinary processes and dynamics that were bound to emerge. It had been agreed (by most) that living with questions, rather than focusing on answers, was an acceptable way forward: a case of 'do and then review'. To expect the notion of 'convergence' to be worked out in theory was unrealistic; it had to be trialled through the reality of course delivery, which is the normal development process for any new teaching programme.

There was an added complication: the school had both an educational and a training responsibility that together created a tension between the delivery of 'orthodox core skills' and the exploration of new methodologies. Balancing these priorities had always been tricky and now it had to be managed within the context of 'convergence'.

Ongoing confusion about what 'convergence' actually *meant* and the method of implementing it continued to bug the school throughout 2006 and into 2007. Poor communication in defining the purpose and the scope of any proposed changes, and a degree of undue haste in enacting some new initiatives, probably didn't help. To a certain extent, the level of disaffection that emerged around 'convergence' was the result of a relatively fast period of growth and diversification at the school rather than being indicative of a systemic breakdown of fundamental ideals. There was arguably no actual need for 'convergence' to be zealously promoted or formalised as a *new* strategy. After all, the students themselves were already experiencing the benefits of a collaborative learning environment and were naturally making their own alliances across the various disciplines. Much of the hostility that developed around 'convergence' can be traced to unrelated matters, or to conflicting departmental priorities within the school.

Annie Ruth and some heads of department presented results from the 2005 visioning sessions to the Toi Whakaari Board of Trustees at its first meeting in 2006. Annie's report was received very positively by the Board, and they concurred with its opinion about the future direction of the school, this was eventually articulated via a sub-committee as a Strategic Plan for the following five years. The Board gave Annie's visioning statement unanimous acclamation and expressed wholehearted support for the staff's enthusiasm about convergence.[3]

However, Miranda Harcourt introduced a note of caution, alerting the Board to the possibility of 'convergence' leading to a certain homogeneity within the school:[4]

> It wasn't that I feared a homogenous school, but I feared a homogenising experience for the actors – and only in the acting department. My major concern always had been for the experience of the actors. The note of caution that I made at that meeting was sensibly made, even though I was in support of that concept at a global level. In my job as head of acting, I was concerned that the actors' experience would get diluted.
>
> This proved to be the case for the first-year actors in 2006, when movement classes became unbelievably crowded. Tom had embraced the whole idea [of convergence] with open arms and everyone in the world seemed to be in the movement classes: designers, directors, techs, stage managers – everyone. As I feared, the actors' experience of 'training' [would mean] they didn't get any private or quiet time for themselves.[5]

Despite a general sense of optimism about 'convergence' reflected in the acting department's report on its own strategic issues, which was presented to the Board of Trustees in March, the report also expressed a note of caution:

> Although convergence will offer us new opportunities and refreshing challenges, this commitment to unifying the courses across the disciplines will have an impact on the culture of the Acting Department. Tom McCrory has opened his first-year Movement and Training classes to [first-year entertainment technology and directing] students. This means that Tom is teaching over 30 students, not all of whom are committed to or skilled in the work as are the acting students, and this will have an impact on the learning journey of the [first-year acting] students.
>
> The benefits of convergence will be seen when the students, beginning their courses in 2006, graduate into the industry, bringing a fresh cross-disciplinary synergy to the performing arts industry of the future.[6]

The Board formed a sub-committee to develop its Strategic Plan and engaged an outside consultant to help pull the document together. In May 2006, a draft Strategic Plan was ratified by the Trust Board: it contained five key development strategies:

> *Positioning – our strategic place,* which talked about re-positioning the school as a centre of excellence within the national and international arts sectors.
>
> *Convergence,* which implied an interdisciplinary approach, with people building on each other' ideas and arriving at new solutions, particularly in the teaching and explorative work. This would culminate in productions. It went on to list a number of initiatives to realise this goal.
>
> *Course Development,* which tabled five new qualifications under consideration, including a postgraduate Diploma in Drama Teaching and a Masters in Performing Arts (Acting.)
>
> *Financial Sustainability,* which outlined the need for more financial resources to enable Toi Whakaari to achieve its vision. This included the need for a coherent fundraising strategy and the establishment of a Foundation to support the long-term financial security of the school.
>
> *Proactive Governance*: a strategy to consolidate the achievements to date, and to guide, manage and resource the next process of strategic change through a series of strategic objectives. The strategic objectives included extending the school's bicultural commitment further into teaching and performances.[7]

In August, a relatively new member of the Trust Board proposed that 'the Board or Director [should] write to the Ministry of Education's Curriculum Division to outline the revolutionary ideas being developed [at the school] through its convergent teaching, as a model for other educational institutions'.[8] Whether or not that recommendation was followed is unclear. What is clear is that those 'revolutionary ideas' had yet to be fully trialled, and any determination at this stage on their success or otherwise was rather premature. Given the exploratory nature of 'convergence', it was neither practical nor timely for the school to give any assessment of outcomes until the end of the year. As it turned out, the Board's early endorsement of convergent teaching faltered the following year when its support for convergence noticeably waned.

In some respects, convergence was unstoppable, driven by students across the disciplines as they increasingly began to work more collaboratively. It was welcomed by most teaching staff in the design, entertainment technology and management, and directing departments, all of which had clear inter-disciplinary teaching structures and evaluation processes in place to support collaboration.

The benefits of 'convergence' were far from clear for the acting department, however. Many of the acting tutors believed the increased level of inter-disciplinary activity at the school endangered the integrity of the acting curriculum and placed undue pressure on the acting course, at a time when they were 'working on unpacking the acting timetable in order to allow the students more breathing space in their learning'.[9]

An additional factor that made this a particularly inopportune time to introduce a major initiative was the number acting staff on professional leave or working on projects away from the school during 2006. Miranda directed *Look Back in Anger* at BATS and later took the production on tour, to the Silo in Auckland. She also worked as an acting coach on *Bridge to Terabithia*, a Disney/Waldon feature film shot in Auckland. Tom toured with Conch Theatre Company, taking their production of *Vula* to the Sydney Opera House and Fiji. Vanessa Byrnes re-worked and toured Sara Standring's 2005 solo piece *Please Don't Feed the Models*, taking it to the Tauranga Fringe Festival. Sylvia Rands spent time in Australia to undertake work associated with voice training; and Annie was also away for five months on long-service leave, engaged in workshops at La Mama in Umbria.

Contract tutors were employed to help cover these absences, including Rawiri Paratene who came in to 'hold the fort' at the start of the year, and Christian Penny who stepped into the breach as acting director during Annie's absence.

Around this time the position of drama school administrator was filled by Bette Cosgrove. She was a trained secondary school teacher, and for the past six years had worked as the administrator of a private-sector dance school in Wellington, as well as being the administrator of the Kapiti WEA (Education for Adults). When she saw the Drama School administrator's job advertised, she knew it was for her:

> That's what I said in my job application, 'You've just advertised my job in the paper, I could send you my CV and all my experience, but really you just need me'. Christine [Richardson] suggested that I'd better go in to talk to her. I came in and had a look around; I'd been into [Te Whaea] since I was about three, so I knew the building and the

Far left: Bette Cosgrove.
Left: Annabelle O'Meara.
Both photos: Philip Merry

> School of Dance, also I'd been six years with Dance Aotearoa New Zealand [DANZ] and their treasurer for three years, so I knew the building heaps.[10]

Vanessa Byrnes had resigned her full-time position as the acting department manager to spend more time with her family, although she remained at the school as dean for the third-year actors and as a senior tutor. Annabelle O'Meara then took over the management of the acting department, after relinquishing her job as drama school administrator:

> There was a certain dizzying dynamic to the Acting Dept in 2006 – it was like this constant whirlwind which – sitting slightly outside of it as my position required – felt both exhilarating and exhausting. I was surrounded by extraordinarily talented, creative people who were unquestionably dedicated tutors, seemingly adored by the acting students, and yet very clearly wanted to inhabit this other world as well – the world of performance, in all its guises. And because the school places strong importance on professional development, I accepted this as the norm. And when you're Desk Woman in an environment like that, it's fair to say you do a fair bit of rescue work. So I was learning a new job and at the same time wondering when we'd reach calm seas, so to speak. I smile now when I recall a workshop we all did as a staff at the beginning of that year, led by an American woman. It was called 'Listen for Change'. How prophetic.[11]

The discontinuity within the teaching faculty at this time did little to assuage the sceptical view of 'convergence' held by some students, particularly the second-year actors. Over the previous year they'd had a great deal of attention lavished on them, especially around *Tough Act*, and they now sensed a decline in tutorial support and pastoral care, making it harder for them to come to terms with the concept of 'convergence':

> *Sophie Hambleton.* Convergence was an easy victim for almost everything else that was going on in the school, and we needed that eruption; we all had hang-ups from the first year.
>
> The whole convergence period of turmoil, for me, boiled down to a communication breakdown. As a class we had stopped communicating with each other because we were quite divided over the issue. We had no idea what was going on and I really think our training suffered during that second year. That was such a shame – because as a concept I was really excited about convergence: I thought, 'Great, this sounds really interesting and exciting'; but our major concern was that although it sounded fantastic as a plan, we didn't feel that the core fundamental skills of an actor fitted in the concept. We were in

> our second year and yet we hadn't had any voice training all term and we were about to do a Shakespeare. If the fundamentals had been delivered, we would have felt much more secure about discussing convergence.[12]

After their involvement in *Chance*, the second-year actors embarked on a major text-based performance project, *Political Agenda*, which comprised two contemporary plays with a political theme. *Myth, Propaganda and Disaster,* directed by Vanessa Byrnes, was a complex and sophisticated work, relating largely to American foreign policy and encompassing themes relating to post-modern cynicism, such as political, sexual and religious beliefs. *The Laramie Project*, directed by Miranda Harcourt, chronicles the life of the town of Laramie following the hate-crime murder of a young gay man. The play has nearly seventy characters, which gave the cast of fourteen a unique opportunity to each perform between three and six characters.

Following *Myth, Propaganda and Disaster* (an unfortunate title under the circumstances), feelings of disquiet re-emerged, causing the second-year actors to write a letter to voice their concerns about the irregularity of their classes. Referring to their recent production, they criticised the lack of time provided for reflection, not just for the actors, but also between them and the twenty or so production/design crew. The acting students also felt strongly that there was a disconnection in some areas between the declared aims of 'convergence' and the ability of the school to sustain those aims within or alongside the core curriculum:

> Where is the time for reflection in the learning? The School has outlined a vision, which aims to create 'theatre makers'. This requires reflection upon the work in its entirety;

Political Agenda, 2005. Dan Musgrove.
Photo: Daphne Eriksen

> we acknowledged and agreed upon the need for this after the *Chance* collaboration. Yet *Political Agenda* is over with no time to consider the plays at a level beyond our own acting. We must find a way together for efficient reflection … the current situation is not a conducive environment [for creative] theatre makers, thinkers or collaborators.
>
> How does the curriculum reflect the need for on-going skills acquisition classes? This feeling of lack of direction arises largely from the irregularity in our learning. How can you train an actor without full, regular vocal training? As well as skill acquisition we must be taught to practise these skills, regularly, daily.[13]

In fact, the acting department had purposefully folded voice and movement into production work, and it was more than likely the students were getting some voice work within the production process. But there was some validity in their other concerns, and there is no denying the massive implosion at the school towards the end of 2006, which resulted in virtually the whole of the acting department leaving, as Miranda Harcourt recalled:

> At the end of that year we called a meeting, because Annie would not acknowledge that there was a problem in her relationship with the acting department. It was the only time in my entire time at the school that the acting department was a hundred percent united about anything; a common understanding that we had a huge communication rift, with the acting department on one side and Annie on the other. We arranged a mediated meeting, when the whole acting department sat down with Annie up in the classroom, with a professional conflict resolution person. That was a disaster. In the end, we all left – for different reasons.[14]

Nevertheless, Annie Ruth continues to believe that one of the most important advantages of 'convergence' was the increased autonomy it gave to the students:

> That has been a very successful thread; but it was something that really frightened and startled some staff: the idea that you would give the students a degree of autonomy in their final year. It's ironic to me that those who resisted it most were those who thought that students learned best by doing. The result of giving more autonomy has since resulted in more doing. And that is defining the roles of how you impart skills – and in what way: whether to do it always in a classroom situation or whether to do it in an interventionist situation around work that students are making. Since 2006, there's been a move to do more interventionist work, particularly in the final year.[15]

The school had other complex issues to grapple with in 2006. Concerns had been raised about the 'raw deal' that some performance design students had at Massey, particularly in relation to their accommodation and course delivery.

The performance design course at Massey was without a head of department for six months in 2005, as Dorita Hannah was in New York undertaking postgraduate study. And when two performance design contract tutors (Kasia Pol and Jim Acheson) left Massey, they were not replaced; instead, a Masters student (Sam Trubridge) was contracted by the university to keep things together until Dorita returned.

The staffing situation was probably manageable, but it signalled a growing inequality in the relationship between the two institutions that Penny Fitt, for one, was aware of:

> By the beginning of 2005, it was clear that Massey had a completely different view of

> what we were in relation to them. They were happy to [adapt] the performance design course to suit their needs, but what they didn't realise was that as a partner institution we were going to have opinions about how that worked. We questioned the benefit of them delivering things in a different way and we were concerned about not doing a proper collaboration that would accept our style of working as well as theirs. There had been no real space made for the course at Massey, and we were always borrowing spaces from other courses at the Design School. James Acheson worked very hard within Massey to get allocations of space and other resources for the performance design students. But in that process, James became very unpopular.
>
> The way Massey had worked out the funding for the course was that we would bring more students in who would then work across other electives at the university. But as soon as we started channelling the students towards the things that we wanted them to do, to get them more specialised, then we were shutting down those other options. Maybe Massey felt we were feeding off them a bit? We started making demands that they accept our voice, as we felt that they hadn't put enough staff, resources and concentration into the performance design students. After a while, it didn't seem to make any sense to Massey to run the performance design course with such a small number of students: it didn't seem right to them that they had to provide this entire infrastructure and yet only get half of the income. As soon as the students saw what they were getting at Toi Whakaari, they also began to question why equal resources were not provided for them at Massey.[16]

Towards the end of 2005, Penny Fitt had reported to the Trust Board that 'There is now, I believe, a marked contrast in the ownership and support of the degree from the two different institutions.'[17]

Toi Whakaari was certainly pulling its weight in the delivery of the performance design programme, with a full-time head of design, and also John Senczuk who had been contracted for six months to teach design papers. Numerous contract tutors were also employed by Toi Whakaari's design department to teach in specialised areas of computer technology, lighting design, prop making, costume design and multi-media studies.

At the end of 2005, Massey delivered a bombshell, declaring that the performance design degree was too expensive for it to deliver, and sought to increase Toi Whakaari's responsibility for the degree. Shortly after that, Massey presented the school with a number of options, including a phased disestablishment of the qualification, as well as a proposal to sub-contract the entire performance design programme to Toi Whakaari. The latter seemed to ignore the essential relationship between Massey and Toi Whakaari: that the two institutions were equal and joint partners in both teaching and awarding the performance design degree.

Massey had clearly started to wind down its commitment to the degree. The promised appointment of a senior performance design tutor had been abandoned, and many performance design classes were taught together with interior design. That solution may have alleviated Massey's immediate resourcing dilemma, but from Toi Whakaari's perspective it did not appear to serve the best interests of the performance design students.

Following a further investigation of the funding model for the design degree, Massey decided it was no longer 'economic' and that the 'funding model' did not support a 'shared delivery with two sets of infrastructure and staff'.[18] A suggestion to increase student numbers to an 'acceptable level', i.e. thirty students in each year of the performance design programme, was discounted because of the additional resources Massey would have to provide to support such a large number of students.[19]

Toi Whakaari and Massey therefore agreed to seek a disestablishment of the Bachelor of Performance Design, and a draft Transition Agreement was developed by both institutions to enable the currently enrolled students to complete their studies and to safeguard the integrity of the degree until it was taught-out in 2010.

It could be argued that the termination of the performance design programme vindicated parts of the 'minority report', which had earlier challenged the establishment of the joint performance design degree when it was accredited in 2002, particularly in its assertion that:

> Massey University offers Interior, Industrial, Transport, Fashion and Textile Design courses with no existing proven or established components of stage design contained within them. In such generic teaching of the disciplines associated with it, the art of performance design, specifically theatre design, will be compromised .... it is probable that there will be conflict, involving design philosophy and the ability of Massey to facilitate the delivery of the course programme to a standard demanded by the theatre industry .... When programmes of study for highly specialised areas such as design for performance, specifically theatre, are being created, the priority must be to provide principles of quality over those of quantity.[20]

For at least the first few years, both institutions were aligned in their philosophy and in their ambition for the Bachelor of Performance Design. Ultimately, what caused the eventual demise of the degree was the harsh economic reality that Massey faced in its attempt to deliver it, a view that was reinforced by the university's bean-counters.

In all other respects, the two institutions maintained a good relationship. It was later agreed that Toi Whakaari could seek approval from its Boards to allow the school to gain accreditation for its own three-year design degree: a Bachelor of Performing Arts (Design). This would be delivered solely by Toi Whakaari with a proposed start date of 2008, and would run concurrently with the existing Bachelor of Performance Design until it was disestablished. To avoid intellectual property issues arising from the disestablishment of the performance design degree, a totally new degree framework had to be developed.

Toi Whakaari had made a considerable commitment in terms of human and physical resources to establish the degree in the first place, and the decision to terminate it was therefore extremely disappointing, particularly for those who had put a lot of time, passion and effort into developing the qualification. It was equally disappointing for the remaining performance design students who were naturally concerned about the ongoing delivery of their course and the long-term value of their qualification. They also needed to be reassured that sufficient resources would be provided until the degree was taught-out.

Yet there was a silver lining. In the process of shaping its own design qualification, Toi Whakaari was able to review the purpose of the degree and then to align it with the school's developing strategic vision. The previous three years had given the school an opportunity to better understand the importance of design and its relationship to other performance disciplines. This had strengthened Toi Whakaari as a multidisciplinary conservatorium.

Because the jointly delivered Bachelor of Performance Design had been established prior to 'convergence', there was no easy framework for delivering or integrating cross-disciplinary projects between Toi Whakaari and Massey. At the same time, a design degree delivered solely by Toi Whakaari would provide much greater flexibility, allowing design students to more easily integrate their training with students from other courses.

The appointment of a head of design at Toi Whakaari had been made *after* the Bachelor of Performance Design was accredited in 2002, and therefore an essential voice had been missing in the initial development of the degree. Penny Fitt was now well-positioned to shape a more focused curriculum, one that would align the teaching programme with live theatre and film, and other qualifications delivered by the school.

In what now seems like an impossible timeframe, Penny Fitt developed and wrote the new design degree in just a few months, at the end of 2006. She used some of that time to gain industry support for its delivery, allowing her to submit an application to NZQA before the Christmas break.

Paradoxically, four cohorts of performance design students attended the school in 2006, significantly increasing the teaching load of the design department. To meet this demand, Claudio Tolusso was appointed at the start of the year as a full-time design tutor. She had studied scenography at Stuttgart Art Academy and had worked in theatre, film and exhibition design in Switzerland for the previous eight years. Claudio brought a contemporary European viewpoint and a broad knowledge of visual art, installation and scenography practices to the design course, setting high standards of rigorous thinking and visual communication.

The two-year Diploma in Costume Construction course officially got under way in April 2006, with an intake of six students from New Zealand – Fiona Brown, Bekky Campbell, Gemma Crouch-Gatehouse, Anna Mahy, Helen Moate and Victoria Young – and one from Texas, Chris McGowan. Chris arrived later than the others as she had to wait for loan approval from a foundation in the USA. As an international student she was paying a full fee of around $20,000 a year, which assisted the financial viability of the costume course at its inception.

Bekky Campbell had completed an acting course at Hagley Community College in 2003, and a year later enrolled in the Toi Whakaari entertainment technology course. At the end of her two years, she decided to transfer into the third year of the newly accredited performing arts management programme to develop her stage management skills. But when she discovered that the costume construction course had also been approved – and was about to start – it triggered a moment of 'self revelation', leading her finally to admit to a much greater passion – costume:

> The best moment for me was being in my garden at home and realising I wasn't going to do the BPAM and realising I desperately wanted to do the costume course, and feeling awesome about it. That was one of the best feelings I've ever experienced, apart from graduating.[21]

It was certainly the right decision; Bekky was clearly in her element for the next two years, evident in her broad grin and the wonderful work she produced. After graduating from the costume course in 2007, Bekky has worked continuously as a costumier and now specialises in theatrical corsetry:

> I just love corsetry. In my first year of the costume course we did Elizabethan foundation garments and it immediately fired within me a passion and hunger for corsetry. In my second year I completed an elective on Victorian foundation garments, I knew then that was what I wanted to do. I now sell corsetry on-line, mainly to customers who wear them as outer garments, or to people who want to create a historic garment and need the right foundation. I also do bridal corsetry and make a few for costume hire businesses.[22]

As soon as the first intake of costume construction students arrived at the school, they hit the floor running to make up the time they'd lost in the first term. Within a few months, they gained some basic costume skills and then threw themselves into their first production as costume assistants on *Political Agenda*. A month later they were making costumes for *Henry VI*.

The increase in design students and the introduction of the costume construction course meant that the student population at the school was now at an all-time high. Excluding the first-year performance design students, who at this time were based mainly at Massey, there were fifty-nine actors, twenty technicians and performing arts managers, thirty-one performance designers, ten directors and seven costumiers: a total of 127 students.

The third-year stream of the performing arts management course expanded the number of management and entertainment technology students at the school. Shelley Irwin, a 2004 graduate of the entertainment technology course, was one of four third-year management students. She was working as the production manager for Centrepoint Theatre and had re-enrolled at the school on a part-time basis to increase her management skills and to upgrade her qualification to a degree.

The school was again very fortunate in finding a group of specialists who were not only leaders in their field, but could also teach. Performing arts managers require a range of skills, different in many respects to those in other commercial or business sectors. Not only do they have to co-exist and function effectively in a collaborative and cooperative relationship with performers, but their work is also central to the realisation of the creative vision.

The stated purpose of the performing arts management degree at Toi Whakaari is to prepare students to operate in a dynamic and fast-changing environment. To deliver that, the school needed visionary tutors who could both inspire students and instil the necessary qualities of leadership. In this and every other regard, the tutors chosen to bed in the management programme were truly excellent. Lani Morris taught one of the central core units, the principles of performing arts management. She had a very direct approach to the subject, based on uncovering latent management potential on which she then focused to develop leadership and/or entrepreneurial skills. Her method recognised that students would eventually operate in a range of performance areas that would often require them to produce their own work. As well as performing arts management students, Lani's classes incorporated MTA directors and performance designers, creating a unique opportunity for the role and purpose of 'management' to be debated from individual perspectives within an evolving learning environment. Discussions are often heated, reflecting the students' engagement with complex questions around management and leadership more than anything else. Many epiphanies occurred as a result of those sessions as students realised their own distinctive management capabilities and began to understand how these could support their future practice. In some cases, the students were led to completely rethink their career path.

Other tutors working in the third year of the BPAM included Jo Hiles, teaching film production management, an intensive hands-on elective over one term. A vital core unit of the degree, calling for a creative approach to what might otherwise seem a dry subject, was financial management. This was taught by Chris Prowse, a highly regarded financial manager who had for many years been the administrative director of Downstage before moving to the New Zealand Film Commission as its financial director. Justine Stuart taught arts funding and sponsorship, again a difficult subject to teach within a single elective, but nevertheless she developed a unique approach that was later expanded by Briar Monro. Jane Chewings (1997 technical production graduate) came on board later to teach marketing and promotions.

Derek Simpson, who had coordinated the production unit in 2005, was unable to fulfil the role for much of 2006 because he had a previous production commitment to take *Vula* to the Sydney Biennale. In the interim, the position was filled by Anneliese Mudge, a 1998 technical production graduate who had recently been working at Victoria University's Studio 77 as a theatre technician.

To create a better alignment between production processes and other teaching activity at the school, a new process was introduced at the start of the year whereby directors were invited to attend staff meetings to discuss their production objectives. This enabled tutorial and administrative staff to give better support to students in their production practice. The benefits of this quickly became evident on the *Henry VI* trilogy, which David O'Donnell directed in August.

Henry VI was chosen for the opportunity it gave to the twenty-two second-year actors, allowing each of them to perform a substantial Shakespearean role or a succession of significant minor roles. Equally important were the many creative and collaborative opportunities provided for the design, entertainment technology and management, and costume students. It also gave audiences the chance to see a full production of *Henry VI*, which had never been staged professionally in New Zealand.

The production coincided with the military conflict escalating in the Middle East and elsewhere, which made some details of the *Henry VI* trilogy resoundingly familiar. The play also raised questions about the nature of power and leadership. For these reasons, David O'Donnell chose to include both modern and historical elements in the production:

> As you experience the story of dysfunctional families, capitalism's greed, factionalism, disappointed egos, and a grand regime turning poisonously upon itself, consider its relevance to current world affairs.[23]

David O'Donnell, 2009.
Photo: David Lewis

▶ *Henry VI*, 2006. L–R Anya Tate-Manning, Stephen Townshend, Evania Vallyon.
Photo: Michael Parrott

David's connection with Toi Whakaari went back to 1978 when he was an acting student at what was then the New Zealand Drama School. His more recent association was as a lecturer in theatre at the School of English, Theatre and Film at Victoria University, where he taught on the MTA directing programme. He was also a member (and later, chair) of the MTA joint Board of Studies. Since 1985, David has directed over fifty productions, and was nominated in the Chapman Tripp Theatre Awards for Best Director, Best Production and Most Original Production in 1999, and again in 2001 for *Sojourns of the Boy* and *Irish Annals of Aotearoa*.

His background as an actor/director/academic clearly helped him to plan and to convey his concept for *Henry VI* to the cast. The amount of care he took, and the time he invested in relating his production ideas to the entire crew, fostered a sense of shared ownership. This came at an opportune time when 'convergence' was still in its infancy and being tested. Sophie Hambleton played three characters in *Henry VI* – Lady Stafford, Joan of Arc and Spirit – and she believes this production gave her class a new insight into the benefits of collaboration, also known as convergence:

> In some respects we felt that convergence was already operating – all disciplines working together – although we understood that most [performance] projects were actor-driven, and knew that had to change. We were working with all the other students: the designers and technicians were working on our shows, yet we weren't actually talking with them about the process. … So we said, 'OK let's talk to them'. But it wasn't until the *Henry VI* production that I felt we were working closely with the students from other disciplines, and they discussed their ideas with us, and suddenly we realised that we were all equally

Images left and immediately below:
Students moving into Te Whaea,
April 1988

Te Whaea Opening Ceremony, 1998

The Threepenny Opera, 1998. Nigel Collins and Jane Donald. *Photo: Simon Clark.*

The Threepenny Opera, 1998. Bjorg Halldorsdottir. *Photo: Simon Clark.*

The Big Game rehearsal, L: Tausili Mose, C : Ian Mune, R: Matt Wilson. *ATL Dominion Post Collection.*

Avalon Studios – fast turnaround TV, 1998. L–R: Rachel Butler, (second year technical production - 2nd AD), John Callen, Kirsty O'Sullivan (second-year actor)s

Avalon Studios – fast turnaround TV, 1998. L–R Karl Drinkwater, Tausili (Mose) Pushparaj, Tama Smith and Pook Berrigan -technical production (in background) .

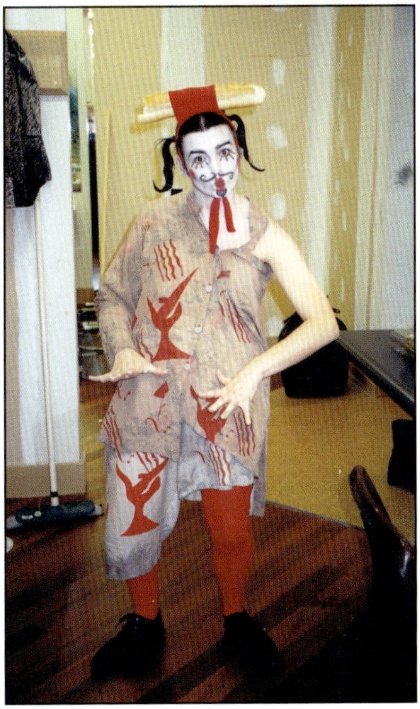

The Tempest, 1999. Nikki MacDonnell.

The Tempest, 1999. Jerome Le'ota (L) and Robbie Hunt (R). *Photo: Matt Grace.*

Great Expectations, 2004.
Photo: Michael Parrott

Penumbra, 2004. Tze Hung Wong and Jessie Alsop. *Photo: Michael Parrott*

Pericles, 2004. Rowan Bettjeman and Tania Nolan. Nathaniel Lees (standing)

Pegasus, 2005. Male dancers (Toi Whakaari) L–R: Martyn Wood, Allan Henry (obscured) Gareth Williams, Ryan O'Kane, performing with dancers from the NZ School of Dance. *Photo: Michael Parrott.*

Accident and Eternity, 2005. L–R: Allen Henry and Ryan O'Kane.

Battles of the Heart cast with director and tutors, 2005

Small Lives, Big Dreams, 2005. L–R: Arthur Meek, Laurel Devenie, Martyn Wood, James Conway-Law, Brooke Williams. *Photo: Daphne Eriksen*

Chance, 2006. *Photo: Derek Simpson*

Peer Gynt cast, 2006. *Photo: Michael Parrott.*

Delicates, 2006. Sophie Roberts. *Photo: Dawn Cheong*

2006 Toi Cabaret at The Big Kumara.
Front L–R: Shaneel Sidal, Byron Coll,
Bryony Skillington, Ahilan Karunaharan. *Photo: Michael Parrott*

White Lie cast (stage production), 2007.
Photo: Michael Parrott

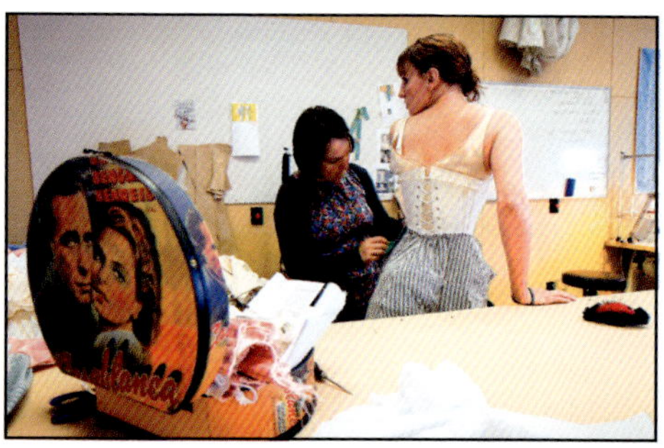

Above left: Costume fitting. *Photo: Philip Merry*
Above right: Costume construction student. *Photo: Philip Merry*

◀ Lighting class with entertainment technology, advanced diploma and performing arts management students. *Photo: Philip Merry*

Acting class with Nathaniel Lees.
Photo: Philip Merry.

A History of American Film, 2007. Salad Girls L–R: Martine Grey, Tansey Hayden, Alix Bushnell, Chelsie Preston Crayford, Mel Firbank. *Photo: Derek Simpson*

Arcadia, 2007. L–R: Stephen Townshend, Bryony Skillington, Sophie Hambleton, Antonia Bale. *Photo: Philip Merry*

Teina leading a Kōiwi session with the entire school. *Photo: Briene Lermitte.*

Toi students and staff at Manutuke Marae, 2008

Macbeth, 2008. L-R: Kay Smith, Juanita Hepi, Aroha White. *Photo: Philip Merry*

▲
Christine Richardson's 'Out of Africa' admin farewell. Standing L–R: Tamara Aluwihare, Jane Clink, Priscilla Gough, Riejke Taljard (School of Dance), Annie Ruth, Tina Alinen (School of Dance), Cathy McCullagh, Dee O'Connor, Virginia Earle. Seated L–R: Christine Richardson, Salesi Le'ota, Bette Cosgrove. Reclining: Steve Stirrat.

Bill Guest send-off, July 2008.
Photo: Bette Cosgrove

A Midsummer Night's Dream, 2009.
James Tito.
Photo: Stephen A'Court

Toi Whakaari 2009

> involved in the production – and that was fantastic. Great friendships and partnerships were made, which still exist between many graduates from that year.[24]

Brian King, then in his final year as a performance design student, was a leading figure in the *Henry VI* creative team, designing the set and costumes. Brian had already completed some impressive commissions, including the set design for Murray Lynch's production of *Niu Sila* in 2004, and more recently for *Doubt* at Centrepoint Theatre. Brian later designed the set for the 2006 graduation production, *Peer Gynt*.

Peer Gynt was directed by John Bolton, a pre-eminent Australian director and teacher of physical theatre. After lecturing at the Victorian College of the Arts from 1985 to 1991, he founded and ran his own theatre school in Melbourne until 1999, and was currently head of acting at the Victorian College of the Arts.

For the Toi Whakaari production, he chose Kenneth McLeish's translation which had been used by England's National Theatre for their 1990 production. With thirty-eight scenes it had a running time of around three hours. A convention allowed the principal role of Peer Gynt to be performed by the entire cast simply by donning a red beanie. John Smythe reviewed the production, and apart from the device of the beanie, which he felt 'rendered the whacky tale of daring do that establishes Peer as a charismatic bullshit artist, less than riveting', he was impressed by the quality of the ensemble work:

> Everything is wondrously executed, with a clear and committed understanding of the sometimes surreal text giving rise to stunning ensemble work that creates place, mood and a supportive context for each scene of the play. In each speaking role – and the odd non-speaking one – all the actors find a centred anchor point that allows them to soar and shine while going with the flow and always remaining part of the overall 'orchestra'.[25]

In addition to the 'mainstream' productions, other performance projects in 2006 clearly demonstrated the underlying principles of 'convergence', especially those that were initiated by students. They included *The Glass Menagerie*, directed by Willem Wassenaar, a second-year MTA directing student. It was first performed in the Garage Space in October, followed by a second season at Circa Two, with a cast of four (2005) acting graduates and a team of production/design students who had 'gravitated' to the production, seduced by Willem's vision for the play. The company worked with the provocation of *The Glass Menagerie* being a subjective memory play, emphasising the language of memory through performance and design to provide 'truth in the pleasant disguise of illusion'. The cast, dressed in white costumes with white 'clown' make-up and eyes and lips emphasised with colour, performed on an all-white set in the middle of the Garage (black) space. To jolt the audience from expecting a semi-realistic or sentimental version of the play, the cast chose to work with quite surreal elements:

> The production is a bit like *The Glass Menagerie* on acid. It's definitely taking the audience into a space where you question what is real and what is not real. I'm not interested in staging a play where people judge these characters as right or wrong: that is simplicity. I think the job of theatre is to provide the audience with something they can think about, to ask questions. With day-to-day life we put things in place to make life simple, which is needed for survival. But in theatre you can put in the complexity of what is happening behind the choices.[26]

In his final MTA year, Willem Wassenaar directed *Delicates*, a site-specific theatre performance in the Riddiford Launderette in Newtown, loosely based on the story of *Alice in Wonderland* which he adapted to create a fantastical journey. The audience was invited into a surreal world, where 'washing powder, raisins and clothes become magical':

> As a theatre director I embrace the childlike quality of human nature. I feel that in art we need to be addressed on that pure and primal level; to be constantly reawakening our curiosity. I do not associate *childlike* with innocence, rather I define this quality as a bare and naked truth, an uncultivated phenomenon that we all carry yet often shield from others for risk of exposing our sensitivity and vulnerability to the world around us.[27]

The Glass Menagerie, Delicates and many other MTA and self-directed projects now being produced by students at the school endorsed the value of unfettered collaboration across the various disciplines. Production students working on *Delicates* or *The Glass Menagerie* were never 'assigned' to those projects; they simply involved themselves, seizing the opportunity to extend their performance skills in areas beyond the 'normal' range, or the formal expectation, of their training at Toi Whakaari.

Karl Jenkins, a final-year performing arts management student, co-directed *Delicates* and was also the director of photography and camera operator for the film. Karl again moved beyond the 'normal range' of his management training when he later produced and directed his own devised dance work, *Dis-pose*, with students from the School of Dance and the assistance of Daniel Williams, a final-year performance design student, together with a team of management and technology students. This 'extra-curricular' project demonstrated the value of self-directed work, particularly when supported by clear learning objectives and backed by resources and training to allow students to follow their passions.

Fishnets, tailcoats, high heels and underwear were the order of the day in October, when the second-year acting students brought a touch of 1920s Weimar Republic decadence to the Big Kumara for the 2006 Toi Cabaret. It was directed by Adrian Barnes with musical direction by Jane Keller. Using songs mostly composed by Kurt Weill, Bertolt Brecht, Kurt Eisner and Wolf Beirmann, the production set out 'to confuse gender and played with the idea of what you see is not necessarily what you get'. As Adrian Barnes put it, 'our aim is also to have as much fun as we can with our clothes on – well, not all our clothes on'.[28]

During 2006 there were some major changes to the Toi Whakaari Board of Studies. Steve La Hood resigned as chair but continued his association as a member of the Board of Trustees. Jean Packman then became the acting chair until Grahame Tetley was appointed to the position in November. Grahame had a particular interest in the school convergence philosophy, as well as taha Māori. And he was keen to clarify the function of the Board of Studies, particularly its relationship to the Board of Trustees and to the recently formed Curriculum Committee. He was also concerned about the imbalance between the number of internal and external members on the Board of Studies and was keen to see that resolved.

The Board of Studies meeting at the end of 2006 was fairly upbeat. Department heads reported a positive outcome for the year, with optimistic predictions for 2007. Christian Penny noted that all MTA students were expected to pass in both years of the directing programme, and 'he had agreement from Victoria University to guarantee the current funding levels for the course in 2007'.[29] This was particularly good news as there had been some doubt about the ongoing financial viability of the MTA programme, brought about by new rules concerning research funding. The Bachelor of Performing Arts Management had just completed its first year of NZQA monitoring and had passed with flying colours; building consent had also been granted for the (much needed) extension to the Costume Workshop. Penny Fitt gave an account of the final-year performance design students' work in film, documentary, exhibition and live theatre. Encouragingly, if not a little surprisingly, Miranda Harcourt reported that the acting department was –

> … united in its ambition to advance the work of the History, Theory and Philosophy of Film and taha Māori programmes within the School in 2007, and we are committed to advancing processes of reflection and assessment for the productions and block courses. The Acting Department is also working towards achieving a Convergent model across the disciplines of the whole school community and we are committed to the process of school-wide discussion and negotiation … in order to re-form Toi Whakaari as a place of cross-disciplinary collaboration and creativity.[30]

The conclusion of the 2006 academic year was marked by a stylish graduation ceremony, this time held in the Plaza and set out in a banquet configuration. It was a particularly auspicious event as it was the first time the school had graduated performance designers and performing arts managers. The whole shebang was designed by Daniel Williams, a performance design student, as his major final-year design project. The graduating designers also set up an exhibition of their work to coincide with the ceremony.

Graduation ceremonies at Toi Whakaari are always special, they each have their own flavour and highlights. This is particularly so for the vanguard of each new course, the 'guinea pigs' who are the first to trial and form the new curriculum. The pioneer graduates of the Bachelor of Performance Design in 2006 are worthy of special mention: Amanda Jelicich-Kane, Brian King, Matt Kleinhans, Laura Nicholls, Rachael Spitzer and Daniel Williams. And the Bachelor of Performing Arts Management graduates were Paul Evans, Charlotte Gordon and Nga Larsen.

They and other graduates were not the only people farewelled by the school in 2006. Sadly, Dr Geoffrey Gibbs, who for a number of years had been the external monitor for most of the degree courses at Toi Whakaari, passed away in August. His wise counselling would be greatly missed, for he had been a strong advocate of Toi Whakaari's academic and cultural ambition. Dr Gibbs would no doubt have approved of the new degree monitor, John Senczuk, as his worthy successor: at that time John was the director of performing arts at WAAPA. The degree monitor for the Bachelor of Performance Design continued to be Tommy Honey.

Miranda Harcourt, who was on maternity leave following the birth of her third child, announced her resignation as head of acting effective from May 2007. A press

◄ 2006 Bachelor of Performing Arts graduates. L-R Paul Evans, Charlotte Gordon, Nga Larsen.

▼ 2006 Bachelor of Performance Design graduates. L–R Rebeka Whale, Dan Williams, Brian King, Amanda Jelicich-Kane, Matt Kleinhans, Laura Nicholls, Rachael Spitzer

release issued shortly after her resignation simply stated: 'Miranda now wished to take on different challenges. She had her own theatre and screen projects underway and also planned to extend a consultancy, which she had established, to develop executive communication and presentation skills.'[31]

As an acting tutor from 1998 and then later head of acting, Miranda had made a valuable contribution to the school. Her overriding ambition during that time was to ensure the actors graduated with a diverse range of practical skills, and in doing so she empowered many to create their own work in an increasingly dynamic performing arts industry. That legacy is particularly evident in Toi Whakaari's screen programme, which Miranda zealously developed and promoted, both within the school and the industry:

> I see that as a major achievement for me. When I got to Toi Whakaari the screen experiences were distancing and disempowering. Whereas later it became about working together to make a product over a period of time, understanding that actors could add something to the product, but also understanding that they were entering into this

> extremely hierarchical set-up; this enabled them to come out better equipped to enter a film set and with a better understanding of what it is to act on film.
>
> What had previously been happening at Toi Whakaari, in terms of acting-for-camera, were little block courses about very arcane aspects of acting for screen, which had nothing to do with the actual practice of acting for screen. So people would walk into a film set out of Toi Whakaari and find that they had no skills about actually being on a film set: they … had no idea about this whole other world called 'screen acting'.
>
> So there were a number of things that we had to institute into the current model of making short films. Key to that is being able to work in the hierarchy of the film industry, but also having the freedom and credibility to bring your best to it.
>
> I'm really proud of the legacy that's been left there and I'm really proud to see the line up of excellent graduates now all graduating with film experience.[32]

Over the past ten years there has been a marked increase in the number of acting graduates working in TV drama and feature films, both nationally and internationally. The six films produced at the school during Miranda's watch have also, at various times, been screened at international film festivals.

When Miranda left, the head of acting position was filled temporarily by Aileen O'Sullivan. This was the second time she'd stepped into the breach as temporary head of acting at the school, although this time she had just come out of hospital after having surgery. Under those circumstances she had every reason to say 'no', but not Aileen. As Annabelle O'Meara recalled:

> Aileen is very much an *anything's possible* person, a classic southern woman, so despite being just out of hospital with a knee joint replacement, she turned up ready to work … along with her rehab 'Exercycle' that sat in our office for the next month or two. Like clockwork, she would abandon her desk and climb on this thing for a prescribed number of minutes. Should a student or tutor want to chat, they did so amidst the pedalling and the whirring of the machine, as Aileen imparted advice or whatever was required of her.[33]

Aileen left after the first term and Robin Payne took over as temporary head of acting, until she too left, in July, to teach actors, directors and drama teachers in Shanghai. Jonathon Hendry was then appointed as the permanent head of acting but was unable to take up the position full time until 2008 as he had projects to complete at Circa, where he was directing *Hollow Men*, and at the Silo in Auckland. When Robin Payne returned to Wellington, she was again contracted by the school as temporary head of acting until the end of 2007.

Student enrolments were now at their highest in ten years and the school had no difficulty in filling its annual quota of acting students from around 150 auditionees. In 2007 there were twenty-two students in each year of the acting course, with five of the first-year students under the age of twenty.

The age requirement for entry into the acting course was lowered from twenty to eighteen in 2006 and came into effect in 2007. This change, first proposed in 2005, was to capture talented young people who were not prepared to wait two to three years after leaving school to apply for Toi Whakaari with many going instead to the National Academy of Singing and Dramatic Arts and UNITEC. Annie Ruth also believed that, for young women at least, the earlier they trained the better: 'Their prime time for a career is during their youth, and it seemed a pity to take up so much of that prime employment time with training.'[34]

This new policy enabled the school to take younger applicants with the maturity and talent to warrant an early acceptance, but it was thought unlikely that a significantly larger percentage of younger people would be taken into the school. Contrary to that belief, there has since been a noticeable increase in eighteen and nineteen-year old students in the first year of the acting course, despite the total number of applicants for the course remaining fairly constant, at around 140 to 150 each year.

Although the lower entry age had no adverse effect on the attrition rate, some tutors felt they could no longer assume that students knew some very fundamental things, which affected the way they taught. There have been other, more profound changes, of which Annabelle O'Meara was very aware in her capacity as the acting course manager:

> Well, the word 'mother' comes up more often than it used to in relation to younger students. It's actually been a surprise, the speed with which the first-year cohort has morphed into this picture of nascent youth. When we first lowered the minimum age, the expectation was that just one or two exceptional school-leavers would be included in the first-year intake, but with so many seventeen and eighteen year-olds now auditioning throughout the country, the flow-on is inevitable. Certainly there is more pastoral care needed than in the past and that's understandable. Coping with actor training is challenging enough, but the double whammy of finding mum's not around to do the washing, shop for and cook tonight's dinner is at best deeply inconvenient for these kids; at worst it can be a precursor to sickness, chronic insomnia, flatting problems and so on. But our department's policies around discipline are designed to really help and hold the actors and I'm proud of that. Another outcome that is more subtle perhaps is our communication with the students and theirs with us as staff. While some of the really young students have a remarkably easy and relaxed way with staff, others struggle with the transition from high school-speak to something more worldly. Often it's not till third year that a more adult connection is made and it's invariably very rewarding. They see you as a true friend and ally as they leave here.[35]

For the first two months of 2007, Christian Penny and Penny Fitt were in Auckland, re-mounting *Penumbra* for the Auckland Festival AK07 at SKYCITY theatre. During their absence, Robin Payne filled the breach as head of directing and Cathryn Monro as head of design.

Penumbra had undergone something of a metamorphosis since it was first conceived in 2004. Whereas the original production had ten actors, the Auckland production had sixteen, but only three were from the original cast as many were now working on other projects. Their roles were taken over by other Toi Whakaari graduates. The crew for the re-staged *Penumbra* included Toi Whakaari graduates, as well as current entertainment technology and performing arts management students, led by Derek Simpson as production manager.

Penny Fitt completely re-designed the AK07 version of *Penumbra*. She and Christian would have preferred to use the fairly intimate Maidment Theatre instead of SKYCITY Theatre, with its vast auditorium and enormous stage, which proved difficult to fill with the allocated budget. The distance between the stage and the audience presented a considerable barrier:

> It's surprising what you can tolerate in a raw space – in a drama school, in a basement – that you cannot tolerate in an end-frame theatre in a professional situation – in a festival. And how do you convey a work that is very much about people's own experiences and their history across a faceless distant audience? Even before you get into the theatre, the whole SKYCITY complex numbs you; it's like being in Vegas or some scenic park. However, we did a whole lot of new different things. I thought we used the [proscenium] frame beautifully; we worked with that in the design and the different transitions between all the 'contacts' in the piece worked fantastically. It also allowed certain theatrical gestures that worked well on the larger stage. We built a whole railway line, with the Van Dooren's house on it which trundled across the stage, and also an illuminated model of the Tangiwai train, which shot across one of the rails at the end of the play when the whole eclipse thing was happening.[36]

Another innovative performance project at the start of 2007 was *White Lie*, devised by Megan Adams with the second-year actors and a team of performance design, costume, entertainment technology and performing arts management students. *White Lie* had a choreographic provocation with a minimum amount of spoken text. All of the physical movement was created by the cast, whose ideas and insights helped to shape the work through a process of devising and improvising. Together the company developed a unique movement vocabulary and a shared understanding of dance. After its season in Te Whaea Theatre, film maker Warren Green and the second-year actors set about translating *White Lie* from stage to screen, to make a short film that was shot on location in Island Bay.

Staff changes in 2007 included the appointment of Kate Robertson as production coordinator. She had been enticed from her job as production manager at Downstage to take on the full-time position when Derek Simpson was unable to continue in that role because of his commitment to *Penumbra*.

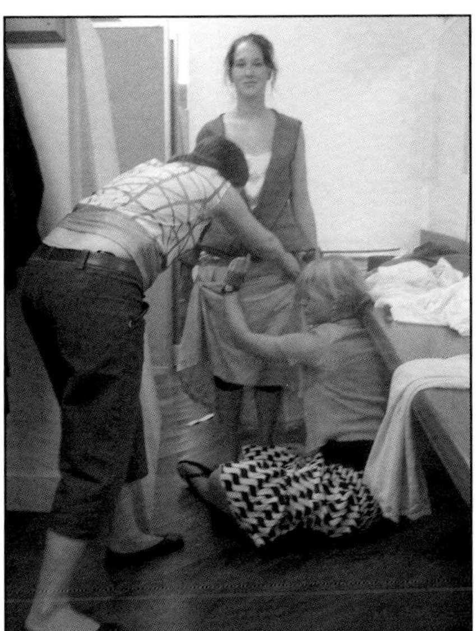

Costume fitting for *White Lie*. L–R: Caitlin Le Harival (designer), Sara Allen (performer), Marina Davis (designer).

Teina Moetara also joined the staff in 2007, replacing Keriana Whati as the taha Māori coordinator. Before she left, Keriana presented the staff with a number of questions to consider on the purpose and delivery of taha Māori, and challenged the school's stated commitment to biculturalism. Her main question to the staff was: Why is [taha Māori] of worth to the school and how will the Industry benefit from this teaching?[37]

There was a growing awareness that, for taha Māori to be truly effective at Toi Whakaari, it had to be re-focused toward the learning objectives of the students' journey – in its entirety. For this reason, the appointment of Teina as taha Māori coordinator was an inspired choice, and timely. He brought with him a wide range of experience and skill as a teacher, composer, choreographer and

◄ Teina Moetara and Keriana Whati

▲ Jade Eriksen. *Photo: Philip Merry*

performer. He had just completed a two-year contract with Disney, performing in *The Lion King* in Australia and Shanghai. Teina is a seminal thinker and his understanding of the process of performance, coupled with his considerable experience as a teacher and his understanding of Māoritanga, enabled him to address many of the core questions around biculturalism, particularly within a performing arts institution:

> In the journey towards asking questions of how we as individuals relate to 'biculturalism' we discover the real working question: *How do we as individuals relate to each other?* This question highlights for us our working nature as individual artists, with all our creative differences, in progressing work with others collegially. Do we work well together? How do we learn with each other? How do we learn from each other?[38]

A way of addressing some of these questions lay in tikanga, a system of principles and rules that allows the learner to engage with another person of difference, and ensures that both sets of mana remain intact. This was particularly timely for Toi Whakaari, as working with difference towards a common goal was at the very heart of collaboration – or 'convergence'. Tikanga was later put into practice through kōiwi sessions, with the whole school community gathering twice a week to learn together.

For Teina, the core foundation that underlies the taha Māori coordination position with Toi Whakaari is encapsulated in the following whakataukī:

> Kii mai ki au, he aha mea nui o teenei ao?
> Maaku e kii atu, he tangata, he tangata, he tangata!
>
> If you were to ask, what is the most important pedagogy of modern times?
> I would answer, it is community, relationships and people.

An equally significant appointment in 2007 was Jade Eriksen. She joined the school as the history, theory and philosophy in theatre (HTP) tutor, replacing Peter Rowlands who had left at the end of 2006. Jade and Teina knew each other well, having gone through primary and high school together at Manatuke near Gisborne. As Jade recalled:

> We weren't the best of friends at that time because he was three years older than me; but I remember he was always a leader within the school, in both Māori and Pākehā worlds. When we found him again, he had a performance background, a teaching degree and his politics were – trying to translate between both worlds.[39]

Jade's association with Toi Whakaari had started as an MTA student in 2002. Her interests lay in intercultural politics and composition, which led her to focus mainly on the devised theatrical form. After working with Christian Penny on *Penumbra* in 2004 and 2006, she had directed and devised other collaborative works, including *Yatra, Stamping Grounds* and *Migrant Nation*, and most recently a STAB-commissioned work,[40] *Arcane*, with her company Theatreheuristic.

Jade immediately set about developing innovative educative models to support the evolving culture at the school. Through this, she believed the school would be more capable of working collectively to strengthen *all* its aims:

> The educative questions within HTP and taha Māori are difficult and specific to Toi Whakaari. The students are not selected on their abilities in either of these subjects, so the teacher is faced with a skill base that spreads from fluent te reo speakers to beginners, students who have Masters degrees and those who have barely made it through high school. As well as this skill-base question, a major difficulty is the students' inability to connect these subjects with their core reason for attending Toi Whakaari.
>
> Toi Whakaari defines itself as a 'bicultural' institution. This definition is illustrative of a commitment to working with the specific cultural questions of our country. However, the term is problematic when applied to the demands of an institution. Biculturalism is not a static descriptive state of being, it is specific to physical human relationships that shift and evolve. Biculturalism is a question the whole country is grappling with. If we can establish biculturalism as a question, not an answer, clearly for ourselves within the school, then we can develop educational structures that serve to foster critical thought in the students.[41]

Both HTP and taha Māori were multi-departmental subjects – delivered across the school. In some respects they were stand-alone subjects, but the values underlying the delivery of both made connections with the other. The two courses were therefore merged to create a single department: cultural and theoretical studies. This amalgamation was very new in concept, but it made practical sense.

What Teina and Jade proposed was not without risk. And because of the recent shake-up over 'convergence', it was not an easy time to introduce 'new ideas'. In fact, their theories and enthusiasms were received by some with a degree of scepticism. However, Annie Ruth saw the value in their proposals, and it is to her credit that she backed them – in spite of dissenting voices:

> When I thought about what they were bringing and the potential for it to transform the learning of the students in a really positive way and to make taha Māori at last an integrated and meaningful part of Toi Whakaari experience for all the students, I felt staunch

> in standing behind them. If we try it for two years and then review it and decide it hasn't worked, then we can change again. But we need to commit and give this a good go.
>
> When Tom came to me with his 'training proposal', I implemented it, over quite a lot of opposition because I saw it was potentially very good for the students even though staff were afraid of the change it signalled. I saw there was an opportunity to discover something new and exciting and empowering for the students and went with it even so.
>
> The current situation with Jade and Teina is similar. I see the potential for a breakthrough in making theoretical studies and taha Māori meaningful to the students and that, if it works, they will have a much stronger skills base on graduation. It is a big change, and again it's placing new people in a central position. So there is considerable disquiet over it, especially since it is a subject area across all courses.[42]

To achieve their aims, Teina and Jade chose to work within a theatrical framework, focusing cultural and theoretical studies toward the specific needs of the student body. Because Toi Whakaari students learn skills appropriate to a degree course, largely through practising their craft experientially, Teina and Jade began to integrate cultural and theoretical studies into the theatre-making process, rather than letting it exist to the side of it. In this way they encouraged the development of independence through critical thinking, and an investigation of theatre within a broad historical, political and social context:

> Rather than being in a 'convincing role' as teachers, our job is to help students understand what they know, as opposed to them coming in knowing nothing, and then we teach them what we know. It is important that they understand and don't undervalue what they do know, and how to build on that. Another thing we are addressing is what exactly of the worlds of te reo Māori and history of theatre and philosophy – of everything – is of use to the students within our school. You can't give them all of that, nor should we be promising it. We are trying to marry practice with those worlds; giving them skills in order to learn those things in the future, we are teaching them the skills of how to learn. That's what our responsibility in tertiary education should be. We are not in the business of just teaching people for two or three years – I feel that's immoral. We have to teach them something for the long term.[43]

These ideas were trialled in the mid-year production of *Twelfth Night*, during which students worked together in course-specific groups, but with a common purpose in the context of collaboration. Focusing their investigation on the needs of their chosen discipline, the students composed a short presentation that they showed at a hui during the run of *Twelfth Night*. This prompted a broader and highly pertinent question: How do we sit with difference?

The Trust Board, the Board of Studies and the staff of Toi Whakaari were grappling with a similar question. At the end of 2006, Jean Packman had stepped down as chair of the Trust Board. During her six year as chair, Jean had seen in the introduction of four new courses, and the school's funding base had been made more secure. She had been particularly supportive of innovation, and her diligence in this regard was much appreciated by many staff and students. This support had been evident in many ways, not least of all her attendance at most performance projects and showings at the school.

Richard Moss, a Board member since 2005, then took over as the new chair. Other

Board members in 2007 were: John Fokerd, Carolyn Henwood, Marion Hobbs, James Johnston, Steve La Hood and Annie Ruth. Tom McCrory was the staff representative and Sophie Hambleton the student representative.

The main agenda item at the first Trust Board meeting in 2007 was 'convergence'. The Board started off by acknowledging its many positive aspects:

> With the growth in the school, and addition of more courses, this was seen as a visionary goal, presented to the Board by the Heads of all courses and enthusiastically adopted by the Board in its Strategic Plan.
>
> The development of other courses provided opportunities for the actors not available hitherto, in developing professional working relationships for their future careers. Convergence has provided opportunities for students to work together on projects and productions, as well as join in each others' classes.[44]

But then things took a different turn when the Board noted that convergence strategy and current staff resignations had created 'a situation of unease':

> There is a concern about whether the school is industry focused and should be serving the needs of the industry at large, or should [the school] be focused on trying to influence and mould the future of the industry. Acting staff believe in serving the needs of the industry.[45]

The Board also noted that the expression of convergence in its Strategic Plan was incomplete, which opened up a number of questions, including: What is convergence? What was its intended impact within the school? Do the changes brought about by convergence alter the nature of what is being taught? Is the emphasis of the school changing and shifting its focus away from what the students expect and are paying for?

To address these and other questions around convergence, the Board decided to review its description in the Strategic Plan: 'to simplify, and clarify the intention of the policy, and to make it more comprehensible to the staff and students'. The Board also set up a subcommittee to investigate and to review 'convergence', whose terms of reference focused mainly on questions that were mainly concerned with the intention and purpose of convergence and the manner in which the strategy had affected teaching and the students' learning. The subcommittee was also asked to advise the Board on whether the 'convergence strategy' should continue, or be renamed, refined, revised and/or communicated in a different manner.

Staff and students were then invited to submit 'their thoughts and comments on the material on convergence [contained] in the Strategic Plan' in writing, to the Board.[46]

An outpouring of opinion and questions resulted from this, mostly from staff who commented on the merits of convergence. The author is in no position to discuss the validity of any substantive points made in submissions to the Board. But, based on anecdotal evidence, it seems highly likely that many of the viewpoints expressed by the staff to the subcommittee, on the value and effects of convergence, exceeded the material on convergence in the Strategic Plan. This would hardly be surprising given the diversity of opinion, the degree of passion and the many unresolved issues that impacted on convergence at that time. As Annie Ruth later put it:

> I felt that convergence had been used as a philosophical hook for internal staff power struggles. It was about staff members disagreeing with each other and not hanging in there and completing the conversation.[47]

Staff, including department heads, and two students who had responded to the Board's request for information on convergence were interviewed by the subcommittee. Annie Ruth was a member of that subcommittee and found it quite challenging. She felt that her involvement on the subcommittee was a terrible mistake, placing her in an invidious situation that threatened her mana within the school. Because of this perceived conflict of interest, and because she wanted to preserve her relationship with her department heads, Annie withdrew from the subcommittee. The heads of department who had their views on convergence interrogated by the subcommittee came away from the process feeling that the investigation was focused on a particular set of rhetorical questions and was biased towards certain predetermined outcomes. The manner in which the review process was carried out was in marked contrast to the Board's extremely positive response to the philosophical and pedagogical aims on convergence in 2006. But the fundamental principles of convergence had not changed since then, and I re-stated those principles in my submission to the sub-committee:

> Convergence is not simply about coexistence, but more significantly about exploring process; developing an understanding of and respect for each other's contribution, and encouraging creative relationships that will continue beyond the students' time at Toi Whakaari. The School also has an important responsibility to encourage our students to explore a broader range of possibilities for a future New Zealand theatre. And to help them identify relationships between ideas and processes that will bring about this change, we need to provide more time and opportunity, across all disciplines, to practise the process of making work together.
>
> … Convergence is *not* (and was never intended to be) about merging, or diluting the integrity of or homogenising the various disciplines at Toi Whakaari.[48]

Statements on convergence within the Strategic Plan may well have been a bit of a 'grab-bag', ranging from visionary to provocative. For example, 'This strategy involves us in re-shaping and re-imagining a performing arts education', and, 'we routinely do what has never been done before'. But these ideals were balanced by other statements, expressing rational, valid, educational aims: 'Education is not a process of transmission. It is a process of enabling; of creating conditions under which people learn and gain ownership and confidence in the work .... We therefore foster leadership from any point within the system, from any discipline or individual.'[49]

The subcommittee reported its findings to the Trust Board in June. Because those findings directly relate to the specific submissions received by the subcommittee, the author is unable to comment on them. The report did, however, put a number of questions to the Board, including: 'What is the School now that it has more diverse students and is offering new courses and a degree? Is [Toi Whakaari] a tertiary institution focusing on the academic and research aspects of performance, regardless of the Industry? How much will the actors' training be dictated by the needs of the others, such as directors or designers [and/or] of the teachers of culture?'[50]

Finally, the report concluded that '"convergence" and "visioning", in our view, had gone a lot further than collaboration in the work place and had crossed over into touching the heart of the school'. It then recommended that 'all visioning and convergence stop at this time and the convergence document be withdrawn from the strategic plan'.[51] That recommendation was later endorsed by the entire Trust Board using more or less the same wording. The Board's decision to withdraw any material on 'convergence' from its Strategic Plan was its prerogative; it had adopted the term and had the authority to remove it.

But there was a fundamental flaw in this dismissal of 'convergence', as Annie Ruth later noted:

> It overlooked the fact that key elements of the school curriculum are delivered in a collaborative way, and that it is a more effective way of delivering core curriculum in certain areas. We are quite clear that we overdid it in that first year and applied it in places where it wasn't well to apply it, but as a methodological approach we are really clear that, for many areas of the school's teaching, it's the right way to go.
>
> However, what was being delivered in the acting course at that time was not what was in the curriculum, and once the acting curriculum review was completed, the subcommittee felt it could present its final report, which it did in 2009. With the new acting curriculum in place, the Board now feel that the school is back on course.[52]

Although the 'C' word was deleted from the Strategic Plan and from the vocabulary of Toi Whakaari, the Board's actions failed to diminish the collaborative ambitions of the school. Interdisciplinary activity was entrenched across most of the courses, benefiting the majority of students at the school. Design, directing and management students continued with their shared core classes and collaborative studio projects. Students across *all* disciplines jointly participated in cultural and theoretical studies, a wide range of performance projects and, of course, mainstream productions.

There is little evidence to support the view that cross-disciplinary activity has weakened the *integrity* of any course delivered by the school. On the contrary, it has reinforced the students' awareness that good and useful collaboration is about working with difference towards a common goal. By equipping students to become innovative and dynamic problem-solvers, it improves their ability to adapt in an evolving theatre, film or entertainment industry.

The central aim of 'convergence' in the Strategic Plan had been expressed with a clear-cut statement of intent:

> We recognise that most creative work is collaborative. Our aim is to get the disciplines working together as often as possible, particularly in teaching and explorative work, culminating in productions.[53]

That ideal seemed reasonable for a multi-disciplinary performing arts school in the twenty-first century. Whether it was a worthy ideal or simply an ill-advised pursuit is still open to debate. But what is beyond dispute is that the ideal was in line with Creative New Zealand's own view of cross-sector collaboration. In 2005, Creative New Zealand had convened a forum, bringing together twenty-five leading theatre practitioners to discuss funding priorities for the period 2006–9: a timeframe that more or less coinciding with Toi Whakaari's own Strategic Plan.

The concluding statement in Creative New Zealand's report on the forum made the following points about collaboration:

> To move towards the vision of a New Zealand theatre that is excellent, distinctive and essential to the lives of all New Zealanders will require a national approach which actively discourages unnecessary duplication of work and resources.
>
> It will require collaboration across the sector built on an awareness of what practitioners are doing and can do. It will also involve an acknowledgement of difference; differences of culture, of genre, of ways of working and of audiences.[54]

The Arts Board's definition of 'excellence' for projects, artists and arts organisations was included in the forum report. This applied equally to emerging and established artists:

- It rises above expectations and sets a new level of achievement – it creates its own climate of expectation and surprise.
- The work is creative, provocative, arresting, innovative, exquisite, disturbing, inspiring, energetic, cutting edge, experimental or paradigm-shifting.[55]

Clearly, not everyone at Toi Whakaari was comfortable with the 'paradigm-shift' that had emerged from recent changes to its more traditional constituency. Without dismissing the broader aspiration of 'convergence', some held the view that its introduction had been rushed, even 'high-jacked' by factions within the school. Tom McCrory, who had in some way instigated the initial concept, later felt that 'convergence' opened up a space that became a 'bloody battlefield for control of the school, and its resources':

> For me, the difficulty with convergence was created by ambition; by some people seizing the day, seeing that open space as an opportunity to advance an agenda that had nothing to do with the initial impetus of convergence.
>
> Convergence became a dirty word for many people. The most important thing to do whenever we create something is to open up, and hold open, an empty space. If we are to look at collaborating together, we have to recognise that none of us must dominate or occupy that open space between us; we have to recognise that whatever we create within that space will take time and has to be painstakingly built out of our meeting, without expressing individual aspirations. That level of communication to hold a space open is difficult to achieve on a human level.
>
> What became convergence is not what I initially envisaged. I supported change and wanted change, but the way it happened I didn't agree with: I thought it was mismanaged and unnecessarily painful. If you believe change is about leaving behind an old model, the danger with that is that some people represent one particular set of values and another group feel they have an absolute right to discard that model in order to move on. People require a lot of care and time, whenever change is taking place. We also needed to make a pathway for it, productively, creatively. Sometimes, certain groups of people who represent something find it hard to let go of a position, especially in New Zealand, because it's a relatively small place and it's been hard to build things up. To let go what they've created and allow change can be difficult.[56]

For Miranda Harcourt, the difficulty around 'convergence' had been more about leadership:

> There was this bizarre mix of democracy and dictatorship that was de-stabilising; it was a management issue not a conceptual issue. It was the way in which decisions were made to institute change. At the end of the day the mistake in 2005 or whenever it was, was in terms of defining leadership. If you wanted there to be change, then, as the leader, you had to forge on and make it happen. Whereas, at the last jump, it became a false idea of democracy and it didn't work.[57]

Tom McCrory, training class.
Photo: Briene Lermitte

The conclusion arrived at by the Trust Board's sub-committee, that convergence and visioning had 'crossed over into touching the heart of the school', and the question this raised for the Board about the actors' training being 'dictated by the needs of the other students such as directors or designers, or the teachers of culture',[58] had the support of many Trust Board members, particularly those who believed the school had sacrificed its status as New Zealand's pre-eminent acting school by diversifying and becoming a multi-disciplinary performing arts academy.

In reality, there was no contest: Toi Whakaari is undeniably 'New Zealand's pre-eminent acting school', but it is *also* New Zealand's pre-eminent multi-disciplinary performing arts school; the two are not mutually exclusive. There is now a high level of co-dependence and synergy across all disciplines at the school. The actors' performance is enhanced by well-considered design elements, creative technology and management, and beautifully crafted costumes. The actors reciprocate by providing a context for the work of the other practitioners. When these joint endeavours are aligned, it can lead to a more successful performance outcome. This integration of skill, together with a shared vision across the disciplines, makes Toi Whakaari distinctive – as New Zealand's pre-eminent performing arts school.

The 2007 degree monitor's report, which encompassed all academic courses at Toi Whakaari, noted that it had been 'a fragile year for the School, with a number of key staff resigning and a number of strategic planning issues dominating the agenda'. The report then went on to reflect on the progress of convergence:

> It was alarming to learn that the *Convergence* initiative, heralded with such enthusiasm last year, was so dramatically excised from the program. It is difficult to understand the reasoning behind the Board of Trustees' decision to bypass normal chains of authority and interfere in a domestic thematic pedagogy. Despite the semantics and the politics, the concept of collaboration, nonetheless, was embraced by students (if not by all staff) and all discipline areas registered their approval of, what they perceive as, a more collegiate, interdisciplinary, mutually supportive, work ethic. The concept of thematic pedagogy occurs with great success in training institutions, such as Toi Whakaari, all over the world

Multidisciplinary production class with Penny Fitt and Annie Ruth. *Photo: Philip Merry.*

> as a mechanism for concentrated periods of activity, or for more flexible and innovative approaches to Teaching and Learning strategies: I would encourage the School to reinvest in the learning discussion concerning such pedagogies.[59]

The subcommittee on 'convergence' recommended that the Trust Board 'speak to the Board of Studies about their role in defining the curriculum of the School':

> The Board of Trustees do not have a full understanding of implications of curriculum matters, and need to understand what level of involvement by the Board of Trustees is appropriate. [As] curriculum matters do not routinely come to the Board of Trustees, except through recommendations from the Board of Studies, should all changes [to the curriculum] be approved by the Board of Studies, and then reported to the Board of Trustees?[60]

The Trust Board invited the Board of Studies to help forge a set of principles to guide the development of curriculum, and to help resolve some of the questions that had been raised about the evolving nature of the school.

The first meeting of the Toi Whakaari Board of Studies, in 2007, was held with its new chairperson, Grahame Tetley, at the helm. The membership of the Board of Studies had recently increased and now stood at twenty-five! There were nine staff representatives, ten industry reps (the maximum number allowed), four student reps and a Trust Board representative, Ray Ahipene-Mercer. Tiahuia Gray also joined the Board of Studies as the kuia, replacing Rangimoana Taylor who had been the kaumātua on the Board.

Teina Moetara and Jade Eriksen delivered a paper on their future strategy for cultural and theoretical studies, and the Board of Studies congratulated them on their continuing work, noting that the aim of cultural and theoretical studies is 'to do less, but more efficiently'.

A recommendation was also made at that meeting to include a cultural and theoretical studies unit in the Diploma in Costume Construction course (an oversight when the curriculum was first developed). Kaarin Macaulay saw this as a crucial area

Stage management class. Entertainment technology and performing arts management. *Photo: Philip Merry*

of inter-disciplinary activity for the costume students, but it was no small matter to accommodate the unit in the costume course as teaching hours had to be reduced in other areas of the curriculum. Nevertheless, the recommendation was passed unanimously by the Board of Studies.

Previously, there had been a lack of clarity concerning the degree of authority held by each of the school's Boards, particularly with regard to curriculum matters. This was complicated further by contention around the concept of convergence. Because the title *Board* of Studies implies certain regulatory powers and a degree of autonomy, it could be argued that it had been established as an academic *committee* of the Trust Board. Had this been the case, there would probably have been far less kerfuffle around 'convergence' – or indeed around other thorny issues concerning the delivery of curriculum.

But some members of the Board of Studies firmly believed they had ultimate 'authority in, and a mandate to, implement academic matters and to sustain academic rigour'. What's more, they believed 'the Board of Studies had, up to now, underestimated its authority'.[61] As the terms of reference for the Board of Studies had not been fully reviewed by the Trust Board since 1997, the trustees decided to appoint a subcommittee to clarify the relationship of the Board of Studies to the Board of Trustees including the scope of the Board of Studies' authority.

Emma Weston had been elected to represent the staff on the Board of Studies and she worked closely with Grahame Tetley to draft a document that was intended to help clarify the lines of communication between the two Toi Whakaari Boards. In essence, this document stated that pedagogical questions relating to the delivery of Toi Whakaari qualifications would be dealt with by the Board of Studies and, *if necessary*, recommendations would then be made to the Trust Board. Conversely, if the Trust Board had any question or requests specifically relating to curriculum matters, these could be conveyed to the Board of Studies via the Trust Board's representative on the Board of Studies for its consideration.

In response to the 2007 degree monitor's report, and the concerns expressed about the Trust Boards' 'excising of convergence', the Board of Studies agreed to 'accept its responsibility for the ongoing monitoring of all aspects of the curriculum, including its convergent aspects'. It further reassured the Board of Trustees that 'this is in active review, and that the above work is progressing in a satisfactory way'.[62]

The appointment of Jonathon (Jonty) Hendry as the new head of acting was clearly a major turning point, one that helped to resolve some of the residual issues around convergence. Prior to taking up his new appointment, Jonty had been the head of acting at UNITEC for three years. He also, of course, had a long-standing relationship with Toi Whakaari, having graduated from the New Zealand Drama School in 1988. In more recent years, Jonty had been a member of the Toi Whakaari Trust Board, had taught at the school and had directed a number of productions, including *Laughing Wild* and *Lute* (1999).

Despite missing out on much of the earlier debate and controversy around 'convergence', Jonty had very definite views on inter-disciplinary collaboration, and the place and function of the acting department within that:

> When I applied for the job, I was very concerned about the 'skills-space' on top of all the other training, and that element being lost. I think that's where we are arriving at now: how do we ensure that this happens? Then in the greater environment of the school, how the actors can be the best that they can be, and collaborate with the other disciplines. I think one of the things that we are now doing better is understanding the complexity of who we are, through our different voices and differences.
>
> What I felt was happening when I arrived at the school [as head of acting] was the identity of the acting department was not aligned to the rest of the school. There was a feeling ... that it couldn't be. There was very much a sense of the acting department trying to be a smaller school within the school or trying to be that [old school] model. There is still lobbying going on about this, the idea that somehow we are being destroyed or we are losing something, and I don't see that. Some of the rhetoric that's bandied around the school actually increases that fear.
>
> Sometimes we are a little inclined in our conversations to try and say that 'we are this', and what I've been recently reflecting on is that 'we are this' and we'll know better what we are when we start to identify with and feel more confident in the difference

Jonathon Hendry. *Photo: Philip Merry*

> within that. It's not about losing anything, it's about actually engaging in collaboration and interdisciplinary activity.
>
> I've seen my way out of the misconceptions of convergence and all that misconstrued emotional tension. There's been a lot of change as a result of convergence, big changes in our area as a result of that period. I see that as an investment. It's important: that tension is now a healthy one in [the acting] department; it sets us up with a strong point of difference.
>
> One of my main priorities now is to bed down the new [acting] degree. We have a responsibility to allow our students the rigours and experiences of a strong training element around the new degree, equipping the students for life-long learning and other educational ideas, and marrying that with the training thrust. If the students are going to go out there and be collaborators, they have that to draw from.
>
> There is an expectation in terms of how the school was originally set up: we are here to further the skills of the best talent in the country, to enable them to go out and work in the industry. We are giving a degree now, so there is a shift there: it's not just about getting up and performing, it's got to be more than that.
>
> George [Webby] had this lovely philosophy, which he based on his background in education. He would say to us, 'You may not end up acting, but you'll be a better person for this experience.' I was strongly influenced by that, and I like that as an idea; but that's not what the [current] climate is about unfortunately. What the students experience and engage in now is infinitely different than it was in George's day: not better than, but tuned to the different pathways that students now choose. We were trained for a particular purpose, and that was theatre.[63]

In July, Toi Whakaari received another piece of good news: NZQA approved the Bachelor of Design (Stage and Screen.) The school immediately opened negotiations with the TEC for funding for the qualification, and began promoting the new degree with the aim of accepting the first intake of students the following year. Yet there was still a dilemma to resolve: there were performance design students enrolled through the Massey University system, which then transferred a proportion of that funding to Toi Whakaari, and it was no easy matter to reallocate that funding to the new Toi Whakaari Bachelor of Design. In fact, it required a considerable amount of lobbying and wooing of TEC officials by the school before funding was finally secured for the new design degree in 2008.

The 2007 production season got into full swing in June with two plays by Christopher Durang. Two-thirds of the second-year actors performed in *A History of the American Film*, directed by Jeff Szusterman (1995 graduate) with musical direction by Jane Keller; the remaining third performed in *Betty's Summer Vacation*, directed by Annie Ruth. *A History of the American Film* crashed through American history and four decades of Hollywood film genres, while the cast of *Betty's Summer Vacation* engaged with America's addiction to reality television.

The second-year actors followed this in August with *Twelfth Night* directed by Vanessa Byrnes. The production was set somewhere 'off the coast of India', emphasising the distinct inter-cultural atmosphere of the play. This Asian theme was reinforced by music composed by Tristan Carter and performed by Sanjay Dixit and Michael

Gavriel, and by the exotic costumes designed by Hermione Flynn and exquisitely constructed by the second-year costume construction students. Lighting for *Twelfth Night* was designed by Chris O'Neill, the first time a performance-design student designed lighting for a major Toi Whakaari production.

By her own admission, Vanessa Byrnes took enormous liberties with *Twelfth Night*, re-working the play from psychological and cultural perspectives to underline her version of 'Illyria':

> I am trying to stretch the play horizontally so that it is anchored in key central values of text, story and structure, but drawn out sideways so that character truths are valued and explored in full capacity. This dimensionality also allowed more performance and technical opportunities and challenges for the nearly *fifty-strong cast and crew*.[64]

Supported by a large pool of students across many disciplines, the scope and calibre of Toi Whakaari productions had clearly now reached a new zenith. Few, if any, commercial production houses in New Zealand could afford to mount works of this scale or to take such artistic risks. Productions at the school not only fulfilled a valuable training need, but were now inexorably linked into the broader teaching practice, extending the possibilities of theatre in Aotearoa through performance research.

New ground was again broken in 2007, when students were invited to pitch ideas and nominate creative teams for an 'alternative' graduation production: a 'G2'. The G2 chosen for 2007 was *Angels in America. Part 1: Millennium Approaches*, by Tony Kushner. It was directed by Willem Wassenaar (2006 MTA graduate) under the auspices of Almost a Bird Theatre Collective. The cast of eight third-year actors and one Toi Whakaari graduate, Martyn Wood (2006), performed for a one-week season at Downstage in October.

The set for *Angels in America* was created by Daniel Williams (2006 Design graduate) out of stacked refrigerators:

> This desert-like interior provides a panoramic landscape, representing the deep freeze of the mind; the kingdom of ice is a place of desolation, refrigeration, and death. The domestic fridge becomes an object of change, transforming from coffins to buildings – although never on its own. Fridges ultimately contain; their job is to preserve and chill, its sterile condition imitates the mood of our scenes; clinical in its appearance the fridge disguising itself as an actor becoming a player in a world dominated by concrete.[65]

Dan had two design assistants working with him on *Angels*, Leanne Stevenson and Emily Smith: final-year design and advanced diploma students. The production was lit by Karl Jenkins; and Pat McIntosh, a second-year performing arts management student, designed the sound and stage-managed the production. The production manager was Lisa Hawken, a third-year performing arts management student

The main (G1) graduation production, Tom Stoppard's *Arcadia,* opened in Te Whaea Theatre shortly after *Angels in America* finished its season. *Arcadia* was cast from the remaining fourteen third-year actors and had a design/production team of twenty-six, led by production manager Karl Jenkins.

Betty's Summer Vacation, 2007. L–R Kristyl Neho, Dawn Cheong, Hadleigh Walker. *Photo: Derek Simpson*

Angel's in America, 2007. Asalemo Tofete and Martyn Wood. *Photo: Philip Merry.*

Arcadia was directed by Tim Spite. After graduating from Toi Whakaari in 1991, he had performed in over seventy shows and had co-written eleven plays; six were created by his group the SEEyD Theatre Company, including *The Remedy Syndrome, The Brilliant Fassah* and *Turbine*. During that time, he also received numerous Chapman Tripp Theatre Awards.

Tim was undoubtedly in his element when directing *Arcadia,* exploring the complex relationship between past and present, chaos and disorder, interwoven with landscape gardening, love, and the nature of evidence and truth. One critic described *Arcadia* as a 'gratuitous intellectual work'.[66] Nevertheless, its intricacies were tackled by the cast of fourteen third-year actors with great conviction, revealing 'contradictory ideas co-existing in the same time and space'. It was clearly an equally demanding intellectual exercise for the audience:

> While there are enough moments of ordinary dialogue in *Arcadia* to provide respite from the otherwise relentless discussion of ideas, it is perhaps best to attend this play when in a sharp mental state; end of week wind down it is not. Rather this production is adeptly directed, convincing and at times impressively performed, worthwhile for its stimulating script and its exhibition of young yet accomplished and inspiring talent.[67]

Chris O'Neill's set design for *Arcadia* featured a huge round table covered with props from both time periods in which the play was set, including a 'crappy remote-control tortoise'[68] that 'intermittently' staggered – and sometimes shot – across the table.

In his review of *Arcadia*, Laurie Atkinson made reference to *Angels in America*, commenting that:

> *Arcadia* is a production that Toi Whakaari, and the students, should be proud of and we should be grateful to have seen two great modern plays so close together and produced on such a lavish scale, and performed with confidence.[69]

Sophie Hambleton, who shared the role of Thomasina in *Arcadia*, had staunchly represented the student body on the Trust Board during a time of change. In her final report to the Board, she affirmed that the school had 'come through' this difficult period and that everyone she spoke to 'felt that they'd ended the year on a high':

> This has been a huge year for the school, a year of much change. Overall, the students are very happy and much of the frustration of earlier in the year has substantially subsided.
>
> The Graduation productions were both an incredible success, with Willem Wassenaar going on to win Best New Director at the Chapman Tripp Theatre Awards for *Angels in America.* Graduating students from all courses have said that the experience of working with an outside director, especially in the case of *Arcadia*, directed by Tim Spite, was very beneficial and a great way to harness their skills in 'just doing the job' before they left.[70]

Not all of the third-year actors were comfortable with the idea of splitting graduation shows, as the student representative on the Board of Studies, Stephen Townshend, reported:

First cohort of costume construction students at Graduation, in 2007. L–R: Gemma Crouch-Gatehouse, Fiona Brown, Helen Moate, Rebekah (Bekky) Campbell

> Having two projects created uneasy feelings in the class in regards to the way pitching and casting was managed. It was a weird scenario having one of our classmates producing and casting one of our graduation shows, and that show getting the first pick in terms of casting. I am pleased to hear that casting will be completely regulated by the school from now on.[71]

The end of the 2007 academic year was marked by yet another extraordinary ceremony celebrating the enormous diversity of talent at the school. There was a record number of forty-seven students graduating from across six courses, including the first cohort of costume construction students: Fiona Brown, Rebekah Campbell, Gemma Crouch-Gatehouse and Helen Moate. At the graduation ceremony, Cliff Curtis was presented with the Toi Whakaari Graduate Award, which been introduced in 2006 when Nigel Scott was the first recipient.

Of the twenty categories in the 2007 Chapman Tripp Theatre Awards, around half of the awards went to New Zealand Drama School/Toi Whakaari graduates, including: 'Most Promising Male and Female Newcomers of the Year', Michael Whalley (*The Cape*) and Jodie Hillock (*Homeland*); 'Most Promising New Director of the Year', Willem Wassenaar (*Angels in America*); 'Weta Workshop Award for Set Designer of the Year', Brian King (*The Hollow Men*); and 'Accolade for Outstanding Performance', Rachel Forman (Blackbird). The author was, much to his surprise, also honoured to receive 'The Mayor's Award for Significant Contribution to the Theatre'.

Twenty-One

2008–2009

'I'm really interested in making theatre that uplifts and surprises an audience and allows them to dream.'

By any measure, the previous decade at Toi Whakaari had been a time of extraordinary growth and change. With a three-year acting degree and the introduction of directing, design, management and costume construction courses in place, the student population at the school had more than doubled. The move from the relatively compact Vivian Street premises to Te Whaea had also brought about a substantial increase in teaching and administrative staff.

Director's Diary, December 2007

Just did a list of our staff for 2008 and discovered we have 21 'equivalent' full-time before you even count the share of Te Whaea Services staff. Amazing proportion of staff to students! We are indeed blessed.

Heads of Departments, April 2008. Front L–R Annie Ruth, Kate Robertson, Bill Guest, Jonathon Hendry. Back L–R Penny Fitt, Christine Richardson, Christian Penny. *Source: Annie Ruth*

▲ Annie Ruth and Gary Trinder at 10th Anniversary of move into Te Whaea

In a relatively short time, Toi Whakaari had gone from being a tightly connected community with an organic flow between acting and technical production courses, to a more traditional departmentalised hierarchy. The changes had been adequately managed, but the shift in the purpose and identity of Toi Whakaari, together with an increase in student and staff numbers, had resulted in a period of unrest and stress. Christine Richardson observed that '150 people are about as much as a community can manage. And we've got about 140 students and twenty staff'.[1] The school was moving into an exciting new phase, with greater emphasis on cross-disciplinary activity across six courses, and a significant increase in integrated teaching practice.

In April 2008, Toi Whakaari and the New Zealand School of Dance celebrated the tenth anniversary of their move into Te Whaea, with showings of work from across all courses of both schools. Key players from the Tertiary Education Commission attended the celebrations, providing an excellent opportunity for Annie Ruth, the heads of departments and Christine Richardson to lobby the TEC over the future funding of the school, particularly with regards to Toi Whakaari's new design degree. The TEC had still not fully grasped Massey and Toi Whakaari's relationship in the delivery of the (old) performance design degree or the circumstances surrounding its disestablishment. But Annie Ruth used the attendance of senior TEC officials at the birthday celebrations to turn this situation around:

> The whole occasion was beautiful and the student work glowed, especially that of the designers ... and the whole of the design studio really engaged them. Finally they understood what had happened to us with the design degree, Massey and student component funding. We were able to make TEC see the difference between equal delivery and delivering the qualification for another institution. When they saw what we were creating here it is not so difficult for them to get our need to be well funded.[2]

Within a few weeks, the school received confirmation from the TEC that the student-component funding for the new design degree had been approved for up to ten students a year – to a total of thirty spread over a three-year period. The seeds planted at the tenth birthday celebrations had indeed born excellent fruit.

As the fortieth anniversary of the founding of the school approached, Toi Whakaari began to enjoy a period of relative stability and consolidation, providing a welcome breathing space for the staff to reflect on a decade of achievement and to reconcile difference. There was also a significant turn-over of staff at this time, bringing with it a new energy unaffected by many of the recent changes – and pressures.

The introduction of the Bachelor of Design for Stage and Screen at the start of 2008 was a significant milestone. The nine students enrolled in the first intake studied alongside the third-year and fourth-year Bachelor of Performance Design students scheduled to graduate in 2008 and 2009. However, Penny Fitt was now the only full-time teacher in the design department: Claudio Tolusso had resigned at the end of 2007 and had returned to Europe, and the school was in the process of recruiting a new senior tutor in design. In the interim, Christine Marfleet from the Royal Welsh College of Music and Drama agreed to join the design department as a tutor for the early part of 2008.

In May, Danielle Schilling was appointed as the full-time design tutor. She had trained at Utrecht School of the Arts in the Netherlands, and then started her own theatre design company, Waterproof Design. She had also worked for Het Syndicaat in Amsterdam as a stage/costume designer; and in art direction for television and film, including Peter Greenaway's *The Pillow Book*. For the past three years, Danielle had been sailing from the Netherlands to New Zealand with her family on a catamaran she and her partner had built.

More support for the design department arrived in October 2008 when Cathy McCullagh, previously the dance administrator with Te Whaea Services, joined the design department as their senior administrator to set up and manage systems for the newly formed Bachelor of Design and to provide pastoral care for the students.

The entertainment technology/performing arts management department also experienced major staff changes in 2008, including my own retirement in July. The past fourteen years at the school as head of department and associate director had been stimulating and challenging. But I felt it was time to move on, having achieved what I set out to do in 1994. Toi Whakaari had now reached a point of equilibrium with the right mix of courses and the school was well positioned to explore fully the interdisciplinary possibilities needed to affect the future direction of theatre in New Zealand.

When I joined the school, my initial goal was to lift the standard of the fledgling technical production course to a level similar to programmes in Australia and the UK. As with the acting course, it seemed logical to extend the two-year technical course to three years, allowing more time for specialisation and for design and management streams to be introduced. I was particularly fortunate in the freedom and support I was given to exercise that ambition, first by Robin Payne and, for the past decade, by Annie Ruth. Without their determination and their considered risk-taking, the expansion and diversification of courses at Toi Whakaari would have remained an impossible dream.

Emma Weston also left early in 2009 to devote more time to her principle interest, events management. During her time at the school, she had taught mostly in the areas of stage, events and production management, helping to bed in the Bachelor of Performing Arts Management programme, and broadening students' thinking around the scope and the opportunities available in events management. She had also demonstrated the value of 'younger blood' in the leadership of the technical and management courses.

Stage management is exceedingly difficult to teach in a theoretical way: it has to be learnt experientially. Emma and I jointly taught the subject by running mock rehearsal sessions, dividing the class into performers and stage managers, me as the 'director' and Emma as the 'uber stage-manager'. Apart from receiving some basic instructions and direction, the students were rarely given immediate solutions to rehearsal or performance problems; instead, Emma continually challenged them to provide their own answers:

> My teaching methodology sat around the idea of maximising the students' potential to communicate with one another, and inevitably to communicate with an audience. The driver was to create a graduate who not only knew their 'borders from their barndoors' but more importantly could initiate dialogue, could hold their own in conversation and articulate something they were passionate about, in a number of ways.

For stage management, there was obviously the element of learning – how to mark out a rehearsal space, how to block, prompt, call a show and so on. We would undertake mock rehearsals and play with the 'comms' systems. I designed a prompt desk, realised by Tony Toufexis, and we played games with the flashing outstations, with chalk lines, tape and pencils, until our fingers were sore and team morale was tested. Students engaged with varying levels of enthusiasm, but all under the mantra that 'you can all be good stage managers if you choose to be'.[3]

That was Emma's style: give them the tools and then confront them with questions – not answers. It was hard work for the students, but an extremely successful learning exercise.

This approach to 'training' was continued with the appointment of Kate Robertson as the new head of entertainment technology and performing arts management. She was absolutely the right person for the job, bringing her remarkable skills as an organiser and teacher to that position. As a student of the school from 1996 to 1997, Kate had valued the sense of community and the relative ease of communication that had existed between the entire student body and staff. This gave her a realistic understanding of the greater communication difficulties that now existed with the much larger school:

At the 'old school', the techs collaborated easily with the actors because they knew each other so well and communication came more easily. The school has only recently come to the realisation that it was still leveraging off that. When you have growth, things like that tend to fall away. I believe the aspirations and the values that we are now trying to build in the school are similar to what we had at Vivian Street, and we are much closer to that model than [we were] two and half years ago. Good collaborative practice relies on effective role modelling and unless [staff] constantly model transparent communication and collaboration, the students just don't buy into it.

It's also about commitment and completion. Having good ideas is great, but we need to drive them and there needs to be greater transparency around systems and production practice. Given its current size, there is a realisation that the school now has to do some engineering around that, and that takes a lot of work.[4]

In June, Pam Hindmarsh and Lisa Maule joined the school as senior tutors in the entertainment technology and management department. Pam had received her formal stage-management training in the 1980s through the New Entrant Training Scheme

Kate Robertson. *Photo: Philip Merry*

Pam Hindmarsh. *Photo: Philip Merry*

Lisa Maule. *Photo: Philip Merry*

and later at the BANFF Centre in Alberta. Her stage management career included working with most professional theatre companies in New Zealand, including Opera New Zealand. In recent years, Pam had been a guest tutor in stage management at Toi Whakaari. Lisa Maule also had extensive professional experience as a lighting designer at Downstage Theatre, Taki Rua, Capital E and the International Festival of the Arts, receiving the Chapman Tripp Lighting Designer of the Year awards in 1998 and again in 2000. She had also taught at Weltec, and Massey and Victoria Universities, and had been a guest lighting design tutor at Toi Whakaari.

When Kate Robertson took up her appointment as head of department, Derek Simpson returned to the school to replace her as production coordinator, having completed a tour of *Vula* to the Barbican in London with Tom McCrory and Nina Nawalowalo.

The school's marketing manager, Ceridwyn Roberts, had been on maternity leave in 2007, and resigned from her position at the end of that year to be at home with her new son:

> In my time at Toi the evolution of the organisation ran through several generations. During that time my job moved away from marketing the productions to communicating the school's courses to potential students. Toi Whakaari joined the world of the internet, with a website customised for all its stakeholders that provided much more information about courses and resources than was previously available. The marketing plan that I instituted focused on word of mouth as key in bringing new applicants for all six courses; it's cheaper and more suited to the specialised niche of Toi's students. By far the most enjoyable part of my job was working with the students, particularly the MTA students, on promoting their shows.[5]

Jo Richardson, who had worked as the school's marketing manager during Ceridwyn's absence, was then appointed permanently to that position. Before she moved to New Zealand in 2005, Jo had been the marketing officer at the Barbican Centre in London, also holding a similar position with Opera North. More recently she had been the marketing manager for Downstage Theatre – that is, until Kate Robertson persuaded her to 'defect' to Toi Whakaari.

Vanessa Byrnes resigned as senior tutor in acting in 2008, after eleven years teaching at the school:

> I reckon I've taught about 300 actors and theatre makers in this time and, as every teacher discovers every day, I've learnt so much from my time at the school. I'm very grateful for my journey there, despite the changing vision of the school, and the negative fallout of 'convergence' pedagogy from 2004 onwards. The currency we work with in theatre – generosity, revealing the truth, developing core skills, trusting an impulse, being specific and being 'in the moment' – are terms I have learnt can have infinite meaning and potential,

> limited only by the size of an actor's imagination, or a designer's vision. The theatre world is changing in terms of taste, quality and form – and I'm proud to have had a part in the journey for New Zealand's most talented theatre-makers at New Zealand Drama school.
>
> For over eleven years I was privileged to work in Te Whaea, the mothership – the unsung diva of Wellington – teaching and directing at the school with a myriad of incredible talent. Toi Whakaari, along with the New Zealand School of Dance and the Film School down the road, are high octane tertiary forces to be reckoned with.[6]

In 2008, Teina Moetara and Jade Eriksen introduced a new strategy to strengthen the sense of community within the school and to open up channels of communication. This was kōiwi, where the entire Toi Whakaari student body and staff gather collectively twice a week throughout the year, to learn from each other as a community:

> When we first started to work with the systems of the school, we had to keep clarifying what it was that we were doing. People working in institutions seem quite comfortable with things Māori on a content level, if it's about changing titles or having a pōwhiri. There's an appropriation in that sense, but people are quite comfortable with that because it's a world view. As soon as you start to relate formal questions, or structure or time, it becomes radical, and you are crossing the line. There was a time when te reo Māori was taught at the school, on Friday afternoon, but that time was terrible and students questioned why we were doing this. So rather than battle things on a Friday afternoon, we suggested beginning in the morning together, to work with the rhythms of a community before classes commenced. By changing the time, a lot of the teaching became obvious and we no longer had those discussions with the students. There would be so many other reasons why that was such a good idea.[7]

Kōiwi provided a forum that enabled students and staff to question openly the purpose and function of biculturalism, and to determine its relationship to the essential work of the school. It also embraced a more immediate question: How do we as individual artists relate to each other, with all of our creative differences, in progressing work with others collegially?

Kōiwi 2008
Photo: Briene Lermitte

Teina believes that tikanga provides a perspective or a way of thinking about this question:

> My understanding of tikanga is that it provides a framework where groups of people can work together, and where they know their role in relationship to each other: that it isn't hierarchy, it's a way of being conscious of each other so that we listen differently. It's also about not being the same: we are not the same. I felt that was very necessary in the school at the time, with the hierarchy of the school being seen as an 'acting school' and somewhere down the list were other courses. I wanted to flip that on its head, so that we all understand that everybody has a mana and a role; that when we listen to each other and are conscious of each other, it doesn't mean that we have to do each other's work, but that listening helps us to collaborate better. Collaboration is in our difference, not in the things that are the same.
>
> Part of that is about knowing why that person is different, which is where kōiwi came in. It provided an opportunity for the different disciplines to show work to the school; to show how they made their craft and to engage in questions with other disciplines. Not just simply for knowledge, but to better understand the role of the other groups in the collaborative process.
>
> Kōiwi is the Māori word for 'bones'. It also means: to address issues face to face.
>
> Through tikanga, we choose the 'bicultural lens' so that we can start to recognise other frameworks, and apply those things to our work when we need to. It's a way of relating to the question. I also wanted to get rid of all the negative connotations associated with using Māori words; to understand what they felt like experientially so that when we used them people understood that it had nothing to do with whether you were Māori or not-Māori; it was just a perspective or a way of thinking about things. It's contextual, so that we can hold a certain way of thinking about our work.[8]

Cultural and theoretical studies fostered kōiwi, bringing a stronger integration of taha Māori and independent research into the general curriculum. By re-focusing the various modules towards the learning objectives of the students' journey, it clarified the place and purpose of cultural and theoretical studies as something other than a generic body of knowledge. One of the modules, tūranga, created opportunities for students to question the value of biculturalism:

> By engaging with the complexity of community and difference, students investigate ideas around their own identity and place in twenty-first-century Aotearoa, and explore the link between creativity and identity, ownership and learning.[9]

This represented a significant shift in Toi Whakaari's engagement with questions surrounding biculturalism. In 1996 and 1998, Alison Richards had visited Toi Whakaari as part of her PhD study on biculturalism in New Zealand, and observed that the specific brand of biculturalism created by the school was a key tool in the 'school's spirit' and corporate identity:

> As such, the question remains as to whether the deployment of Māori culture in this context is appropriate or simply strategically appropriate. The answer must lie in the benefit other individuals and groups can derive from it and its generative potential inside and outside the immediate environment of the school.
>
> Unsurprisingly, such excursions into the new territory of biculturalist practice are

complex and uncertain. In both years of my observation and from subsequent conversations with participants, it is clear that the programme at Toi Whakaari remains in an experimental mode.

As Trevor James has pointed out: 'Since it seems that Māori tradition is not closed but open, reinvention may in fact be a natural communal process and part of tradition' …. The bicultural allegiances maintained by Toi Whakaari are therefore not static, but are themselves contributors to social change.[10]

Since it was first adopted in the 1980s, the bicultural orientation of the school had been under constant development. However, not all students had readily accepted some of the more performative aspects of taha Māori. With the introduction of kōiwi, and through tūranga, students from every discipline have been able to express their views on the significance of a bicultural context, but in relation to performance and in the broadest possible sense of the word.

In their delivery of cultural and theoretical studies, Teina and Jade believed that by transposing some taha Māori practice into a non-Māori setting, students could better understand the principles and purpose of its function in the school. To explore this idea, and to work with questions of culture, history and identity, they made a piece of theatre, *Pakiwaitara*. The project involved a team of creators from various disciplines in the school, who collaborated to explore the histories and stories housed within the Museum of Wellington City and Sea on Queens Wharf:

It seemed crucial to us that we had to blend theoretical work, or the things that we were trying to share in class, into something practical so that we could translate all the things we had been exposing students to in their first year through something practical. What we were finding was [that] those satellite areas that we were teaching were going to remain peripheral to the reason they came [to Toi Whakaari], until we could get them inside a production and actually work backwards. It's an interesting way to go about things; they couldn't do *Pakiwaitara* until we grounded them in certain principles, and that we needed to put them in the thick of a creative conversation with each other, and then say, 'That's what we're talking about.'[11]

Pakiwaitara, 2008
Photo: Philip Merry

The method adopted for this project was part of a greater investigation into performance research. *Pakiwaitara* was not a simple re-enactment of historical events: it honoured the past, and the cast worked with it to create something new in the present. As the audience travelled through the Museum, they were invited to actively create for themselves rather than passively to receive information, in order to 'stimulate an engagement with the histories'.[12] The performance culminated in a forum discussion in which the audience was encouraged to ask questions, share experiences, and debate thoughts and ideas stimulated by the work.

This, and other experiences in cultural and theoretical studies, began to reveal to the students different ways in which they could structure work:

> In the past, in terms of devising, the students were often working under a devising director, so they weren't necessarily presented with structures, or knew how that deviser was constructing a creative methodology; they were within it. You might end up with a really strong 'product', but in terms of their learning as students, how much of that do they know in order to continue, or build on? We're trying to seed practitioners for fifty years from now. And if you get too panicked in terms of a result or fixing up all the bits, for me, that's when my practice – or my taste as a director – gets in the way of my job as a teacher. Instead, I know that this will have fruits later on. I think the trick of devising is not to come out overtly with the reason, but keep moving through the process. To stand up as the 'expert' and list what you are going to take them through and teach them is crazy – in terms of theatre. You can't get them to work through the phases and then be the facilitator through those phases. It's an ephemeral art, so to work in those moments is pretty important.
>
> Actors don't necessarily understand theatrical relationships; rather they think, 'What does light or space do in relation to this?' And designers often come to the school with little realisation of what actors do; they may come with some understanding of television and film, but they rarely know what's possible in terms of theatre. So, in order to reveal metaphor to them, and to deal with questions of identity and difference, we need to be in the thick of theatrical production. Otherwise we run the risk of students leaving the school with no understanding of what they are part of, within that art form.[13]

The link between creativity and identity within a bicultural context was further explored when the majority of the school visited Manutuke Marae near Gisborne in May for a week-long intensive. The focus of the visit was on 'community'. Teina hailed from Manutuke, Tūranganui-a-Kiwa, and was largely responsible for organising the visit:

> After a long trip, then meeting the local marae people, eating the first meal, and initial nerves settled, we witnessed relationships develop and firmly root throughout the duration of the stay, both across disciplines and year groups. Toi Whakaari morphed into a living entity, and everywhere you turned were activities happening, not just at the marae but across the Manutuke community, and into Gisborne itself.[14]

The school engaged in a large amount of activity during the visit to Manutuke, including performances of *Scene/Unseen* by the second-year actors, seeding of rehearsals for the *After Democracy* season of plays, workshops by staff and students at various local schools, mau rakau training and movement, and harakeke flax and weaving sessions.

Staff and students also visited Matapuna Training Centre and Toihoukura, the Māori School of Visual Arts in Gisborne.

The marae visit provided an opportunity for staff and students to redefine and affirm their working relationships through a true cultural exchange within a Māori community. This cultural exchange was reinforced a month later when Tūranga Wahine/ Tūranga Tane Kapa Haka, predominantly made up of people from Manutuke, visited Toi Whakaari to perform for the school during kōiwi.

The year before, Toi Whakaari had applied to the New Zealand Screen Council to receive a *ScreenMark* accreditation for the acting course. This prestigious stamp of approval is not given lightly, and is awarded only for high quality practical tertiary courses that meet the needs of the screen industry. Following a stringent appraisal of Toi Whakaari's screen programme and the resources available to deliver it, the school received its *ScreenMark* accreditation in April 2008, providing a clear endorsement of the quality of screen training the school had developed and is delivering. To this day, Toi Whakaari remains the only acting programme in the country to have received the accolade.

Shortly after receiving its *ScreenMark*, the school was given a further boost to the screen training programme when Nathaniel Lees was appointed senior acting and screen tutor to continue and develop the pioneering work that Miranda had earlier introduced.

Nathaniel, a New Zealander of Samoan heritage, had built a substantial career over thirty years as a stage, television and screen actor, and as a director. He is a leading figure in the Pacific theatre movement in New Zealand, having directed groundbreaking plays such as *Think of a Garden*, *A Frigate Bird Sings* and *The Songmaker's Chair*. His film and television work famously includes *The Matrix Trilogy*, *Lord of the Rings*, *30 Days of Night* and *The Tattooist*, as well as films reflecting the Pacific influence: *No 2* and *Sione's Wedding*.

Nathaniel also had a long association with Toi Whakaari, having previously taught on courses in the acting department. Shortly after taking up his appointment, he was asked what advice he would give to someone wanting to be an actor, to which he replied:

> Have a really good think about it. Acting is not to be entered into lightly, or something easy to do to fill the time. Acting is a craft, a very difficult craft even for those who have a passion for it. But you will be joining a family of like-minded people, creative people coming together to tell stories of New Zealand, and that is something very special indeed.[15]

Nathaniel Lees. *Photo: Philip Merry*

When the second-years returned from Manutuke, they began the principal rehearsals for *After Democracy*, a season of political one-act plays by British playwrights Edward Bond, Caryl Churchill and Harold Pinter. The productions were directed by Christian Penny, Rachel More, Bill Guest and David Nevell, who had been contracted by the school as voice tutor after Sylvia Rands resigned from that position.

The cast of *After Democracy* were asked to focus their learning questions around truly living the moment-by-moment life of the characters on stage; this was further reinforced by the growing familiarity of the complex political issues within each of the plays. The need to manage the logistics of four productions within a single programme also provided a particular challenge for the technical/management/design team.

After that, the second-year actors embarked on a Shakespeare double-bill, with half the group working on *The Tempest* with John Bolton in Te Whaea Theatre, and the other half, an all female cast, working on *Macbeth* with Jonathon Hendry at the Garage Theatre.

The productions were approached very differently. *The Tempest* group chose to explore themes of 'revenge, power and desire' in order to make the play relevant to today, shaping their production through a process of devising and uncovering the work through negotiation. The designers, crew and cast of *Macbeth* worked with the ambience of the Garage to create a performance environment that reflected their current world. They explored different approaches to the text to capture the 'movement of thought' in Shakespeare's verse:

> Where does evil spring from? Is it an external force or something more sinister? *Macbeth* is Shakespeare's shortest and darkest tragedy. A play that can still shock as it speaks of the demons within us all. We're perfectly placed in the Garage Theatre space – it has a dark brooding bunker atmosphere that is magic.[16]

The productions were performed concurrently, with a crew of over forty students and graduates, including ten designers, two production managers, four stage-managers, eight costumiers, eight set builders, four prop makers and a host of technician/operators.

Toi Whakaari's international profile had significantly increased over the previous decade, largely as a result of student and staff exchanges. In September, Annie Ruth attended the World Conference of Theatre School Directors and the World Festival of Theatre Schools in Barcelona. The conference was run by the UNESCO International Theatre Institute, and participation was by invitation, aimed at including top training providers from each of twenty-five different countries. Annie ran a master-class with students from the Ukraine, Germany, Japan, Mexico, Costa Rica, Iran, South Africa and Romania:

> My class was an introduction to 'viewpoints', with a final section looking at movement and spatial relationships as they are articulated in different cultures. Towards the end of the class I asked the participants to gather in national groups and create a five-movement sequence based on dance from their area. I then paired them with another culture so that the final piece they created was a combination of two cultures. The fusion of Japan and South Africa was particularly amazing for its successful integration of two very different movement vocabularies.[17]

As a direct result of Annie's work at the conference, and Toi Whakaari's involvement in establishing the Masters of Theatre Arts in Directing programme, the Chair of UNESCO ITI invited her to plan and set up a one-year intensive International Masters Programme in directing under the auspices of UNESCO ITI, to be delivered in Bu-

The Tempest, 2008. L–R Emmett Skilton, Timothy Carlsen, Guy Langford. *Photo: Philip Merry*

charest as a pilot programme to test international interest in such an initiative.[18]

Other benefits of Toi Whakaari's participation in the conference lay primarily in relationship-building; important connections were made with major players from key training institutions in the UK, Australia and China. One immediate outcome was an invitation from the Shanghai Theatre Company for Annie and other staff and students from Toi Whakaari to attend a regional festival and conference in Shanghai in June 2009.

Production activity at the school continued apace. Unlike 2007, when there had been just two graduation productions, there were now four. In 2008, the main (G1) graduation production, performed in Te Whaea Theatre at the end of October, was Kevin Kerr's *Unity (1918)*, directed by Conrad Newport. This was bracketed by three (G2) productions: Sarah Kane's *Blasted,* directed by Kat Tomas, a second-year MTA director; *The Pillowman* by Martin McDonagh, directed by Stuart Handloff, also a second-year MTA director; and Jo Randerson's *AoTERRORoa*, directed by Geoff Pinfield, a 2003 MTA directing graduate. *Blasted* and *AoTERRORoa* both performed in the Garage Theatre, and *The Pillowman* at Circa Two.

Nine graduating actors appeared in *Unity (1918)*; others appeared in *AoTERRORoa* and/or *The Pillowman*, although *Blasted* and *The Pillowman* had mostly Toi Whakaari graduates in their casts.

With four productions now being mounted at the same time, the resources of Toi Whakaari were stretched, with each project vying for technical crews, designers, managers and costumiers. The very fact that a workable outcome was achieved was a clear endorsement of the sophisticated level of collaboration occurring across all courses at the school. This was noted by Laurie Atkinson in his review of the Toi Whakaari graduation season:

> University students simply write exams. The poor old drama student has to put on plays for public scrutiny during a month-long graduation season. The graduating acting students were up to the usual high standards of the school, but what stood out for me this year was the sophistication of the technical side of theatre: the three stages and

> accurate settings (all created in six weeks) for *AoTERRORoa*, the menacing sound effects of the grim reaper and the spaciousness of the setting evoking the Canadian prairie in *Unity (1918)*, the terrifying explosion that destroys the smart hotel bedroom in *Blasted*, and the dank, underground interrogation room and cell of *The Pillowman*: all of a very high standard.[19]

Unity (1918) is set in Saskatchewan, Canada, immediately after the First World War. Just as rehearsals were about to begin, D'Arcy Smith, a voice and speech specialist from Canada, arrived to take over from David Nevell as the school's voice and speech tutor. This allowed him to coach the cast in the subtleties of the Canadian accent. D'Arcy is a graduate of Toronto's York University and has worked extensively in Canada and the United States as an actor, teacher, and voice, speech and dialect coach.

Toward the end of 2008, Christine Richardson, the business manager for Toi Whakaari and Te Whaea Services for the previous seven years, resigned to take on volunteer work at the Moshono Campus of the School of St Jude in Arusha, Tanzania, as office manager.

Christine had contributed enormously to the development of school and had been a stabilising influence during a difficult period in its history. Modest by nature, Christine always insisted that none of her achievements was accomplished independently and that there was always a team effort. Nevertheless, she deserves full credit for the numerous schemes that she initiated and implemented that significantly increased the effectiveness of the school's operation, including a service agreement model that more clearly defined the services provided by Te Whaea Management to Toi Whakaari and the New Zealand Dance School. She put much needed processes in place around human resources, and encouraged the various departments within the two schools to take greater responsibility for their own budgeting, which in turn resulted in greater transparency around process. And with the support of Tamara Aluwihare, Christine finally managed to get the Trust Board's and the school's finances into a good state. Getting Toi Whakaari onto a three-year NZQA audit cycle was also a major achievement for Christine, and an equally rare achievement for a private training establishment. Above all, she saw the 'big picture', enabling her to appreciate where gains could be made, often by hooking up with the right people and pushing the right buttons.[20]

Steve Stirrat succeeded Christine Richardson as general manager of Te Whaea Management Services. He had initially trained as a teacher at Wellington Teachers' College from 1973–75: his lecturers included George Webby, Laughton Pattrick and Ralph McAllister, giving a certain synchronicity to his latest employment at Te Whaea, thirty-four years on. In the intervening years, Steve had worked as a teacher and more recently as a building contractor.

My full-time connection with Toi Whakaari also ended in July with a magnificent send-off, themed on *The Great Escape*: it had been rumoured that the only way I would eventually leave Te Whaea would be via a tunnel, 'under the wire'. The occasion was very theatrical and, much to my relief, jovial. To signify my 'graduation' from the school, I received a 'Doctorate of Phenomenological Theatre' (with high distinction!), and two magnificent cloaks crafted by Kaarin Macaulay and the 'costume girls'; one of the cloaks was emblazoned with patches, individually made by staff and students.

Along with the memory of that surprising and touching farewell, the cloaks will be forever treasured.

In April 2009 the school returned to Manutuke Marae, and again performed at schools in Gisborne and Tolaga Bay, bringing a greater awareness of Toi Whakaari and the courses offered to those areas. If anything, this visit was even more successful than the previous year, having benefited from lessons learned through kōiwi, as Annie Ruth noted:

> Manutuke Marae was an extraordinary experience … partly due to the increased ease between us and the people of the marae, and partly because the students have absorbed the lessons of kōiwi at a deeper level and therefore were better prepared for the community-building challenges and to recognise the learning when it came. They are getting so articulate about this and I find it utterly moving.[21]

Absent on the marae this time was Jade Eriksen; she had taken maternity/parental leave for a year and was replaced by Heather Timms. Before coming to New Zealand, Heather had been head of drama at John Curtin College of the Arts in Freemantle. She had subsequently collaborated with Jim Moriaty at Te Rakau Hua, working and touring with them, which had helped her to find a new place in New Zealand. Heather later set up her own company in Wellington, Eko Theatre, working with Māori and Somali communities. The combination of her academic experience in developing curriculum, and her artistic practice within various ethnic communities in Africa, Australia, the UK and New Zealand, imbued her with a strong awareness of context, and the politics of relationships and community:

> It came as a real surprise to me to come to New Zealand and to see a lot of artistic work trying to do what was being done elsewhere. It wasn't valuing what is here and what's really potent about this place. When in fact it can compete on an international scale, because what you're bringing forward is different and specific. I see the bicultural frame as an incredible gift to this country, but there is so much misunderstanding about it.
>
> When I saw what Jade and Teina were doing at Toi Whakaari, I realised it was very similar to my previous theatre work, but within an institution. And the more I heard

D'Arcy Smith
Photo: Philip Merry

Heather Timms
Source: Heather Timms

about what Jade and Teina were building here, the more I saw parallels between that and the things that I was interested in. How artistic work can better reflect the community from which it's grown so that it doesn't exist in isolation, and how do you use the two degrees of separation in New Zealand to your benefit, rather than something that's a negative? That interested me.

How then do we set up this provocation for exciting innovation? I was excited by what Jade and Teina were doing and I believe things happened for a reason. There's great value in a new face coming into the school. I had no agenda, so I was able to hear things in a new way and build some relationships that had perhaps been problematic before.

When I arrived, the 'department' was cultural and theoretical studies; but it still divided the two, even though they were together. We were asking the students to translate and make connections, but as a subject area – we weren't. I see the usefulness of the Māori framework as a way of encountering difference. And you need to be really strong in your difference, because it's creatively exciting. When you butt real differences against each other, you're going to have something really explosive. Honouring that and knowing how you're going to deal with that is important, so that you can then build.

Then there is the understanding of our role as tutors. We are not part of acting or design, but really the movement through which different facets of the school can translate and make sense of [it all] when the work is about serving an industry that's already here and creating a new industry, and the different responsibilities required. This has got to be a place where students can test out their ideas, dream huge, but connect with rigour. And if it's difficult, try harder.[22]

Dr Raymond Boyce, arguably New Zealand's most seminal stage designer, had gifted a collection of his set models to Toi Whakaari. His career had paralleled the development of professional theatre in this country over the past forty years, from the pioneering touring with the New Zealand Players to the full realisation of an indigenous and vital New Zealand theatre. To acknowledge Dr Boyce's generosity publicly, and to celebrate his contribution to and his influence on theatre design, the school decided to mount an exhibition of his work at Te Whaea. The exhibition, Sculpting the Empty Space, which included models loaned by the Royal New Zealand Ballet and Victoria University, opened in May 2009 with a large turn-out of theatre practitioners in attendance; many were contemporaries of Dr Boyce, including Richard Campion and Sunny Amey.

The Shanghai Theatre Company's invitation at the 2008 UNESCO ITI resulted in Annie Ruth, Jonathon Hendry and four final-year students – Guy Langford, Shadon Meredith, Kate McGill and Emma Ransley – attending the Asian Pacific Expo of Theatre Schools and the Fifth Shanghai International Experimental Theatre Festival. During the festival, the students performed *Tapu Toru*:

The process we went through to make the work really challenged us to make a purpose for taking this overseas. Why are we doing this, what do we show and who are we? To take something that represents the school and New Zealand based on *The Caucasian Chalk Circle* or *Romeo and Juliet*. It was a hard struggle to get to that. We came to the conclusion that we needed to show that we were 'in work': that we were making work, not trying to get it right, but trying to work it out. This approach was in direct contrast to the Beijing Opera's production of *Oedipus* which we saw, and how trained their gestures are: that

Top three images: Launch of Sculpting the Empty Space exhibition.
These three photographs by David Lewis

Above left: Richard Campion (L) and Dr Raymond Boyce (R)

Above right: Penny Fitt and Dr Raymond Boyce.

Right: Bill Sheat (L) and David Carnegie (R).

Below: UNESCO ITI Conference in Shanghai. L–R: Jonathon Hendry, (?), Shadon Meredith, Annie Ruth, Guy Langford, Katharine McGill, Emma Ransley

> they denote something, and you are already in the world of it. We were different from everybody else at the conference. Most other groups were doing fairly safe twenty-minute versions of *The Caucasian Chalk Circle*, mainly in the style taught by particular academies, such as the Shanghai Theatre Academy, with teachers mainly making the work. Whereas at Toi Whakaari we don't learn one style, instead we find what form works for what we are trying to do. We don't have a single form at Toi Whakaari, and that struck me as a major difference. So that when we made *Tapu Toru* we asked, 'What is going to work to get us there, and what do we want to work with?' Annie brought her viewpoints work and Jonty his text methodology, and we all had our questions.[23]

As well as the opportunity it provided to showcase Toi Whakaari on the international circuit, the expo and festival ratified the school as a full member of the Asia Pacific Bureau of the World Federation of Drama Schools. Annie Ruth also signed bilateral agreements with the National Drama School of India and the Shanghai Academy of Dramatic Arts to facilitate exchanges of staff and students between the schools. This provided an important stepping-stone in the creation of a distinctive identity and a connection between theatre schools in the Asia-Pacific region.

A month later, Toi Whakaari's relationship with UNESCO ITI was further enhanced when Annie travelled to Sinaia in Romania, and Burghausen in Bavaria, to teach in an International Acting Master Class. Workshops at both centres were based on the work of Eugene Ionesco, involving participants from Romania's National Theatre School, Shanghai's Drama and Central Academies, and individuals from Tehran and Japan. Ironically, the Romanian workshops were held in what had once been the King of Romania's Casino; Annie Ruth's classes took place in offices that had previously been occupied by Nicolae Ceausescu and his wife, Elana. As Annie later commented, 'It was quite an environment for working on the theatre of the absurd.'[24]

The much-needed and long-awaited design studios in Te Whaea eventually came to fruition in 2009 after the Trust Board agreed to the construction of a design wing to provide a separate studio for each year of the Bachelor of Design programme. It included an exhibition space and a new props workshop for the design, costume and technical students. In consultation with the architects, Aonui Architecture, the decision was made to locate the new design wing on the north-facing side of Te Whaea to complement the architecture of the Plaza and acting studios, and to bring life to the street-facing wall of the building. Two studios situated on the upper level connect the design wing to the Plaza and to the school's administration area via a suspended bridge.

A building contract for the design wing was signed in April, but as the building had to be financed by a loan, the school again faced the ongoing difficulty of borrowing without any real equity in Te Whaea. This was eventually resolved through an arrangement with Te Whaea Management Services and the Premises Management Trust. The new design wing was completed in August and officially launched by Prime Minister John Key in October. He entered into the spirit of the occasion, donning costumes that were being prepared for the upcoming production of *The Caucasian Chalk Circle*.

When Jonathon was appointed head of department in 2007, one of his first priorities was to rewrite the curriculum document for the acting degree. The curriculum and

▲ Performance Design model-making class 2009. L: Helen Boebel, C: Vibol Moeung (Tutor from WETA), R: Violet Wilson-Baird. *Photo: Philip Merry*

Launch of new design wing, October 2009. Prime Minister Right Honourable John Key, and Emma Ransley (4th year Performance Design student) at rear. *Photo: Philip Merry*

Launch of new design wing, October 2009. Rt. Hon. John Key and Penny Fitt (extremely happy). *Photo: Philip Merry*

the purposes outlined in the original (now moribund) 1997 acting degree document bore little resemblance to what was currently being delivered, and no longer accurately described the scope or the core teaching objectives of the qualification. Throughout 2008, the acting department met to more precisely define the three-year structure of their degree and to articulate the modes of delivery and assessment procedure. A fully revised version of the curriculum document was then presented to the Board of Studies for its approval in March 2009.

Feedback from the Board of Studies was mostly positive. The new curriculum document clearly reflected the values of Toi Whakaari, effectively articulating what was currently being delivered by the school. The Board did, however, request that greater emphasis be placed in the document on the importance of risk and failure (in a constructive way) to ensure staff and students continued 'to be experimental and pushed the boundaries, while supporting those who fail'. Arguably, the most significant change to the acting curriculum was in the third year of the course, now described as 'an outward looking year in preparation for a life-long career'.[25]

The third year of the acting course had evolved to include individual self-defined projects and secondments, as well as the development of research and independent practice. This was not clearly articulated in the earlier curriculum document, whereas the new documentation stated the broader purpose of the degree, in which students are 'encouraged to develop other skills to sustain self-employment; such as time-management, individual responsibility, reflection and self analysis'.[26]

Importantly, the acting degree update was a living document that could be used as a framework to allow individual unit modules to be adapted to reflect an evolving programme. The aims of the acting degree were reduced to just three: 'Teaching – to develop actors who are skilled, professional and creative; Training – to forge and sustain an acting career in the performing arts; and Support – so that the individual may learn from failure and success.'[27] Importantly, these aims relate well to those of other courses at Toi Whakaari.

A major factor that has helped the school to achieve its pedagogical aims and to weather the storm of recent structural change has been the strength of support provided to tutorial staff and students by the administrative staff. Bette Cosgrove who had arrived at a critical time during that change is particularly aware the way it has affected the school:

> The growth and changes in the school over the past five years have been extraordinary across all the disciplines and with a big growth in student numbers. It's now a true drama school, whereas before, I guess people used to think they'd come here to do either acting or technical production. That's quite a significant directional change. I know that's exactly what was written in the 2006 Strategic Plan, which had been worked on, and you can see how that's come to fruition and how the school has settled into being a cross-disciplinary tertiary deliverer. I'm a process person, and lots of processes have been tightened up. Before, I think, a lot was just reactionary with phases of 'OK, this works well, let's use that again', or 'This doesn't work so well, so let's discard that'. Whereas now, rather than everybody trying to reinvent the wheel every time there is a question, we tend to go, 'Let's be flexible enough, yet let's not discard what works'. We can still allow that

essential creativity and know that there's a reasonable structure we can fall back on. It's much clearer for the students and for the staff.

The school's administrative structure is respected because it has a really vital role in providing concrete structures to underpin the training. Without that, the creative stuff can't happen. It's a constant support structure and there's always going to be integrity around it.

When I started and for much of the past five years, Christine Richardson was the lynchpin in providing the infrastructure in that process. It's absolutely extraordinary how she achieved that, and probably quite revolutionary in terms of how the administration team work. I have never worked in an environment that is as innovative as this, particularly in the way it responds to things, it's always looking outside the square and testing new ways of working and solving a problem. It's completely ongoing, everyone in the team has the authority and flexibility to make and instigate changes, to try and find better or more efficient ways that work, and to then share them.

We work in an environment where people have such creative ideas, but there has to be someone there asking, 'Why are we doing that?' I guess it's our job to go, 'OK, if you imagine it that way, then if we do this, this and this, it could work better.'[28]

Performance projects at Toi Whakaari in 2009 included two epic productions. The first, *A Midsummer Night's Dream*, was directed by Josette Bushell-Mingo, a leading UK Afro-Caribbean actor and director. The production had a cast of second-year actors and a crew of thirty-six design and production students. Josette Bushell-Mingo had previously been nominated for a Laurence Olivier Award in 2000 for her performance in the West End production of *The Lion King*. She had also established a multidisciplinary black-led arts festival PUSH, with the aim of inspiring diversity and promoting more black artists into mainstream British arts.

Josette Bushell-Mingo negotiated designs and casting for Toi Whakaari's production of *A Midsummer Night's Dream* via the internet from her base in Sweden, where she worked as artistic director for Tryst Theatre, the National Deaf Theatre of Sweden. One of her aims for the production was to give 'Shakespeare a decent shake-up', some of her inspiration for this coming from metaphors of dreams and magic, combined with symbols of circus production – illusion, magic and transformation:

My productions are often epic, visual and sensual. I am greatly influenced by films and we have been watching stuff from *Hero* to *Pan's Labyrinth*, *Moulin Rouge* to Buster Keaton, each differently tapping emotions that are seen in the play. I want the audience to have a theatrical experience, to hear and see Shakespeare through his imagery and visual landscape, to leave knowing they have been in a theatre caught up in a dream.[29]

Although Josette Bushell-Mingo is a fairly radical director, she is also very traditional in her approach, bringing a kind of mischief and irreverence to Shakespeare through her 'theatrical' production methods. Her circus-based *A Midsummer Night's Dream* was extremely theatrical, with the cast acquiring an impressive range of circus skills: stilt walking, fire breathing, rope walking and acrobatics, under the guidance of the circus director, Deborah Pope. The circus theme was further reflected in the beautifully executed and colourful costumes made by the costume construction and design

The Caucasian Chalk Circle, rehearsal. L–R: Veronica Brady, Matariki Whatarau, Christian Penny, Shadon Meredith, Amelia Reid.
Photo: Philip Merry.

The Caucasian Chalk Circle, rehearsal. Front: Sophie Lindsay (L) Aroha White (R), behind L–R: Ricky Beirao (DSM), Emmet Skilton, Dan Hannah.
Photo: Philip Merry.

The Caucasian Chalk Circle, performance. L–R Romy Hooper, Juanita Hepi, Matariki Whatarau.
Photo: Philip Merry

students, and in Rose Morrison's set, based on a large circus ring surrounded by audience seating.

Heightened theatricality was again evident in the second 'epic' production of the year, Frank McGuiness's adaptation of Brecht's *The Caucasian Chalk Circle*. This graduation production, for the third-year actors and for some design, costume construction and performing arts management students, encapsulated much of the learning that had taken place in the kōiwi sessions over the previous two years, and for the actors through their solo performances. To fulfill his aims for *The Caucasian Chalk Circle*, Christian Penny encouraged the cast and crew to assume roles of leadership and to work to their strengths. The company operated more like a collective, with the cast directing each other in groups, quickly sketching out scenes and devising around the text. The results were then played back to the entire company at the end of the day's rehearsal:

> Putting us in places of leadership was very smart because it meant by the end of the rehearsal process we owned the production. That's quite important in theatre: you can smell it a mile away if the cast don't believe in what they are doing on stage. It also gave us a whole set of other tools to leave the school with; not just as actors. The skills we learned could be honed and focused in so many different aspects to support our work.
>
> As a collective we were very aware that our core characters were going to shift, but we had a real sense of our goals in the piece. There were variables every night [where] things would change because of the audience – because of the child, there were things that were completely unpredictable, and we simply had to go with that: it forced us to be alive in the moment. *The Caucasian Chalk Circle* is a complex story, and it was great to have a production that permitted us to deal with the unpredictable in this way.
>
> We had a real sense of testing things: what are we trying to work out? This allowed the audience to come along with us, and their inclusion in that process made the production work – on several levels. There was a real sense of company, of community working with the designers and tech crew. Through the rehearsal process we played games and worked things out together: the stage manager (Ricky Beirao) helped us with a lot of the acting.[30]

Students involved in *The Caucasian Chalk Circle* had all joined the school since 2007 and valued the level of collaboration now occurring across the various disciplines. In many ways, they embodied the continuing spirit of 'convergence' that had more recently emerged in the school and saw it as a distinct advantage:

> Convergence has happened – but it's no longer called convergence. Today, in the school the 'converging' of all disciplines is happening, we're just not giving it that name. For us, it started with *Pakiwaitara* where we worked with the designers, and those relationships continued. In *The Caucasian Chalk Circle* we worked with some of the same management students who had worked with us on *After Democracy*: those relationships build. It was fantastic because we could more easily communicate with them.
>
> It's like politics: you talk and talk and don't necessarily get anywhere, but if you do it – then you see results. You need to put it into practice, and *Pakiwaitara* worked: it had lots of faults, but like *The Caucasian Chalk Circle* it worked. We can use that experience as an example when we speak to convergence, whereas before it was just an idea around a table.
>
> It's not about 'I' but 'We'. It's an understanding of the whole, that's what convergence achieves. We now understand where we fit in the 'whole', and where we stand in relation

Canopy of ribbons, 2009 graduation ceremony.
Photo: Melissa Spratt

to that. If we go back in time, then it was really actor biased, there was a lack of balance and understanding of the whole: it's not realistic to the world we now work in.

Without the other courses at the school, it limits the work you produce, particularly in the context of performance. We are leaving Toi Whakaari not just as skilled actors, but as skilled and creative practitioners and learners. Which is particularly relevant to the New Zealand industry: to be able to make and to know where our job as a performer fits in the 'whole' so that we can be more useful.

Everything we say has been developed in kōiwi: it's been subtle. Developments such as the marae visit, department presentations and the graduation ceremony have fostered working relationships. It is the glue that holds everything together and challenges us to ask why we are here, and what we stand for. What is our purpose in our art form, and who stands behind you? Why are we here? How do we make this thing better as a team? They're all important in the field in which we work: these are life-skills.

At our recent graduation we knew every one of [the other graduates] and we'd had a professional relationship with each of them, and we were celebrating each other. It really felt that this year group had embraced this thing – convergence – and had really worked at it. It hasn't been easy; there were a lot of prejudices that needed to be broken, but it felt that we got there, especially with *Caucasian Chalk Circle*.[31]

So what of the future? The introduction of kōiwi has created a platform and a stimulus for students and staff collectively to address the place and purpose of Toi Whakaari and its relationship to the wider performing arts community. Kōiwi has also helped to inform the collaborative process of the school.

The 2009 intake of students, unaware of some of the earlier barriers around questions of community, immediately accepted the culture of kōiwi. Because of that, they operate at a different level of listening to community, more so than in previous years:

> Kōiwi is a 'norm' for new students. This was reflected in the recall weekend this year, where the first-years competently talked about the community of the school, and that reflected again on that group of auditionees. They felt, 'Wow, this is such a strong place to be in' and I assume that will continue to build next year.
>
> This year's graduates also hold that relationship of community in their work, developed through their learning in cultural and theoretical studies. It strengthens our purpose in what we do when we practise community; but we can get better and clearer about that. We now do an event, then unpack it and reflect on it to see what we've learned, and in some ways it's excessive and over-engineered. We need to be more organic in terms of creating and in moving naturally together as a school.[32]

In recent years, kōiwi has been strongly promoted by Teina, Jade and Heather, and in its development has revealed different ways of working together, as Jade recalled:

> I remember somebody saying to me, I want you to know that everything that's in the school has been approved of by a kaumātua, and I said, 'Isn't that interesting – because what's right for one kaumātua is not always right for another.' I think this is part of a movement in terms of a nation's understanding of Māoridom, that it's not about one rule, nor can it be lumped into one. The students coming through today are not interested either, they don't see themselves in one box, like the Samoan students, who don't want to represent a culture that's imposed on them. I think that's an interesting shift in the school. Rather than focusing on possession, it's actually about the complexity of us as Pākehā – or whatever. What's our culture – what's the language for that in terms of how it relates to their work? You don't just go off and play a Chekhov character and think you can just slip into their shoes. It's got to be full of human complexity and experiences, and you need to come to the part with a question, as opposed to proficiency, which is a kind of arrogance.
>
> … Do we honour a tradition by repeating, or do we honour it by actually looking at what the principles are of that tradition? For theatre and for culture to shift and change, it has to move in relation to that context. In the past, cultures have been fixed and a lot of theatre represents that thing of those cultures. But it's also meant that Pākehā are left with a sense that they no longer have one. So the question for us is, how do these cultures learn from each other? We have the potential to translate these human terms to do with relationship instead of becoming fixated on the idea of information, and being right or wrong.[33]

The value of Toi Whakaari's interdisciplinary culture was further endorsed at the 2009 graduation ceremony as the six disciplines or strands of the school were symbolised by a canopy of six ribbons woven together above the Plaza. At the ceremony, Simon Phillips was (in absentia) presented with the Toi Whakaari Graduate Award for Excellence. This was most fitting: as a trainee director at the New Zealand Drama School in the 1980s, Simon was one of the first students of the school to explore an additional strand. He has since received a raft of awards for his work as a director, both internationally and as artistic director of the Melbourne Theatre Company. In his acceptance speech, given on his behalf by Sarah Pierse, Simon Phillips had this to say about his time at the school:

> My own life was lit up by the deep humanity and heedless wit of George Webby, the canny instincts of Grant Tilly, the long-suffering leotarded love of Erica Stephenson and the raunchy ululations of Jane Waddell among many other truly inspiring forces.

Simon Phillips
Source: Melbourne Theatre Company

Tanea Heke

> I don't know what it is about New Zealand; maybe its isolation provides a cocoon in which people feel safe to explore their individuality and find a voice, a style, a point of view relatively uncluttered by the noise from the world at large. Which, needless to say, is a macrocosm for a good drama school – you feel safe to explore, fail, discover your strengths and increase your dexterity, without being judged by the world that's hanging around to do so when you leave.[34]

When I arrived at Toi Whakaari in 1994, the school had been operating for twenty-three years essentially as an acting school, and had produced around 220 graduates. Although the core business of the school was identified as actor training, for all intents and purposes it was far more than that. George Webby certainly had a broader view of the school: he was principally interested in training people for the theatre, and was well aware that many graduates would eventually move into areas other than acting:

> Our job at the school, surely, was to see that graduates left us well-grounded in *all* those areas needed for success in whatever branch of stage, film or TV they intended to work in. As I saw it, the training of some of the graduates would, I hoped, lead to more specialised theatre work, and any group wanting to further their interests of one particular culture would be well trained to pursue that.[35]

Around half of those who graduated from the Drama School between 1970 and 1994 still work as actors in theatre, television or film, in New Zealand and overseas. Many of those have become 'household' names, including Tim Balme, Cliff Curtis, Dave Fane, Kerry Fox, Michael Galvin, Robyn Malcolm, Rawiri Paratene, Jacob Rajan and Katie Wolfe. Many others from that time have diversified to take on different roles in the performing arts, for example:

Guy Boyce (festival director)
Stephanie Creed (PA to Nica Burns, CEO of Nimax Theatres in London)
Frances Edmond (screen writer/playwright/theatre critic)
John Godfrey (administrator for the Edinburgh Festival)
Hone Kouka (playwright)
Rachel Lang (script writer)
Prue Langbein (programme producer with Radio NZ)
John McDavitt (CNZ Strategy Advisor)

Christina Milligan (TVNZ producer)
Danny Mulheron (writer/director)
Liz Mullane (casting director and actors' agent)
Jan Prettejohns (writer/script editor)
Eva Radich (broadcaster and radio drama producer)
Annie Ruth (Director of Toi Whakaari)
Sima Urale (screen writer and director)

Tanea Heke, a student at the school from 1986 to 1987, is a prime example of a graduate who has since diversified in her career. For many years, she was on the Toi Whakaari Board of Studies and this has given her a good overview of the way the school has changed and advanced its purpose in recent years:

> My year was the last of the diploma course, and we were the last lot to come through completely at Vivian Street. I think I was lucky in that I had a degree before I went to Toi Whakaari. I'd come directly from Victoria and also Wellington College of Education where I'd got my teaching diploma.
>
> It's different now, and I'm not sure how I can compare it. I'm pleased to hear the school has integrated more, and that the disciplines are actually working together because that's how it works out in the industry. I don't think we had that sort of synergy at the time that we were there. Also, the purpose is different now. While I was there, I didn't think the staff or the students, or even the Board at times, were objective enough, or had enough distance from what they were trying to achieve. Some of the staff and most of the Board members also seemed to have their own agendas because they came from or represented the industry. Of course that's very important, but I wondered if we'd lost our way for some time there. I felt for a while that the focus was too narrow, with an emphasis on churning people out for film or TV, and whatever the industry needed or required. I couldn't see the point. If the industry wants Shorty Street actors, then they should train them.
>
> It's actually not about that, it's about finding out what the students – or our people – need. I can see that a balance has now returned to Toi Whakaari, they're not actually trying to churn out 'Shortland Street kids'.
>
> To have an enduring career, you've got to have a wealth of knowledge, which you only touch upon over three years. Essentially, what we came away with were the tools and we were responsible for how we used those, and which area we moved into. Students need to have the ability to move seamlessly from one thing to the next. Sometimes there is an expectation that when you come out of Toi Whakaari you'll never stop working and when/if that doesn't happen it can be very easy to get resentful. Even if you get kicked out it really doesn't matter; you take what you're given and you work at it, but by Christ you've got to work at it.
>
> There are a number of graduates who continue to do what they were trained to do, and are happy in that. Then there are those of us who are very strong script writers or have gone on to work in arts administration. I will always be grateful to Toi Whakaari for putting me in contact with some amazing people, and for giving me the skills to identify how the industry works – or in some instances, doesn't. I went on to work at Taki Rua until that burned me out – which ultimately running a theatre company that's strapped for money and the work is hard – does. Then I spent time at Te Papa as a project manager,

> which really helped me as a producer. I thought I'd left the theatre sector behind, but actually the visual arts and exhibitions are exactly the same; essentially you are given a lump of money, a project with an end date – and a disparate team, much like a theatre production. I then moved to Creative New Zealand and I'm now the Senior Adviser for the International Team. People at CNZ have an interesting relationship. Many have worked through the sector and through the industry and have now moved on. Some are senior practitioners with work of a standard that's been shown at the International Festival here in New Zealand and overseas. The International Team at CNZ and its international strategy ensures that the best of the best go overseas; otherwise our market's too small.[36]

The 2009 graduating actors were undeniably resilient, and in their own way refuted a previously held notion that 'change' had somehow disadvantaged students or had been sole driver of discontent within the school. In fact, many of the 2009 graduating actors credited their changing circumstances at the school with having fostered a greater sense of independence.

So, how have the 2009 graduates been changed and supported by Toi Whakaari? And what values and ambitions do they now hold? Those questions were put to a random selection of them:

> *Guy Langford, Bachelor of Performing Arts (Acting).* I came to the school wanting to be a good actor and am leaving the school as an artist. There is a difference. I have a whole lot more ownership of my craft; of why and what I'd doing, and how to continue to learn, this is very empowering. I have also learned to embrace change that you have to let things move and you have to adapt, and to trust that: a huge thing for me. I'm passionate about theatre and really enjoy the relationship between the actor and a live audience. For my secondment I went to Paris and worked with Philippe Gaulier, and also through my work with John Bolton on *The Tempest* and with Christian on *Caucasian Chalk Circle*, I have been inspired by the factor of play and having pleasure with an audience. I'm really interested in making theatre that uplifts and surprises an audience and allows them to dream.

> *Sophie Lindsay, Bachelor of Performing Arts (Acting).* Having come from Auckland University, which is very cerebral, and to now get learning in my body has had a huge impact on the way I see things, and the way I understand and relate to others. What I want to do now is to create theatre, and I've been stimulated by what people can create together. I'm really excited about where New Zealand is as a country: it's like a lab – we can test things here. We are quite fortunate in that sense.

> *Amelia Reid, Bachelor of Performing Arts (Acting).* When I first arrived at Toi Whakaari, I stood up in orientation and said, 'I want to change the world with theatre.' At the time I didn't really know what that involved, but now I have a clearer sense of my purpose.
>
> In 2008, I went to Cambodia with two of my classmates: Shadon Meredith and Matariki Whatarau. What that gave to us was a framework, to discover how we work together; it was somehow easier to do that in a foreign context where we were all New Zealanders. We held a devising workshop with the Khmer community, with the aim of empowering the 'performers' by instilling the devising process, to enable them to speak to their community. We worked as facilitators, in a similar way to *Pakiwaitara*, but around the provocation of Angkor Wat, relating that to modern Cambodia.

Images L–R:
Guy Langford,
Sophie Lindsay,
Amelia Reid.
Photos: Philip Merry.

We have since formed a collective with Ngapaki Emery (MTA student) and we hope to work with a range of communities to learn how best to work with our difference. The power of theatre is that it can often start conversations that can't otherwise be had, which we can do through metaphor, movement and design to open a window for something to talk to: it's so exciting.

Ian Hammond, Bachelor of Performance Design. *Pakiwaitara* was the project where our whole [design] class completely shifted. At the end we were so different – so were the actors – we began to understand how we could start to make work together. At the beginning of the process, we were all on the same level, at the end we had collective ownership of the work.

My fourth-year major project was *Quarters*, a collaborative film project made with three other performance design students. The film was in four inter-related parts, with one central research question on the notion of 'home', which we responded to individually. I started by doing a whole lot of personal research and design tests using film, and attempted to translate that into a narrative for a short film. But in trying to do what you are 'meant to do' with film, I finished up with this really awful epic-looking film; I had lost the integrity of my research and all the initial modesty. So I went back and re-shot the film honestly. I now want to continue developing our own way of working, together with the other designers who worked on *Quarters*. We are interested in forming a collective, where we can make film projects with design informing the direction, as well as other projects, such as installation work, music events and theatre.

The performance design course has been unlike any other degree. We've been involved in developing the course, which has been shaped around us and where we as individuals wanted to go, giving us more control around our learning. We were also fortunate in being a relatively small cohort. Lots of my friends are now coming out of Massey with beautiful work that they've slaved over. But few of them

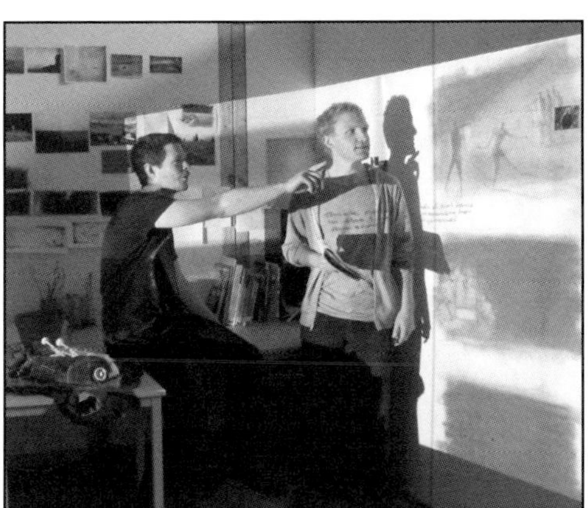

Ian Hammond (R) with Rowan Pierce

can get jobs as there is currently so little work in the architectural or advertising area, whereas we have lots of job offers, mainly because we've been taught and have been working with the people who are in a position to employ us. They know us, and how we work.

In 2010 I will be working with Malia Johnston on Wearable Arts, and also with one of our tutors, Kate Hawley, who I worked with on *Lovely Bones*. Shc is now designing the costumes for *The Hobbit* movie and has asked me to assist her.

Stuart Handloff, Master of Theatre Arts (Directing). I enrolled in the MTA from the United States, which is where my early background in theatre was, in stage lighting and as a technician. I chose Toi Whakaari because I wanted to make it a full-life experience, not an academic exercise; there were also no schools with directing programmes in the States that engaged my interest. When I enrolled in the directing course I thought it would confirm and affirm what I already knew. But I soon realised that I would learn stuff well outside my comfort zone. I thought as a director I could take almost any piece of work and develop it into good theatre. Now I have a much more specific voice and strength, and a better perspective on what I do well. I'm particularly interested in classic text work: in Shakespeare, in being able to transfer the written word into beautiful images that are accessible.

I'm now working on developing a Summer Season programme at Steamboat Springs, Colorado. They have no performing space, so I decided to take advantage of that – and do theatre outdoors, which I've called Picnic Theatre Festival. The venue is over a kilometre away from the carpark – in the woods: so it's a true outdoor experience. This year I did *Taming of the Shrew* as part of the Picnic Theatre Festival, with two Samoan actors who are Toi Whakaari graduates. We also performed a work that was a combination of Māori myth and music, in repertoire with an original piece of American folk theatre, specifically commissioned for the outdoor theatre complex. We've merged indigenous New Zealand with the culture of small-town America to develop an interesting and successful way for each to see each other through a different lens.

The summer programme epitomises what I really do well. I produce well, I engage people, I attract people to my vision and it gets them excited. The ability of a director to graduate from any programme and then go, 'Oh thank you, I'll work for you' is unlikely – anywhere. I believe it's important to do one's own work and be capable of producing it. For me that's where most of the satisfaction comes from.

Austin Mather, Diploma in Entertainment Technology. Before coming to Toi Whakaari I'd done the lighting for a couple of community groups in Warkworth and also helped out the lighting for the Music Mountain event in Matakana. I had no idea what to expect when I first came to Toi Whakaari, although I've since focused mainly on lighting. This year, I've designed lighting for the Choreographic Season and *Caucasian Chalk Circle*. The tech course has exceeded my expectations. I not only learned more about theatre craft, but also communication and time management, especially how to work in a collaborative way – it's about attitude. I've just scored a job as a technical operator with TVNZ. There were 170 applicants for the position and I was told that personality and attitude were important qualities, also how I related to others.

One of the biggest things I've learned at Toi is making decisions; decision-making is everything. My decision got me here. I had the opportunity to enroll in a similar course in Auckland, but instead I decided to take a risk and to move to a city I'd never lived in

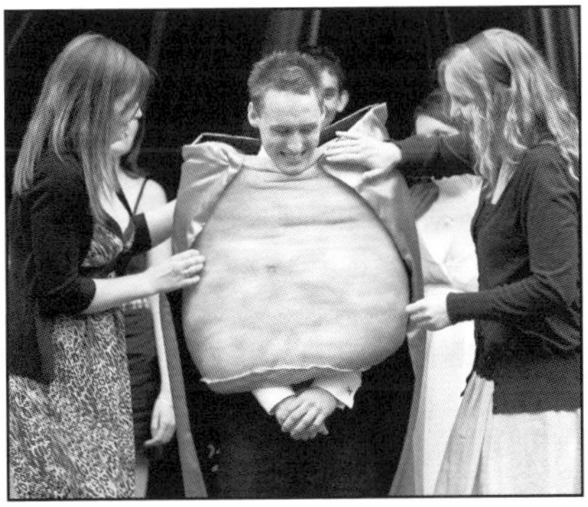

Left: Stuart Handloff *(photo: Philip Merry)*. Centre: Austin Mather receiving his cloak from Jade Turrall and Monique Webster *(photo: Philip Merry)*. Right: Jane Boocock (r) with Kaarin Macaulay.

before. Also, the entertainment technology course at Toi seemed more 'open-ended', less prescribed.

When we visited Manutuke Marae earlier this year, I was given the job of sausage-roll-maker. And I realised I wasn't just making a sausage roll; it was part of something bigger. I was just one individual working as part of a community and to be part of that community I had to pull my weight. In a way, it was a metaphor for working in the theatre, where each department and each discipline has to work collaboratively to pull off a production. If one part is slacking off, it affects the whole. The 'sausage-roll incident' became sort of folklore at Toi, and at my graduation I was presented with a giant sausage-roll cape in recognition of my efforts.

I've had a very rich experience at Toi. Perhaps one of the biggest things I've learned is to be flexible, to adapt your working methods to the given circumstances. Once you get out into the 'big bad world', there are a million and one ways of doing things.

Jane Boocock, Diploma in Costume Construction. I'd enjoyed sewing as a hobby but had never thought of it as a career. Before coming to Toi Whakaari, I majored in film and television studies and art history. When I graduated, I worked in the art department on several short films in Auckland. But that seemed to involve a lot of heavy lifting, with very little opportunity to create stuff; it was also a bit of a 'boys' club'. So then I thought, why not make a hobby a career, and applied for the costume construction course – and got in. I didn't have any expectations about what the costume course was going to teach me, it's more about what you put into it rather than what's given: you have to go after what you want. I've learned a lot since, not just technical stuff, but also working with other people and different ways of thinking. Everything I've learned has been really useful; a lot of people want to specialise when they graduate but I don't.

When I started the costume course all I wanted to do was make costume for films, but when I worked with the School of Dance on the Choreographic Season, I discovered I really enjoyed making dance costumes. I now see a lot more opportunities opening up, even outside film, theatre and dance, and eventually I would like to move into design. The most important thing about building a career is making and maintaining contacts in the industry. I'm quite lucky, because my tutors are able to help me out there: Kate Hawley is designing *The Hobbit*, so she will know my work if I apply for a job on the film. Previous graduates of the course also let me know what's happening in the industry.

Ellis Thorpe. *Photo: Philip Merry*

> *Ellis Thorpe, Bachelor of Performing Arts (Management).* I came to Toi Whakaari from Otaki, where I had been involved in theatre at school and with the local theatre society: more in acting than technical. When I enrolled at the school, I initially wanted to work as sound operator; I really enjoy music and it was a way into that world. Since then I've completely changed, and am more interested in lighting design and event and production management. I production-managed *Caucasian Chalk Circle* in my final year. It was pretty crazy and a big show to manage; being a devised work within an existing play, it was forever changing right up to and after opening night. Flexibility was the key, so I ran the production in a way that allowed the production team to remain really open, and I communicated a lot. My worry was not about the adaptability, but more about keeping the crew on task. It worked in the end and we achieved what we wanted within the time available to us.
>
> The BPAM has given me the ability to manage; this is supported by the range of craft and technical skills that I gained in the first two years of the course. My ambition is to get into tour management. I will be working with Capital E for most of 2010 as their technical manager, touring *Endgame* and *The Farm at the End of the Road* from Keri Keri down to Invercargill.[37]

Toi Whakaari is not only an elite institution, it is also rare. The school's bicultural and multicultural aspirations, and its educational pedagogy and artistic endeavour are now explored and steered through a process of 'context and practice', until recently known as 'cultural and theoretical studies'. Context and practice is a consolidator, in that it assists students and staff to make connections across the various disciplines and to develop creative relationships. It also guides learning by asking questions to promote the students' thinking about what it is that they as individuals bring to the school. This in turn helps them to re-vision the way things can be, and to push the relationship between audience and performer.

With the digital and multi-media age advancing in leaps and bounds, the pattern of diversification within performance will surely intensify as the move from traditional theatre forms into more interactive environments, further blurring the boundaries between performance disciplines. That scenario is readily acknowledged by many of the school's directing, design, management, technology and costume students, and is fast becoming a reality for the acting students. There is a real tension in the way actors are now being trained that is evident in the evolving teaching methodology at the school, which includes a significant focus on the development of entrepreneurial skills. Actors, as well as other practitioners, have become increasingly aware that to survive in the industry they have to make work, build companies and find their own performance spaces.

Bill Sheat, who played a major role in helping to found the QEII Drama School in 1970 and later argued vehemently for its retention in Wellington, has been a strong supporter of the school. He believes Toi Whakaari is now strongly positioned to affect the future of theatre in New Zealand:

> It's doing exactly what I wanted it to do, which is to provide advanced training for those wanting to make a career in the theatre. In the late fifties and early sixties, when I was with Wellington Repertory and doing things at university, I knew that I could do better, but had neither the time nor opportunity to do it.
>
> What has motivated me ever since is the desire to make it possible – particularly for young people – to live and work in their own country and provide excitement and enlightenment in their own way. We tend to do things in a different way in New Zealand; that's the strength we should build on. I think Toi Whakaari is achieving all of those things. In some ways it's taken a long time for the school to understand and acknowledge that we are training people here for New Zealand, primarily – that there's a New Zealand story to tell.
>
> The way in which biculturalism came into the school's ethos, post-George Webby, has helped it to address that, and to find a direction for New Zealand drama within that context.
>
> But it went wrong footed for a while by adopting biculturalism as though that would be the answer. It's a model of working that you can reference if you like, in terms of the students' training, it's another way, but it doesn't have to be the only way.
>
> Identifying the talent and making it possible for them to maximise it is a vital part of the process. Of course, creating situations where there are employment opportunities for graduates is the hardest part. For a long time, the work at the school was directed towards servicing the existing industry; there is now an acknowledgment that the industry needs to grow. As a result of that, there are students going out and creating their own opportunities, and to me that's fantastic: that's been the big shift.[38]

Now more than ever, acting graduates are their own producers, writers and managers. This expansion of skill is clearly illustrated by the recent work of Toi Whakaari graduates including Arthur Meek (2006 graduate) and Sophie Roberts (2007 graduate). Arthur Meek wrote *Collapsing Creation*, an exploration of Charles Darwin's courage in publishing *On the Origin of the Species*. The 2009 production of *Collapsing Creation* received the Chapman Tripp Award for Production of the Year, and Arthur Meek received the Peter Harcourt Award for Outstanding New Playwright of the Year. It was directed by David O'Donnell (1979 graduate), and featured Peter Hambleton (1982 graduate) as Darwin and Cathy Downes (1973 graduate) as Emma. At the same ceremony, Sophie Roberts received the Chapman Trip Award for Most Promising Female Newcomer of the Year for her outstanding performance in *Wolf's Lair* as Traudi Junge, Hitler's personal secretary, a work she devised and created with director Willem Wassenaar (2006 MTA graduate). Writer/director Louis Sutherland (2003 acting graduate), with co-director Mark Albiston, continue to pull in awards for *Six Dollar Fifty Man*, and their first full-length feature *Shopping* is in development and well on the road to being produced.

From its beginnings as a 'prototype' acting school in 1970 with just eight students, Toi Whakaari now has an annual intake of around 150 students. It is a place where performance artists from a broad range of disciplines can effectively collaborate to determine a context for their craft: in doing so they imagine and shape the future direction of 'theatre' in Aotearoa. Well – in fact, anywhere.

Appendix One

List of Graduates

Abbreviations:

Adv. DET	*Advanced Diploma in Entertainment Technology*
BPA	*Bachelor of Performing Arts (Acting)*
BPD	*Bachelor of Performance Design*
BPM	*Bachelor of Performing Arts (Management)*
CA	*Certificate in Acting*
DA	*Diploma in Acting*
DCC	*Diploma in Costume Construction*
DET	*Diploma in Entertainment Technology*
DTP	*Diploma in Technical Production*
Grad DTA	*Graduate Diploma in Theatre Arts (Directing)*
MTA	*Master of Theatre Arts (Directing)*

QEII ARTS COUNCIL DRAMA SCHOOL GRADUATES

1970	Jean Betts	CA
1970	Elizabeth Coulter	CA
1970	Jennifer Ludlam	CA
1970	Denise Maunder	CA
1970	William Petley	CA
1970	Darien Takle	CA, and BPA 2005
1970	Bevan Wilson	CA
1971	Stephen Crane	CA
1971	Ross Duncan	CA
1971	Roslyn Everett	CA
1971	Marion Gottlieb	CA
1971	Anthea Harper	CA
1971	Christopher Howell	CA
1972	Patricia Birdling	CA
1972	Griselda Goring-Johnstone	CA
1972	Rex Merrie	CA
1972	Rawiri Paratene (David Broughton)	CA, and BPA 2005
1972	Kathryn Rawlings	CA
1972	Annie Ruth	CA
1972	Linda Sexton	CA
1973	John Black	CA
1973	Greta Campbell	CA
1973	Anna Campion	CA
1973	Cathy Downes	CA
1973	Janet Findlay	CA
1973	Peter Hayden	CA
1973	Geraldine Holmes	CA
1973	Bernard McBride	CA
1973	Peter McCauley	CA
1973	Stephen McElrea	CA
1973	Ruth (Osbaldstone) Pretty	CA
1973	Peter Sakey	CA

NZ DRAMA SCHOOL GRADUATES

1975	Frances Edmond	DA
1975	Charles Hambling	DA
1975	Christopher Harding	DA

1975	Peter Land	DA
1975	Prue Langbein	DA
1975	Christina Milligan	DA
1975	Claire Oberman	DA
1975	Jan Prettejohns	DA
1975	Gary (Rangimoana) Taylor	DA, and BPA 2004
1975	Jane Waddell	DA
1975	Celia West	DA
1976	Margaret Campbell	DA
1976	William Kircher	DA
1976	Michael McGrath	DA
1976	Lorae Parry	DA
1976	Duncan Smith	DA
1976	Tony Ward	DA
1977	Philippa Campbell	DA
1977	Peter Dennett	DA
1977	John Godfrey	DA
1977	Michael Hyde	DA
1977	Peter Nicoll	DA
1977	Wiki Oman	DA
1977	Sandra Reid	DA
1977	Paul Shirriffs	DA
1977	Mary Spencer	DA
1977	Timothy Toye	DA
1977	Maria Vlassova	DA
1977	Michael Williams	DA
1978	Vivienne (Laube) Aitken	DA, and BPA 2003
1978	Laurie Couchman	DA
1978	Janet Fisher	DA
1978	James Heyward	DA
1978	John McDavitt	DA
1978	Mark Prain	DA
1978	Eva Radich	DA
1978	Mary Regan	DA
1978	Ashley Sumner	DA
1979	Katherine (Platt) Beasley	DA
1979	Pip Byrne	DA, and BPA 2005
1979	Mark Cubey	DA
1979	Denise O'Connell	DA, and BPA 2002
1979	David O'Donnell	DA
1979	David Pringle	DA
1979	Lani John Tupu	DA
1979	William (Bill) Walker	DA
1980	Louise Dunne	DA
1980	Rob Jayne	DA
1980	Georgina Monro	DA
1980	Blair Park	DA
1980	Simon Phillips	DA
1980	Fiona Samuel	DA
1980	Joanne Simpson	DA
1980	Alexander van Dam	DA
1980	Kate Ward	DA
1981	Heather Bolton	DA, and BPA 2004
1981	Robert Colhoun	DA
1981	Philipa Dann	DA
1981	Peter East	DA, and BPA 2003
1981	Mark Everton	DA
1981	Fiona Johnstone	DA
1981	Kerry O'Reilly	DA
1981	Merfyn Owen	DA, and BPA 2005
1982	Jon Brazier	DA
1982	Jan Fisher	DA
1982	Peter Hambleton	DA
1982	Rachel Lang	DA
1982	Michelle Leuthart	DA
1982	May Lloyd	DA
1982	Colin McCulloch	DA
1982	Augusta McDonald	DA
1982	Perry Piercy	DA, and BPA 2002
1982	Alison Routledge	DA
1982	Lucy Sheehan	DA
1982	Craig Thaine	DA
1983	Guy Boyce	DA
1983	Ruth Dudding	DA
1983	Ross Girven	DA
1983	Stephen Judd	DA
1983	Jeff Kingsford-Brown	DA
1983	Danny Mulheron	DA
1983	Rima Te Wiata	DA
1984	Brett Alcock	DA
1984	Michele Amas	DA, and BPA 2002
1984	Tim Bassett	DA
1984	Vivien Bell	DA
1984	Jo Briant	DA
1984	Eteuati Ete	DA
1984	Nick Farra	DA
1984	Miranda Harcourt	DA
1984	Natasha Hay	DA
1984	Patupatu Ripley	DA
1985	Elizabeth Brimilcombe	DA
1985	Theresa Healey	DA
1985	Murray Keane	DA
1985	Michael McLeod	DA
1985	Katherine McRae	DA

1985	Liz Mullane	DA
1985	Peter Shearer	DA
1985	Roy Ward	DA
1985	Mark Wright	DA
1986	Simon Creasey	DA
1986	Richard Finn	DA
1986	Tim Homewood	DA
1986	Stephen Lovatt	DA
1986	Annabel Newman	DA
1986	Robert Pollock	DA
1986	Louise Tourelle	DA
1986	John Wraight	DA, and BPA 2002
1987	Sean Allan	DA
1987	Jed Brophy	DA
1987	Stephanie Creed	DA
1987	Kerry Fox	DA
1987	David Geary	DA
1987	Robyn Malcolm	DA
1987	Peter Manuel	DA
1987	Tina Regtien	DA
1987	Cameron Rhodes	DA
1987	Emma Robinson	DA
1987	Jessica Wilcox	DA
1988	Simon Bennett	DA
1988	Tina Cleary	DA
1988	Jonathon (Jonty) Hendry	DA
1988	Emma Kinane	DA
1988	Colin Kitchingman	DA, and BPA 2004
1988	Andrew Laing	DA
1988	Katherine Mitchell	DA
1988	Micheala Rooney	DA
1988	John Vakidis	DA
1988	Darren Young	DA

TE KURA TOI WHAKAARI: NZ DRAMA SCHOOL GRADUATES

1989	Carol Smith	DA
1989	Hori Ahipene	DA
1989	Tim Balme	DA
1989	Marton Csokas	DA
1989	Cliff Curtis	DA
1989	Julie Edwards	DA
1989	Michael Galvin	DA
1989	Emily Perkins	DA
1989	Sarah Preece	DA
1989	Sima Urale	DA
1990	Toni Gordon	DA
1990	Neil Holt	DA
1990	Hone Kouka	DA
1990	Larissa Matheson	DA
1990	Angela Jane Meiklejohn	DA
1990	Amanda Rees	DA
1990	Mick Rose	DA
1990	Erik Thomson	DA
1990	Stuart Turner	DA
1990	Katie Wolfe	DA
1990	Stelios Yiakmis	DA
1991	Stephen Bain	DA
1991	Nancy Brunning	DA
1991	Joe Conway	DA
1991	Frances Kewene	DA
1991	Sue Morrison	DA
1991	Donna Muir	DA
1991	Allen O'Leary	DA
1991	Andrew Scott	DA
1991	Tim Spite	DA
1991	Erina Toi-Paku	DA, and BPA 2005
1991	Mairanga White	DA
1991	Stephanie Wilkin	DA
1992	Damon Andrews	DA
1992	Bronwyn Bradley	DA
1992	Bradley Carroll	DA
1992	Matthew Chamberlain	DA
1992	Dale Corlett	DA
1992	Peter Daube	DA
1992	David Fane	DA, and BPA 2003
1992	Kirsty Hamilton	DA
1992	Lucy Schmidt	DA, and BPA 2006
1992	Johanna Smith	DA, and BPA 2003
1992	Leighton Young	DA
1993	Shane Bartle	DA
1993	Aimee Belton	DA
1993	Nicola Blackman	DTP
1993	Sarah Boddy	DA
1993	Bridget Brady	DA
1993	Paul Burns	DA
1993	Sean Coyle	DTP
1993	Hera Dunleavy	DA
1993	Elisabeth Easther	DA
1993	Simon Ferry	DA, and BPA 2003
1993	Rebecca Hobbs	DA
1993	Rachel House	DA
1983	Nicola Murphy	DA

1993	Kate Peters	DTP
1993	Lyndee-Jane Rutherford	DA, and BPA 2003
1993	Jeremy Scrivener	DA
1993	Antonio Te Maioha	DA, and BPA 2005
1993	Leanne Watkins	DA
1994	Iaheto Ah Hi	DA
1994	Stephen Butterworth	DA
1994	Vanessa Byrnes	DA
1994	Gregor Cameron	DA
1994	Suzie Everard	DA
1994	Nicola (Kawana) Flynn	DA
1994	Ali Harper	DA
1994	Anna McPhail	DA, and BPA 2002
1994	Craig Muller	DA
1994	Jacob Rajan	DA
1994	Tamati (Rice) Te Nohutu Patuwai	DA, and BPA 2005
1994	Kirk Torrance	DA, and BPA 2003
1994	Scott Wills	DA
1994	Eryn Wilson	DA
1994	Tandi Wright	DA
1995	Neill Bryce	DTP
1995	Glen Drake	DA
1995	Georgia Duder	DA
1995	Grace Hoet	DA, and BPA 2004
1995	Michael Leger	DTP
1995	Vela Manusaute	DA
1995	Fi McCormick	DTP
1995	Eliza Meldrum	DTP
1995	Malcolm Murray	DA
1995	Fiona Ofamo'oni	DA, and BPA 2004
1995	Karl Kite Rangi	DA
1995	Neill Rea	DA
1995	Nigel Scott	DTP
1995	Sally Stockwell	DA
1995	Jeff Szusterman	DA
1995	Gavin Todd	DA
1995	Claire Waldron	DA, and BPA 2004
1995	Gary Young	DA
1996	Cheryl Bartlett	DTP
1996	Adam Brookfield	DA
1996	Jo Bunce	DTP
1996	Janine Burchett	DA
1996	Joshua Carvell	DTP
1996	Nicole Cosgrove	DTP
1996	Richard Edge	DA
1996	Ben Farry	DA
1996	Jane Fullerton-Smith	DA
1996	Jane Gratkowski	DA
1996	Hone Katipa	DA
1996	Toby Leach	DA
1996	Scott Macky	DA
1996	Clea Matthews	DTP
1996	Paul McLaughlin	DA
1996	Steven Moore	DA
1996	Anne Nordhaus	DA
1996	Helen Pearse-Otene	DA
1996	Mark Sant	DA
1996	Greg Smale (Justin Gregory)	DTP and MTA
1996	Brett Tompkins	DTP
1996	Konstantina Tina) Tsinas	DA
1997	Kate Bartlett	DA
1997	Jane Chewings	DTP
1997	Lynette Crawford-Williams	DA
1997	Kate Louise Elliott	DA, and BPA 2006
1997	Ross Gibbs	DTP
1997	Luanne Gordon	DA
1997	Tanea Heke	DA
1997	Kelson Henderson	DA
1997	Waimihi Hotere	DA
1997	Juliette Howard	DTP, and Adv. DET 2000
1997	Genevieve McClean	DA
1997	Kirsten McIver	DA, and BPA 2009
1997	Rhys Morgan	DA
1997	Vanessa Rhodes	DA
1997	Kate Robertson	DTP
1997	Victor Rodger	DA
1997	Matthew Sunderland	DA
1997	Mitch Thomas	DA
1997	Misa Tupou	DA
1997	Heidi Simmonds	DTP, and Adv. DET 2000
1997	Kieth Walker	DTP

No Acting Graduates in 1998 as 3 year degree introduced in 1997

1998	Pornsupasri Berrigan	DTP and Adv. DET 2000
1998	Dion Boothby	DTP
1998	Rachel Butler	DTP
1998	Matthew D'Herville	DTP
1998	Stacey Merrifield	DTP and Adv. DET 2000
1998	Anneliese Mudge	DTP
1998	Tama Smith	DTP
1998	Janice van Rooyen	DTP

1999	Nyree Andrews	DTP
1999	Kylie Banks	DTP
1999	Nick Brown	BPA
1999	Nigel Collins	BPA
1999	Jane Donald	BPA
1999	Karl Drinkwater	BPA
1999	Peter Edge	DTP
1999	Bjorg Halldorsdottir	BPA
1999	Anna Hewlett	BPA
1999	Jason Hood	BPA
1999	Joshua Judkins	DTP
1999	Van Locker	DTP
1999	Cath McWhirter	BPA
1999	Emily Mowbray	BPA
1999	Kirstie O'Sullivan	BPA
1999	Tausili (Mose) Pushparaj	BPA
1999	Susannah Radford	BPA
1999	Gareth Reeves	BPA
1999	Richard Samuel	BPA
1999	Alice Tinning	DTP, and Adv. DET 2000
1999	Robert Tripe	BPA
1999	Matthew Wilson	BPA
2000	James Amos	BPA
2000	Sefton Bates	DTP
2000	Marlena Campbell	DTP, and Adv. DET 2002
2000	Glen Crighton	DTP
2000	Deana Elvins	BPA
2000	Kayte Ferguson	BPA
2000	Natalie Gyles	DTP
2000	Rosella Hart	BPA
2000	Natasha James	DTP
2000	Kenny King	BPA
2000	Jerome Leota	BPA
2000	Miranda Luxford	DTP
2000	Nikki MacDonnell	BPA
2000	Heather O'Carroll	BPA
2000	Anapela Polataivao	BPA
2000	Barbara (Carey) Power	BPA
2000	Olivia Robinson-Falconer	BPA
2000	Tipene Te Rore	DTP
2000	Hadley Thomson	DTP
2000	Simon Vincent	BPA
2001	Aaron Alexander	BPA
2001	Ben Barrington	BPA
2001	Fraser Brown	BPA
2001	Thomas Clarkson	DTP
2001	Fiona Collins	BPA
2001	Vicki Cooksley	DTP
2001	Nigel Edgecombe	Grad DTA
2001	Marc Edwards	DTP
2001	Matt Fraser	BPA
2001	Claire Gilligan	DTP
2001	Cohen Holloway	BPA
2001	Brian Hotter	BPA
2001	Lauren Jackson	BPA
2001	Maria (Poppy) James	BPA
2001	James Kearney	DTP
2001	Dena-Marie Kennedy	BPA
2001	Ian Leslie	DTP
2001	Kristan Mulcahy	DTP
2001	Ciara Mulholland	BPA
2001	Biddy O'Donnell	BPA
2001	Peter Rutherford	BPA
2001	Matthew Saville	BPA
2001	Callum Stembridge	BPA
2001	Jann Tarrant	DTP
2001	Jason Te Kare	BPA
2001	Julian Wilson	BPA
2002	Genevieve Bowers	BPA
2002	Melinda Brown	DTP
2002	Jacqueline Coats	MTA
2002	Emma Deakin	BPA
2002	Sarah Feely	DTP
2002	Ines Ferrer-Bergua	BPA
2002	Angela Green	BPA
2002	James Hadley	MTA
2002	Tamsin Lakeman	DTP
2002	Salesi Le'ota	BPA
2002	Danielle Mason	BPA
2002	Miriama McDowell	BPA
2002	Nathan Meister	BPA
2002	Rachel More	MTA
2002	Daniel Northcott	BPA
2002	Toby Papazoglou	DTP and MTA 2008
2002	Talya Pilcher	DTP
2002	Jarod Rawiri	BPA
2002	Mark Ruka	BPA
2002	Shannon Small	BPA
2002	Laura Staples	DTP
2002	James Sutherland	MTA
2002	Amy Tarleton	BPA
2002	Curtis Vowell	BPA
2002	Maia Whittet	DTP
2002	Lucy Wigmore	BPA
2002	Marie Williams	BPA
2002	Sonia Yee	BPA

2003	James Ashcroft	BPA
2003	Andrew Ausage	BPA
2003	Noa Campbell	BPA
2003	Nicola Colson	BPA
2003	Jean Copland	BPA
2003	Erina Daniels	BPA
2003	Nick Dunbar	BPA
2003	Jade Eriksen	MTA
2003	Timothy Foley	BPA
2003	Sonia Hardie	DTP
2003	Lynley Hill	DTP
2003	Jodie Hyland	BPA
2003	Brian King	Adv. DET, and BPD 2007
2003	Francis Kora	BPA
2003	Tahi Mapp-Borren	BPA
2003	Johnny Moffatt	BPA
2003	Matu Ngaropo	BPA
2003	Kerryn Palmer	MTA
2003	Rina Patel	BPA
2003	Rashmi Pilapitiya	BPA
2003	Geoff Pinfield	MTA
2003	Kristin Smith	MTA
2003	Louis Sutherland	BPA
2003	Alasdair Watson	DTP
2004	Jessie Alsop	BPA
2004	Amanda Baker	BPA
2004	Anna Brothers	BPA
2004	Jade Daniels	BPA
2004	Laurence Dean	DET
2004	Semu Filipo	BPA
2004	Shelley Irwin	DET, and BPM 2007
2004	Laughton Kora	BPA
2004	Ngahuia (Nga) Larsen	DET, and BPM 2006
2004	Abby Marment	BPA
2004	Madeline McNamara	MTA
2004	Leo Gene Peters	MTA
2004	Kate Prior	BPA
2004	Robert Ringiao-Lloyd	BPA
2004	Amelia (Sam) Selliman-Layne	BPA
2004	Vaughan Slinn	BPA
2004	Jessica Sutherland	MTA
2004	Gareth Tiopira-Waaka	BPA
2004	Te Kohe Tuhaka	BPA
2004	Claire Van Beek	BPA
2004	Katlyn (Tze Hung) Wong	BPA
2005	Veialu Aila-Unsworth	MTA
2005	Thomas Beauchamp	MTA
2005	Rowan Bettjeman	BPA
2005	Penni Bousfield	MTA
2005	Daniel (Dan) Caddy	BPA
2005	Aaron Cortesi	BPA
2005	Anna Drakeford	DET
2005	Ngapaki (Marama) Emery	BPA
2005	Rachel Forman	BPA
2005	Justin Gregory	MTA
2005	Natala Gwiazdzinski	DET
2005	Jarren Jackson	DET, and Adv. DET 2006
2005	Richard Knowles	BPA
2005	Julie Noever	MTA
2005	Tania Nolan	BPA
2005	Kylie O'Callaghan	BPA
2005	Beatrice Papazoglou	BPA
2005	Maaka Pohatu	BPA
2005	Thomas Press	DET
2005	Jessica Robinson	BPA
2005	Blair Ryan	DET
2005	Renee Sheridan	BPA
2005	Pedro Ramos Ilgenfritz da Silva	MTA
2005	Sara Standring	BPA
2005	Kate Tarrant	MTA
2005	Michael Whalley	BPA
2006	Francis Biggs	BPA
2006	Chantelle Brader	BPA
2006	Rebekah (Bekky) Campbell	DET, and DCC 2007
2006	Tina Cook	MTA
2006	Harriette Cowan	MTA
2006	Kerina Deas	MTA
2006	Laurel Devenie	BPA
2006	Paul Evans	BPM
2006	Katie Fletcher	DET
2006	Caroline (Boo) Frost	DET
2006	Charlotte Gordon	BPM
2006	Allan Henry	BPA
2006	Jodie Hillock	BPA
2006	L'Hibou Hornung	MTA
2006	Amanda Jelicich-Kane	BPD
2006	Miriama Ketu	BPA
2006	Brian King	BPD
2006	Matthew Kleinhans	BPD
2006	Ngahuia (Nga) Larsen	BPM
2006	James Conway Law	BPA
2006	Bradley McCormick	BPA
2006	Fraser McLeod	BPA
2006	Arthur Meek	BPA
2006	Laura Nicholls	BPD

Year	Name	Qualification
2006	Brittany (Bree) Peters	BPA
2006	Yvette Reid	BPA
2006	Sally Richards	MTA
2006	Emily Smith	DET, and Adv. DET 2007
2006	Sam Snedden	BPA
2006	Rachael Spitzer	BPD
2006	Amy-Louise Waller	BPA
2006	Willem Wassenaar	MTA
2006	Rebekah Whale	BPD
2006	Steven Whiting	MTA
2006	Brooke Williams	BPA
2006	Daniel Williams	BPD
2006	Gareth Williams	BPA
2006	Martyn Wood	BPA
2007	Antonia Bale	BPA
2007	Fiona Brown	DCC
2007	Rebekah Campbell	DCC
2007	Byron Coll	BPA
2007	Laurel Collins	MTA
2007	Helena Coulton	BPM
2007	Gemma Crouch-Gatehouse	DCC
2007	Brad Cunningham	DET
2007	Colleen Davis	BPA
2007	Natasha Falconer	BPA
2007	Hermione Flynn	BPD
2007	Meggan Frauenstein	BPD
2007	Sophie Hambleton	BPA
2007	Lisa Hawken	BPM
2007	Shelley Irwin	BPM
2007	Karl Jenkins	BPM
2007	Ahilan (Ahi) Karunaharan	BPA
2007	Natano Keni	BPA
2007	Caitlin Le Harivel	BPD
2007	Cameron Lithgow	DET
2007	Maria Rose MacDonald	BPA
2007	Andrew McKenzie	MTA
2007	Natalie Medlock	BPA
2007	Claire Middleton	BPD
2007	Helen Moate	DCC
2007	Daniel Musgrove	BPA
2007	Christopher O'Neill	BPD
2007	Megan Peacock	MTA
2007	Kyle Potter	BPM
2007	Ryan Richards	BPA
2007	Sophie Roberts	BPA
2007	Shaneel Sidal	BPA
2007	Bryony Skillington	BPA
2007	Lee Smith-Gibbons	BPA
2007	Sarita So	BPA
2007	Leanne Stevenson	BPD
2007	Anya Tate-Manning	BPA
2007	Alana Tisdall	BPM
2007	Asalemo Tofete	BPA
2007	Stephen Townshend	BPA
2007	Paul Tozer	DET
2007	Evania Vallyon	BPA
2007	Hollie Weir	BPA
2007	Matthew Whelan	BPA
2007	Robin Yee	BPD
2008	Sarah Allen	BPA
2008	Seamus Arnel	Adv. DET
2008	Yvonne Autridge	DCC
2008	Michael Blockley	DET
2008	Sam Bunkall	BPA
2008	Sarah Burrell	BPD
2008	Lucie Camp	BPM
2008	Danielle Casey	BPD
2008	Donna Chapman	MTA
2008	Dawn Cheong	BPA
2008	Kylie Clow	DCC
2008	Chelsie Preston Crayford	BPA
2008	John Coddington	BPD
2008	Julia Croft	BPA
2008	Marina Davis	BPD
2008	Adam Donald	MTA
2008	Melanie Firbank	BPA
2008	Chloe Forbes	BPM
2008	Barnaby Frederic	BPA
2008	Hannah Goldblatt	DCC
2008	Esher-Rose Green	BPA
2008	Paul Harrop	BPA
2008	Tansy Hayden	BPA
2008	Sera Henare	BPA
2008	Gina Hitchcock	BPD
2008	Rosie Horsley	DCC
2008	Yu-San Kang	BPD
2008	James Kupa	BPA
2008	Nathan McEndry	BPM
2008	Pat McIntosh	BPM
2008	Samantha Mott	DET
2008	Kristyl Neho	BPA
2008	Tureiti Nelson	BPD
2008	Toby Papazoglou	MTA
2008	Kirsty Peters	BPA
2008	Sarah Prestidge	DET
2008	Asher Smith	BPA
2008	Ruth Swift	DCC

2008	Hazelle Tailby	DCC
2008	Adam Tatana	BPA
2008	Chris Ulutupu	BPD
2008	Maria Walker	BPA
2008	Hadleigh Walker	BPA
2008	James Winter	BPA
2009	Rachel Baker	Adv. DET
2009	Jane Boocock	DCC
2009	Elizabeth Boyle	DCC
2009	Veronica Brady	BPA
2009	Lindsay Broomfield	DCC
2009	Timothy Carlsen	BPA
2009	Liz Carpenter	BPD
2009	Kylie Clow	Adv. DET
2009	Rennee Dennison	BPD
2009	William Donaldson	Grad. DTA
2009	Jamie Dorner	MTA
2009	Emma Draper	BPA
2009	Martine Gray	BPA
2009	Ian Hammond	BPD
2009	Stuart Handloff	MTA
2009	Juanita Hepi	BPA
2009	Romy Hooper	BPA
2009	Ashleigh Kane	BPD
2009	Rose Kirkup	BPD
2009	Guy Langford	BPA
2009	Richard Larsen	BPD
2009	Sophie Lindsay	BPA
2009	Tara Low	DCC
2009	Austin Mather	DET
2009	Katherine McGill	BPA
2009	Shadon Meredith	BPA
2009	Suli Moa	BPA
2009	Rose Morrison	BPD
2009	Theo Nettleton	DET
2009	Kelly Nicholl	DCC
2009	Mike Norman	BPM
2009	Emma Ransley	BPD
2009	Amelia Read	BPA
2009	Helle Rosenberg	DCC
2009	Jessica Sanderson	BPD
2009	Emmett Skilton	BPA
2009	Jessica Grace Smith	BPA
2009	Kay Smith	BPA
2009	Manda Smith	BPM
2009	Ruth Swift	Adv. DET
2009	Katherine Thomas	MTA
2009	Eliza Thompson-Munn	DCC
2009	Ellis Thorpe	BPM
2009	Adam Walker	BPM
2009	Ellen Walsh	BPM
2009	Aiden Weekes (Dan Hannah)	BPA
2009	Matariki Whatarau	BPA
2009	Aroha White	BPA
2009	Cian White	BPA

Appendix Two

Select Productions

Major Toi Whakaari Productions 1970–2009

Abbreviations:

Dir	Director/s
Facil	Facilitator/s

1970

Suddenly Last Summer	Tennessee Williams	Dir: Anne Flannery
Lunch Hour	John Mortimer	Dir: Nola Millar
Happy Haven	John Arden	Dir: Nola Millar

1971

Effort at Speech Between Six People	Improvisation	Dir: Grant Tilly
Lines from Mother Courage	Bertolt Brecht	Dir: Anne Flannery
That Total Pink Look Suits You, Sir.	mime	Dir: Jacqueline Burt
Underground Lovers	Jean Tardieu	Dir: Nola Millar

1972

An Exploration in Sound	devised	Dir: Caroline Ormond
Actors in Search of a Character; based on Who's Afraid of Virginia Woolf	Edward Albee	Dir: Anne Flannery
The Nonentity	mime	Dir: Jacqueline Burt
Lysistrata	Aristophanes	Dir: Anne Flannery
The Madwoman of Chaillot	Jean Giraudoux	Dir: Nola Millar
The Seven Faces of Cressida	Shakespeare	Dir: Nola Millar

1973

Why Can't Everyone Else Be More like Us?	work in movement and sound	Dir: Jacqueline Burt
On the Eighth Day	body and voice work	Dir: Caroline Ormond
Scenes from Blood Wedding	Garcia Lorca	Dir: Nola Millar

1974

Trevor	John Bowen	Dir: Jan Prettejohns
Comings & Goings	improvised	Dir: Grant Tilly
View from the bridge	Arthur Miller	Dir: Anne Flannery
Playing Favourites	compilation	Dir: George Webby

1975

Futz	Rochelle Owens	Dir: Jan Prettejohns
The Way of the World	William Congreve	Dir: Elric Hooper
Superdoops on the Loose	devised	
Spin Off	devised/compilation	
Orison	Fernando Arrabal	Dir: David Smiles
The Problem	A.R. Gurney	Dir: David Smiles
Scenes from Shakespeare	compilation	
An Evening of Tennessee Williams.	compilation	Dir: George Webby, Anne Flannery, Jan Prettejohns

1976

The Birthday Party	Harold Pinter	Dir: George Webby
The Mother	Bertolt Brecht	Dir: George Webby
Twelfth Night	Shakespeare	Dir: Anne Flannery

1977

Under Milkwood	Dylan Thomas	Dir: George Webby
Merely Players	compilation	Dir: Jane Waddell Grant Tilly, Debbie Hunt
The Cherry Orchard	Chekhov	Dir: Sabin Epstein

1978

Standard Safety	Julie Bovasso	Dir: George Webby
After the Rain	John Bowen	Dir: Meriol Buchanan
Lord Byron's Love Letter	Tennessee Williams	Dir: Meriol Buchanan
Harlequinade	Terence Rattigan	Dir: Grant Tilly
The Shadow Box	Michael Cristofer	Dir: George Webby

1979

What if you died tomorrow?	David Williamson	Dir: George Webby
The Borage Pigeon Affair	James Saunders	Dir: Simon Phillips
A Family & a Fortune	Ivy Compton-Burnett Adapted, Julian Mitchell	Dir: George Webby

1980

The Maids	Jean Genet	Dir: Simon Phillips
Living Quarters	Brian Friel	Dir: George Webby
Barbarians	Barrie Keefe	Dir: Simon Phillips
The Kid	Robert Coover	Dir: Grant Tilly
Women Beware Women	Thomas Middleton	Dir: Simon Phillips

1981

Return of the International Troubadours	devised, compilation	Facil: Aileen Davidson
Fanshen	David Hare	Dir: George Webby
Don Juan Comes back From the War	Odon von Horvath translated by Christopher Hampton	Dir: Rhys McConnochie
Henry V	Shakespeare Adapted by George Webby	Dir: George Webby

1982

Today's Bay	Craig Thaine	Dir: Derek Nicholson
Lavender Blue	John MacKendrick	Dir: George Webby
The Twelfth Man	Jeffrey Thomas	Dir: George Webby

1983

Marat/Sade	Peter Weiss	Dir: Simon Phillips
The Rimers of Eldrich	Lanford Wilson	Dir: Grant Tilly
Lunch-time Concerts	Student led	
Quartermain's Terms	Simon Gray	Dir: George Webby

1984

Look at Me, Look at You	compilation	
The Skin of our Teeth	Thornton Wilder	Dir: Stuart Devinie
Taking Our Time	Red Ladder Th. Co.	Dir: Phillip Mann
Lunch-time Concerts	Student led	
The Workroom	Jean Claude Grumberg	Dir: George Webby

1985

World Service	Roy Ward	Roy Ward
The Seagull	Anton Chekhov	Dir: George Webby
The Water Engine	David Mamet	Dir: Grant Tilly
Lunch-time Concerts	Student led	
The Sea	Edward Bond	Dir: George Webby

1986

The Homecoming	Harold Pinter	Dir: Susan Wilson
Oh What a Lovely War	Theatre Workshop	Dir: Richard Campion
Welcome Home	Tony Marchant	Dir: George Webby
Lunch-time Concerts	Student led	
Salt & Honey	Greek poetry & texts	Dir: Louise Tourelle, Annabel Newman,

1987

Philistines	Maxim Gorky	Dir: Jane Waddell
Stags & Hens	Willy Russell	Dir: Colin McColl
Lunch-time Concerts	Student led	
A Midsummer Night's dream	Shakespeare	Dir: George Webby
Your Attention Please	Karl Buckley	Dir: Simon Bennett

1988

Sonnets	Shakespeare	Dir: Jane Waddell
Tartuffe	Moliere	Dir: Jane Waddell, Sylvia Rands
The Fortunes of Punch	Lunch-time Concerts	Student led
The Three Sisters	Anton Chekhov	Dir: John Anderson

1989

Ten Stories High	improv. based	Dir: Stuart Devenie
Reflections	devised monologues	Facil: Andrew Noble
Falstaff	Shakespeare/ Vaughan Williams	Dir: Andrew Noble
Pantalone Moves House	improvised comedy	Dir: Ralph Johnson
Happy End	Bertolt Brecht/Kurt Weill	Dir: Colin McColl
The Cherry Orchard	Anton Chekhov	Dir: Lisa Warrington

1990

Roomers	devised work	Dir: Murray Lynch
The Beaux' Stratagem	George Farquar	Dir: Rhys McConnochie
Blood Wedding	Garcia Lorca	Dir: James Beaumont
Reflections	Devised Monologues	Facil: Sunny Amey, Jane Waddell

1991

What's Bred in the Bone	Improvised Performance	Dir: Annie Ruth
Reflections	Devised Monologues	Facil: Robin Payne, Annie Ruth, Jane Waddell
Sonnets & All that Jazz	Shakespeare	Dir: Jane Waddell, Robin Payne
Mad Forest	Caryl Churchill	Dir: Robin Payne
Who Killed Richard Cory	A R Gurney	Dir: George Webby
A Long Walk off a Tall Rock	Stuart Hoar	Dir: Michael Hurst

1992

Separate Tables	Terence Rattigan	Dir: James Beaumont
The Body	Nick Darke	Dir: Murray Lynch
Reflections	Devised Monologues	Facil: Anna Marbrook, Christian Penny
The Two Gentlemen of Verona	Shakespeare	Dir: Colin McColl
Swords, Songs & Sonnets	Shakespeare compilation	Robin Payne, Annie Ruth

1993

Acting naturally	Turn of the century naturalism (Extracts)	Dir: Stuart Devine

Romeo & Juliet	Shakespeare	Dir: Christian Penny
Reflections	Devised Monologues	Facil: Annie Ruth
Summer of the Aliens	Louis Nowra	Dir: Susan Wilson
Words of Love	Fiona Samuel	Dir: Murray Lynch
Tungoungou/Metamorphoses	Vincent O'Sullivan, Apirana Taylor, Virgil	Dir: Bert van Dijk
Accidental Death of an Anarchist	Dario Fo	Dir: Murray Lynch
House of Bernardo Alba	Garcia Lorca	Dir: Colin McColl

1994

Shakespeare to Go	Shakespeare compilation	Dir: Robin Payne, KC Kelly, Annie Ruth, Murray Lynch
Reflections	Devised Monologues	Facil: KC Kelly
Born in the RSA	Barney Simon & Co.	Dir: Murray Lynch
The Island	Athol Fugard	Dir: Robin Payne
Statements After An Arrest	Athol Fugard	Dir: Annie Ruth
Just Like Home	Pieter-Dirk Uys	Dir: Whetu Fala
The Caucasian Chalk Circle	Bertolt Brecht	Dir: Murray Lynch
The Rover	Aphra Benn	Dir: Roger Hodgman

1995

Blarney Bullets & Blessings	Irish Plays – extracts	Dir: Annie Ruth, Hone Kouka, Jonathon Hendry
Out of Space	5 devised plays	Facil: Bert van Dijk
A View from the Bridge	Arthur Miller	Dir: KC Kelly
All My Sons	Arthur Miller	Dir: M. Johnson- Chase
Spring Awakening	Frank Wedekind	Dir: David Latham
A Midsummer Night's Dream	Shakespeare	Dir: Murray Lynch

1996

The Wild Man	Bert van Dijk & co	Dir: Bert van Dijk
Siren	David Williamson	Dir: KC Kelly
Lanarch Castle of Lies	Michelanne Forster	Dir: Stephen Bain
Mixed Lollies	5 devised works	Facil: Gary Henderson
Human Cannon	Edward Bond	Dir: Annie Ruth
Pentecost	David Edgar	Dir: Robin Payne

1997

Mind Your Manners	Comedy of Manners Compilation	Dir: Raymond Boyce,Bill Guest, Jane Waddell, Murray Lynch, Roy Ward
McCahon by Numbers	Devised work inspired by McCahon paintings	Facil. KC Kelly
Ornithes: Nga Manu: The Birds	Aristophanes	Dir: Robin Payne, Rangimoana Taylor, Tolis Papazoglou
Passion Plus Treachery, Minus Doublet & Hose	Shakespeare Compilation	Dir: Murray Lynch, Annie Ruth, Vanessa Byrnes, Cameron Rhodes, KC Kelly
Insurrection: Holding History	Robert O'Hara	Dir: Timothy Douglas
Vinegar Tom	Caryl Churchill	Dir: Murray Lynch

1998

The Crucible	Arthur Miller	Dir: Christian Penny
Between a Rock & A Hard Place	Transatlantic Contemporary texts	Dir: Murray Lynch, Annie Ruth, Vanessa Byrnes, Simone Lourie, Miranda Harcourt, Bill Guest.
The Threepenny Opera	Bertolt Brecht/Weill	Dir: Murray Lynch
Under Southern Skies	Contemporary NZ Women writers	Dir: Murray Lynch, Cameron Rhodes, Annie Ruth, Simone Lourie, Rangimoana Taylor, Vanessa Byrnes

1999

Translations	Brian Friel	Dir: KC Kelly
Bondagers	Sue Glover	Dir: Vanessa Byrnes
The Love of the Nightingale	Timberlake Wertenbaker	Dir: Annie Ruth
NZ Monologues	Devised	Facil. Tom McCrory
The Tempest	Shakespeare	Dir: Murray Lynch
Social Disorder	Scenes compilation	Dir: Bill Guest, Jonathon Hendry, Rawiri Paratene, Vanessa Byrnes.
The Three Sisters	Anton Chekhov	Dir: Timothy Douglas

3rd year co-operatives

Laughing Wild	Christopher Durang	Dir: Jonathan Hendry
Burn This	Lanford Wilson	Dir: Murray Lynch
Elvis was a Coconut	Devised work	Dir: Damon Andrews
Cowboy Mouth	Sam Shepard	Dir: Cameron Delaney
The Swan	Elizabeth Egloff	Dir: Tony McCaffrey

2000

Whatu/Weave	Celtic/Maori devised work	Dir: Tom McCrory
The Mysteries	Wakefield & Chester Mystery Cycles	Dir: Annie Ruth, Bill Guest Vanessa Byrnes & Larry Rew
Ophelia Thinks Harder	Jean Betts	Dir: Annie Ruth
Lovelock's Dream Run	David Geary	Dir: Murray Lynch
Go Solo & Gone Solo	devised monologues	Facil. Jude Gibson
The Bare Essentials	turn of century Naturalism compilation	Dir: KC Kelly, Rawiri Paratene, Simone Lourie, Jude Gibson
Into the Woods	Stephen Sondheim	Dir: Miranda Harcourt
Mr Whatnot	Alan Ayckbourne	Dir: Bill Guest

3rd year co-operatives

A Space Without Boundaries	devised work	Dir: Nina Nawalowalo
Faultline	devised work	Dir: Tom McCrory
Sweet Phoebe	Michael Gow	Dir: Robin Payne

2001

Who Needs a Vespa	Devised work based on the films of Fellini	Dir: Jude Gibson
Southern Lights	NZ South Island texts (selection)	Dir: Miranda Harcourt Annie Ruth, Tom McCrory Simone Lourie, Karl Kite- Rangi

Transitions

Orpheus Descending	Tennessee Williams	Dir: Miranda Harcourt
Go Solo	devised monologues	Facil. Jude Gibson
The Cook, the Thief, his Wife & her Lover	Peter Greenaway	Dir: Jude Gibson

3rd year co-operatives

I am Me	devised work	Dir: Vendula Prager
East	Steven Berkoff	Dir: Ralph McAllister
Cooking with Elvis	Lee Hall	Dir: Vanessa Byrnes

2002

Hollywood Combo	Bill Guest	Dir: Bill Guest
Mother Courage	Bertolt Brecht	Dir: Miranda Harcourt
Same Wind, Different Times.	devised works based on NZ short story writers	Dir: Miranda Harcourt, Annie Ruth, Stephen Bain Nina Nawalowalo
Go Solo	devised monologues	Facil. Vanessa Byrnes, Perry Piercy, KC Kelly
The Rover	Aphra Benn	Dir: James Beaumont

3rd year co-operatives

Spinning Tale	devised work	Dir: Bert van Dijk
The Prophet	Hone Kouka	Dir: Hone Kouka & Kirk Torrence
Road	Jim Cartwright	Dir: Larry Rew

MTA graduation productions

Women Beware Women	Howard Barker & Middleton	Dir: James Hadley
Speed the Plough	David Mamet	Dir: Rachel More
A Despoiled Shore	devised by director	Dir: Jacqueline Coats
DSCH: The Conscience of Music	James Sutherland	Dir: James Sutherland

2003

Memories for Tomorrow	devised with NZ School of Dance	Dir: Miranda Harcourt, Wendy Wallace
The Gentleman from Olmedo	Lope de Vega	Dir: Tom McCrory
Book of Hours	Langford Wilson	Dir: KC Kelly
Troilus & Cressida	Shakespeare	Dir: Annie Ruth, Rangimoana Taylor
Solos	devised	Fasc: Mirada Harcourt, Jude Gibson

3rd year co-operatives

Desdemona		Dir: Rachel More, Jacqui Coates
Quills	Philip Kaufman	Dir: Karen Lamb
Wholly Grain	devised	Dir: Vanessa Byrnes

MTA major productions

The Maids	Jean Genet	Dir: Jade Erikson
The Three Birds	Joanna Laurens	Dir: Geoff Pinfield
The Real Inspector Hound	Tom Stoppard	Dir: KJ Smith
When Sun & Moon Collide	Briar Grace-Smith	Dir: Kerryn Palmer
Black Square	devised installation	Dir: Justin Gregory

2004

Dead Friend	devised work	Dir: Andrew Foster
Great Expectations	Simon Phillips	Dir: Miranda Harcourt & Tom McCrory
Pericles	Shakespeare	Dir: Peter Hambleton
Solos	devised	Fasc: Jude Gibson
Penumbra	David Geary & company devised work	Dir: Christian Penny Des: Penny Fitt

3rd year co-operatives

Couch	Taylor	Dir: Sue Ott Rowlands

MTA major productions

Blue Kettle	Caryl Churchill	Dir: Madeline McNamara
One Flesh	Fiona Samuel	Dir: Kate Tarrant
Shifting	devised	Dir: Leo Gene Peters
One Youth's Tragedy	Larry Thompson	Dir: Jessica Sutherland

2005

Pegasus Moon	Devised with NZ School of Dance	Dir: Jude Gibson, Tom McCrory, Wendy Wallace Paula Steeds-Huston
Battles of the Heart	Devised	Dir: Aileen O'Sullivan
The Seagull	Anton Chekhov	Dir: Miranda Harcourt
Small Lives, Big Dreams	Anne Bogart & SITI Co.	Dir: Annie Ruth
Solos	devised	Fasc: Jude Gibson
Jack Manning Trilogy	David Williamson	KC Kelly

MTA major productions

The Play About the Baby	Edward Albee	Dir: Penni Bousfield
Attempts on her life	Martin Crimp	Dir: Steven Whiting
Endgame	Samuel Beckett	Dir: L'Hibou Hornung
Girls, suitcases, highways & wide open spaces	devised	Dir: Julie Noever
The Spot	devised clown	Dir: Pedro Ilgenfritz
Plunge	Devised/dance/arial/circus	Dir: Thomas Beauchamp
Nga Pou Wahine	Briar Grace-Smith	Dir: Tina Cook
Blue Willow	devised film	Dir: Veialu Aila-Unsworth

2006

Chance	devised	Fasc: Tom McCrory, Annie Ruth & Penny Fitt
Myth Propaganda and Disaster	Stephen Sewell	Dir: Vanessa Byrnes
The Laramie Project	Moises Kaufman	Dir: Miranda Harcourt
Henry VI, Parts 1,2 & 3	Shakespeare	Dir: David O'Donnell
Solos	devised	Fasc: Christian Penny & Jade Erikson
Peer Gynt	Henrik Ibsen	Dir: John Bolton

MTA major productions

The Glass Menagerie	Tennessee Williams	Dir: Willem Wassenaar

You Want Me To Do What.	devised cabaret	Dir Kerina Deas
The Lead Wait	Jo Randerson	Dir: Hariette Cowan
Top Girls	Caryl Churchill	Dir: Megan Peacock
Brimstone & Treacle	Dennis Potter	Dir: Sally Richards
Squatter	Stuart Hoar	Dir: Andrew McKenzie

2007

White Lie	dance devised	Dir, Chorographer: Megan Adams
A History of the American Film	Christopher Durang	Dir: Jeff Szusterman
Betty's Summer vacation	Christopher Durang	Dir: Annie Ruth
Solos	devised	Fasc: Jade Erikson
Twelfth Night	Shakespeare	Dir: Vanessa Byrnes
Arcadia	Tom Stoppard	Dir: Tim Spite

G2 (Alternative grad. prod)

Angels in America	Tony Kushner	Dir: Willem Wassenaar

MTA major productions

Stones in His Pocket	Marie Jones	Dir: Toby Papazoglou
Finders Keepers	documentary film	Dir: Laurel Collins

2008

Pakiwaitara	devised	Dir: Jade Erikson & Teina Moetara
Party Time	Harold Pinter	Dir: Bill Guest
Far Away	Caryl Churchill	Dir: Rachel More
Chair	Edward Bond	Dir: Christian Penny
Mountain Language	Harold Pinter	Dir: David Neville
Macbeth	Shakespeare	Dir: Jonathon Hendry
The Tempest	Shakespeare	Dir: John Bolton
Go Solo	devised	Fasc: Jade Erikson, Annie Ruth & Sophie Roberts
Toi Cabaret	Cole Porter & Gershwin	Dir: Lyndee-Jane Rutherford
Unity	Kevin Kerr	Dir: Conrad Newport

G2 (alternative grad. prods

Blasted	Sarah Kane	Dir: Kat Thomas
Pillowman	Martin McDonagh	Dir: Stuart Handloff
AoTERRORoa	Jo Randerson & Co. devised	Dir: Geoff Pinfield

MTA major productions

Vita & Virginia	Eileen Atkins	Dir: Donna Chapman
The Illusionist	Tony Kushner	Dir: Adam Donald
Appetite	devised film	Dir: Alyx Duncan

2009

Her Naked Skin	Rebecca Lenkiewicz	Dir: Annie Ruth
Manawa Pou	devised site specific work	Fasc: Teina Moetara & Heather Timms
Go Solo	devised	Fasc: Sophie Roberts
A Midsummer Night's Dream	Shakespeare	Dir: Josette Bushell-Mingo
The Caucasian Chalk Circle	Bertolt Brecht	Dir: Christian penny

MTA major productions

The Land of Nonsense	Jaime Dormer	Dir: Jaime Dormer
Bedlam		Dir: Robin Kerr
Interface	devised work	Dir: Chad Hansing
Mates and Lovers	Ronald Nelson based on Mates and Lovers by Chris Brickwell	Dir: Ronald Nelson

Notes

Prologue

1 George Webby, *Just Who Does He Think He Is? A Theatrical Life*, Steele Roberts, Wellington, 2006, p. 283.

Chapter One

1 E. Martin Browne, 'Antipodean Adventure', *Drama*, September 1951.
2 *Ibid.*
3 *Ibid.*
4 *Ibid.*
5 Edith Campion (née Hannah) inherited a considerable fortune from her grandfather, Robert Hannah, who founded the Hannah shoe empire in Wellington and, by the 1940s, had around forty-two retail outlets in New Zealand. In the 1960s the Hannah Playhouse was named in honour of the family whose shoe-shop fortunes made it possible.
6 Nola Millar, 'A Future for the Players', *Landfall*, vol. 14, no. 4, December 1960.
7 Nola Millar, Review of *A Survey of the Arts in New Zealand* by E. C. Simpson, *Landfall*, vol. 15, no. 3, 1961.
8 Old Tote Theatre Company became an independent organisation in 1968 and the resident theatre company at the new Sydney Opera House from 1973–78. The Tote was the precursor to the Sydney Theatre Company that was established in 1989.
9 'Drama and the Ballet', *New Zealand Official Yearbook 1964*, 69th Issue, Department of Statistics, Wellington, 1964.
10 Elric Hooper, 'Making Our Own Mistakes', *Landfall*, vol. 116, December 1975.
11 Don Farr, 'Drama and the Universities', *New Zealand Stage*, vol. 1, no. 1, February 1967.
12 John Kim and Jonathon Hardy, 'Kim and Hardy on Theatre – Part II', *New Zealand Stage*, vol. 1, no. 2, March 1967.
13 Bill Sheat interviewed by Bill Guest, February 2010.
14 Letter from Bill Sheat, chair, QEII Arts Council, to Basil Potter, Wellington Polytechnic, 28 April 1969.
15 B. Mason and J. Pocock, Letter Six, Chapter VI, *Theatre in Danger: A Correspondence between Bruce Mason and John Pocock*, Pauls Book Arcade, Hamilton, 1957.

Chapter Two

1 Sarah Gaitanos, *Nola Millar: A Theatrical Life*, Victoria University Press, Wellington, 2006, p. 12.
2 J. M. Mason and M. J. Staffan, *Unity Theatre Presents*, Unity Theatre (Inc.), Wellington, February 1966.
3 Letter from Shirley Maddock Easther to Ruth Graham, September 1989.
4 Nola Millar, 'Plays by New Zealand Writers', *New Zealand Drama*, September 1951.
5 Nola Millar, *New Zealand Listener*, 22 May 1959.
6 John Callen, recollections of his association with Nola Millar and as a part-time tutor at the New Zealand Drama School from 1996. John Callen went on to become an award-winning actor and director for theatre, radio and television, including many years with South Pacific Pictures directing *Shortland Street*. He also directed numerous fast-turnaround TV projects with acting students at both the school and at Avalon Studios.
7 Grant Tilly interviewed by Bill Guest, November 2009.
8 Letters from Nola Millar to Margaret Turnbull, reporting on her travel to the UK from May to July 1967.

9 Letters from Nola Millar to Margaret Turnbull, reporting on her travel to the UK from May to July 1967.
10 *Ibid.*
11 *Ibid.*
12 Nola Millar, Report to the QEII Arts Council on her Overseas Travel, May–September 1967, MS-paper 1563-08, Alexander Turnbull Library.
13 *Ibid.*
14 *Ibid.*
15 Nola Millar, public lecture, MS-paper 1563-08, Alexander Turnbull Library.

Chapter Three

1 Darien Takle, 'History Theatre Project – 127 Cuba Street', thesis for Toi Whakaari Bachelor of Performing Arts (Acting), 2005, Nola Millar Library.
2 Jennifer Ludlum interviewed by Bill Guest, September 2009.
3 *Ibid.*
4 Bill Sheat, chair, QEII Arts Council, Drama Panel, address, February 1970.
5 Letter from Nola Millar to David Peters, director, QEII Arts Council, February 1970.
6 Letter from Grant Tilly to Darien Takle, August 2005.
7 Grant Tilly interviewed by Bill Guest, November 2009.
8 Unattributed press clipping, 'Acting Bursars Study TV Methods', 1970.
9 Bevan Wilson interviewed by Darien Takle, 'History Theatre Project'.
10 Bill Sheat interviewed by Bill Guest, February 2010.
11 Nola Millar, report on the first term of the 'New Theatre – Arts Council Training School', to David Peters, director of the QEII Arts Council, April 1970, Archives NZ.
12 *Ibid.*
13 Graduates interviewed by Darien Takle, 'History Theatre Project'.
14 *Ibid.*
15 *Ibid.*
16 *Ibid.*
17 Jennifer Ludlum interviewed by Bill Guest, September 2009.
18 Report of the QEII Arts Council of New Zealand for the year ended 31 March 1971.
19 Letter from Nola Millar to David Peters, 4 February 1971, AANV 972 9/3/3, Archives New Zealand.
20 Darien Takle returned to Elam in 1972 to complete her fine arts degree and join the Living Theatre Troupe in Auckland, followed by three years with Mercury Theatre and then Theatre Corporate. She later worked in England, touring with *Godspell*, and also at the Haymarket Theatre Company in Leicester, before forming the Centre Theatre Company in London. She returned to New Zealand, working for a while in TV, film and theatre ('lots of musicals') before moving to Australia to play the lead in the TV drama series *Possession*, and a year in Melbourne performing in *Les Misèrables*. She returned again to New Zealand, in the early 1990s, to continue her work in theatre, film and TV, and to teach singing and acting. Darien is also (famously) known for the role she played for seven years in the TV series, *Xena*, as Xena's mother.
21 Letter from Michael Nicolaidi to Nola Millar, 9 December 1971.
22 Rawiri Paratene interviewed by Sarah Gaitanos, September 1995, Toi Whakaari New Zealand Drama School, Oral History Project (OHP).
23 *Ibid.*
24 *Ibid.*
25 Annie Ruth interviewed by Bill Guest, January 2009.
26 Rawiri Paratene interviewed by Sarah Gaitanos, September 1995, OHP.
27 Annie Ruth interviewed by Bill Guest, April 2010.
28 Annie Ruth interviewed by Bill Guest, January 2009.
29 Rawiri Paratene interviewed by Sarah Gaitanos, September 1995, OHP.
30 Annie Ruth interviewed by Bill Guest, January 2009.
31 Article 6, *Mai Review*, 2008.
32 Parliamentary Petition 1972/42, ABEX, W3706, p.3, box 72, session 3, Petition of H Jackson, NA Wellington, p. 3.
33 Rawiri Paratene interviewed by Sarah Gaitanos, September 1995, OHP.
34 Annie Ruth interviewed by Bill Guest, January 2009.
35 Elric Hooper, 'Making Our Own Mistakes', *Landfall*, vol. 116, December 1975.

Chapter Four

1 Letter from Nola Millar to Mike Nicolaidi, March 1973, Archives New Zealand.
2 Sunny Amey, Meriol Buchanan, David Carnegie, Raymond Hawthorne, Johnny Johnston, Tony Richardson, David Smiles and Mervyn Thompson.
3 Memo from W. B. Sutch, chair, to M. T. Nicolaidi, director, QEII Arts Council, 12 June 1973, Archives New Zealand.
4 The summary and quotations that follow all relate to George Webby, *Report to the QEII Arts Council on Observations Concerning Professional Drama Training in Australia*, 4 June 1973, Archives New Zealand.
5 At that time, NIDA's recurrent expenditure was in excess of $400,000, not including accommodation, plant, library and other facilities provided by the University of New South Wales. Of this amount, approximately half went on wages and salaries.
6 The following account of the 'Wellington meeting' is taken from the minutes of the meeting, 26 June 1973, Archives New Zealand.
7 Letter from W. B. Sutch, chair, QEII Arts Council to Rt. Hon. N. E. Kirk, Prime Minister, 25 July 1973, Archives New Zealand.
8 *Ibid.*
9 'Memo: Rationale for Transferring the Drama School to Auckland', from M. T. Nicolaidi, director, to W. B. Sutch, chair, QEII Arts Council, 10 August 1973, Archives New Zealand.
10 *Ibid.*
11 Letter from the Auckland Theatre Trust [unsigned] to W. B. Sutch, chair, QEII Arts Council, 23 August 1973, Archives New Zealand.
12 Bill Sheat interviewed by Bill Guest, February 2010.
13 'Memo: Rationale for Transferring the Drama School to Auckland'.
14 'An Interim Proposal to Site the [Drama] School at the Wellington Polytechnic', QEII Arts Council, 20 September 1973, Archives New Zealand.
15 Sarah Gaitanos, *Nola Millar: A Theatrical Life*, p. 326.
16 David Tinkham, 'Nola Millar 1913–1974', *ACT*, Issue 24, 1974.
17 Grant Tilly interviewed by Bill Guest, November 2009.
18 Letter from Grant Tilly to Darien Takle, August 2005.
19 Jack Shallcrass interviewed by Rona Bailey and Ruth Graham, September 1991, Nola Millar Archive, New Zealand Drama School.

Chapter Five

1 Robin Payne interviewed by Bill Guest, December 2008.
2 George Webby, *Just Who Does He Think He Is?*, p. 216.
3 Letter to new students (1974 intake) from George Webby, undated but probably late 1973.
4 Cathy Wylie, 'What Are They Teaching Them?', *ACT*, vol. 25, December 1974.
5 George Webby interviewed by Bill Guest, March 2009.
6 George Webby, *Just Who Does He Think He Is?*, p. 214.
7 Jane Waddell interviewed by Sarah Gaitanos, 7 February 1996, OHP.
8 Frances Edmond, recollections of her time at the New Zealand Drama School, 1974–75.
9 Rangimoana Taylor interviewed by Hilary Halba, 'Let Me Feel the Magic', in Marc Maufort and David O'Donnell (eds), *Performing Aotearoa: New Zealand Theatre and Drama in an Age of Transition*, Peter Lang, Brussels, 2007.
10 Jane Waddell interviewed by Sarah Gaitanos, 7 February 1996, OHP.
11 Frances Edmond, recollections.
12 Jane Waddell interviewed by Sarah Gaitanos, 7 February 1996, OHP.
13 Frances Edmond, recollections.
14 Jane Waddell interviewed by Bill Guest, 14 December 2009.
15 Erica Stephenson interviewed by Bill Guest, January 2009.
16 George Webby interviewed by Mike Nicolaidi, 'Outward Bound Actors', *Sunday Herald*, 19 October 1974.
17 George Webby, *Just Who Does He Think He Is?*, p. 288.
18 Jan Prettejohns, recollections of her time at the New Zealand Drama School, 1974–75.
19 *Ibid.*
20 *Ibid.*
21 *Ibid.*

22 Letter from George Webby to the QEII Arts Council, undated.
23 *Ibid.*
24 Letter from QEII Arts Council to George Webby, 4 October 1974.
25 George Webby interviewed by Sarah Gaitanos, August 1995, OHP.
26 'There's More Than Just Comings and Goings', *Evening Post*, 23 November 1974.
27 Cathy Wylie, 'What Are They Teaching Them?'.

Chapter Six

1 George Webby, *Just Who Does He Think He Is?*, p. 221.
2 Letter from Mervyn Thompson to George Webby, 1975 (undated).
3 Letter from George Webby to M. Rickard, director, QEII Arts Council, 24 April 1975, Archives New Zealand.
4 Letter from M. A. Rickard, director, QEII Arts Council, to George Webby, 1976.
5 Letter from M. A. Rickard, director, QEII Arts Council, to Professor John Roberts, 28 July 1975, Archives New Zealand.
6 Minutes of the Board of Studies, 6 December 1976.
7 Extract from a Roberts Report text, dated September but no year (c. 1991 or 1992), National Library of New Zealand.
8 Minutes of the New Zealand Drama School Board of Studies, 6 December 1976.
9 Charles Hambling, recollections of his time at New Zealand Drama School, 1974–75.
10 Bruce Mason, 'With Fan Spread and Money Well Spent', *Dominion*, 25 August 1975.
11 Letter from Hamish Keith, chair, Arts Council, to George Webby, 9 July 1975.
12 Jane Waddell, recollections of her time at New Zealand Drama School, 1974–75.
13 Charles Hambling, recollections.

Chapter Seven

1 Minutes of the Board of Studies, 6 December 1976.
2 *Ibid.*
3 Editorial, *Evening Post*, 10 August 1977.
4 Miranda Harcourt interviewed by Bill Guest, December 2009.
5 Mike Nicolaidi, 'Tiros Meet Towering Challenge of Chekhov', *The Press*, 23 November 1977.
6 Bruce Mason, 'Sauce Brings Out Piquant Flavour', *Dominion*, undated.
7 George Webby, 'NZ Drama School Third Year Annual Report, 1976', July 1977.
8 Letter from John Roberts, chair, Board of Studies, to the chair, QEII Arts Council, 18 October 1977, Archives New Zealand.

Chapter Eight

1 George Webby, *Just Who Does He Think He Is?*, p. 279.
2 Letter from George Webby to new students (1974 intake), undated but probably end of 1973.
3 Viola Spolin, 'Creative Experience', *Improvisation for the Theatre*, Pitman Publishing, London,1973, p. 7.
4 Interview with George Webby, 'What Are They Teaching Them Now?', *ACT*, December 1979.
5 George Webby interviewed by Sarah Gaitanos, August 1995, OHP.
6 Peter (White) Land, recollections of his time at the New Zealand Drama School, 1974–75.
7 John McDavitt, recollections of his time at the New Zealand Drama School, 1977–78.
8 'Fast and Funny Affair from Drama School', *Evening Post*, 27 October 1979.
9 Bruce Mason, 'Family Talk … Mean Worried', *Dominion*, 5 December 1979.
10 George Webby, *Just Who Does He Think He Is?*, p. 230.
11 The final sentence in the Arts Council letter lacked a question mark.
12 Grant Tilly interviewed by Bill Guest, November 2009.
13 *Ibid.*
14 Ruth Graham interviewed by Sarah Gaitanos, November 1995, OHP.

15 Ruth Graham interviewed by Bill Guest, February 2010.
16 Ruth Graham interviewed by Sarah Gaitanos, November 1995, OHP.
17 Ralph McAllister, 'An Excellent Way of Feeling Sick', *Dominion,*19 September 1980.
18 Ralph McAllister, 'Imaginative Play Farewells School', *Dominion*, 28 November 1980.
19 Bruce Mason, 'Remarkable Close to Two Years of Study', *Evening Post*, 2 December 1980.
20 Jane Clifton, 'Drama Student Finds the Right Direction', *Dominion*, 2 December 1980.

Chapter Nine

1 'An Interview with George Webby', *ACT*, vol. 6, no. 2, April 1981.
2 Ralph McAllister, 'Drama School Fare Delights in Despair', *Dominion*, August 1981.
3 Bruce Mason, 'Don Juan in War's Wake', *Evening Post*, 21 August 1981.
4 Peter Hambleton interviewed by Sarah Gaitanos, October 1995, OHP.
5 Ralph McAllister, 'Sixth Form Mansfield Smells a Bit Fishy', *Evening Post*, 1 April 1982.
6 Bruce Mason, 'Another Bite of the Cherry', *Evening Post*, 10 April 1982.
7 Extract from interview with Rachel Lang by Christine Nikiel, 'The Storyteller', *Weekend Herald*, 9 May 2009. Rachel Lang is now one of New Zealand's most respected and prolific scriptwriters. Her credits include *Go Girls*, *Jackson's Wharf*, *Mercy Peak*, *Outrageous Fortune* and *Shortland Street*. Rachel's work was recognised at the 2008 NZ WIFT Awards where she won the TV3 and C4 Award for Success in New Zealand Television. At the 2008 Qantas Film and Television Awards, she also won the Best Script (Comedy/Drama Programme) award for series three, episode 11 of *Outrageous Fortune*.
8 George Webby interviewed by Eric Papps, 'Drama School like a Jungle', *Truth*, 27 October 1982.
9 Letter from George Webby to James Booth, QEII Arts Council, 8 April 1982.
10 Jeffrey Thomas interviewed by Neil Nelson, *The Tribune*, undated.
11 Mike Nicolaidi, '*The Twelfth Man* Shows Why Theatre Outlasts Alarmist', *Evening Post*, 3 December 1982.
12 Miranda Harcourt interviewed by Bill Guest, December 2009.
13 Jim Curran, 'OBE Adds to Drama', *Dominion,* 31 December 1981.
14 Erica Stephenson interviewed by Bill Guest, January 2009.
15 Ruth Graham interviewed by Bill Guest, February 2010.
16 Ruth Graham interviewed by Sarah Gaitanos, November 1995, OHP.
17 Ruth Graham interviewed by Bill Guest, February 2010.
18 Final statement from Erica Stephenson, in her report, *The Second Fire at 5 Vivian Street,* 5 February 1984.
19 Information for the Board of Studies Meeting, held at 5 Vivian Street, 7 February 1984.
20 John Roberts, Board of Studies report, 5 March 1984.
21 *Ibid.*
22 Reported in an article by Danny Mulheron, *Salient*, 5 March 1984.
23 'Training for Professional Technicians', NZATT Draft Report, June 1984, published in *Profile*, the newsletter of the New Zealand Association of Theatre Technicians, Issue 9, September 1984.
24 Letter from Michael Fowler, chair, QEII Arts Council, to Professor John Roberts, 17 May 1984, Archives New Zealand.
25 Miranda Harcourt interviewed by Bill Guest, December 2009.
26 *Ibid.*
27 Application for an increase of the New Zealand Drama School bursary, letter from George Webby to QEII Arts Council, 10 November 1982, Archives New Zealand.
28 Michael Clad, 'Enthralled by Theatre', *Evening Post*, 1 March 1986.

Chapter Ten

1 Jean Sabatine, *The Actor's Image: Movement Training for the Stage and Screen*, Prentice Hall, 1983.
2 Rona Bailey interviewed by Sarah Gaitanos, July 1995, OHP.
3 George Webby, *Just Who Does He Think He Is?*, p. 211.
4 Nerissa Moore interviewed by Bill Guest, April 2009.
5 *Ibid.*
6 Aileen Davidson interviewed by Bill Guest, May 2009.
7 Emma Kinnane, recollections of her time at New Zealand Drama School, 1987–88.
8 *Ibid.*

9 David Geary, recollections of his time at New Zealand Drama School, 1986–87.
10 Simon Bennett, recollections of his time at New Zealand Drama School, 1987–88.
11 Minutes of a meeting between Ruth Harley, Rona Bailey and Jane Waddell, QEII Arts Council, 26 February 1986.
12 Letter from Ruth Harley, chief executive officer, QEII Arts Council, to Phillip Mann at Victoria University, 14 March 1986.
13 Professor Don McKenzie, memo on the operating principle of drama studies at Victoria University of Wellington, 1968, Vice Chancellor's File 792.
14 Vinod Dahya, 'Drama Students Join Up', *Evening Post*, 3 October 1986.
15 Ralph McAllister, 'Harsh Brilliance in Grim Falklands Tale', *Dominion*, November 1986.
16 Annie Ruth interviewed by Bill Guest, September 2009.
17 George Webby, *Just Who Does He Think He Is?*, p. 275.
18 Programme note, 'Oh What a Lovely War', October 1986.
19 Jonathon Hendry interviewed by Bill Guest, September 2009.
20 George Webby interviewed by Sarah Gaitanos, July 1995, OHP.
21 'Director Webby Vacates His Chair', *Evening Post*, 8 August 1987.
22 Jonathon Hendry interviewed by Bill Guest, September 2009.
23 Jan Colosimo, 'Joyful Adventure into the Realms of Fantasy', *Dominion*, November 1987.

Chapter Eleven

1 Simon Bennett, recollections of his time at New Zealand Drama School, 1987–88.
2 Vincent O'Sullivan, 'Foreword' to George Webby, *Just Who Does He Think He Is?*
3 Nerissa Moore interviewed by Bill Guest, April 2009.
4 George Webby, *Just Who Does He Think He Is?*, p. 288.
5 Robin Payne interviewed by Bill Guest, January 2009.
6 George Webby, 'Theatre Attracts Few Maoris', *Evening Post*, June 1982.
7 Sima Urale interviewed by Sarah Gaitanos, 10 July 1996, OHP.
8 Philip Wakefield, 'Theatre for Change', interview with Andrew Noble, *On Film*, No. 6, 1988.
9 Rona Bailey, 'Some Thoughts on Bi-culturalism in Relation to the [New Zealand Drama] School', March 1988.
10 Philip Wakefield, 'Theatre for Change'.
11 Jonathon Hendry interviewed by Bill Guest, September 2009.
12 Resolution of QEII Arts Council meeting, 22 September 1988.
13 Andrew Noble, 'Preliminary Statement of Goals and Implications of Implementation of Three Year Training', 1 September 1988, p. 44.
14 *Ibid.*
15 Jonathon Hendry interviewed by Bill Guest, September 2009.
16 Grant Tilly interviewed by Bill Guest, November 2009.
17 Letter from Grant Tilly to Darien Takle, August 2005.
18 Grant Tilly interviewed by Bill Guest, November 2009.
19 Jonathon Hendry interviewed by Bill Guest, September 2009.
20 Laurie Atkinson, 'Checkhov a Challenge to Drama Graduates', *Evening Post*, 6 December 1988.
21 Mary Lochore, 'Critique Criticised', Letters to the Editor, *Evening Post*, 12 December 1988.
22 *Ibid.*
23 Simon Bennett, recollections.
24 Rona Bailey interviewed by Sarah Gaitanos, July 1995, OHP.
25 His partner, Jenny Pattrick, was a student at teachers' college at the same time.
26 Rona Bailey, 'Paper on Bi-culturalism for the NZDS Trust Board', 6 March 1989.
27 Programme notes from 'Reflections: Portrayal of 10 NZ Faces', 6–9 June 1989.
28 Tim Balme interviewed by Melanya Burrows, *New Zealand Herald*, 29 September 2004.
29 Sima Urale interviewed by Sarah Gaitanos, 10 July 1996, OHP.
30 After leaving drama school, Emily studied creative writing with Bill Manhire at Victoria University, before moving to London where she wrote her first collection of short stories, *Not Her Real Name*, which won Best First Book Award for Fiction at the 1996 Montana New Zealand Book Awards. She has since edited and published numerous works including *The Picnic Virgin* (1999), *Leave Before You Go* (1998), *The New Girl* (2001) and, most recently, *Novel About My Wife* (2008), which won both the fiction category and the overall Montana Medal for Fiction or Poetry in the 2009 Montana New Zealand Book Awards. Emily returned to New Zealand in 2008 and lives in Auckland with her family.

31 Sarah Gaitanos, *Nola Millar: A Theatrical Life*, p. 174.
32 Jane Waddell interviewed by Sarah Gaitanos, 7 February 1996, OHP.
33 Sunny Amey interviewed by Bill Guest, March 2009.
34 David Larsen, 'Happy End', *Salient*, 14 August 1989.
35 Patricia Cooke, 'Watch Out for the Magnificent Ten', *Dominion Sunday Times*, 13 August 1989.
36 Hone Kouka interviewed by Sarah Gaitanos, March 1996, OHP.
37 Robin Payne interviewed by Bill Guest, January 2009.
38 Jonathon Hendry interviewed by Bill Guest, September 2009.
39 Denis Welch, 'Mysterious Attractions', *Listener and TV Times*, 29 January 1990.
40 Shane Rangi deferred his training during 1988 and returned in 1989 to recommence his first year.
41 Sunny Amey interviewed by Bill Guest, March 2009.

Chapter Twelve

1 John Roberts, 'The Importance of Theatre', 1994, re-published in *The Roberts Report*, compiled and edited by Margaret Clark, Victoria University Press, Wellington, 1999.
2 Ruth Graham interviewed by Bill Guest, February 2010.
3 Emma Neale, review of *The Beaux Stratagem, Salient*, August 1990.
4 James Beaumont interviewed by Ruth Nicholl, *Salient*, 25 November 1990.
5 Robin Payne interviewed by Bill Guest, January 2009.
6 *Ibid.*
7 Robin Payne interviewed by Marion McLeod, *The Listener*, 5 August 1991.
8 Robin Payne interviewed by Sarah Gaitanos, July 1996, OHP.
9 Robin Payne interviewed by Bill Guest, January 2009.
10 Robin Payne interviewed by Sarah Gaitanos, July 1996, OHP.
11 *Ibid.*
12 Sunny Amey interviewed by Bill Guest, September 2008.
13 George Webby, *Just Who Does He Think He Is?*, p. 300.
14 Nancy Brunning, 'An Actor's Tribute', Letters to the Editor, *Dominion*, December 2008.
15 Robin Payne interviewed by Bill Guest, January 2009.
16 Minutes of the Toi Whakaari Trust Board, 1989.
17 In February 1990, a carnival billed by promoters as 'New Zealand's biggest event ever' opened in Wellington to mark New Zealand's Sesquicentenary, its 150th birthday. The six-week carnival known as Sesqui was a joint venture between the Wellington Show Association and the 1990 Trust, and the Wellington regional and city councils jointly underwrote the event by $1.4 million. It was launched by fireworks worth $150,000 and 30,000 visitors a day were expected, but Sesqui struggled to attract visitors and it closed after only two weeks with debts of $6.4 million.
18 Robin Payne interviewed by Bill Guest, January 2009.
19 Norman Kingsbury was director of tertiary education for the Ministry of Education from 1991–93.
20 Robin Payne interviewed by Bill Guest, January 2009.
21 Annie Ruth interviewed by Bill Guest, December 2009.
22 *Ibid.*
23 Pam Hindmarsh interviewed by Bill Guest, May 2009.
24 Robin Payne, 'Notes on Proposed Technicians' Training Course for Toi Whakaari: New Zealand Drama School', 1992.
25 Robin Payne interviewed by Bill Guest, January 2009.
26 Donald R. Holder, review of *A Long Walk Off a Tall Rock*, *Stage and Radio Record*, no. 6, Summer 1991–92.
27 *Ibid.*
28 Laurie Atkinson, 'Bold Work in *A Long Walk*', *Evening Post*, December 1991.

Chapter Thirteen

1 Letter from Nonnita Rees, QEII Arts Council, to Robin Payne, 18 February 1992.
2 The staff were arguing that members of the Trust Board should be appointed for their expertise and should include: the director, a staff representative, a student representative, a kaumātua, and five members whose credentials covered law, accounting, education, the theatre industry and business.
3 Letter from Nonnita Rees, QEII Arts Council, to Robin Payne, 24 March 1992.

4 Sean Coyle interviewed by Bill Guest, January 2009. Sean now mostly designs for TV and is currently the programme leader at the Pacific Institute of Performing Arts.
5 Laurie Atkinson, 'Verona Gents Act Witty Tale', *Evening Post*, December 1992.
6 Pauline Swaine, 'Class Act by Drama School Graduates', *Dominion*, November 1993.
7 Vanessa Byrnes, recollections of her time at Toi Whakaari, 1993–94.
8 Robin Payne, 'Possible Amalgamation with the New Zealand School of Dance', May 1992.
9 Robin Payne, 'Summary: The Current State of Staff and Effectiveness in Teaching the Core and Academic Subjects at Toi Whakaari: New Zealand Drama School', undated (possibly 1991–92).
10 Director's programme notes, *Tungoungou/Metamorphoses*, October 1993.
11 Bert van Dijk interviewed by Bill Guest, July 2009.
12 'Viewpoint', Toi Whakaari Friends Newsletter, no. 23, 1993.
13 Toi Whakaari archives.

Chapter Fourteen

1 Jacob Rajan, 'The Festival Revisited', *Toi Whakaari Friends Newsletter*, no. 27, May 1994.
2 Miranda Harcourt interviewed by Bill Guest, December 2009.
3 Vanessa Byrnes, recollections of her time as a student at Toi Whakaari, 1993–94.
4 Bill Guest, 'Brief for WW1 Project', July 1994.
5 Bill Guest, 'General Assessment of WW1 Project', 19 August 1994.
6 Eliza Meldrum, 'Life and Love in the Technical Department', *Toi Whakaari Friends Newsletter*, no. 35, November 1995.
7 Minutes of Premises Management Trust, September 1994.
8 Eliza Meldrum, 'Taranaki Festival', *Toi Whakaari Friends Newsletter*, no. 32, May 1995.
9 Susan Budd, 'Student Inspiration Wide-ranging', *Dominion*, 25 May 1995.
10 *Ibid.*
11 Laurie Atkinson, '*Out of Space* Full of Vigour Across Town', *Evening Post*, 27 May 1995.
12 Director's programme note, 'All My Sons', July 1995.
13 Anna Fyfe, 'Shakespeare Staged With Island Touch', *Dominion*, 24 November 1995.
14 Susan Budd, 'Polynesian Dream Lively But Flawed', *Dominion*, 28 November 1995.
15 Sarah Griffiths, recollections of her time at Toi Whakaari, 1993–96.
16 Fax from Fiona Samuel and Murray Keane to the 'New Zealand Drama School 25th Birthday Bash', August 1995.
17 Robin Payne, 'Robin's Report', *Toi Whakaari Friends Newsletter*, no. 34, September 1995.

Chapter Fifteen

1 Ruth Graham interviewed by Bill Guest, February 2010.
2 Board Membership and Procedures Working Party, Toi Whakaari: New Zealand Drama School, July 1995, included in Trust Board minutes, August 1995.
3 'Nga Tiriti Whakahoa Kaupapa Treaty Partnership Policies', Toi Whakaari: New Zealand Drama School, May 1995.
4 Letter from Terry Kilminster to Toi Whakaari Trust Board members, 2 November 1995.
5 Minutes, Toi Whakaari Trust Board, 20 May 1996.
6 Susan Budd, '*Wildman* Gorgeous and Bizarre', *Dominion*, April 1996.
7 Laurie Atkinson, 'Tale Told with Style', *Evening Post*, April 1996.
8 Tolis Papazoglou, 'Dance and Drama PMT Brief: General and Area Specification', 14 March 1996.
9 Lidia Zatorski,'Artists Take Over Show Building', *Evening Post*, 17 May 1996.
10 Simon Vita, 'End of Winter Shows', *City Voice*, 23 May 1996.
11 'Show Building's Petition', *City Voice*, 18 July 1996.
12 Laurie Atkinson, 'Dramatic Bag of Good Allsorts', *Evening Post*, 24 August 1996.
13 Robin Payne, Letter, *Toi Whakaari Friends Newsletter*, no. 39, November 1996.
14 George Webby, Letters to the Editor, *The Listener*, 14 October 1995.
15 Jenny Pattrick interviewed by Bill Guest, January 2009.
16 Item (7), Premises Trust Board Meeting minutes, 7 November 1996.
17 Robin Payne interviewed by Bill Guest, January 2009.

18 Robin Payne interviewed by Bill Guest, January 2009.
19 Annie Ruth interviewed by Sarah Gaitanos, 27 November 1996, OHP.
20 Sarah Gaitanos, 'Top Dramatic Role for Former Pupil', *Sunday Star Times*, 4 May 1997.
21 *Ibid.*
22 *Ibid.*
23 Jenny Pattrick interviewed by Bill Guest, January 2009.
24 Jane Chewings, 'Report', *Toi Whakaari Friends Newsletter*, no. 41, May 1997.
25 Tanea Heke interviewed by Bill Guest, December 2009.
26 Jody Hopkinson, 'Revolution Time', interview with Timothy Douglas, *City Voice*, 20 November 1997.
27 *Ibid.*

Chapter Sixteen

1 Vanessa Byrnes, recollections of her time as a student at Toi Whakaari, 1993–94.
2 Miranda Harcourt interviewed by Bill Guest, December 2009.
3 Board of Studies responsibilities as originally laid down by the Trust Board and recorded in the (acting) degree documents approved by NZQA, 1997.
4 Jenny Pattrick interviewed by Bill Guest, January 2009.
5 Simon Vincent interviewed by Bill Guest, January 2009.
6 Extract from Sir Michael Hardie Boys' speech given at the official opening of Te Whaea, June 1998.
7 Jenny Pattrick interviewed by Bill Guest, January 2009.
8 Lynn Freeman, review of 'The Threepenny Opera', *Capital Times*, 2 December 1998.
9 NZQA Degree Monitoring Report. 3 December 1998.
10 Tom McCrory interviewed by Bill Guest, September 2009.
11 Bronwyn Tweddle, 'Where Grotowski Meets Lecoq. "Flow" in Training at Toi Whakaari: New Zealand Drama School', in Marc Maufort and David O'Donnell (eds), *Performing Aotearoa: New Zealand Theatre and Drama in an Age of Transition*, Peter Lang, Brussels, 2007.
12 Jenny Pattrick interviewed by Bill Guest, January 2009.
13 Letter from PhilipTremewan, theatre and dance arts adviser, Creative New Zealand, to David O'Donnell, Theatre Studies, Victoria University, 16 November 1999.
14 Glen Crotskey, 'Elvis was a Coconut', *Capital Times*, 21 July 1999.
15 Helen Lehndorf, 'Tales from the City', *City Voice*, 1 July 1999.
16 Miranda Harcourt interviewed by Bill Guest, December 2009.
17 Lynn Freeman, '*The Three Sisters*', *Capital Times*, 1 December 1999.
18 John Smythe, 'New Crop Faces Uncertain Future', *National Business Review*, 10 December 1999.

Chapter Seventeen

1 Miranda Harcourt interviewed by Bill Guest, December 2010.
2 Tom McCrory interviewed by Bill Guest, September 2009.
3 Susan Hilferty, 'Special Report: Education', *Entertainment Design*, vol. 3, no. 9, 1999.
4 *Ibid.*
5 Helen Todd and Nina Nawalowalo, Process Notes, *He Kore Te Wiwia* programme, 15 June 2000.
6 Jennifer Shennan, 'What a Little Trove of Taonga', *Evening Post*, 22 June 2000.
7 Tom McCrory interviewed by Bill Guest, September 2009.
8 Lynn Freeman, 'Exciting Moments, but Less is More', *Capital Times*, 19 July 2000.
9 Tom McCrory interviewed by Bill Guest, September 2009.
10 'Drama School Looks at Feature Film Possibility', *Evening Post*, 12 December 2000.
11 Priscilla (Cilla) Gough interviewed by Bill Guest, February 2010.
12 Mark Lipman, recollections of working on *Into the Woods*, 2000.
13 Quotation from Wellington City Council, Steve Rendle, 'Show Goes on Following Injection of Council Cash', *Evening Post*, 24 February 2001.

14 Lyn Ferguson, 'Performance Schools Near Final Act', *Sunday Times*, 4 March 2001.
15 *Ibid.*
16 Ruth and Peter Graham carried out their ambition to produce olive oil, winning a gold medal in 2009 for their stellar product, 'Atutahi Extra Virgin Olive Oil'.
17 Ruth Graham interviewed by Bill Guest, February 2010.
18 'Ruth Graham', *In the Limelight*, Issue 3, May 2001.
19 Peter Edge, Composer's Programme Note, *Who Needs a Vespa*, March 2001.
20 'Vespa Anybody?', *Capital Times*, 28 March 2001.
21 Bill Guest, 'Background Paper and Proposal for a Bachelor of Performance Design', May 2001.
22 Miranda Harcourt interviewed by Bill Guest, December 2009.
23 'Students Set for Silver Screen', *Independent Herald*, 25 September 2001.
24 See Zenolith website: www.zenolith.info.
25 *Ibid.*
26 Frank MacShane (ed.), *The Notebooks of Raymond Chandler*, Weidenfeld and Nicholson, London, 1976, p. 48.
27 Minutes of Toi Whakaari Board of Studies, 10 December 2001.
28 *Ibid.*

Chapter Eighteen

1 'Report on the Performance Design Hui', College of Design, Fine Arts and Music, Massey University School of Design, 26 January 2002.
2 'Performance Design Joint Venture', *Massey News*, issue 3, 4 March 2002.
3 *Ibid.*
4 Christine Richardson interviewed by Bill Guest, December 2008.
5 Robbie Warwick, recollections of her time teaching at Toi Whakaari, 2002–4.
6 Christian Penny interviewed by Bill Guest, August 2009.
7 Rachel More interviewed by Bill Guest, August 2009.
8 NZQA Degree Monitoring report, 30 November 2000 (delivered 4 July 2001).
9 'Student Secondments', *In the Limelight*, issue 2, August 2002.
10 Minutes, Acting Advisory Panel, August 2001.
11 Bachelor of Performance Design, Minority Report, NZQA approval and accreditation panel documents, 23 July 2002.
12 Sadly, Amy Szostak passed away in March 2008, having written a book called *Radar the Viking*, which was serialised by Access Radio in 2006. Her work was also featured in the Australian exhibition, Without Borders: Outside Art in an Antipodean Context, in 2008.
13 Ceridwyn Roberts, reflections on her time as Toi Whakaari's marketing manager, 2003–7.
14 Bill Guest, 'Background and Discussion Paper for the Bachelor of Performing Arts Management', March 2003.
15 Miranda Harcourt interviewed by Bill Guest, December 2009.
16 Tom McCrory interviewed by Bill Guest, September 2009.
17 Annie Ruth interviewed by Bill Guest, December 2009.
18 *Ibid.*
19 John Smythe, 'Drama: A Truly Trojan Horse', *National Business Review*, 18 September 2003.
20 Annie Ruth interviewed by Bill Guest, December 2009.
21 John Smythe, 'Drama: A Truly Trojan Horse'.

Chapter Nineteen

1 This figure includes salaries for the director and one other full-time staff member covered by the Department of Education.
2 Helen Clark, *Launch of the Tertiary Education Commission*, government media release, 13 February 2003.
3 *The Next 10 Years 2004–2014*, Toi Whakaari visioning document, published in 2004.
4 Toi Whakaari: New Zealand Drama School, Strategic Plan, 1 July 2006–30 June 2011.
5 Academy Awards winner for costume designs on *The Last Emperor* (1987), *Dangerous Liaisons* (1988) and *Restoration* (1995).
6 'Just When You Least Expect It', *Capital Times*, 1 December 2004.
7 Programme notes for *Penumbra*, 'The Steps and Stages Towards Performance', 2004.

8 Penny Fitt interviewed by Bill Guest, September 2009.
9 In an eclipse of the moon, a larger area is dominated by the 'penumbra', the partial shadow where the moon and sun aren't in complete alignment.
10 Kim Knight, 'Counting by Penumbras', *Sunday Star-Times*, 4 March 2007.
11 Eleanor Bishop, 'Shifting', *Salient*, issue 23, 2004.
12 Open letter from Stuart McKenzie (director) and Jeanie Davison (producer) to the first-year actors (2005 intake), 2004.
13 *Ibid.*
14 Miranda Harcourt interviewed by Bill Guest, December 2009.
15 Annie Ruth interviewed by Bill Guest, September 2009.
16 Jane Clifton, 'Another Good Show Squandered', *Dominion Post*, 23 May 2006.
17 *Ibid.*
18 'Tough Slot to Justify', Editorial, *On Film*, 23 June 2006.
19 Stuart McKenzie, 'The Director Responds', Letters to the Editor, *Dominion Post*, 27 June 2006.
20 Jane Bowron, 'Tough Act at the Boot Camp for Thespians', *Dominion Post*, 17 June 2006.
21 Sophie Hambleton interviewed by Bill Guest, September 2009.
22 From *Battles of the Heart* company notes compiled for Gaylene Preston, Judith Fyfe, Alison Parr and Allen O'Leary, May 2005.
23 *Ibid.*
24 *Ibid.*
25 *Ibid.*
26 *Ibid.*
27 *Ibid.*
28 Programme note, Toi Cabaret, 2005.
29 Pedro Ramos Ilgenfritz da Silva, recollections of his time as an MTA directing student at Toi Whakaari, 2004–5.
30 Media Statement by Rt Hon. Helen Clark and Hon. Trevor Mallard, 2 August 2005.
31 Emma Weston, reflections on her time as a tutor at Toi Whakaari, 2005–8.
32 Sir Ken Robinson, 'All Our Futures: Creativity, Culture and Education', Report from the National Advisory Committee on Creative and Cultural Education for the [UK] Secretary of State for Education and Employment and the Secretary of State for Culture, Media and Sport, London, May 1999.
33 Sir Ken Robinson, Keynote Speech, Mini-summit on Arts Education, Melbourne, 12 September 2005.
34 Minutes, Acting Advisory Panel meeting, 5 May 2005.
35 Emma Weston, reflections.
36 Notes from Toi Whakaari staff visioning sessions, December 2005. (These statements were later incorporated in the 'Strategic Plan 2006–2011' under 'Statement of Purpose and Vision', 8 May 2006.)
37 'A Tribute to Rona Bailey', *DANZ Quarterly*, no. 2, October 2005, edited address by Jan Bolwell, Te Whaea, Wellington, 31 October 2005.

Chapter Twenty

1 Tom McCrory interviewed by Bill Guest, September 2009.
2 Sophie Hambleton interviewed by Bill Guest, September 2009.
3 Minutes, Toi Whakaari Board of Studies meeting, 16 February 2006.
4 *Ibid.*
5 Miranda Harcourt interviewed by Bill Guest, December 2009.
6 Report, Acting Department to Board of Trustees, March 2006.
7 'Our Strategies: The Way Forward', Toi Whakaari: New Zealand Drama School, Strategic Plan, 1 July 2006–30 June 2011, pp. 10–14.
8 Director's report, Toi Whakaari Board of Trustees meeting, August 2006.
9 Report on the Acting Department, 'Structure and Vision for 2006', 2005.
10 Bette Cosgrove interviewed by Bill Guest, February 2009.
11 Annabelle O'Meara interviewed by Bill Guest, February 2010.
12 Sophie Hambleton interviewed by Bill Guest, September 2009.
13 Letter from the second-year acting students, 'To the Staff' [signed Natalie Medlock, representing her class], undated.
14 Miranda Harcourt interviewed by Bill Guest, December 2009.
15 Annie Ruth interviewed by Bill Guest, December 2009.

16 Penny Fitt interviewed by Bill Guest, September 2009.
17 Report, Head of Performance Design to Toi Whakaari Board of Trustees, October 2005.
18 'Relationship with Massey University: Bachelor of Performance Design, 2006', Report to Toi Whakaari Board of Trustees, March 30, 2006.
19 Briefing document on the current status of the Bachelor of Performance Design, Toi Whakaari Board of Studies, 17 July 2006.
20 From 'Minority Report', Toi Whakaari application for approval and accreditation of a jointly awarded Bachelor of Performance Design, July 2002.
21 Bekky Campbell (now Coburn) interviewed by Bill Guest, November 2006.
22 *Ibid.*
23 Director's programme notes, *Henry VI*, August 2006.
24 Sophie Hambleton interviewed by Bill Guest, September 2009.
25 John Smythe, 'Brilliant if Flawed Play Done Brilliantly', *Theatreview*, 24 October 2006.
26 Willem Wassenaar interviewed by Kate Orglas, *City Life*, 3 October 2006.
27 Director's programme notes, *Delicates*, 2006.
28 Programme Notes, Toi Cabaret, 2006.
29 Minutes, Toi Whakaari Board of Studies meeting, November 2006.
30 *Ibid.*
31 Media Release, 'Toi Whakaari Farewells Miranda Harcourt', Toi Whakaari: New Zealand Drama School, 8 February 2007.
32 Miranda Harcourt interviewed by Bill Guest, December 2009.
33 Annabelle O'Meara interviewed by Bill Guest, February 2010.
34 Letter from Annie Ruth to Toi Whakaari Board of Studies members, 23 February, 2000.
35 Annabelle O'Meara interviewed by Bill Guest, February 2010.
36 Penny Fitt interviewed by Bill Guest, September 2009.
37 Notes for presentation at Toi Whakaari staff hui (visioning meetings), November 2006.
38 Teina Moetara, 'Key Question proposed for Kōiwi 2008', 2007.
39 Jade Eriksen interviewed by Bill Guest, November 2009.
40 The STAB (BATS in reverse) commission was set up in 1995 as part of BATS to allow theatre artists to experiment in a supportive environment, pushing the boundaries of New Zealand performance.
41 Jade Eriksen's paper for the Toi Whakaari Board of Trustees, 'On Issues of Convergence', 2007.
42 Annie Ruth, Directorag's Diary, 2007.
43 Jade Eriksen interviewed by Bill Guest, November 2009.
44 Minutes, Board of Trustees, Other Business, 20 February 2007.
45 *Ibid.*
46 Toi Whakaari Convergence Review, Terms of Reference.
47 Annie Ruth interviewed by Bill Guest, September 2009.
48 Bill Guest, 'My Viewpoint on Convergence', 14 March 2007.
49 'Strategy on Convergence, Our Strategies: The Way Forward', Toi Whakaari: New Zealand Drama School, Strategic Plan, 1 July 2006–30 June 2011, p. 11.
50 Toi Whakaari Trust Board sub-committee report on convergence, June 2007.
51 *Ibid.*
52 Annie Ruth interviewed by Bill Guest, September 2009.
53 Toi Whakaari Strategic Plan, 2006–2011.
54 Report on Creative New Zealand Theatre Forum, 25 November 2005.
55 Arts Board working definition of excellence, December 2004.
56 Tom McCrory interviewed by Bill Guest, September 2009.
57 Miranda Harcourt interviewed by Bill Guest, December 2009.
58 Report to the Board of Trustees – Toi Whakaari: New Zealand Drama School, from the sub-committee to review submissions made by students, staff and heads of department regarding 'Convergence', 5 June 2007, pp 1–3.
59 NZQA degree monitor's annual report, 2007.
60 Toi Whakaari sub-committee Report on Convergence, June 2007.
61 Minutes, Toi Whakaari Board of Studies, 26 April 2007.
62 Minutes, Board of Studies, 27 March 2008.
63 Jonathon Hendry interviewed by Bill Guest, October 2009.
64 Director's notes, *Twelfth Night* programme, August 2007.
65 Designer's notes, *Angels in America* programme, October 2007.
66 Melody Nixon, 'Arcadia', *Lumiere Reader*, 25 October 2007.

67 Melody Nixon, 'Arcadia', *Lumiere Reader*, 25 October 2007.
68 Thomas La Hood, 'A Rich Theatrical Dish', *Capital Times*, 26 October 2007.
69 Laurie Atkinson, 'Up for Challenge of Comedy' , *Dominion Post*, 22 October 2007.
70 Minutes, Toi Whakaari Trust Board, 5 December 2007.
71 Minutes, Third-year acting student representative report, Board of Studies, 15 November 2007.

Chapter Twenty-One

1 Christine Richardson interviewed by Bill Guest, December 2008.
2 Annie Ruth interviewed by Bill Guest, August 2009.
3 Emma Weston, recollections of her time as a tutor at Toi Whakaari, 2005–8.
4 Kate Robertson interviewed by Bill Guest, July 2009.
5 Ceridwyn Roberts, recollections of her time as Toi Whakaari's marketing manager, 2003–7.
6 Vanessa Byrnes, recollections of her time as a tutor at Toi Whakaari, 1998–8.
7 Jade Eriksen interviewed by Bill Guest, November 2009.
8 Teina Moetara interviewed by Bill Guest, November 2009.
9 Cultural and Theoretical Studies outline, Toi Whakaari: New Zealand Drama School, 2008.
10 Alison Richards, 'Bicultural Bodies: The Production of Nation at Toi Whakaari/The New Zealand Drama School', in H. McNaughton and A. Lam (eds), *The Reinvention of Everyday Life: Culture in the Twenty-first Century*, Canterbury University Press, Christchurch, 2006.
11 Jade Eriksen interviewed by Bill Guest, November 2009.
12 Jade Eriksen and Teina Moetara, 'Proposal for Collaborative 2nd Year Production, The Museum of Wellington City and Sea', undated [2007].
13 Jade Eriksen interviewed by Bill Guest, November 2009.
14 Teina Moetara, 'Toi Whakaari Marae Noho 2008, Broad Objectives', Report to the Toi Whakaari Board of Studies, June 2008.
15 'Nathaniel Lees joins Toi Whakaari: NZ Drama School', *The Big Idea*, 26 May 2008.
16 Jonathon Hendry, 'Media Release on Macbeth Production', July 2008.
17 Annie Ruth, Report, UNESCO World Conference of Theatre School Directors and the World Festival of Theatre Schools, Barcelona, 2008.
18 *Ibid.*
19 Laurie Atkinson, 'All The Drama of Exams', *Dominion Post*, 3 November 2008.
20 Christine Richardson returned from Tanzania at the end of 2009 and was re-appointed Toi Whakaari's business and strategy manager. The School of Dance had its own business manager, and Steve Stirrat remained the business manager for Te Whaea Services.
21 Annie Ruth, Director's Diary, 2009.
22 Heather Timms interviewed by Bill Guest, December 2009.
23 Shadon Meredith and Guy Langford, on *Tapu Toru* at the 2008 UNESCO ITI Asian Pacific Expo.
24 Annie Ruth interviewed by Bill Guest, September 2009.
25 Minutes, Toi Whakaari Board of Studies, 14 March 2009.
26 The [new] Curriculum for Bachelor of Performing Arts (Acting), Toi Whakaari: New Zealand Drama School, March 2009.
27 *Ibid.*
28 Bette Cosgrove interviewed by Bill Guest, February 2010.
29 Josette Bushell-Mingo interviewed by Tom Fitzsimons, 'Shaking up Shakespeare', *The Dominion Post*, 12 August 2009.
30 Guy Langford, Shadon Meredith, Amelia Reid and Sophie Lindsay interviewed by Bill Guest, October 2009.
31 *Ibid.*
32 Teina Moetara interviewed by Bill Guest, November 2009.
33 Jade Eriksen interviewed by Bill Guest, November 2009.
34 Extract from Simon Phillips' acceptance speech on receiving the 2009 'Toi Whakaari Graduate Award for Excellence', read on behalf of Simon Phillips by Sarah Pierse, 11 November 2009.
35 George Webby, *Just Who Does He Think He Is?*, p. 288.
36 Tanea Heke interviewed by Bill Guest, December 2009.
37 2009 students, written comments on their time at Toi Whakaari.
38 Bill Sheat interviewed by Bill Guest, February 2010.

Index

Bold references refer to illustrations. Colour Section C1 is after page 180. Colour Section C2 is after page 308.